EEDS OF YOUTH

ll Youth Have in a Democratic Society

e educational program in the secondary school

all youth adequately.

6 All youth need to understand the methods of science, the influence of science on human life, and the main scientific facts concerning the nature of the world and of man.

7 All youth need opportunities to develop their capacities to appreciate beauty in literature, art, music, and nature.

8 All youth need to be able to use their leisure time well and to budget it wisely, balancing activities that yield satisfactions to the individual with those that are socially useful.

9 All youth need to develop respect for other persons, to grow in their insight into ethical values and principles, and to be able to live and work co-operatively with others.

10 All youth need to grow in their ability to think rationally, to express their thoughts clearly, and to read and listen with understanding.

AMERICAN
HIGH SCHOOL
ADMINISTRATION
Policy and Practice

Rinehart Books in Secondary Education

WILLIAM M. ALEXANDER AND PAUL M. HALVERSON
Effective Teaching in Secondary Schools

WILLIAM M. ALEXANDER AND J. GALEN SAYLOR
Secondary Education: Basic Principles and Practices

R. WILL BURNETT
Teaching Science in the Secondary School

WILL FRENCH, J. DAN HULL, AND B. L. DODDS
American High School Administration: Policy and Practice,
REVISED EDITION

LUCIEN B. KINNEY AND C. RICHARD PURDY
Teaching Mathematics in the Secondary School

J. PAUL LEONARD
Developing the Secondary School Curriculum, REVISED EDITION

J. GALEN SAYLOR AND WILLIAM M. ALEXANDER
Curriculum Planning: For Better Teaching and Learning

WILLIAM L. WRINKLE AND ROBERT S. GILCHRIST
Secondary Education for American Democracy

So the role of an indigenous American secondary school— free, public and state-supported—becomes that of producing, as far as school education can, healthy, self-supporting, socially conscious, morally upright and rationally behaving young men and women who as home-makers, as workers and as citizens of their school, community, state, nation and the world are able and willing to defend, maintain and improve our American way of life. The historical secondary school being exclusive, selective and authoritarian in spirit could not and did not have such a major function. Our high schools—inclusive, adaptive and democratic—today are engaged in the process of freeing themselves from the chrysalis of the past and—too slowly and uncertainly—are taking on a form and program which can more effectively perform the function of a truly American high school.

From "The Role of the American High School," NASSP *Bulletin*, February, 1955.

AMERICAN

HIGH SCHOOL

ADMINISTRATION

Policy and Practice

REVISED EDITION

WILL FRENCH

Emeritus Professor of Education, Teachers College
Columbia University

Executive Editor, General Education Project
Educational Testing Service, Princeton, New Jersey

J. DAN HULL

Director, Instruction, Organization and Services, Office of
Education, U.S. Department of Health, Education and Welfare

B. L. DODDS

Dean, College of Education, University of Illinois

RINEHART & COMPANY, INC., NEW YORK

Preface

ANYONE WHO THINKS that the secondary school in America is a static institution should undertake to revise a textbook dealing with it. Even in the relatively short period of five years he will discover many new developments, problems, and shifts in emphasis. These are the earmarks of a dynamic, not a static, institution.

Behind these changes is America's basic desire to make each junior and senior high school a place where each boy or girl has an opportunity to become all that within him lies. As Frank H. Bowles, Director of the College Entrance Examination Board, put it at the Board meeting in the spring of 1955, "We have adopted the principle that all Americans are entitled to the opportunity of finishing secondary school as part of the process of becoming of age in America and have structured the secondary school curriculum to match that concept." The changes one sees in high schools are their more or less effective efforts to develop structure essential to the achievement of this relatively new and unique function. Not all the changes lead, of course, in this direction: some are plus and some minus. But the moving mean of change over the years points in the direction indicated by Bowles.

It is the intention of the authors that this book shall accept this trend, and their hope that the volume will help principals, prospective principals, and other students of secondary education to become more expert in the process of assisting communities to redesign their high schools into more effective instruments for serving American youth. Abraham Lincoln once said, "In the end the people wobble right." We believe that left to themselves the people of any community will eventually develop the kind of high school which they feel is best for their boys and girls. But the skillful leadership of a good high school principal can help them achieve their goal more completely and expeditiously. Reducing the "wobble" and producing more nearly straight-line progress is the real test of educational leadership today and one which the authors hope this book will help secondary school leaders to meet effectively.

In the writing of the text for the first edition of this book and in this revision of it the authors have been helped by the criticisms and suggestions of a large number of their friends and colleagues. The authors are especially grateful to President Hollis L. Caswell and Dean Stephen M.

Corey of Teachers College, Columbia University, for their help on the original manuscript, and to Professor David B. Austin of Teachers College, Columbia University, and Professor Raymond P. Harris of the College of Education, University of North Dakota, for suggestions for this second edition.

WILL FRENCH
J. DAN HULL
B. L. DODDS

New York
January, 1957

Contents

Part One is designed to provide students with some orientation for the high school principalship. This position needs to be seen as one exercising executive functions shared in common with all executive positions in all large enterprises and institutions, both public and private. It also needs to be seen in relation to the whole of public education in the United States and in relation to the whole of youth education in the community. The authors believe that such orientation will help in the development of a better understanding and appreciation of the functions of the position than would otherwise be reached.

Part One

THE EXECUTIVE FUNCTION AND YOUTH EDUCATION

Chapter 1

ORGANIZATION AND ADMINISTRATION
IN EDUCATION

SCHOOL ADMINISTRATORS, unlike the members of most other professions, live in what amounts to solitary confinement. In a typical town, with its one superintendent of schools and its high school principal, there will be several lawyers, ministers, doctors, bankers, and store owners or managers. The members of these groups have many opportunities to discuss with their fellows the common problems and concerns of their several professions. They have more opportunity than schoolmen do to meet in the community in mixed groups representing two or more of these professions, where matters of common concern to several professions and businesses may be discussed and information and ideas exchanged. Other business and professional people create their own local groups or associations, such as the retail merchant group or the city medical association, in whose meetings special problems can be discussed in confidence. These people have learned that the problems facing the superintendent of a hospital or of a flour mill are essentially and basically the same as those facing the man who operates a lumberyard or a laundry. Through their contacts with each other they have a chance to see the broad aspects of organization and administration.

The school administrator, by contrast, is a somewhat isolated man. He may belong to a luncheon club to which some of the community's business and professional leaders belong, but the members usually spend their energy and time on civic affairs rather than on the common professional problems of executives. Granted that he has many people within the public school organization with whom to confer; such contacts, however, tend to be narrowing rather than broadening. The heads of the public schools of a community ought to, but seldom do, meet with those who head the community's parochial schools, private schools, or commercial colleges in order to exchange and develop ideas. Instead, the public school administrator tries to offset his isolation by belonging to county, state, and national school administrators' associations, but their infrequent meetings do not afford him anything like the chance that other community leaders have to see the various aspects of the administrative process at work.

An ideal solution for the local school administrator, at least, would be the formation of an executives' club by the heads of the community's institutions and business enterprises. In such a club the common duties, responsibilities, and problems of its members could be discussed and studied. Here schoolmen would find that other executives are frequently plagued by problems that are only slightly different from their own. For instance, the solutions to basic problems relating to employed personnel are fairly similar, whether the employees are machinists, truck drivers, bank clerks, or schoolteachers. The members of such a club could improve their techniques of management by a study of their common problems in terms of the broad principles of organization and administration.

BETTER ORIENTATION TO ADMINISTRATION NEEDED

Membership in a community club composed of the executives of various business and professional groups would break the shell of the school administrator's isolation and give him a basis for orienting himself to the whole field of administration in business, labor, public-service institutions, and government. During their years of professional education and while they are at work, school administrators tend to regard educational administration as something rather separate and apart from other types of administration. They study books written by authorities in *educational* administration; they read articles written by other *educational* administrators; they visit and inspect the work of other *educational* administrators in other school systems. Is it reasonable to believe that all the best books, articles, and work in administration have been produced by that small segment of administrators who are working in educational institutions? Is it not more reasonable to believe that out of the vast experience of executives generally, and of those who have studied organization and administration especially, as it can be seen in operation in a great variety of enterprises, a great deal may have been learned from which school administrators could profit?

To the authors of this book the typical approach to a study of school administration seems too narrow and too limited to the field of education; they feel that students of high school administration should see their special field of administrative work in relation to the work of administrators generally. Hence this first chapter seeks briefly to orient these students, to some extent, to the whole field of administration as it functions in the life of the modern social, political, and economic world. Just as a psychiatrist, or a brain surgeon, though a specialist in a particular field, sees himself first as a member of the medical profession, so should the high school principal, though a specialist in a particular field of administration, see himself first as a member of a new and increasingly important profession of administration. This chapter thus seeks to sketch the principal relationships that a student of high school administration must recognize if he sees his own work in proper perspective in relation to that of other administrators who are helping to organize and administer the varied work of the world today.

Organization and Administration in Modern Institutions

Whenever men engage in purposeful activity—play, games, or work—they organize it, either to lighten the effort involved or to improve or increase whatever is produced. Even in simple work situations where a man is working by himself, there will be evidence of organization. Work that is almost exclusively repetitive, in that it involves nothing but the repetition of a single act on the part of a worker, involves the least organization. For instance, if a worker is sorting sixpenny nails from eightpenny nails, little in the way of organization is involved. But even here, how he places himself in relation to the unsorted nails and where he puts the sixes and eights probably are at least unconscious efforts at organization. If the man's job is not wholly repetitive but requires a succession of different acts, he will decide upon the essential movements and an order of doing them. If he is just learning to do the job, he may try several ideas before deciding which seems best. Whatever these decisions are, they represent efforts at organization. In industrial plants these decisions are sometimes put to rigorous tests to find out if better organization cannot be secured and thus either increase the output or lessen the strain on the worker or both. Job analysis studies break work down into its simplest essential parts. Motion pictures are made; time studies are conducted; and, in the end, the placement of the "raw" materials to be used, the amount and kind of space to be used by the worker, his position in relation to the materials and the work space, the movements he needs to make, their order of performance, and the best speed at which to work may all be reliably established. Such studies may even result in some kind of decisions as to the kinds of persons who should be employed to do this particular job most easily and effectively. The result is a better organization of the work to be done than previously existed.

If careful organization of the work of a single worker can produce remarkably better results in amount and ease of production, it is not hard to see how important organization can become as two or more people are associated in the accomplishment of a particular job. The play of a football team is an example of sound or weak organization of the work of eleven players. Eleven good players whose play is not organized will not give us as good an example of teamwork as will less spectacular players who have been coached in the elements of team play. Industry and the military, as well as coaches of athletics, are aware of the advantage of teamwork and of the fact that it contributes to the successful accomplishment of desired results, usually with more satisfaction to the workers. Thus as the number of workers who must work together on a job grows, the need for and the importance of organization increases.

DIVISION OF LABOR AS A FORM OF ORGANIZATION

A group of workers can work together on a project with each worker doing everything that any worker does. No effort need be made to give different kinds of essential tasks to different workers, but instead, all can join in doing what needs to be done next. For example, at an old-time barn-raising in which all the neighbors participated, everyone present could have helped hew the logs, raise the beams, lay up the logs for the sides, split shingles for the roof, and close up the chinks between the logs. When the barn was raised, each person might have done some part of every operation necessary to its completion. Because they were all fairly good general mechanics, it might have been possible to proceed entirely in this way. All that was really necessary was that they agree upon what needed to be done and upon an order of procedure. They worked "as one man," the gain being that they multiplied one man's strength by the number of workers and decreased the amount of time required for the completion of this piece of work.

But the chances are that in any such group some of the workers would be better at certain jobs than at others and that the owner-host would suggest that they divide up into teams, each to work on a different kind of job. The lack of enough tools of a kind required for one operation or the lack of space in which to do one operation if all worked on it might be another reason for breaking up the whole group into subgroups for special jobs. When a project is more complex and is made up of a variety of jobs—some requiring much more skill than others, and requiring many workers—it is very likely that division of labor with the accompanying specialization of workers will increase the part played by organization in the success of the project. In present-day production and, in fact, in almost every type of institution today, division of labor and specialized workers are taken for granted. The industrial revolution, the factory system, or our high level of technological development did not, however, bring into existence the idea of division of labor. They simply made an old technique of work accomplishment more important than it had ever been before. As a by-product of this one kind of specialized work, that of the organizer—the foreman or supervisor, for example— gained new importance because if labor is divided among specialized workers, then he who plans on how the work will be divided, and who decides on the kinds of specialized abilities needed and how the different groups of workers will be related to each other, becomes a much more important element in the work process than ever before.

SIZE AND COMPLEXITY MAGNIFY PLACE OF
ORGANIZATION AND ADMINISTRATION

Enterprises in a technological world differ from those of the period before the industrial revolution in that their operations are now on a larger scale and are more complex than could be undertaken at an earlier time. Both of these factors magnify the importance of good organization. The canning of fruit in a canning factory is probably no more complex a process than it would be if equally well done in a kitchen. But if fruit canning is to be industrialized and put on a factory basis, a good deal more time, money, and ability has to be spent in proportion on good organization than would be the case if the enterprise were on a smaller scale. As size increases, the importance given to the work of the organizer must increase if the full benefits of large-scale production are to be fully attained. Wherever large-scale operation is really good, one may be sure that good organization enters in a large degree to make it so.

When work is of a very complex nature, as many processes carried on by present-day institutions and enterprises are, good organization is especially essential. One could not build with efficiency even one automobile unless the undertaking has been very well organized. The complex nature of the completed car requires much more in the way of organization than would be required to build a cart. If the purpose is to build many automobiles in a plant so that complex operations are to be combined with large-scale operations, a high order of organizational ability is required. If one has watched the operation of the assembly lines of a large automobile plant from which a completed car emerges every few minutes, he cannot help but be impressed with the amount of detailed organization required. Organizational planning brings to the main assembly line from a number of subassembly lines the various parts of the automobile all ready to add to other parts just at the right time and in the right amounts. Organization has placed at each station on the lines the right number of men, with the right kind of skills and tools, supplied in correct amounts with the right kind of materials, properly placed for use to add at a coordinated rate a particular part to the car being assembled. Every detail has been planned beginning with the point or points where workers put together the first two parts, which when added to by a score of other groups of workers results in a particular subassembly unit and finally in a completed automobile with its myriad of parts. The highest level of ability to organize for production is needed to plan such a complex undertaking and without it the enterprise would degenerate into a madhouse. The increase in automation, or the use of machines to control other machines, while it may reduce or change the manpower needs, increases the over-all organizational planning required. Where size and complexity combine, as they tend to do in our modern world in schools and other service agencies, as well as in industry, one may be sure that unless high levels of organizational ability are present, the potential benefits of large-scale enterprises are lost.

It is true that there is considerable study in industry, government, and education concerning the benefits of decentralization and the optimum size of operating units, such as a school, a production unit, or an agency, to avoid the problems of massive concentration, but this in no real sense reduces the problems of organization. Rather, the problems of organization in the proper coordination of decentralized units probably demand an even higher order of organizational and administrative ability.

What has just been said about the current importance of good organization can also be said for the related process of administration. As will be shown soon, these two processes are closely interrelated; and so, when it is shown that organization plays a most important part in today's large-scale and complex enterprises, it is not necessary to make a detailed case for the increased importance of administration. Even when it is very well organized, the conduct or operation of a big, complex enterprise requires more in the way of administrative ability than a small, simple undertaking requires.

ADMINISTRATIVE ABILITY UNEQUALLY DISTRIBUTED

This all adds up to the fact that big business (here used to include "big" business, "big" labor, "big" agriculture, and "big" government as Chase does in *Democracy under Pressure*) today requires a very large number of workers whose specialized ability and training are in the field of organization and administration. All people do not have an equal amount of the abilities and traits which, taken together, we call ability to organize and administer. Some have much ability to develop a good organization for their own personal work, whereas others will not even seem to be conscious of the fact that the reason their work is not better and more easily done is due to their not having organized it well. It is not likely that one who shows little or no ability to organize his own work well will be able to organize well the work to be done by a large group of workers. Higher levels of competence are required to organize and administer the work of others than for one's own work, and the level required increases as the number of workers for whom one is responsible increases. Since the modern trend toward more and more large units of organization draws upon the relatively small number of people who have the training and ability to organize and administer, the competition for their services is sharp. Most people have some of the abilities to organize and administer. Relatively few have them in the degree required of those who head up large enterprises. Many who are above average in these abilities have not had much training. Hence, in the face of the trend toward larger units of organization, there is a relatively decreased supply of competence.

ADMINISTRATIVE TRAINING AND EDUCATION NEEDED

Training, education, and practice, as well as natural ability, are all factors in the development of a high level of managerial ability. Of these, natural ability is perhaps the most important, for the degree to which it is present determines how much an individual will profit from education, training, and experience. In a technological world that makes a heavy demand for high levels of ability to organize and administer large enterprises, every effort should be made to discover and educate those who possess natural ability. The skill of the administrator determines the maximum levels of effectiveness of the whole enterprise. A poor high school principal, for example, can make it impossible, or at least most difficult, for the faculty of a school to make it an outstanding one. A good principal can make that task much easier. Only the most competent in organization and administration, and only those who, in addition, have had the best type of training, should be placed in positions where they have the power to make or break the work of a whole organization, including the happiness and welfare of all connected with it.

ADMINISTRATION PLAYS AN INCREASINGLY IMPORTANT ROLE

As pointed out above, "bigness" and complexity are not characteristics of the present world that apply only to business. They apply equally to nearly all of our organized and institutionalized life. The small corner grocery gives way to "chains" or becomes incorporated within them. The local union becomes a small part of an international brotherhood. The one-room school becomes the big school system. The local children's aid society becomes first a unit in the local community chest and then, in turn, part of the national community chest organization. Not only in business and industry do we find the trend toward large-scale organization but in education, in social service, and even in government itself. A world that applies science and technology to affairs will find such a trend inevitable. It may have been overdone or have proceeded too rapidly in some instances so that reaction sets in, but the general tendency holds and, once started, will not be permanently reversed. Science gives the world as a whole and everyone in it new levels of freedom and opportunity and yet creates a "one world" situation that makes us all more interdependent and thus, in a way, less free than ever before. Individuals find it increasingly necessary to live and work as members of a group, small groups find it necessary to ally themselves with larger ones, and so on up the scale until, at the top levels, we find sovereign national states faced with the problem of deciding whether or not to surrender some sovereignty to a United Nations organization and thus to begin creating a governmental unit at the world level. If and as such a unit is developed, we shall then have reached the top level of organization everywhere, for we already have world-wide business, religious, and social-service agencies. And if world government is attained, the present need for many highly competent men and women to organize and manage large-scale and complex enterprises will be still further sharpened. Government will then be "big" also in the full meaning of the term and, in proportion to its size and to the complexity of its work, will require more and more administrative personnel of the highest skill.

Only within recent years has our representative democracy begun to compete on a large scale for high levels of administrative ability. Our early small-scale and relatively simple governments made little use of specialized administrative talent. In fact, the elements of our population who most favored democracy were suspicious of any plan that gave anyone with any specialized ability any prior claim to consideration for governmental service. Anything that smacked of qualifications for office beyond the reach of anyone was frowned upon by those who were willing to go the furthest in democratizing our early American local and state governments. Appointment to office was less popularly favored than direct election by the people. In the Midwest, for example, county and state superintendents of schools were generally made elective officers with almost no qualifications prescribed for office. Among this large segment of the people who most favored democracy an outright suspicion of the "natural aristocracy" of people with ability supported constitutional provisions and legislative enactments that tended to make any public officer having specialized responsibility directly dependent upon the will of the people.

This historic fear and distrust is reflected today in this country in a tendency that many people have to restrict, to belittle, and to hamper the work of a public official with specialized training for a technical responsibility. If a well-qualified public health official wants to make changes that all in the profession agree are necessary for good organization and administration of a public health service, lay officials in government are quite likely to discount his professional recommendations, making their decisions on the basis of lay opinion and receiving popular support and approval for doing so. Many men who employ experts in their own businesses, and who depend upon them for advice in making their business decisions and for skill in the conduct of their business, distrust government's use of experts in administrative positions where they can supply technical information and skill in the improvement of public service. But as government, too, has become big, as it has become increasingly active and constructive in its work, the trend has necessarily been for it to undertake activities in which technical and professional competence is required and in which high levels of ability to organize and administer are essential. At the local, state, and federal levels, governments are now tending to branch out into a wider range of constructive enterprises and so are making larger and larger use of administrators. The trend in this direction is no more likely to reverse itself than it is in the world of business.

So, at present, in all aspects of the work of all types of institutions and enterprises, the place of the organizer, the administrator, the manager, continues to grow. More and more the owners of stock in a business concern, the union worker in industry, the lay board members of educational and social-service institutions, and the citizens of the state become dependent upon those who head the organization and administration of their company, their union, their schools, or some activity of their government. The typical enterprise becomes so vast and so complex that only a trained person who is in direct, daily contact with all that happens can exercise any good judgment about what course of action ought to be taken. These executives are really employees in an organization who are supposed to be subject to the will of their employers. Yet, under present circumstances, the employers hardly dare exercise any will of their own except as it is created by their managers. James Burnham, in his *Managerial Revolution,* points out that we may get our world into a situation in which we are dictated to by the managers of our enterprises—both public and private. Then we would be ruled not by an aristocracy of blood, or by the owners of land or other forms of capital, or by the people with their votes, but by a group of managers who, once in the seats of power, would take advantage of the situation to entrench themselves until, in the end, no one would dare unseat them.

To whatever extent these dangers are real and not fancied, it becomes increasingly important that those who organize and administer our enterprises and institutions have moral and ethical standards as well as natural ability. Our programs of professional education for administration should strive to develop high levels of moral and civic integrity as well as high levels of technical skills. Such a course of action is probably more promising than any plan to reverse the trend toward the creation of large-scale and complex enterprises, a trend that is inherent in our application of science and technology to the various aspects of life. Our task is not to create a world that tries to get along with little or no resort to skilled managers because it is afraid of them, but rather, a task of developing processes of democratic government that, while permitting the full use of all the fully trained technical competence we can discover in our people, nevertheless makes them always the instruments of the popular will—never its masters.

The Administrative Function

Organization and administration are two phases of the process of effectively accomplishing purposes whose achievement requires the continuous physical or mental activity that we call work or play. Both are necessary aspects of the complete process. If an enterprise is organized for the achievement of a purpose but the administrative phase is never entered upon, the purpose will not be accomplished, or at best will be accomplished on momentum only for a brief space of time, after which the enterprise will become less and less efficient. It would be like building a house for a home and then never beginning to live in it. Ordinarily, one never voluntarily stops such an enterprise at the point where its organization has just been perfected. Under normal conditions we do not enter upon the administrative phase of the process of achieving purposes without going through the organizational phase. In an emergency situation we may be forced to do so—in fact, that is why we call it an emergency. The organizational phase may take but a moment in a simple enterprise, in larger affairs a longer period of time; but in both cases, and irrespective of the amount of time required, organization does occur.

The organizational phase is chiefly concerned with making arrangements that permit the beginning of purpose realization. It may also be a process of making new arrangements to replace old ones. In this case we call it reorganization, but it is actually the same process as when it is called organization. In fact, most of what we call organization is really reorganization. Properly speaking, only when a new enterprise is originally undertaken is pure organizational work done. The construction of Hoover (formerly Boulder) Dam gives us an instance of organization in its pure form. Arrangements were then being made to achieve a purpose where there had been no effort or arrangement for doing so. In most typical situations that confront an executive, there are some arrangements for achieving the institution's purposes. If it seems that different arrangements would result in increased or more economical purpose achievement, then the executive may be authorized to reorganize. This reorganization process is ordinarily under way constantly, because of (1) discovery of defects in the original arrangements, (2) modification or extensions of purposes to be realized, (3) change in conditions external to the enterprise that force a change in its arrangements, or (4) invention of new techniques or discovery of new facts or processes. Only in a perfectly static situation and only when the original organizational work had been perfect, could the head of an institution be sure that he needed only to administer and to give no thought to organization. Since such a condition never exists, the executive is constantly both organizing and administering.

ORGANIZATIONAL PHASE INVOLVES COORDINATION

Making the arrangements that permit purpose realization usually involves consideration of money, site, plant, supplies and materials, personnel, scientific discovery and invention, and legal and governmental regulations. But it goes further than merely considering each of these separately. It involves coordinating each with all the others. In fact, the most intricate aspect of organizational work is this matter of coordination. If one word were to be used to show what we mean by organization, it would be the word "coordination." "The major purpose of organization is coordination," says Luther Gulick in his chapter in *Papers on the Science of Administration.*[1] Unless each need involved in the accomplishment of purpose is met in proportion to all other needs, no real job of organization has been done. No ability to organize would be credited to a man who planned to build a house if he merely sat down at a telephone and called up a real-estate dealer, the bank, the lumberyard, and the carpenters' union to say to each, respectively, that he wanted enough land, money, materials, and help to build a house. Detailed and specific requisitions covering all the necessary items are required if good organization is to be provided. When a good job of organizing is completed, it must be evident that materials, time, and money were economically used and the right amounts of specific skills were provided and utilized in ways that were reasonably satisfactory to the workers. Beyond all this, it must be evident that a plan of operation is contemplated that can result in the effective, continuous achievement of the purposes whose accomplishment is sought.

ADMINISTRATION CONCERNED WITH MANAGEMENT

The second and purely administrative phase of the process of purpose achievement is concerned with the conduct, operation, and management of the enterprise as organized so that the purposes continue to be effectively achieved. For reasons stated above, this stage includes de-

---

[1] Luther Gulick and Lyndall Urwick, eds., *Papers on the Science of Administration* (New York: Institute of Public Administration, Columbia University, 1937), p. 33.

termination of the need for such reorganization as will maintain or improve the effectiveness of purpose achievement. Good arrangements for purpose achievement through good organization supply only the possibility for achieving the desired results. Good administration is required to ensure continuous realization of the possibilities of good organization. Poor administration, on the other hand, may easily prevent a well-organized enterprise from producing what it is capable of producing. All the high schools in a state may be very much alike in organization but, because of differences in the quality of administration, may differ from each other markedly in the effectiveness with which they achieve their purposes. It is a tragic spectacle to see a well-planned and well-organized enterprise like a school put in the charge of such a poor administrator that all of its potentialities are frittered away day after day.

On the other hand, it is very difficult, if not well-nigh impossible, for even the best of administration to overcome serious defects in organization by trying to better the administration of the enterprise. If a machine is poorly designed to accomplish a certain operation, one cannot greatly improve the situation by paying more for a better operator. What is needed is a better-designed machine. In like manner, a poorly organized institution cannot be brought to maximum effectiveness by providing it with an extremely competent administrator unless he is given full authority to restructure its organization so that the good administration he is capable of providing will have a chance to succeed.

It is thus evident that in evaluating the work of a school or other enterprise it is important to try to discover whether any failure to achieve its purposes is due to poor organization or to poor administration, or to both. Sometimes the recommendations should be for more reorganization, sometimes for better administration of an existing organization. The executive head of an institution, therefore, not only must be competent to evaluate both its organization and its administration, but must be a good organizer (or reorganizer) and a good administrator. At least he must recognize more clearly than some school administrators appear to do that there is a difference between organization and administration and that the lack of one cannot be compensated for by a superabundance of the other. They are two distinct phases of the one process of purpose achievement through work. Unless both phases are well cared for, maximum results from any institution or enterprise are not to be expected.

ORGANIZATION AND ADMINISTRATION INTERRELATED
AND INTERDEPENDENT

It is clear from our previous reference to Hoover Dam that in the launching of wholly new enterprises the organizational phase precedes the administrative phase; yet it should also be clear that in typical on-going enterprises the two are so interrelated that it is easy to see how the layman fails to distinguish between them. This, however, is no excuse for the failure of an administrator to make this distinction. The typical administrator constantly turns from the organizational phase of his work to its administrative phase, and though we call a person a school *administrator,* we are not implying that he is not also responsible for improved organization. For such reasons Arthur B. Moehlman, in his *School Administration,* uses the term "executive" and refers to the "executive function" rather than to the administrative function. The general practice, however, seems to be to use the term "administrator" even though it seems to stress one phase of the work for which an administrator is responsible at the expense of the other.

To what extent both phases of the process enter into the work of administrators is evident by a study of the analysis made by Gulick:

Planning, that is working out in broad outline the things that need to be done and the methods for doing them to accomplish the purpose set for the enterprise;

Organizing, that is the establishment of the formal structure of authority through which work subdivisions are arranged, defined and coordinated for the defined objective;

Staffing, that is the whole personnel function of bringing in and training the staff and maintaining favorable conditions of work;

Directing, that is the continuous task of making decisions and embodying them in specific and general orders and instructions and serving as the leader of the enterprise;

Coordinating, that is the all important duty of interrelating the various parts of the work;

Reporting, that is keeping those to whom the executive is responsible informed as to what is going on, which thus includes keeping himself and his subordinates informed through records, research and inspection;

Budgeting, with all that goes with budgeting in the form of fiscal planning, accounting and control.[2]

This analysis was made without reference to the character of the enterprise in which the executive works. Schoolmen who read it will see that it applies to top-level administration of all other types of enterprises. No matter what the character or purpose of an enterprise is, its chief executive will be responsible for all these functions. In a given enterprise one function may be more important than in another, but all will be found to be present in some form in any enterprise that operates as a complete independent unit. Some of these functions in some instances may be wholly delegated to a subordinate, but such delegation

[2] *Ibid.,* p. 13.

does not indicate that they are still not responsibilities of the chief executive. A high school principal, however, may find that he is not responsible in any degree for one or more of the executive functions. Though he is the chief administrative officer of his own school, he is a subordinate administrator in the system of which his school is a part. It does not operate as an independent enterprise and he therefore bears responsibility for only part of the executive function, sharing it with others in the system: an assistant superintendent in charge of high schools, the school system's business manager, the superintendent of schools, for example.

BASIS FOR A SCIENCE OF ADMINISTRATION

These functions may be considered as "universals" in that wherever administration is carried on all over the world, they will be found to be present. Whether it is a military or business organization, or a school, church, labor union, or government agency; whether the enterprise is being carried on under democratic or autocratic forms of government; whether it is an ancient institution or as new as the Atomic Energy Commission, a study of its administration will reveal the exercise of these functions by its administration. These functions show that both organization and administration are involved in the work of the administrator; they show the interrelatedness of the two phases of his work; they show, furthermore, that the administration of a particular type of enterprise such as a school system cannot be considered as something wholly different from the administration of other enterprises. Instead, those who look beneath the surface of things administrative, as a professional man is supposed to do, will see that the work of an administrator anywhere has more in common with that of other administrators everywhere than the less trained eye of the layman would lead him to believe.

To the extent that these functions are exercised everywhere that organized enterprises operate, it is possible that laws and principles can be discovered which should act as controls on the work of all administrators. To whatever extent such principles can be discovered, then, there is, or can be, a science of administration. For example, in the field of personnel administration ("staffing" on Gulick's list) there are some underlying principles that ought to be utilized by anyone attempting to develop or improve any plan of personnel administration. These principles apply with equal force to the work of any administrator, whether his particular personnel is made up of schoolteachers, taxi drivers, clerks, nurses, or coal miners. They apply because all of these are people—human beings—before they are workers in particular occupations. They are "warmed and cooled by the same winter and summer," and good personnel administration will develop practices in any particular situation based upon the general principles underlying all good personnel administration. So we may, in time, identify and validate the laws and principles that underlie all other phases of the work of the administrator. As this is being done, a new social science in the field of administration is being developed that will guide the work of all kinds of administrators and rank it with that of the other professions.

The school administrator, then, should learn to think of himself as a practicing social scientist. His particular social science is the science of administration. His specialty is educational administration, which is an applied social science. Like all social sciences, it is an inexact science in that mathematical measurement plays a minor part in solving its problems. But if any social science can be called a science, then administration deserves to be. But it will not be so recognized until those who study educational administration have an opportunity to see their work in school administration in relation to the work of administrators generally, and are encouraged, as they study their own particular variety of administration, to relate it and its problems to those who have a similar role in other types of enterprises.

Educational Administration: A Type of Public Administration

Educational administration in the United States may be classed as public administration along with the administration of all other non-profit-making enterprises, as opposed to private administration, which is concerned with the organization and administration of enterprises primarily conducted for private profit. Some "private" schools of the proprietary type are doubtless conducted primarily for profit, but these are so far in the minority that the general statement classifying educational administration as public in nature is still true. Educational administration, therefore, along with the administration of social-service organizations of an educational, religious, or philanthropic nature, quasi-public in character, may be regarded as in the same class as governmental administration and may be considered as public administration. Public schools, of course, are governmental agencies, and therefore their administration falls wholly and clearly in the area of public administration. The term "public administration" will be used to apply to the administration of public agencies, and "private administration" to apply to the administration of private enterprises where the term "business administration" is commonly used. This distinction avoids the implication that good "business administration" is not as necessary a part of good administration of governmental enterprises as it is of private enterprises.

PRIVATE ADMINISTRATION EMPHASIZED IN UNITED STATES

In this country private enterprises have been accorded a degree of freedom of operation that has made their ownership or management or both very attractive to men and women of wealth, ability, and ambition. These enterprises have, as a result, drawn many very able persons into management positions that usually command rather high salaries. Salaries in public administration are generally lower than those in private administration, though it is by no means evident that the former's value to the general public is not greater. During the depression of the thirties, when private enterprise was unable to absorb the young men and women with administrative ability as rapidly as they were being trained by schools and colleges, and during more recent years, when the scope of governmental activities was being largely expanded, public administration of public-service agencies attracted many able young administrators. There is thus some reason to hope that education may also be able to interest more people with a high level of administrative ability.

It is a part of the tradition of this country to offer the individual every opportunity to make his way in private enterprise. It is thus not surprising to find colleges and universities providing good educational training for those interested in private ("business") administration, or to find the public willing to pay for such education in state schools, and business itself willing to underwrite business education and schools of business administration in the private colleges and universities. The youth of the country have therefore had greater opportunity and encouragement to be educated for some aspect of private administration than for public administration. Scattered throughout the land are many business and commercial schools and colleges. On the campuses of most of the larger universities, large and imposing schools of business administration are to be found. By comparison, the amount of money and ability devoted to public administration is insignificant; as a people we have been rewarded in proportion, for we find private business richly endowed with many men and women of administrative talent, whereas public business, such as schools, government, and social-service agencies, is not so fortunate.

PUBLIC ADMINISTRATION NOW OF GROWING IMPORTANCE

But within the last quarter century there has been a change. Government from the local to the world level has begun to engage in an ever wider range of constructive activities, each of which requires organization and administration. Public health, education, and agricultural and industrial services have been expanded. Public corporations, such as the

Tennessee Valley Authority and many others, have come into being. The place in our community life of social-service agencies and activities has also become enlarged. Critical national and world conditions have concentrated public attention on the need for high levels of ability in governmental positions and have found us lacking in men and women educated to lead in activities at the world level. Within recent years a number of new schools and institutes of public administration have been added to the pitiably few already in existence. New organizations for the study of public affairs and world politics are being created, and new courses of advanced study able to deal with problems of public enterprises are being developed. It looks as if that part of the people's business that the public decides it will organize and operate for and by itself is to be given more attention, and that youth will have more opportunity for the advanced professional education needed in the organization and administration of such activities. This is a tardy recognition of a public need that has long been felt in this country but did not become acute until the depression of the 1930's. The opportunities available to those who enter activities requiring ability and training in the administration of public enterprises may perhaps be more fully appreciated by us all and be more fully taken advantage of by young people seeking life careers. Salaries, of course, lag, and will continue to lag, behind those paid to administrators of private enterprises, but there are offsetting advantages, so that the differential may not penalize public enterprise in the future as much as it has in the past.

EDUCATIONAL ADMINISTRATION MOST COMMON
TYPE OF PUBLIC ADMINISTRATION

The early commitment of this country to public education, coupled with the proliferation of schools as a result of westward expansion and a rising standard of living, has made educational administration one of our most rapidly developing and most widely practiced types of public administration. Educational administration did not, of course, spring into a full-fledged profession in this country overnight. Nevertheless, as schools increased in number and size at a rapid rate, so did the profession of educational administration. High school principals or "headmasters" who were heads of schools and assigned a degree of administrative responsibility and authority have existed from the last half of the eighteenth century. The first city school superintendencies were created in Buffalo, New York, and Louisville, Kentucky, in the year 1837. We had in 1951–1952, 20,716 elementary school principals, 13,242 high school principals, 25,215 superintendents of schools and professional assistants in all types of districts, and 3,623 professional workers in state school offices, not to mention a growing number of other assistants to those who help with the processes of school organization and administration. [3]

More people "work for the government" in educational enterprises than in any other one type of activity except the military service. This, coupled with the fact that education in the United States is so largely organized on a local basis, means that more people are needed in its administration than in any other single type of public administration. As education was one of the earliest kinds of positive, constructive governmental activity widely carried on by governments in the United States, it is only natural that educational administration should be one of the few types of public administration recognized as such and practiced throughout the country.

The same reasoning accounts for the fact that "schools of education," each with its courses of study leading to educational administration, constitute, on many campuses, the only type of professional education offered, with its use in public administration as the primary reason for providing it. The schools of law, medicine, business, and engineering, for example, have chiefly had private enterprise and its needs for administrative ability in mind, and have considered entirely as a by-product the satisfaction of any need by public enterprise for their particular types of administrative services.

In some respects this situation has had an unfortunate effect upon education for educational administration. As almost the only form of professional education for public administration offered on the campus, it has developed its courses with its eye fixed only upon administration in education—and even in public schools—without giving any attention to the common interests and activities of those who engage in other types of public administration. The school of education has not generally taken any advantage of the fact that some of the professors in the schools of business and law could have contributed something about administration in other types of business or professional activity that would have been a valuable addition to the professional equipment of their students of educational administration.

In fairness to the faculties of schools of education, however, it should probably be said that had they seen this need for the larger view of administration, and had they sought to integrate the basic courses offered students interested in administration as a career, neither their view nor their interest would have been shared by their colleagues in the other professional schools. As a result, professional preparation for educational administration has been inbred, paying almost no attention to

[3] Data derived from U.S. Office of Education, *Biennial Survey of Education in the United States, 1950–52, Statistical Summary of Education, 1951–52* (Washington, D.C.: Government Printing Office, 1954), Chap. 2, Tables, 2, 3, 6.

any common interests, abilities, duties, and points of view that ought to be the property of all who administer institutions and enterprises, both public and private, in this country. This narrow view harms education and educational administration, as well as the country as a whole, and ought to be abandoned in favor of a kind of basic professional education for administration as a life career; on top of this, special types of courses designed to provide the kinds of administrative competence required in particular kinds of situations in public and private administration should be provided. Since such a plan seems unlikely to be adopted in any near future, about the best we can do now is to see that in courses in educational administration offered in schools of education, and in texts written for use in these courses, more effort be made to relate educational administration to the profession of administration generally. There are hopeful indications that some progress in this line is being made as students of school administration draw more heavily on the research and experience in the total field of organization and administration. When this is done, educational administrators will have a broader point of view and a broader base of experience with administration, as a result of taking courses in educational administration, than is now generally the case.

The High School Principalship as a Specialized Type of Educational Administration

The high school principalship represents a specialized kind of educational administration. The general pattern of organization of education the world over calls for a secondary school to be attended by at least some pupils who have completed the elementary school. In this country the high school is a secondary school only in the sense that it is the second level of education offered to the children and youth of this country. In theory and law it is as open to all as is the elementary school. This condition makes the professional responsibility of the high school principal more difficult, and, in the judgment of the authors, more important than if the high school were a selective secondary school. It also makes the position more akin to the elementary school principalship than would be the case if the high school were a selective institution.

The school principalship, whether elementary or secondary, is perhaps the most important administrative position in our school system. This statement assumes that the purpose of educational administration is to organize and manage the education of pupils, that this process will be centered in what we call schools, and that someone (the principal) will be in charge in each school who will work under the *general* direction of the superintendent's office. The most important element in the job of educating pupils is the quality of teaching service provided. The next most important element is the quality of administrative service provided in the school. No amount or quality of administrative service provided elsewhere in the school system—at the city superintendent's office, in the county superintendent's office, or in the state department of education— can make up for its lack at the level of the school principalship. This is the point at which administrative service actually goes into action to facilitate the work of teachers with children, and unless the person immediately in charge of the enterprise is professionally competent, a poorer result will be obtained than could have been achieved under wise direction. As in a military operation, where the achievements of the carefully laid plans of the over-all command depend, in the final analysis, upon the competence of the men on the line—each of whom is in charge of a relatively small group of men, and each of whom is able to lead his group to the attainment of its particular objective—just so in a school system, the success of the program hinges upon competent leadership and direction in the school where that program actually is to be carried out. As in industry, where the success of an enterprise depends upon the ability to organize and manage possessed by those in the plant who are in direct charge at the points where skilled workmen come into contact with raw and unfinished materials, so in an educational system the school principal is the difference between outstanding and mediocre results. This is true of all schools, both elementary and secondary, but it is especially true of the high school principalship, where, despite the existence of many small high schools, the principal is often in charge at the point at which a relatively large and complex operation is under way.

NO SUCCESSFUL SUBSTITUTE FOR GOOD PRINCIPALS

Nevertheless, the fact is that many high school principalships are held by persons with almost no special professional training for the position. Boards of education and superintendents of schools have either failed to sense the folly of staffing the front line with weak officers or have trusted too much to hoped-for strength in and around the superintendent's office to offset weakness in the high school principalship. Such principals have then learned by practicing on their schools, which have suffered much through mistakes that could have been avoided if the principals had had more adequate professional training in educational administration. Where incompetent principals have not tried to overcome their faults, or where their efforts have not been successful, some superintendents have gradually withdrawn responsibility and authority for the school from the principal, leaving him in charge of a few clerical routines.

Thus, in some situations, assistant superintendents in charge of high schools and directors and supervisors of various fields and activities directly responsible to the superintendent's office are permitted to enter a high school to organize and manage various aspects of the program. If a superintendent of schools were charged with having done this, he would either deny the charge or would defend himself by saying that he had tried to get the high school principal to take responsibility and authority without success and so had been reduced to the necessity of adopting this plan of bypassing the principal. In many school systems this process of undermining the high school principalship is under way, even though it is not a matter of stated policy and even though it is denied. One has only to observe how many city school systems are organized and to watch their operations to know that, in fact, the authority for what goes on in a high school is being so dissipated among numerous individuals that it is impossible to fix responsibility. Any scheme of organization that fails definitely to assign responsibility and to delegate authority may succeed over a short period but is destined to wind up in confused and hopeless failure. There is no successful alternative to competence in the high school principal's office.

GOOD HIGH SCHOOL ADMINISTRATION
MOST URGENTLY NEEDED

Never before has it been so important that those who organize and administer secondary education in the United States have the highest degrees of professional competence. Changes in social and economic conditions have increased the pressure on conventional secondary education and schools. An institution under pressure always needs daring and farsighted leadership. Many high schools in the United States have had such leadership and are changing their philosophy and their practices and procedures. Many have resisted change, and many, in making changes, have floundered about to a greater extent than seems necessary. High school principals and students of secondary school administration who aspire to become principals need a more highly specialized and at the same time a more comprehensive professional education than ever before. Part of this needed education can come from individual reading and study on the job. Part can come from an open-minded study of social, economic, and political trends in our country and the world today, and of their meanings in terms of education for American youth and its organization and administration. Part can come from association with other wide-awake citizens engaged in other types of important works, and from association with other high school administrators in conferences, forums, discussion groups, and workshops where there is open, free, and unhampered consideration of problems of American life and education. Local, state, and national associations need to be active in furthering such activities. A part of this education, especially for younger and less experienced members of the profession, can come from more formal study in colleges and universities.

The high school principal, as has been pointed out in this chapter, needs a more broadly based professional competence than has been required of him in the past. Assuming that he is a kind of practicing social scientist, his professional education needs to help him to be a keen student of the society in which his school functions. Above all, he must be sensitive and alive to the goals and purposes sought by our democratic society and to the role of education and of the school in helping such a society achieve its purposes. He must know what learning is, what a democratic society wants and needs to have all its youths learn. He must know how to get learning to occur in the maximum amounts in unselected student bodies. And, of course, his professional education must help him to be a competent administrator—he must know a great deal more about the techniques and practices of organization and administration as it is practiced in and out of education than his general experience can have provided. He can be a good educator by being an advanced student of his life and times, of education and its place in our society, and of the psychology of learning; but if, in addition, he is to be an educational administrator, then he must be able to apply to education the principles and practices of organization and administration.

The readers of this book will find implicit in what is said about the high school, and the principal's work in it, an effort to look at each aspect from the points of view of society, education, and administration —to encourage and enable the principal to see with the eyes of the social scientist, the educational psychologist, and the administrator. The points of view, policies, and practices proposed seem to the authors to be approved by high school principals who may be said to be social scientists and educational psychologists as well as administrators. Thus Part One tries to create a feeling for the social setting of school administration. The succeeding parts of the book and various chapters in them stress one or more of these aspects, depending on what part of the work of the school they discuss. The fact that educational administrators are constantly absorbed in situations that involve working with other people and developing and maintaining good working relations with people accounts for the emphasis on personnel problems in three major sections of the book. Even Part Five, dealing with the management of the school plant, stresses the importance of good group relationships among those who care for and use it. The central importance of the principal's work as leader in efforts to evaluate and improve the school's educational program accounts for Part Three being the longest of the book's six parts. Parts Three and Four, in which the school's program and those administrative practices most directly related to it are under consideration, make up approximately half the entire book.

In the final analysis, however, being expert as an administrator is of major importance. Without destroying the case that they have attempted to develop for the high school principal's bringing to his position the skills of the social scientist and the educator, the authors can point out that the principalship is essentially a "doing" job. Unless a principal is effective in helping a community, the faculty, and the students bring into being a high school in which the fine concepts that his ability as a social scientist and an educator has helped them visualize and desire, he has failed in the most important aspect of the position.

Good organization and administration is usually the difference between a high school that means well and one that does well. Administration may be compared to a lens that brings everything about the school into focus for community, faculty, and students. If it is a poor lens, the image is fuzzy and obscure, and no one in the school or community gets a clear picture of what the school is trying to do. If it is a good lens, the school becomes a clear-cut and vivid projection of the ideals and ideas that all hoped to bring into being.

Some Points to Consider

1. Many people, including the authors of this book, think that school administration now has many of the weaknesses of business administration. What is to be gained, then, by proposing, as this chapter does, that students of school administration should know more about nonschool organization and administration?

2. Can you name a piece of work for which a high school principal is usually responsible in which he shows good or poor ability to organize?

3. What are some of the weaknesses in school organization and administration that begin to appear as the size and complexity of schools increase?

4. Should a high school principal receive more salary than a teacher in that school? Why? Under what conditions?

5. What do doctors call an unprofessional member of their profession? lawyers? school executives? What weakness does the lack of an equivalent term for unprofessional school executives indicate?

6. Take some task usually performed by high school principals and break it down into aspects that are principally organizational and others that are principally administrative in character.

7. In the United States, should the standards for deciding on expertness in private (business) administration be different from those for deciding on expertness in public administration?

8. What does the word "policy" mean as used by executives? What purposes do policies serve in school administration?

9. What is the difference between a policy and a practice in school administration? How are they related? Illustrate.

Further Reading

Burnham, James. *Managerial Revolution.* New York: John Day Co., Inc., 1941.

Chase, Stuart. *Democracy under Pressure.* New York: Twentieth Century Fund, 1945.

Donham, Wallace B. *Education for Responsible Living.* Cambridge, Mass.: Harvard University Press, 1944.

Gulick, Luther, and Lyndall Urwick, eds. *Papers on the Science of Administration.* New York: Institute of Public Administration, Columbia University, 1937.

Koopman, G. L., Alice Miel, and P. J. Misner. *Democracy in School Administration.* New York: Appleton-Century-Crofts, Inc., 1943. Chaps. 1, 2, 3.

Lynch, Douglas C. *Leading and Managing Men.* New York: The Ronald Press Co., 1950.

Miller, Van, ed., National Conference of Professors of Educational Administration. *Providing and Improving Administrative Leadership for America's Schools.* Fourth Report; New York: Bureau of Publications, Teachers College, Columbia University, 1951.

————, and Willard B. Spalding. *The Public Administration of American Schools.* Yonkers, N.Y.: World Book Company, 1952. Chap. 21.

Moehlman, Arthur B. *School Administration.* 2nd ed.; Boston: Houghton Mifflin Company, 1951. Parts I, II.

National Society for the Study of Education. *Changing Conception in Educational Administration.* Forty-fifth Yearbook; Chicago: University of Chicago Press, 1946. Chap. 1.

Newlon, Jesse H. *Educational Administration a Social Policy.* New York: Charles Scribner's Sons, 1934. Chaps. 10, 11.

Shane, Harold, and Wilbur A. Yauch. *Creative School Administration.* New York: Henry Holt & Co., Inc., 1954.

Stryker, Perrin. "Who Is an Executive?" *Fortune Magazine,* 52 (Dec., 1955), 107.

Tompkins, Ellsworth, and Galen Jones. *Keystones of Good Internal Administration.* U.S. Office of Education, Misc. No. 20; Washington, D.C.: Government Printing Office, 1955.

Chapter 2

LOCAL, STATE, AND FEDERAL PARTICIPATION IN YOUTH EDUCATION

As THE RESPONSIBLE HEAD of a high school, the principal finds himself both aided and restricted because he operates within a framework of secondary school organization that extends from the federal government in Washington to his state government in the capital city and into the local school system. Whatever his plans are for this high school or whatever the desires of the local community with respect to its high school are, they will have to be realized within the possibilities of a national, state, and local framework of relationships.

Presumably this framework of organization has been developed as a means of assisting high schools to do the work of educating American youth. But in an expanding and developing situation the existing organization always needs to be evaluated, and probably to be changed, if it is to be most effective in helping schools perform their tasks. This chapter will examine the existing organizational framework within which American high schools operate, approaching the problem so that students of secondary school administration may be intelligently and constructively critical of this organization and thus be prepared to work within it and to improve it.

Background of the Present Situation

The three levels of general government in the United States are reflected in our educational organization. The federal and state levels are rather easily discernible, both in general and in school government. The local level is less sharply defined, for we have a variety of "local" school governments: county, township, city, and special districts. The Bureau of the Census reports that in 1954 there were 59,631 independent school districts and 2,409 school systems administered by county and municipal governments or a total 62,040 local government school units.[1] These

[1] Department of Commerce, Bureau of the Census, *School Districts in the United States in 1954* (State and Local Government Special Studies, No. 40; Washington, D.C.: The Bureau, 1955).

many local government school units present enormous variations. There may be some disagreement about the proper function of the federal and state levels in education, but at least we know what each level is. At the "local" school level, however, we have county, city, town or village, township, and unified, central, or consolidated districts. Local school units may exist to operate a one-room school for a few pupils or a city system serving thousands of pupils. The county may operate as a complete local administrative unit, as a secondary type of intermediate local unit providing certain supervisory and special services to subsidiary local units, or continue as a vestigial unit of educational organization after practically all of its territory has been reorganized into independent local districts.

Unified, central, or consolidated districts may be organized in an area to administer only a high school. Hence in that area local school government is carried on by two or more boards of education: one for the high school and one or more for the elementary schools. The present chaotic situation, both in local general and in local school government, calls for drastic reorganization to eliminate small and unnecessary administrative units and to consolidate functions. Both economy and increased efficiency could result from such a movement. While much reorganization of local administrative units has taken place in recent years, much remains to be done. Modern means of communication have enlarged the scope of the term "local" so that today much more area and many more people are included in what is a local community than were included a few decades ago. A reorganization of the administrative units of local government that took this into account would reduce the number and variety of such units and give us a more practical and functional concept of the term "local" school government.

LOCAL SCHOOL GOVERNMENT AND LOCAL
GENERAL GOVERNMENT

Experts in municipal government have recognized this need and have been active proponents of the reorganization of local government. Among the changes some of them have proposed is the abolition of the school district as something apart from the local unit of general government. Under this plan the local unit of general government would also administer the schools. The functions of the board of education would be absorbed by the local board of commissioners or by the city council, and the head of the local schools would become the head of a department of local government as the heads of the park, fire, or police departments now are. The municipal government experts can make a fairly logical case for such a plan if one overlooks or agrees to waive the fact that education in this country has always been regarded as a function of the state governments, and that therefore a local board of education is in reality part of the state government and not a division of the general local government. As will be shown later in this chapter, we have developed a tradition of education as a state function. Also a strong case can be made that education has a unique function to perform and as such should be organized and administered independently of other governmental units. Only when we abandon this theory of education as a function of the state, and repeal the constitutional enactments supporting it in the several states, can we logically make the local school administration a department of local school government. In time the people could, of course, decide to make such a change, but until they do and until we have many more examples of highly professionalized municipal government to compare with the many examples of professionalized local school government, school executives will continue to consider that the best interests of public education are better served where the local school administration is free and independent of local general government. In the meantime, however, it would be good policy to reduce the number of small, overlapping, and unnecessary local units of school administration to the number now needed in each state to provide for the effective and economical operation of the schools of the state. Thus the opponents of the local independence of schools would be deprived of one of their most cogent arguments in favor of consolidating the local school unit of government with general local government.

This tradition of education as a peculiar responsibility of the governments of our states, usually discharged by authorizing local boards of education to organize and conduct schools, is not one, however, that is confirmed by the facts concerning the founding of schools in this country. As a matter of history, there were local schools in the colonies and early states before there were colonial or state systems of education of which they could be a part. The tradition is one that has been carefully nurtured by those who believed strongly in public education and who took advantage of the provisions of the federal constitution and of the Supreme Court's interpretations of it to build a theory and a supporting body of state law upon which now rests the tradition of education as a function of the government of our states. As intelligent students of school organization and administration we all now support the tradition of education as a function of the state; yet we need to see this modern theory in the light of historical fact if we are to keep our balance when confronted with the arguments over the proper relationships and responsibilities of local, state, and federal government in the field of education.

In early colonial days, education was generally regarded as a matter of family and church concern rather than a matter with which government—either at the colonial (state) or local level—was to be concerned. The earliest "local" schools were local in the sense that they served some of the families of a locality or the members of a particular church, but they were not "local" in the sense of being part of the local town government. They were not required to be established by the colonial legislature nor to be authorized by it or the town governments. Later, when largely at the instance of church leaders—who feared the effects of ignorance—parents were required by action of colonial legislatures to see that their children (including children apprenticed to them) could read and write, it was still not required that public schools be established or that children attend them. All that was specified was that parents or adults responsible for children were ordered to teach them or have them taught. Churches or private individuals sometimes performed the task for fees. Masters sometimes taught their young apprentices. Sometimes groups of families set up a school on a cooperative basis. Newton Edwards and Herman G. Richey comment on this slow recognition of education as a proper function of government as follows:

> Corresponding stages in the progress toward acceptance of the idea of universal education supported by a tax on all property were reached at widely varying times in the different states and regions, but everywhere the movement was slow. Certain states moved more rapidly than others, but differences between states with respect to this development were perhaps no greater than differences found between communities within a single state. Educational historians have professed to see the origins of free schools in the legislation enacted in Massachusetts in the fourth and fifth decades of the seventeenth century—a series of laws which provided that the cost of government and church should be met by a tax upon the inhabitants according to their means (1638); that children should be taught to read (1642); and that towns of fifty householders should provide a teacher of reading and writing and towns of a hundred householders should maintain a grammar school to fit youth for the university (1647). It should be noted, however, that the idea of taxing wealth for the support of church and state was not new; that the purpose of the law of 1638 was to compel all inhabitants to support the Puritan church; that schools were not contemplated under the law of 1642; that the law of 1647 did not require tax support for schools; and that no legislation of the period was based on the assumption that education should be provided freely to the children of parents who were able to pay.
>
> The claims put forth that the right to tax for the support of schools open without charge to rich and poor alike and that the several other principles upon which the present free, compulsory, and secular systems of education rest sprang from acts of the General Court of Massachusetts acting for the Puritan church, even though they may have a small measure of validity, have tended to obscure the fact that these principles evolved slowly and painfully, and were only recognized and accepted in much later times. Outside Massachusetts, and perhaps one or two other New England states, the principle of public support

of education through taxation was rejected during the first half-century of the national period.[2]

So it can be seen that not only were early schools on this continent not established as part of a system of state (colonial) education, but not even as part of the well-recognized responsibility of local government. Rather the general feeling was that education was a family responsibility. If it were to concern anyone beyond the family it was the church rather than the government. The church, at least in New England, was partly responsible for getting government into the business of education because church leaders believed that thus some families whom the moral suasion of the church could not induce to educate their children would be compelled by the government to do so. Also it can be seen that the colonial legislation in Massachusetts, which required towns with fifty householders to provide a teacher of reading and writing and those of one hundred householders to maintain a grammar school to fit youth for the university, did not necessarily require that there be a local public school or that it be under the control or at the expense of local government. Some of these towns chose, however, to meet the requirements of this law by establishing town schools supported by local taxation. So we have here historical bases for the claims of present-day proponents of (1) local autonomy in education, (2) schools as a part of local general government, and (3) colonial (state) responsibility for education. We do not have clean-cut historical precedent exclusively for any one of these points of view. Our present sound tradition of education as a responsibility of the state has been developed by those who saw the importance of education in a democratic society in spite of historical precedent as well as on account of it. It was also developed under the influence of the "residual powers" interpretation of the Constitution. Convinced that public education was a matter of great social importance in our representative democracy, many of those most interested in education did not propose that it be left wholly to the decision of the family, to the discretion of the local community, or to the philanthropy of any or all churches. Supported by the popular theory of "residual powers," the largest and best units of government to which they could turn were those of the states. Thus fortunately we have developed the tradition of education as a recognized governmental activity that is chiefly a responsibility of the forty-eight states.

The early tendency not to regard education as a matter for governmental action is further illustrated by the fact that public education is

[2] Newton Edwards and Herman G. Richey, *The School in the American Social Order* (Boston: Houghton Mifflin Company, 1947), pp. 362–363. Reprinted by permission of the publishers.

not provided for in the federal Constitution. There were those in the Constitutional Convention who favored some provision for public education, but their influence and their concern were not great enough to put provisions for public education into the Constitution. Subsequently, it has been reasoned that the convention intended to leave education to the states. However, in other matters that they considered of great importance, positive action that assigned the matter either to the federal government or to the states was taken. Only because of the general provision that what was not specifically assigned to the federal government belonged to the states does education as a state responsibility become a constitutional fact. One might say, therefore, that by omission rather than by intention were we later able to expound the theory that education was a responsibility and function of state government and to begin building state systems of education.

THE DEVELOPMENT OF STATE SYSTEMS OF SCHOOLS

We have developed the theory that there should not be a federal system of schools and that we should not have federal control of schools except in areas where there is nothing corresponding to the state level of government to carry the responsibility. An equally logical deduction from the legal fact of state responsibility for schools is that local government does not have the responsibility for education. Under the theory of state responsibility neither the federal nor the local levels of government can or should bear any responsibility for education except that which the states may want them to carry. It has been popular in this country to decry federal control of schools and to elaborate on the wisdom of concentrating responsibility for education at the state level. It has not been so popular to argue that since education is a state function, local general governments ought not to exercise control over local schools, or that local boards of education and local school executives were in reality agents of the state enjoying only such freedom and independence as the state saw fit to provide for. The logic of the argument is, however, irrefutable.

When men like Horace Mann undertook to implement the theory of education as a responsibility of the state by creating state school systems, they ran head on into opposition from proponents of local autonomy for schools. For a hundred years and more along the eastern seaboard, local schools had generally operated under the control of local groups—the town, the church, or private owners. In the more westerly states the provisions for public school lands administered by the state laid the foundation for the functioning of the states in education. Yet, as a matter of actual fact, local schools enjoyed such a measure of unrestricted freedom that they did not relish the creation of the strong state departments of education that were a corollary to the theory of education as a responsibility of the states. Many states, therefore, have not even yet developed the well-rounded systems of public education that our constitutional theories make possible and that the importance of educating all children and youth in a democratic society makes necessary.

PRESENT ORGANIZATION A STAGE IN A CONTINUING PROCESS

It is evident that the present organization of education in this country does not represent the culmination of a well-conceived plan for handling federal, state, and local relations in education. Rather, it is the result of the last series of compromises among powerful forces with interests in education. In the process of reaching the present stage we have, however, developed a strong tradition—education as a function of the state—which even the federal government needs to respect. In World War II, when the emergency could have been used to break that tradition, the federal government decided to use the existing schools and the state-local chain of relationships as a means of training workers in war industries instead of setting up special federal centers for that training. It is not so clear that the responsibility of the state in education, as opposed to the local level of government, has been established, but the probabilities are that circumstances will cause us to decide to develop more well-rounded and coordinated state school systems rather than the host of independent uncoordinated systems that is the probable alternative if education is not clearly recognized as a responsibility and hence a function of the state level of government.

Students of high school administration, however, need to examine our present organizational patterns in education, not so much to determine whether they conform to previously approved ideas of what these patterns and relationships should be, as to determine to what degree these patterns promise to be effective in helping this country to provide the adequate and appropriate educational opportunity for each youth, a goal that all agree is not only desirable but essential. Students in this field need to analyze the events of the present and to appraise them as the modern offshoots of conditions, pressures, and movements long at work in our society. They need to have thought their way through to an educational philosophy that gives them a sense of direction and helps them to decide what positions to take on issues involving federal, state, and local relationships in the face of present conditions and those with which the future is likely to confront us.

CURRENT CONFUSIONS AND CONTRADICTIONS

The crux of the present ambiguous situation can be studied best, perhaps, if we regard it as an issue between those who, on the one hand, favor centralizing the responsibility for and authority over education at the federal and state levels, or at either, and those who, on the other hand, favor decentralizing this responsibility and authority and placing it in the hands of the local school units. In actual fact, the situation is not as clear-cut or simple as this. There are few, if any, school executives who favor centralization over education at the federal level. There are few, if any, who favor a high degree of centralization at the state level. Nor are there any who favor complete decentralization to the local level with no responsibility or authority left at either the state or federal level. No proponent of local control, for example, would argue that the states should not pass compulsory attendance laws and that this matter should be left to action by the local district. Nor would any proponent of state control in education argue that the enforcement of state attendance laws should be taken away from local districts and placed in the hands of a state enforcement agency. Yet the arguments often used in supporting or opposing federal and state financial aid or school consolidation, for example, if carried to their logical conclusion, would mean that we must accept either complete centralization or complete decentralization. The proponents of state action speak as if no good could come out of Nazareth, and the proponents of local schools cry out against "encroachment" of the state on their rights. Each makes his own point of view an unmitigated virtue and makes the position of the other wholly evil. Is the present chain of federal, state, and local relationships in education something that should be broken in order that responsibility may be completely centralized or decentralized? Or is it something to be preserved and improved upon by intelligent action so that the best possible organization of education is developed? If the answer to the first of these questions is in the affirmative, then we have to decide whether to centralize or to decentralize, at the same time developing a new organization of education that implements our decision. If the answer to the second question is in the affirmative, then we need to examine the present relationships to see if the best distribution of responsibility and authority is provided, and if not, then what changes should be made.

Students of youth education and high school administration should study this problem carefully and decide whether they think education should move toward or away from centralization, and what should be centralized or decentralized, and when, because their collective decisions will have a most profound effect on the development of youth education. These decisions, in fact, will affect all education, but the necessary variety, scope, and costs of education for older youth make it especially important that wise decisions on these points be reached and appropriate plans and programs developed. The basic positions held by the proponents of each group will therefore be examined in terms of their implications for the education of youth.

THE LOCAL AUTONOMY POINT OF VIEW

It is not necessary for those holding this point of view to deny that the nation and state have deep interests in education. In fact, they *claim* that such is the case. But, they argue, these interests are best furthered when each local school is free from any state or federal control. The concern of parents for their own children is greater than that of the general public for all children; hence if the parents whose children attend each particular school are free to do as they think best about the education of those children, all children will be better educated by and large than would otherwise be the case. "Home rule" in education is therefore the best rule. Education should be kept "close to the people."

Throughout most of our history, local schools have been relatively free; consequently present tendencies for the federal and state governments to exert any pressure on them are regarded as "encroachment" on the "rights" of local schools. Such actions, it is argued, usually restrict "local initiative" in education and thus tend to keep schools from developing the variety of programs that has been one of the most worthwhile features of American education. The advocates of local autonomy point to evidence that "adaptability," or the tendency and capacity of a school to change, is best where schools are free to exercise their local initiative. The ideal situation, therefore, exists where education is left entirely free to be developed in each locality as the parents of that locality see fit. This ideal situation being impossible, the state and federal governments should take as little action in education as possible, leaving to local schools all the freedom and initiative that can be bestowed upon them.

This leads to a compromise wherein it is held that the state governments should concern themselves with the setting of "minimum standards" below which no local school will be allowed to go, and to attain which the state or federal government may "assist" a local district if necessary. For instance, the minimum qualifications for a teaching certificate may be set by the state, no public school being permitted to employ teachers who do not hold state certificates. If a local school is financially unable to employ an adequate number of such teachers, the state may assist it to do so. It is claimed that it would be the rare community that, given freedom, would exercise its initiative to operate a poor or cheap school, but to meet the emergency that might occasionally develop, the state should have authority to compel compliance. Usually the state's action would be made necessary by lack of financial ability to meet the minimum standards—not by lack of willingness. Thus we find an application of the theory that, the least government is the best government, although state and federal actions are allowed to concern themselves with minimum standards.

LOCAL AUTONOMY AND STATE AND FEDERAL AID

In the face of obvious inequality of financial resources among local schools in a state and among the local schools of one state as compared with those of another, equalizing federal and state financial aid to schools is accepted as essential by those who believe in local autonomy for education. The fact that any aid required to be given by a rich state or district to a poorer one actually interferes to that degree with its freedom to develop its own schools as it may wish is ignored in the general interest, but in order to respect as far as possible the theory of local autonomy it is argued that this aid should come to the schools with "no strings," or at least as few as possible, tied to it. Thus the value of having each local school able to do as it pleases about its program is protected to some extent. An extension of this line of reasoning brings us to the proposition that any federal or state money should not be earmarked for any special purpose such as vocational or health education. Rather it should be a free grant to the local school to be used by it as it thinks best. Actually, if federal or state money is appropriated for education in general, it is earmarked for education as opposed to good roads or soil conservation, for example, but the objection to earmarking is not carried this far.

Thus by carefully hedging state and federal action in the field of education all the benefits that may be derived from it are thought to be attained for the local schools with the minimum loss of freedom for local initiative in education.

Basically the proponents of this point of view hold to a political philosophy derived from Rousseau. All government, at least above the local, face-to-face level, is a necessary evil: the least governed are the best governed; weak central governments are desirable because more democratic small local units of governments are better than larger, non-local units. They conceive of federal and state government as necessarily that of the police state—autocratic, bureaucratic, and restrictive. The virtue that they see in local autonomy for schools reflects only a part of a whole political philosophy. If they are consistent, they favor local-ism not only in school government but in all government.

THE STATE RESPONSIBILITY POINT OF VIEW

The proponents of the second alternative stated in preceding sections of this chapter believe that education, and especially youth education, will be best provided when the principal responsibility for its organization is borne by the state, with the federal and local levels of government playing auxiliary roles. There should be a planned, defi-nite distribution of responsibility among the three levels, with an appro-

priate and proportionate authority to act, but, since in this country education is recognized as a responsibility and hence as a function of state
government, the states should play the leading roles. The advocates of
state responsibility therefore hold that local schools should not be autonomous but should enjoy only the freedom the state recognizes to be
necessary to the development of a good state program.

The members of this group are often accused by those in the "local"
camp of being autocratic, undemocratic opponents of popular government, who obviously have no faith in the people and want to take the
schools away from them. The rejoinder to this accusation usually is that
the people act through the state and federal government just as they do
through local governments, and that to locate a governmental power
with these larger units is not taking it away from the people. It is also
claimed that local control, home rule, or local initiative is not opposed
in principle, but that the purposes of popular government will be best
achieved when this local initiative is exercised in the light of clearly
expressed national and state concerns for education.

Just as there are no proponents of local autonomy in education who
deny to the federal and state governments any responsibility or authority
in education, so there are no proponents of the opposing philosophy
who deny to the local level of government all power over education.
No one in the latter group wants a completely centralized system of
education either at the state or the national level. No one wants a
completely nationalized system of schools. But between the two groups
there is a real disagreement as to how much responsibility for education
should be placed in the lower and higher levels of government. We are
not dealing with a situation in which the difference in degree of control
is so little that it makes no difference which point of view prevails. The
difference between the freezing and the boiling point of water is only a
matter of the degree of temperature, but no one claims that there is not
a real difference. The difference between local autonomy and state responsibility in education is only a matter of the degree of responsibility
to be borne by the various levels, but no one can say that it makes no
real difference which point of view eventually becomes accepted as
standard practice in American youth education.

STATE RESPONSIBILITY AND FEDERAL INTERESTS IN EDUCATION

Those who advocate greater state responsibility for education do
not deny to the federal government a deep interest in education. If
anything, they tend to accept more easily than does the local autonomy
group the tendency for the federal government to become increasingly
active in the field of education. The trend of events seems to show how

important education can be to the safety and welfare of a people. It is to be expected, therefore, that the people's government will be concerned to see that good education is provided. As conditions make it increasingly evident that education is indispensable to national existence and welfare, the federal government may be expected to take more frequent and more positive action with respect to education. The educational provisions of the "G.I. Bills" may be the forerunner of a continuous recognition of the need for federal support and encouragement of the education of older youth. In any situation except that of dire national emergency, the advocates of state responsibility expect the federal government to be able fully to protect its interests by helping the state systems of education to do their job well. They claim that if federal assistance is continuous and ample, the need for resorting to any other way of organizing education in the United States will become less and less likely.

Those who urge greater state responsibility readily accept the need for a strong federal Office of Education as the agency of the federal government in education. They are not satisfied with simply a passive service role on the part of this office that would confine itself to research and exhortation. This office should, of course, collect statistics and do research work. It should interpret the results of research to the workers in education everywhere. Its officers should discuss with state and local school groups new techniques for the improvement of education. But the interests of the nation in education are fully protected and advanced only when the Office of Education plays an active and constructive part in helping the states so to organize their programs as to promote national interests and welfare through education. For instance, when it seemed to some in 1946 that it was time to develop a better program of "life adjustment education," the Office of Education could have been content with taking a position of "willingness" to help if and when the chief state school officers wanted such a program pushed. It could have been content with conducting some research to show a need, and perhaps suggesting to the states that they consider such a program. Actually, the Office of Education did all this, but it went further and took the initiative. After conferring with the chief state school officers, it called regional and national conferences of all the groups with interests in youth education, and at these conferences the need and the ways of meeting it on a national level were discussed and acted upon. The result was a more immediate, a better-integrated, and a more positive action on the program than could otherwise have been secured. The theory of the responsibility of the states for education was not violated by these actions of the Office of Education but the "leadership" function of the federal level of government was raised to what we have called above "an active, constructive" level.

The White House Conference on Education program initiated in 1954 by the federal government, whatever may be the ultimate outcome of the undertaking, illustrates recognition of the fact that the national government inevitably must be concerned over the future development of education throughout the country. Neither would it be violating the principle of education as a function of the states if the federal government were to invest much larger sums in research and other active leadership functions of the U.S. Office of Education. Certainly there are other areas of endeavor, such as agriculture, where the national government has invested large sums in research and related activities independent of any attempt to control operations in the field. Only in the field of education have we apparently extended the principle of nonfederal control to the point of almost questioning any but the most minimum of federal activities and expenditures.

Those who advocate state responsibility accept the fact that education under the federal Constitution is a function of the states, whether or not it was the intent of the founding fathers. The fact that education is, under the Constitution, a function of the states does not mean, however, that the federal government must wash its hands of all responsibility for or interest in education. It means only that the federal government is committed to the policy of recognizing the state governments as the proper points for its contact with education throughout the country and as its proper agencies of action in education. It also means that the federal government is prevented from establishing its own set of public schools and from dealing directly with local schools in matters of education.

Thus it is clear that adherence to the theory of state responsibility does not mean denial of the nation's interest in education or insistence that the federal government take no action in the field of education. On the contrary, the theory holds that our establishment of state systems of education merely means that the federal government is committed to a policy of protecting and promoting the nation's interests in education through these state systems of education. Moreover, the states, by accepting the responsibility for education, assumed an obligation to the nation. The states do not have the responsibility for education within their boundaries in order that they may be free to conduct programs of education detrimental to the nation as a whole, should they so desire. Instead, they have the obligation to the nation to educate their children and youth well enough to enable them to become not only good citizens of the state, but of the nation as well. Whatever the reasons for leaving education to the states, these state systems were expected to operate in the national interest.

STATE RESPONSIBILITY AND LOCAL SCHOOLS'
INTERESTS IN EDUCATION

Anyone who believes that the states have accepted these responsibilities and obligations in education will find it practically impossible to accept the theory of extreme local autonomy in education. He must, instead, think of the local school as a part of a state system of education and as an instrument through which the state discharges its responsibilities and obligations in education. The local school does have freedom, it does exercise local initiative, and it does have that degree of autonomy necessary for the satisfactory discharge of its share of the state's responsibility for education. The local school works, or should work, within a broad framework of purposes agreed upon by the state. Since communities differ sharply in their needs for education and in their ability to carry out their share of a desirable program, the part each is to play in that program and the help it requires, and how each is to achieve this program, can best be determined by the local educational executives working with a legally constituted local board of education and with the help of local groups interested in education. The concept of the community school as an institution serving children, youth, and adults and adapted to the needs of that particular community is not in conflict with the principle of state responsibility. The state under positive leadership should do all that it can to encourage and support the development of the community school. No one who supports the theory of state responsibility in education is blind enough to think that it means a strait jacket for every local school. If they are aware of the problems of organization and administration they know that such thinking on the part of a school executive would mark him as an administrator who is heedless of the intangibles in his organization—the mind and spirit of all who are working with him. As Gordon R. Clapp has said,

Democratic administration must accept the tendency of the individual to act for a purpose and his desire to exercise his own will in choosing to act or to be idle. It tries to remember that the energy of persons, singly and in groups, is made available to an organized purpose only through the will of the participant.[3]

SETTING STATE STANDARDS

Planning and purposing at the state level will have disappointing results if the state is satisfied to set up only the bare minimum standards

[3] Gordon R. Clapp, "TVA Learns As It Teaches," *Phi Delta Kappan*, 29 (1948), 235.

below which no school can go but which most are expected to exceed if the state is to have a good average program. The state's standards must be high enough so that if they are attained a reasonably adequate program of education for all children and youth will be assured. If public education were a charity, then the voters of a state could legitimately decide how benevolent with the younger generation they wanted to be. But since we know that public education is a sort of insurance that a state takes out on its future security and well-being, then it is shortsighted for it to provide a "minimum" program that is less than it needs or can afford. (If a program is all a state can afford, then it actually is not a minimum program but its maximum program.) In any case, if there is any virtue in taking out a little insurance, there is more virtue in taking out all that is required. And in a nation that has only begun to provide appropriate youth education, or to tax its ability to do so, there can be little reason to be satified with "minimum" state standards.

The argument for the adoption of fully adequate state standards rather than minimum standards rests on the theory that if education is a responsibility of the state, this responsibility is not fully discharged when the state's educational office exercises only a sort of police function over laggard communities, when it exercises merely a custodial, prudential function over the state's educational concerns and activities. This responsibility is adequately discharged only when the state, through its educational office, takes the positive, active, and forward-looking part that enables—and requires where necessary—each local school to do its full share toward meeting the state's need. Since it is unlikely that at any time the standards set by the state represent the ultimate of what can or should be attained, the state authority should be continually at work to improve or raise standards. This in the long run is a type of leadership activity with local communities being encouraged and assisted in improving their educational programs. Standards are not typically raised by fiat, but rather by encouraging individual schools to go beyond the requirements of the moment to a point that a practice becomes sufficiently recognized and accepted and then can become drafted into state standards and at this point made mandatory for the laggard or static school community. The state must concern itself with developing the over-all purposes of the educational program in terms of its need, with outlining the educational program required, with building the state school organization necessary for this program, with determining the costs of providing this program under a good organization that evenly distributes this educational opportunity over the state, and with evaluating the results on a state-wide basis.

All the arguments that support an active interest on the part of the United States Office of Education, because of the nation's interest in education, are even more cogent in support of an active, positive type of work on the part of state offices of education because education is a primary responsibility of state government. To endorse this line of reasoning is not to endorse an arbitrary, dictatorial, undemocratic administration of education, either at the federal or at the state level. It is just as possible to have what we call "democratic" administration at the federal and state levels as at the local level. If we cannot organize and administer the relatively narrow field of public education democratically on the state level, then what hope have we that in the broader, more complex area of general government we shall ever be able to develop satisfactory patterns of democratic action? To lose faith here is to lose hope of achieving democratic organization of our society through our representative form of government.

The authors believe there is no reason to surrender this hope, and so far as education is concerned, hold that the weaknesses now exhibited at the state level are largely the result of our failure fully to recognize the implications of having made education a state function; hence a few states have not accepted or discharged this responsibility adequately. Many states have failed to staff their state departments of education at a level that permits them to operate above a minimum "police" basis. These conditions exist largely because of the insistence of some that local schools should be almost autonomous, unhampered by state action in education. Whatever weaknesses are now exhibited at the state level in education cannot be used as evidence that state action in education is bad for education; they are largely the result of the fact that state officers of education have unconsciously or unwillingly accepted a minimum, regulative function instead of an active, positive, creative function. Even the best of our state departments have operated under these pressures, and although they begin to illustrate at their best what might be done on the state level as they are permitted an enlarged function, still it can be said that we have not yet had a good example of what could be done in education by a state that fully accepted—and was freely permitted by local school leaders to discharge completely—its primary responsibility for education. The present weaknesses in the administration of our state systems of education are not to be regarded as forerunners of the evils that will result if the states really begin to carry out their responsibility for education, but rather as the remaining evidences produced by their failure fully to accept—or to be allowed to accept—their responsibility for education.

SUMMARY: STATE RESPONSIBILITY

Basically, the advocates of greater responsibility for the states in education also support the modern political theory of the "positive" state actively and constructively at work in various fields of human endeavor—agriculture, public health, air safety, radio, commerce, and education, for example—promoting public welfare and well-being. They believe that our people can organize themselves in large units as well as small for the effective satisfaction of group needs. They think that large units of governmental operation need be no less democratic or efficient than small ones, and that modern developments have enlarged geographic and social areas far beyond the physical boundaries of many existing local units the past has bequeathed us. They believe that planning and action in the public interest can and must be carried out on a large-unit basis by the representatives of the people in a democratic society if their institutions and their freedoms are to be preserved and promoted. They hold that public education is one of the most vital of these large group interests because it plays an ever more important part in the life of our nation and is so increasingly necessary to our security and welfare that to leave it almost wholly to the uncoordinated and unorganized activities of thousands of local school districts is to invite disaster. Finally, they hold that it is better policy to recognize some national and large state responsibility, as well as some local responsibility for education, and to provide for a distribution of authority among the three levels, each bearing what appears to be an appropriate share in our modern democratic society when we start from the realistic assumption that we are committed to the principle of education as a function of the government of the forty-eight states. The most fundamental question now is therefore one of what constitutes a sound basis for reaching decisions on a wise redistribution of authority and responsibility for education among the three levels of government.

Applying Knowledge of Organization and Administration to the Situation

Chapter 1 pointed out the differences and the relationships between organization and administration. The term "organization" was shown to apply to activities designed to develop a structure or an organism through which certain desired results or ends could be effectively reached. The term "administration" was shown to apply to activities involved in the operation or functioning of this structure or organism. The point was made that good organization is essential to good administration: that it is difficult and sometimes impossible effectively to administer what has been poorly organized. Experienced executives, therefore, in evaluating an enterprise, are always studying it to see if its effectiveness—or lack of it—is due to inherent strengths or weaknesses in the organizational structure or whether it is due to extraordinarily competent or incompetent skill in administration. When they have reached an opinion on these points, they are ready to begin considering what improvements or modifications are necessary both in structure and in function.

In considering the status of youth education in the United States, it is now proposed to apply these principles of organization and administration to decisions about proper relationships between and among the federal, state, and local levels and about an appropriate redistribution of responsibility among them. The discussion should project a sound basis for reaching decisions pertaining to the improvement of present over-all organization and administration. It should also make clear that by applying our technical knowledge of how best to organize and administer large enterprises to the problem of improving federal, state, and local relationships in education we shall be able to reach better solutions than if we follow uncritically the promptings of either the proponents of local autonomy or of state responsibility.

PRESENT STATE AND FEDERAL ORGANIZATION ONLY A
POINT IN A PROCESS—NOT ITS END

The pattern of the present organization of education at the federal and state levels shows traces of a design that grew out of the older concepts of secondary education. Local organization has the same defects, also as has been shown in this chapter. How appropriate this design would have been had we not shifted our concept of youth education from one of selective education for the few to one of education for all youth is beside the point. The present organization of the United States Office of Education and that of the state departments of education show both the remnants of the old and evidence of the new. For example, the large staffing of some of the subject areas is out of proportion to that of some other areas when compared to the importance now attached to them. Again, certificate requirements still overstress knowledge of highly specialized subject fields at the expense of broad fields of study and knowledge of child growth and development, which we now know are important for the teacher. Organization at the federal and state levels also illustrates, as we have seen, the effect of the traditional resistance of the proponents of local autonomy to strong federal and state action in education. Organization at the state and federal levels also exhibits to a lesser extent the effect of the newer concept of universal youth education that made necessary a larger participation in education at both levels. Organization at these levels has not, however, succeeded in redesigning itself so that it represents what would be created were we able to start out anew with a clear concept of universal youth education and a full awareness of modern principles of organization. As a result of our not having been able to remake our educational structures as rapidly as changes made redesigning desirable, it is now more difficult than it should be to provide good educational administration at any of the three levels.

Plans for improving the over-all organization of education should start with the assumption that the states are intended to be "prime movers" in the area of public education. The state departments of education would then be well enough financed and staffed to supervise whatever programs of education each state needed—for children, for youth, and for adults—of generalized, specialized, and professionalized types. Such a program would assume that the federal government would take an active interest in education and, when national interest was involved, would urge and assist and even press the states to fulfill their obligations toward public education. It would also assume each local unit to be an integral part of the state organization—the basic unit of *operation* in childhood and youth education and in general adult education with all the freedom required—but still everywhere recognized as a unit of a larger organization. The acceptance of these assumptions would let us move toward a clean-cut, over-all organization that would clarify working relationships among the three levels and would thus open the way for decisions about location of responsibilities for the administration of education in each state. To picture the situation graphically, we might think of public education as a grove of forty-eight trees growing in federal soil. Each tree represents a state educational organization, the trunk and roots represent the state level, and the branches and leaves represent the local level, the leaves being compared to operating units upon which the life of the whole state organization depends. A biological organism has to be well "organized," with the necessary specialized functions provided for and performed if the organism is to live and be healthy. Social organisms are no different.

DISTRIBUTION OF RESPONSIBILITY IN LARGE ENTERPRISES

If we look at what is known about good administration of large enterprises we may observe that some of the executive functions are centralized in the hands of the chief executive and his assistants and some are decentralized. Decisions as to what shall be centralized and what decentralized are not made on any theory that all centralization of responsibility and authority is bad and all decentralization good, or vice versa. Nor does the chief executive decide that since he likes or is good at finance or selling he will head that up. It is not a matter of the personal likes of the chief executive. Instead, decisions are based upon the nature of the executive function and its relation to the enterprise as a whole. These considerations decide what ought to be centralized, and very likely the board of directors then selects an executive who can handle these functions well.

So in a large enterprise like public education we must let the nature of the undertaking help us to decide what functions should be centralized in the hands of the state as the chief center of educational organization, and to a lesser degree centralized in the hands of the federal government, and what should be decentralized to the local level. For instance, teacher certification is a function now largely centralized at the state level. It is good not to center this function at the local level, but it would be better to move toward centralizing some aspects of this function at the national level, or at least toward coordinating through federal initiative the certification policies of the various states. In any case with reference to any function, it is not likely that the function will be completely centralized or decentralized, but the major responsibility will be likely to fall to central or local administrators, with others still bearing a minor responsibility for it. Both levels may have a part in all functions, but that part will vary from major to minor according to the function being considered. In a preceding paragraph it was indicated that the advocates of state responsibility for education held that the state should bear the major responsibility for developing over-all purposes, for outlining the needed program, for building the necessary state organization, for determining and providing for costs, and for evaluating results in terms of the stated purposes. In this respect, they are applying to public education experiences in the administration of other large enterprises. In education these goals can and should be the responsibility of the chief executives if we are to develop sound and economical state programs of education. Again let us repeat that local school executives are not thus deprived of any part of the exercise of these functions. They should share with the state executives in the process of reaching these decisions, but the *major* responsibility for the achievement of these goals may well be centralized. To see the wisdom of this, one has only to take any of the functions mentioned earlier in the paragraph and imagine it to be chiefly decentralized with the state school executives playing only a minor part. The result would be the virtual disappearance of anything resembling state organization. If this development is defended as sound in a democratic society, one wonders why we bother with a public educational system at all, for in the end, planning, organizing, financing, and evaluating would all be determined on local bases. In fact, if the theory is sound at all, it undermines local as well as state school systems and makes it possible for each principal and his patrons to argue that all decisions should be made at the level of the local attendance unit, not at the level of the local administrative unit. If public education is to be in the public interest, then some centralized, controlling organization representing major units of public action (in the United States, the states) should be expected to exercise major organizational responsibility with reference to purposes, plans, organization, finance, and evaluation.

IN EDUCATION, OPERATIONAL RESPONSIBILITY
MUST BE CHIEFLY LOCAL

On the other hand, the nature of education as a process dictates that the major responsibility for those functions primarily operational or administrative in character should be borne by those in authority close to the points where the actual work of educating is done. In most societies, the nature of education is such that it must be a decentralized operation whose chief activities are carried on near the homes of its students. In contrast, there is nothing about the making of shoes that requires the process to be carried on in the area in which the wearers live. Shoes are therefore manufactured at points determined by other factors. Education is different. It requires a highly decentralized administration and must be organized to provide for a large measure of such administration. Decisions in matters closely related to the school, as a center where children and youth learn, need to be made by those who are in direct contact with these pupils. Hence the conduct and the operation of schools as learning centers should rest in the hands of executives who are on the job in the local school community. Such matters as staffing, instructional methods and materials, improvement and adaptation of the educational program, pupil safety, health, and welfare, and others of a similar nature must be left in the hands of those in charge of the school centers where the business of learning goes on. To attempt to conduct such matters from distant, central points would, in the nature of the educational process, be poor administration. It may even be said that more of the responsibility for such matters should be centered in the hands of school principals and school faculties at the level of the attendance unit rather than at the level of the local school system, although most of the advocates of decentralized administration of education would not carry the theory much further than to be sure that it supports the autonomy of the local school *system*. The nature of the activity that organized public education is expected to carry on thus indicates that if well done it will not tend to be administered wholly on a centralized basis or wholly on a local basis. Instead, each aspect of the executive function will be considered by itself, and the decision whether mainly to centralize or decentralize it will be made as the nature of the educational goal suggests. For example, even in school finance practically everyone is willing for the federal government to exercise enough control to assure that federal money is spent by the states and local districts for the purpose for which it was appropriated. So also practically everyone agrees that it is a good thing for the state to equalize the costs of schools on a state-wide basis and to equalize the support of schools. Practically everyone wants the local community to exercise the principal control over the expenditure of any

federal or state funds and to have power to provide for additional local
financial support. Almost no one wants all the control over school
finances located at any one level. Certain aspects of this function may
properly be located at each of the levels. Current organization and administration of education at all three levels could be improved upon
much more rapidly than is now the case if these relationships were more
frequently examined in the light of the latest additions to our growing
body of knowledge about the successful organization and administration
of large undertakings.

BETTER PROFESSIONAL LEADERSHIP MEANS
BETTER AND MORE RAPID CHANGE

It is, of course, impossible and even undesirable completely and
suddenly to redesign national, state, and local educational organization.
It is not here proposed that school administrators should undertake to
do so. On the other hand, if more school executives were better
grounded in the theories and principles of organization and administration than they now are they would be better able to exercise the wise
leadership that is so greatly needed. There would be fewer cases where
the recommendations of one school executive or group of executives
contradicted those of other groups. We could expect to find a public
unconfused by such contradictions and more ready to understand and
accept the reasons for change in the educational system.

The really professionally competent school executive, by reason of
the completeness of his education in organization and administration,
ought to be able to keep his sense of direction in the midst of present
confusions and contradictions in federal, state, and local educational relationships because he clearly recognizes these points:

1. The nation has a great stake in the education of all children and
youth and cannot therefore afford to be unconcerned about education.
2. The federal Constitution by indirection makes education a function of
the States; we therefore have forty-eight state system of education.
3. With education so vitally related to national security and welfare, as it
is in the modern world, the federal government must be concerned to see
that these forty-eight systems of education are enabled and, if necessary, required to provide for national security and welfare as well as or better than a
national system of schools could possibly do.
4. Since we do have forty-eight legally constituted state systems of education, local schools are subordinate parts of these systems and not independent
units.
5. Since local schools are parts of a state system of schools, they cannot
properly be a phase of local, city, or county general government.
6. The nature of education, as well as the best theories of organization

and administration, requires that many of the functions of the executive be localized or decentralized.

7. Local control, home rule, and local initiative, however, are not unqualified virtues of which we can never have too much.

8. By the same token, centralization at the federal and state levels is not an unqualified evil.

9. A degree of centralization at these levels of some functions of administration is desirable.

10. The many who regard the assumption of any function in education by the federal or state levels of government as an "encroachment" either are ignorant about organization and administration or have ulterior motives to serve.

11. The few who urge a completely or a highly centralized organization of education at the state or federal levels of government are either ignorant or hypocritical.

12. Since education is legally a function of the state, the state's department of education must be sufficiently developed and staffed to discharge this function fully.

13. Many present state departments of education are incompletely developed and inadequately and poorly staffed because of failure or reluctance to recognize that education is really a function of the state.

14. Present tendencies for state departments to operate at the negative, custodial, prudential, restrictive level are due largely to our failure to recognize or fully to accept education as a function of state government.

15. Some of this "minimum" approach to the task of education in the state departments of education is due to the fact that when any organization is inadequately or incompetently staffed it always tends to reduce its functions to the "police" level and usually tends to discharge these functions in an arbitrary and dictatorial manner.

16. The remedy for the evils of this present situation is not to weaken further or destroy the states' educational arm but to build it up to the strength and standing that a complete acceptance of education as a function of the state and an adequate recognition of the importance of education in a democratic society require.

17. A very inadequate and incompetent discharge of the state's responsibility for education through a weak department of education invites the federal government to institute a system of federal schools.

18. This condition also tempts the local schools to go ahead with the task of education on an independent, unorganized, and uncoordinated basis.

19. In youth education especially, where such a variety of offering is required, strong, active state leadership in planning, organizing, and financing of education is the only way to provide an adequate amount of appropriate educational opportunity, well enough distributed over the state to be available to all at the least cost for each pupil.

20. The alternative to this strong and active state leadership in these aspects of youth education is a concentration of enriched educational opportunity for the youth living in relatively well-to-do urban areas and a correspond-

ing dearth of educational opportunity in the other areas of the state; other results are needless and unplanned duplication of facilities for some kinds of specialized educational opportunity, excessively high costs for each pupil for such educational opportunity as is provided, and failure to realize the goal of education for all youth.

21. Local school executives charged with the education of youth therefore have a particularly heavy responsibility for making their colleagues and laymen in general understand the need for rapid improvement in federal, state, and local relations in education.

Summary

Today both liberals and conservatives are aware of the urgency of the need for education for the sake of national security and welfare. The need for education for all, both in the techniques of science and in those of democratic citizenship, is generally accepted. The problems of improving our education tend to come to a head at the level of youth education. They will not be solved by our people as well or as speedily as they should be unless public education has the benefit of professional leadership of a high order. In public administration, and especially in public education, there is no place for the professionally incompetent or the personally unprincipled executive. Leadership of personal integrity, social vision, and professional competence alone will give this nation a well organized and administered program of public education.

Some Points to Consider

1. What do you understand by an "attendance unit," as the term is used in reference to schools? An "administrative unit"? Should they usually coincide?

2. If it is the policy of the board of education of a large city to provide equal educational opportunity for the city's youth, should it permit free access of any youth to any of its high schools? How else could it implement this policy?

3. Can you cite actual examples of unequal educational opportunity for youth in a state due to excessive "localism" in education? What are some of the practices by which such inequalities can be reduced?

4. Under what conditions should it be easy, difficult, or impossible for a high school student to transfer by the interdistrict transfer process from one administrative district to another? How is this arranged for in your state?

5. Cite examples of state department of education practices that are restrictive, custodial, regulative, or prohibitive on local districts. Cite some that are stimulative, creative, or enabling in their effect on local districts. Are there places for both types? Which now predominates? Which should?

6. Is your state department of education adequately staffed to exercise

constructive, creative leadership among the local school executives of the state? Can you give examples of good or bad effects of adequate or inadequate staffing of this department?

7. When did our federal government first participate positively in education in this country?

8. Give some examples of the effects of the participation of the federal government on any high schools with which you are familiar. In what respect are these effects good? bad?

9. Is the federal government well organized for effective participation in education or not? Should it be?

10. What are some of the gains and losses in the United States from our not having a centralized national school system? What are some of the things we must do to get as many of the benefits and reduce the evils of decentralization?

Further Reading

American Association of School Administrators. *The American School Superintendency.* Thirtieth Yearbook; Washington, D.C.: National Education Association, 1952.

————. *Paths to Better Schools.* Twenty-third Yearbook; Washington, D.C.: National Education Association, 1945. Chap. 7.

————. *Schools for a New World.* Twenty-fifth Yearbook; Washington, D.C.: National Education Association, 1947. Chap. 4.

Beach, Fred F., and Robert F. Will. *The State and Education.* U.S. Office of Education. Washington, D.C.: Government Printing Office, 1955.

Caswell, Hollis L., ed. *The American High School.* John Dewey Society Yearbook, 1947; New York: Harper & Brothers, 1946. Chaps. 11, 12.

Educational Policies Commission. *Policies for Education in American Democracy.* Washington, D.C.: National Education Association, 1946.

Moehlman, Arthur B. *School Administration.* 2nd ed.; Boston: Houghton Mifflin Company, 1951. Chaps. 10, 11, 24, 25, 35.

Mort, Paul, and William S. Vincent. *Introduction to American Education.* New York: McGraw-Hill Book Co., Inc., 1954. Chap. 4.

National Society for the Study of Education. *American Education in the Post-War Period: Structural Reorganization.* Forty-fourth Yearbook; Chicago: University of Chicago Press, 1945. Chaps. 3–5, 9, 10.

————. *Changing Conception in Educational Administration.* Forty-fifth Yearbook; Chicago: University of Chicago Press, 1946. Chaps. 2, 4.

Chapter 3

YOUTH EDUCATION IN OUR
DEMOCRATIC SOCIETY

Eᴅᴜᴄᴀᴛɪᴏɴ ɪs ᴀ ᴄᴏɴᴛɪɴᴜᴏᴜs ᴘʀᴏᴄᴇss. Repetition has made this statement
commonplace, without, however, in any degree decreasing the significance of the fact. From birth to death the individual is participating in
continuous experiences that modify subsequent behavior, which in turn
represents learning or education. In early childhood, education centers
largely around the informal life of the home. Through childhood and
adolescence in our modern society the school as a social institution
attempts to provide organized sequential educational experiences. The
learning experiences of adult life comprise the multitude of organized
and unorganized, formal and informal, planned and unplanned experiences that constitute life.

Any particular period of education must of necessity be based upon
previous experience in other periods and be directed toward the needs of
subsequent stages. Any sharp differentiation or compartmentalization of
education into neatly defined stages or periods is contrary to the facts
of human development. However, it is desirable to organize education
into certain broad areas, based in general upon periods of human growth
and development. These stages are reflected in the structure and program
of organized education today. Whether the current structure is that best
adapted and most appropriate for meeting the needs of children and
youth is a problem for later consideration. The first period of organized
education for children is that comprehended by the elementary school,
which is responsible for education beginning from four to six years of
age and extending to the age of approximately twelve years. Youth
education usually covers the adolescent and immediately post-adolescent
period from twelve to twenty years of age or, in terms of conventional
school organization, grades 7 to 14, inclusive. Higher education and
various programs of organized adult education are directed toward the
needs of older youth and adulthood. It is futile to consider the relative
importance of these various stages of education since they are all

necessary links in any complete educational system. This chapter is directed specifically to the consideration of a comprehensive program of youth education with such consideration of the preceding and subsequent stages of education as is necessary to define and plan youth education as a stage in a continuous educational process.

Any consideration of youth education naturally will place its major emphasis on the analysis and description of educational programs provided by the high school, since it is the social institution created for the organized education of youth. This emphasis upon organized education has, however, resulted in the too frequent failure of both the professional educator and the lay public to recognize the educational significance of much of the out-of-school experience of youth. In the broad sense, the total experience of youth at school, at home, at church, at play, at work, in school hours and in out-of-school hours and vacation periods—all these experiences represent what society can provide for the development of youth. Organized education must be viewed within the total context of youth experience if it is to be the functional, integrating, developmental experience it should be. Not until organized education is fully recognized as a social invention of recent origin, established to provide what could no longer effectively be obtained by direct experience, is it possible to formulate a total educational program for youth. Much of our current confusion concerning secondary education arises from a very limited understanding—if not a complete lack of understanding—of the development and changing function of youth education in a constantly changing society.

EDUCATION A SOCIAL IMPERATIVE

Organized schools are characteristic only of fairly advanced and complex societies, but education in the broad sense must take place wherever any form of structured and self-perpetuating society exists. Any society, be it ever so primitive, has its devices and means for transferring its culture to the young. In the simple society this process of education may be largely informal, unplanned, and incidental to other activities. Education is largely a process of learning by doing, as the young are gradually taught by their elders to assume the responsibilities of adult life. The skills necessary for survival are learned from parents or other adult members of the group. The revered beliefs and the accepted customs and mores of the group are learned incidentally from parents and elders. As a society increases in complexity and its knowledge accumulates, these incidental means of education become inadequate, and the long, slow development toward the elaborate organized system of modern education begins. In its first stages certain selected elders of the tribal group may undertake the responsibility of imparting to the young the special lore, secrets, mythology, and skills held precious and essential by the group. These may be associated with the ceremonials of induction into adult status. As the complexity of a society increases, the body of culture that must be transmitted by formal means becomes greater, and it becomes necessary to increase the scope and extent of planned organized education.

The rate of change in the world today increases our need to stress organized education, for not only is there more to learn, but each year there are more *new* things to learn—and some things to unlearn. As democracy, which is inherently dynamic, modifies group living, organized education not only assumes the function of transmitting the past culture in order that it may be relived by future generations, but also begins to function as a means for improving and developing the culture in the light of its democratic ideals.

The invention of the alphabet and later the invention of printing and the mechanical production of books vastly increased the body of accumulated knowledge that society could transmit from generation to generation and made it more easily possible for all to be educated, thus increasing the size of the task undertaken by organized education. The history of the development of organized education in any social group is characterized by all the variations of social belief, social organization, geographic and chance differences that distinguish each group from others. Education may be organized in many different forms and patterns. Typically, the responsibilities and advantages of organized education are first available to only a selected few, who carry the special responsibility and prestige of being the perpetuators and transmitters of the precious heritage. Few societies have been able or even willing to extend organized education to all.

The significance of these sociological commonplaces for the student of secondary education lies in the fact that the story of the development of the American secondary school can have little meaning and the contemporary institution can have little pattern unless viewed against the background of a society attempting to transmit its cultural heritage and to teach the young to meet new contemporary problems by organized education as it recognizes the growing inadequacy of any system of incidental unplanned education.

THE PHENOMENAL DEVELOPMENT OF ORGANIZED EDUCATION

The development of organized education in the world has been a long and slow process, paralleling the development of man's mastery over nature. As science, the industrial revolution, and technology have revolutionized the methods of man's control over his environment at an ever-quickening rate, so has the development and expansion of organized education constantly accelerated until one of the major social problems of this age is the adaptation and expansion of education to meet the imperatives of a dynamic society. Viewed in this perspective, the amazing expansion of American secondary education is not a chance growth arising from a theoretical or humanitarian belief in education; it is the result of the efforts of a people to find a practical means of transmitting, perpetuating, and further developing an enormously complex culture.

The rapidity of that development has led to much of the confusion, contradiction, and controversy that characterizes American secondary schools today. Within a few generations greater adaptations have been forced upon organized education than in any equal number of previous centuries. In colonial America the large part of the education of the vast majority of children and youth was provided through the informal but very effective medium of direct experience. The home, the farm, the church, and the intimate life of the small community were the practical school of the day. At best, the school provided for the majority a supplementary education for the attainment of elementary literacy and the broadening of the individual's horizon beyond that of the restricted community in which he lived. Only a selected few were able or found it necessary to undertake formal education of any extended nature, and these few sufficed to fill the small number of positions in the society that required specialized or professional knowledge. This relatively simple pattern of education characterized American education until well into the nineteenth century. However, science and technology were at work laying the bases that were to revolutionize the American way of life. The relatively simple occupational pattern of the past disappeared as the work of the world segmented into an ever-growing number of specialized jobs and professions. Urbanization transformed the way of life of an increasing proportion of the population. Farming changed from a simple method of work largely learned by practical experience to a field of business and scientific management. The health of the individual became a cooperative and community problem. An interdependent economy created situations calling for group understanding and planning. Complex social problems of national scope affected the welfare of each individual. The story of the development of our contemporary industrial economy has been recounted and documented many times. The significance of the developments as they affect schools lies in the fact that more and more the informal, unorganized means of education became inadequate. No longer was it possible to attain by direct experience in the home, the farm, or the community the skills and understandings necessary for survival and success. Specialization and industrialization tended to bar youth from direct experience. Individual and group welfare demanded that the understandings of the young go beyond that which could be gained by direct observation and experience. The expanding program and enroll-ment of the secondary school in the twentieth century are the direct results.

Many educators and lay citizens have looked askance at the new responsibilities assumed by the schools. The controversy over vocational education, extracurricular programs, recreational activities, and health ed-ucation are current examples. Contrary to the assumption of many critics, these additions to the schools have not been occasioned by and large by the ambitious ideas of teachers or school administrators. They have found their way into the school because other social devices for providing youth with the necessary skills, understandings, and attitudes for modern life have not proved adequate. Certainly it is pertinent to question the effectiveness with which the school may be discharging its new responsi-bilities. The more effective use and coordination by our society of other means of education besides the school undoubtedly need to be explored and developed more fully. These are real problems of educational plan-ning for today. To raise such questions, however, does not discount the basic need for organized education. The need for organized, planned ed-ucation of a scope and extent undreamed of in past generations is an in-escapable part of modern existence.

The Unique Responsibility of Education in a Democracy

THE DEVELOPMENT OF DEMOCRATIC CITIZENS

Schools in a democracy have a particular responsibility to develop the type of independent, free, responsible citizen that this kind of so-ciety urgently requires. Obviously the schools of any society, be it demo-cratic or authoritarian, will attempt to mold the children and youth to support and contribute to its stability. To assume that a society will sup-port or long tolerate an educational system that does not agree with the controlling social philosophy is nonsense. In our democratic society, com-mitted as it is to the "promotion of the general welfare," stability does not imply absence of motion or progress. Instead, it implies controlled mobility, for since democratic living is by nature dynamic living, the present and its problems are not conceived wholly in the light of the past but in the light of our democracy's goals and purposes. If change seems to offer a better promise of attainment of these than stability does, then change will be insisted upon. Democracy therefore expects the school to guide society's movement toward its only partly realized goals and pur-poses.

In a democracy the school does not act as a brake to ensure the *status quo* but as a gyroscope to help keep it on the path toward its goals and ideals. However, the actual problem of developing an effective program of education for the potential citizen of the democratic state is in many ways more difficult and critical than in the more authoritarian society. In the latter the major function of education is to indoctrinate the many to follow blindly the decisions of the few. The contrary is true in a democracy. Each citizen participates in the long run in the determination of the governing policies of the nation. Each citizen is assumed to have the right and the competence to contribute his judgment to the making of the critical decisions of his time.

The compelling need for universal education as a prerequisite for sustaining and developing our democracy was recognized by the more farseeing of the founding fathers, as is evidenced by the statements and activities of such men as Jefferson, Washington, and Franklin. They clearly recognized that a democracy which places its trust in the wisdom of the group judgment of all men must ensure that all men have an opportunity to secure the information and understandings needed for making intelligent decisions. Only a system of common schools available to all can possibly hope to attain this objective. In our earlier history the major goal was to provide all men the opportunities of becoming literate, for it was assumed that, with the tools of reading and writing, the truth could be discovered. This goal no longer appears adequate, partly because of the increasing complexity of modern social organization and the consequently more complex problems that the citizen of today must understand. Education for citizenship today requires far more than elementary literacy. Although the nature and extent of what may be termed the essentials of civic education may be controversial, our democracy depends more than ever before upon an adequate and effective program of education.[1]

EDUCATION AND EQUALITY OF OPPORTUNITY

Education plays an increasingly important role in attaining what has long been a goal of our democracy: the provision of equality of opportunity for all. Equality as a basic ideal has not been interpreted in the same way by different groups or in different periods of our country's history, but the varied definitions have had this in common: All youth should be given the opportunity to achieve, without artificial restrictions of class, race, color, or creed, whatever position of influence, prestige, or standing they can win with their given ability, talents, and industry. The cynic, observing the numerous cases where equality of opportunity does not exist because of race or economic class, may question the actual ex-

---

[1] For a more complete treatment, see Educational Policies Commission, *Public Education and the Future of America* (Washington, D.C.: National Education Association, 1955).

istence of a real belief in equality of opportunity and conclude it is largely a pious and timeworn expression of little real meaning today. But the existence of social ideals cannot be affirmed or denied in terms of their absolute achievement in practice. In an imperfect world, ideals are goals toward which progress is slow. American practice contains many indications of our awareness of the ideal of equality. It is in the tradition of "from log cabin to the White House," of "from office boy to president." It is evident in our eagerness to recognize the achievement of those who start from humble beginnings, in our inclination to distrust or at least disparage those who have had the initial advantage of wealth and social position. It is part of our emphasis upon fair play. In a more tangible way, much of the motive behind the popular support of the public schools has arisen from a not always articulated but very real desire to give all children and youth a fair chance at education and whatever rewards it can bring.

There are many aspects to the implementation of the ideal of equality of opportunity, but the provision of equal educational opportunity, if not the most important single aspect, ranks among those at the top. Students of the American social and economic structure have shown greater awareness, in recent years, of the indispensable role of education in a program that seeks to establish a real equality of opportunity. In their natural setting the early periods of American settlement and expansion provided in a rough way for a fair measure of equality of opportunity. A frontier society, with its new population, placed all on a relatively equal footing. Success went to those with the necessary industry, foresight, and skills, and these attributes were either potential in the individual or obtainable through direct experience. Class, family, and even formal education, in and of themselves, carried no extreme advantage for any individual. An expanding economy provided new opportunities for the ambitious and made America known throughout the world as the land of opportunity. But many characteristics of this period have disappeared. No longer is it possible for a young man to plunge directly and freely into the occupational world and assume that he will have the same chance of success as one with greater educational attainments. The prized positions in a highly industrialized society dominated by technology and characterized by complex commercial patterns and intricate political structures, demand extensive and systematic education. Hence free and available education of an appropriate nature for all is today a prerequisite for the maintenance of equality of opportunity. There have been numerous studies in recent years of the American class structure and the means by which "social mobility" or the chance to improve one's lot in life are maintained. While education is certainly one of the chief means of providing the opportunity for social mobility, the evidence indicates the degree to which the school serves that role depends very much upon the nature of the program of that school and the awareness of the professional staff of what is necessary for the school to serve well that function. Certainly the principal and staff of any secondary school can profit from careful study of recent research on the role of schools in providing for social mobility and equality of opportunity.[2]

EDUCATION AND THE GENERAL WELFARE

Education contributes to the public welfare. Concern for the welfare of the individual is implicit in the democratic faith, which also holds that the ultimate good of all is served by the development of the individual. America's investment in public education is based upon the belief that this investment yields dividends for the total group. Briggs, writing on this thesis, states,

The doctrine of education as an investment by the state that it may perpetuate itself and promote its own interests, carries with it far more concern for the individual, for all pupils as individuals, than is shown now for the few who are fortunate enough to have special advocates. The state can profit only as it recognizes whatever is unique, whatever is distinctive, in each boy and girl and develops that as far as it promises to be profitable to do so! [3]

French, in *Education and Social Dividends* writes as follows:

A proportional-opportunity society will recognize as no other type of society does that education is its means of creating both economic and cultural wealth. Education in such a society will be the instrument by which its human resources, consisting of the individual abilities and capacities of its members, are both refined and multiplied. When so refined and multiplied by education, not only will the power to produce increasingly large quantities of both economic and cultural wealth be enhanced but in addition, the power and desire to consume larger and larger amounts of these kinds of wealth will be provided. In brief it is the function of education in such a society to develop on the part of all the power to produce and maintain and the capacity to use and enjoy increasingly higher standards of living and life. In a society of proportional opportunity with given aggregates of natural and human resources, the measure of the effectiveness of the educational program is the rate of gain in the society's standards of cultural and economic life.[4]

That education contributes to the general welfare is accepted as

[2] Among others the following are recommended for study: James Bryant Conant, *Public Education and the Structure of American Society* (New York: Bureau of Publications, Teachers College, Columbia University, 1946); August B. Hollingshead, *Elmtown's Youth* (New York: John Wiley & Sons, Inc., 1949); W. Lloyd Warner, *American Life* (Chicago: University of Chicago Press, 1953); and W. L. Warner, R. I. Havighurst, and M. B. Loeb, *Who Shall Be Educated?* (2nd ed.; New York: Harper & Brothers, 1944).

[3] Thomas H. Briggs, *The Great Investment* (Cambridge, Mass.: Harvard University Press, 1930), p. 64.

[4] Will French, *Education and Social Dividends* (Kappa Delta Pi Research Publications; New York: The Macmillan Company, 1935), p. 29.

axiomatic by the majority of people. Common sense and casual observation provide evidence of a type. However, there is a growing body of systematic evidence that demonstrates that education is directly related to different aspects of the general welfare. Studies have consistently revealed a positive relation between the level of education of a community, a region, or a nation, and its standard of living and economic productivity.[5]

There are many indications that such factors as community health and juvenile delinquency are directly related to the level of education made available by that community. Certainly none of these factors is entirely determined by education alone, but its influence is great, and improvement in its quality is the strategic point of attack for any social program looking toward the improvement of human welfare.

The Present Status of Youth Education

THE GROWTH OF YOUTH EDUCATION

The phenomenal growth of organized youth education is known to all who have even a general familiarity with education in the United States. This growth has involved an increase in the proportion of youth enrolled in schools, the retention of a greater number of youth until later age, and a parallel expansion of school facilities and of variety of educational offerings.

Until recent decades, youth education was largely limited to a selected few. The Latin grammar school, which may be considered the first secondary or youth school of this country, was available to, and served the needs of, only a small minority of boys. It is estimated that the number of these schools never exceeded forty, with a total student body of less than one thousand. The academy which followed contributed in limited but significant ways to the popularization and democratization of youth education. In 1850, the more than six thousand academies in existence enrolled over a quarter million of youth. In only a very limited way did those predecessors of the high school serve as instruments of popular and democratic mass education. Not until the closing years of the nineteenth century did the popular will and the economic and social conditions prevail which were necessary for the creation of our extensive contemporary system of youth education. The statistics that record the amazing growth of the American high schools (Tables 1 to 5) portray the physical expansion of the high school as well as indicate far-reaching changes in American society itself, changes that called for youth education of a nature different from and more varied than that of previous periods. They are, moreover, an indication of America's unsatisfied appe-

[5] See Education Department, *Education—An Investment in People* (Washington, D.C.: Chamber of Commerce of the United States, 1954).

tite for youth education. As each decade has witnessed a rise in the average standard of living, so it has registered the will of parents to keep more of their children in school for a longer period. These statistics should be read in dynamic terms. They trace the path of a moving finger that has not yet stopped. There is nothing to show that the desire of the American people for more and better education for all youth is satisfied. Not only these five tables, but also the increasing percentage of youth continuing their education beyond grade 12, show that the common people intend that whatever benefits youth education has bestowed in the past upon a limited few shall, as the years go on, be increasingly enjoyed by all their children. Peter F. Drucker, writing in *Harper's Magazine* in March, 1955, suggests that we will witness a popularization of higher education in the next twenty years similar to the popularization of secondary education in the decades following World War I.[6] This possibility will have a direct impact on the secondary school system since this popularization may require a phenomenal expansion and development of local or community junior colleges.

The immense gain in high school enrollments, shown in Table 1,

TABLE 1. SECONDARY SCHOOL ENROLLMENT AND POPULATION, 14–17 YEARS OF AGE, 1889–1890 TO 1951–1952

Year	ENROLLMENT, PUBLIC AND PRIVATE SCHOOLS		POPULATION, 14–17 YEARS OF AGE		*Number enrolled per 100 population 14–17 years of age*
	Number	*Per cent increase over 1889–90*	*Number*	*Per cent increase over 1889–90*	
1889–90	357,813		5,354,653		7
1899–1900	695,903	94.5	6,152,231	14.9	11
1909–10	1,111,393	210.6	7,220,298	34.8	15
1919–20	2,495,676	597.5	7,735,841	44.5	32
1929–30	4,799,867	1,241.4	9,341,221	74.5	51
1939–40	7,113,282[a]	1,888.0	9,720,419	81.5	73
1941–42	6,923,538[a]	1,835.0	9,418,613	75.9	74
1943–44	6,020,890[b]	1,582.7	9,118,049	70.3	66
1945–46	6,227,349[b]	1,640.4	8,780,020	64.00	71
1951–52	6,585,151[c]	1,840.1	8,472,000	58.03	77

[a] Does not include 9,727 children in residential schools for exceptional children. Data for such schools are not available for earlier years.
[b] Does not include 9,784 children in residential schools for exceptional children.
[c] Does not include 11,200 children in residential schools for exceptional children.
Source: U.S. Office of Education, *Biennial Survey of Education in the United States, 1944–46, Statistical Summary of Education, 1945–46* (Washington, D.C.: Government Printing Office, 1949), Chap. 1, p. 11; and *1951–52*, Chap. 1, pp. 7, 8.

[6] Peter F. Drucker, "America's Next Twenty Years, Part I, The Coming Labor Shortage," *Harper's Magazine*, 210, No. 1258 (March, 1955), 27–32.

reflects increases in both the number of potential high school pupils and the number of actual high school pupils. A study of the percentage columns in relation to each other makes it obvious that the growing popularity of more extended educational opportunity accounts for the major share of the gains registered in high school enrollments.

TABLE 2. PER CENT OF THE SEXES OF VARIOUS SCHOOL AGES
ATTENDING SCHOOL, 1951

Age	Male	Female	Both sexes
10 to 13 years	99.1	99.3	99.2
14 and 15 years	95.1	94.5	94.8
16 and 17 years	74.3	75.4	74.9
18 and 19 years	32.4	21.3	26.2

Source: Biennial Survey of Education in the United States, 1950–52, Statistical Summary of Education, 1951–52, Chap. 1, p. 8.

The significance of Table 2 in relation to this discussion is that it shows the present sharp drop from 74.9 to 26.2 per cent in school attendance at the eighteenth year. This age approximates the age of graduation from high school when public education too generally ceases to be locally and freely available. As indicated in the preceding paragraph there is every reason to believe that if facilities can be made available, we may expect this sharp drop to be substantially reduced.

TABLE 3. NUMBER OF PERSONS GRADUATED FROM PUBLIC AND PRIVATE HIGH
SCHOOLS, PER 100 PERSONS 17 YEARS OF AGE, 1869–1870 TO 1950–1951

Year	Number graduated from high school	Number 17 years of age[a]	Number graduated per 100 persons 17 years of age
1869–70	16,000	815,000	2.0
1879–80	23,634	946,026	2.5
1889–90	43,731	1,259,177	3.5
1899–1900	94,883	1,489,146	6.4
1909–10	156,429	1,786,240	8.8
1919–20	311,266	1,855,173	16.8
1929–30	666,904	2,295,822	29.0
1939–40	1,221,475	2,403,074	50.8
1941–42	1,242,375	2,531,553	49.1
1943–44	1,019,233	2,384,040	42.8
1945–46	1,080,033	2,374,234	45.5
1950–51	1,045,633		

[a] U. S. Bureau of the Census and estimates.
Source: Biennial Survey of Education in the United States, 1944–46, Statistical Summary of Education, 1945–46, Chap. 1, p. 14; and 1951–52, Chap. 1, p. 31.

TABLE 4. HISTORICAL STATISTICS OF PUBLIC SECONDARY DAY SCHOOLS, 1890–1952

[Junior high schools are included, beginning in 1920; ungraded schools and schools with less than 10 pupils, beginning in 1938]

Item	1890	1900	1910	1920	1930	1938	1946	1952
1	2	3	4	5	6	7	8	9
Number of schools on file	2,526	6,005	10,213	14,326	23,930	25,308	24,146	23,757
Schools reporting					22,237	25,091	24,146	23,757
Pupils in grades 7–12	202,963	519,251	915,061	1,999,106	5,212,179	7,458,045	6,861,030	7,693,140
Boys	85,943	216,207	398,525	891,469	2,522,816	3,633,319	3,248,960	3,797,550
Girls	117,020	303,044	516,536	1,107,637	2,689,363	3,824,726	3,612,070	3,895,590
Per cent girls	57.7	58.4	56.4	55.4	51.6	51.3	52.6	50.6
Teachers	9,120	20,372	41,667	97,654	213,306	274,163	[1]286,512	332,106
Men	3,695	10,172	18,890	34,396	74,532	113,249	104,886	151,575
Women	5,425	10,200	22,777	63,258	138,774	160,914	181,626	180,531
Per cent women	59.5	50.1	54.7	64.8	65.1	58.7	63.4	54.4
Average number of teachers per school	3.6	3.4	4.1	6.8	9.6	10.9	11.9	14.0
Average number of pupils per school	80.3	86.5	89.6	139.5	234.4	297.2	284.1	323.8
Average number of pupils per teacher	22.3	25.5	22.0	20.5	24.4	27.2	23.9	23.2
Pupils in last 4 years of high school [2]	202,963	519,251	915,061	1,851,965	4,135,171	5,926,722	5,417,122	5,695,514
Boys	85,943	216,207	398,525	821,015	1,986,246	2,852,539	2,615,658	2,785,553
Girls	117,020	303,044	516,536	1,030,950	2,148,925	3,074,183	2,801,464	2,909,961
Per cent girls	57.7	58.4	56.4	55.7	52.0	51.9	51.7	51.1
Population, aged 14–17 years [3]	5,354,653	6,152,231	7,220,298	7,735,841	9,341,221	9,908,000	8,897,000	8,728,000
Percent of population, aged 14–17 years in last 4 years of high school	3.8	8.4	12.7	23.9	44.3	59.8	60.9	65.3
High school graduates	21,882	61,737	111,363	230,902	591,719	1,030,216	[1]1,011,173	[4]1,045,633
Boys	7,692	22,575	43,657	90,516	267,298	481,457	442,214	496,087
Girls	14,190	39,162	67,706	140,386	324,421	548,759	568,959	549,546
Per cent girls	64.8	63.4	60.8	60.8	54.8	53.3	56.3	52.6

[1] Includes teachers and also, in the 24 ungraded schools, other professional staff (principals, supervisors, counselors, etc.). [2] Includes special or unclassified pupils of high school grade. [3] Bureau of the Census. Data for 1938–52 estimated by the Bureau. [4] Data for the school year 1950–51.

NOTE.—The figures in italics represent revisions of previously published data. The data have been revised to exclude postgraduates from "Pupils in the last 4 years of high school," 1920–46; to include schools enrolling fewer than 10 pupils, 1938 and 1946; and to exclude evening schools, 1938 and 1946. The data for 1930 and presumably for prior years include some evening schools.

Source: Biennial Survey of Education in the United States, 1950–52, Statistical Summary of Education, 1950–51, Chap. 5, p. 6.

Again it is shown that the major part of the high school's growth has come from the fact that more youths were able and willing to stay in high school longer. The figures show, however, that we are still far from reaching our hope that "all" American youth will attend high school while they are of high school age.

Some of the preceding tables give figures that are the sum of public and private secondary school enrollments. Table 4 is included because it summarizes a number of statistical facts for public high schools only.

Table 5 is significant because it shows that educational opportunity beyond the twelfth year has been greatly expanded in recent years and

TABLE 5. JUNIOR COLLEGES AND THEIR ENROLLMENT: CONTINENTAL UNITED STATES, 1917–1918 TO 1951–1952

	ALL JUNIOR COLLEGES		PUBLICLY CONTROLLED		PRIVATELY CONTROLLED	
Year 1	Number 2	Enrollment 3	Number 4	Enrollment 5	Number 6	Enrollment 7
1917–18 . . .	46	4,504	14	1,367	32	3,137
1919–20 . . .	52	8,102	10	2,940	42	5,162
1921–22 . . .	80	12,124	17	4,771	63	7,353
1923–24 . . .	132	20,559	39	9,240	93	11,319
1925–26 . . .	153	27,095	47	13,859	106	13,236
1927–28 . . .	248	44,855	114	28,437	134	16,418
1929–30 . . .	277	55,616	129	36,501	148	19,115
1931–32 . . .	342	85,063	159	58,887	183	26,176
1933–34 . . .	322	78,480	152	55,869	170	22,611
1935–36 . . .	415	102,453	187	70,557	228	31,896
1937–38 . . .	453	121,510	209	82,041	244	39,469
1939–40 . . .	456	149,854	217	107,553	239	42,301
1941–42 . . .	461	141,272	231	100,783	230	40,489
1943–44 . . .	413	89,208	210	60,884	203	28,324
1945–46 . . .	464	156,456	242	109,640	222	46,816
1947–48 . . .	472	240,173	242	178,196	230	61,977
1949–50 . . .	483	242,740	256	187,695	227	55,045
1951–52 [1] . . .	480	229,991	265	182,870	215	47,121
Per cent of all higher education	26.2	10.0	41.3	15.8	18.1	4.1
Average enrollment per institution		479		690		219

[1] Excludes 26 public junior colleges (designated as normal schools) having a combined enrollment of 1,184.

Source: Biennial Survey of Education in the United States, 1950–52, Statistics of Higher Education: Sec. 1, Faculty, Students, and Degrees, 1951–52, Chap. 4.

that when such opportunity is more freely and easily available, older youth attend in increasing numbers. It would seem that the amount of educational opportunity for older youth which this country can and will use if it is available has not even been approached.

The years following 1940 produced some changes and fluctuations in secondary school enrollments. The decrease in total high school enrollments in the 1940's and early 1950's reflected the decreased birth rates of the 1930's, but even casual examination of the birth statistics following 1940 reveals that this decrease is only a temporary recession before the coming of a new surge of increased enrollments. There appears no reason to believe that these fluctuations will in any way substantially alter the long-term trends that produced the changes up to 1940. These trends in school enrollment arise out of far-reaching social and economic changes. Intelligent projection of past trends requires an examination of these forces.

SCHOOL ENROLLMENTS RELATED TO SOCIAL
AND ECONOMIC FACTORS

It has been customary to attribute the growth of American education in large part to the belief and faith of American people in education. It is true that without this faith and belief education would not have expanded to its present state. Yet this faith could not have accounted for this growth and development of American education without an economic or productive system able to provide the basic resources and the leisure time for schooling. An economic system that requires the labor of the large part of the population, both young and old, to produce the basic necessities of life, cannot, no matter what the faith of its people, release from directly productive labor any substantial proportion of its youth to attend schools. Such was colonial America, and not until science and technology enabled man to produce by machinery what had formerly been produced largely by his strength alone, could any significant part of the youth population be freed from productive toil for long years of systematic education. The fundamental reason why about 70 per cent of the youth population is in school today, as contrasted with less than 5 per cent previous to 1890, is revealed in a few relatively simple statistics supplied in Tables 6 and 7, which portray the increase in productive capacity of the individual man during the last century. The average family is thus now able to keep its children in school longer.

In *America's Needs and Resources: A New Survey*, Dewhurst continues,

Mechanization has been taking place at an accelerating rate, and productivity has been making parallel gains during the past century. Today we produce more than three times as much per worker in a 40-hour week as our grand-

TABLE 6. ESTIMATED PRODUCTIVITY PER MAN-HOUR, 1850–1960

Year	Productivity per man-hour in 1950 prices	Year	Productivity per man-hour in 1950 prices
1850	33.7	1910	89.6
1860	40.6	1920	93.2
1870	42.6	1930	106.9
1880	44.4	1940	131.5
1890	61.1	1950	193.5
1900	75.5	1960	240.0

Source: J. Frederic Dewhurst and Associates, *America's Needs and Resources: A New Survey* (New York: Twentieth Century Fund, 1955), Table 14, pp. 40, 41. Reprinted by permission of The Twentieth Century Fund.

TABLE 7. INDEX OF AGRICULTURAL PRODUCTION PER MAN-HOUR, 1910–1952
(1935–1939 = 100)

Year	Production per man-hour	Year	Production per man-hour
1910	74	1940	112
1920	81	1950	163
1930	90	1952	175

Source: Adapted from data presented in Dewhurst and Associates, *America's Needs and Resources: A New Survey*, Appendix 22–27, p. 1080. Reprinted by permission of The Twentieth Century Fund.

parents did working 70 hours a week a century ago. This means that average output per man-hour for the economy as a whole is six times what it was in the middle of the nineteenth century. But productivity little more than doubled during the second half of the nineteenth century while it has almost trebled since 1900, and the increase during the 1940's seems to have been greater than in any earlier decade. But even the average rate of increase over the past century would yield fabulous results if long continued. By 2050 we would be able to produce and earn as much in one 7-hour day as we do now in a 40-hour week, and as we did in 1850 working more than three weeks at 70 hours a week.

These great advances have been achieved by harnessing inanimate energy on a lavish scale to displace animal power and multiply human effort. Gasoline-powered trucks and buses have long since displaced the horse in transportation, and the tractor is fast displacing him in agriculture. Coal-generated steam power long ago became the dominant source of energy in industry, as in rail and water transportation, but technological progress is now fast displacing coal by fuel oil in ocean transport, by diesel power on the railroads, and by central-station electricity in industry. In the home a widening variety of mechanical devices and electrical equipment is easing housework and making life more pleasant.

All of these technological changes involve heavy and expanding capital investment and growing use of mechanical power.

. . . . .

Nearly all the back-breaking tasks of industry have already been taken
over by mechanical power. Mass production has become increasingly automatic,
since any repetitive operation can be done better by machines than by men.
Electronic controls are now opening a new era of "automation," which has
already brought the automatic factory in such processing industries as petroleum
refining and promises soon to automatize machining and even assembly operations. These new electronic laborsavers relieve the worker of routine mental
tasks just as power-driven machinery has taken over physical tasks. And just as
machines are more efficient than muscles, electronic computers and controls
are more sensitive and dependable and far speedier in performing routine
mental tasks than the human brain. The various industrial applications of elec-
tronics in computers, industrial TV, and instruments for measurement, communication, inspection and control open a revolutionary new field for further en-
hancement of labor productivity.[7]

The net effect of this increase in productive power of the average
man is revealed in many ways. It has resulted in a decrease in the hours
of labor and an increase in the leisure time of the worker. It is revealed
in the decreasing proportion of the population engaged in basic production in agriculture. But it is revealed even more strikingly in the release
from productive labor of the extremes of age groups of the population;
namely, youth at one end of the scale and the elderly at the other end.
Thus the amazing increase in the hourly productive capacity of the individual worker, as shown in Tables 6 and 7, has actually contributed to
the fact that over sixty times as many youths attend secondary school
today as in 1870 since a proportionately larger share of the release from
labor has been channeled to the youth group.

The effects of technology have touched every aspect of social life.
It is not the purpose here to attempt to review these changes except as
they relate to the general status of youth education. It is important to
emphasize that as technology has released youth from labor and furnished
the resources needed by modern educational facilities, it has also vastly
increased the need for education. The technological society, with its specialized vocations, its demand for technical knowledge, and its resultant
complex social and economic life, is dependent upon an extensive and
highly varied educational program. Thus we have the situation of a technology that makes universal youth education possible and in turn depends for its own continued existence and development upon that educational system.

[7] J. Frederic Dewhurst and Associates, *America's Needs and Resources: A New
Survey* (New York: Twentieth Century Fund, 1955), pp. 942–943. Reprinted by permission of the Twentieth Century Fund.

There is no reason to believe that the present technological or in- dustrial situation is static. As it adds to its stock of accumulated knowl- edge, science, the foundation upon which this situation rests, provides an ever larger base for the projection of new discoveries and their ap- plications. Actually such expansion may be limited only by our inability or failure to provide adequate and appropriate social organizations and institutions to direct and exploit it.

A LOOK TO THE FUTURE

Our society today has the potential productive capacity to provide the time and resources for education of a larger proportion of youth to a late age and, as noted above, in turn requires this expanded education successfully to carry on its line of development. On the basis of these facts it appears inevitable that the expansion and upward extension of youth education will continue. Only in the context of conditions long past, or by postulating a social-political revolution that will completely alter the trend of American events, can any other prediction be logically defended. The actual rates of extension and expansion and the precise number of years needed to reach a given condition are certain to be influenced by the various short-term factors that influence our economic and social life. But in the long run these do not substantially affect the ultimate ends toward which our society is moving. Youth education today must be planned toward the *end of serving all youth through the years of the conventional high school to approximately the age of eighteen years and the time for planning for a majority of youth to continue their education beyond this stage, either in higher education or in the growing number of part- and full-time terminal educational programs of less than university extent, is at hand.* The nature of the educational program for youth, the administrative arrangements, the control and support of youth educa- tion are problems that will need to engage the best and fullest efforts of educators and public. The time has passed, however, when there is really a genuine issue concerning whether this country can or should provide universal secondary education and an expanding program beyond that level. The nature and needs of our society and our times leave no real choice.

It is pertinent to note that the American secondary school system faces the need for a major expansion and development in the years fol- lowing the middle 1950's. The increase in the number of students re- sulting from the phenomenal increase in the birth rate following 1940 will demand a tremendous increase in staff and facilities. The number of youth from fourteen to seventeen years of age in 1954 approximated 9 million. In 1965 the number will exceed 14 million.[8] There should still continue to be some increase in the percentage of the age group remaining in school. An estimate of approximately 12 million secondary school students (grades 9 to 12) in 1965, as contrasted with an enrollment on the order of 7.5 million in 1955, is reasonably conservative. To this must be added an increase in local junior college enrollment which as has been previously suggested may be phenomenal. All of this indicates that educational leadership of the highest order will be needed to meet the challenge of these demands.

THE IMPLICATIONS OF UNIVERSAL SECONDARY EDUCATION

The concept of secondary education for all youth is neither an innovation nor an impractical ideal. An accomplished fact in numerous communities and nearly achieved in others, its implications for secondary education have not been fully realized by the profession or, especially, by the general public. The increased heterogeneity of the student body of the secondary school, the inevitable result of the increased proportion of youth in attendance, has forced an expansion and differentiation of the secondary educational program. However, many people regard much of the recent adaptation in secondary education as regrettable concessions made to a heterogeneous student body whose members vary widely in interests, aptitudes, purposes, and abilities. The philosophy of selective secondary education, mixed with the reality of universal secondary education, has contributed to much of today's confusion concerning youth education. Even when the ideal of universal secondary education has been accepted verbally or nominally, the full implications of what must necessarily follow have not been fully faced or accepted. Thus secondary educators, rather than developing a genuinely positive program for the education of all youth and eliciting the kind of support that this democratic ideal can secure from the public, have often reluctantly and even apologetically made unavoidable adaptations in the prevailing program. Universal secondary education has implications for every aspect of the educational program that must be fully accepted if a consistent positive program of universal youth education is to be developed.

For example, it must be assumed and genuinely believed that education is feasible, desirable, and necessary for all youth. Regardless of his capabilities, every youth is assumed to have potentialities that education can help to develop. In spite of numerous opinions to the contrary, the great weight of American public opinion has steadfastly if not always

[8] From estimates presented in National Citizens Commission for the Public Schools, *Financing Public Education in the Years Ahead* (2 West 45th Street, New York: The Commission, 1954), Table 4, p. 45.

systematically supported the extension of education to all people. As stated early in the chapter, the demands of our times and of our society have created a need for universal youth education. The systematic evidence and arguments that can be marshaled to support this view are impressive.[9] It is clear that as a nation we are embarked upon a program of universal youth education.

The facts—and they are certainly indisputable facts—of individual differences must be realistically and completely accepted if any positive and imaginative program of universal youth education is to be developed. This acceptance implies the recognition that while education can contribute to the development of common attitudes, it cannot reduce the differences among students in interests, abilities, and aptitudes. On the contrary, continued education will actually contribute to increasing the range of differences as potential abilities in different fields are developed through education. No classroom techniques or educational programs will miraculously cause individual differences to disappear and enable all people to achieve any specific goal with equal success. This fact, along with the fact of universal secondary education, means that the secondary school must accept with equal willingness the responsibility for educating all types of youth. There can be no single selected group to which the secondary school should give primary service. There can be no type of ability or any particular combination of abilities in which the secondary school should undertake to make all students alike.

Corollary to the facts of individual differences is the fact that in a school for all youth there can be no single uniform program for all students, no defined and single body of content for all, nor even any common body of skills in which all will achieve uniform excellence. Only if a school selects its students and rejects or discards those who will not or cannot conform to its established programs and standards can a single course of study and single standards be maintained. A school for all youth must be willing to take youth with whatever abilities, achievements, and interests they possess and to develop a program that starts at the level they are in and best provides for their needs for further growth and development. The implication of such terms as "high school work," "high school curriculum," and "high school standards" are often misleading in their implication of uniformity. In a school for all youth, high school work can only be defined as anything that a high school teaches. That, in turn, can be anything that judgment and study indicate to be profitable for any group of youth in attendance.

The attempt to apply uniform standards of achievement in any part

<hr />

[9] See Committee on Orientation of Secondary Education, "Issues of Secondary Education," National Association of Secondary School Principals of the National Education Association (hereafter abbreviated to NASSP), *Bulletin*, No. 59, January, 1936.

of an educational program for all youth in a heterogeneous student body is likewise a futile endeavor, no matter how seriously the pretense of doing this is maintained. Standards of achievement based upon the individual youth's capabilities may be logically established. Minimum standards of acceptable achievement may also be established in the various differentiated programs within a school, and such standards, insofar as they are consistent with the purposes of the differentiated program, may be defended as just and desirable. The high school record of achievement which defines and describes the particular work and success of the individual student can and should be meaningful. The high school diploma in a school for all youth cannot in itself be testimony to the mastery of any highly defined body of content or any uniform level of achievement in given skills, and is not so regarded by universities and the majority of large employing agencies today that secure the high school record of work done and achievement level for use in their appraisal and selective processes. In brief, what is needed are not more futile efforts to apply selective standards to a universal school but a clear recognition that American youth education must provide programs of work of all types and levels, and that differing standards must be applied in terms of the purpose of the individual student. Moreover, the high school diploma should be regarded as simply a certificate that the individual youth has completed that program of work which has been judged to be most appropriate to his purposes and abilities. These are not conditions for which secondary school teachers and administrators need apologize; they are the realities of universal youth education which need to be explained and interpreted to the public because its understanding and acceptance are prerequisite to the development of a functional and positive education for all youth by any modern secondary school.

The Major Functions of Youth Education

The public and those who work in the field of education ordinarily accept without question the fact that youth education has a number of important and valuable functions. These functions are often only vaguely defined in ordinary practice or by inference in terms of what the school does. Certainly, if youth education is to have orientation and direction, its major functions periodically need systematic and careful definition. The most comprehensive recent study directed toward defining and analyzing the functions of secondary education is that carried on by the Committee on Orientation of Secondary Education of the National Association of Secondary School Principals of the National Education Association.[10]

[10] See Committee on Orientation of Secondary Education, "Functions of Secondary Education," NASSP *Bulletin*, No. 64, January, 1937.

More recently published are the related documents, *Education for All American Youth: A Further Look* (Educational Policies Commission) and *Planning for American Youth* (NASSP), both of which include parallel statements of "needs" to be served by secondary education and therefore delineate its functions. Older statements running back to those listed by Inglis in his *Secondary Education* show a remarkable degree of unanimity as to the functions to be performed by secondary education. This agreement is illustrated in the accompanying chart in which the items in each set of statements that tend to be identical are placed under each other. If, for instance, one reads the explanatory statements made by each writer in support of the first item in each statement he will find that each is only expressing the same idea in his own way. And so for the second item, and on through the list. Some are further subdivided than others, but an analysis of the documents from which these items are drawn will show a remarkable degree of agreement persisting over the years during which the statements have been developed.

From these one may deduce that there are four principal major functions which modern secondary education must perform: (1) the integrating function; (2) the developmental function; (3) the exploratory and guidance function; and (4) the differentiating function. Although these four functions may be defined into a greater number by detailed analysis (see Chart 1), yet they are adequate for a working definition of the scope of secondary education and provide practical guides for the selection and organization of the activities of the secondary school.

THE INTEGRATING FUNCTION

One major function of youth education is to contribute to the cultural integration of students.[11] In any group of people, the social stability and the ability to act cooperatively fundamentally depends upon everyone's possessing a measure of common understandings, attitudes, beliefs, skills, and purposes. This does not preclude the development of individuality, but it does postulate the development of a common core of shared beliefs, attitudes, values, and underlying knowledge. The Report of the Committee on the Orientation of Secondary Education puts it thus:

The aims of social integration can be stated simply. It is an old axiom that there can be no social progress worthy of the name unless individuals are able and willing to work together—unless they have common backgrounds of experience and culture, common purposes, and the cooperative spirit. . . .

In general terms, the aim of social integration on the secondary school level—as on all levels—is to enable and encourage individuals to cooperate in

---

[11] See Chart 1, Spencer, 3, 4, 5; Inglis, 3; Cardinal Principles, 4, 5, 6, 7; Bobbitt, 7, 8, 10; Koos, 3, 4; North Central, 3, 4; Spaulding, 1, 3, 4; and Educational Policies Commission, 1, 3, 4.

	Health	Economic / Vocation	Fundamental / Calling	Nonvocational practical	Home / Social / Human relations	Parenthood / Civic-social-moral	Social-civic / Living with others	Citizenship	Ethical / Religious / Social-political	Leisure
I SPENCER	1 Self-preservation	2 Securing necessities of life			3 Parenthood				4 Maintaining social and political relations	5 Leisure and culture activities
II INGLIS	1 Physical efficiency underlies all objectives	2 Economic vocational					3 Social-civic			4 Individualistic avocational
III CARDINAL PRINCIPLES	1 Health	2 Vocation	3 Fundamental processes		4 Home membership			5 Citizenship	6 Ethical character	7 Worthy leisure
IV BOBBITT	1 Health	2 Mental sufficiency	3 One's calling	4 Nonvocational practical activities	5 Language; social communication	6 Parenthood	7 Living with others	8 Citizenship	9 Religious activities	10 Spare-time activities
V KOOS	1 Physical efficiency	2 Occupational efficiency				3 Civic-social-moral efficiency				4 Recreational and aesthetic participation and appreciation
VI NORTH CENTRAL ASSOCIATION	1 Health and physical fitness	2 Participation vocationally			3 Social relationships including domestic, community, civic, moral, religious					4 Right use of leisure time
VII SPAULDING NEW YORK REGENTS	1 Social competence includes health	2 Vocations						3 Citizenship		4 Further learning and wholesome recreation
VIII EDUCATIONAL POLICIES COMMISSION	1 Self-realization includes health	2 Economic efficiency			3 Human relationships			4 Civic responsibility		5 Self-realization includes leisure use

CHART 1. SOME STATEMENTS OF PURPOSES FOR EDUCATION

using for the welfare of all the knowledges and skills which they acquire individually. This aim requires that pupils possess certain characteristics of mind and view in common.[12]

This integrating function is not performed alone by the secondary school. The elementary school, dealing with all children at an earlier and more impressionable age, plays the crucial part in the achievement of this end. The out-of-school life, in its varied aspects, also plays an important part. The complexities of modern life, with their critical demands for group action and common understandings, place upon the secondary school a responsibility to contribute in its way to the development of the more complex and interrelated understandings necessary for social integration today.

The achievement of this integrating function is not as simple as a superficial examination of the statement might indicate. Common understandings do not necessarily grow out of a uniform educational program. In fact, the diversity of a student body precludes a uniform program even to achieve common ends. The achievement of the integrating function requires that the necessary common understandings, attitudes, and skills be determined, and differing methods and programs to achieve these selected purposes be devised for the various types of students enrolled in our youth schools.

THE DEVELOPMENTAL FUNCTION

Education in a democracy has a responsibility to assist in developing the unique qualities of each individual, who should have the opportunity of self-development in those areas that will contribute to self-adjustment, personal happiness, and the satisfaction of personal interests.[13] More specifically, around this function may be grouped those educational activities that can contribute to the individual's personal health, satisfaction and skills in the arts, social adjustment, and personal philosophy. It is not easy exactly to designate which part of a school's program performs this function because almost any part of the program may serve this function for some particular student.

The developmental function of education is in general less recognized and understood than are the other functions. Many people who are impressed with the real need for group social education and practical specialized education are unimpressed with those school activities that appear superficially to have little purpose beyond the personal satisfaction they give the individual. Those who suggest that there is little justification for expending public funds for such purposes overlook the

[12] See Committee on Orientation of Secondary Education, "Functions of Secondary Education," *loc. cit.*, pp. 23–24.

[13] See Chart 1, Spencer, 5; Inglis, 4; Cardinal Principles, 3, 6, 7; Bobbitt, 2, 4, 5, 9, 10; Koos, 3, 4; North Central Association, 3, 4; Spaulding, 1, 4; and Educational Policies Commission, 1.

fact that every individual has an existence apart from group life and vocational activities. In our highly organized contemporary life the uniqueness
of the individual may find its greatest, perhaps its only, expression in
those highly personal activities that must be carried on outside group
vocational and civic life. A democratic social philosophy must support
educational activities that give everyone the opportunity to enlarge his
particular interests and talents and so develop into a unique individual.
In a practical sense the adequate performance of an individual in all his
spheres of activity is dependent upon his satisfactory personal development.

Nonschool youth and educational agencies assist in this function.
Such agencies as the Boy Scouts and Girl Scouts, YMCA, YWCA, 4-H
Clubs, and the numerous other youth and special groups attract groups
of like interests and often in informal ways provide opportunities for
developing special interests and talents. The fact that other agencies can
perform this function to some extent does not relieve the school of its
responsibility. Human interests and needs are so varied that they require
the joint effort of all agencies for their satisfaction.

THE EXPLORATORY AND GUIDANCE FUNCTION

Students emerge from the elementary school with a more or less
common background of educational experience. During the period of secondary education the student faces the problem of determining and crystallizing his own particular interests and purposes.[14] As a given class progresses through the secondary school the program must be increasingly
differentiated to meet the diversified vocational and special interests of
its various members. Much of the effectiveness of the specialized education of his later years in secondary school depends upon the effectiveness
and the wisdom with which the individual student isolates and determines his life purposes and selects the appropriate special field of education. Related to the differentiating functions, but preliminary to and
somewhat independent of it, is the exploratory and guidance function
of the school. The wisdom of the choices the student makes depends in
large part upon the breadth and variety of experience he has had and
upon the aid he receives in recognizing, interpreting, and acting upon
that experience. Therefore the secondary school, particularly in its lower
classes, has the responsibility of providing for each youth a broad range
of educational activities that will permit him to explore his potentialities
and discover his aptitudes and interests. That the junior high school has
particularly emphasized the exploratory function is reflected in a program
of broad general courses covering the academic and practical fields. As

---

[14] See Chart 1, Spencer, 5; Inglis, 4; Cardinal Principles, 6, 7; Bobbitt, 2, 4, 9,
10; Koos, 4; North Central Association, 3, 4; Spaulding, 1, 4; and Educational Policies
Commission, 1.

youth remain longer in school and as the age of entering employment tends to be delayed, with the result that specialized education also tends to be delayed until the last year of the conventional secondary school or the junior college, it should be recognized that the exploratory function is continuing further into the period of youth education. Furthermore, this function is not principally concerned with school grades or ages but varies with the individual student. For many youth the whole of secondary school experience may be largely of an exploratory nature. Associated with exploratory experience, then, is adequate counseling and guidance to enable the student to profit by and interpret the exploratory experience that the school offers. The two together constitute one fundamental function of youth education.

THE DIFFERENTIATING FUNCTION

The secondary school must finally attempt to provide the appropriate types of differentiated education that a heterogeneous student population requires.[15] The secondary school is a terminal institution for the large majority of youth. Differences in ability, interests, and purposes of students crystallizing into markedly different patterns as youth mature make it imperative that youth education provide within its general framework different systematically organized programs of education appropriate to the needs of different groups of youth. The differentiating function as discussed in this paragraph in its broadest aspects is closely related to the developmental function, since both are primarily concerned with meeting the individual and varied needs of students. It is useful, however, to distinguish between two aspects of this differentiation: that which consists of organized sequences of courses required of all students enrolled in a given vocational program, for example, and that which consists of free electives as in the arts or other fields of personal interests whose main purpose is to satisfy individual inner needs for self-development and realization.

This function has been increasingly recognized in recent years as various types of terminal vocational programs have been developed. The traditional college preparatory program, regardless of the general value claimed for it, represents in considerable part a specialized prevocational program similar in intent to, although differing in content from, the more immediately terminal program of vocational education. There is much controversy today concerning the relative merits and the place of general education and specialized education including vocational education. This controversy often leads to a mistaken inference that education

[15] See Chart 1, Spencer, 5; Inglis, 4; Cardinal Principles, 6, 7; Bobbitt, 2, 9, 10; Koos, 3, 4; North Central Association, 3, 4; Spaulding, 1, 4; and Educational Policies Commission, 1, 3.

should be primarily one or the other. There are genuine problems regarding the amount of differentiated education that should be provided, the grade and age level at which different programs may be most effectively introduced, the relative emphasis to be given the different stages of growth, but all of these problems need not be interpreted as leading to the conclusion that the secondary school should provide either entirely common or entirely differentiated education. Rather, the problem is the development of a balanced program that serves the four functions described above. If the program fulfills these functions it will in some respects be general and in others specialized; it will in some respects be integrating and in others differentiating; and it will in some respects be terminal but in others it will lead on to further education in college or to adult education. But it will never be wholly any one of these as opposed to any other one of these. The facts of social life in America today and of educational psychology preclude any easy "either-or" solution to the problem of the educational program of the secondary schools.

Some Points to Consider

1. If a man owns a profitable business, should he complain if it costs something to run it? When may he legitimately complain about its costs?

2. When may a community or state legitimately complain about the "costs" of its schools?

3. Does the Briggs thesis (listed for further reading) mean that a nation could continuously increase its expenditures for education and expect a corresponding increase in returns from this "investment"? If not, where is the limit?

4. What special needs has the United States that would warrant an increase in expenditure for education?

5. Should youth be encouraged to think of educational opportunity as a right, a privilege, an obligation?

6. Are publications, radio, television, and motion pictures as well as schools to be regarded as educational agencies? If so, what obligations do these other agencies have in common with schools?

7. Under what reasoning can the childless and corporations be legitimately taxed for the support of public schools?

8. What special obligations do high schools have in the face of the social class differences discussed by Warner et al., and by Davis (listed for further reading)?

9. When is a high school a really good high school?

Further Reading

Bogue, Jesse P., ed. *American Junior Colleges, 1948.* 2nd ed.; Washington, D.C.: American Council on Education, 1948.

Bowles, Frank H. "Social Demands on Schools and Colleges," *College Board Review,* No. 26, Spring, 1955, pp. 4–9.

Briggs, Thomas H. *The Great Investment.* Cambridge, Mass.: Harvard University Press, 1930.

Committee on Orientation of Secondary Education. "Functions of Secondary Education," NASSP *Bulletin,* No. 64, January, 1937.

———. "Issues of Secondary Education," NASSP *Bulletin,* No. 59, January, 1936.

Conant, James Bryant. *Public Education and the Structure of American Society.* New York: Bureau of Publications, Teachers College, Columbia University, 1946.

———. "The Unique Features of Our American Schools," NASSP *Bulletin,* No. 220, May, 1956.

Davis, Allison. *Social Class Influences upon Learning.* Cambridge, Mass.: Harvard University Press, 1948.

Dewhurst, J. Frederic, and Associates. *America's Needs and Resources: A New Survey.* New York: Twentieth Century Fund, 1955.

Drucker, Peter F. "America's Next Twenty Years, Part I, The Coming Labor Shortage," *Harper's Magazine,* 210, No. 1258 (March, 1955), 27–32.

Education Department. *Education—An Investment in People.* Washington, D.C.: Chamber of Commerce of the United States, 1954.

Educational Policies Commission. *Public Education and the Future of America.* Washington, D.C.: National Education Association, 1955.

———. *The Purposes of Education in American Democracy.* Washington, D.C.: National Education Association, 1938.

Edwards, Newton, and Herman G. Richey. *The School in the American Social Order.* Boston: Houghton Mifflin Company, 1947. Part III.

French, Will. *Education and Social Dividends.* Kappa Delta Pi Research Publications; New York: The Macmillan Company, 1935.

———. "The Role of the American High School," NASSP *Bulletin,* No. 214 (February, 1955), 1–62.

Hollingshead, August B. *Elmtown's Youth.* New York: John Wiley & Sons, Inc., 1949.

Russell, John Dale. "High School and College for All?" *Phi Delta Kappan,* XXXVII, No. 4 (Jan. 1956), p. 153.

U.S. Office of Education. *Biennial Survey of Education in the United States 1950–52.* Washington, D.C.: Government Printing Office, 1955. Chaps. 1, 2, 3, 5.

———. *Junior High School Facts.* Misc. No. 21; Washington, D.C.: Government Printing Office, November, 1954.

Warner, W. Lloyd. *American Life.* Chicago: University of Chicago Press, 1953.

Warner, W. L., R. J. Havighurst, and M. B. Loeb. *Who Shall Be Educated?* 2nd ed.; New York: Harper & Brothers, 1944.

Chapter 4

SCHOOL ORGANIZATION FOR
AMERICAN YOUTH

It is difficult to define secondary education precisely in terms of age span, grade levels, or even educational program. Roughly it is that intermediate level of education lying between elementary education for children and higher education for young adults. It is purportedly designed to serve the needs of the age group from the period of immediate preadolescence through adolescence. In terms of the educational program the lower level is at times defined as that period when the emphasis shifts from the pupil's mastery of the tools of learning to the use of those tools in achieving functional ends. Thus Morrison has argued that secondary education begins with the fourth grade. Henry C. Morrison's definition in his *Practice of Teaching in the Secondary School*[1] is a sort of final rear guard action on the part of those who believe that elementary or primary schools should enroll pupils of whatever age, who were working at the beginning levels of the educational process—learning to read, for example. He defined secondary education as beginning at about the fourth grade because then pupils generally had enough mastery of the techniques of learning to use them for further learning. They were therefore working at a secondary level of education. All pupils, of whatever age, working at this secondary level should be regarded as belonging in a secondary school. Schools were thus organized to fit the educational process. Subsequent studies of child growth and development have caused us to move in the direction of organizing schools around the pupils and not the process.

In practice, the boundaries between elementary, secondary, and higher education have been somewhat vague. Perhaps logically they should be, since from the standpoint of the individual, education as a continuous process and movement through the school years should not involve abrupt changes in educational procedures or purposes. As the idea of universal youth education is accepted, those differences not related to

[1] Henry C. Morrison, *The Practice of Teaching in the Secondary School* (Chicago: University of Chicago Press, 1926), p. 12.

the age needs of the pupils become less and less significant. The traditional delimitation of secondary education to grades 9 through 12 is generally accepted today as unnecessarily restrictive. It tends to exclude both younger and older pupils whom we regard as in the youth group as opposed to the child and the adult groups. Secondary education is more generally considered today as involving the range from grade 7 to the present post-high school grade 14. Roughly this extends secondary education from the preadolescent age of twelve to approximately nineteen or twenty. It thus includes those whom we no longer consider to be children and yet to whom we do not accord full adult status.

The division of the total school system into units by years has its basis in more than an arbitrary division for administrative convenience. It is an attempt to establish educational units approximate to the somewhat unique needs and characteristics for broadly defined age periods. Consideration of possible units of school organization in any locality should be guided by the educational and developmental needs of children and youth. Administrative or financial convenience or necessity may cause a community to adopt a particular organization without adequate consideration of the needs of the pupil groups thereby created, but to whatever extent these needs are sacrificed this organization becomes increasingly indefensible.

CHARACTERISTIC EDUCATIONAL NEEDS OF DIFFERENT AGE GROUPS

An analysis of all the precise educational needs of any age level requires detailed and careful study. However, certain broad needs, which in considerable degree determine the general school environment and the educational facilities required for defined age groups, can be distinguished without undertaking a comprehensive analysis or without assuming that age groups have only needs peculiar to themselves.

CHARACTERISTICS OF CHILDREN'S SCHOOLS

The young child enters school from the relatively simple social situation of the family. Since he usually has not had extensive experience in being with other children, one of his major needs is learning to adapt to, live with, and cooperate with his contemporaries. The formal educational program for young children is nonspecialized, and it is increasingly being recognized that a sharply organized subject matter approach to learning activities is psychologically unsound for young children. Rather learning needs to be flexibly organized around certain major centers of interests or themes appropriate to the maturity and experience of the child.

For the foregoing and other reasons the characteristic school organization for the young child should provide (1) a relatively simple social situation where the child remains largely with the same group throughout the school day and with the same teacher, and (2) a flexible educational program planned and directed by one teacher. A typical elementary school situation, then, is simple: a small school relatively close to the home if possible; a single group working together with a teacher and educational facilities that provide a classroom laboratory where the major activities of the group may be carried on. Rooms for school activities and special teachers to aid the group teacher are needed for a complete or enriched program, but the basic program is organized around the single group, room, and teacher. In brief, it should be a situation in which young children are most comfortable.

CHARACTERISTICS OF SCHOOLS FOR OLDER
CHILDREN AND EARLY ADOLESCENTS

As the child grows and matures, the need for broader social experiences develops. Accompanying this is also a need for educational experience that begins at least to explore the many specialized and semispecialized fields of learning. These wider social interests require a school organization that offers opportunity for organizations and groups broader in scope than those within the more self-contained room group of the elementary school. School interests begin to develop that may call for activities cutting across the room group. The need to explore different fields of learning produces a need for special building equipment in the nature of science laboratories, general shops, expanded library facilities, home economics laboratories, art rooms, and other special facilities. The variety of fields to be explored requires the introduction of more specialized teachers. Although the special equipment need not be elaborate in the beginning stages, it is in general beyond the resources of the single classroom. We have here a situation appropriate for *older* children that grows slowly into what may be termed the beginning of secondary education.

The development of this need for expanded and more varied educational facilities and for a change in educational organization is, in practice, gradual, and there is no precise age or grade level at which any abrupt transition should be initiated. The necessities of school organization and the physical plant require in practice, however, that some average point be selected. In general, experience and study indicate that by the end of grade 6 or at age twelve the simpler elementary school pattern begins to fail to provide the stimulation and enrichment needed. Thus secondary education, defined in terms of the more varied and expanded social pattern, greater maturity of pupils, increased special facilities, and the introduction of some measure of specialization, begins at about grade 7 and with the preadolescents at age twelve or thirteen.[2] The basis of organization thus shifts to one satisfactory to *younger* adolescents.

CHARACTERISTICS OF SCHOOLS FOR ADOLESCENT YOUTH

The older adolescent's social and educational needs represent a gradual expansion from those outlined for the early adolescent. The exploratory experience provided in the beginning period of secondary education may mature into definite interests that require specialized programs and facilities. Expanding social and civic interests create the need for more extensive and more highly organized social and recreational activities that may involve larger groups of students. Increased maturity makes possible and desirable increased responsibility for participating in and directing the general organizational life of the school. The development of defined special interests creates the need for special curricular offerings as well as for special interest activity groups. The educational facilities for a comprehensive educational program require an expansion and increased specialization in shops, libraries, and laboratories. The school thus becomes an environment suitable to *older* adolescents who will soon be accepted as young adults.

Since this is the period when full-time education for the majority of youth will terminate, the substantial general education needed for modern life as well as special differentiated education must be emphasized. With the increased need for both general and special education on the part of all people and the increase in the average amount of education that pupils normally anticipate in this country, there is good reason to believe that the time is rapidly approaching when the extension of secondary education to grades 13 and 14 and to approximately age twenty will be commonly accepted. As this happens we shall see the idea of universal educational opportunity extended to include those whom we regard as young adults. In the transition period between the general acceptance of a twelve- to a fourteen-year period of universal educational opportunity, we shall no doubt see many instances where these two upper years are regarded as secondary education and many where they are regarded as higher education and organized accordingly. Variations among individuals in maturity and in types of post-secondary educational programs give some logic to this dual approach in the organization of older

[2] Detailed discussions of the function of the junior high school appear in several excellent bulletins and books, such as William T. Gruhn and Harl R. Douglass, *The Modern Junior High School* (New York: The Ronald Press Co., 1947); The State Education Department, *A Design for Early Secondary Education in New York State* (Albany, N.Y.: The University of the State of New York, 1954); and U.S. Office of Education, *Junior High School Facts . . . A Graphic Analysis* (Washington, D.C.: Government Printing Office, 1954).

youth education. However, the great increase in college enrollments, which is ahead, along with the increased emphasis upon professional and graduate education in many universities may mean that the two years beyond grade 12 will increasingly be regarded as a responsibility of the secondary school.

This points up the belief of the authors that in the organization of secondary education, adolescence should be considered from a sociological point of view as well as from a biological or psychological point of view. Members of the society exhibiting whatever levels or degrees of immaturity regarded by that society as associated with childhood should be grouped into a children's school probably subdivided into units for younger and older children. For those members of society who are regarded as too mature to be any longer considered children, but who by no means are accepted by the society as adults, there should be a youth school. Again subdivisions into a school for younger and older groups are indicated. The attitudes of society toward these younger groups, the society's willingness or reluctance to accord or deny to them certain rights and privileges, duties and responsibilities, and to fix for each age group a status in reference to all other age groups, ought to be a major determinant of school organization with biological and psychological aspects of maturity playing a larger part in relation to the guidance and educational programs of the schools.

TYPICAL SCHOOL ORGANIZATION LARGELY UNPLANNED

The conventional organization of the public schools provides for a twelve-year system with an eight-year elementary school (seven years in selected states) followed by a four-year high school. This particular division appears to have been accidentally established. The elementary and secondary schools arose from different beginning institutions that developed more or less separately. With the addition of the high school to the public school system, the form and organization of previously organized secondary schools were largely adopted. Thus a three- or four-year high school was to a considerable degree superimposed upon an existing "common" school system of up to nine years. The trend was to settle on an eight-year elementary unit and a four-year secondary unit. There was little more of planning in it than this. The 8–4 organization is therefore entitled to no profound respect. Although, as will be indicated, there arose a strong reorganization movement relatively soon after the high school developed, nevertheless the 8–4 plan remains today a rather frequent form of school organization. Much basic school legislation initiated during the period of general acceptance of the 8–4 organization differentiated between elementary and secondary education on this basis. Separate school district organizations for elementary and secondary on the 8–4 basis are by no means unusual. This situation has tended legally to recognize the elementary school as the first eight years and the secondary school as the last four and has increased the difficulty of reorganization.

REORGANIZATION OF SECONDARY EDUCATION

The movement to reorganize secondary schools arose in the late 1800's and has continued to this day. A number of reasons contributed to it. For example, the fundamental basis for this reorganization must rest with the educational needs of the pupils to be served. As has been briefly sketched in the beginning sections of this chapter, observation and careful studies of child and adolescent development have produced substantial evidence of the need for a more varied and a broader type of school experience as the child approaches adolescence. In general, then, it appears desirable that what may be termed secondary education should begin at approximately age twelve or grade 7. Other reasons have contributed to the reorganization of secondary education as well. The Committee of Ten recommended in 1893 the introduction of certain subjects previously appearing in the high school course of study into the educational program of grades 7 and 8.[3] The primary purpose behind this recommendation appears to have been to provide for greater acceleration of the student completing his work for college entrance. Some of the earlier recommendations for beginning secondary education at an earlier age seem to have developed because of the need to introduce some specialization for the benefit of students who formerly completed their school attendance by age fourteen. With a growing proportion of students remaining in school until age sixteen or eighteen, reorganization plans for the purpose of economizing on time or introducing specialization at an earlier age have less validity, and may even be seriously questioned as a desirable educational policy. The recent increased attention to the gifted child where the nurturing and development of special interests and abilities appears desirable may again bring increased attention to certain types of specialization which can be aided by reorganization.

The Commission on Reorganization of Secondary Education, whose reports have had an enormous effect on the development of secondary education, in 1918 presented systematic recommendations for the organization of a six-year elementary school to be followed by a secondary school of six years that might appropriately be organized into a junior and senior unit.[4] Out of these proposals grew the reorganization of secondary education and the junior high school.

[3] Committee on Secondary School Studies, *Report* (Washington, D.C.: Government Printing Office, 1893).
[4] U.S. Office of Education, *Bulletin*, No. 35 (Washington, D.C.: Government Printing Office, 1918).

Paralleling this extension of the period of secondary education by lowering the age of entrance has been consistent recognition of the need for extension of secondary education upward to comprehend what has been termed the junior college. The theory of this upward extension has in general received wide acceptance because it tends to make the period of secondary education cover the full period of adolescence sociologically defined. Although not overlooking the function of college preparation for a substantial number of students, the primary justification for this upward extension rests upon the need to provide full-time general, vocational, and semiprofessional education for a large number of students who wish to continue their education beyond what is usually offered in a twelve-year system but who for various reasons will not become students in higher educational institutions. The resources and facilities needed to serve the needs of the rapidly expanding secondary school enrollment to grade 12 have absorbed this country's major efforts and attention to date, with organization beyond grade 12 still relatively infrequent. This upward extension is one of the challenges of the future, and it may well be the most marked educational achievement of the next few decades.

The principles and theories sketched in the preceding paragraphs underlie the development of several specific plans of organization and reorganization of the public schools. The particular plans of reorganization adopted in various communities have been varied and in all probability will continue to be. Local conditions, total enrollments, geographical distribution of pupils, and available building facilities have combined to make variation necessary and desirable. Comment on some of these principal variations follows.

THE DEVELOPMENT OF THE JUNIOR HIGH SCHOOL —THE 6–3–3 SYSTEM

The early movement to extend secondary education downward resulted in the development of the junior high school, most frequently comprehending grades 7 through 9. The present junior high school development appeared around 1910. It is difficult to isolate "first" schools in this category since precisely what degree of reorganization marks the establishment of a separate institution is a matter of judgment. The following period of marked growth of the junior high school was a time of rapidly growing enrollments, particularly in urban areas, and the consequent building of new schools. Many cities adopted the 6–3–3 plan of organization: a six-year elementary school, a three-year junior high school, a three-year senior high school. Minor variations of this general plan have appeared (6–2–4, 7–2–3). Since at least several hundred pupils must be available to justify economically the special facilities and organization of a separate junior high school, these schools have become typically city school organizations. In its biennial survey of 1950–1952, the Office of Education reported the high schools of various types and the pupils enrolled in each type as shown in Table 8. Although the pro-

TABLE 8. NUMBER AND ENROLLMENTS OF SCHOOLS BY
TYPE OF ORGANIZATION, 1952

Type of School	Number	Number of pupils	Enrollment of median school
Junior high school . . .	3,227	1,526,996	361
Junior-senior high school . .	8,591	2,696,707	215
Senior high school . . .	1,760	1,528,006	634
Regular high school . . .	10,168	1,937,210	95
Total	23,746	7,688,919	1305

Source: U.S. Office of Education, *Biennial Survey of Education in the United States, 1950–52, Statistics of Public Secondary Day Schools, 1951–52* (Washington, D.C.: Government Printing Office), 1955, Chap. 5, p. 26.

gram and even the purposes of the junior high school have been considerably modified since the inauguration of the plan, it has become an established and accepted part of the public school system.

THE JUNIOR-SENIOR HIGH SCHOOL—6-6 SYSTEM

Even a casual inspection of the data on the size of high schools in the United States and on the total number of pupils to be served by a given school system reveals that a very considerable number of school systems cannot establish separate junior and senior high schools without creating schools of exceedingly small enrollment with consequent inefficiency and high costs in terms of each pupil. One of the essential purposes in the organization of the junior high school is to offer a broader educational program and an enrichment of experience. This requires the provision of some special building facilities along with some degree of specialization in the total staff. In general these need not be as elaborate or as highly developed as those for the senior high school adolescent, but they are of similar nature. To provide these facilities without an enrollment that will occasion their full use is extremely costly. These considerations account for the junior-senior high school organization that in one unit takes care of grades 7 to 12 and provides for the joint use by these grades (or by occasional variations such as 8 to 12) of special facilities and specialized staff.

In practice there is much variation in the degree in which the junior-senior high school operates as one integrated unit. In many cases the units use a single building, to some extent jointly using special facilities while having separate staff and administrative organizations. At the other extreme is the completely integrated six-year school with a common staff and common administration. In practice most junior-senior high schools fall somewhere between these two. That the junior-senior high school organization is appropriate to the conditions faced by many school communities is evidenced by the fact that this type of organization has been growing in recent years and, in 1952, 8,591 such schools enrolling 2,696,707 pupils were reported, as is shown in Table 8. That the junior-senior high school is primarily developed in smaller school systems is indicated by the median enrollment of 215 pupils, noted in Table 8.

Although there are critics of the entire junior-senior high school organization, the further development of the six-year high school has been the subject of the most careful examination. No precise enrollment figure can be given indicating where it is feasible to establish separate junior and senior high schools, but it is clear that as enrollments drop below a thousand pupils in grades 7 through 12 it becomes increasingly costly to provide separate schools. Even with rapid progress in the needed organization of larger administrative units, it is obviously impossible to assemble secondary attendance units of this size in many nonurban sections of this country. If the expanded, enriched program of secondary education is to be provided for all younger youth, the six-year organization must be further extended.

PRESENT STATUS OF 8–4 SYSTEM

Examination of Table 8 reveals that in 1952 there were 10,168 regular four-year high schools enrolling 1,937,210 pupils, an average of less than 200 pupils a school. Thus after forty years the reorganization of secondary education has modified the structure of something over half of our high schools. It is to be noted that the total number of pupils enrolled in reorganized schools (junior high schools, senior high schools, junior-senior high schools) exceeds considerably that of the regular four-year high school, indicating that the reorganized schools are typically those of larger enrollment. As has been noted, district organization and legislation have tended to structure the school system with the 8–4 setup. Furthermore, reorganization is often difficult with buildings planned for the 8–4 grouping. The trend has definitely been toward some form of secondary school organization for grades 7 and above. The extent of reorganization of further schools may in a considerable degree be dependent upon the creation of large secondary school attendance units and the development of new building programs.

OTHER FORMS OF SECONDARY SCHOOL ORGANIZATION

The secondary school organization of the future may well be a modification of those already discussed. As has been stated, the extension upward of secondary education is apparently imminent. To date the so-called "junior" college has ordinarily been a two-year unit operated some-what independently of the rest of the secondary school organization. If this upward extension is to be truly a part of the secondary school, it must be integrated with it. Educational and pupil personnel programs need to be planned for the entire school period. The best organizations of older youth education replace the "junior" college with a community college that offers older youth and adult education to all, sometimes in a four-year unit of grades 11 through 14. Koos has offered evidence to show why he believes four-year units of grades 7 through 10 and of grades 11 through 14 are both superior to the 3–3–2 plan.[5]

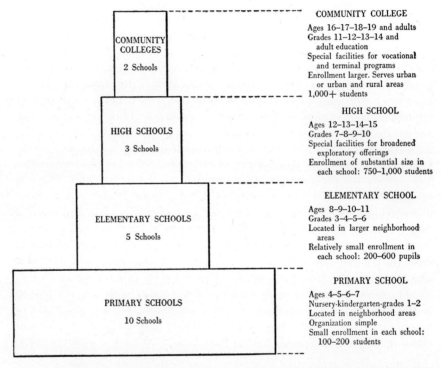

COMMUNITY COLLEGE
Ages 16–17–18–19 and adults
Grades 11–12–13–14 and
    adult education
Special facilities for vocational
    and terminal programs
Enrollment larger. Serves urban
    or urban and rural areas
1,000+ students

HIGH SCHOOL
Ages 12–13–14–15
Grades 7–8–9–10
Special facilities for broadened
    exploratory offerings
Enrollment of substantial size in
    each school: 750–1,000 students

ELEMENTARY SCHOOL
Ages 8–9–10–11
Grades 3–4–5–6
Located in larger neighborhood
    areas
Relatively small enrollment in
    each school: 200–600 pupils

PRIMARY SCHOOL
Ages 4–5–6–7
Nursery-kindergarten-grades 1–2
Located in neighborhood areas
Organization simple
Small enrollment in each school:
    100–200 students

COMMUNITY COLLEGES — 2 Schools

HIGH SCHOOLS — 3 Schools

ELEMENTARY SCHOOLS — 5 Schools

PRIMARY SCHOOLS — 10 Schools

CHART 2. SCHEMATIC REPRESENTATION OF SCHOOL ORGANIZATION SHOWING THE NUMBER OF SCHOOLS AT EACH AGE GROUP LEVEL WHERE SCHOOLS OF GIVEN SIZES EXIST

Although it is not a part of the problem under discussion, it should also be noted in passing that there are genuine reasons for extending public education down to children of ages four and five. Students of school organization have suggested that a complete school system should include a sixteen-year program organized on a 4–4–4–4 plan. Chart 2 presents a

[5] Leonard V. Koos, *Integrating High School and College* (New York: Harper & Brothers, 1946).

picture of the number and major levels of schools in a community of five hundred children or youth at each grade level when no withdrawal occurs and when schools of the sizes specified on the chart are established. Such 4–4–4–4 reorganization or variation of it (6–4–4, and so on) is a matter of long-term planning since usually a given community has not anticipated such a distribution of pupils and cannot replace its school buildings quickly. However, consideration of general plans can guide long-term planning as buildings are replaced and schools are reorganized. The plan here presented—or minor variations of it—provides a pattern for the achievement of an integrated eight-year program of secondary education.[6]

ORGANIZATION ONLY ONE ASPECT

In reality statistics indicating the number of schools that have been reorganized in terms of certain grade groupings present only part of the true facts. The fundamental purpose of extending secondary education to grades 7 and 8 is to provide a broader educational program, exploratory experience, special facilities to implement the above, and a social setting appropriate to the growing interests of young adolescents. Organization of a separate school in a separate building does not guarantee that this fundamental purpose will be attained. Contrariwise, an organization of grades 1 through 8 under one administration and in one building may nevertheless provide the desired educational experience if it is planned. There is no question but that certain cities, where available buildings and their distribution have made an 8–4 organization necessary, have nevertheless established an effective breadth of experience and educational program for the upper grades. Observations of the junior high school programs in some purportedly six-year secondary schools, on the other hand, reveal a circumscribed program particularly at the seventh- and eighth-grade levels. Too often we have accepted the external organization as the evidence of the fact, rather than the experiences provided for the pupil. Systems that have reorganized have, however, tended to expand their seventh- and eighth-grade offerings more rapidly than those that have not reorganized.

Types of High Schools

The American high school has typically been a general school presumably set up to serve all youth who were economically and intellectually able to attend it. It was never the property of any particular class to the exclusion of youth of all other classes, but in its original development the high school was largely an academic institution devoted to providing

[6] See Educational Policies Commission, *Education for All American Youth: A Further Look* (rev. ed.; Washington, D.C.: National Education Association, 1951); and President's Commission on Higher Education, *Higher Education in American Democracy*, Vol. 3, *Organizing Higher Education* (Report; Washington, D.C.: Government Printing Office, 1947), pp. 5–15.

for a selected minority, a considerable proportion of whom were preparing for further education. The early high schools thus usually had but a single educational program and a single purpose, but it was believed that this purpose served all youth of ambition and that this program had substantial value for all.

The expansion and diversification of high school enrollments accompanying our increasing industrialization created the necessity for providing differentiated programs at the secondary school level. This differentiation could theoretically have been afforded either by the creation of separate schools to serve specific functions or by the organization of comprehensive high schools to offer different programs under one organization. Both methods have been and are being used, but either by accident or by design the comprehensive high school has been largely preferred in this country. There are implications involved in its development that merit special consideration. The specialized high school, however, is found in many large cities and in some areas.

The Specialized High School

The European pattern of secondary education has been primarily that of specialized schools, with one type of school preparing for higher education and a variety of other schools of a terminal nature preparing for various trades and subprofessions. This pattern was never entirely adopted in the United States, but as demands arose for the inclusion and extension of vocational programs in secondary education, specialized high schools did develop in many if not most cities. The genesis and original purpose of such high schools is revealed in such common names as the "Technical High School," the "High School of Commerce," the "Vocational High School," the "Manual Arts High School," and the "Polytechnic High School." Some areas established regional high schools for agriculture; in others may be found schools emphasizing work in selected academic fields such as music, arts, and sciences. It is interesting to note, however, that even in those cities where specialized schools have been most effectively promoted, a parallel system of comprehensive high schools has enjoyed equal popularity. It is difficult, if not impossible, to determine in any precise manner the number of specialized high schools because the specialized schools have typically expanded into comprehensive schools while presumably maintaining some particular emphasis upon their named specialization. It is not unusual to find a manual arts high school or a technical high school with a college preparatory program in which may be enrolled more students than in its specialized course of study. On the other hand, the comprehensive high schools in the same city will frequently be found to provide vocational programs comparable to those of the specialized high schools. In most communities it has thus been very difficult to keep a specialized high school true to type.

Obviously only in very large cities or in smaller cities dominated by one trade or industry can specialized high schools be developed. Although any generalization is subject to many exceptions, the general trends even in the large cities appear to be the further development of the comprehensive high school. Highly specialized programs that cannot be economically provided in all high schools may be centralized in a certain comprehensive high school open to qualified students from all sections of the city. Thus we may see developing a city pattern of a series of comprehensive high schools with certain specialized programs distributed among them. The specialized high school may have been a necessary step in the process of broadening and popularizing universal youth education, but it does not appear to have secured a dominant position in American secondary education. There is little indication that it will do so or that it is in the best interests of America that it should.

THE COMPREHENSIVE HIGH SCHOOL

As indicated, the comprehensive high school, established to serve many different special needs, is the typical secondary school institution in this country and is a peculiarly American institution. A scattered population and the existence of many small communities account in part for the development of a single secondary school; nevertheless, the comprehensive high school is congenial to and in harmony with some deep-rooted American democratic beliefs. There is a genuine belief that it is right and desirable for children from all classes, economic levels, and occupational groups to associate together. Although differences in abilities and occupational goals are recognized and accepted, the American public rejects the too early and too arbitrary classification of pupils on the basis implicit in separate and specialized high schools. This belief in equality which insists that all children ought to attend a common high school may appear naïve and unrealistic to some, but it is a very real belief and may provide an avenue for social integration of a people which is overlooked by those who profess to be impressed by the supposed educational efficiency of the specialized high school.

Recent studies cited at the conclusion of this chapter, which purport to show to what a large extent the experience of youth is affected by the economic level of the family, the occupational status of the father, and the area of the city in which the family lives, make it all the more important that this country's high schools shall be so patterned as to help offset these tendencies toward social cleavage. It is the deep-seated conviction of our people that differences of race, religion, and economic ability shall not come to dominate American life. Those of our social institutions that greatly influence the growth and development of children and youth, and especially the schools, must not be allowed to develop patterns of organization or practices that even unconsciously tend to emphasize and encourage arbitrary and undemocratic differences. Indeed, every effort should be made to be sure that positive and effective methods be found to discourage such developments. Among these means the comprehensive high school, with its common required program of general education, supplemented by the variety of specialized offerings necessary to serve all the youth of the community, is probably second to none, and its organization should be extended and improved as the needs of democratic life in this country demand.

The development of the truly comprehensive high school is thus at once one of the great achievements and one of the great challenges of American public education. Because it takes youth from all segments of American life it contributes to the social integration so badly needed. It offers the challenge of meeting this social need well at the same time that it meets the individual, specialized needs of each youth. Perhaps the major limitation of our comprehensive high schools has been that they have remained too closely attached to their original academic orientations. It has also been claimed that their specialized programs were not effective in producing the necessary technical competence in the students. The fact that secondary educators have not always fully realized the potentialities of the comprehensive American high school should be a stimulus for further study and effort. A common high school for all youth was only the dream of idealists a few generations ago; today that dream is being realized in what is one of the great experiments in education in the world's history. One of the criteria of whether a country is at heart democratic or autocratic is what it does about the education of its youth. If a nation's policies and practices in youth education magnify and perpetuate accidents of birth it is essentially autocratic and will become more so. If, on the other hand, its youth education deliberately eradicates these accidental differences while magnifying and cultivating intrinsic personal ability and worth, the nation is inherently democratic and will continue on that path. To such a goal and purpose high school administrators have a chance to make a substantial contribution.[7]

Size and Effectiveness of Secondary Schools

The need for the development of a comprehensive offering in the typical high school has focused attention on the enrollment size of high schools, since under prevailing conditions it is impossible to provide an

[7] David B. Austin, "The Potential of the Comprehensive High School," NASSP *Bulletin*, No. 198 (December, 1953), p. 74.

extended program in a small high school without raising the cost in terms of each pupil. A small student body may actually have the same diversity of educational need that a large student body has. It may have but one student whose needs are best served by a special educational program, whereas in a large high school there will be a whole class of pupils enrolling in this special program. A small student body thus makes the provision of these special facilities, used only a fraction of the day, an extremely expensive procedure. The costs of auxiliary services will also be correspondingly high. For this reason and others the matter of size of secondary attendance units and schools has come under sharper study.

The approximately 24,000 high schools in the United States range from urban high schools enrolling in excess of 5,000 students to isolated rural high schools with fewer than 10 students. Table 9 shows the number

TABLE 9. NUMBER AND PERCENTAGE OF PUBLIC HIGH SCHOOLS
BY SIZE OF ENROLLMENT, 1946 AND 1952

Enrollments	1946			1952		
	Number	Per cent	Cumulative per cent	Number	Per cent	Cumulative per cent
1–9	234	1.0		184	.8	
10–24	975	4.0	5.0	640	2.7	3.5
25–49	2,685	11.1	16.1	1,896	8.0	11.5
50–74	3,116	12.9	29.0	2,311	9.7	21.2
75–99	2,547	10.6	39.6	2,086	8.8	30.0
100–199	5,917	24.5	64.1	6,025	25.4	55.4
200–299	2,641	11.0	75.1	3,103	13.0	68.4
300–499	2,370	9.8	84.9	3,106	13.1	81.5
500–999	2,200	9.1	94.0	2,757	11.6	93.1
1,000–2,499	1,303	5.4	99.4	1,536	6.5	99.6
2,500–4,999	122	.5	99.9	97	.4	100.00
5,000 or more	12	.1	100.00	5	(Less than .05 per cent)	
Total	24,122	100.00		23,746	100.00	

Source: Biennial Survey of Education in the United States, 1950–52, Statistics of Public Secondary Day Schools, 1951–52, Chap. 5, p. 14.

and percentage of high schools by size of enrollment. It is to be noted that over 5,000 high schools enroll seventy-five or fewer pupils and that over one half of all high schools enroll two hundred or fewer pupils. While it certainly is true that the majority of pupils now attend high schools moderate or large in size, there is still a substantial number of secondary school pupils attending schools of relatively small enrollment.

The number of schools of small enrollment is accounted for in part by the sparsity of population in some areas and hence is unavoidable.

However, the principal reason for the numerous schools of small size is the fact that secondary school districts were established by small local communities before the era of modern transportation. Local community pride, admirable in itself, has tended to resist vigorously the reorganization of high school units to provide larger schools. Numerous studies have indicated the feasibility of consolidating small units into schools that can provide a more adequate program of secondary education at a reasonable cost.

A DESIRABLE MINIMUM ENROLLMENT
FOR A SECONDARY SCHOOL

All the evidence points to the need to develop secondary schools that will enroll a sufficient number of students to justify the offering of a reasonably broad and varied educational and activity program at a cost for each pupil that the public can afford. The minimum enrollment desirable to provide such breadth of offerings will vary somewhat with the nature of the special fields needed in a given community. Nevertheless, it is possible to cite approximate figures of enrollment that can be defended as desirable minima. Without question further increases in the size of enrollment, up to at least 1,200, permit more economical operation and a further enriched program. Presumably there is a point in enrollment beyond which there is little gain by further increases. This optimum size will vary somewhat with the degree of specialization that is desirable in a given community. The increased demands upon secondary schools for programs of broader scope tend to increase the enrollment necessary for efficient operation. It seems safe to say that comprehensive high schools of not less than five hundred in enrollment, and extending perhaps to two thousand students, would support broad programs of general education and services along with a reasonable variety of specialized offerings. In general it remains to be established whether any advantages, financial or otherwise, which may be found in schools of more than two thousand students, are not offset in whole or in large part by other disadvantages. The reduction in the number of very large high schools enrolling in excess of five thousand pupils in recent years would tend to indicate that there is a question of the desirability of organizing extremely large high schools.

It must be recognized that the desirable minimum enrollments cannot be achieved in all localities where high schools must be maintained, but it is equally true that reorganization and consolidation could eliminate a large fraction of very small high schools. Where really small high schools are unavoidable, the state should provide extra support so that a good program can be offered in spite of high costs in terms of each pupil. Anyone familiar with the intricacies of school consolidation and the understandable reluctance of the people in local areas to give up their local high school will realize that progress in this direction will be slow and somewhat troubled. The pressures for consolidation are, however, growing with the increased public demand for a generally broad program of secondary education and the prohibitive cost of providing such a program in the small high school. The accumulated evidence and pressures of recent years, as is noted later, is producing a substantial amount of reorganization.

ADAPTATION OF ORGANIZATION
AND TYPE TO LOCAL NEEDS

A large amount of unity of purpose and common understanding is necessary in the proper development of secondary education in the United States, but this is not to say that schools must have the same kind of organization and administration. Part of their vitality has arisen from the fact that states and local communities are free to experiment and adapt school organization to local conditions as new ideas present themselves. Conditions vary widely throughout the country, and facilities and resources are far from similar. Certain trends in organization are appearing and certain patterns of organization can be educationally justified, but these patterns will be adapted to the varying needs of local communities. Although the policy of extending secondary education through the junior college period may be accepted throughout the nation, each community should be allowed to choose which of the various types of organization seems best adapted to it. Again although the comprehensive high school is the kind generally to be encouraged, there are now and will continue to be some situations in which specialized high schools are more appropriate. The small high school is not something to be generally favored in this country, but still there are situations in which they must be retained and when retained they must be financed adequately so that they can provide a really good program. Adaptation to the local situation must be the rule, and although the simplicity that comes from identical organization and administration may be attractive to some educators, it is not as important as the vitality inherent in a system that encourages diversity and intelligent innovations.

A Look Ahead

There is much to suggest that the years ahead will offer a great and strategic opportunity to effect an organization of secondary education more nearly in line with best educational theory and practice. As has been noted, while there have been trends toward reorganizing secondary education, developments have often seemed to be controlled more by the exigencies of financial and building needs than by any educational design or belief. After an initial period of enthusiasm in the development of the junior high school, there appeared a period when apparently little new thought was given to this phase of the educational program. Often the education of older children and early adolescents appeared to be regarded as something to be shifted about in the organization to meet the particular pressures of the moment. Thus in the 1930's, when elementary school enrollments dropped while high school enrollments were still increasing, in many cases grade 7 and sometimes grade 8 remained or were reattached to the elementary school organization in order to use available building space. In the 1940's, when a reverse trend became established, the tendency was of course in the other direction. Certainly the practical demands of a given moment will necessitate flexibility in organization and, as noted, the particular organization does not automatically indicate the nature or quality of the educational program. However, a community should have a long-time master plan of educational organization as a goal if education is to be more than continual improvisation.

In a somewhat similar fashion the junior college has been all too frequently a marginal operation. While in some few states and in some communities the junior college has become established as a recognized integral part of the community school organization, all too frequently it has been a limited operation borrowing facilities from the regular secondary school and operating with inadequate financial resources.

There is evidence, as we move into the middle 1950's, that extensive reorganization of secondary education has been under way since 1945, and that the pace of change may well be accelerating. Table 10 presents some striking evidence of the reorganization that has taken place in the short space of six years. In this period there has been a decrease of 568 in the total number of high schools presumably because of reorganization and the elimination of many small schools. The actual decrease in the number of small high schools may be larger than indicated since actually there have been new high schools organized in areas of population growth. This is substantiated in part by the fact that, as reference to Table 10 will show, there has been a decrease in the number of high schools in all size categories enrolling less than one hundred pupils and an increase in all size categories above that figure until the size category of 2,500 is reached. The most striking fact revealed in the comparison is an increase of 3,241 in the number of reorganized high schools with an accompanying decrease of 3,676 in the number of regular high schools (grades 9 to 12).

There are parallel indications of a renewed interest in examination of the important educational role of the junior high schools. Local, state, and national studies have appeared appraising and redefining the broad

TABLE 10. COMPARISON OF NUMBER OF PUBLIC SECONDARY
SCHOOLS BY TYPES, 1946 AND 1952

Type of school	1946	1952	Increase	Decrease
Junior high schools	2,654	3,227	573	
Junior-senior and undivided high schools	6,366	8,591	2,225	
Senior high schools (grades 10 to 12)	1,317	1,760	443	
Regular high schools (grades 9 to 12)	13,844	10,168		3,676
Other	133			133
Total	24,314	23,746		568

Source: Biennial Survey of Education in the United States, 1944–46, Statistics of Public High Schools, 1945–46, Chap. 5, pp. 8–9; and 1950–52, Statistics of Public Secondary Day Schools, 1951–52, Chap. 5, p. 26.

function and purposes of education for early adolescents.

In similar fashion as the growing surge of enrollments advance into the secondary school and the institutions of higher education, there will be increasing need to examine the possibilities for an expanded program of community junior colleges. For instance the President's Commission on Higher Education, in a forward-looking report in 1947, states, "The time has come to make education through the fourteenth grade available in the same way that high school education is now available."[8]

Predictions are hazardous as witness the predictions made in the 1930's of a continued static or decreasing birth rate, but the authors are convinced that the late 1950's and the 1960's will be a period of extensive development and continued reorganization of secondary education perhaps equal or surpassing that in any past comparable period. Certainly the opportunity will exist. Expanding enrollments have required and will continue to require an enormous school building program. This provides an opportunity for re-examination of school organization and for long-time planning of the systems along the lines of good educational theory. The pressure of need for more diverse and complex school programs will continue to encourage district reorganization and consolidation. The need for more education should hold more youth in school for more years. Demands for adult education will likewise increase. A highly productive economy, moving—according to all prediction—into even higher levels of efficiency, can provide adequate resources to support an expanding educational system. The opportunities and challenges of a dynamic period will demand high level and imaginative leadership. The opportunities for the improvement and further development of secondary education will constitute a great challenge.

[8] President's Commission on Higher Education, *Higher Education in American Democracy*, Vol. 1, *Establishing the Goals*, p. 37.

Summary

The organization of schools into administrative units is fundamentally an attempt to create schools that can best serve the age and growth periods and the educational needs of children and youth. Growth is a continuous process, with wide variations among individuals, so that any division by ages and grades must be to some extent arbitrary and at best can be only an average time for transition into a different educational setting. Statistics of child development have indicated that as the child approaches adolescence around the twelfth year he needs a broadened and wider exploratory educational experience. These are the grounds for establishing the beginning of secondary education at grade 7 and extending it until the youth either ceases his school experience at eighteen to twenty or moves on to institutions of higher education.

The eight-year elementary school, followed by the four-year high school, which developed apparently somewhat by accident, has been recognized as less well adapted to the educational needs of children than an organization that will introduce secondary education earlier. The reorganization movement has resulted in the establishment of the junior high school and the 6–3–3 organization and the junior-senior high school and the 6–6 system. Also as a result of the movement, the junior college has become a part of the secondary school system in such organizations as the 6–6–2, the 6–4–4, or the 4–4–4–4 groupings. Although previously established patterns of school district organizations, existing legislation, and buildings in use explain the fact that the 8–4 organization is still frequent, there has been a steady increase in the number of reorganized schools.

Specialized schools have developed in many areas, primarily urban, but the comprehensive type of school serving all youth and offering a wide program within one institution is the dominant and characteristic secondary school. Specialized high schools have a function to perform in selected areas; nevertheless, the comprehensive high school is more in harmony with our democratic beliefs in equality and in the social intermingling of all youth.

The demand for a broad program of secondary education has brought more attention to the problem of the small school. Over half of the high schools in the United States have less than two hundred enrolled. This figure is below that at which it is feasible to provide adequate educational opportunity. Consolidation and reorganization of attendance areas can eliminate most of these small schools. There is evidence that we are moving into a period characterized by dramatic developments and extensive reorganization. Although certain patterns of organization can be suggested as most desirable, in general, American high schools should continue to show the diversity in organization that has been one of their characteristics and a source of their growth and strength.

Some Points to Consider

1. If organizing schools on the basis of age-mates is a good idea, should the plan be extended to a separate school for each age? What are the practical limits of such a basis of organization?

2. Do you think you can see in a typical small community how in one way or another the adults let youth know that they are not yet fully accepted as adults? What are some of the methods used?

3. Is it true that older adolescents put younger ones "in their places"? How? How can a younger adolescent win his place among the older ones?

4. When younger youth are separated from older youth by school organization, is the younger group left without adequate leadership?

5. What are some of the methods a school faculty can use in a junior-senior high school to assure that the younger youth in such a school are not crowded out of school life by the older youth?

6. Should youth be required by law to attend school, and for how long?

7. Is older youth education popular because there is little else for many of them to do except go to school? Can all older youth continue in school full-time with profit to themselves and to society? On what conditions besides the native ability of youth does your answer depend?

8. What can the school do to help youth move from full-time attendance in school to a responsible place in adult life without too abrupt a transition?

Further Reading

Austin, David B. "The Potential of the Comprehensive High School," NASSP *Bulletin*, No. 188, Dec., 1953.

Bogue, Jesse P. *The Community College*. New York: McGraw-Hill Book Co., Inc., 1950. Chaps. 10, 11.

Caswell, Hollis L., ed. *The American High School*. John Dewey Society Yearbook, 1947; New York: Harper & Brothers, 1946.

Davis, Allison. *Social Class Influences upon Learning*. Cambridge, Mass.: Harvard University Press, 1948.

Educational Policies Commission. *Education for All American Youth: A Further Look*. Rev. ed.; Washington, D:C.: National Education Association, 1951.

Fretwell, E. K., Jr. *Founding Public Junior Colleges*. New York: Bureau of Publications, Teachers College, Columbia University, 1954.

Gaumnitz, Walter H., and J. Dan Hull. "Junior High Schools versus the Traditional (8–4) High School Organization," NASSP *Bulletin*, No. 201, March, 1954.

Gruhn, William T., and Harl R. Douglass. *The Modern Junior High School*. New York: The Ronald Press Co., 1947.

Hollingshead, August B. *Elmtown's Youth.* New York: John Wiley & Sons, Inc., 1949. Parts III, IV.

Indiana School Study Commission. *An Evaluation of Indiana Public Schools.* Indianapolis: The Commission, 1948.

Keller, Franklin J. "What We Know about Comprehensive High Schools," NASSP *Bulletin,* No. 211, May, 1955.

Koos, Leonard V. *Integrating High School and Colleges.* New York: Harper & Brothers, 1946.

————. "The Junior High School after a Half-Century," *The School Review,* October-December, 1953.

National Association of Secondary School Principals. "The Modern Junior High School," *Bulletin,* No. 130, April, 1945.

National Society for the Study of Education. *American Education in the Post-War Period: Structural Reorganization.* Forty-fourth Yearbook; Chicago: University of Chicago Press, 1945. Chap. 2.

President's Commission on Higher Education. *Higher Education for American Democracy.* Report; Washington, D.C.: Government Printing Office, 1947.

Sexson, J. H., and J. W. Harbeson. *The New American College.* New York: Harper & Brothers, 1946.

State Education Department. *A Design for Early Secondary Education in New York State.* Albany, N.Y.: The University of the State of New York, 1954.

Sunderland, Albert, and Leland N. Drake. "The Junior High School, Yesterday and Today," NASSP *Bulletin,* No. 208, February, 1955.

Texas Study of Secondary Education. *Criteria for Evaluating a Junior High School.* Research Study No. 5; Austin: University of Texas Press, 1954.

U.S. Office of Education. *Biennial Survey of Education in the United States, 1950–52, Statistics of Public Secondary Day Schools, 1951–52.* Washington, D.C.: Government Printing Office, 1955.

————. *Junior High School Facts . . . A Graphic Analysis.* Prepared by Gaumnitz & Committee; Washington, D.C.: Government Printing Office, 1954.

Warner, W. L., R. I. Havighurst, and M. B. Loeb. *Who Shall Be Educated?* 2nd ed.; New York: Harper & Brothers, 1944.

The importance of good personnel relationships to the effective operation of any organization is more clearly recognized now than ever before. Part Two deals with the principal professional relationships that must be maintained by the high school principal. A good deal of stress is put on the democratic, cooperative quality of these relationships, since it is increasingly evident that unless this quality pervades the whole area of professional relations the staff-team will operate at much less than its best potential.

Part Two

STAFF PERSONNEL RELATIONSHIPS, RESPONSIBILITIES, AND ORGANIZATION

Chapter 5

THE HIGH SCHOOL PRINCIPAL, THE
SUPERINTENDENT OF SCHOOLS, AND
THE BOARD OF EDUCATION

O NE OF THE UNIQUE ASPECTS of school organization in America is the degree to which the local citizens of any community can influence and control the local school through their board of education. In many other countries there is nothing to correspond to our local boards. In others the local "council" has practically nothing to say about staff, program, policies, or practices. The head of the local school and his staff operate the school under the direction of a state authority. The profession moves into the community and conducts the school as it thinks best on the theory that technical and professional matters ought to be decided and handled entirely by the professional staff, which is not required to get local approval of basic policies. Such an arrangement produces a professional oligarchy in education that would not be tolerated in the United States.

In this country, good local high school administration requires that broad policies within the framework of the state's over-all program be understood and accepted not only by the local profession but by the community as well. It requires that allocations of authority and responsibility be those that the local community, through its board of education, has approved. It is therefore most important that the three main controls of a community's high school program—the board of education, the superintendent of schools, and the high school principal—work together in the greatest harmony and understanding. This entails clean-cut agreement on the functions each is to perform and on the resulting areas of responsibility and the limits of authority each is to have. Without such coordination the program of any high school, large or small, will suffer.

Board of Education and the Superintendent

The board of education represents the people of the state in their exercise of control over the local public school. Within the broad framework established by the state, the local board responds to the pressures of the community and provides the kind of school, in its judgment, that the community wants and can afford. Hence it is important for school workers to keep the community informed and maintain an intelligent public opinion that will demand and support an effective school.

PRESENT CONCEPT OF BOARD'S FUNCTION

In the earliest days of school boards and committees in this country, it was the practice for members to carry out specific acts of school administration, such as selecting teachers, textbooks and supplies, and supervising instruction. Occasionally members of boards of education still meddle in school administration, but they should delegate school administration to school specialists, and in general they tend to do so. This does not mean that the responsibilities of boards of education have been decreased. They are still entirely responsible to the state and to the community for the kind of school the community has. But they can best meet their responsibilities by functioning as legislative, evaluative, and policy-forming bodies. As such they are freed from the personal influences and petty distractions attached to detailed work and are able to devote their energy, thought, and judgment to the larger and more important problems of school control. Determining the annual budget and tax levy, providing the best of school leadership, considering recommendations for expansion of the schools, and evaluating evidence concerning the effectiveness of school practices—all these are examples of larger problems worthy of the time and best efforts of the board of education.

The board is effective as a body and not as individuals. Unless the board has legally and temporarily delegated authority to an individual member, that member alone has no more legal control over the schools than has any other citizen. Even when the board is in session, individual members have only the authority arising from their right to cast their own votes. Their control over the schools is exercised through this voting procedure, which indicates the policies and decisions adopted by majority vote.

The morale of teachers is greatly dependent upon the friendliness, integrity, and devotion to the schools of school board members. As individuals, members of the board should be friendly with all employees and considerate of them. They should guard carefully, however, against the impression that they are playing favorites among employees or bypassing the superintendent in dealing with any employee.

BOARD SELECTION OF SUPERINTENDENT

One of the most important duties of the board of education is the selection of a superintendent of schools as an executive officer. The board should sit in judgment upon his recommendations, demand of him any information that will aid them in making decisions, and charge him with the responsibility of carrying out the policies they have determined. At intervals the board should review and evaluate his executive acts, and either encourage him to move forward with renewed confidence and an improved sense of direction or employ someone to take his place whom the board can entrust with large responsibilities for executive action. Only in a somewhat less degree is it important that the board assure itself that the policies it has approved for the conduct of the high school program are being carried out under the general direction of the superintendent of schools by a thoroughly competent high school principal.

THE SUPERINTENDENT'S RELATIONSHIP WITH THE BOARD

As the educational leader of the community, the superintendent is responsible for building an alert and informed public opinion that will support and even demand effective schools. If they are properly informed, his two greatest allies in this enterprise will be the board and the professional staff. Hence the superintendent should spend much of his time with both in developing the educational program. Members of the board cannot be expected to make wise decisions unless they have had an opportunity to study all the facts and issues involved. Many superintendents find that they can best inform board members by spending time with them individually; others prefer to present oral and written reports at one time and in one manner to the whole board. Skillful superintendents do not press for decisions or determination of policies by the board until the members have acquired seasoned insights into the issues involved. A premature decision may block the progress of an educational program, whereas a board can move steadily forward in successive short steps so long as it moves with complete understanding. As new members come on to the board of education, it is necessary for the superintendent and other members of the board to acquaint them as soon as possible with the educational program as well as with their duties and responsibilities.

The superintendent will often find it helpful to invite the high school principal and other members of the staff to attend board meetings and report on particular school activities. However, no member of the staff, as such, should attend a meeting unless invited by the superintendent; and since the superintendent is the executive officer of the board, members of the staff are responsible to the board only through the superintendent. All business between staff members and the board should be cleared through the superintendent, who is responsible for building mutual understanding between the board and the members of the staff and for interpreting the actions of each group to the other.

THE SUPERINTENDENT'S RELATIONSHIPS
WITH THE SCHOOL'S STAFF

The superintendent is the educational administrator and leader of the members of the staff. As an effective administrator he should assign duties definitely and evaluate results fairly. However, as a leader he should aid members of the staff to look forward and to plan activities that can be achieved with benefit to boys and girls and with satisfaction to themselves. Staff members will carry on with greatest intelligence and understanding those activities that they have had some part in initiating and planning. Since effectiveness in classrooms depends not alone on duties assigned and results checked, but upon the enjoyment of working conditions as well, it is the duty of the superintendent to arrange working conditions so that staff members will enjoy their work. Job satisfaction in teaching as well as in industry is known to depend on many things besides financial return. Teachers who think they will be better satisfied by getting more money for teaching where the working conditions are bad are doomed to disappointment, though one cannot blame them for wanting an extra compensation for bad working conditions. School administrators who think that if the teachers of a community are only paid enough they will be satisfied and happy are also doomed to disappointment. School administrators should work for higher teachers' salaries in order to get the kinds of persons into education that are needed, but they also have it within their power to create other conditions of work that are at least equally effective in getting the best from teachers. Not until school administrators drop their patronizing attitudes toward teachers and move beyond the stage of "cordial" or "friendly" relations with teachers will staff relationships be what they should. The most advanced stage is based upon the administrator's sincere and wholehearted acceptance of staff members as full partners in the processes of school organization and administration. Only as this is done through the institution of such arrangements as are illustrated in other chapters of this book, where various aspects of high school organization and administration are dealt with, can we hope to have high school administration that is at once democratic, effective, and educative. Unless such staff relationships and arrangements exist, the school is not so organized or administered as to deliver its highest potential to its pupils or the community.

The Allocation of Responsibility and Authority to Principals

In 1932 the National Survey of Secondary Education reported wide variations in the responsibilities of high school principals and great variations in the judgments of principals and superintendents concerning the authority and responsibility that had been allocated to the former. Practically all stages in the development of the high school principalship were found. Some principals, even in large high schools, were merely carrying on as did the principal-teachers of a hundred years ago. Others, occasionally even in small schools, had attained a professional status as leaders of importance and influence in their local communities. The responsibility and authority of principals tended to be least in junior high schools and greatest in four-year high schools. There was also a tendency for superintendents to retain some responsibility for many of the duties and functions of the principal's office. Generally the superintendent was responsible for the maintenance of buildings, the ordering and distribution of supplies and equipment, and the operations of the budget. In schools enrolling as many as three hundred or more students, the principal was generally responsible for the internal administration of his school, including pupil personnel, the guidance program, the schedule of recitations, extracurricular activities, and the assignment of duties to teachers. In more than half the schools the principal was authorized to recommend teachers to the superintendent, who appointed all teachers or recommended them to the board of education, and who determined all teaching loads. Usually the principal and superintendent shared the responsibilities for supervision, textbooks, research, educational program, and public relations.

In his investigation of the principalship in large cities Reavis found many evidences of strength in the professional status of the position, but in at least three areas there were weaknesses as well. Generally, the principal was held responsible for his building and its condition, but he was given no authority over the custodial service. The principal was held responsible for the quality of instruction in his school but often he had to accept any teacher sent him by the central office. The principal was expected to interpret the educational program to the teachers in the school, but his influence at the time it was drawn up was insignificant in most of the cities studied. Evidently there were large schools as well as small ones in which a redefining of the authority and responsibility of the high school principal was needed.[1] Probably the situation has improved considerably since these studies were made. In the next chapter is presented some indirect evidence that this is so.

THE PRINCIPAL AND THE SMALL HIGH SCHOOL

In 1950 the U. S. Office of Education reported, "Regular 4-year and junior-senior 6-year high schools have a full-time principal when en-

[1] William C. Reavis, "Relations of School Principals to the Central Administrative Office in Large Cities," NASSP Bulletin, No. 66 (April, 1937), pp. 366–367.

rollment reaches the 200-size group. The separate senior high school has a full-time principal in the 100–199 enrollment range."[2]

In some states "supervisory principalships" have been created which are in reality superintendencies. Each of these supervising principals is in charge of a group of small high schools each with a full- or part-time principal. He may also be responsible for the elementary schools that send pupils to these high schools. This plan reduces the number of small superintendencies in the state and at the same time creates more economical attendance and administrative units. It also has the advantage of leaving someone constantly in immediate charge of each high school building; whereas if the superintendent acts as high school principal, his duties in connection with board business and with the elementary schools often require his absence from the building for a considerable time.

Occasionally administrators in small high schools make the mistake of copying organizational practices and procedures from larger schools. A complex organization for the guidance of pupils which is quite effective in a large school may be a hindrance in a small school because already existing in the small school is the situation which the complex organization is designed to bring about. In the same way it is not advisable to adopt courses of study in business subjects merely because they have been useful in larger schools. It is not advisable to divide administrative responsibilities among a number of persons in a small school merely because that procedure may be essential in a large school. In small schools which have made the greatest progress, responsibilities for administration and supervision have been assigned to a single individual. In the smallest school districts this individual is usually the superintendent with someone serving on a part-time basis as assistant principal while teaching the other part of the day.

Insistence upon the centralizing of administrative responsibilities does not in any way decry the importance of the small high school. The administration of any school, however small, is of sufficient importance and difficulty to challenge the capacities and resources of a single well-trained administrator. However, an unnecessary division of responsibilities is inefficient and in the smallest schools the individual best equipped to administer the high school is probably a superintendent who has had training in high school administration. In an assistant principal or assistant superintendent the high school may well have the leadership of a young person of recent professional education at the high school level who is able and willing to work closely with the youth of the community in affairs of particular interest to them.

[2] Ellsworth Tompkins and Walter H. Gaumnitz, *High School Staff and Size of School* (Washington, D.C.: U.S. Office of Education, Government Printing Office, 1950), p. 16.

More than half of our high schools enroll fewer than two hundred students each. In most of these schools costs are exorbitant and instructional programs are meager. Efforts to effect consolidations should be continued. Some improvement can come through the attaining of larger districts for taxing and administrative purposes while retaining community high schools even though they are small.

Other improvements can be made through direct attention to the opportunities and problems of the small high school. Small schools offer unusual opportunities for teachers and pupils to know each other and for both to know the community. Small schools ordinarily recruit young and flexible teachers. It is possible for in-service educational programs to be more effective with these teachers than they often are with teachers who are more mature and settled. The principalship or the assistant principalship of the small high school offers opportunities for dealing in an intimate and personal way with most situations and problems which face the administrator of a large school. Thus for the novice who is ambitious there is the opportunity of a worth-while apprenticeship, and for the experienced worker who chooses to remain in a small school there are opportunities for many personal and professional satisfactions.

THE HIGH SCHOOL PRINCIPAL AND THE SUPERINTENDENT

In the larger schools the high school principal is responsible to the superintendent for the administration of the high school, and generally a harmonious professional relationship exists between them. The principal is in a key position since the superintendent is dependent upon him for the execution of board policies in the high school. He is the personal selection of the superintendent—sometimes, in large cities, from an eligible list determined by examination or by agreement of the superintendent's associates and assistants. The principal recognizes the leadership of the superintendent in the matter of the policies of the school system, but often the principal contributes to the modification of old policies or to the creation of new ones as he acquaints the superintendent with the problems and needs facing his own school. The superintendent recognizes the principal as the responsible head of the school who has wide freedom of judgment and action so long as he follows the general policies of the school system, but who can be counted on to secure the approval of his superior when contemplating any departure from established procedures. Reavis believes that the status of the principal in the local school is the reflection of the administrative theory of the superintendent.

If the central office wants the principal to be the intellectual and professional leader of his school, responsibilities will be accorded to the principal commensurate with the influence the central office desires him to wield. If, on the contrary, the principal is conceived by the central office as a "super" clerk, he will be weighted with routine responsibilities, deprived of clerical assistance, and regarded only as the titular head of the local school.[3]

Upon the attitude of the superintendent and the ability of the principal depends the professionalization of the principalship. Principals who have the greatest influence and who have developed the principalship into key positions are those who have demonstrated a capacity for leadership and have been allowed great freedom by superintendents.

There are some areas—providing for articulation between the high school and lower schools is one—where the duties and responsibilities of superintendent and principal are in danger of overlapping. To avoid such confusion, in many school systems principals, in cooperation with the superintendent's office, have developed rules and regulations to be used as guiding principles in administration. They have great value but are sometimes so detailed that they hamper resourcefulness and contribute to perfunctory or routine administration on the part of principals. Opportunities for leadership vary with schools and with the personalities involved. In the absence of regulations, it is wise for the principal and superintendent, at the beginning of their service together, to draw up a written statement distinguishing their duties. Such a statement may be revised from time to time, but practice and experience are more effective than written words in establishing clear understandings and eliminating confusion.

Ordinarily, the experience and training of the superintendent will be broader than that of the principal, and he should be the latter's professional adviser, stimulus, and counselor. The superintendent is a busy man, but if he is interested in the execution of his policies he has no more important work than that of providing the motivating force for the professional development of the principal. Fortunate is the beginning principal whose superintendent is available for professional guidance but at the same time careful never to make himself indispensable. There is no fairer way of estimating the effectiveness of a superintendent than by the success of the principals and teachers whom he has appointed and to whom he has given in-service training.

On the other hand, the high school principal will usually be a younger person than the superintendent and his experience with high school administration and his often more extensive professional education at the high school level are likely to be more recent. The high school principal, therefore, should be expected to bring strengths to the school system beyond those possessed by the superintendent. If the high school principal's professional education has been what it should have been, he will regard the position as making him one of the most important leaders in the life of the youth of the community. He will expect to play a lead-

[3] Reavis, *op. cit.*, p. 366.

ing part in coordinating the activities of all the youth-serving agencies in the community to the end that each of them, and especially the high school, will be able to do a better job. He will not think of his position as limiting him to work in education narrowly conceived and restricted to a high school building. Rather, the total life of the community's youth is his concern, and he should be expected to make a more substantial contribution to this area than anyone else in the school system and, oftentimes, in the whole community.

The principal should also be a specialist in secondary education more narrowly defined. He therefore has an obligation to help keep the superintendent informed not only of the achievements and problems in his own school, but also of developments in the entire field that might have a bearing upon the school in which he is working. If the principal has done everything within his power to remedy weaknesses in the instructional program of the school and is being frustrated by deficiencies in personnel or equipment or physical facilities beyond his control, it is his duty to bring these matters to the attention of the superintendent with definite recommendations for their improvement.

The principal and the superintendent owe each other candor and frankness. When it is possible, they should spend time together informally discussing their common problems and attempting to work out common aims. They should learn to disagree in friendly fashion while presenting a united front to the public. If the principal should be overruled by the superintendent in a matter of major policy and find himself unable to support the superintendent's decision, he should find another position. For his part, the superintendent should do everything possible to magnify and dignify the prestige of the principal's position. All communications between the superintendent and the teachers or pupils of the school should go through the hands of the principal. The superintendent should refer to the principal all questions of patrons concerning the high school. All complaints about the school should be settled by the principal or in his presence. However, the principal should understand that an appeal to the superintendent from his decisions is always in order.

THE HIGH SCHOOL PRINCIPAL AND
THE SUPERINTENDENT'S STAFF

Even in large cities the responsibility and efficiency of the high school principal are enhanced by making his relations with the superintendent as direct as possible. However, the superintendent appoints his assistants and defines their duties. If the principal is responsible to the assistant superintendent in charge of high schools, their relationships should be the same as if the latter were the superintendent, except that the principal should be able to appeal to the superintendent if he deems it necessary. The principal should not be forced to go through an intermediary to whom he is not responsible, and an intermediary officer should be either administrative or supervisory. For instance, if there is an assistant superintendent for secondary schools, he should have real authority over the principals and not be an officer to whom a principal goes only to be told, "You ought to see the superintendent." If the assistant superintendent cannot decide the matter, he should say, "I will have to take it up with the superintendent and will let you know." Assigning both administrative and supervisory responsibilities to an intermediary officer or setting up a buffer between superintendent and principal, with little or no power to act, is more likely to lead to delay and confusion than to the efficient dispatch of business.

The history of the high school principalship indicates that at times there has been conflict between principals and supervisors of special subjects such as art, physical education, and music. However, P. R. Pierce reports that "since about 1900, superintendents as well as principals have, by and large, been satisfied that principals should be mainly responsible for special subjects." [4]

Principals themselves are seldom qualified as special supervisors, but they are most effective in improving instruction when they bear full responsibility and have access to the counsel and professional guidance of the special supervisors. There is developed between the supervisor and principal a common interest and a spirit of cooperation which serve to improve instruction in the local school and unify the work of the entire school system in the special field of the supervisor.

Failure to develop this common interest and spirit of cooperation between high school principals and supervisors appears to be in part a matter of deliberate attempt on the part of the central administration to minimize the instructional functions of the high school principalship. The confusion that results from poor organization grows out of failure on the part of the superintendent or assistant superintendent in charge of high schools to define the functions and relationships of special-subject supervisors in the central office and of high school principals. The supervisors get the idea that they are responsible for improving instruction in their particular subjects—over the dead body of the high school principal if necessary. They therefore tend to operate in a high school not as supervisory (staff) officers but as administrative (line) officers. In such a situation, administrative responsibility in a high school is divided among several supervisors and the principal, violating the sound administrative principle that at one time and one place one person and one person only must be in charge. The resulting confusion and inefficiency as well as ill

[4] Paul R. Pierce, *The Origin and Development of the Public School Principalship* (Chicago: University of Chicago Press, 1935), p. 216.

will between principals and supervisors can be corrected if it is agreed that the principal is in full charge at the school and the supervisors serve in an advisory (staff) relationship.

The confusion arising from a deliberate though generally unannounced attempt to minimize the responsibility of the high school principal in the instructional area is even more serious. It appears to result from a loss of confidence in the high school principal's leadership in the field of the educational program. He is considered competent to organize and operate such a program but not to lead in improving it. He is therefore reinforced in the instructional area by special supervisors or directors at the central office who are specifically put in charge of the school's educational program. The principal is thus in the position of a cook who is considered thoroughly competent to work over the hot stove but not to plan the menu. It may be true that some high school principals do not have the insight into instructional problems that they should, but it is still a question as to whether the remedy is to divide the responsibility for the high school among several workers, part attached to the central office and part to a particular high school. The one-time-one-place-one-person principle supports those who argue that the superintendent should insist that the principal become competent in the educational program or give way to one who is. If for any reason the high school principal needs assistance in the educational program, a full- or part-time specialist in this area should be provided for the high school and made responsible to the principal. The fact that many good high school principals are able to exercise competent leadership in this field is an argument for requiring each good high school principal to do so. Evading the issue by curtailing the principal's functions and assigning responsibility in the instructional area to others attached to the superintendent's staff, if carried to its logical conclusion in the local high school, means that the school system has principals who are order takers and rule followers with no privilege or expectation of exercising any initiative. This is bureaucracy at its worst—and no less bad because it occurs at the local level of school administration than if it occurs at the state or federal level. The only sound basis for action is to make the principal of each school solely and fully responsible to the superintendent of schools for all that goes on at the school and then requiring him to be or to become fully competent to perform all his duties acceptably.

In school systems where noneducational executives—business managers and their assistants—are responsible to the superintendent of schools, the relationships of high school principals with these executives are functional and direct in nature. However, in badly organized systems where noneducational executives are directly responsible to the board of education, communications between the principal and the noneducational executives are often routed through the superintendent or an intermediary educational executive. This routing is done in order to maintain the lines of authority in the organization, but it often results in confusion, friction, and delay. Clear differentiation should be made between matters that are routine and those that are exceptional. In routine procedures such as those concerned with the requisitioning of budgeted supplies where office policies are clearly defined and established, there should be direct communication between the high school principal and the noneducational executive. In exceptional procedures such as the requisitioning of special supplies not included in the budget, requests should be channeled through a superior educational executive.

THE HIGH SCHOOL PRINCIPAL AND THE SCHOOL STAFF

The earliest high schools were small schools and the principals were principal-teachers. It was the function of the principal to know the interests and abilities of every student in the school. The ablest and most energetic principal knew the family of every student and something of the ambitions and out-of-school experiences that conditioned him and were responsible for his total personality. In larger schools today it is not possible for the principal to have this personal knowledge, but it is his function to select and organize a staff that will know every student and provide learning experiences for him in terms of his needs.

The principal will find it necessary to assign tasks and delegate authority, but he will still bear the ultimate responsibility. In making some decisions, he may choose to accede to pressure from without or within the school, but he will not escape responsibility. The pressure groups which importuned him will not hold him blameless if the outcomes of their requests, to which he has yielded, are unsatisfactory. They are not responsible. He is. He will find it advisable to seek a group judgment and develop a consensus of the staff, but he still bears the responsibility of leadership.

In these days of so much discussion of democracy in school administration, some critics of school administrators argue for a situation in which the principal has no more responsibility for the school than any other member of its staff. He is simply the person who, having no classes to teach, has time to do some of the work of the school that the staff thinks needs to be done. They do not recognize that he as principal has any more responsibility for the school than has any other member of its staff. He has no more important responsibilities than they have—just different ones. His status in the group is different from but equal to theirs. The position of principal does not mean that its occupant has any leadership privilege or responsibility except when the groups want him to act as leader. In the name of "democracy" they argue that the group be left to find its own leadership, to recommend who should be principal, and to decide when he should cease to be principal. Administration as a specialized kind of service requiring the possession of particular abilities and distinct kinds of professional education is practically denied. Wilbur Yauch, in his book *Improving Human Relations in School Administration,*[5] takes a saner view of the matter. Without in any way defending arbitrary or autocratic school administration or without justifying any principal in attempts at leadership based wholly upon his status as principal, this writer shows that recognized leadership is an essential to effective group action, illustrates from practical experience how a principal can use his position to get full and free participation by all in the process of conducting the school, yet maintains that, as principal, he has a specialized and particular responsibility for the success of the institution.

In order to fulfill his responsibility, it is necessary in an emergency for the principal to be the final authority in the school, as he legally is. He should display his status-authority upon as few occasions and with as little ostentation as possible. He should recognize that need to resort constantly to it is a reflection on his leadership ability. His influence in the school should depend not upon his position but upon his friendliness and enthusiasm, upon his genuine acceptance of his co-workers as full partners in the enterprise, upon the fairness of his decisions, upon the depth of his general knowledge and the expertness of his professional skill. Still on occasion he will need all these resources plus the knowledge that his authority can be overriden only by the superintendent of schools if he is to meet his responsibility of organizing and administering the school as effectively as possible for the boys and girls within his charge. The price of leadership in an organization is willingness to bear responsibility, and, like General Eisenhower before the Normandy invasion, to be prepared in advance to accept the full responsibility for failure if one expects, in case of success, to be accorded his share in the glory.

Some Points to Consider

1. "This board of education was elected by this community to conduct the local schools. We know our community and what it wants its schools to do. We do not need any help from the state, and we do not want any interference from its department of education." What would be your comment on this quotation from a member of a local board of education?

[5] Wilbur A. Yauch, *Improving Human Relations in School Administration* (New York: Harper & Brothers, 1949). See also American Association of School Administrators, *Staff Relations in School Administration.* (Thirty-third Yearbook; Washington, D.C.: National Education Association, 1955), Chap. 1.

2. A high school principal asked the superintendent to have his duties officially defined by the board of education. The superintendent said he did not think it necessary to do so. As this principal, how would you support your request? As this superintendent, how would you defend your position?

3. A board of education of a city school system takes the position that it employs an expert superintendent of schools, furnishing him with a good staff to work under his personal direction, and that therefore it need not employ especially well-trained principals. Is the board's position weak or strong? Why?

4. A city superintendent of schools sent out a notice to all high school principals saying that the supervisor of physical education for the city schools would be responsible in the following year for the conduct of the interscholastic athletic programs of the city's high schools. What difficulties would you anticipate? What purposes could he have had? How else could he have handled it?

5. A committee of high school teachers visits you as superintendent of schools saying that the faculty thinks that you should recommend to the board of education a person whom they name to fill the vacancy in the high school principalship. You want to be a "democratic" school superintendent; what will your attitude toward their suggestion be?

6. When questioned about the obviously bad management of the opening of a school year at the high school, the principal said, "I am not responsible. The superintendent of schools has urged us to be democratic in our school administration, involving the faculty in the process as much as possible. The plans for school opening were all laid by a committee appointed by the faculty. The committee's plans evidently were not very good." Is the principal right? Is it better to be less efficient and democratic than the reverse? Must one make this choice?

Further Reading

American Association of School Administrators. *The American School Superintendency.* Thirteenth Yearbook; Washington, D.C.: National Education Association, 1952, pp. 65–102.
——. *Schools in Small Communities.* Seventeenth Yearbook; Washington, D.C.: National Education Association, 1939.
——. *Staff Relations in School Administration.* Thirty-third Yearbook; Washington, D.C.: National Education Association, 1955. Chaps. 1, 2.
Department of Supervision and Curriculum Development. *Group Planning in Education.* Washington, D.C.: National Education Association, 1945.
Elsbree, Willard S., and E. Edmund Reutter, Jr. *Staff Personnel in Public Schools.* Englewood Cliffs, N.J.: Prentice-Hall, Inc., 1954. Chap. 1.
Hoslett, Schuler D. *Human Factors in Management.* Rev. ed.; Harper & Brothers, 1951. Chap. 7.
Jacobson, Paul B., William C. Reavis, and James D. Logsdon. *Duties of School Principals.* Englewood Cliffs, N.J.: Prentice-Hall, Inc., 1950.
Johnston, Eric. "He Must Be More Than a Business Man," *New York Times Magazine,* January 25, 1953.

Koopman, G. R., Alice Miel, and P. J. Misner. *Democracy in School Administration.* New York: Appleton-Century-Crofts, Inc., 1943.

Meyering, Harry R. "The School Principalship," NASSP *Bulletin* No. 134, December, 1945.

Morrisett, Lloyd N. "How Can We Solve the Problems of Administration in the Small High School?" NASSP *Bulletin,* No. 269, March, 1950.

National Society for the Study of Education. *Changing Conceptions in Educational Administration.* Forty-fifth Yearbook; Chicago: University of Chicago Press, 1946. Chap. 4.

———. *The Community School.* Fifty-second Yearbook; Chicago: University of Chicago Press, 1953. Part II, Chaps. 6, 7, 8.

Pierce, Paul R. *The Origin and Development of the Public School Principalship.* Chicago: University of Chicago Press, 1935.

Reavis, William C. "Relations of School Principals to the Central Administrative Office in Large Cities," NASSP *Bulletin,* No. 66, April, 1937.

Reeder, Ward G. *School Boards and Superintendents.* New York: The Macmillan Company, 1954, Chaps. 1–3.

Tompkins, Ellsworth, and Walter H. Gaumnitz. *High School Staff and Size of School.* Washington, D.C.: U.S. Office of Education, Government Printing Office, 1950, p. 16.

Yauch, Wilbur A. *Improving Human Relations in School Administration.* New York: Harper & Brothers, 1949. Part IV.

Chapter 6

THE HIGH SCHOOL PRINCIPALSHIP

THE DEVELOPMENT OF THE HIGH SCHOOL principalship corresponds rather closely to the growth of the movement to open the secondary schools of America to all youth. During the eighteenth century, the Latin grammar school was the typical secondary school. It was a small school undisturbed by democratizing influences and usually taught by one master. During the latter part of the eighteenth century and the first half of the nineteenth century, demands for a less selective and less aristocratic secondary school stimulated the growth of the academy, a private or semipublic institution. Since the early academy was intended to be less selective, a broader educational program was provided. This tended to increase the size of the academies and necessitated several teachers. One of the teachers was generally designated as headmaster or principal, although he was primarily a teacher and often taught a full schedule of classes. In addition, he was responsible for discipline and administered the routine of the school as outlined by the regulations of the governing board.

With the rise of the high school in 1820 began the development of the public secondary school and also the growth of the modern secondary school principalship. The high school was directed and supervised by the local school committee, and in schools large enough to employ two or three instructors one of them was appointed "principal-teacher" to aid the committee in administering the school. Like the headmaster or principal of an academy, he was primarily a teacher who kept records, cared for the school plant, and disciplined pupils.

THE PRINCIPALSHIP EVOLVES

As school enrollments grew larger and less highly selected, it became necessary to free the principal from his teaching duties for part of the time. He was assigned the responsibility of visiting the classrooms and giving instructions to assistant teachers, since teachers were not educated for their work. The principal began to regulate classes and courses of instruction, to devote time to public relations, and to function as the real head of the entire school. As the population increased, cities grew larger, and the burdens of school committees became greater, there appeared a tendency to recognize specialists in the public school area. By 1835 the superintendent of schools was beginning to be recognized as the administrative and supervisory head of school systems in larger cities. Sometimes the superintendent was also principal of the high school. Often he had no connection with the high school, but the very fact that the superintendent was being recognized as a specialist made it easier for the principal to be regarded as a specialist also. By 1875 this tendency to recognize school management as a task for experts rather than for laymen or regular teachers had grown to such an extent that it began to be the practice for the authority over school systems to be centralized in the office of the superintendent of schools, and it was common practice also for the principals of the largest high schools to devote all their time to supervising their own schools.

Increasingly, as schools have grown larger and more complex, principals have been freed from teaching duties so that they could devote greater efforts to professional leadership. In the larger schools, where principals do no teaching, many responsibilities are assigned to assistant principals, counselors, and department heads. The principals serve as leaders for the study of educational problems and as coordinators of the efforts of all in solving those problems.

The steadily increasing high school enrollment has provided a constant spur and pressure to the professionalization of the principalship. From 1890 to 1930 the high school enrollment doubled every decade. From 1890 to 1940 the high school enrollment increased approximately 2,000 per cent while the population was increasing less than 100 per cent. Each decade saw greater variations in the home backgrounds, ambitions, abilities, and interests of high school students. As teachers sought to provide profitable learning experiences for types of students who had never before attempted to do their growing up in school classrooms, their resourcefulness and ingenuity were severely taxed and there was greater and greater need for the leadership of the principal.

The changing life outside the school also complicated the problems of the high school and increased the need for full-time, professionally educated principals. In 1890, there was little need to provide occupational information for high school students. Most of them had to begin work early and to take whatever work was available. Those who were able to choose vocations had no need of being informed by the school. They could see the work of the merchant, the lawyer, and the physician, and they could talk with these people about their work. By 1950, however, there was a great need to provide occupational information for high school students. Laws restrained their early entrance into vocations so that they were forced into a waiting period that could be used for choosing a vocation. Urban life was so specialized that they could not see clearly the work of different professions and industries. Moreover, in 1950, the schools faced problems of health, safety, leisure time, and citizenship that had not existed in 1890.

To help increasingly heterogeneous student bodies adjust to a changing and increasingly complicated life outside the school, high school educational programs were broadened and new subjects were added to programs of studies. New techniques were developed for organizing and administering schools and for helping students learn in classrooms. There was need for thoughtful study of the school and its problems under the leadership of a full-time and well-educated administrator. The principal was forced to grow into professional leadership.

Although the years 1890–1950 saw a steady growth in the authority and responsibility of the principalship, it is only in the larger high schools that the position can be termed professionalized. There are many schools in which the principal is still the principal-teacher. About 30 per cent of the approximately 24,000 public high schools in the United States enroll fewer than one hundred students each, and in these schools the origin of the principalship can be clearly seen. Other larger high schools in the United States exhibit every stage in the development of the responsibility and authority of the high school principalship.

Although principals are better educated today than ever before, the challenge and tasks facing them are greater. The principal of 1849 had little formal preparation for his administrative tasks, but he dealt with a highly selected student body that had common goals and that was learning to live in a simple and comparatively static society. The high school principal of today works with almost all the youth of the community as they are learning to live in a complex and changing society. The principal must manage routine details and operate the school as it is. This is a task of considerable size, but chiefly it is the work of an office manager. In addition, the principal needs to plan and work continuously to make the school over into what it ought to become. This is the work of a policy maker and leader. The high school principal should be not only an office manager but also an educational statesman.

THE PRINCIPAL'S TASKS

In an address made before the North Central Association of Colleges and Secondary Schools in 1923,[1] when he was principal of the

---

[1] Milo Stuart, in Proceedings of the Twenty-eighth Annual Meeting of the North Central Association of Colleges and Secondary Schools, March 15, 16, and 17, 1923 (Hotel Sherman, Chicago), Part II, pp. 79–86.

Arsenal Technical High School in Indianapolis, Milo Stuart, one of America's successful high school principals, expressed his conception of the principal's task which he later summarized as follows:

The relation of the principal to his teachers should be the most intimate of any. If a teacher fails, the principal fails; if the teacher succeeds, the principal succeeds. To sum up what the principal's job is, I should call him a referee —the captain of the ship—the boss of the firm—a juvenile judge before whose tribunal come not only the culprits but the adults who frequently contribute to the pupils' shortcoming. He is a promoter who must project the future of his institution and convert the public to his plan. He is social physician to every parent who has a wayward son who needs attention. He is a friend-in-need to pupils and to all the homes in which misfortune comes. His power, his activities, even the good he does, cannot be measured by a material yardstick.

After considerable deliberation a national committee on training and experience standards for principals of secondary schools reported that

Each of us has a particular part to play in secondary education. The principal of the American secondary school has in some measure all the responsibilities of the secondary classroom teacher, the custodian, the cafeteria worker, the clerical staff, the nurse, and all other school employees. In addition, the principal has three kinds of responsibilities which are over and beyond those of other school workers.

First, the principal has the responsibility for leading the entire staff of the secondary school in developing as guiding principles the objectives of the school. . . .

Second, the principal has the responsibility for coordinating all those activities which grow out of a dynamic program of secondary education. . . .

Third, the principal has the responsibility for making decisions. . . .[2]

The committee held that in order to meet these responsibilities the principal needs an understanding of education's major responsibilities in a democracy for the development of the individual and for the advancement of the general welfare.

Under the authority of the Pennsylvania Branch of the National Association of Secondary School Principals, a group of graduate students at Lehigh University collected statements of specific duties of the high school principal from about two thousand teachers, administrators, laymen, and students. These returns were analyzed and summarized into the thirteen categories of duties listed below. "Leadership in the professional improvement of the staff" was mentioned most frequently as a principal's duty by teachers, administrators, and laymen and was the item mentioned second most frequently by the students.

[2] Dan Harrison Eikenberry, "Training and Experience Standards for Principals of Secondary Schools." NASSP *Bulletin*, 35, No. 181 (November, 1951), 16.

Duties	RANK IN IMPORTANCE				
	Total	Teacher	Admin.	Layman	Student
Leadership in the Professional Improvement of the Staff	1	1	1	1	2
Improving the Classroom Instruction	2	2	2	2	4
Building and Improving the Curriculum	3	3	3	4	8
The Maintaining of Order and Discipline	4	5	10	7	6
Building and Improving the Extra-curricular Program	5	6	6	9	7
Self-improvement and Growth on the Job	6	7	9	3	5
Informal Relations of Principal-Students	7	11	13	8	1
Public Relations and Community Responsibility	8	8	5	6	9
Making the Schedule of Classes	9	4	4	13	11
Guidance and Adjustment of Pupils	10	12	7	5	3
Desk Work, Supplies, Correspond-ance	11	9	8	12	10
Provision and Upkeep of Building	12	10	11	10	12
Relations to Superiors	13	13	12	11	13

Source: National Association of Secondary School Principals, "A Study of the High School Principalship in Pennsylvania," Bulletin, 37, No. 198 (December, 1953), 118. Reprinted by permission.

CHART 3. RANK OF IMPORTANCE OF DUTIES OF THE HIGH SCHOOL PRINCIPAL AS RANKED BY TEACHERS, ADMINISTRATORS, LAYMEN, AND STUDENTS

Attitudes toward the High School Principalship

Two comprehensive and thoughtful studies of attitudes toward the high school principalship were reported by David B. Austin and James S. Collins.[3] In each of twenty-five communities in the metropolitan area of New York City, a high school teacher, a school superintendent, a lay citizen who had been closely associated with the school, a high school senior, and a high school principal were interviewed. The purpose of the interviews was to collect reports of effective and ineffective job behaviors of high school principals which were judged to have made the difference between success and failure in observed work situations. Each interviewer was asked to respond in detail with descriptions of actual incidents to the following question: "Thinking back over your

[3] David B. Austin and James S. Collins, "A Study of Attitudes toward the High School Principalship," NASSP Bulletin, Vol. 40, No. 215, January, 1956.

observations and experiences in connection with the high school, what do you believe the high school principal must do or avoid doing to meet your expectations?" The data collected through the interviews were analyzed and classified under eleven interrelated areas of job performance:

1. Organizing, Managing, and Coordinating Components of the School
2. Improving Curriculum and Teaching
3. Gaining Confidence and Support of Staff Members
4. Winning Respect and Approval of Students
5. Enlisting the Support and Cooperation of the Community
6. Delegating Authority and Responsibility
7. Increasing His Professional Competence
8. Participating in Community Affairs
9. Making Policies and Decisions
10. Working with Higher Administration
11. Executing Policies and Decisions

Altogether in the eleven areas, ninety-one acceptable practices and sixty unacceptable practices were identified as having an important influence on the success or failure of the principal. Examples of acceptable practices identified in the area of organizing, managing, and coordinating components of the school were "Bases all plans and courses of action on a purpose consistent with accepted goals of secondary education" and "Makes arrangements to insure intercommunication among students, staff members, parents, and the administration, regarding proceedings of the school." In the same general area examples of unacceptable practices were "Makes changes without deliberately studying, planning, and organizing affairs of the institution" and "Emphasizes certain aspects of the school in which he has strong interest but neglects other parts." The 151 acceptable and unacceptable practices deserve the careful consideration of students who propose to be high school principals and of high school principals interested in improving their competencies.

As a basis for the second study reported by Austin and Collins, juries of high school principals aided in developing from the acceptable and unacceptable practices a list of thirty-two activities judged to be critical items contributing to the success of high school principals. Questionnaires designed to find out these principals' attitudes toward the thirty-two activities were mailed to twelve thousand high school principals, superintendents of schools, teachers, students, school board members, and Kiwanis club secretaries in all the states of the nation. Each respondent was asked to check in appropriate columns whether he believed that each of the activities was (1) of greater or lesser importance, (2) considered important or unimportant by the community, or (3) that he had no opinion on the matter. Forty-two per cent of the twelve thousand persons to whom the instrument was addressed returned usable replies. Most replies came from principals and superintendents, but there were hundreds of respondents in each category.

In general, the activities regarded as important by principals were regarded as important by the community also. Actually community opinions concerning a number of the principal's activities were apparently higher than the principals expected them to be. The reported practices of principals were closely related to their own attitudes toward the practices. The authors summarized the study as follows:

As this study has collected information concerning the attitudes and expectations concerning the principalship, certain fairly clear conclusions have emerged. They include the fact that the principal's modern role is first and foremost that of leading in the instructional program. Further, managerial responsibilities can be delegated when necessary to further the effectiveness of the principal in his major work without fear of lack of support or understanding on the part of his fellow-workers and the community to be served. The role of the principal in the school includes responsibility for improving the educational program of the school, for counselling with pupils and their parents, for understanding and helping the teaching staff with the solution of personal and professional problems.

As a citizen in the community, the principal is expected to live within the community and enjoy its social and civic life freely. He is not expected to announce his views on political and civic issues to any unusual degree, but is expected to serve on civic planning groups, be a member of a service club, participate in church life, and lead in the study of school and community by community study groups. On the other hand, he is not expected to leave his school building frequently to participate in civic organization activities to any great extent, and is not looked upon with great enthusiasm as the appropriate person to lead in the coordination of youth-serving agencies within the community.

As a member of a profession, the principal is expected to attend professional meetings of a local, state, or national scope, and his reimbursement for part or all of his expenses for such attendance apparently seems reasonable. To a slight extent he is expected to do some writing for publication, and to represent the best interests of the school and the teaching staff in conference with the superintendent.

These generalizations, of course, are based upon expressions of attitude and opinion volunteered by over two thousand principals and hundreds of superintendents, teachers, Kiwanians, board members, and students.[4]

These statements and reports concerning the work of the high school principal suggest a job of considerable significance.

Certainly the task is worthy of our ablest talent. Even in our best schools that can afford high school principals as full-time professional

[4] *Ibid.* (This part of this article draws upon data from unpublished doctor's degree studies made by Dr. Russell Clark, Dr. Harry Brown, and Dr. Howard Strong. New York, Teachers College Library, Columbia University, 1956, pp. 138–139. Reprinted by permission.)

leaders, there is a need for dignifying the position as a career in order to retain administrators now serving and to attract able leadership in the future. Too many high school principals are drawn into business and industry, into the superintendency, or into the college professorship. We need able men to influence the behavior of high school boys and girls, even as we need them to manufacture breakfast foods, soft drinks, and ladies' ready-to-wear. An intelligent society will not by design attract its ablest workers into activities that deal with material resources and its least able workers into activites that deal with human resources. We need able high school principals, even as we need able school superintendents and college professors. But to neglect the potentialities of our youth is the surest road to national suicide. We need to create a situation that makes good high school principals feel that they can afford to regard the post as worth while in itself and not merely as a steppingstone to another position. The work to be done through the years with the boys and girls of high school age in any community is challenging enough for the best efforts of a lifetime, and ordinarily the longer a principal remains in one school the greater are the dividends that reward his efforts.

Personal Qualifications of the High School Principal

As a leader of the instructional staff and the community, the principal is in need of the qualities sought in all teachers. He should be respected for his general scholarship and for his special competence in at least one area of learning. He should have had successful experience as a teacher. He should be able to express himself accurately and stimulate others effectively. He needs mental and physical health and their accompanying energy. Society has no right to expect the principal to be a paragon of all virtues, but qualities such as fairness, patience, buoyancy, flexibility, sympathy, persistence, and native ability must in some degree belong to all successful teachers. As a teacher among teachers, if he is to be effective, the principal cannot be inferior in these personal characteristics. Many teachers who can successfully complete graduate courses that prepare for the principalship should not aspire to that position. Superintendents of schools, high school principals, and college professors have a guidance responsibility toward ambitious high school teachers to the end that only the most promising counselors of youth and leaders of youth education may be drawn into the high school principalship. In addition to general personal qualities needed by all teachers, the high school principal should acquire a basic philosophy of education, professional knowledge and understanding, an interest in ideas and professional literature, an interest in people and especially in boys and girls, and devotion to the highest ideals that will enable him to lead a faculty and community to the highest levels of cooperative work with youth.

A BASIC PHILOSOPHY OF EDUCATION

By careful thinking he should decide what his educational aims are and how he proposes to achieve them. As a leader of a school he should know where he is going. His aims should be continuously reevaluated and subject to change in emphasis in the light of new evidence, but unless he keeps his ultimate goals constantly in view, he is likely to be distracted by the pressure of routine duties, the weight of the machinery of the school, and the conflict of competing ideas and forces that press in upon the school. No principal is able to meet all the demands upon his time, and necessarily he has many routine duties, which are like a habit-forming drug in that they protect him from the discomfort of thinking, and constantly tempt him to escape more and more into routine responsibilities that could be assumed by others. The machinery of the school operates on its own momentum in well-established paths, and changes are disturbing to everyone concerned. The principal is busy and tempted to let well enough alone. People who are selfish and reformers who mean well all hope to achieve their aims through the schools. Often their schemes are in line with the objectives of the school. Often they are not. The principal who has not thought out and in some degree popularized his educational aims is ineffectual in coping with these pressure groups. He has no measuring sticks with which to judge their proposals and no backing from the community on his decisions. He needs a frame of reference that he has made for himself or thought through and accepted from someone else which will guide all his efforts toward ultimate goals and protect him from his own desire for comfort, the inertia of the school, and the aggressions of forces that would use the school for their own ends.

A SOCIAL PHILOSOPHY

The school operates in a social situation. If its educational philosophy is to be sound and is to make its strongest appeal to a principal, it must be rooted in a social philosophy in which he deeply believes. Education has always grown out of the needs of a social group in its life setting. Longfellow in his "Hiawatha" gives a good picture of the education of an American Indian youth for life in his social group. In more complex social situations where education has been institutionalized and made more largely the business of the school and its teachers, it still gets its validity from the goals, purposes, and ideals of the society in which it exists. Briggs has stated the idea well with relation to education in our democratic state when he says that our schools exist "to make the state a better place in which to live and in which to make a living."[5] Before one can be sure of his concept of the function of our schools, he must be sure of his concept of the function of our democratic society. He has to be sure that the protection and perfection of our democratic organization of society are not only worth dying for but worth living for. He has to recognize that despite our noteworthy gains, the level of general welfare we have attained still falls far short of our hopes and our potentialities. Unless one believes in democracy as a way of life that holds out to all peoples everywhere their maximum possibility for individual self-realization and self-development, and unless one recognizes education as the democratic society's chief instrument for achieving these levels of individual welfare and well-being, one cannot bring to his lifework in education the convictions, the loyalties, and the devotion needed to sustain and guide him in the maze of confusions and contradictions in which school men and women customarily work.

PROFESSIONAL KNOWLEDGE AND UNDERSTANDING

In order intelligently to formulate his goals and his methods for reaching them, the principal must have a knowledge of the schools below and above the secondary level, an understanding of the history and philosophy of educational movements and social institutions, and insights into the psychology and learning processes of adolescents. He should know principles of curriculum construction, practices of school administration, and methods of research and teaching. In working with pupils, teachers, and the community, the principal with little professional training is decidedly handicapped in comparison with fellow principals who understand sound and effective practices in administering schools. Indeed, well-trained men of mediocre ability are often able to achieve where brilliant, untrained men have failed.

INTEREST IN IDEAS AND PROFESSIONAL LITERATURE

No matter what his training and experience, unless the principal maintains a constant interest in professional books and magazines, his usefulness will soon be impaired. Many of the best books in the field of secondary education are of comparatively recent date. Moreover, any book or idea that has significance for society has significance for secondary education; hence the principal's search for ideas will be over a wide area. It will be necessary for him to be selective in his reading, for he cannot read everything even in the field of secondary education, but only a genuine interest in all ideas that bear upon his work can keep him abreast of his rapidly changing problems. He can stimulate his interest by oc-

[5] Thomas H. Briggs, *The Great Investment* (Cambridge, Mass.: Harvard University Press, 1930).

casionally writing professional articles or contributing to professional conferences. He can learn from people as well as from professional literature. The probation officer, the judge of the juvenile court, the educational director of an industrial concern, the college dean, the employer who employs the product of the school, and other laymen of the community who are interested in education and youth may have helpful ideas for the high school principal.

The National Association of Secondary School Principals' Committee on Training and Experience Standards for Principals of Secondary Schools emphasized especially the individual responsibility of the principal for his own continuing professional growth through the use of facilities of educational institutions, activity in professional associations, travel, participation in community activities, research in education, participation in workshops or educational conferences, reading, television, radio, lectures, and hobbies. The Committee also recommended that school budgets include financial provisions to encourage the in-service growth of the secondary principal through attendance at professional meetings and the devotion of summer vacations to educational opportunities rather than noneducational employment.

INTEREST IN PEOPLE AND ESPECIALLY IN BOYS AND GIRLS

Unless the principal has a real interest in people and a strong sympathy and even affection for young people, his work will seem to himself, and to others as well, cold and mechanical. It is impossible either to feign or to conceal such a genuine interest, and patrons, teachers, and pupils distinctly sense the absence or presence of sympathetic concern. In their trial-and-error methods of achieving their developmental tasks, adolescents are often annoying and irritating. They recognize scorn and intolerance of their efforts but respond readily to those who attempt to help them solve their problems. The high school principal will not be happy and useful if he is repelled by the boisterous exuberance of youth. Many of his satisfactions will be found in sharing the discouragements and enthusiasms of young people and in helping them grow into mature adults.

DEVOTION TO HIGHEST IDEALS

The principal must have the highest ideals for himself, the school, the community, and his profession. Thoroughly honest and possessing a strong moral sense, he must also be imbued with a spirit of service. He may have splendid ultimate goals for the school and even know how to achieve them, but he will not do so unless he is willing to sacrifice personal comfort, time, and effort. At times he may need to risk or even sacrifice his position for the best interests of the young people in his community. It is difficult to isolate precisely the motives of educational leaders, but it appears that those who have influenced secondary education most have been driven by something of the missionary spirit and the desire to achieve through service.

CHARACTERISTICS AND PRINCIPLES OF LEADERSHIP

A new type of educational leadership will be demanded of the high school principal of the future. The positive role of education in shaping the personal and social ideals of youth and thus achieving the goals of our democratic society is more clearly evident than ever. Moreover, the position of the principal is central in the improvement of our educational program. Far-reaching plans may be developed on the national, state, and community level, but they can only be made effective by principals who work with teachers, students, and patrons in particular schools.

This does not mean, however, that the principal as an individual should always be the director, stimulator, or helper of others. Educational leadership enlists the abilities, drives, and interests of many people and brings them together in a common effort. A large part of the principal's leadership should be in identifying leadership qualities of other staff members or in recognizing and developing their leadership potentials. Most individuals have qualities which will enable them to serve as leaders in some particular situations. Mackenzie and Corey define leadership as "a name for the activities of people who are perceived by an individual or a group as providing maximum help, actually or potentially, with the means which the individual or group desires to use to attain its goals."[6] They show that leadership characteristics vary with the situation in which leadership is exercised and make the following observations to explain this situational aspect of leadership behavior:

1. The person perceived by an individual or a group as able to provide help for the achievement of one goal may be unable to help the same individuals or group reach another goal. . . .

2. The person who may be perceived by one individual or one group as being able to help achieve a certain goal may not be perceived by another individual or group as useful in the attainment of the same goal. . . .

3. The individual thought to be most helpful in respect to control of one means toward a given goal might not be perceived as providing help in respect to another means toward the same goal. . . .

4. The person who is perceived by an individual or a group as being able to help them at one time may not always be so regarded. . . .[7]

[6] Gordon N. Mackenzie and Stephen M. Corey, "A Conception of Educational Leadership," NASSP *Bulletin*, 36, No. 183 (January, 1952), 10.

[7] *Ibid.*, pp. 11–12.

One of the outgrowths of a series of studies designed to improve the quality of educational leadership was the development of a number of generalizations about certain aspects of human behavior which help explain why people behave as they do and how they change. The statements were drawn chiefly from experiences with teachers and administrators, but the authors hold that they are equally applicable to all staff members and to teachers working with youth. The generalizations which deserve thoughtful consideration from students of the high school principalship are as follows:

Proposition I—Most of our behavior, particularly as it involves relations with others, can be explained as our attempt to preserve our integrity, our self-respect—to maintain or build our self-esteem.

Proposition II—At the time of our action, our behavior is determined by our private, personal perception of the situation and its requirements.

Proposition III—At the time we act, we do what seems justified to us according to our view of the situation.

Proposition IV—People behave differently because their perceptions of the situations to which they react differ.

Proposition V—Changed perceptions lead to changed behavior.

Proposition VI—We feel satisfaction when we realize that our perceptions and our consequent behavior are considered correct and right by others of the group or groups to which we want to belong.[8]

Educational Qualifications of the High School Principal

During the past thirty years there has been a steady increase in the amount of professional training acquired by high school principals in the United States. This trend indicates a deepening appreciation of the responsibilities of the principalship on the part of high school principals, employing officials, certifying agencies, and the general public as well.

The Office of Education published in 1925 a bulletin entitled, "The Status of the High School Principal," of which D. H. Eikenberry was the author.[9] In 1947 Floyd M. Farmer made a study of the public high school principalship, basing it upon a sampling of the membership of the National Association of Secondary School Principals.[10] To some extent the Farmer study parallels that by Eikenberry, so that we may note some

[8] Stephen M. Corey, A. Wellesley Foshay, and Gordon N. Mackenzie, "Instructional Leadership and the Perceptions of the Individuals Involved," NASSP *Bulletin*, 35, No. 181 (November, 1951), 83–91, *passim*.

[9] Eikenberry, *Status of the High School Principal* (U.S. Office of Education, Bulletin No. 24; Washington, D.C.: Government Printing Office, 1925).

[10] Floyd M. Farmer, "Public High-School Principalship," NASSP *Bulletin*, 32, No. 154 (April, 1948), 89–91.

changes that have occurred in the intervening twenty years. The following statements are based either on the medians of the two groups or on the modal practices. The median age reported in the Farmer study is forty-three years as compared with thirty-three years in the previous study. This increase is largely accounted for by the fact that the principals of smaller high schools were older on the average than they were in 1925. The median high school principal in 1947 taught an average of 1.4 periods each day as compared with 3.0 periods previously reported. In 1947 he was generally a member of the various educational associations—city, county, regional, state, and national—with about 30 per cent having recently held an officership in one of these organizations.

In 1947 he had twenty-three undergraduate hours of education to his credit and twenty-eight graduate hours, compared to thirteen and four, respectively, in the previous study. About half had earned graduate credit within the five years preceding 1947. The typical high school principal in 1947 held a master's degree, whereas Eikenberry reported the bachelor's degree as typical. This master's degree was generally earned between 1931 and 1941. Generally, the high school principal entered his first principalship from a high school teaching position in which he had served for a median of 4.3 years, as compared to 3.2 years in the Eikenberry study. He was generally a principal in the state in which he received his educational preparation. In 1947 the median length of time he had been in the present principalship was four years as compared to three in the previous study. He was thirty years of age when he entered his first high school principalship, whereas Eikenberry's principals were twenty-six years of age.

The typical high school principal in 1947 usually attended church and was possibly an active member of the church. He was a member of various civic organizations, of a luncheon club, and of lodges. He read such professional magazines as were published by the state and national educational associations and the *School Executive, Clearing House, American School Board Journal,* and the *Nation's Schools.* He read such nonprofessional magazines as *Reader's Digest, Time, Life,* and the *Saturday Evening Post.* He also read two or three professional books every year. He reported himself as being moderately liberal in his educational philosophy as measured by the Cooperative Study of Standards, though moderately conservative with reference to pupil participation in determining content and activities of school experiences. He was, however, generally the principal of a school in which the curriculum was of the conventional, college preparatory type, with some commercial work and household and industrial arts offerings.

In general, the chief gain in the period between the two studies has been in moving from a bachelor's degree to the master's degree. In 1947, professional reading was not very generally done, nor was it done in very large amounts. Nonprofessional reading, both magazines and books, tended to follow the typical level of the community as measured by the best sellers and the size of magazine subscriptions.

IMPROVED CERTIFICATION STATUS

In recent years state certification agencies have, in increasing numbers, provided certificates for high school principals which require more training than do those for high school teachers. In 1951, according to a committee of the National Association of Secondary School Principals, Massachusetts was the only state not issuing certificates for all principals and only thirteen states issued the same types of certificate for secondary school principals as for teachers.[11]

For the initial certification of secondary school principals fifteen states required the master's degree or its equivalent. Eleven states required courses in addition to the bachelor's degree but less than one full year of graduate study. Twenty-four states issued initial certificates which required only the bachelor's degree. Only Colorado and Oklahoma issued initial certificates for secondary school principals with requirements which amounted to less than a bachelor's degree.[12]

For initial certification the amount of professional work required ranged from none to sixty semester hours, the average being twenty-six semester hours. In some states certain courses were required, usually educational psychology, guidance, and courses in high school teaching, curriculum, administration, and supervision. Eight states required administrative experience for initial certification and in all but nineteen states some experience was required.

The NASSP Committee on Training and Experience Standards for Principals of Secondary Schools proposed definite standards for the certification of high school principals.[13] Included were a basic general educational background, specialized professional preparation equivalent to the master's degree, required renewal of the initial certificate after a minimum service of three years, and an advanced professional certificate renewable in periods of from five to ten years.

Instructional Leadership Does Not Just Happen

The sampling of attitudes toward the work of the high school principal reported earlier in this chapter is encouraging. It shows that

---

[11] Eikenberry, "Training and Experience Standards for Principals of Secondary Schools," *loc. cit.*, p. 9.

[12] *Ibid.*, p. 12.

[13] *Ibid.*, pp. 59–61.

the principals themselves accept their modern role as that of improving the instructional program and that selected laymen, Kiwanis club secretaries and school board members, probably attach more importance to this role than the principals do. The study indicates a favorable climate of opinion for the further professionalization of the principalship. It is certain, however, that improving the instructional program is a difficult task and not an easy one. It is a task demanding careful planning and persistent effort.

HOW THE PRINCIPAL SPENDS HIS TIME

A number of studies have shown that high school principals spend more time on administrative problems than on improvement of instruction, especially during the school day.[14] There is evidence also that much of the time principals spend on improving instruction has to do with the development of new courses rather than the reorganization of present courses within the curriculum. A study involving five hundred high school principals in an eastern state indicated that the greatest block of their working time outside the school day was spent on "athletics."[15] The second consumer of working time outside the school day was "teacher, parent, and student conferences" and the third was "checking on buildings, equipment, etc." Among those who have given thought to the problems and tasks of educating American youth there is general agreement that the high school principal has not yet assumed his ultimate role in improving instruction. Obviously, the principal's most important job is a difficult one.

FINDING TIME FOR IMPROVING INSTRUCTION

The principal who would find time for improving the instructional program must realize that many administrative duties of minor importance can and should be delegated to others. In the case of the principal, his most important responsibility is that of improving instruction. Just as he sets up a classroom schedule for a teacher and holds it inviolate, he should set up a schedule for himself that is calculated to improve instruction. This will keep him out of the way of many minor administra-

[14] See Charles W. Boardman, Harl R. Douglass, and Rudyard K. Bent, *Democratic Supervision in Secondary Schools* (New York: Houghton Mifflin Company, 1953), p. 95; John W. Eckhardt, "The High School Principalship in Its Relation to Curriculum Development," NASSP *Bulletin,* 32, No. 154 (April, 1948), 103; Fred Engelhardt, William H. Zeigel, Jr., and Roy O. Billett, *Administration and Supervision* (U.S. Office of Education, Bulletin No. 17, Monograph No. 11; Washington, D.C.: Government Printing Office, 1933), Table 48, p. 117; and A. J. Lynch, "The High School Principalship," NASSP *Bulletin,* 38, No. 201 (March, 1954), 27.

[15] National Association of Secondary School Principals, "A Study of the High School Principalship in Pennsylvania," *Bulletin,* 37, No. 198 (December, 1953), 119.

tive activities which find their way to the principal's office and present
themselves as problems to be solved.

This is not to say that the principal should seldom be accessible, or
that he should keep himself buried continually in professional literature. At times, improving instruction may involve improving the morale of teachers, or the afterschool activities of students, or the understanding of patrons. However, improving instruction, broadly but not
vaguely defined, should constantly be the chief goal of the principal,
and he should budget his time thoughtfully and spend it intelligently to
that end. He should make a schedule for himself and learn to maintain it
by delegating less important matters to others and by dispatching
promptly all business that he undertakes. His energies should not be at
the mercy of the ongoing machinery of the school. During most school
days he should be the master of his own schedule.

FACTORS IN PLANNING

After he has found time for improving instruction the high school
principal still has a challenging and demanding task ahead. Careful planning and a determination not to be deflected from the attainment of
his goals are essential. In his planning, three factors should be taken into
account. First, American schools have found it difficult to break away
from the patterns and traditions of the selective European secondary
schools. These schools have been aristocratic in character and have been
designed to train leaders for a certain class of society. They have indeed
produced scholars and leaders and have acquired great prestige. It has
been hard for us to understand that a secondary school operating in
full harmony with the meaning and purposes of democracy must be
different from the secondary school planned to preserve and maintain a
more static society. James B. Conant, now Ambassador to Western Ger-
many, phrased it thus when he was president of Harvard.

Let it be agreed by the professors in our colleges and universities that the
high schools of the country today have a job to do which is not to be measured
primarily in terms of their success or failure in the formal education of the
specially gifted youth.

Let it be admitted that by and large a good job has been done in providing an education for a large proportion of American youth and that the
present movement along such lines as those indicated in the recent volume,
Education for All American Youth, published by the Educational Policies Commission, is in the right direction.

On the other hand, let the faculties of education and the superintendents
of schools and those concerned with secondary education agree that in attempting to solve the terrific problems of the last fifty years they have neglected a

number of important problems which concern the type of youth who should in the best interest of the nation go on to college.[16]

Second, high school principals and teachers have been reluctant to question the basic psychological concepts of the educational process. They have been willing to try new paths in such areas as building and equipment, extraclass activities, or even classroom methods, but they have assumed that their basic understandings and aims were above question and that their only opportunities for improvement lay in attaining increased efficiency. They have thought of education as the storing of the mind with information to be kept in reserve for possible future use. The newer concept that learning is the modification of behavior as the result of experience presents the school with a more complex task, but it offers principals and teachers challenging opportunities to determine what behavior is desired and what experiences will bring it about.

Finally, the concept of the principal's responsibility held by a vocal portion of the public has served to limit his own conception of his job and his activities as a policy maker. Many patrons of the school are not inclined to criticize him or the school for failure to adjust to new situations; rather, they are likely to be critical of innovations and variations from procedures to which they as school children became accustomed. As he attempts to meet new responsibilities within the school he creates problems for himself outside it. Hence the situation does not encourage the principal to assume additional responsibilities. On the contrary, since he must accept the responsibility for everything that happens in the school, his burden is heavy and always present, and he is often tempted to lighten it by limiting his activities.

Instead of meeting his responsibilities in full, he may be tempted to operate the school in such a way as to evade them. The standards of achievement may be raised so that slow learners or troublesome students are eliminated. The afterschool use of the school building may be curtailed so that school property is more easily protected. The social program may be limited so that the school can deny responsibility for excesses and indiscretions committed by youth in the social program that they build for themselves away from the school. All these are evasions. The school and the high school principal have some measure of responsibility for the education, care, and welfare of all youth in the community whether they are in school or not. The question the principal should ask himself is not, "How can I limit the activities of the school so that I can escape blame for the mistakes of youth?" but rather, "How can I extend or redirect the activities of the school so that all youth can profitably stay in school

---

[16] James Bryant Conant, "A Truce among Educators," *Teachers College Record,* 44 (December, 1944), 162–163.

and so that the school can be most helpful in improving the behavior of all youth in the community?"

Some Points to Consider

1. In an informal conference with the superintendent, members of a board of education were discussing their ideas of the qualifications needed by the candidates for the vacancy in their high school principalship.

"We have a big plant, costly equipment, a large budget, and a $25,000-a-year student activity program in that high school. We need a man with a good business head for that job."

"Above everything else I think we need a scholar for high school principal. One whose scholarly reputation in some field will inspire those teachers to do their best teaching."

"What that high school needs more than anything else is a good disciplinarian."

"The high school needs to be sold to our community leaders. They don't understand what we are doing out there. We need a popular sort of man who is a good mixer and can inspire confidence downtown."

If you were superintendent, and the president of the board said, "Mr. Superintendent, what do you think?" what would be your answer?

2. Consider some high school that you know well. Is the principal working along steadily on something calculated to "improve the school," as this chapter says he should be? What? How is he going about this job?

3. From what you know of the school what "improvements" ought he to be trying to bring about?

4. Suppose a high school principal says, "This is a pretty good high school. I cannot see that this community wants it to be a better one. Why should I go to the bother of trying to get these folks to want a better one?" What is your answer?

Further Reading

Austin, David B., and James S. Collins. "A Study of Attitudes toward the High School Principalship." NASSP *Bulletin,* Vol. 40, No. 215, (January 1956), 104–140.

Boardman, Charles W., Harl R. Douglass, and Rudyard K. Bent. *Democratic Supervision in Secondary Schools.* New York: Houghton Mifflin Company, 1953. Chap. 4.

Bossing, N. L. "Wanted: A New Leadership for the Secondary Schools," NASSP *Bulletin,* No. 138, April, 1946.

Bowles, Frank W. "Social Demands on Schools and Colleges," *College Board Review,* No. 26, Spring, 1955, pp. 4–9.

Briggs, Thomas H. *The Great Investment.* Cambridge, Mass.: Harvard University Press, 1930.

———, and Joseph Justmam. *Improving Instruction through Supervision.* New York: The Macmillan Company, 1952. Chap. 2

Conant, James Bryant. "A Truce among Educators," *Teachers College Record,* Vol. 44, December, 1944.

Corey, Stephen M., A. Wellesley Foshay, and Gordon N. Mackenzie. "Instructional Leadership and the Perceptions of the Individuals Involved," NASSP *Bulletin,* 35, No. 181 (November, 1951), 84–90.

DeZafra, Carlos. "What a High School Teacher Looks for in Principals," *Clearing House,* 26, No. 2 (October, 1951), 87–91.

Douglass, Harl R. *Modern Administration of Secondary Schools.* Boston: Ginn & Co., 1954. Chaps. 1, 2, 3.

Eckhardt, John W. "The High School Principalship in Its Relation to Curriculum Development," NASSP *Bulletin,* Vol. 32, No. 154 (April, 1948).

Eikenberry, Dan Harrison. *Status of the High School Principal.* U.S. Office of Education, Bulletin No. 24; Washington, D.C.: Government Printing Office, 1925.

———. "Training and Experience Standards for Principals of Secondary Schools," NASSP *Bulletin,* 35, No. 181 (November, 1951), 5–62.

Engelhardt, Fred, William H. Zeigel, Jr., and Roy O. Billett. *Administration and Supervision.* U.S. Office of Education, Bulletin No. 17, Monograph No. 11; Washington, D.C.: Government Printing Office, 1932.

Farmer, Floyd M. "The High School Principalship," NASSP *Bulletin,* 32, No. 154 (April, 1948), 82–91.

Gorman, Burton W. "Some Characteristics of a Successful High School Principal," *American School Board Journal,* 118 (June, 1949), 28.

Hoshall, C. E. "High School Principals Suggest Changes in the Pre-service Education of Principals," NASSP *Bulletin,* 35, No. 181 (November, 1951), 63–67.

Jacobson, Paul B., William C. Reavis, and James D. Logsdon. *Duties of School Principals.* Englewood Cliffs, N.J.: Prentice-Hall, Inc., 1950, pp. 727–756.

Kyte, George C. *The Principal at Work.* Rev. ed.; Boston: Ginn & Co., 1952.

Lynch, A. J. "The High School Principalship," NASSP *Bulletin,* Vol. 38, No. 201 (March, 1954).

Mackenzie, Gordon N., and Stephen M. Corey. "A Conception of Educational Leadership," NASSP *Bulletin,* 36, No. 183 (January, 1952), 14.

———, and Associates. *Instructional Leadership.* New York: Bureau of Publications, Teachers College, Columbia University, 1954.

National Association of Secondary School Principals, "A Study of the High School Principalship in Pennsylvania," *Bulletin,* 37, No. 198 (December, 1953), 118–120.

Rice, Theodore D. "The Principal," NASSP *Bulletin,* 34, No. 174 (December, 1950), 28–35.

Tanner, H. Jeanne. "The High School Teacher Looks to the Principal," *School Review,* 63, No. 2 (February, 1955), 96–97.

Trecker, H. B. *Group Process in Administration.* New York: Womans Press, Whiteside, Inc., 1946.

Chapter 7

THE PROBLEM OF SCHOOL
AND STAFF ORGANIZATION

THE PRINCIPAL IS RESPONSIBLE for organizing the school, but the project is a group affair rather than an individual one. Each member of the staff may have some part in the tasks involved in the organizing and the continuing reorganization of the school. These tasks may be divided into five categories: (1) defining the purposes of the school; (2) determining the organization for achieving the purposes; (3) selecting the personnel; (4) instructing and integrating the personnel; and (5) evaluating the results. These five categories will be considered in this and the following chapter.

In the performance of these tasks no member is constantly in a superior or a subordinate position. At times when he can serve the group enterprise as a specialist, each member may serve as a leader; at times each will serve as a follower. To the extent that the principal is successful in enlisting the participation of all staff members, each one will make his particular contribution to the group enterprise by performing any task that he can achieve more effectively than anyone else in the group.

THE PRINCIPAL AS LEADER

To the extent that a principal realizes, and other staff members recognize, that a school is best organized and administered when the leadership function is as widely shared as the professional abilities and interests of the staff permit, will a school have a chance to become distinctively good. If a principal feels that his legal status as principal permits or requires him to monopolize the leadership function, the school will not be as well organized or administered as it could be. The legal status, which is essential to the initiation of the process of organizing a school, is like yeast in bread. It is a necessary ingredient, but yeast is not bread and too much of it spoils the bread. The laws of the states and the actions of boards of education under these laws endow the principalship with certain responsibilities and hence certain authorities. These are what a principal starts with, but if he does not bring to the position trained administrative ability of a high order, the school will always be mediocre. If he is well trained, he should have learned long since that the institutions of a democratic society are well organized only when those who legally head them recognize that leadership opportunity and responsibility must be as widely dispersed among all those who are connected with the institution as their abilities and interests will permit. Only thus can administration in the long run be really efficient, for only thus can the institution capitalize fully upon the resources of those who make it up. Only thus can administration be really democratic, giving to each the full part that his abilities, as recognized by the group, make him competent to play. Only thus can administration be really educative, for only through responsible participation in the affairs of an institution does the staff become better educated for work in it and thus able to help it reach still higher levels of institutional success. Administration cannot be really efficient without being democratic. If it is democratic it will be educative. Each one of these elements is an essential link in the chain that leads to the highest levels of organization and administration. Hence we start with the assumption that though the principal may be legally responsible for organizing the school, yet the proper discharge of this responsibility requires that it become a group affair in which all members of the staff have an opportunity and responsibility for participation.

Defining the Purposes of the School

A good starting point for defining the purposes of the school may be found in Chart 1, *Some Statements of Purposes for Education*. An examination of the chart shows clearly that the emphasis on purposes for education has been an evolutionary development. It does not represent a sharp break with the past. Because they know more about the functions of organization and administration, educators are increasingly recognizing a close relationship between the type of organization developed and the achievement of purposes. As they become increasingly concerned about the achievement of purposes they will probably develop organizations based upon the purposes they hold.

To avoid an unwieldy set of aims, many schools have classified their ultimate objectives under four headings: health, citizenship, leisure time, and lifework. Each school staff should either find a statement of aims that it can accept or make one of its own. As is illustrated in *Education for All American Youth: A Further Look*, this process of delineating purposes is one in which the lay public and pupils may well have a part. It may be that the principal and staff know the community well enough to decide without any help from laymen what purposes should be stressed in the school. But even so, since the rate of progress made by a local school is determined by the understanding of its public, it is wise to have lay participation not only in an original consideration of purposes but in their subsequent implementation and in the evaluation of results. If "a little learning is a dangerous thing," the antidote is not less learning but more. In any case, each of the purposes finally accepted will probably receive a varying emphasis at different times and in different places. Good mental and physical health has always been important, but it had a special prominence during wartime. Immediately after the war, in the divorce rate, in black markets, in industrial strife, in criminal records, and in other similar evidences of social disintegration, there were signs of breakdowns in the character and moral sense of our people. At that time, laymen and educators alike felt the need for a renewed emphasis on education for ethical character.

WHAT PURPOSES SHALL BE STRESSED?

By studying the characteristics of the student body the staff can determine the purposes that need emphasis. The socioeconomic background, physical characteristics, abilities, attitudes, educational achievements, learning difficulties, and study habits of students all provide clues for needed educational emphasis. No general educational aim can be analyzed and defined except in terms of a particular student body and community. Education for lifework may be chiefly preparation for college in one community, preparation for distributive occupations in another, and preparation for heavy industries in another. Education for citizenship may involve teaching table manners in one school and restraining the practice of wearing orchids to school dances in another. The members of the staff should study the community and the students of the school and decide what their most important tasks are at a particular time and place. Such study will not lead to the discovery of unique and wholly different sets of tasks for each high school because there are some fairly common needs that all youth have, one statement of which has been developed by Corey in *The American High School:*

> Coming to Terms with Their Own Bodies
> Learning New Relationships to Their Age Mates
> Achieving Independence from Parents
> Acquiring Self-confidence and a System of Values[1]

[1] Stephen M. Corey, in Hollis L. Caswell, ed., *The American High School* (John Dewey Society Yearbook, 1947; New York: Harper & Brothers, 1946), pp. 75–83. See also Robert Havighurst, *Developmental Tasks and Education* (Chicago: University of Chicago Press, 1948).

Thus while each school should build its goal around its own student body, it will not be surprising to find that high schools in this country still have many common goals.

Although a general statement of ultimate goals will serve as a starting point for the staff in defining the purposes of the school, it is not enough. The purposes should be so specific that they help in determining the experiences to be provided for students and so definite that the staff can reach decisions as to whether or not they have been achieved. For example, preparation for lifework is generally accepted as a purpose of the secondary school. However, it has more meaning and provides better guidance if we say that the school should equip every student either (1) to fill successfully a position on a rung of some occupational ladder or (2) to continue successfully his schooling in some other educational institution. This statement in some measure suggests the kind of educational experiences that should be provided, and if we are willing to make the necessary effort, we can ascertain whether or not the purpose has been achieved. In the field of mental and emotional health, if we say we wish to help each student to learn to work and to play happily and successfully with his fellow students, we have some sense of direction for our efforts and one criterion for judging their effectiveness. Often members of a faculty have a cynical spirit as they approach the task of defining their purposes. They fear that they are doing busywork which must ultimately conform to a statement of the principal or of some accepted educational authority. They see little relationship between a statement of purposes and the practical activities of the classroom. This attitude can change to one of interest and concern as teachers come to see that they are defining their purposes in terms of student behavior so that they can plan learning activities intelligently and later evaluate them in terms of outcomes. As a result of the evaluation, faculty members may change the learning activities or purposes or both. The defining of purposes is an integral part of the educational process.

A good example of why a school not only should state or accept such a general purpose as lifework, but should focus it sharply on the local community, is to be found in the experience of the Springfield (Missouri) High School. Here the lifework purpose was studied with particular reference to the group in the school not bound for college. The postschool occupational careers of these students and the job opportunities that actually existed in the community were studied carefully. As a result, the lifework educational program of the school was changed to offer broadened opportunities for experiences in the practical arts and in actual work. Classes in English and social studies gave increased attention to the problems of students and of the community. When teachers actually use the results of such studies of purposes in their teaching, and when they see how a particular study has affected the education of particular boys and girls, they will not be so likely to regard defining purposes for a school as a sheer waste of time.

Bases of Organization

The coach of an athletic team plans his system of play to make the best possible use of the material he has available. There is no one system of play that is best under all circumstances, but there is usually one system that is best for a team at a particular time, and there are some general principles that underlie all good play. In the same way there are methods of teaching and of organizing a staff, and the best ones will vary with time and place. The lengthened period may increase the effectiveness of one group of teachers and decrease the effectiveness of another. In one situation a single dean of girls may very effectively direct the counseling program for the girls of the school. In another school or in the same school at a different time, the work may best be done by a number of girls' counselors serving coordinately.

The staff should be so organized that it utilizes its strength to the fullest in these different situations. In fact, the organization of the school should be adaptable enough to adjust readily to changing problems, novel conditions, or new personnel. Simple machinery is more likely to be flexible than a complicated organization which may easily grow to be an end in itself rather than a means to an end. However, even the simplest of machinery can become an end in itself. For example, twenty-five years ago vocational guidance was emphasized quite generally in the ninth grade because great numbers of pupils could be reached there before they dropped out of school. Since that time most pupils are persisting in high school much longer, and vocational information can be provided more effectively for some pupils in the eleventh and twelfth grades. Yet many schools by force of habit still confine their vocational guidance to the ninth grade. Similarly, some schools retain the machinery of mid-year promotions even though these schools no longer have any particular need for them. This is not to say that no school should retain mid-year promotions, but that they require much time and effort and are justified only if they contribute to the objectives of the school that uses them.

The greatest contributions toward flexibility are an open-mindedness and a conviction on the part of the staff that improvement is both possible and desirable. For good morale a staff needs to have satisfaction and even pride in the achievements of the school, but care should be taken to see that this pride does not grow into a feeling that past and present practice is the acme of perfection and that new procedures are dangerous.

ORGANIZATION BASED UPON PURPOSE

The type of high school pictured in *Education for All American Youth: A Further Look*[2] and in the parallel publication, *Planning for American Youth*,[3] raises a question regarding the conventional basis of high school organization in which subject-teaching departments are the chief element. If the school, to be effective, must subordinate departmental teaching to the purposes of secondary education to the extent implied in these publications, justification for the prominence given to departmentalization in the school's organization in the future is required. A close study of the effects of these publications on school organization suggests that a more forthright acceptance of basic *purposes* as determinants of high school organization is demanded. Accordingly, it is here proposed that high schools should be "purpose-organized."

In any institution that is to function effectively one basis of organization must predominate. A small, simple enterprise usually uses but one basis of organization; in larger and more complex enterprises there is need for more than one basis of organization, but one usually takes priority over all others. Where this is not the case, the enterprise is not well organized and is therefore difficult to administer.

The following four bases of organization are most commonly found if one examines enterprises and institutions of various types.

1. *Purpose*. In city government there is a law enforcement function, so there is a police department. A different function or purpose accounts for the organization of a fire department.

2. *Process*. A chemical company manufacturing or processing a particular drug might organize its workers chiefly according to the process in which they were expert, and subordinate everything else to these technical skills.

3. *People or things*. We have a Bureau of Indian Affairs to deal with all affairs of the Indians in which the federal government is concerned. To use a quite different example, a junk dealer may organize his business according to the kinds of things bought and sold.

4. *Place*. The nature of some businesses—perishable products, for instance—decrees that geographical location must be the chief basis of organization. So a company has a New York, a Chicago, and a West Coast branch, at each of which a complete plant operates.

[2] Educational Policies Commission, *Education for All American Youth: A Further Look* (rev. ed.; Washington, D.C.: National Education Association, 1951).
[3] National Association of Secondary School Principals, *Planning for American Youth* (Washington, D.C.: National Education Association, 1951).

In any large organization all four of these bases, as well as less usual ones, may be found to operate. The major executive assistants to the chief executive are therefore chosen according to one of these bases, with other assistants subordinate to them, or, if the latter are responsible directly to the chief executive, recognized as operating in an auxiliary capacity to the major executive assistants.

ORGANIZATIONAL WEAKNESSES IN HIGH SCHOOLS

If we evaluate the organizational pattern in common use in secondary schools as an expert in institutional organization would do, we can identify two weaknesses that may well make us feel that we should begin to shift this organizational pattern toward a clean-cut, purpose basis. The first of these two weaknesses is that, for the major part of the program—the "academic" part—schools are organized on a process basis although there is good reason to believe that the institutions exist primarily to achieve purposes which are not identical with the processes now being stressed. The second weakness is that we do not retain this process basis throughout the whole institution, but shift toward a purpose organization when we enter the areas of "nonacademic" and vocational education. This procedure causes an institutional fracture, running from top to bottom of the organization between these two aspects of the work of the school, which can but weaken the entire educational structure. Both of these weaknesses should be eliminated by centering on the purpose basis of organization and by giving it priority throughout the institution.

HOW PURPOSE ORGANIZATION WOULD
CHANGE HIGH SCHOOLS

If our high schools in general were to begin to unify their organization around the major purposes of youth education, we might expect to find more schools in which some of the following changes were being made. This list, which is not meant to be an inclusive one, will suggest the kind of institutional structure that might develop.

1. Under the immediate supervision of the principal would be four or five "coordinators," each representing a major purpose of secondary education that the school intended to stress.

2. The coordinators or the coordinating committees or both would each study the school's work to see that everything possible was being done to achieve the major purposes of the school.

3. Courses of study would be developed in which content was evaluated in terms of its usefulness in achieving one of the major purposes with the students for whom the course of study was intended.

4. The requirements and electives under each of the school's curriculums would be reconsidered in terms of the purposes of each curriculum for its students.

5. The registration of students for a new year would be under the supervision of the coordinators.

6. The present practice of requiring students to secure a given number of credits in certain departments or subjects before graduation would be abandoned as fast as the organization of the school in terms of purposes could be effected.

7. When the school's educational program is in the direct charge of coordinators who are responsible for the achievement of major purposes through that program, we may expect each coordinator to be concerned about evaluating the pupils' growth in terms of the purpose for which he as coordinator is responsible.

8. A trend toward the purpose organization of secondary schools will modify programs for the education of teachers.

EVIDENCES OF PURPOSE ORGANIZATION

Almost every comprehensive high school is organized in part upon the purpose basis. All vocational programs—business, agriculture, printing, and auto-mechanics, for example—are developed to meet as well as possible a particular lifework purpose that particular students desire. Where a functional health education program prevails that is not merely a study *about* health, one may find a purpose-organized department of health. Elective courses in art and music open only to those with particular interest or ability are indicative of some attempt at purpose organization. Some schools have created a position of "coordinator," or "director," or "supervisor" or "coordinating committee" for one or more of the principal purposes accepted by the school. Few schools, however, have played up their purpose organization to the point where it has an unchallenged priority over all other bases of organization.

In such schools there are supervisors or coordinators of citizenship objectives, of aesthetic objectives, of health objectives, and of lifework objectives. Each supervisor is charged with the responsibility of helping every teacher in the school attain the educational outcomes desired in each subject with relation to his particular objective. The staff members in a number of schools have assigned themselves to committees to promote the major objectives of education in their schools. Instead of a supervisor or coordinator of citizenship, there is a committee on citizenship education, another on health education—one for each purpose they stress.

Although few high schools are fully purpose-organized, the fact that the plan has strong logical justification and the fact that the staffs in other schools tend to use it in proportion as they become seriously interested in improving the educational programs of their schools suggest that purpose organization will be used increasingly by forward-looking and professionally minded staffs in the future. Without disturbing the existing departmental organization in a large school, an assistant principal, a dean of girls, a dean of boys, and a director of guidance could readily undertake the tasks of leading teachers and department heads in achieving the major objectives of that school. Types of relationships that might exist in schools stressing purpose organization are illustrated in Charts 4a and 4b.

The appointment of coordinators for major objectives will be especially helpful in schools that are developing correlated or core programs. In the former, school experiences are organized to transgress subject matter boundaries in order to present a better picture of life to the student. Classes may remain separate, but teachers work together out of class to articulate the work. In the core program, students remain with a teacher for two or three periods at a time for the common learnings that may come from several subject matter fields. In both programs, the necessity for teachers from different departments to work together should be facilitated by the leadership of four or five purpose coordinators. Where schools are highly departmentalized along subject (process) lines and where such departmentalization cannot be abandoned, the need for the coordination that can be secured through purpose coordinators is even more acute if a school is seriously interested in a better achievement of its purposes.

SUBORDINATE ADMINISTRATIVE OFFICERS

Most schools of more than average size employ, at least on a part-time basis, administrative officials such as assistant principals, deans of girls, counselors of boys, directors of guidance, directors of extracurricular activities, and heads of departments. Many assistant principals perform the duties of deans of girls or counselors of boys, and many deans or counselors perform the duties of assistant principals in schools where no one is given that title. If a school is small enough, the principal can perform the duties carried by all such functionaries in larger schools, but as the enrollment of a school grows larger, the need becomes greater for the principal to delegate responsibility to subordinate officers. In some schools it is the practice to employ several girls' counselors instead of a dean of girls, and several boys' counselors instead of a dean of boys. Counselors generally spend their time in dealing directly with students and are seldom charged with disciplinary responsibilities. They may be directly responsible to an assistant principal or to a director of guidance.

Many studies have been made of the teacher's student load, but

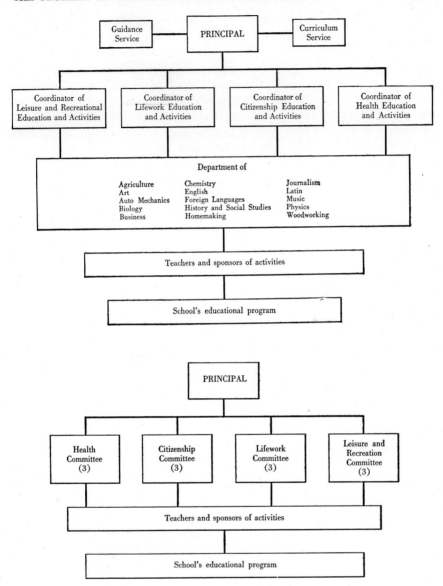

CHARTS 4A AND 4B. ILLUSTRATIVE TYPES OF ORGANIZATION: PURPOSE-ORGANIZED
HIGH SCHOOLS

few have been made of the administrative student load. R. E. Boyles[4] investigated the ratio between the enrollment and the administrative staffs (teachers and administrators doing administrative work) of second-

[4] Robert E. Boyles, "What Is a Satisfactory Pupil-Administrator Load?" NASSP Bulletin, No. 103 (January, 1942), pp. 107–109.

ary schools in cities with a population between 10,000 and 25,000. From data secured from 291 schools in forty-six states he found considerable variation in administrative loads. Ten schools enrolled more than 1,000 students each for the equivalent of each full-time person doing administrative work. In one school the equivalent of five full-time administrators dealt with 825 students. In schools of different types, the median enrollment for each full-time administrator was as follows: four-year high schools, 570; six-year junior-senior high schools, 550; and three-year senior high schools, 450. These results also show the traditional tendency to lighten the load as students grow older and advance in grades. This tendency as well as the practice of assigning as many as 450 students for each administrator in the senior high school may well be questioned. In all probability in very few schools is the administrative load light enough for securing optimum results.

THE ASSISTANT PRINCIPAL

Studies of the duties and activities of assistant principals indicate considerable growth in the professional stature of this important position. At one time the assistant principal was chiefly concerned with clerical duties and the supervision of extraclass activities.[5] Comparatively recent studies show the assistant spending the largest percentage of his time in the area of administration and school management.[6] He is also taking a part in developing supervisory programs although he spends little time in activities concerned with community affairs.[7] The investigators believe that as assistant principals improve their professional preparation and establish their worth, they will be given greater responsibilities in performing the more critical and significant of the principal's duties such as improving instruction and meeting parents.

In a school large enough to require a principal it is desirable to have an assistant principal. He may be only a regular teacher who has been appointed to carry on in the absence of the principal, but such an arrangement provides for stability and allows the principal to multiply his activities and broaden the areas in which he works. It is to be expected that an assistant principal will be chosen to complement the principal in many ways. Few if any individuals are equally able in all fields. Hence it is reasonable for the principal to choose an assistant who works with

[5] Charles R. Van Ewan, "The Function of the Assistant High School Principal and Other Assistant Executives," *Educational Research Bulletin* (Ohio State University), March 31, 1926, pp. 148–150.

[6] C. W. Boardman, J. M. Gran, and Agnes E. Holt, "The Duties and Responsibilities of the Assistant Principal in the Secondary School," NASSP *Bulletin*, No, 137 (March, 1946), pp. 3–11.

[7] George A. W. Weiss, "The Duties of the Secondary-School Vice-Principal," NASSP *Bulletin*, No. 198 (December, 1953), pp. 109–117.

great effectiveness in areas where he himself is least skillful. However, such a choice obligates the principal to provide his assistant increasing opportunities for growth as he is able to take advantage of them. Most individuals grow under responsibility and should be guided so that they grow in effectiveness. The assistant principal should have opportunities to grow into the responsibilities of the principalship and in his turn select an assistant whose qualities and characteristics complement his own.

HEADS OF DEPARTMENTS

As schools increase in size, the departmental form of organization is the usual one, although it occurs in some of the smallest schools and is by no means obligatory in many of the largest. Department heads have these duties:

1. Conducting departmental meetings
2. Budgeting supplies and instructional materials
3. Visiting, rating, assigning, and conferring with teachers
4. Selecting textbooks
5. Planning courses of study
6. Recommending teachers for appointment
7. Evaluating achievement

A study by F. M. Raubinger[8] in 1946 shows that the situation reported by H. C. Koch[9] had not changed greatly in the intervening years. Over three fourths of the high schools reporting in the more recent study said that departmental heads were officially appointed. About 5 per cent of the schools reported the existence of rotating plans for appointment instead of permanent appointment. Over half of the principals reporting stated that they were dissatisfied with the organization of the high school by the traditional subject fields represented by the existing department heads. The chief reason they gave for continuing this organization was "tradition," but when asked how they would organize a high school if freed from the pressures of tradition, 80 per cent of those replying said they would organize by subject departments with department heads. This might raise a question as to the nature of the basic reason for the continuance of an unsatisfactory practice.

Although department heads still serve in the large majority of schools, there has been a trend to replace them with chairmen appointed for a year at a time or with chairmen of groups that cut across the traditional departmental lines.

[8] Frederick M. Raubinger, "Certain Aspects of Departmentalization in High Schools" (A Type B project, typewritten; New York: Teachers College, Columbia University, 1946), 101 pp.

[9] H. C. Koch, "Some Aspects of the Department Headship," *School Review*, Vol. 30, April, 1930.

There are several reasons for this incipient tendency to abandon the departmental organization. In the first place, as was pointed out earlier in the chapter, it is a process rather than a purpose organization. The department head is under a great temptation to concentrate on building the vested interests of the subject rather than upon changing the behavior of boys and girls. For example, competing departments are tempted to strive for large enrollments even at the expense of the optimum growth of pupils. This condition is especially likely to exist in schools where department heads are appointed by seniority, and where, as a consequence, some of them have much the same proprietary attitude toward their positions that they have toward a piece of real estate they own. They think of their posts as personal possessions to be exploited until death or retirement and not as opportunities to stimulate the growth of students. Moreover, many department heads have looked for leadership to college specialists who have been interested in knowledge for its own sake and not as a means for influencing student behavior. As a result, department heads often cling tenaciously to traditional methods of teaching and to autocratic methods of working with other teachers.

Some principals and school staffs wish to develop programs that will cut across subject matter lines and allow students to see problems as wholes rather than as isolated parts. Many wish to develop less static and more flexible program patterns that will more readily permit the introduction of new ideas and allow greater teacher participation in administration. Hence the tendency to abandon the departmental organization is likely to grow stronger although it may spend itself in an effort to improve the existing situation.

The objections to the present departmentalization in high schools have led some students of high school administration to decry all departmentalization as bad and to conclude that good schools were not departmentalized. Although it is true that present high schools, in general, suffer from excessive and inefficient departmentalization, it does not follow that departmentalization is altogether bad. Many high schools, too small to raise any problem of overdepartmentalization, should continue to operate as "a school-of-the-whole" with only a trace of any departmentalization. But large schools, like any other large institutions that carry on complex programs, require departmentalization. They need, however, to be departmentalized along lines directly related to the achievement of the various purposes for which any institution exists. For instance, if local city government exists to protect the property, life, and health of citizens, it needs departments of police, fire, health, sanitation, parks, and so on, each of which is concerned with fulfilling a purpose of local municipal government. It may also need such other purpose departments as personnel and purchasing, but these two will be recognized as subordinate to the former group, whose work they assist. The latter are typical of the "service" departments that are subordinate to the departments directly concerned with the achievement of the major purposes to be served.

So in a school there should be both major and service departments. The major departments should bear a close relationship to such major purposes as health, citizenship, and lifework, for example; that is, they should be purpose-organized departments. There should also be such service departments as guidance service and curriculum improvement. These latter are subordinate to the former and exist not to decide what the major departments should do but to furnish such service in their special fields as is needed by the major departments in the discharge of their functions. Every large school needs such departmentalization; the present fault lies not in having departmentalized high schools but in having departments that center not on purposes but on processes which perhaps were once necessary to achieve the school's purposes. The high school principal's function in relation to this situation is not to abolish all departments, and thus bring into being a nondepartmentalized school, but rather to lead the school and community to be willing to reorganize the school in terms of its major accepted purposes, and then to coordinate the work of the major and service departments so that maximum levels of purpose achievement are more effectively and easily reached than would be possible without such coordination.

In fairness to present department heads, it must be said that many have been effective leaders in improving instruction in their departments. They have tried to do what they were told they were to do by those who appointed them. Some have been especially effective in stimulating teacher participation in administration and have been active in influencing student behavior, even though their efforts required the overstepping of departmental lines. Many have carried heavy loads of teaching, in addition to administrative detail. However the problem of departmentalization is solved, clerical assistants should relieve department heads of harassing administrative details, and teachers should relieve them of heavy teaching loads. Principals must also provide time for department heads or committee chairmen or purpose coordinators to exercise professional leadership and should help them become open-minded and resourceful teachers influencing student behavior and achieving the fundamental goals of the schools.

In large and small schools alike, some of the most effective work is done by committees. Committees of the faculty often deal with such matters as curriculum revision, scholarships, professional study, and faculty welfare. Special committees of the faculty are concerned with such problems as improving the marking system, establishing memorials, determin-

ing salary increments, evaluating achievements, and even selecting personnel. Committees of faculty members and students work together on
athletics, school assemblies, social affairs, afterschool activities, health,
safety, citizenship, and beautification of the school. Because there is a psychological value in arranging for everyone to have a part in any group
project, committees are sometimes created which have small reason for
existence. There is no justification for thus straining to achieve the form
of a vigorous organization. There are plenty of important tasks to be performed in any school, and if the needs are developed clearly in faculty discussions, the problem will be one of securing personnel to carry on important work and not one of finding busywork for committees that have no
real function.

Such committees and their work should be evaluated by the committees themselves and by the faculty each spring. No committees should
be continued beyond the year which the staff cannot see as essential for
the work of the following year. Committee membership and the chair-
manship should be on a rotating basis so that some new members replace
the old ones each year and a new chairman takes charge. This prevents
a member of the staff or a whole committee from "getting in a rut"; it also
means that staff members get a broader experience with the work of the
school and hence are progressively better able to participate effectively
in helping to plan and carry on the work of the school.

Selecting New Staff Personnel

For many individuals the vocation of high school teaching has
always been one of short duration. During the past fifty years the situation has improved and the average tenure of high school teachers is now
longer than it was in 1890. However, except in periods of economic depression, the financial and educational loss caused by the turnover of high
school teachers is considerable. It is expensive because of the time and
effort that must be spent in selecting, orienting, and supervising new
teachers. It is expensive, also, because society receives no return on its
investment when individuals who have been trained at public expense
for teaching serve in the profession for a short time and leave it. Administrators can well give careful thought to the matter of securing longer
tenure on the part of staff members.

Undoubtedly improving salaries is the chief means of lengthening
the stay of teachers in their present positions; hence administrators
should do everything in their power to secure the most attractive salary
schedules. And yet salaries alone cannot explain the efforts of teachers to
move from smaller communities to larger ones. Salaries are generally related to living costs, and real wages are not always highest in communities that pay the highest salaries.

There are other factors which affect tenure. Administrators should be aggressive in improving the conditions under which teachers work, in improving their status in the community, in protecting them from unreasonable demands on the part of the public, and in making it possible for teachers to achieve professional recognition without moving from one community to another. Administrators should use all possible opportunities to strengthen and utilize whatever advantages their schools and communities have over others in making high school teaching positions therein attractive. Many high schools and school systems are generally considered desirable places in which to work because of staff morale, or because of community appreciation or opportunities for professional growth, or because of the effectiveness of the staff as judged by the achievement of students. These conditions seldom exist in isolation but are usually found together and are one explanation of why teachers remain in the profession.

STAFF SELECTION A PROFESSIONAL TASK

For many years authorities in school administration and superintendents of schools have earnestly attempted to bring local school boards to accept the point of view that the selection of teachers is a technical task to be performed by an educational expert, the superintendent, and not by a lay board of education. Information gathered in the National Survey of Education indicated that their efforts have been generally successful and that only occasionally does a school board appoint teachers without the official participation of the superintendent. In the same survey it was found that in high schools enrolling fewer than two thousand pupils, the principal has a significant part in the selection of teachers in approximately four fifths of the schools. In schools with higher enrollments the proportion is almost three fifths. In very small high schools where the high school principal is in reality an assistant principal, he has very little to say about the selection of teachers, the superintendent of schools assuming practically all of the responsibility. In larger, one-high-school communities the principal of the high school carries a larger share, perhaps even the full responsibility for nominations to the superintendent of schools. In urban multiple-high-school communities, the degree of responsibility for teacher selection carried by high school principals tends to fall, for here centralized personnel officers are often a part of the superintendent's office and draw up recommended lists of qualified candidates. The high school administrators are required to accept or select from the top name or names on these lists. A limiting factor is the transfer of teachers between high schools of the system. A principal cannot expect to have the right to ask for a teacher new to the system when an unassigned teacher is already employed in the system. Thus the freedom of choice of some high school principals in large cities is less than that in communities with but one high school. In any case, great care should be used not to assign teachers to a high school in such a way that the principal feels that he cannot be held responsible for the failure of that teacher. Moreover, the assignment should be so made that the new teacher feels that the principal and the staff of the school or department really wanted him to join the staff.

The principal cannot be held responsible for the conduct of the high school unless he has an active part in selecting the staff. The judgment of assistant principals, department heads, and teachers who expect to work with a new appointee can be helpful to the principal in making wise choices. A principal and his staff have no responsibility more important than that of selecting new members of the staff. If they can do that one task well enough, the success of the school is assured.

SELECTING GOOD CANDIDATES

When vacancies occur, administrators should be aggressive in searching out new personnel. They should determine staff needs as early as possible and search for the persons most likely to complement the abilities of those already on the staff. Occasionally the members of a staff are so young that age and maturity are needed. Often the reverse is true. To provide lifelike experiences for boys and girls there should be a balance between men and women. There should also be a balance in achieving the purposes of the school. Leisure time activities, represented in art, music, dramatics, and athletics, should be emphasized but not at the expense of citizenship activities. Staff members should have intellectual interests and attainments but not at the expense of a broad interest in the activities of those with whom they work. The staff should represent as many localities, educational institutions, and experiences as possible.

"Other things being equal, the school should employ only a limited number of home-town teachers. Home-town teachers tend to lead to cultural inbreeding." [10] Although this statement by Lee Thurston, the late United States Commissioner of Education, receives much professional support, shortages of qualified teachers often force administrators to great dependence upon local applicants for teaching positions. Sometimes it has been necessary to recruit housewives who are college graduates and provide them with special training for temporary positions. Citizens in the community have sometimes been recruited for part-time teaching. Where such expedients cannot be avoided they should be regarded as temporary measures which are to be discarded at the earliest possible moment.

The matter of acquiring and maintaining a staff balanced to achieve the purposes of the school is a subtle problem that presents itself each time an addition or replacement is made. If an instructor of mathematics

[10] Lee M. Thurston, "Personnel Policy Development" (Bulletin No. 411; Lansing, Mich.: Superintendent of Public Instruction, 1948), p. 96.

is being added, should he be selected on the single basis of skill in the classroom or upon the two bases of classroom skill and usefulness in stimulating and guiding extraclass activities? If both criteria are used, should the opportunity be utilized to secure an assistant coach of football or to strengthen the dramatic activities? Overemphasis of one aspect of the school, generally an unwitting result of wholehearted enthusiasm, is not so likely if principals are aware of the implications of each appointment.

Many administrators who have given much thought to the selection of teachers upon the basis of traits that are intangible and difficult to measure, but essential to teaching success, have been impressed by the apparent maturity of high school students in judging teaching effectiveness. A few students always express admiration for a teacher not regarded highly by administrators; a few students always fail to appreciate a stern taskmaster however well thought of by administrators; but generally, in the judgment of administrators, high school students are discerning and not easily deceived.

Through the acts of their legislatures and the rulings of their state boards of education, all states have set up minimum requirements for secondary school teachers. The regional accrediting associations have set up minimum standards for teachers as well. These standards and requirements eliminate some kinds of failure in teaching but they do not insure success. It has been difficult to define good teaching, and as a result difficult to determine the characteristics that predict success in teaching. Nevertheless, experienced administrators regard as highly significant any information about prospective employees that pertains to the factors of health, kinds of experience, scholarship and professional preparation, intelligence, personality, and training for the direction of extraclass activities. Probably the most important quality a teacher can have is a capacity for growth, but it is difficult to detect the presence or absence of this characteristic in a young or prospective teacher. It is not difficult to learn about three additional significant items, however—general intelligence, success in practice teaching, and the manner in which a candidate is regarded by his peers.[11]

The most reliable sources of data concerning prospective teachers are references, interviews, and visits to the classroom. All three have their weaknesses. Prospective candidates ask for references only from those persons who are likely to write favorable ones. If the employing official knows personally a reference to whom he can write (with the permission of the candidate if need be), he should write asking specific questions. Knowing the reference, he will know how to evaluate the answers. Some

[11] Willard S. Elsbree and E. Edmund Reutter, Jr., *Staff Personnel in the Public Schools* (Englewood Cliffs, N.J.: Prentice-Hall, Inc., 1954), Chap. 3.

candidates appear at their very best in an interview or when being visited in the classroom. Other equally strong candidates are at their very worst in similar situations. The employer is safest when securing a candidate whom he knows or who is well recommended by someone whose judgment he trusts or by a teacher-training institution known for its ability to identify promising professional prospects. Lacking these, he must use his own judgment, supported perhaps, in the words of a successful administrator with many years of experience, by "a hunch, a hope, and a prayer."

Movements have started for the more careful selection of students of education by schools of education and for the early elimination of the least fit during the training period. The development of a workable plan by which the schools of education can bear more of the responsibility for providing better candidates from which high school principals may choose is a task that will require much time and research. Until then the responsibility of selecting new staff members who are properly qualified will have to rest pretty largely upon the judgment and experience of the superintendent, the high school principal, and their assistants.

Some Points to Consider

1. What purposes do parents have when they send their children to high schools? Youth, when they attend? Teachers, when they teach? A community, when it supports a public high school? To what extent are these sets of purposes identical with or related to each other? Which should be given greatest weight by a faculty in deciding what purposes are important? Should a faculty decide what the purposes of any high school are to be?

2. Consider the organization of a fairly large business or store. Is it departmentalized? Should it be? Why? Is each department necessary if the purposes of the enterprise are to be realized?

3. Are large high schools "too" departmentalized or wrongly departmentalized, or both? If so, what would you do about it? Abolish all departmentalization? Create different ones? What ones?

4. When, if ever, should a high school principal use the facilities of a private teachers' agency in filling a staff vacancy? What are the arguments for and against doing so?

5. How, in the college you are attending, may superintendents and high school principals become acquainted with the qualifications of seniors interested in teaching? Do the records on each prospective teacher that are available to them show what his qualifications are, and are they complete enough to help the school executives decide on the merits of each?

6. How important is it for a high school principal to observe the teaching of a prospective teacher? Is it fair to the teacher to be asked to undergo such a visit? Is it fair not to have a chance to show what he can do in the classroom?

7. What do you as a student like and dislike most in teachers? Should principals take these characteristics into account?

Further Reading

Boardman, C. W., J. M. Gran, and Agnes E. Holt. "The Duties and Responsibilities of the Assistant Principal in the Secondary School," NASSP *Bulletin*, No. 132 (March, 1946), pp. 3–11.

Boyles, Robert E. "What Is a Satisfactory Pupil-Administrator Load?" NASSP *Bulletin*, No. 103 (January, 1942), pp. 107–109.

Caswell, Hollis L., ed. *The American High School.* John Dewey Society Yearbook, 1947; New York: Harper & Brothers, 1946. Chap. 5.

Committee on Orientation of Secondary Education, "Functions of Secondary Education," NASSP *Bulletin*, No. 64, January, 1937.

———. "Issues of Secondary Education," NASSP *Bulletin*, No. 59, January, 1936.

Elsbree, Willard S., and E. Edmund Reutter, Jr. *Staff Personnel in the Public Schools.* Englewood Cliffs, N.J.: Prentice-Hall, Inc., 1954. Chap. 3.

Hamrin, Shirley A. *Organization and Administrative Control in High Schools.* "School of Education Series." Evanston, Ill.: Northwestern University Press, 1932.

Havighurst, Robert. *Developmental Tasks and Education.* Chicago: University of Chicago Press, 1948.

Herriott, M. E., and others. "Organizing the Junior High School," NASSP *Bulletin*, No. 35 (December, 1951), pp. 3–157.

Kilpatrick, W. H. "A Reconstructed Theory of the Educative Process," *Teachers College Record*, March, 1931.

National Society for the Study of Education. *American Education in the Post-War Period: Structural Reorganization.* Forty-fourth Yearbook; Chicago: University of Chicago Press, 1945. Chap. 3.

Research Division, National Education Association. "Teacher Personnel Practices, 1950–1951: Appointment and Termination of Service," *Research Bulletin*, Vol. 30, No. 1, February, 1952. Chaps. 1–3.

Thurston, Lee M. "Personnel Policy Development," Bulletin No. 411; Lansing, Mich.: Superintendent of Public Instruction, 1948, p. 96.

Topp, Robert F. "Let Your Teachers Evaluate You," *School Executive*, December, 1953.

Van Ewan, Charles R. "The Function of the Assistant High School Principal and Other Administrative Executives," *Educational Research Bulletin* (Ohio State University), March 31, 1926, pp. 148–150.

Weiss, George A. W. "The Duties of the Secondary-School Vice-Principal," NASSP *Bulletin*, No. 198 (December, 1953), pp. 109–117.

Yauch, Wilbur A. *Improving Human Relations in School Administration.* New York: Harper & Brothers, 1949. Parts IV, V.

Chapter 8

STAFF LEADERSHIP AND
SCHOOL IMPROVEMENT

No principal can do his professional duty to his country or his community by doing only the "shopkeeping." Until his high school is as good as it can be expected to be, that principal's major responsibility is its *improvement*. As the last chapter indicated, this is also a group responsibility of the whole staff in any high school, but in this area particularly the principal is expected to show the high qualities of leadership well illustrated by Yauch in his book referred to in Chapter 5. But no principal has organized his school well merely because it is organized to *operate* well. It is only really well organized when it is organized for its own *improvement*. The present chapter stresses this aspect of high school organization.

INTEGRATING STAFF PERSONNEL

In any cooperative enterprise it is necessary to define the functions of the various units in order to prevent overlapping and misunderstandings. This means that everyone on the staff of the school should understand the purposes of the institution and the part to be played by each group and each individual in their achievement. However, it is possible for a group of workers to spend a disproportionate amount of time in trying to define duties too sharply and in allocating responsibilities too rigidly. Neither individuals nor groups should develop possessive attitudes toward their work, and all should expect occasional innocent duplications of effort. If all have common ultimate goals and a general understanding of duties, it is possible to develop a spirit of give-and-take and of sacrifice for the common good. However, if instructions are hazy, or if two individuals or groups both believe they have been assigned the same task, confusion, friction, frustration, and lack of teamwork are inevitable.

The members of the staff should have a large part in determining the policies and making the programs of the school. In a sense faculty participation in school administration is like student participation in school government. The principal is the legal source of all authority in the school, but in order to attain the highest level of organized student life and to give students practice in self-government, he defines a limited area, and in this area for a definite length of time he delegates all authority to the students. This gives reality to the student government experience and provides students with responsibility that promotes their growth. They may make mistakes in using their authority, but in the judgment of the principal the damage done is a small price to pay for the student growth achieved. In general, teachers as well as students grow when they are given responsibility, and principals have often been amazed at the development of professional interest, enthusiasm, willingness to work, and willingness to sacrifice when teachers' committees have been given real responsibilities in determining issues vital to them and to the schools.

WHY TEACHERS SHOULD PARTICIPATE IN ADMINISTRATION

Promoting their growth by giving them responsibility is a valid reason for encouraging teachers to take a large part in determining the policies of the school, but it is by no means the only one. Principals find that better programs are built when teachers take part in their development than could possibly come out of the thinking of the principal alone. The principal has a broader point of view than the teacher. He is likely to see problems in clearer perspective and to take more factors into account in reaching a decision. However, the teacher has the closer view, for he can see the effect of a policy on the individual student. Both views are needed for the formulation of the best educational policies. All views and all kinds of ability are needed, as well, for the making and carrying out of specific programs. Doubtless in every high school there is at least one small area in which each member of the faculty may be a more effective specialist than the principal. The best interests of the school and of the staff demand the full utilization of all these talents.

In addition, principals find an advantage in wide teacher participation because teachers carry out more effectively and understandingly a policy that they have had a part in determining than they do one that has been handed to them. It is essential that teachers have understanding, sympathy, and even a sense of authorship toward the educational plans with which they are entrusted. Many worth-while innovations have failed because teachers did not understand them or had no real interest in seeing them succeed.

It is true that the principal is the legally constituted source of authority in the school, subject to the superintendent and the board of education, and cannot by delegating it absolve himself from responsibility. He may find it wise to delegate authority only in definite areas and for limited lengths of time. In an extreme case he might find it necessary to overrule (veto) the acts of the entire faculty. In such a case the faculty still has the right of appeal. If in a particular school a principal finds it increasingly necessary to resort to the legal authority of his status as a principal, if he feels frequently called upon to veto directly or indirectly the expressed will of the staff, if he finds it increasingly necessary to resort to the techniques of the dictator in order to keep the school going, then he has reached the extreme limits of usefulness in that school. He should recognize this sooner than anyone else and should take steps to bring the relationship to an end. It may not be easy or convenient for him to do this, but it is better for him and for the school if he takes the initiative instead of waiting until the superintendent or the board of education takes it.

In most schools he will succeed best by being a coordinator and director of cooperative activities. His effort should be to stimulate and release initiative rather than stifle it. He should promote free trade in ideas and talent so that the best ones can be adopted by the school. As he and his staff grow in their interest and understanding of professional problems, he will probably come to behave as though it were the chief source of his inspiration.

DELEGATING RESPONSIBILITY AND AUTHORITY

With each assignment of responsibility the principal should delegate authority to carry out that assignment. In fact, it may be said that responsibility has been assigned or delegated only in name unless authority goes along with it. In a democratic society no one has authority unless he has responsibility, which is the first to be acquired and is the reason for the authority. Even the principal would have no authority in a school if he had not been given responsibility by the state through the local board of education and the superintendent's office. The principal, in turn, delegates authority if he really delegates responsibility; not to do so makes such delegation a mere pretense. It is not possible or desirable for the principal personally to administer all the details connected with the management of a secondary school, but unless he really delegates both authority and responsibility, he may find himself faced with such a task. Most people—teachers, pupils, and patrons—prefer dealing with the principal rather than with the assistant principal, director of guidance, director of extracurricular activities, department head, or individual teacher charged with a particular responsibility. When the principal is approached concerning a matter that has been delegated to another, his reply should be, "Have you seen the assistant principal?" (Or "the girls' counselor," or whoever has charge of the problem.) He should be reluctant to overrule a decision of one to whom he has delegated responsibility. Unless the decision is patently wrong or unfair, it should be sustained. Otherwise, the principal will find that the responsibilities he delegated to others are finding their way right back to his desk. However, here again the spirit is more important than the letter. In any big organization, definite limits must be set for all large units of administration in order to avoid the overlap and duplication of functions.

DEVELOPING UNITY AND DIVERSITY

Systematic efforts should be made to improve the morale of the teaching staff. In the first place, in the making of group decisions a consensus should be secured wherever possible. Some decisions will have the opposition of a considerable minority group, but as long as some forward progress is being made it is worth while to proceed slowly in order to maintain wholehearted and enthusiastic support. Second, in making any innovation it is important to achieve success; hence initial projects in a new program should be so planned that they will have every chance of succeeding. Moreover, whenever possible, successful achievements of any kind by any staff member or committee should be recognized publicly, but such recognition should not persist long enough to evoke jealousy or ill will. Praise often repeated, even though deserved, has contributed to the professional jealousies that divide some faculties into two or more militant and mutually suspicious groups. Finally, no one expects a leader to place his worst foot forward, but few will accept the leadership of anyone who is preoccupied with covering up his own mistakes. An open and aboveboard policy which holds that all school business is the rightful concern of teachers, patrons, and students is likely to build confidence and group morale.

Unless they are socially undesirable, individual differences of students and teachers should be respected. A dynamic society does not try to mold all individuals to a pattern; rather, it wants individuals to grow as individuals in the hope that some of them will vary enough to make distinctive contributions to the progress of the group. A school that is preparing for future democratic living by means of its present practices will have a staff whose members have professional training and professional interests and who are without snobbishness in dealing with the ideas advanced by others. The ideas and ideals of the principal, for example, will be accepted or rejected on their merit and not merely because they were presented by the principal. And in dealing with students, teachers will give their ideas and points of view the same hearing and courteous attention they would give to those of adults. Suggestions that have no merit need not be tolerated, but they are accepted or rejected on their own face value alone. They are not rejected merely because they come from people who can be imposed upon because of their inexperience. Democratic practices in a high school also mean that the principal will respect teachers as he wishes them to respect young people. In a democratic school the ideas of all individuals will compete for status on an equal basis.

The staff should cultivate not only an understanding of youth but a faith and confidence in them as well. A certain lack of understanding is inevitable between any two generations, for their different experiences have given them different points of view. This has perhaps never been more noticeable than it is today, with rapidly changing conditions. Young people now have the same matter-of-course attitude toward the airplane that their grandparents had for the horse and buggy. As always, many adults have difficulty in understanding youth and easily resent even their vigor and enthusiasm. Teachers must remember that Mother Nature is not shortchanging the human race, that young people are educable and are merely the product of their experiences. They are in need of our confidence, good will, and sympathetic understanding.

ORIENTATION PAYS DIVIDENDS

In inducting the beginning teacher into the staff, school officials and experienced teachers have one of their greatest opportunities to improve the effectiveness and morale of their school. A genuine spirit of helpfulness will develop in the beginner a feeling of security at a time when he is under a great strain. In some schools, teaching schedules that all dislike are assigned to the beginners as a kind of hazing procedure until they have served apprenticeships and attained seniority. The procedure should be, on the contrary, to assign the lightest schedule to the beginner, who needs it most.

Help should be afforded to newly appointed teachers in finding suitable living accomodations, in becoming acquainted with the school and community, and even in making personal adjustments. With some encouragement from the principal many persons can be interested in carrying out such orientation procedures. The local teachers' association can collect and interpret information on the local housing situation. The chamber of commerce or the automobile dealers' association can take new teachers on a tour of the community. Some experienced teacher can serve as a professional guide and counselor for each newcomer during the first year of service.

There are not many persons to whom the principal can delegate responsibility for helping beginning teachers plan their classwork. He or his assistants, including department heads where they exist, should provide aid especially for beginners in selecting and organizing materials of instruction, in choosing and using instructional methods, and in judging the effectiveness of plans which have been followed.

ASSIGNMENTS AND LOADS ARE IMPORTANT

Although state departments of education and regional accrediting associations have done much to reduce teaching loads, the tasks of American secondary school teachers are still much too heavy. In most schools, for optimum effectiveness, they probably should be reduced by at least one third. Principals should attempt to reduce the teaching loads that are assigned. In addition, they can lighten the burdens of teachers in other ways. They can arrange that committee meetings and staff meetings are held on school time, even if the school is dismissed early upon occasions. They can cultivate a respect for the authority of the teacher and protect him from the unjustified attacks of critics. They can use student assistants and office clerks to relieve teachers of clerical duties. They can take every opportunity to eliminate red tape and at the same time help teachers to systematize their work. They can seek better practices in assigning teaching loads.

The National Commission on Teacher Education and Professional Standards proposed that "twenty-five pupils should be the maximum number enrolled in any class or grade taught by one teacher. The total number of pupil-class enrollments taught by a teacher of academic subjects in secondary or departmentalized schools should not exceed one hundred per day." [1] In the opinion of the authors, it is more important to reduce total teaching loads than class size. Some teachers can teach large classes successfully, but there is a definite limit to the number of pupils who can be provided by any one teacher with the personal conferences and individual instruction which are essential in most subjects. Teachers in junior high schools often teach great numbers of pupils because so many of their classes meet one or two or three days each week. Thus the teachers meet different pupils on alternate days instead of the same pupils every day of the week.

In every secondary school it is necessary to have a definite policy relative to the combination of duties assigned to teachers. In some schools it is considered desirable for all teachers to carry equivalent loads and efforts are made to equalize all teaching loads. In other schools it is held that varying loads are desirable and some teachers are paid extra for extra duties in athletics, music, speech, chess, or dramatics. A few schools and school systems have made detailed analyses of the load problem. They have usually found the teachers spending about forty hours a week

[1] Research Division, National Education Association, "Teaching Load in 1950," *Research Bulletin*, 29, No. 1 (February, 1951), 47.

in teaching and other regular assigned duties. The Douglass formula is helpful in understanding the factors involved in the equalizing of loads.[2]

Often the effectiveness of the staff can be increased merely by a shift in assignments. It is the business of the principal or his assistants to know the capacities and interests of teachers so that each one can perform the tasks that he can do with the greatest effectiveness. A survey of teachers' interests, hobbies, and work experiences may serve, as well as a study of academic records, in providing information that will be useful in planning staff assignments. Sometimes the sponsor of a dramatic club has a greater interest in a debating or current affairs club. Some teachers can instruct large groups successfully in social studies or in "appreciation" subjects. Others are least effective in large groups and most effective in individual instruction or counseling. One teacher of English may succeed in building appreciation of literature, whereas another is a skillful teacher of composition. Each one should serve where he can serve best.

Evaluating Results

In every school there is need for continuing re-examination and evaluation of what is being done. Many aspects of the school situation change from semester to semester and from year to year. The personnel of the staff and the pupil body changes, the community which the school serves does not remain static, and our society as a whole changes in many respects. This means that continuing vigilance is needed to make sure that the objectives of the school program are appropriate and that the plan of organization and the activities of the staff are contributing to the achievement of these objectives. In trying to find out the extent to which the objectives of the school program are being realized, the principal can appraise the work of teachers and pupils and he can lead the staff and the pupils in cooperative efforts to appraise the whole school program. At periodic intervals under the leadership of the principal the school staff should systematically attempt to find out the extent to which the objectives of the school program are being realized.

EFFECTIVENESS OF STAFF

Satisfactory service should be the basis for retaining a teacher on the school staff and allowing him or her to receive a salary increment. Likewise, outstanding service should be the basis for assigning increased responsibilities and awarding promotions. Thus it follows that the principal will always carry a responsibility for evaluating the effectiveness of

[2] Harl R. Douglass, "The 1950 Revision of the Douglass High School Teaching Load Formula," NASSP *Bulletin*, 35, No. 179 (May, 1951), 13–24.

the teaching staff. In no other way could he make intelligent assignments of teaching loads or adjustments in those loads. However, this does not necessarily mean that every individual on the staff should be assigned a periodic comparative rating. Both unsatisfactory and outstanding services come to the attention of the principal in many different ways and can be identified rather easily. If the individuals on the staff are to be rated periodically, the intervals between ratings should be as wide as possible since cumulative judgments made over a long period of time are more valid than those made on the basis of a short period.

Approximately one sixth of the city school systems require at least one formal rating per year of each teacher's performance.[3] A comprehensive rating form can be used for formal ratings, for helping beginning teachers, or for encouraging all teachers to analyze their own performances with a view to improvement. Such a form is the *Ohio Teaching Record Anecdotal Observation Form*,[4] which was developed by specialists in evaluation and has been used widely. It is organized around the following eight questions:

1. What were the materials of instruction?
2. What was the function of the subject matter used?
3. What methods of instruction were employed?
4. How effective were the materials and methods employed?
5. How did the teacher help students with their own personal problems?
6. What was done to promote better school-community relations?
7. How were democratic attitudes and relationships fostered?
8. How were good human relationships furthered?

Teachers generally are opposed to being rated by administrators and as yet no rating scheme has been devised which is both valid and reliable. It is probable that teacher rating will be a controversial issue for many years to come. Until it is determined whether merit rating does more good than harm, administrators should probably spend a minimum of their energies in rating the performance of individual teachers and a maximum of time and energy in helping the teachers appraise themselves, the achievements of pupils, and aspects of the program of the school as a whole.

APPRAISING PUPIL PROGRESS

The time-honored means of judging pupil growth include essay tests, achievement tests, and teachers' estimates of pupil achievement.

[3] Research Division, National Education Association, "Teacher Personnel Procedures, 1950–1951: Employment Conditions in Service," *Research Bulletin*, 30, No. 2 (April, 1952), 49.

[4] *The Ohio Teaching Record Anecdotal Observation Form* (2nd ed.; Columbus, Ohio: Ohio State University, 1945).

All three are valuable. The organization and character of a pupil's writing on an essay test tell something about him that could be learned in no other way. Knowing the standing of a pupil or a pupil body on a widely used achievement test is generally helpful as a matter of diagnosis. The teachers' estimate of pupil achievement is generally the best single predictor of future success in school. Procedures which have more recently proved their usefulness as aids in evaluating pupil growth include adjustment inventories and the systematic observation of pupil behavior. In spite of the fact that these useful means of judging pupil growth are available, many teachers have great difficulty in appraising the growth of some of the competencies which they say they are trying to develop.

In the Kansas Study of Education for Citizenship, it was shown that twelfth-grade high school pupils knew more about government and about the communities in which they lived than did ninth-grade pupils. However, twelfth-grade pupils had not made significantly greater progress in acquiring skills in critical thinking than had the ninth-grade pupils.[5] In a survey of St. Louis (Missouri) schools, it was found that twelfth-grade pupils who had taken both general science and biology were not appreciably better in dealing with everyday health problems than were those who had had no science.[6] These are just two of numerous examples which might be cited to show that schools are more effective in helping pupils to acquire factual knowledge than they are in helping pupils to acquire social competencies.

Pupil appraisal practices are in part responsible for this situation. Pupils prepare to meet the school's tests, and, therefore, the school teaches what it tests. If tests ignore entirely the skills of critical thinking and the understandings of everyday health problems, any attention which pupils give to these neglected areas will be entirely incidental. If pupils are to give systematic attention to the development of social competencies, these competencies must be involved in appraisal practices. This point of view is developed in Chapter 19 where it is urged that for each subject objectives should be stated in terms of behavior so that teachers can more readily determine the extent to which the objectives have been achieved.

Each pupil's progress toward educational objectives should be appraised in terms of his capacity as well as his achievement. Most progress in the acquiring of social competencies will be judged by observation and other nonstructured procedures. The principal should work with teachers in the actual process of evaluating individual pupils and in helping these

[5] *An Evaluation of Citizenship Education in the High School* (Manhattan, Kan.: Kansas State College Press, 1950), p. 37.

[6] Division of Field Studies, *Report of Survey of the Public Schools of St. Louis, Missouri* (New York: Bureau of Publications, Teachers College, Columbia University, 1939), p. 44.

pupils to evaluate themselves. Paul B. Diederich has outlined the steps in the development of a total program of pupil appraisal.[7] An excellent and practical guide for the classroom teacher is *Evaluating Pupil Progress.*[8]

A new gauge of pupil progress should be developed in terms of the kinds of outcomes in which good secondary schools are now primarily interested. It needs to meet the demand for methods and measures of evaluation and appraisal that are closely concerned with the kinds of growth and development that good secondary schools now generally seek to effect in their youth. It should be so designed as to be useful in administration of pupil guidance, programing, promotion, marking, graduation, and college and job placement; and if so it will revolutionize all these processes and the whole attitude of youth (and of many teachers) toward the schools' programs of education. No more powerful impetus to curriculum reform and reconstruction at the youth level could be provided than would result if pupils and teachers gradually began to realize that what was marked and recorded, what was used for promotion, guidance, graduation, and placement was not the older familiar units of credit in subject matter learned. For a good decade schools have been getting themselves into a frame of mind to appreciate and to use new measures and methods for evaluating the results in which they are really interested; hence now is the time to start the research work necessary to develop and validate such measures. With no more effort than has gone into the development of our most elaborate plans for measuring our students' knowledge we could create new measures of much more significance in American secondary education than those now commonly used.

The Carnegie unit credit is a measure of time spent and ground covered but, in many respects, it is inadequate as an instrument for indicating the achievement of high school pupils.[9] The tests of General Educational Development used to evaluate experiences in the armed services are illustrative of the measures of growth that are needed; whenever possible, high school principals and teachers should cooperate with test makers in developing a wider range of evaluation techniques to measure some of the less commonly appraised objectives. Until more adequate instruments are available, teachers can do their best to select and use tests and other appraisal instruments which measure the objectives they have set up. They can also make and use their own tests,

[7] Paul B. Diederich, "Design for a Comprehensive Evaluation Program," *School Review,* 58 (April, 1950), 225–232.

[8] Bureau of Education Research, *Evaluating Pupil Progress* (Bulletin No. 6; Sacramento: California State Department of Education, 1952).

[9] Ellsworth Tompkins and Walter H. Gaumnitz, *The Carnegie Unit: Its Origin, Status, and Trends* (U.S. Office of Education, Bulletin No. 7; Washington, D.C.: Government Printing Office, 1954).

check lists, and observation records, which will aid in indicating the extent to which their objectives are being achieved.

EVALUATING THE SCHOOL

It is more difficult and more complex to evaluate a school than it is to evaluate a business enterprise. If a business has made a profit, it is usually said to be successful. If it has not made a profit, it is a failure. The school, however, exists for many purposes, some of the most important of which are difficult to measure. Evaluation of all the objectives of the school is too big a task to be accomplished at one time. Yet the magnitude of the task is no reason for avoiding it; and when it is necessary, as it often is, to decide which objective of a school activity shall be accepted as the most important one, an idea of the success or failure of the activity in terms of that objective can be obtained.

Members of the staff of a typical high school are not as competent to evaluate their own achievements as were the staff members who worked on the evaluation program of the Eight-Year Study. Yet the school staff is more competent than the patrons of the school who are daily forming judgments about the school and every activity in it. No amount of academic seclusion will prevent the community from evaluating the school program. The staff of every high school has the responsibility of evaluating its achievements in terms of its own objectives. If the objectives are definite and specific enough to aid in determining what educational experiences are to be provided for youth, they will also be definite enough for the staff to decide whether or not it has made progress in achieving its goals.

EVALUATIVE CRITERIA

The evaluative criteria, devised by the Cooperative Study of Secondary School Standards, are helpful to any staff interested in evaluating the whole school. From 1933 to 1940 the six accrediting associations of the nation cooperated in developing evaluative criteria for secondary schools. A check list of more than a thousand items was made, and the records of more than twenty thousand pupils in two hundred schools were studied intensively. Items on the check list were weighted by judgments of two hundred principals and eighty-seven professional staff members. From these data were prepared criteria for evaluating secondary schools as to curriculum, library, pupil activities, guidance, instruction, outcomes, staff, plant, and administration. The result is a comprehensive check list that can be used in surveying every aspect of a school.

The evaluative criteria are universally used in accepting or rejecting applications for accreditation in the associations. A school applying for membership must first fill out its own report, which means that the school must evaluate itself. Over a period of from several months to more than a year, members of the staff prepare a statement of the purposes and philosophy of the school, describe the pupil population and school community, secure objective data where they are demanded, and form judgments on all aspects of the school as outlined under the different standards.

After a school has evaluated itself, a committee of from five to twenty-five schoolmen visits the school and reviews the self-evaluation. The committee divides into subcommittees to study all aspects of the school's work. The visitors confer with staff members, pupils, patrons, and school board members. Before they leave, they write a report for the local staff, pointing out the strengths of the school, making recommendations for improvement, and revising where necessary the staff's own self-evaluation. The evaluative criteria have improved greatly the inspections administered by the accrediting associations, but their greatest value has been in providing an outline of procedure for schools that wished to evaluate themselves. The 1950 edition[10] of these evaluative criteria improved the section related to curriculum by devoting attention to the separate subject matter areas. In view of long-term plans for periodic revisions, it is expected that these evaluative criteria will be of continuing service to American secondary schools.

A few sets of evaluative criteria which were developed by local and state groups have been useful to high school staffs throughout the nation. An example is found in the *Criteria for Evaluation of Junior High Schools* developed by a committee consisting chiefly of Texas junior high school principals.[11] Included are nine criteria for self-appraisal and improvement.

CHECKING THE IMPERATIVE NEEDS OF YOUTH

A plan developed by W. L. Ransom under the direction of the Committee on Curriculum Planning and Development of the National Association of Secondary School Principals makes available to high school faculties assistance in evaluating a high school in terms of the "imperative needs of youth" as stated in *Education for All American Youth*. Ransom says,

For the past three decades educators of vision have worked unceasingly to help guide the schools toward educational programs more in keeping with

[10] Cooperative Study of Secondary School Standards, *Evaluative Criteria* (rev. ed.; Washington: American Council on Education, 1950).

[11] Texas Study of Secondary Education, *Criteria for Evaluation of Junior High Schools: Preliminary Statement* (Research Study No. 15; Austin: University of Texas Press, 1954), 142 pp. See also California Association of Secondary School Administrators, *Procedures for Appraising California High Schools* (Sacramento: The Association, 1954).

known facts about human growth and emerging trends in the modern social, economic, and political scenes. By the middle thirties it became evident that the secondary schools of this country were divided on a number of fundamental issues which were brought sharply into focus by the Report of the Committee on the Orientation of Secondary Education. All of these issues are not yet resolved. Resolution of the seventh issue, as posed by the Committee, seems of primary importance if the American High School is to fulfill the role generally ascribed to it by the people who render it support. Issue VII of the Committee's Report reads as follows: "Shall secondary education accept conventional school subjects as fundamental categories under which school experiences shall be classified and presented to students, or shall it arrange and present experiences in fundamental categories directly related to the performance of such functions of secondary schools in a democracy as increasing the ability and the desire better to meet socio-civic, economic, health, leisure-time, vocational, and pre-professional problems and situations?" [12]

He therefore makes the following proposal in another study:

A good idea of whether a school can be characterized as strong or weak with reference to each need may be gained if a member of the faculty, a faculty committee, or the entire faculty rates a school on each of the items listed under that need. It is proposed that 5 be given as a high rating and 1 for a low rating for each of the characteristics, and N for situations in which an item or characteristic does not apply. Then, by connecting the scores on the items under each need with a line drawn from top to bottom of the page, one can see whether the school has been rated as strong or weak on the need as a whole. The weakest characteristics will also thus be easily identified, and consideration can then be given to what can be done to raise these low points. Schools get better faster when their weaknesses are identified and when there is a school-wide and community-wide effort at eliminating these specific weaknesses.

The value of the checklist lies in the fact that its use will enable a school more easily to identify the weak spots in its program as a means for meeting the imperative needs of youth. If a school's program is good when it meets the imperative needs of its youth, as many people are on the record as believing, then the only really valid criteria by which a school's program can be legitimately judged are those which measure it in terms of its success in meeting these needs. [13]

An idea of how Ransom's method of evaluation may be used is suggested by the following extract, which deals with the first of the ten imperative needs:

[12] William L. Ransom, "Meeting the Imperative Needs of Youth in the American High School, A Checklist" (Unpublished doctoral project; New York: Teachers College, Columbia University, 1949), pp. 1–2.

[13] Ransom, "How Well Does Your School Rate on the Ten Imperative Needs of Youth?" NASSP *Bulletin*, No. 164, October, 1949.

Imperative Need No. 1: All youth need to develop salable skills and those understandings and attitudes that make the worker an intelligent and productive participant in economic life.

	N	1	2	3	4	5
1. The school seeks to develop in all students an understanding of the interdependence of workers and the contributions of all workers to the social and economic welfare of the nation.						
2. The school has a plan by which students, employers, parents, and community agencies work together in developing the student work program.						
3. The school stresses the dignity of both essential and creative labor, giving equal recognition to all work that is well done.						
4. The school strives to develop in pupils an adaptive attitude toward technological developments and the occupational changes brought about by new inventions.						
5. The school provides for all students who plan to go to work before completing high school, or immediately after graduation, instruction in such pertinent areas as the channels through which jobs may be secured and the techniques of applying and being interviewed as an applicant.						
6. The school provides for experiences through which students may develop understandings of the individual's role, responsibilities, and methods of functioning in labor and management organizations: talks by employers and employees, study of community groups, motion pictures, and so on.						
7. The school gathers much information about each individual student's interests, abilities, aptitudes, and personal characteristics for use in helping the student determine a field of work in which he may be successfully employed: diversified occupations program, tests, observation, and so on.						
8. The school provides opportunity for students to evaluate critically, in terms of their purposes, interests, and capabilities, employment opportunities and requirements of many occupations through study, field trips, job surveys, discussions with labor and management personnel, and so on.						
9. The school emphasizes the development of abilities in basic occupational processes and with basic tools and machines.						
10. The school maintains contact with major occupational fields to keep its vocational program up to						

date in regard to new methods and procedures and
technological developments.

	N	1	2	3	4	5

11. The school enlists employer and parent cooperation in evaluation of pupils' work experiences in terms
of student growth in attitudes toward work and fellow
workers and toward quality of work.

12. The school helps to arrange for supervised work
experience, in terms of individual purposes, interests,
and capabilities, for an increasing number of youth
regardless of academic, economic, or social status.

13. The school bases its program of vocational education on continuing studies of present and probable
future types of work available to youth in the local and
regional community.

14. Space and equipment are available in school or
community or in both for an increasing number of
youth to receive training in work for the production
and distribution of goods and as a civic service.

15. The school uses the work experiences of its
students to enrich the instructional programs of both
employed and unemployed youth in school.

16. The school evaluates its program for developing
salable skills in terms of pupil ability to find and hold
jobs suited to individual interests and abilities.[14]

ADDITIONAL WAYS OF EVALUATING

The persistence of students in remaining in high school until graduation has been used as a measure of the school's success. During the past
forty years the percentage of elimination from the high schools of the
United States has been greatly reduced, but even now almost half our
youth fail to graduate.

The success of students in doing the work of the school has been
studied as another index of the achievement of the school. Throughout
the nation, failures have been steadily reduced during the past forty
years, but some of our students still experience failure in school, and to
those who believe in universal secondary education, the percentage seems
much too large.

Most schools have pointed with pride to the records made in college by some of their graduates. Of the many careful studies made of
success in college, the most significant is that made by the Progressive

[14] Adapted from Ransom, "How Well Does Your School Rate on the Ten
Imperative Needs of Youth?" loc. cit., pp. 13–15. By permission of the National
Education Association.

Education Association as a part of the Eight-Year Study.[15] This investigation reveals that (1) students who had superior success in high school usually succeeded in college; (2) there was no pattern of subject preparation for college superior to any other pattern of preparation; (3) students from the experimental schools had slightly greater success in college than did the pupils from the traditional schools; and (4) the more the students' high school programs had departed from the conventional college preparatory pattern, the greater was their success in college.

Many schools have interviewed employers of graduates to secure evidence of the success of former pupils and possible indications of adjustments which should be made in the educational program. There are available instruments for securing opinions held about the school by pupils, parents, and others in the community.[16] In Chapter 25 are described procedures for studying the community and its youth. Many of these procedures can be useful in evaluation projects.

In the New York Regents' Inquiry[17] the young people themselves were used in evaluating schools. They were asked to describe the characteristics of their schools that they liked least and those they liked best. They were asked what changes they would like to see made in their schools. Recent graduates were asked if they had been given educational guidance when they were in school and what their current chief problems were. A large proportion of the answers to many questions were vigorously critical of schools and their divorcement from normal life. A weakness in using the opinions of youth to evaluate the school is that, as adults, we lack confidence in their judgments. However, as teachers we must be interested in their opinions. Even though they are wrong, they are the starting point for any changes in pupil opinions that we may hope to bring about.

The Regents' Inquiry in the state of New York also turned its attention to the social competence of pupils when they leave school. Among the significant findings of F. T. Spaulding were these: (1) The high school's opinion of its pupils' vocational competence bears little relation to the actual success of these boys and girls in getting jobs, and (2) the general citizenship and leisure-time activities of pupils who have left school bear no apparent relation to the curricula they have followed.[18]

---

[15] Dean Chamberlin and others, *Did They Succeed in College?* (New York: Harper & Brothers, 1942).

[16] Harold C. Hand, *What People Think about Their Schools* (Yonkers, N.Y.: World Book Company, 1948).

[17] Ruth Eckert and Thomas A. Marshall, *When Youth Leave School* (The Regents' Inquiry; New York: McGraw-Hill Book Co., Inc., 1938).

[18] Francis T. Spaulding, *High School and Life* (New York: McGraw-Hill Book Co., Inc., 1939).

These statements imply a vigorous criticism of traditional secondary schools. They also suggest points of attack for any secondary school staff interested in evaluating its own effectiveness.

Such evaluations make interesting reports to parents and serve as a means of introducing them to all aspects of the work of the school. Staff members, for their part, need interested audiences to whom they can report their plans and achievements. Most teachers who are failing to do their best work are not lacking in technical information; they are merely neglecting to use it in making wise choices of the means to employ in working toward the school's objectives. They are faced with a plethora of activities to carry on, and it seems to them that no one appreciates the distinction between activities that are important and those that are not. They need the stimulus of understanding parents and administrators.

Every competent workman in any field of endeavor is constantly asking himself "What am I trying to do?" and "How can I do it more effectively?" In every division of the entire school and in every class or group activity, the members of the staff should ask themselves a continuous stream of questions such as these: "What are our aims?" "How shall we achieve them?" "How well did we succeed?" "How shall we revise our aims and procedures?"

Evaluation thus becomes not a culminating activity but a constant feature of the work of a school staff and an integral part of the planning and replanning of all activities in the school. It is an appropriate and essential part of planning an assembly program, a unit of work in the classroom, the work of a school for a year or for several years. Without intelligent evaluation there is no assurance that the school is making real progress. Without the active leadership of the principal in organizing the high school staff for school improvement it is not likely that the best rate of progress will be attained.

Some Points to Consider

1. If it is the business of the high school principal to see that teachers get "in-service education," whose business is it to educate the high school principal in service?

2. A high school principal said, "We are so busy in our school working on problems which the faculty think we must solve if our school is to be a better one that we do not have time for an in-service education program." If he said this seriously, what is wrong with his idea of "in-service" education? Should he be told to conduct a formal in-service education program each year?

3. If you were principal of a high school in which the faculty was satisfied to let you run the school as you wished, would you want to change this attitude or be glad to have a chance to carry out your ideas without interference?

4. How does some high school with which you are familiar rate on the check list for Imperative Need No. 1 as given in the text of this chapter? What, if anything, should this school do to improve its standing?

5. Will a cursory inspection of a car enable you to decide how good or bad it is? What assumptions do you make in such an inspection if you conclude from it that the car is good or bad?

6. If you have evidence to show that a certain make and model of car has an excellent performance record, is it as important for you to check its exact specifications as if you did not have this evidence?

7. Is it best to judge a high school by its specifications (what it has) or by its performance record (what it does)?

8. Can two high schools serving very different communities be exactly alike and be equally good? Why or why not? Do most of the ways of evaluating high schools used by state departments of education and other accrediting agencies tend to encourage uniformity in high schools? Should uniformity or individuality be encouraged?

Further Reading

American Association of School Administrators, *Staff Relations in School Administration.* Thirty-third Yearbook; Washington, D.C.: National Education Association, 1955.

Association for Supervision and Curriculum Development. *Better Than Rating: New Approaches to Appraisal of Teaching Services.* Washington, D.C.: National Education Association, 1950.

Briggs, Thomas H., and Joseph Justman. *Improving Instruction through Supervision.* New York: The Macmillan Company, 1952, pp. 232–266.

Bucher, Dwight. "Judging the Effectiveness of Teaching," NASSP *Bulletin* 34, No. 174 (December, 1950), 270–281.

California Association of Sunday School Administrators, *Procedures for Appraising California High Schools.* Sacramento: The Association, 1954.

Chamberlin, Dean, and Others, *Did They Succeed in College?* New York: Harper & Brothers, 1942.

Department of Supervision and Curriculum Development. *Leadership at Work.* Fifteenth Yearbook; Washington, D.C.: National Education Association, 1943.

Eckert, Ruth, and Thomas A. Marshall. *When Youth Leave School.* The Regents' Inquiry; New York: McGraw-Hill Book Co., Inc., 1938.

Educational Policies Commission. *Education for All American Youth: A Further Look.* Washington, D.C.: National Education Association, 1951.

Elsbree, Willard S., and E. Edmund Reutter, Jr. *Staff Personnel in the Public Schools.* Englewood Cliffs, N.J.: Prentice-Hall, Inc., 1954, Chaps. 4, 5, 9.

Eye, Glen G., and Willard R. Lane. *The New Teacher Comes to School.* New York: Harper & Brothers, 1956.

Federal Security Agency, U.S. Office of Education. *High School Staff and Size of School.* Washington, D.C.: Government Printing Office, 1950.

Findley, Warren G. "Educational Evaluation: Recent Developments," *Social Education*, 14 (May, 1950), 206–210.

Gunkle, Mennow M. "Teacher Orientation in Selected High Schools of Cook County," *North Central Association Quarterly*, 27 (January, 1953), 313–326.

Leonard, J. Paul. *Developing the Secondary School Curriculum*. Rev. ed.; New York: Rinehart & Company, Inc., 1953.

McCall, William A. *Measurement of Teacher Merit*. Raleigh, N.C.: State Superintendent of Public Instruction, 1952.

Ransom, William L. "How Well Does Your High School Rate on the Ten Imperative Needs of Youth?" NASSP *Bulletin*, No. 164, October, 1949.

Research Division, National Education Association, "Teaching Load in 1950," *Research Bulletin*, Vol. 29, No. 1, February, 1951.

Spaulding, Francis T. *High School and Life*. New York: McGraw-Hill Book Co., Inc., 1939.

Texas Study of Secondary Education. *Criteria for Evaluation of Junior High Schools: Preliminary Statement*. Research Study No. 15; Austin: University of Texas Press, 1954.

*Since obviously the high school's program of education is
the basic reason for having such an institution, what the
principal does to improve this program and to facilitate its
operation is the most important aspect of his work. Part
Three presents a broad concept of what the high school's
educational program really is, and then shows how high
schools can be organized and operated to get the maximum
out of the program in the way of growth and development
of students.*

Part Three

THE PRINCIPAL AND THE EDUCATIONAL PROGRAM

Chapter 9

LEARNING AND GENERAL EDUCATION

Tʜᴇ ᴡʜᴏʟᴇ ᴇʟᴀʙᴏʀᴀᴛᴇ and complicated organization of the public school system and of individual schools exists for only one purpose: to provide the most completely favorable learning situation possible for children and youth. School administration is the process of organizing and directing the resources of the school to provide effective learning situations. Administrative procedures should never become an end in themselves, although the complexities of procedure and organization at times make them almost seem so. Fundamentally, the educational program, with the learning experiences it provides, is the heart and the whole of the school; all else is subsidiary and important only as it contributes to the educational program.

The body of contemporary educational literature dealing with the elementary and the secondary educational program is immense. Even a casual review of this literature will reveal that educators whose points of view are similar frequently differ, however, in their solutions to educational problems. The lack of a standard terminology is at times confusing, as newly coined terms are used with entirely different meanings by different authors. Fundamentally, the study of the educational program requires the study of everything that affects human life and organization today: the individual's development and behavior, the social and economic scene, and the interaction between the individual and his environment. Faced with this complexity, it is no wonder that the secondary school administrator may be reluctant to engage in a study of a fundamental revision of the educational program. Yet such a revision is necessary if youth education is to be a vital and directing influence in our society; hence the continuous development and adaptation of the educational program must be the primary concern of the secondary school principal. He need not be, and probably cannot be expected to be, expert in all of the specialized aspects of the educational program. The resources of the entire school staff are required for a comprehensive revision of the school's program, but the principal himself must have a genuine understanding of the forces affecting the educational program, the principles of its organization, and the methods of giving leadership to a total staff in its study of learning and the educational program.

Nature of Learning and the Educational Program

The educational program comprises all the actual experiences of the pupil under the influence of the school. The ready acceptance or rejection of this concept of the program depends upon one's basic concept of the nature of learning and of the conditions under which it takes place. The study of human behavior and development has led to a gradual broadening and more inclusive concept of the whole nature of the learning process. Learning earlier was conceived to be a highly intellectual process through which what was vaguely termed the "mind" was strengthened and developed. The evidence of learning was the ability to respond in verbal or written symbols, although those verbal responses might mean little in terms of understanding or the behavior of the individual. Experimental work has revealed no basis for the concept of the mind as a separate entity or as something strengthened by practice, particularly if that practice is irrelevant to the problems and needs of the individual. The studies of human behavior and development have provided the evidence for a much more inclusive and functional concept. The individual from birth is continually meeting new situations and undergoing experiences through which new responses are acquired. This process is obviously the manner by which the individual or organism learns to live in, and adjust to, his environment and adapt it to his needs. The evidence that this adjustment learning is taking place is the change in behavior of the individual. *Learning is the process of acquiring new responses or adjustments and is evidenced by changes in behavior.*

Where the organism faces a novel situation, old responses will not suffice. A new response is called for or failure confronts. If fortunate, the organism will contrive a response new to it and adequate to cope with the novel difficulty. Such a contriving we call "learning." . . . In such a case the restoration (return to equilibrium) is not to the prior state. The organism is different by the new response and all that it brings. Each act of learning adds a certain change and increment to the very structure of the organism itself.[1]

Two aspects of this concept of learning are important for the student of the curriculum. First, it removes the impression that learning is a mysterious process going on in and strengthening a postulated and equally mysterious something called the mind. Rather, learning is the adjustment of a total being, and the only evidence of it is the change in behavior. It is not necessary or particularly fruitful to postulate a local or

[1] William H. Kilpatrick, "A Reconstructed Theory of the Educative Process," *Teachers College Record*, 32 (March, 1931), 532–533.

separate entity, the "mind," for learning is much more adequately explained in terms of the integrated response of a total organism. Second, learning involves the total responses of the individual: emotional, physical, and verbal. Learning thus includes the total behavior of the individual rather than primarily the narrow and stereotyped verbal response.

The individual in and out of school is continually facing new experiences. Obviously, therefore, learning is not confined to the school. However, learning through the simple process of growing up and meeting situations by trial and error as they occur is sporadic and unorganized. The role of the school is to provide many planned and selected experiences through which the individual can learn more fully, efficiently, and effectively than by unplanned experience. These experiences are expected to provide the opportunity for more complete and more desirable growth of the student through controlled modification and change of his behavior than would occur were there no school.

Although all learning results in change in behavior, the latter must be interpreted broadly. Learning may be the process of acquiring the meaning of symbols and then being able to speak, read, and write. It may be the development of certain skills in shops and laboratories. It may be the change of attitudes that results in different responses and behavior. It may be the learning of methods and processes for the solution of problems.

The educational program thus becomes all of the experiences that the school provides or allows to exist in the environment under its control and through which the individual learns new modes of behavior. This means that what goes on in the playgrounds, in games, in social events, in the classroom, and in all the activities of the school constitutes the educational program. Such a definition is not based upon an arbitrary classification of certain experience as educational and other experience as noneducational. Rather, it arises from an acceptance of the inevitable fact that students will learn from all of their experiences. All those that are provided by the school thus become part of the educational process for which the school must be responsible. The principal's responsibility for improvement of the school's educational program, then, in its broadest sense, involves him in an effort to provide a better total experience for the students while under the supervision of the school. The over-all purpose is to help all youth to be and to become happier, better adjusted, more successful in their personal lives, and as young citizens better able and more willing to defend and develop our democratic social order.

Factors Affecting the Educational Program

Since the educational program should provide learning experiences that enable the student to adjust more successfully to the environment in which he lives, and to be more skillful in improving it, the program itself should be affected by all the forces and factors that affect both the learner and the environment. The experiences comprising the program should provide activities conducive to learning, should reflect the problems and situations relevant to the social and economic scene in which the student lives, and should be directed toward goals that are real and important to the student. The development of the educational program should be based upon consideration of the general principles of learning, the major social and economic characteristics of the society, and the broad purposes to be achieved by secondary education.

SOME GENERAL PRINCIPLES OF LEARNING

A comprehensive analysis of the experimental work on learning and the subsequent general principles that might be derived from it is far beyond the scope of this review. Numerous comprehensive volumes on the subject are available,[2] but certain general principles are sufficiently broad and universal and pertinent to the development of the educational program to be stressed here.

One fundamental principle is that *the individual learns only through his own activity. What is learned is only what the learner experiences through his own activity.* True activity is of a widely varied nature and need not necessarily be overt and obvious. The significance of this principle is that the teacher cannot pour knowledge or learning into a passive student. The measure of the effectiveness of the school's offering is not the outline of the course or the activity of the teacher. The activity of the teacher, the whole plan of the classroom procedure, the content of the educational program have only one purpose and point: to stimulate activity on the part of the student. The essential core of the educational program, then, is the learning activities it stimulates.

Learning leads to the development and understanding of new relationships. The meaning and significance of new understandings depends upon how closely they are related to the past understandings and experiences of the learner. The earlier experimental work in educational psychology, with its study of the single stimulus and response, led to the inference that learning was primarily the accumulation of a multitude of discrete responses. The more recent work and studies of the so-called Gestalt and organismic psychologists have emphasized that responses are essentially stimuli in a total context, that for each student, learning is basically the fitting of new adaptations into his total pattern of thinking or behavior, and that initial responses are to this total pattern and not to single, isolated stimuli. Consequently, one phase of learning for each person is concerned with attempts to relate his past experience to the components

[2] For example, see William H. Burton, *The Guidance of Learning Activities* (rev. ed.; New York: Appleton-Century-Crofts, Inc., 1952).

of the total new pattern or situation. The significance of this principle for curriculum construction is pervasive. It establishes the need to organize instruction into blocks or units around some central problem theme or to utilize a student interest around which numerous and varied specific learnings can be related. It denies the validity of organizing instruction and the educational program around a series of drills and rote learnings that may have little significance in themselves.

The learning situations must have some degree of resemblance to the life situation in which it is presumed the student is being prepared to think and act. Thorough review of this principle would require examination of the whole literature on generalization and transfer of learning. It is sufficient to state that the assumption that the student will automatically transfer to life situations what is learned in school is extremely doubtful. Only as the school situation resembles the outside situation can students generally be expected to make such application. It is true that the intelligent or bright student will transfer from situations where the resemblances are more remote than will the slower student, but it is also probable that the ability of even the bright student in this regard has been overestimated.

> . . . if one wants youth of all levels of ability and interest generally to learn in the sense of becoming more and more competent to think and act as responsible young citizens, the teaching and learning situations of the school must be seen by the pupils as similar to those in life in which they are expected to use what they have learned in school. The most able of these youth *can* make the deductions, generalizations, and applications of what they learn in school under the subject-organized curriculum to the aspects of their living to which this learning applies, no matter how remote the connections and associations with life-use are. The average students cannot easily make these associations. The least able hardly do so at all. Even the best pupils learn more when the connections between school-learning and life-use are easily and directly made. But the best plan for use in the high school . . . must be one effective with *all* youth. As one goes down the scale of educability from this upper ten or fifteen per cent of most able youth, the need for relating the learning situation used by the school to the use-situation in life where we want the learning to affect conduct becomes more and more essential.[3]

The significance of this principle for the development of the educational program is the need it establishes for the learning activities to be drawn from problems with which students are familiar in their environment, to use the community as a laboratory for instruction, to utilize all visual and auditory means for establishing relationships, and to provide many applications for students.

[3] Will French, "The Harvard Report and the High School," NASSP *Bulletin,* No. 138 (April, 1946), p. 7.

Real learning must grow out of the experience of the learner and must deal with material that he can relate to his own efforts for self-preservation and self-realization. L. Thomas Hopkins states that "all good learning is seeking satisfaction for personal goals." [4] The highest type of learning activity cannot go on unless the learner has some purpose in view. A purpose will not be effective if the activity is so remote from the previous experience of the individual that he is unable to relate it in any way to his own needs and aims. Real interest, concerning which so much has been written in recent years, is not something that exists apart from an activity, something extrinsic that the ingenious teacher can attach to this or that unit of instruction. Genuine interest comes into existence only when a proposed activity or learning unit is seen by a learner as being related to his own interest and welfare. The learner must feel that the proposed activity will contribute to his own efforts to adjust to his environment and to those ends that he conceives to be essential to his development, that is, to his self-preservation and self-realization. It does not follow that instruction must cater to the passing whims and fancies of the student, but from whatever source the instruction arises, the learner must see and feel its relation to his own development. Certainly the teacher should guide the student in selecting those learning activities that are effective.

The principle that the learning activity must grow out of the experience of the learner and must contribute to his own felt needs is not a new one. Largely as a result of the teaching of John Dewey[5] and his followers, it has received wide acceptance today.

A tremendous amount of effort and experimentation in recent curriculum work has gone into attempts to implement these principles in order to overcome the difficulty of translating them into actions in practical situations. Involved is a consideration of the maturity and characteristics of the learner, the experiences the environment has provided, and the life purposes of the learner. The application of these principles means the development of the educational program around problems that are drawn more nearly from current problems and from life. It means that we recognize that logically organized subject matter will not necessarily provide effective learning situations. The acceptance of this criterion of effective learning has provided the curriculum worker of today with his greatest challenge.[6]

[4] L. Thomas Hopkins, "Emerging Emphasis as to Learning," *Teachers College Record,* 40 (November, 1938), 119–128.

[5] John Dewey, *Experience and Education* (New York: The Macmillan Company, 1938).

[6] For a forthright statement of this view of the curriculum and of learning, see *A Framework for Public Education in California* (Sacramento: California State Department of Education, 1950).

SOME SOCIAL AND ECONOMIC FACTORS

The ends that are to be achieved by education must always be related to the needs of the social groups to which the learner belongs, and those needs will be affected by the particular conditions of that social order and culture. Also, learning experiences, to be vital to the student, must be related to the problems that he recognizes as those encountered by people in his own cultural age and group. Basically, then, the content of the educational program must grow out of the social, economic, and personal situations in which people live. The curriculum worker should be a constant student of the social environment. Social change, always a characteristic of this country, has been continually accelerating. Significant changes in almost every phase of living have occurred in the past two generations which have most profoundly modified the role of the school. Although many aspects of these changes might be considered, only a few of the more salient ones are presented here.

The school curriculum must aid in preparing youth to live in an industrial, urban, and interdependent economy. The implications of this simple fact are many. It means that even youth who live in one of our predominantly agricultural states grow up in a culture that is becoming increasingly urban. This urban culture provides many stimulating experiences and many educational resources, but it does not provide the opportunities for direct learning experiences that a rural environment often can. Even boys and girls who live in rural areas have less opportunity for work experience and for working in partnership with their parents than was once the case. Experience in lifework activities is less easily gained by gradually working into it as the youth grows up; hence more dependence must be placed upon the preliminary training and experience that the school can provide. The interdependence resulting from a complex, industrial, money economy places greater demands upon youth who are learning to work as members of business, labor, and professional groups and creates a genuine need to understand vexing political and social problems. Housing, transportation, community health, and recreation, for example, are among those that affect almost all people. Our culture has thus placed much heavier burdens on the school, but at the same time it has provided a rich and stimulating laboratory for the school's educational program.

The school's offering must prepare youth to face increasingly complex problems of democratic citizenship. The complexity of our industrial economy has produced its problems of citizenship. The democratic face-to-face relation of our earlier, simpler culture has changed to the organized groups of today. Although democracy may have the appearance of a static concept, actually it has been continually reinterpreted and expanded with each generation, for part of its vitality has been due to its dynamic nature. Civic problems that were predominantly national in character have, after two world wars, become international. Once our chief problems grew out of man's relation to nature; now they grow out of man's relation to other men. The crucial responsibility of the school and the central purpose of its program must revolve around the development of intelligent, democratic citizens. The conditions of today provide enormous problems, but they also provide one of the greatest of educational adventures for those who work with the high school's educational program.

The school's program must prepare youth to live in a world dominated by the methods and products of science. The discoveries and applications of science are the foundation of our technology from which have come our productivity and wealth. Although science is commonly associated primarily with the so-called natural sciences (physics, chemistry, biology, and related fields) and assumed to be a method of study characteristic of these fields, the revolutionary concept for which science is responsible is actually a *method* of study, of studying problems, and of arriving at the truth. As such, it is applicable broadly to all fields of human activity. The products of scientific discovery have revolutionized our ways of living and have created new social conditions, but the methods of science have provided us with a powerful intellectual tool whose ultimate effect on man may exceed all the material benefits derived from science.

The school's educational program not only must provide experience in the so-called scientific fields, but must also develop an understanding of the social implications of scientific discoveries as well as a skill in applying scientific method to all of the broad fields of human endeavor. A full recognition of what science and its methods mean to us must be reflected in our educational program if it is to be realistically oriented to the problems of the twentieth century.

The school's program must prepare youth to deal with a vastly increased body of knowledge in all fields. Scientific study, the printing press, and the increased amount of research has accumulated an enormous body of facts and information in a wide array of fields from which those who plan and select the content of the school's offering today must choose. Where a few generations ago a few simple courses might present the main facts available in the whole field of natural science, today a similar amount of time can hardly deal with the elementary principles in one small specialized branch of the sciences. American literature has developed innumerable specialized areas, as has mathematics. New fields of study (health, conservation, psychology, sociology, and many others) have appeared. Whether or not the curriculum worker accepts the concept of subject organization, he must still face the problem of selecting from the vast storehouse of contemporary knowledge.

The concept that youth education or education in any particular field must be survey and mastery of available knowledge becomes impractical and even fantastic. A major problem of education is thus one of establishing criteria for the selection of the most pertinent experiences that will best prepare youth in methods of approaching new problems and of securing information when needed, rather than attempting to develop encyclopedic knowledge, an approach that probably never was functional and is certainly impossible today.

The school curriculum must provide educational experiences for youth of all interests, abilities, and life purposes. Previous chapters have described the development of the secondary school into a school for all youth. Numerous studies indicate that the heterogeneity of the student body has increased steadily in all respects as the proportion of youth enrolling and remaining in high school has increased.[7] These differences in the abilities and interests of the student body have created a need for an educational program vastly more flexible and diversified than is generally available today. The requirements of students may be broadly similar, but the means by which they are met must be varied. The special fields of study must be modified in numerous ways if a heterogeneous school population is to have genuine educational opportunities. To continue trying to meet this problem by adding new subjects for each new interest, ability, or purpose found in a student body is obviously impossible. Present trends toward a more unified, integrated approach with provision in the classroom for individual differences seem to offer more hope, but they call for fundamental reconstruction of the educational program.

THE NEEDS OF YOUTH

Planning the organization and selection of learning experiences must be guided by the ends to be achieved: the development of certain understandings, skills, and attitudes in youth. Without a clear concept of the ends to be achieved, curriculum planning at best is opportunistic improvising. The practical administrator may be occasionally impatient with what appears to be a theoretical review of major purposes of education or major needs of youth. Yet the theoretical approach is fundamental to any sound program.

Numerous excellent studies have reviewed and summarized the major purposes and objectives of secondary education. A particularly fruitful approach is to think of the purposes of secondary education in terms

[7] See B. L. Dodds, "That All May Learn," NASSP *Bulletin*, No. 35 (November, 1939), Chaps. 1, 2.

of the needs of youth for which the school should provide learning and developmental experiences. This approach from the standpoint of the needs of the learner is in harmony with the concept that the effective learning situation arises when learning experiences are designed to meet students' interests and fundamental objectives.

The publication of the Educational Policies Commission, *Education for All American Youth: A Further Look,*[8] and the related report of the National Association of Secondary School Principals, *Planning for American Youth,*[9] have had a substantial influence in secondary school curriculum adjustment and have focused attention on "the ten imperative needs of youth." These appear as the end papers of this book.

The Committee on Curriculum Planning and Development of the National Association of Secondary School Principals has subsequently further implemented these reports by identifying the characteristics needed by high schools if their programs are likely to be able to meet these needs.[10]

The Organization of the Educational Program

Organizing an educational program that attempts to respond to the pressures for needed changes is no longer a simple matter. The fields of study that may contribute to the meeting of any particular youth need or to the attainment of any specific social purpose may be numerous. Indeed, the special fields of knowledge that have developed in recent decades make an impressive accumulation of separate course offerings in many high schools. J. Paul Leonard reports that in 1930–1931, the Los Angeles high schools offered 469 separate courses.[11] In this maze of possible offerings the curriculum worker may easily get lost without a pattern of organization or criteria for selection of offerings. In a preliminary consideration of the high school's educational programs it is useful to recognize two major phases: one for general education, and another for specialized education.

GENERAL EDUCATION

Although the imperative needs of youth are common to all young people, the programs to meet some of these needs cannot be uniform.

---

[8] Educational Policies Commission, *Education for All American Youth: A Further Look* (rev. ed.; Washington, D.C.: National Education Association, 1951).

[9] National Association of Secondary School Principals, *Planning for American Youth* (Washington, D.C.: National Education Association, 1951).

[10] William L. Ransom, "How Well Does Your High School Rate on the Ten Imperative Needs of Youth?" NASSP *Bulletin*, 33, No. 164 (October, 1949), 4–86.

[11] J. Paul Leonard, *Developing the Secondary School Curriculum* (rev. ed.; New York: Rinehart & Company, Inc., 1953), p. 37.

Those to meet the needs for vocational skills, vocational pursuits, leisure time activities, and appreciations, for example, must vary according to the interests and talents of the individuals. The need for competence and understandings in democratic citizenship, family life, and health and physical fitness, on the other hand, requires common or similar experiences for all youth. The area of the curriculum that is directed toward providing common or similar experiences for universal needs may be termed "general education." It may be defined as the program to meet the educational needs that every individual has by virtue of being a person and a member of a social group regardless of his particular position and professional or vocational goal.

The elementary school program is almost entirely directed toward general education and so, increasingly, is that of the junior high school. Although differences in emphasis exist among high schools, examination of the required work in the typical high school reveals that approximately half of the programs are in this category. This presumably is the work regarded as universally needed and by inference represents general education. Whether or not it is the best program of general education is another matter, but at least the presence of constant, required subjects means that high schools now have a program of general education.

The present emphasis upon education for citizenship and other common needs would indicate a trend toward greater emphasis on general education in the senior high school and a consequent concern for the effectiveness of this program. The upward extension of secondary education is likely to bring with it the postponement of some specialized education into these later years and a consequent greater emphasis upon general education or the common learnings in the present senior high school years. This would require a greatly enriched program of general education.

Although the need for general education may be common to all people, it must be recognized that even here there are different levels to which the program can be carried, rather than a standard level for all youth. The same ends are sought, much common content is used, but a broader range of generalizations and inferences is attempted with some students than with others. Thus youth who continue their education in college, and who will work in professional fields in many cases, will in general have positions of leadership in the civic, cultural, and social activities of their communities. Thus the undergraduate college programs should continue in part the program of general education for students who will need and desire a more advanced level of education in both common and special fields. The development of an effective program of general education that will facilitate the kinds of growth and development necessary for all our young people is the central curriculum problem of American youth education.

SPECIALIZED EDUCATION

One of the functions of secondary education is to provide opportunity for students to develop their special talents, meet individual needs, and progress toward individual vocational goals. A dynamic democratic society cannot afford to miss any chance to develop through education all of the specialized capacities its youth may have. For this reason youth education must provide specialized courses and sequences of courses to meet these special needs. This body of work, which is not required of all students but is elected by the student, under guidance, is the strand or area of the educational program that may be termed "specialized education." Although the needs of each youth may be unique and the planning of each student program should be an individual problem, the area of specialized education is most feasibly organized into special sequences for groups with similar purposes and interests. Specialized education has at times been considered to be primarily vocational in character, but anyone with an insight into the purposes to be served by it will see that it must encompass much more than this. The typical college preparatory program beyond the level required of all students is specalized education, in fact quite highly so. The elective courses in the academic areas should be recognized as specialized offerings for those with appropriate interests and abilities. Much of the advanced work in the arts also consists of specialized offerings.

The scope and extent of the school's program in specialized fields should properly be limited only by the interests and needs of the students, but in practice the resources of the particular school are often the limiting factor. Theoretically, any field of study which a group of students has a genuine interest in and need for, and which is directed toward a socially acceptable goal, is a legitimate offering in specialized youth education. For the increasingly specialized world of work that now exists, with its rich variety of avocational interests, the comprehensive secondary school needs to furnish a broad and diverse offering in the field of specialized education if it is to serve the needs of youth. The principal problem here is how in small high schools we can provide for the wide range of worth-while abilities and interests to be found in a typical student group.

NEED TO DISTINGUISH BETWEEN GENERAL
AND SPECIALIZED EDUCATION

The curriculum planner needs to distinguish between the two areas of the educational program, that of general or common education and that for special needs. Because of the failure to make this distinction, much confusion has developed on the part of some people concerning cur-

rent curriculum reorganization. Different methods of subject organization, grading standards, and even teaching procedures may be indicated
in these two areas of the total program. Thus organization by subjects
may prove not to be the most functional presentation of content for
general education and yet be effective and appropriate in a specialized
field that students may be permitted to elect because of a special ability
or interest. In a class in the field of general education, which all youth are
required to take regardless of ability, the satisfactory progress and
achievement of the individual student can be fairly measured only in
terms of that student's ability. In a specialized field, which the student
elects and which may be for the purpose of preparing for a vocation or
further study where a specific level of competence is required, a degree
of achievement needed for initial employment in the industry or for
further study of the subject can justifiably be required for credit in
that course. In a broad course in general education, much of the content
for study may grow out of the planning of the students and teacher,
while in a class established to provide competence in a specialized skill
such as typing, such group planning will serve little purpose. Here recognized need, individual interest, and desire to achieve can be assumed
from the fact that the course has been voluntarily elected by those enrolled in it.

Much of the program reorganization described in recent literature
has been concerned with the field of general education. Reconstruction
of the integrating, required part of the high school's educational program, rather than the differentiating, specialized part, is the heart of
the current curriculum problem. The remainder of this chapter, therefore,
deals with developments in the field of general education, including the
attempts to solve this critical curriculum problem.

The Organization of General Education

The conventional high school program has presented three categories of course offerings: "the constants," courses required of all students; "the variables," courses required of certain groups of students;
and the "free electives." The program for the individual student consists
of the constants plus the variables required for the field of specialization
he has selected (preparation for commercial college, vocational training,
and so on), plus whatever free electives the student may want to include
to bring his program to the total number of credits or units required for
graduation. The "constants" or required courses represent the traditional
solution to the problem of education for common needs or for general
education.

The particular sequence of courses required as general education varies among states and among different schools. In some states a minimum program is required by state regulation, the individual school being allowed to add further required subjects. In some states the requirements are largely the responsibility of the individual schools. Although particular regional and local interests may be evidenced in state requirements and although many minor variations exist among schools, the similarity of the general body of requirements among the thousands of secondary schools is much more impressive than the miscellaneous differences. Several strong influences explain this similarity. The academic orientation of the high school, particularly in its early development, has given the academic subjects a predominant place in the program of required general education. The colleges have in general reinforced this tradition. Educational associations and accrediting organizations, although not always under the spell of this academic orientation, have nevertheless operated to bring about considerable homogeneity. The more diverse student population, the development of new youth problems and needs, and public demand as expressed in legally required courses have tended to reduce some of the academic emphasis and to bring about some introduction of new courses. Thus ancient and modern languages and advanced mathematics are less frequently required in the high school program today, and new courses in physical education, modern problems, and driver education have been introduced. Nevertheless the required program today is still primarily academic in orientation, and American high schools, as a whole, have been requiring students to spend at least half of their time on the study of a limited range of academic subjects.

Although specific requirements vary, there is something resembling a nation-wide program. For example, this minimum program required by the state of Indiana for graduation from a four-year high school is fairly typical.

TABLE 11. HIGH SCHOOL GRADUATION REQUIREMENTS

Course	Units
English	3
Social studies—citizenship	1
United States history	1
Mathematics	1
Science	1
Health, safety, and physical education	1
Total Required	8
Elective	8
Total	16

Source: State of Indiana, *The Administrative Handbook* (Bulletin 200; Indianapolis: Department of Public Instruction, 1948), p. 165.

If the general education program is organized as a sequence of subjects, examination of this listing and similar ones reveals that most of the work is drawn from the fields of English, social studies, mathematics, and science, usually in the order named.[12] Six, and often eight, units of work are required in these four fields, so that the bulk of whatever results are now sought from current programs of general education must be expected to derive from the study of these subjects. There has therefore been a question as to whether a different program of general education could not attain better results with more students than can be expected from this program.

DEMANDS FOR REORGANIZATION OF GENERAL EDUCATION

The subject organization of general education has had certain advantages: it is an organization with which teachers and parents are familiar; the program is easily modified by the addition of organized courses; and the sequence of work is the relatively clear-cut, logical organization of courses and sequences of courses in the recognized academic fields.

Increasingly, however, certain disadvantages have become apparent. The subject organization, with its highly logical content arranged into relatively narrow fields of learning, is essentially an artificial division of the world's knowledge. Moreover, that content is likely to be remote from the life problems the student faces. The learning activities are largely determined by the demands of logical subject organization rather than by the needs of youth or by their contribution to the ends of general education. Each subject is automatically oriented to preparing the student for more study in that field, an orientation that is not the primary function of general education. The organization of the program is likely to be so rigid that it is difficult to introduce the new and needed problems and areas of study that changing social conditions may demand. Although logical organization of subject matter may be an appropriate learning sequence for the skilled adult learner and the specialist in a given field, evidence has steadily accumulated that it is not necessarily a functional learning sequence for the adolescent and the nonspecialist. Learning activities and situations dealing with the common life problems of all youth, which general education hopes to enable youth to meet better, seldom demand content falling wholly within one of the conventional subject fields. Usually content from several subject fields is required, the logic of the arrangement deriving from the relation of these selected contents to the solution of the problem in hand. The increased hetero-

---

[12] The high concentraton of enrollments in the required subjects listed in Table 11 is shown in U.S Office of Education, *Biennial Survey of Education in the United States, 1950–52, Offerings and Enrollments in High School Subjects* (Washington, D.C: Government Printing Office, 1951), Chap. 5.

geneity of the present-day student body, with its larger number of students who require a close relationship between the learning situation and the use situation, has served to bring the limitations of strict subject organization into sharper relief. Increased public and professional realization that under present-day world conditions this country needs to have the most effective program of social, economic, and civic integration it is possible to develop has also created a demand for fundamental curriculum reorganization. Numerous studies and systematic reviews of the past forty years present a comprehensive and well-documented story of the demand for it.[13]

Numerous national studies, reaching as far back as to that of the Committee on the Reorganization of Secondary Education, which issued the Cardinal Principles Report in 1918, have been conducted. Educational associations and state departments of education have sponsored experimental programs in selected schools. Individual schools have undertaken reorganizations ranging from minor adaptations to rather sweeping revisions. This reorganization movement has affected in some degree the educational program of all high schools, although, as stated, the academic and subject orientation is still characteristic of the majority of secondary schools. Even where the movement has produced but minor alterations in the subject organization of the school's offering, it has resulted in changes in content, in methods of teaching, and in classroom activities. A complete survey of the programs of curriculum modification and experimentation would need to summarize literally hundreds of works, ranging from books, reports of national and state study groups, bulletins of state departments, and courses of study and pamphlets from individual schools. The attempt to place the various programs of reorganization into a few categories would oversimplify the problems. However, in spite of numerous differences in the programs proposed or adopted, it is profitable to distinguish two fundamentally different approaches. One approach has sought the reorganization of existing subjects; the other has sought to build a curriculum based upon the problems and needs of youth. The issue was stated by the Orientation Committee of the NASSP in 1936 as Issue VII in the following words:

Shall secondary education accept conventional school subjects as fundamental categories under which school experiences shall be classified and presented to students, or shall it arrange and present experiences in fundamental categories directly related to the performance of such functions of secondary schools in a democracy as increasing the ability and desire better to meet socio-

[13] Hollis L. Caswell, ed., *The American High School* (John Dewey Society Yearbook, 1947; New York: Harper & Brothers, 1946), Chap. 7; and Leonard, *op. cit.*

civic, economic, health, leisure-time, vocational, and pre-professional problems and situations? [14]

REORGANIZATION OF SUBJECTS

The reorganization of subjects has been directed primarily toward introducing newer functional content, reducing the detailed specialization of conventional courses and developing more comprehensive courses, breaking down subject lines within a given broad field of study, and selecting content more closely related to youth needs and present-day problems. The introduction of new material into conventional courses, which has been the simplest and least disturbing step, has occurred to some extent in practically all high schools. Frequent examples are the introduction of speech activities into the study of English, the development of applied problems in mathematics and science courses, and the inclusion of content from economics and sociology into history and civics courses. Textbooks of today, contrasted with those of twenty years ago, markedly reflect this type of change.

Reorganization going somewhat beyond the mere introduction of new material into established courses has been the extensive development of the survey and so-called "fused course." Although somewhat difficult to define precisely, in general the survey course has resulted from the telescoping of a sequence of specialized courses into one comprehensive course. As the name implies, such courses become less specialized and detailed and are assumed to give a general understanding of a field rather than preparatory knowledge for another course to follow. A familiar example is a general course in world history to replace a sequence of courses in ancient, medieval, and modern history. Courses in American and English literature have more and more assumed the characteristics of survey courses. The survey course has been particularly popular at the junior college level. It is to be suspected that the force of circumstances has been more responsible for the development of survey courses than has any desire really to improve the educational program. The limited amount of time for general education that can be allotted to any one subject field and the impossibility of covering any complete sequence of specialized courses in that time has forced even the most subject-minded curriculum maker, often very reluctantly, into reorganization involving condensation of content material into survey courses.

Very closely related and often associated with the development of the survey course is the fused course. This represents an effort to bring together into one what may have been two parallel courses. Thus civics,

---

[14] Committee on Orientation of Secondary Education, "Issues of Secondary Education," NASSP *Bulletin*, No. 59 (January, 1936), p. 257.

history, and economics may be brought together into one social studies course. Biology, as typically offered in the high school today, grew out of a fusion of botany and zoology. General science in the junior high school is a familiar example. A course in physical science may be developed by drawing material from physics, chemistry, astronomy, and earth science. The degree of actual fusion that may be undertaken in such reorganization can vary tremendously. Thus the reorganized course may actually be but a series of shortened versions of the original special courses, or it can be drastically reorganized to draw content simultaneously from the different specialized courses as needed to deal with certain situations involving the use of a particular field of knowledge.

Somewhat apart from these developments have been the numerous attempts to develop so-called "correlated courses," which organize two courses in different fields in such a way that common problems can be studied simultaneously. Thus colonial literature and colonial history may be studied in the English and history classes at the same time. Problems of family living and the home may be studied in a series of classes such as home economics, science, and social studies. The obvious purpose in correlation is to break down the strict compartmentization of courses. Useful and desirable as correlation of subjects may be, there are several limitations implicit in this approach. If the logic of subject matter is advanced as the basic principle of organization of courses in the high school curriculum, it is very difficult to find more than occasional and incidental instances where the materials of two courses actually integrate. Relationships forced into such programs often become more fancied than real. Subject organization of the curriculum is fundamentally in conflict with real correlation.

Another type of reorganized subject approach to general education is the so-called "broad fields curriculum." It is the survey and fused course organization, with attention to sequence, carried to its logical end. In the complete broad fields program the subject matter organization is accepted insofar as the broad fields of study are concerned, with, however, the lines between the separate subjects within these broad fields largely broken down. Thus general education may be considered to include English (or the communication arts), the social sciences, the natural sciences, the fine and practical arts, and physical education and health. Within each of these five broad fields a sequence of courses, each consisting of a series of units of study, may be planned which draws material from the separate subjects usually thought of as belonging in that field. Thus the social studies sequence may be composed of units of work around common problems of people or around social needs, each of which may draw material from what to the specialist is a separate subject in the field of the social sciences.

Numerous examples of development of excellent programs of the broad fields program are available.[15] There is no question that a much more functional program of general education has resulted from such program reorganization. Whether the attempt to retain the subject approach is fundamentally sound or not is one of the genuine controversies in American secondary education today. Some pattern of organization of knowledge is necessary and some pattern from which to build sequences is necessary. Many able students of the curriculum contend that the organized bodies of knowledge developed and arranged by scholars throughout time represent the most effective and feasible basis of organization for general education. They do not deny, however, the possibility of introducing new material, applications to current problems, or reorganization, within limits. The Harvard report[16] is a competent presentation of this point of view.

LIFE ADJUSTMENT EDUCATION

Recent examination of the population of the secondary school, and of both the general and the specialized programs of education, has led to the conviction that a sizable fraction of the school population is not adequately served by either. This problem was effectively presented by Charles A. Prosser in 1944, at a conference of committees studying the problems of vocational education for the Vocational Division of the United States Office of Education. He held that this fraction should be provided with a life adjustment program.

The program of study and planning that developed from this proposal has been termed "Life Adjustment Education."[17] Life adjustment is, of course, the goal of all education for all youth. Observation and study indicate, however, that the present school program markedly fails to meet the needs of that group of youth who are neither academically inclined nor blessed with interests and aptitudes for the skilled occupations. Every teacher and school administrator is familiar with this group of students. The general education program is frequently too academically oriented to be functional for them, and the vocational programs are too specialized to be useful or appropriate. From this group comes the largest proportion of those who drop out. Those who remain in school find meager success in a collection of courses that prepare neither for general living nor for specialized work. Consequently they often leave the school with little preparation for any life goals.

[15] See H. H. Giles, S. P. McCutchen, and A. N. Zechiel, *Exploring the Curriculum* (New York: Harper & Brothers, 1942).

[16] Harvard Committee Report, *General Education in a Free Society* (Cambridge, Mass.: Harvard University Press, 1945).

[17] J. Dan Hull, *A Primer of Life Adjustment Education for Youth* (Chicago: American Technical Society, 1949), Foreword.

One of the most significant features of the life adjustment proposal was the fact that it brought together personnel from the general and vocational fields to consider the joint development of a better program of education. Although there are no ready-made, simple solutions to the problem of life adjustment education, it demands a type of functional, general education oriented around common problems of living and a vocational education of a less specialized nature. Factors of occupational adjustment related to securing employment in the semiskilled trades and the attitudes and attributes necessary for success on a job need to be isolated so that appropriate programs in vocational education may be developed.

A program for these neglected youth should start with an analysis of the needs and possibilities in the local community. Here the local school has almost complete freedom of action, since the oft-cited restrictions of college entrance requirements or the conventions of organized vocational programs do not exist. There are many isolated examples of specific adjustments in individual schools that suggest what can be done.[18]

The life adjustment proposal thus provides a new attack on the problem of adapting secondary education to the needs and abilities of a substantial group to which little special attention has thus far been given. A vigorous group of students of the secondary school's educational program maintains, however, that fundamentally these various subject approaches cannot provide the most effective means for achieving a really functional general education for unselected groups of learners of the levels of maturity found in today's high school student bodies. Rather, the basis for the development of the general education program must be the organization of learning experiences around the needs and interests that youth feel and have as they grow up in our kind of a society.

NEWER PATTERNS OF GENERAL EDUCATION

Those who have doubted the validity of the logic of organized subjects as the basis for the selection of learning experiences and for program organization have looked with favor upon another basis upon which to build a better program of general education—the common needs and recurring problems of the students. Such an approach assumes that in their growth and development in our society youth face certain common personal and social problems and therefore have certain common interests; that these common interests and needs can be defined; and that the curriculum of general education can be developed by organizing study and

[18] B. L. Dodds, "That All May Learn," NASSP *Bulletin*, No. 85, November, 1939. See also, U.S. Office of Education, *A Look Ahead in Secondary Education* (Bulletin No. 4; Washington, D. C.: Government Printing Office, 1954).

learning experiences around them. Reference to the "imperative needs of youth" reprinted on the end papers of this book will show one currently popular statement of these needs. Some of the needs are common to all youth in America because they are a part of trying to grow up and to become competent to carry on one's life in our American setting. Competence involves ability and willingness to use knowledge, ideals, and skills in the satisfaction of life needs. General education ought to aim at producing this kind of competence by giving youth a chance to learn how to use knowledge drawn from any and all fields as it helps them to solve these types of common problems and needs.

This approach, carried to its ultimate end, means that the so-called subject matter of study ("knowledge") in a given program will be drawn from different subject fields because the problems of youth are broad and varied and do not neatly fit into the fields of the conventional academic subjects. Likewise, the sequence of learning experiences will not have subject matter with the internal logic of the organized academic course. It is argued that the curriculum organized around the real problems and interests of youth will possess a type of psychological organization and sequence to the student that will be much more real and meaningful than the academically logical organization of subject courses. In this second type of general education program the youth is integrating new experience into his total pattern of past experience because the educational program deals with problems and situations that he has encountered either directly or indirectly. Thus the organization and sequence, unlike those that have been established to facilitate mastery of a field of knowledge, continually contribute to the developmental needs of the student.

The program of general education built upon this basis abandons the concept of any fixed bodies of knowledge as the core of general education. Nor is a fixed course of study equally appropriate in all schools or even in the same school over any period of time in harmony with this concept of the high school's educational program. Although there will be similarity in the problems of study, since youth have common needs and since the central purposes of general education each year will be the same, the content of study necessary to develop the desired concepts and understandings, and thus to build the levels of competence sought, may not necessarily be the same or constant from year to year. Students and teachers planning together are expected to select learning experiences in terms of the interests and needs of their own group so that it may best achieve the end it seeks. Instruction is organized as a group project, but a wide range of flexibility in the operation of any class is assumed to provide for individual projects and the special interests of the individual students.

To those secondary school administrators or teachers who find satisfaction in clear-cut, predetermined design, this approach to the general education program may seem amorphous, vague, and impractical. Actually only a few secondary schools have achieved anything like a complete reorientation of general education from the subject-organized basis to the youth-needs-and-problems basis, yet there have been numerous developments in this direction which evaluation has proved to be educationally effective.[19] Administrative and class organization to implement this concept of the curriculum has generally involved the development of the so-called "core curriculum" or "block program."

Although these types of programs as developed in numerous schools have varied, particularly in the degree to which the subject matter approach has been abandoned, certain common characteristics have been present. Characteristic organization of such programs makes these provisions:

1. The allocation of a larger block of continuous time for the core class, usually two to three periods with some possible reduction in the last year or two of senior high school, instead of the single period usually provided for in a subject-organized program
2. A wide degree of freedom for student-teacher planning in selection of content and activities for the class
3. The use of a wide variety of classroom procedures with the classroom as a learning laboratory rather than a recitation room
4. The use of a variety of classroom materials rather than dependence upon a textbook
5. The inclusion in the classroom program of many activities conventionally appearing in home rooms and in the activity programs
6. The integration of group and individual guidance activities in the classroom program
7. The use of broad evaluation techniques (student self-appraisal—evaluation of work habits, attitudes, and problem-solving abilities) rather than only measurement of information gained

In practice the organization of core programs has ranged from those that have used the fused content of perhaps two courses as basic, to those that have evolved units of study from the common problems that adolescents typically face. Resource units used in the latter are extremely varied, but they generally fall in the fields of civic, economic, home life, health, and leisure time education. The particular center of interest may be boy-and-girl relationships, planning a school program, health problems, relationships to parents, spending and saving money, evaluation of the individual aptitudes and abilities involved in choosing a

[19] See Wilford M. Aikin, *The Story of the Eight-Year Study* (New York: Harper & Brothers, 1942).

vocation, or such social and community problems as recreation or housing. A complete catalogue of such units would present the problems of contemporary America from the standpoint of the adolescent.

The reaction of a layman who has had a chance to become acquainted with a core program as a board member is shown by the following which he wrote in 1952 for *Building Together in Garrett County* (Maryland), a mimeographed publication of that county school system:

As I observe core and understand it, core involves committee meetings, talking over pros and cons of a problem in small groups, actually seeing a situation in lifelike settings, learning by doing, attacking a problem of large scope and sticking with it until completion, evaluating progress, in-service education for teachers.

All of this entails planning together to enrich the experience. Skills of grammar, spelling, writing, arithmetic, composition, speaking, etc., are involved in the problem being solved by students. Basic skills of respect for others' rights, getting along well together, ethical character, principles of democracy, etc., are also outcomes of core teaching. To make core work, many more teaching aids are necessary because youth learns by doing.

Core, as I see it, is no different from work experiences of adulthood in industry or profession. In my automotive place of business, my employees and I operate in a similar manner: large problems to be solved, many tools with which to work, basic skills in operation, traveling to a distant plant to witness at first hand a new operation, in-service meetings with my employees, harmonious working together, respect for fellow-man, developing personnel to assume greater responsibility in larger jobs, and evaluation of our progress.

Briefly, to me, core means working daily in a realistic manner which prepares a student for assuming his responsibility as a member of a household, as "bread-winner" in a position or profession, and as an American citizen who can contribute in cooperative planning in his community and country for the welfare of mankind.

The school principal and faculty seeking to develop an experience program of general education cannot find a ready-made pattern to follow. A clear concept and acceptance of the basic approach is a fundamental first step. Contemporary educational literature provides a rich source of suggestions on approach and procedures.[20]

COMMON EMPHASES IN CURRENT PROGRAM DEVELOPMENT

Educational programs for the general education of youth may be developed in various ways and may be fundamentally different in method and organization. Nevertheless, certain concepts about the learning activities of the student are basic.

[20] See, Educational Policies Commission, *op. cit.;* Giles, McCutchen, and Zechiel, *op. cit.;* Leonard, *op. cit.;* and Harold Spears, *The Emerging High School Curriculum* (2nd ed.; New York: American Book Company, 1948).

The recognition of the need to provide unity and a basis for relationships in learning has led to *the development of the comprehensive unit of instruction* as the basis for organization. Thus we have the attempt to supplant the segmented daily lesson and isolated learning of facts with the study of a central problem, theme, or focus of interest. Around this central problem facts and information are studied as needed, and skills and understandings are developed in relation to the central problem. Although unit topics as used in some schools may be questioned in terms of their reality for the student, the principle of using facts and developing skills in relation to a large central problem, theme, or need is a sound learning principle. The chance of being able to develop a comprehensive unit as it should be developed is better when there is no need to keep it within one field of knowledge as would be expected under the reorganized subject approach.

The recognition of the importance of student purpose and motivation has led to the development of a greater degree of *flexibility in the organization of the activities of the class and of the individual student and to a greater degree of student participation in program and course planning.* Although the basis upon which the educational program is organized will obviously determine the range and degree of freedom for student planning, even in the more conventional class organization some freedom can exist. The acceptance of the concept of student participation has in general characterized recent curriculum developments. The likelihood of free, vital, and general student participation is increased as the units tend to center about youth needs rather than about details of a logically organized subject.

There has also been a growing acceptance of the idea of *utilizing in the classroom a much wider variety of activities and materials.* Studies of learning have presented convincing evidence that purely verbal methods are relatively ineffective in many situations. Technology has brought many new classroom aids. Today classroom activities—in spite of many existing single-textbook courses—frequently include field trips, visual aids, a wide variety of reference materials, and a general classroom laboratory situation. Increasingly it has been recognized that the class period is a learning period and the classroom a laboratory workroom rather than a "teaching" period and a recitation room.

Related to greater flexibility of procedures and variety of materials is the attention to methods for dealing with the differences in interests and abilities of students within a class. Learning activities that provide opportunities for direct experiences, dramatic and constructive as well as verbal activities, together with a wide range of adaptable reference materials and individual projects, offer a framework for serving the rather heterogeneous class groups that are characteristic of the comprehensive high school. Much remains to be done, however, large classes, inadequate rooms and materials, and professional and public resistance present difficulties; nevertheless, substantial progress in practice as well as in theory has been made.

The broadened concept of the outcome of education, which is concerned with the growth of attitudes, skills, and the ability to solve problems and to be self-directive as well as with the accumulation of information, has called for the *development of a more comprehensive method of evaluating or appraising student learning and growth.* Obviously tests measuring mastery of information can effectively appraise only one aspect of student development, and are inadequate in the evaluation of an educational program with broader goals. Recent curriculum development has served to focus attention on this fact. The development of evaluation devices has lagged behind the general program, partly because of the difficulty of producing devices for measuring some of the more elusive learnings and partly because schools have neither the time nor the staff needed for detailed evaluation. Recognition that the student has a part to play in appraising learning has increased. There is also a more general acceptance of the need for teachers' observations of student behavior and for anecdotal records of student performance in varied situations. As a result of the greater awareness of the need for a systematic and careful evaluation of the new programs, we may expect to see scientific study and invention produce appropriate measuring devices and techniques.

Organizing the School for Program Study and Development

The major responsibility of the principal and the total staff of the secondary school is the study, organization, and direction of the educational program. All else is subsidiary and important only as it contributes to the fundamental purpose of providing the most effective total program. Since it concerns all of the learning activities of the school, the study of the educational program is the responsibility of all who work in that school. But any program must have leadership if it is to be coordinated and maximally effective, and it is the principal's responsibility to supply it while he draws on the resources of the entire staff.

Though the principal should supply leadership in program development, it is not a function of the principal and his administrative assistants to develop a program that the teachers will then use. To assume such a division of responsibility in relation to the school's educational program is to presume an impossible division, since by definition how the school is administered must inevitably affect the teaching and classroom situation.

Leadership in the study and development of the curriculum is not a role that can be outlined in neat steps. Nor could an outline be made that will work in all the varied contexts of the different secondary schools in the United States. Leadership is not synonymous with a dependence upon static rules of procedure; it always requires imagination and judgment and the intelligent application of general principles to specific situations. What are the general principles that should guide the secondary school principal as he leads his staff in surmounting the problems of working out an effective educational program for their school?

SOME PRINCIPLES IN CURRICULUM DEVELOPMENT

Important as are extraclass activities and situations in learning, in the final analysis most of the students' time is devoted to learning activities that go on primarily in the classroom. Outside direction and student reaction may have some effect, but the teaching staff is the single most influential force in determining the nature of learning activities. It follows from this *that any comprehensive program of curriculum study, reorganization, and adaptation must involve the group planning and individual work of all teachers.* A real program reorganization cannot be master-minded by the principal or by a director of curriculum by the simple process of producing and handing out a new course of study. The whole modern concept of program development is that it is basically a joint project of students and teachers working together to achieve certain accepted ends and goals. A written course instituted by administrative order will at best result only in a nominal modification; more probably it will produce little change unless the individual teacher has had a part in the development of that material and, with the students, genuinely accepts the goals and ends it proposes. Chart 5, which originally appeared in "The Role of the American High School" (listed in the chapter references), is an attempt to picture adults, youth, guidance workers, and teachers all contributing to the decisions which modify the educational program of the school as it is to be presented in the schools' classrooms.

Fundamental to any integrated attack upon the problems in the development of the educational program is consideration of a basic philosophy that is to guide the program. Although within any school staff there will be differences and variations in points of view, an educational program without some common areas of agreement will make little progress. Agreements need to center on the role of youth education in our society; on a concept of learning and how to bring it about; and

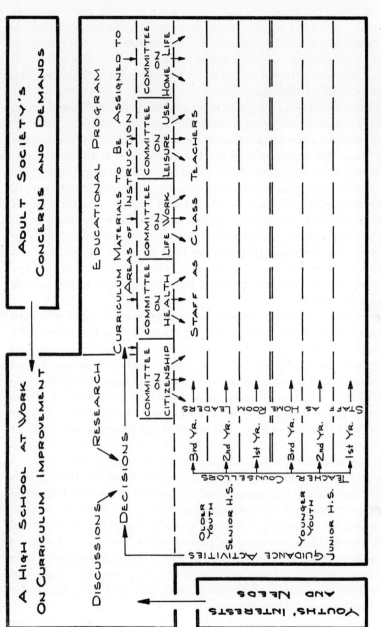

CHART 5. ORGANIZATION FOR DEVELOPMENT AND USE OF AN EDUCATIONAL PROGRAM BASED ON THE DEMANDS OF SOCIETY AND THE NEEDS OF YOUTH

Source: Will French, "The Role of the American High School," NASSP *Bulletin,* 39, No. 1 (February, 1955), 57. Reprinted by permission.

on areas of learning that need emphasis in a particular community at a particular time.

Whether or not the point of view presented in this particular chapter is accepted in part or in whole is not as important as the searching study that any faculty group must make in an effort to define principles and crystallize plans. Without such a study any program will be sporadic, contradictory, and self-defeating.

Any vital curriculum program must continuously evolve and grow. It is a natural human tendency to look for final answers that, once secured, can provide a comfortable, secure course of action. In the field of the curriculum this is represented by the attempt to institute administratively a particular program as of a certain date which can be universally followed until at least some future date, when again superior wisdom will supply another answer. The whole concept of a vital curriculum directed by people of different personalities in a dynamic culture negates this approach. Only a people of completely identical philosophy in a perfectly static culture can legitimately hope for final answers. Since even authoritarian societies are not completely static, *final* answers are always impossible everywhere. Why, then, should they be expected in the schools of a democratic order?

In our culture, with its tremendous tensions and changes, the high school program must be continually evolving; hence the curriculum worker must accept the difficult role of working to provide experiences and to achieve ends that, by the very nature of the environment, can never remain fixed. Likewise, since any program of curriculum development will largely represent the point of view and development of the teachers who guide it, changes, adaptations, and evaluations will occur only as teachers themselves grow and adapt. Thus program development is not accomplished by administrative fiat. It occurs only as the teachers grow; like all growth, it is a continuous and variable process.

The task of providing leadership in program development is primarily that of providing stimulation and opportunity for the individual teacher to grow and exercise initiative. Since the curriculum is what the individual teacher makes it, it follows that the individual teacher and his class are central to any program of improvement. The role of the leader is to provide stimulation, suggestions, and freedom for development. The principal must work to achieve conditions that can provide opportunity for and encouragement of maximum growth and real opportunity for individual initiative of all concerned.

SOME STEPS IN PROGRAM PLANNING

The principal seeking to organize the school for a program of curriculum study may be guided by the experience and organization of

other schools, but any plan decided upon must be adapted to the particular needs and characteristics of his school. Some general suggestions follow to implement the principles stated above.

An educational program can well start with a consideration of the
needs and interests of the students being served. Examination of their
family background, their vocational destination, and their practical
problems is a realistic base for further work. The particular techniques
used in such a study can be varied. A study of the holding power of the
school will provide information on the degree to which the educational
program is adapted to all youth.[21] A systematic follow-up of graduates,
as well as of those who have dropped out of the school, will provide
valuable and often unexpected and illuminating information. A canvas of
the judgments of present and former students concerning their needs
may be useful. Study groups concerning adolescent or youth development
should help develop fundamental understandings. The individual teacher
can be encouraged to study individual students, visit their homes, and
collect broad information relative to the conditions under which they
live and work. Illustrative of such an approach is the recent Illinois effort
to get basic information from parents, students, and teachers. The effect
of all such activities is to focus the attention of the school staff on what
ought to be, but too often is not, the central concern of the school—
the welfare and development of the individual students attending it.[22]

The maximum number of the staff—ideally, all the members—
should be drawn into the study of the student and the curriculum. Participation through coercion will not produce particularly effective results,
but wise leadership and organization should make coercion needless. An
expanding curriculum study will develop many types of work and responsibility that will provide numerous opportunities for all staff members
to make some kind of contribution. A central, steering, or coordinating
committee will be necessary to integrate and harmonize the many
groups that will be formed once the study is under way. Such a committee should include parents as well as teachers, and to them will be delegated special assignments. Production of instructional materials may also
be assigned to small groups or to individual teachers. The review and try-
out of such materials, however, may involve a much larger group. Naturally the particular pattern of organization and the number and kinds

[21] See Charles M. Allen, *How to Conduct a Holding Power Study* (Illinois
Curriculum Program, Bulletin No. 23; Springfield: State Superintendent of Public
Instruction, 1955).

[22] Illinois Curriculum Program, *The Nature of the School Population in the State
of Illinois* (Illinois Curriculum Bulletin No. 24; Springfield: State Superintendent of
Public Instruction, 1955). See also Harold C. Hand, *How the Illinois Secondary
School Curriculum Program Basic Studies Can Help Your School* (Illinois Secondary
School Curriculum Program, Bulletin No. 13; Springfield: State Superintendent of
Public Instruction, 1951).

of committees required will vary from school to school, since local needs and conditions will govern these matters.

Relatively early in a planned program, a statement of general philosophy, points of view, or guiding principles should be evolved, with the staff participating as completely as possible. Such a statement may not be unique or original, but the process of evolving it is important. Without some crystallization of the basic principles upon which the group can operate, a cooperative curriculum program will be difficult to develop. The philosophy and values of all members of a given staff need not be identical. There is genuine strength in individuality as well as stimulation in differences, but there must be at least some defined areas of agreement upon which to base action. The statement does not need to be complete. If it covers some of the important issues, work can start. As further agreements are needed they can be hammered out.

Practical implementation of program adaptations in terms of introducing new courses, new materials, and new instructional procedures need not be initiated upon a school-wide basis. There is much merit in encouraging individual teachers who possess particular interests and talents to undertake experimental, trial, or pilot programs. The convictions and enthusiasms of the teacher undertaking the experimental program are much more likely to carry it through to a point of value than would be possible were a large group, many of whose members lacked enthusiasm for or interest in the project, to attempt it. The successful program started by a single teacher or a small group can provide an example that will gradually influence other teachers and other schools to undertake real changes and adaptations. The problem here is one of popularizing the idea so rapidly that the new program is never regarded as the personal property of the teacher who initiated it.

The improvement of the high school's educational program should draw on the resources of the students, parents, and citizens of the community and must be related to the needs of the community and the students.

The more technical problems of program organization are the responsibility of the professional staff, but the general areas to be included in the school's program are the concern of the interested public and are areas in which the student and the citizen can give valuable aid to the professional staff. Local advisory committees working with the principal and with the teachers are important developments in many recent programs of curriculum study and school improvement. School programs must have public support at the outset and must be careful to retain it. The school's public relations are important, and administrators should guard against the temptation to regard the school's patrons as too uninformed on educational matters to understand them. The principal will have the strong support he needs if citizens actually participate in the study of the school and have an active part in the formulation of its policies and practices. Furthermore, the program gains by the contributions of able citizens.

Finally, any staff organization for program development must be so flexible that it can be altered as new problems arise and as personnel changes. A school staff may wish to undertake a particular area of study during a given year. This may lead to the consideration of other areas. Leadership that provides the setting for this type of fluid and dynamic organization is much more fundamental to progress in program improvement than any particular pattern of organization of supervisors and committees at any given time.

THE PRINCIPAL AND THE CLASSROOM

It should be clear by now that the principal's task of leading a school community program of curriculum improvement is a complicated and complex one. But there are also many other duties for which the principal must find time, including the task of program leadership touched upon in Chapter 6. No amount of remote-control work on the school's educational program nor any amount of time devoted to it by assistants and specialists in curriculum work can be substituted for the principal's direct and personal attention to daily classroom activities.

In the smaller schools, where there is little or no administrative or supervisory assistance provided for the principal, he must do whatever class supervision is done. On the other hand, this very lack of assistance makes it the more difficult for the principal to find the time and energy required to make it clear to students and teachers that he is actually interested in what they are doing. In larger high schools, where some assistance is provided and where usually there are department heads, all too frequently the principal is inclined to leave the daily work of the school to them. He meanwhile attends to other duties, which students and teachers naturally assume are to be regarded as of greater importance. Another chapter stressed the harmful effect on the principalship of placing the responsibility for program leadership outside the building in the superintendent's staff. In the end it is clear that there is no desirable substitute for attention to classroom work by the principal. There is no convincing way to explain why the head of the school gives little or no direct personal attention or time to the school's major activity.

As he visits the classrooms of his school the principal can see for himself what is being done there, can find out how the ideas and plans he has helped stimulate and develop are working out. He is usually not so much concerned to discover whether the teacher is a good teacher or not as he is to find out how students react to some of the school's new ideas. He wants to see what they are doing rather than what the teacher is doing. He wants a chance to show them his interest in their personal and group successes. He wants to see if he can learn something that will help him in future work on program improvement. He wants to give just as sincere approval to the good work done by boys and girls in their shop-work as he gives to those who work in the laboratory, studio, or regular classroom. He wants to see for himself how certain proposed new equipment or supplies will be used to supplement what is there. He wants to respond to special invitations given him to see certain exhibits, demonstrations, and group projects that have grown out of classwork.

Occasionally the principal may go to a classroom—by invitation of a new and inexperienced teacher—because this teacher wants some help from the principal with his class teaching. Occasionally he may find it necessary to visit classes to get more firsthand information about a teacher's ability to teach. But such reasons for class visiting will be the unusual rather than the usual ones. Mostly he is there because he is interested in what is going on and because it is a very good way to let his interest in and concern for classwork be known to all. How many classes he visits, how long he stays, and the proportion of his time the principal spends in direct contact with the ongoing educational activities of the school are all determined by the local situation. Increasing the proportion of time, stepping up the frequency of coverage of each class, or prolonging each visit does not necessarily help. It is obviously impossible for the principal of a large high school to get into each class each semester. Perhaps it is entirely unnecessary. But there should be no doubt in anyone's mind in any high school as to the interest and concern felt by the principal for the daily work of the classroom, as manifested by the time and attention he gives to it.

Summary

The educational program of a high school is the sum total of the learning experiences that the school provides for its students. Learning is the process of mastering new responses and adaptations that the individual gains from his experience in the school. It is essentially a process arising from the activity of the student, motivated by purposes real to that student; it is also a process of fitting new experiences and understandings into a present pattern of understanding.

The experiences provided in the school must be related to the needs and problems that arise in the environment of the school. The purpose of having schools and of trying to get pupils to learn is to help them become healthy, happy, and successful persons capable of maintaining and improving our type of democratic life. The youth school of today must therefore prepare youth to live in an industrial, urban, interdependent economy, to deal with an increasing body of knowledge in all fields, and to meet complex problems of a social and civic nature.

Two major areas must be provided in the total program: a program designed to meet common needs, or general education; and a program for specialized interests and individual needs. There is increasing evidence that conventional subject organization is not the most effective pattern for general education. Program reorganization, involving as a first step at least the reorganization of subjects and, in the more advanced programs, the organization of study around the problems and needs of youth, has been definitely developing.

The single most important responsibility of the secondary school principal is that of providing leadership in program development. To it the good high school principal wants to give his personal time and attention. A comprehensive program of curriculum improvement must draw upon the resources of the total staff, must seek the aid and interest of the community, and must be a continually evolving and never-ending program.

Some Points to Consider

1. If learning were defined as "committing to memory through study," what would be some examples of school procedures designed to get pupils to learn?

2. If learning is conceived of as this book does, what are some examples of school procedures designed to get pupils to learn?

3. Can you give an illustration of the teaching of a "subject" as it might be done if the teacher were guided by the "memory" concept of learning? by the "behavior" concept?

4. Why have state legislatures made it compulsory for American history, for example, to be taught to all students during their high school career? What ought the teacher of history do if he is to accomplish his state legislature's purpose with all youth with any degree of effectiveness?

5. Try out one of the tests appearing in Hand's book (see below) in a high school to which you have access. What is to be learned by studying the returns?

6. Do you think the Gilchrist booklet (see below) could have been developed by high schools you know about? What would have to be the principal's part if it were done?

Further Reading

Aikin, Wilford M. *The Story of the Eight-Year Study.* New York: Harper & Brothers, 1942.

Alberty, Harold. *Reorganizing the High School Curriculum*. New York: The Macmillan Company, 1953.

————. "A Sound Core Program," *NEA Journal*, January, 1956.

Burton, William H. *The Guidance of Learning Activities*. Rev. ed.; New York: Appleton-Century-Crofts, Inc., 1952.

————. "A Symposium on the Status and Role of Curriculum Assistants and Department Heads . . . in Instructional Improvement," *California Journal of Secondary Education* (March, 1955), pp. 157–187.

Caswell, Hollis L., ed. *The American High School*. John Dewey Society Yearbook, 1947; New York: Harper & Brothers, 1946. Chaps. 7–9.

————. "Progressive Education," *NEA Journal*, 44, No. 8 (November, 1955), 474–476.

Corey, Stephen, and others. *General Education in the American High School*. Chicago: Scott, Foresman & Company, 1942. Chaps. 3, 5, and Part II.

Dewey, John. *Experience and Education*. New York: The Macmillan Company, 1938.

Dodds, B. L. "That All May Learn," NASSP *Bulletin*, No. 85, November, 1939.

Doll, Ronald C. *Organizing for Curriculum Improvement*. New York: Bureau of Publications, Teachers College, Columbia University, 1953.

Educational Policies Commission. *Education for All American Youth: A Further Look*. Rev. ed.; Washington, D.C.: National Education Association, 1951.

Fair, Jean. "The Comparative Effectiveness of a Core and a Conventional Curriculum in Developing Social Concern," *School Review*, 62, No. 5 and 6 (September and October, 1954), 274–282 and 346–353.

French, Will. "The Harvard Report and the High School," NASSP *Bulletin*, No. 138, April, 1946.

————. "The Role of the American High School," NASSP *Bulletin*, 39, No. 1 (February, 1955), 1–62.

Gilchrist, Robert S., and others. *A Primer for the Common Learnings*. Minneapolis: Minneapolis Public Schools, 1948.

Giles, H. H., S. P. McCutchen, and A. N. Zechiel. *Exploring the Curriculum*. New York: Harper & Brothers, 1942.

Hand, Harold C. *What People Think about Their Schools*. Yonkers, N.Y.: World Book Company, 1948.

Harris, Norman. "Jack Be Nimble," *Phi Delta Kappan*, February, 1956.

Harvard Committee Report. *General Education in a Free Society*. Cambridge, Mass.: Harvard University Press, 1945.

Hill, Gladwin. "A Father Looks at Progressive Education," *Atlantic Monthly*, December, 1954.

Hopkins, Thomas L. "Emerging Emphasis as to Learning," *Teachers College Record*, 40 (November, 1938), 119–128.

Hull, J. Dan. *A Primer of Life Adjustment Education for Youth*. Chicago: American Technical Society, 1949. Foreword.

Indiana, State of. *The Administrative Handbook*. Indianapolis: Department of Public Instruction, *Bulletin* No. 200, 1948.

Kilpatrick, William H. "A Reconstructed Theory of the Educative Process," *Teachers College Record*, 32 (March, 1931), 532–533.

Leonard, J. Paul. *Developing the Secondary School Curriculum*. Rev. ed.; New York: Rinehart & Company, Inc., 1953. Chaps. 3, 4, 8, 11.

National Association of Secondary School Principals. *Planning for American Youth*. Washington, D.C.: National Education Association, 1951.

Oklahoma Secondary School Curriculum Commission. *A Guide for the Improvement of Curriculum in Secondary Schools*. Oklahoma City: Oklahoma State Department of Education, 1953.

Ransom, William L. "How Well Does Your High School Rate on the Ten Imperative Needs of Youth?" NASSP *Bulletin*, No. 164, October, 1949.

Skogsberg, Alfred H. "Organizing for Staff and Student Growth," *Teachers College Record*, 57, May, 1956.

Spears, Harold. *The Emerging High School Curriculum*. 2nd ed.; New York: American Book Company, 1948.

———. *Some Principles of Teaching*. Englewood Cliffs, N.J.: Prentice-Hall, Inc., 1949.

U.S. Office of Education. *Core Curriculum*. Bulletin No. 5; Washington, D.C.: Government Printing Office, 1950.

———. *Core Curriculum Development—Problems and Practices*. Bulletin No. 5; Washington, D.C.: Government Printing Office, 1952.

Wisconsin, State of. *Guides to Curriculum Building*. Madison: State Department of Education, 1950.

Chapter 10

THE ORGANIZATION OF
SPECIALIZED EDUCATION

IF A TOTAL EDUCATIONAL PROGRAM is to be effective, the different parts of that program must be planned and coordinated to provide a balanced and comprehensive offering for the individual student. The common learning or general education program furnishes a core of educational experiences for all students, and many of the student activities considered in the succeeding chapter supplement and contribute to this general education. A comprehensive educational program must, however, provide for differentiation; that is, provide for meeting the special vocational, avocational, and developmental needs of its students. By definition this area of the educational program is not a constant or single program but rather a series of special offerings and sequences of offerings for groups with similar interests. The good educational program gives individual students both the common experiences they need and the specialized experiences their individual interests require. Ideally, perhaps, the special educational experiences of each student should be a separate program for each student; certainly this should be the basic assumption in the counseling and guidance of students concerning their educational program. But in practice, the organized educational offering of large schools provides planned specialized programs for groups of students of presumed like special interests and goals. Education dealing with large groups of students must necessarily be organized in this manner. However, group organization must not degenerate into rigidity that neatly classifies students and expects them to stay within boundaries imposed by those who planned the particular program. There should always be sufficient flexibility to permit modifications and variations for the individual student.

The selection and organization of the areas of special education is one of the major problems of curriculum planning. As noted in the discussion in the preceding chapter, in some states specialized education accounts for nearly one half of the programs of many students in the senior high school. The numerous programs in this category will vary from time to time and from place to place. Although communities with similar characteristics may have similar specialized programs, the field as a whole cannot be standardized among secondary schools. A flexible, dynamic part of the program of each school, specialized education should grow out of the needs of the school community and the interests of students. There are certain general principles that should guide curriculum development in the special fields and certain general areas of specialized education that have their particular problems of organization and administration. These the secondary school principal should be prepared to understand, but too often the typical high school principal, having an academic background, is not as well prepared to develop and administer a good program of specialized education as the principal of a comprehensive high school should be.

THE FUNCTION OF SPECIALIZED EDUCATION

The purpose of the special offerings and elective areas of the educational program is relatively simple: it is to meet the unique educational needs of each student. Theoretically, the scope of the special offerings in any school is determined by the extent of the interests of the youth attending it, provided, of course, that their interests may be expected to be met by education. Practically, it is limited by the resources and facilities of the typical high school. Any field of educational experience that is a socially desirable and acceptable activity and can contribute to the development of youth is a legitimate undertaking for youth education. Perhaps the principal advantage of the large high school is the fact that it has a sufficient number of students in many different areas of vocational and avocational interests to justify economically and to make possible the development of many specialized educational offerings.

As more and more older youth go beyond the high school, it may be desirable to place at higher levels some of the specialized courses now offered in high school. Hence the schools at the higher levels should be large enough so that they can afford to offer more enriched programs of specialized education than many high schools now can.

The specialized offerings in the secondary school are roughly of two types: courses organized into a defined sequence of work in preparation for a vocational field or for entrance into an institution for further study, and more flexible courses that satisfy avocational or personal interests. The college preparatory and the various vocational programs are examples of the former; the elective offerings in the fine and practical arts, as well as the free electives in most of the academic fields and most phases of the work in physical education, are typical of the latter. The organization of the curriculum in vocational education is unusual enough to call for a special consideration of its problems.

Vocational Education

As an earlier chapter noted, vocational education of some kind is necessary in even the simplest of societies, for the young must be instructed in the crafts and skills through which the society satisfies its basic wants. Throughout most of history and in many parts of the world even today this education is of an informal nature, with parents and the elders of the group teaching the young. The necessary skills are learned in the practical work situations in which children and youth participate.

Apprenticeship, a somewhat systematic, organized method of instruction, appeared early in history as a means of transmitting the special skills of definite crafts and guilds. Apprenticeship education was brought to America in early colonial times. Although some of the early youth schools founded in this country were presumably to prepare for occupational life, and some of the offerings of the first academies had a practical flavor, the academic emphasis and the college preparatory purpose dominated the secondary school almost completely until well past the beginning of the twentieth century. It was not until 1917, with the passage of the Smith-Hughes Act, that anything approaching a national interest and program of vocational education in the secondary school appeared. The academic orientation of the early secondary school may have accounted in part for the relatively late introduction of vocational education; nevertheless, changing economic and occupational demands have stimulated the growing emphasis on vocational education. Occupations have become increasingly specialized in huge, complex industrial and business establishments and require scientific and technological information for their satisfactory performance. Apprenticeship and learning by direct experience are important elements in mastering vocational skills and will continue to be, but the need for supplementary vocational education in the school has grown as more technical knowledge has been required of workers. At the same time, thanks to our highly organized industries, the opportunity for informal direct experience by growing youth has practically disappeared. Consequently, whatever prevocational and vocational education they receive must be provided by the schools.

DEFINING VOCATIONAL EDUCATION

Although vocational education is today generally accepted as a normal and desirable part of secondary education, there is no agreement on its exact nature or on its place in the total program of secondary education. Vocational education has been developed under special legislation and to a considerable extent by special personnel and supervisory staff, a fact which has contributed to an unnecessary degree of separation of staff in vocational and nonvocational education.

F. Theodore Struck offers this definition of vocational education: "Vocational education deals with knowledge, skills and attitudes that fit an individual, wholly or in part, for a definite occupation or vocation, the pursuit of which equips him for successful living." [1] Interpreted literally, this may suggest that all fields of study are vocational in the sense that they incidentally make some contribution to vocational competence. Thus English and mathematics are presumably helpful in any field of work. This type of analysis has not only led to much fuzzy thinking but has sought to justify the failure to undertake genuine study of what is required to prepare youth for vocational competence. It is much more realistic and conducive to clear analysis if the term "vocational education" is confined to those offerings whose central purpose is preparation for defined occupations, and whose content has come from an analysis of the knowledge and skill required for competence in the occupations for which they prepare. Although many areas of the academic curriculum may contribute incidentally to vocational competence in the same way that they contribute to the general competence of youth, their central objective and purpose is not preparation for a given field of work. When grouped into a college preparatory curriculum, academic subjects are a part of special education, but they are not vocational education because they do not directly prepare for lifework. Delimiting vocational education to preparation for specific, defined occupations does not imply that the field is extremely narrow and limited to mastery of only motor skills. Many fields of vocational education require the development of attitudes, problem-solving abilities, and mastery of a considerable range of information as well as motor skills. In fact, a broad program of vocational education will contribute to the general education of the student, but again, in spite of the claims of some enthusiastic adherents, vocational education is not a substitute for general education any more than general education alone can serve the purposes of vocational education.

Another element of confusion concerning vocational education has arisen from the tendency of many people to classify as vocational any course dealing with motor or manual skills. Thus, any type of general shop, industrial, or practical arts course is assumed to be vocational. Such courses serve an important purpose, but although they may provide useful prevocational exploratory experience, by intent they prepare for no specific vocation and must be considered a part of the program of broad

---

[1] F. Theodore Struck, *Vocational Education for a Changing World* (New York: John Wiley & Sons, Inc., 1945), p. 5.

general education. Whether or not a field of study involves manual skills or verbal understandings, the criterion of distinction should be the central purpose of that work; only if it is directed toward competence in a defined occupation can it be truly said to be vocational.

SOME COMMON MISCONCEPTIONS

It is perhaps unfortunate that vocational education has in many respects developed as a separate educational movement from the total field of secondary education. This may be accounted for in part by the separate funds and provisions which the federal acts established, but at the beginning of the movement secondary school administrators and teachers in the dominating academic fields often exhibited, if not downright opposition to it, very little sympathy. A generation of experience with vocational education has closed some of the distance between the academic and the vocational programs, but sweeping and generalized statements and discussions are responsible for many lingering misconceptions concerning the latter's nature and place.

Vocational education is not a substitute for broad general education, or vice versa. No responsible educator interested in either field would contradict this statement. However, arguments over the relative importance of each are vigorous. Some of the highly specialized vocational programs that have absorbed a large proportion of the students' time have been defended on the basis that occupational competence is the primary factor in the development of the good citizen. On the other hand, many general curriculums provided for secondary school students completing their educational program at grade 12 or before have not prepared students to enter any vocational field. There is a place for both programs in the comprehensive high school, which has the broad resources required to develop a balanced program of both general and specialized education, each program strengthening and supplementing the other. In typical American communities the comprehensive high school is the ideal type. The development of specialized types of high schools should be opposed in most typical communities as a form of segregation that has no place in schools for children and youth.

Vocational education is not a field of study designed primarily for the academically maladjusted. Certain of the vocational fields of study provide a type of direct experience in which students lacking in academic interests and verbal adaptability may find relatively more satisfaction and greater success than they would find in an academic program; however, the organized vocational curriculums characteristically offered in secondary schools prepare largely for selected skilled trades and business occupations. Success in these programs requires special aptitude in that field and general adaptability of at least an average level. Actually today vocational curriculums are of a selective nature appropriate to only a minority of students. This fact has led to the development of the so-called "life adjustment education."

There is no general formula for the organization and direction of vocational education. Much of the discussion about occupational preparation sweeps back and forth in windy generalizations that have slight validity in an enormously varied occupational world. Educational literature staggers under the weight of endless arguments over such generalized questions as these: Should or can vocations be learned on the job or in schools? At what ages and grades should vocational study be introduced? Should vocational education be limited to adult ages? With the growing number of semiskilled routine jobs that can be learned on the job, is it necessary or possible to offer vocational education in the secondary school? Can facilities be provided in school that are sufficiently similar to work situations to make vocational education effective?

These time-wasting questions can never be settled definitely or finally; the occupational world is too complicated. Some skills can be learned easily on the job with relatively little supplementary school experience. Others require long programs of training that school facilities and instruction can effectively provide in the form of situations closely similar to industrial or business conditions. But in some fields, of course, the school will be quite unable to furnish the necessary training. Where youth have already had direct contact and responsibilities in an occupational field, as in agriculture, vocational education can be introduced effectively at an earlier age and grade than in fields in which students have had little if any experience. Vocational education for adults, in order that people may improve their performance and advance themselves, is important—but does not remove the school's responsibility for providing the experience and skills needed by youth when they begin to work.

The task of developing fundamental programs of vocational education demands that particular jobs and communities be analyzed and studied so that vocational programs offered youth be realistic. This approach, which is certainly more laborious than the armchair method described above, is also more fruitful, for it recognizes that vocational education must be as varied, flexible, and dynamic as the occupational world for which it prepares youth.

SOME GUIDING PRINCIPLES

Obviously, no precise specifications for a program of vocational education can be attempted, but certain general methods have characterized successful programs. They can be sufficiently defined to serve as guiding principles for other effective programs of vocational education. *The primary purpose of real vocational education is to prepare each student to enter and progress in socially useful employment.* This principle may appear obvious, but it is the essential orientation of a functional program. This is not to belittle concomitant outcomes of genuine importance or the usefulness of programs directed to other purposes. Direction and guidance will be derived from the specific definable goal of competence in selected occupations.

Vocational education is a continuous program directed at providing youth in the secondary school with the initial competence necessary to enter an occupation, and older youth and adults with experience to enable them to progress and improve on the job. Although this particular discussion is primarily concerned with youth education and the secondary school, vocational education is broadly organized to serve and meet the educational needs of people throughout their vocational life. In fact, some of the most extensive and effective programs in vocational education have been with out-of-school youth and adults as in the tremendous program of training carried on during World War II. Many of those who have been doubtful of the ability of the secondary school to provide adequate vocational education in the school setting have failed to recognize that final competency is not postulated or intended. Gaining an initial level of competence that can give youth a foothold in the occupational world is the primary intent, for this initial step or foothold is tremendously important and crucial in the life of any youth. Improvement and progress on the job is often a simpler task from a practical standpoint than securing the job originally.

Vocational education must draw its content of study and the educational experiences it provides from analysis of occupations. This has been perhaps the major distinguishing feature of effective vocational programs. Techniques for the job analysis of many occupations have been developed, and advisory groups drawn from workers in a given occupation have been extensively consulted. A realistic program of occupational preparation is not a matter of a program determined by the judgment of experts, a review of the literature, or philosophical speculation. The approach recommended here may seem narrow to those who forget the basic purpose of vocational education. It should be added, however, that occupational analysis does not limit the range of vocational activities; it is needed to give them direction.

Vocational education should be broad enough to include all of the factors that contribute to occupational adequacy. Vocational education has been criticized for giving too much attention to the development of skills and not enough to attitudes, related information, satisfactory personal adjustment, and relations with others. All these factors must be recognized and experience in them provided insofar as possible if the program is to escape the charge of narrowness.

Vocational education must be flexible and dynamic. Technology and invention continually modify occupations, create new ones, and actually eliminate others; hence a fixed program, no matter what its adequacy on some given date, cannot remain effective unless it is continually modified to meet the demands of time and change.

Current educational literature provides more detailed and specific guiding concepts.[2] Those presented here, which stress not only the orientation of vocational education to the specific purpose of occupational preparation but also the actual analysis of occupations, are the core from which other principles are developed.

Major Areas of Vocational Education

The secondary school can provide some degree of preparation for many occupations, which may be classified into four major areas or groups: (1) agricultural education, (2) business education, (3) home economics education, and (4) trade and industrial education. The first and the third categories represent broad areas of work or ways of living and are examples of the blending of aspects of general and vocational education. Business education includes those occupations involving clerical, accounting, and sales skills. Trade and industrial education contains a broad range of occupations characteristic of modern industrial organization. In it are the major crafts or skilled trades plus the occupations associated directly with specific industries and public services.

Each of these major fields of vocational education provides several types of educational programs organized primarily for groups of different ages and different vocational needs. The so-called day school program is for youth regularly enrolled in secondary school and is directed toward providing the competence necessary to enter an occupational field. Part-time programs for out-of-school youth are primarily concerned with improving the initial adjustment on the job for those who have left school. Finally, evening classes for employed adults have as their main purpose the improvement of skills used on the job or training in new skills for those who wish to transfer to other occupations. The secondary school administrators must be concerned with this total program. Although the secondary school is organized primarily for youth, the dynamic and really effective school provides continuous service and is the educational center for all age groups in the community. The best means of securing the support of the community for youth education is to serve it in all areas of educational activity.

Each of the fields of vocational education listed above has its unique problems and patterns of organization. The following brief comment on

[2] *Ibid.,* Chap. 7.

each can provide no more than meager orientation. The high school administrator whose school offers work in these areas must be familiar with the very considerable body of literature dealing with specific policies and problems. Without a thorough knowledge of this vast field he will be unable to counsel and work with those of his staff engaged in it.

VOCATIONAL EDUCATION IN AGRICULTURE

Vocational education in agriculture, as would be expected, is concerned with the development of those skills and understandings necessary for success in farming. Farming is more than an occupation in the restricted sense; it is a whole way of life. Success in farming requires a knowledge of the application of scientific principles, managerial and business ability of a high order, and many skills of a specialized nature. Programs in vocational agriculture are most appropriate for schools serving rural areas; indeed, they are often one of the few specialized programs in the offering of the small high school.

Characteristic of these programs is the fact that their students are farm youth who since childhood have had practical experience at some level in farm work and in farm problems. The school program is thus able to combine theory and practical experience. The school can furnish supplementary scientific information and direct attention to managerial problems that will be new to those whose experience has thus far been entirely practical. Supervised farm practice or the home farm project that the boy carries on under the supervision of the teacher further strengthens this relation between theory and practice.

Since farming activities vary widely in different sections of the country, the curriculum in vocational agriculture has necessarily varied in content. This flexibility has enabled the individual school and teacher to develop a program fitted to the local community. The typical school has had to create its own program through the cooperative efforts of teacher, students, and experienced adults in the community. This system, whatever its limitations in individual cases, has kept vocational agriculture dynamic and flexible and has furnished a setting more in harmony with modern educational theory than that of some other programs.

Another characteristic of vocational agriculture has been the close relation between school and community. Advisory committees of experienced farmers have usually aided in guiding the program. Through his supervision of students' farm projects, the teacher comes to know and work with parents in the community. Adult evening classes, often conducted by this teacher, have a similar result. Year-round employment of the teacher has closely identified him with the community.

The Future Farmers of America, a national organization of farm boys who are enrolled in vocational agriculture in the public secondary schools, has been widely praised for the outstanding work of its members.

The total setting for education in agriculture has thus been favorable for the application of good educational principles. Although too often the work has been narrowly interpreted and its potentialities have not been fully realized, the field is so flexible and dynamic that it has developed programs exemplifying the best principles of vocational education.

BUSINESS EDUCATION

Business education was one of the first fields of vocational education to be introduced into the program of the secondary school. Today the commercial curriculum appears more frequently in high school offerings than does any other vocational program. The reasons are obvious. The equipment and facilities required for at least a limited program are not as difficult to plan or as expensive to provide as are many specialized industrial programs. Furthermore, it is to be suspected that originally the business curriculum preparing for so-called "white-collar jobs" was welcomed and accepted by secondary schools more readily than educational programs preparing for the skilled trades and crafts. This glamour of office work also seems to have a powerful attraction for students.

But in spite of the popularity of the commercial program, a considerable vagueness of purpose and organization has characterized some of its offerings. There has been a lack of definition between the offerings of a rather general educational nature that provide skills and understandings useful to the individual in his personal life and those designed to provide skills necessary for employment in the business world. Introductory courses in such fields as typing, bookkeeping, and business practices may be useful to individuals who are not occupationally interested in the business field. As such they are justifiable offerings of the school, and the standards for such courses should be adjusted to the needs of the students. Offerings designed to provide vocational competence should be systematically planned as a sequence of work. The content should be drawn from the practices of the business world, and the standards should be those required for actual employment in the types of positions open to youth of graduating ages.

The number of youth who have entered business employment as a result of their education in this field in high school is evidence that commercial education has been functional. For one thing, the school is able to reproduce a situation reasonably similar to that in the business world. The development of more specialized business machines, however, means that the traditional battery of typewriters is not sufficient equipment for the comprehensive program needed today. Possibilities for a cooperative work-and-school program are good, and although many examples of such cooperative programs exist, it is doubtful whether all their possibilities have been utilized. Good programs have been developed in many schools, but the continued success of the proprietary business college suggests that the public schools have not fully developed their programs of business education.

Commercial education, as typically offered in the high school, has not come under the federal vocational acts that have furnished aid for vocational education in many fields. However, recent federal acts have provided aid for vocational education in the distributive occupations, which are related to the management, sale, and distribution of goods and services. These do not include clerical occupations, such as bookkeeping and stenography. Examination of occupational data reveals that the proportion of workers engaged in the distributive as compared with the direct production fields has been steadily increasing. The vocational programs in the distributive occupations have thus far been largely confined to part-time and evening classes for adults employed in this field. Cooperative training programs that provide for paralleling experience on a job with related education in school have been developed in many larger high schools. These programs have been almost exclusively planned for older youth who are in their last years of high school. It appears reasonable to predict that current occupational trends emphasizing the sale and distribution of goods and services will bring expansion and development of this particular program.

HOME ECONOMICS EDUCATION

Home economics education is directed toward better preparing youth for the responsibilities of family life and homemaking. The general recognition of the importance of this goal is revealed by the fact that the large majority of the high schools in this country provide curriculums in home economics education. Education for homemaking actually involves almost all aspects of living—the particular skills needed in the home, as well as attitudes, the understanding of human development and human relations, community service, child care, business management, and so on. Thus much of the program in home economics can be regarded as general education of a vital and functional nature. In fact, the core of work required for girls in the junior high school or in the beginning years of senior high school has assumed the character of a broad general education organized around the common problems and needs of family life.

Of the two more or less distinct divisions characteristic of the typical home economics program, the first provides broad general experiences appropriate for all girls (and perhaps boys as well), regardless of their specific plans and occupational goals. The second is that part of the program devoted to specialized work leading to competency in some particular skill. In practice, the program actually does not sharply divide into two neat categories. Rather, it may be better represented along a continuum, with the broad, general, all-purpose courses at one end and certain very specific occupational courses at the other, the middle area being filled by a block of work that provides for the development of a few specialized skills and understandings.

The approach in home economics education has broadened considerably in the period of its existence. The early emphasis upon training in skills in cooking and sewing has been modified by the introduction of experiences dealing with problems of social relations, health, home management, and related topics organized into courses in home life or education for family living. Students of all types of interests and abilities have been attracted to the program, many aspects of which are now recognized as appropriate and useful for boys. Although the proportion of boys enrolled is still negligible, the fact that it is increasing is evidence of the breakdown of convention that home economics is of concern only to girls.

As in other vocational and vocationally related fields, there has been a consistent attempt to plan and develop the program around the home problems of students actually enrolled in a class. The result has often been an unusual flexibility as well as teacher-student planning of a functional nature. As a matter of fact, no vocational field has been so genuinely and consistently concerned with building its program around the needs of its students, with encouraging and maintaining flexibility, and with establishing close relationships with the community. The very real national concern over the stability of the family and the home may be expected to add impetus to the development of education in the homemaking field.

TRADE AND INDUSTRIAL EDUCATION

Trade and industrial education is concerned with preparing students to enter occupations in the skilled trades and in manufacturing or industrial establishments. In 1950, the industry divisions of mining, manufacturing, construction and transportation, communication and public utilities utilized 42 per cent of the experienced labor force.[3] The occupations covered in this classification are so varied that a realistic program in vocational education must be adapted to the industries and employment needs of the local community. Education in the trades and industries is not confined to a single group, but to perhaps as many as five, which Struck identifies as follows:

[3] J. Frederic Dewhurst and Associates, *America's Needs and Resources: A New Survey* (New York: Twentieth Century Fund, 1955).

1. Students who are getting ready to enter trade and industrial occupations and who are attending full-time, all-day schools
2. Young men and women who have left school and who need additional instruction of a refresher or of a conversion type in order to get a job
3. Employed persons, male and female, who, because of technological change or other conditions, need training to fit them for emerging job requirements
4. Employed persons of all ages who need upgrading training to fit them to perform their jobs better or to enable them to qualify for higher and more difficult jobs in their line of work
5. Persons injured in the armed forces, in civilian life, or congenitally handicapped who need industrial training to enable them to earn their living as self-respecting, self-supporting members of society[4]

Broadly speaking, all these programs come under the general scope of secondary education and are the concern of the school administrator.

The program for the full-time day students has ordinarily included three types of courses: applied work, supplemental or related work, and the regular work in general education required of all students in the school. The applied work may not be the same in all schools, although typically education for the common trades has been characteristic of most programs. The day school program will in some cases provide for a cooperative work-school program. The development of cooperative programs in diversified occupations has expanded in recent years. The cooperative work-school program sponsors part-time experience on a job or jobs paralleled by a study in school of the problems and skills related to it. The teacher or coordinator has the responsibility for selecting and making the arrangements for working positions of educational value, for partially supervising the student on the job, for developing appropriate materials for the related work in school, and for finally evaluating the outcome of the work experience. In the program in diversified occupations, cooperative programs including a wide variety of jobs are planned under its supervision. This in effect has resulted in something approaching an individual program for each student. The diversified occupational program is particularly feasible for the smaller community where the number of openings for students in any single occupation will be small. Probably the principal factor limiting such programs has been the relatively small number of students whom the teacher or coordinator can supervise and the resulting cost.[5]

As indicated by Struck's list of groups served, vocational education

[4] Struck, op. cit., p. 448.
[5] For a thorough discussion, see Clarence E. Rakestraw, Training High School Youth for Employment (Chicago: American Technical Society, 1947).

in trades and industries includes programs for out-of-school youth and adults. Apprenticeship training, trade extension, and many specific training courses are possible. In general the success of these courses depends upon cooperative and close relationships with the industries and with trade and craft groups in the community, which in turn require the closest coordination of the educational program with the needs of the community.

Trade and industrial education and, in fact, all vocational education are variously administered in different school systems throughout the country. There is no standard pattern and perhaps there should be none. Trade and industrial education has developed largely in urban school systems of considerable size. In some states and cities, vocational education has been organized and administered independently of the rest of the school system. Whatever the incidental merits of such a plan, it divorces one part of education from the total, and on that basis may be seriously questioned. The development of specialized schools in some city systems has provided for their more or less separate operation under the general, single, over-all supervision of the city superintendent. In the comprehensive high school, the vocational program may be nominally under the direction of the principal, although again in actual practice a system-wide administration of vocational education may exercise a considerable amount of the direction.

The variations in practice and the systems followed suggest that much remains to be done before vocational education is completely integrated with the secondary school. Vocational education, particularly in the field of the trades and industries, makes its personnel responsible for coordinating the program with the industries of the community and with those of other agencies. Nevertheless, there is sound reason for insisting that the secondary school administrator have the responsibility for supervising and directing the total school. But if he is to do so he must generally understand and be competent to administer vocational education as well as the other parts of the school program. The current separation in the administration of secondary and vocational education can be accounted for in no small degree by the lack of background and often the lack of interest on the part of the secondary school principal, who typically comes into his position with experience only in the non-vocational areas of education.

As noted before, trade and industrial education, like the other vocational fields, maintains close relations with the work situations in the community for which it prepares. The techniques of job analysis, which are the basis for course planning, have been highly developed. The concept of the purpose of vocational education has broadened with the passage of time and with the professionalization of teachers in the program, but vocational education often is still not as closely integrated with the rest of the school's program as it should be.

THE VOCATIONAL ACTS

Much of vocational education has developed under the stimulus of special federal grants of funds and under the specific supervision and administration provided for in the enabling acts. These provisions and particular administrative procedures for implementing the acts in different states are such that the school administrator must give special study to the factors in the local situation that may require modifications in the state-wide regulations. The general purposes and policy provisions, however, need to be understood in advance. The basic legislation is the Smith-Hughes Act passed in 1917, the purpose of which is stated in the preamble to the act:

An Act. To provide for the promotion of vocational education; to provide for cooperation with the States in the promotion of such education in agriculture and the trades and industries; to provide for cooperation with the States in the preparation of teachers of vocational subjects; and to appropriate money and regulate its expenditure.[6]

The Smith-Hughes Act provided for education in agriculture, home economics, trades, and industry, and for teacher training in these fields. The basis for the disbursement of funds and the general administrative provisions of the Smith-Hughes Act have established the pattern for the operation of the program in vocational education. Since 1917, a series of acts has provided additional funds supplementing those provided in the Smith-Hughes Act. In each case these grants have been enacted for a limited period of years and have been followed by a similar law modified in accordance with Congressional appraisal of the current need. These acts have followed the general pattern established in the Smith-Hughes Act, although modifications have been introduced. The George-Deen Act, passed in 1936, provided aid for vocational education in the distributive occupations, including service occupations. The George-Barden Act, passed in 1946 and which has been modified in some details from time to time, provides for funds substantially in excess of those appropriated in the original act. Although numerous specific details govern the operation of these acts, their major policy provisions are reasonably simple.

In accordance with the announced purpose of promoting vocational education in cooperation with the states, funds are not appropriated directly to the schools but are made available by grants to the states, the amount depending upon certain specified population ratios

[6] Public Law No. 347, 64th Cong., S. 703. Approved, February 23, 1917.

among the states that are presumed to measure needs in the various fields.

Each state is eligible to receive grants of funds upon the organization of a state board of vocational education to formulate a plan for the administration of the program in that state in accordance with the provisions of the act and to provide for the actual administration. The administration of the act within the state becomes the responsibility of the state vocational education authority; the personnel for state administration and supervision are employees of the state.

The funds provided by the federal government must be matched with funds from state and local sources. Funds must be expended on costs of instruction, administration, and supervision rather than on capital expenditures. The funds available for supervision have provided for more comprehensive in-service teacher training and supervision than has generally been possible in nonvocational fields. Actually in well-established programs of vocational education the local and state funds expended far exceed the amount derived from federal sources.

The desirability and the wisdom of the policies and subsequent practices established by the Federal Vocational Education Acts have been the subject of serious debate and consideration. Grants-in-aid for special fields have been questioned because they tend to stimulate only specific fields instead of providing flexibility by allowing the expenditure of funds where the need is thought to be the greatest. The stipulation that funds must be matched may favor wealthier school corporations rather than those in greatest need of financial assistance. Programs of special aid may have a divisive effect on the school. In short, opposition to the real or fancied perils of federal control hidden in the vocational acts has been vigorous.

Nevertheless, these factors deserve serious consideration if the federal government is to have a permanent role in education. Thirty years of operation of the vocational education acts reveal the following facts. The program has resulted in the development and growth of an expensive field of education to a point that an entirely local group would have been unable to reach. A system of state teacher training and in-service teacher training has provided service and stimulation in a manner that other fields might profitably copy. After years of operation, public confidence in and support of vocational education have been gained to a degree to suggest that the present program of aid will be continued and even increased as time passes. The problem of rigidity and overcentralized control, however, remains, although a considerable part of the responsibility for the administration of its program rests in the hands of each state, which is permitted a good deal of leeway in setting up its plan of operation. It is quite possible that some of the rigidity and excessive regulation often laid at the door of the federal government actually originates at the state level and should be attacked there. There is little or no evidence that federal regulation has increased during the years the acts have been in force. The time spent on uncritical opposition to the whole idea of federal participation in vocational education would be more profitably used if it were devoted to an effort to secure flexibility at state and local levels.

WORK EXPERIENCE

During the 1930's, a period when there was a dearth of job opportunities, both of a part-time nature for those in school and of a full-time nature for those out of school, the public became concerned with the problem of providing work experience for youth. The current economic situation has remedied the situation in part, although it seems probable that modern industrial employment, which delays admission to a job until eighteen years of age or later, and modern urban life, with its limited number of part-time jobs suitable for youth, will control the long-term trend by restricting job opportunities for youth under eighteen. Because the responsibility of holding a job is a desirable educational and developmental experience for youth, a great many schools have attempted to provide types of work experience for students.

In practice, the work experience programs that have been evolved have had widely different purposes. They have ranged from organized efforts to employ youth in community and school projects, through encouragement and aid to youth in securing any and all kinds of part-time jobs, to cooperative programs aimed at the development of specific skills. All, perhaps, have their place if their purposes are realizable and clearly recognized for what they are.[7]

The experience of working on a real project and the assumption of responsibility that such work entails are a valuable preparation for learning to accept the responsibilities of adult life. However, this is not to say that all jobs represent valuable experience. Certain cautions must be observed.

The value of work experience is increased if a youth is given supervision, counsel, and related experience to enable him to analyze his experience, recognize its learning opportunities, and evaluate them. Experience on just any job is no guarantee that the student will make an intelligent vocational choice or even a better selection when he chooses another work experience. Vocational skills that can be learned through work experience on part-time jobs of the type ordinarily available to youth can be greatly overestimated. Vocational skills through job ex-

[7] Caroline E. Legg, Carl A. Jessen, and Maris M. Proffitt, *School and Work Programs* (Joint Publication of Federal Security Agency, U.S. Office of Education, and U.S. Department of Labor, Division of Labor Standards, Bulletin No. 9; Washington, D.C.: Government Printing Office, 1947). See also Stuart Anderson, "The Case for Work Experience," *American Vocational Journal*, 25 (December, 1950), 7–8.

perience will be achieved only when jobs are carefully selected and supervised. Once the general responsibilities of being employed have been realized, a point of diminishing educational returns may be rapidly reached in a routine job.

These limitations are cited to illustrate the need for planning, counselling, and related education to help youth realize the educational values to be derived from work experience. Present trends suggest that the school will be depended upon more and more to aid youth in securing work experience and later the first job. The type of work experience that the school can sponsor alone or with other agencies may vary from community and school projects, to supervised part-time work, to cooperative programs in order to develop specific skills. The details of all such projects should be worked out with great care so they may have the greatest educational value to the student.

It need hardly be added that the whole field of occupational education and adjustment is still a relatively new one for the secondary school, and that much needs to be done to integrate it with specialized and general education so that the school's total program may be as effective as possible.

Other Areas of Specialized Education

The vocational fields represent programs of highly specialized study. Other parts of the total school program are also specialized, although many of them are less well defined and organized.

The college preparatory curriculum is, of course, the oldest and most widely recognized of the special curriculums. Whether or not in a broad sense it may be considered a type of prevocational education, since it prepares for further education that may be professional or occupational in nature, it certainly belongs in the category of special education rather than in that of general education. The college preparatory curriculum has been specifically defined, its sequence of work being largely determined by the logic of the subject matter content of the courses presumed to be essential for entrance to college. Although incidental variations exist among colleges, the major part of the required pattern has been the same for all colleges. This program may once have been presumed to be reasonably appropriate for college preparatory students, but recent investigations have thrown doubt upon the validity of these assumptions. Numerous studies, the most notable being the Eight-Year Study of the Progressive Education Association, have revealed that the particular pattern of subjects taken in high school has little to do with success in college.[8]

Success in college is largely contingent upon the possession of in-

[8] Wilford M. Aikin, *The Story of the Eight-Year Study* (New York: Harper & Brothers, 1942).

terest and ability, adequate verbal skills, and effective study habits, rather than upon the special sequence of specific subjects taken in high school. Students who have special interests in given subject fields and who plan to continue to study them in college are not precluded from electing these fields in high school. The Eight-Year Study suggests that the conventional college preparatory curriculum is not sacred and that its revision and adaptation to provide more functional education for high school youth may be freely undertaken without endangering their future chances of success.

Certainly it is true that in the years ahead much concern will be exhibited about the adequacy with which secondary schools prepare youth for further education. An increasing percentage of the high school graduates are now continuing beyond grade 12. The percentage of college-age youth attending college has risen from 4 per cent in 1900 to more than 30 per cent in 1955. It is not unreasonable to assume that this percentage may reach 40 per cent or even approach 50 per cent in the years ahead.[9] The secondary school has passed the stage when it is assumed that its sole function is preparation for college. Certainly even with the increase of college-bound youth it should not return to this orientation nor attempt blindly to emphasize a precise academic pattern upon the assumption that it will serve best even the preparatory function. Rather there is a need for a more rigorous analysis of the skills that are necessary for continued education and the provision of special opportunities to master these skills.

Specialized offerings and opportunities in the arts, music, physical education, extracurricular activities, and the practical arts are typically provided more frequently as free electives than as organized sequences of work. The purpose and intent of such offerings make this practice entirely appropriate. Except for a relatively few highly specialized schools and programs, such offerings are not intended to provide technical competence for occupations or employment but rather to provide for avocational interests and developmental experiences. The students' current needs and interests are the primary guiding factors. Thus the comprehensive high school should offer a variety of special courses in these fields and encourage students to elect them. Exploratory in nature for some, they often reveal unsuspected talent. For the gifted students they provide an essential element of education, the lack of which would be disastrous for both the individual and society. No high school's program can pretend to adequacy unless it offers basic general integrating education to all and a rich variety of specialized education to each.

Many high schools tend to neglect the nonvocational type of spe-

[9] See American Association of Collegiate Registrars and Admission Officers, *The Impending Tidal Wave of Students*, 1954, p. 20.

cialized education. They may offer the required general education program consisting mostly of academic subjects—which are really, as has been shown, specialized in character—but only a little in the way of prevocational or vocational education. Sometimes there are no specialized offerings at all, or they may be crowded out of most students' schedules by the number of required subjects or by conflicts in the schedule. Music is an example of specialized education whose increasing popularity has won it a place in the programs of most schools. Every effort is made to schedule these classes so they are available to many students. Other types of nonvocational electives have not won the place they deserve in the schedule, although they are equally important in the education of those who really desire to take them.

If the American people do not exhibit the range of well-developed cultural and aesthetic interests that critics of our culture would wish, perhaps part of the cause lies in the culturally poverty-stricken "minimum essentials" type of elementary and secondary education still too popular in this country. A good, well-balanced high school program will provide a program of the "common learnings" type described in the preceding chapter; a program of preprofessional and vocational education for lifework; and a specialized program of offerings that do not prepare for lifework but meet the avocational needs and interests of different members of the student body.

EDUCATION OF THE GIFTED

The particular problems of education of the atypical students are not precisely a feature of specialized education since curricular modifications may need to be effected in both general and special fields. However, they may be appropriately considered in this context since many of the adaptations will relate to specialized offerings and programs. While concern for a program which would most effectively stimulate and develop the potentialities of the gifted student has always been felt, the mid-years of the 1950's have tended to bring particular attention to this need. The current crucial need to develop our talented youth to meet effectively our national manpower shortages in the sciences and professions has been increasingly recognized. Our future national progress and development demands this. Certainly in all of these considerations of special groups within the high school enrollment there has been a philosophy which emphasizes the necessity of some common general education and some common experience which would tend to integrate the diverse population of a comprehensive high school. This, however, does not preclude the possibility of special programs which might be directed toward the most effective development of the talented boy or girl. It is impossible for high schools to develop any one specific program of special education which will meet the educational needs of students who differ so widely from each other. Each type of talent requires its own differentiated program. However, it is possible to outline a few developing trends and characteristics of programs which would seem to be most promising in this particular area of concern.

One of the problems that always demands consideration when the education of the gifted and able youngster is discussed is the degree to which accelerated progress through the school should be encouraged or endorsed as a matter of policy. It is obviously possible for the gifted youngster to advance through the elementary and high school programs and enter into a program of higher education at an early age as compared to the average student. However, these types of proposals have always met with the objection that, while able youth may be able to progress at an accelerated pace through the academic curriculum, in matters of physical and social maturity, such acceleration is not possible. Serious social maladjustment may therefore result from the acceleration of such immature youth early into the more mature society of the institution of higher education. However, this problem has been studied to some extent and there is no evidence to show that accelerated students are maladjusted. There is still a question of whether any great amount of acceleration of the very young into college is necessary in order to meet the needs of the talented. Enrichment of typical high school courses coupled with a plan for offering in the secondary school courses and special programs that were ordinarily associated with the colleges or universities seem to make early admission to college unnecessary. The experimentation in permitting selected groups of students to pursue certain fields of study to a level which would ordinarily be beyond that considered a part of the regular high school program and into programs which might comprehend materials taught in the freshman and sophomore years of college offers great promise. Certainly there is no question but that selected students in the high school are capable of pursuing specialized work in the sciences, in mathematics, in languages, in the arts and in other selected fields to a level not ordinarily comprehended in the high school program. Arrangements have been developed with some colleges and universities which permit youth to enter these universities at a normal social age but with advanced standing in some of the academic areas. With the pressing demand for manpower in certain of the selected scientific and professional fields, these students faced with the possibilities not only of normal college programs but of advanced programs into the graduate fields certainly should, whenever possible, be offered this possibility of advanced progress within the high school.

There is another factor to which the curriculum worker interested in the education of the talented in the secondary schools needs to give serious consideration. There is no question but that as the school could count upon the average youth remaining in school an increased number of years, the period of general education has tended to be extended upward in the high school. This is appropriate as a major emphasis. However, the facts of individual growth and development make it desirable to parallel this field of general education with many highly specialized offerings for the most able students. They should have not only an enriched general education but also specialized courses not open to less gifted students. Gifted youth often discover at an early age interests in science, mathematics, languages, or other particular fields which they wish to pursue as a matter of individual interest at a relatively early age; and certainly there is nothing in the current emphasis upon general education which would preclude the possibility of gifted youth undertaking at an early age, along with their general education, specialized courses suited to their talents. The talented should be identified at an early age so that under the guidance of the school, the right kind and degree of specialized education can be provided and so a proper balance between general and special education can be attained for each one. The demands of our expanding social and cultural life, of the specialized professional world and of the specialized research and development fields now current in modern America mean that here again is a new challenge for the secondary school administrator in designing programs which will not be in conflict with the general intent and purposes of the high school and still will offer rich opportunities to these youth, so that a larger percentage of our most able youth will be able to make more nearly their maximum contribution to American life.[10]

SOME PROBLEMS FOR THE PRINCIPAL

Implicit in the foregoing discussions of specialized education are a number of problems of organization and administration that will confront the principal and the staff of any high school that attempts to provide an adequate program of such education.

1. *The comprehensive versus the specialized high school.* Where it is possible, most communities should move toward the former rather than toward the latter. Democracy, efficiency, practicality, and economy are on the side of the comprehensive high school.

2. *Adapting the program to the community.* Successful programs of vocational education have kept close to reality and have been continually aware of local needs. They have consulted advisory committees and have made occupational surveys so that their offerings fit the work life of a community.

[10] A. Harry Passow, "Talented Youth: Our Future Leaders," *Teachers College Record*, December, 1955.

3. *The small high school's program.* Even in a "one industry" community, the small high school has difficulty meeting youths' needs for specialized education for all its youth should not enter that one industry. There are also recreational and avocational needs to be met by specialized education. With its small budget, the typical small high school is hard pressed to offer an adequate, balanced program.

4. *Grade-level placement of vocational programs.* Part of the difficulties of small high schools could be solved if the trend toward offering specialized vocational education at the higher grade levels continues to be justified. If these offerings eventually settle at the junior college level and if regional or area colleges are developed, the small high school will be expected to offer only the nonvocational special education courses, most of which can be more easily and cheaply offered in small schools. Good grade-level placement of vocational programs now tends to vary with the type of industry and the economic level of the community. The higher these are, the higher the grade level can be.

5. *Vocational and educational guidance.* Any enrichment of the educational program calls for an extension of guidance services. The more specialized an offering is the worse it is to let pupils elect it indiscriminately. Adequate guidance services are a necessary adjunct to a good program of specialized education.

6. *School shops versus work in industry.* Both types of experience have their places in the same program. Much good use of industrial plant facilities can be made if management will allow it under conditions that best promote the education of the youth involved. On the other hand, many industries favor periods of school shop experience for younger students, even though they open their plants to the older ones.

7. *Adequate facilities.* Buildings, equipment, and supplies for many types of specialized education cost more than those for an academic education. This accounts at least in part for the fact that many schools with small budgets concentrate on the academic program. A school that undertakes an improved program of specialized education should expect to find its operating costs increased.

8. *Relation to general education.* Actually a pupil's general education program and his vocational program should be integrated; hence the term "related subjects." Integrating these with the vocational program without narrowing them down to the point where they are in reality just added specialized offerings is the problem to which good over-all curriculum planning and good teachers with broad points of view are probably the answers. Leaders in specialized education are as much concerned to see that students also get a good general education as are educators generally.

9. *Status for vocational education.* In many communities, voca-

tional education is not accorded the status that academic education receives. Most of the members of many high school faculties represent
what amounts to a vested interest in academic education. The result on
the students and teachers of vocational subjects is bad. Both types of
offerings have their places, and it is the principal's problem to see that
vocational education is built up to the point where its offerings and
teachers have a status equal to that of the academic program.

10. *Vocational work that competes with industry.* Good programs
of work education produce marketable goods, but industry occasionally
objects to their sale. Unions may want to control not only the number of
students who take certain vocational courses but also the details of these
courses. The school must insist on being free to do whatever is essential
to the best education of its students. If a program requires students to
perform certain kinds of personal services to the community without
charge, or if it produces marketable goods, then the services must be performed and the goods made and sold on a nonprofit basis or supplied free
to charitable nonprofit institutions. They should not be destroyed merely
to get them "off the market." The school, however, has no right to render
personal service or make goods merely for profit. They should be nothing
more than a by-product of a good educational program. This is a problem
on which good advisory committees may help.

11. *Federal and state regulations.* Many schools chafe under the
regulations imposed from above. They may indeed be galling or badly
administered by state and federal personnel. On the other hand, sometimes communities want state and federal aid while making no effort to
supply the best education this money will buy. The proper sphere of
federal and state action in education is delineated in an earlier chapter
in this book, and the principal has to insist as earnestly as possible that
these authorities stay in the proper zone while he does a good job in his.

12. *Duality of control at state and federal level.* A high school
principal may be able to do nothing about the way general education
and vocational education programs are administered at the federal and
the state levels, where they may be administered as if they were unrelated to each other. But at least at his own level he can bring them under his own administration and supervision, thus eliminating the division,
rivalry, and separation that are as inefficient in education as they are in
any institution and about which we now hear a great deal.

Some Points to Consider

1. Can you describe some practice in a high school you know that reflects
one of the misconceptions of vocational education listed in this chapter?

2. Do you think segregated high schools are essential if good work in
either general education or specialized education is to be done?

3. What types of special educational programs are available to students in high schools near you? Do you think what each high school offers meets the needs of its student body? How can you tell?

4. After examining the booklet *Education for Family Living* (see Further Reading), do you think such education is appropriate for both boys and girls in high schools you know? Are they getting it? Why not?

5. Do graduation requirements in a high school with which you are familiar encourage or discourage students from selecting its special educational offerings? How should the requirements be changed?

6. What gives such organizations as the Future Farmers and the 4-H Clubs the vitality they have? How could we get more of that into all phases of school life?

7. Make a list of types of jobs in some town or school neighborhood you know that might be used as work experience. Why would it be a good thing to use them? Why are they not used?

8. Do you agree that college preparatory courses are a form of special education? Should any of them be required of all students? None of them? To the extent that you would cease requiring them of all students (if you would), what would you substitute? More general education? More special education? Or both?

9. To the extent that vocational education courses are moved up toward the years after high school, will not a vacuum be created in the high school years? How would you fill this so as to have as profitable and interesting a program for some students as they now have?

Further Reading

Aikin, Wilford M. *The Story of the Eight-Year Study.* New York: Harper & Brothers, 1942.

Annual Report of the Superintendent of Schools to the Board of Education, 1944–1945. *Education for Family Living.* Highland Park, Mich.: Highland Park High School, 1945.

Dodds, B. L. "That All May Learn," NASSP *Bulletin,* No. 85, November, 1939.

Gilbert, A. W. "Work Experience for Secondary School Pupils," NASSP *Bulletin,* No. 123, May, 1944.

Hamlin, Herbert M. *Agricultural Education in Community Schools.* Danville, Ill.: Interstate Printers and Publishers, 1950.

Havighurst, Robert J., Eugene Stivers, and Robert F. DeHaan. *Survey of Gifted Children.* Chicago: University of Chicago Press, November, 1955.

Jacobson, Paul B., and B. L. Dodds. "Work Experience and Secondary Education," NASSP *Bulletin,* No. 120, February, 1944.

Keller, Franklin J. *Principles of Vocational Education.* Boston: D. C. Heath & Company, 1948. Chaps. 2, 3, 13–16.

Legg, Caroline E., Carl A. Jessen, and Maris M. Proffitt. *School and Work Programs.* Joint Publication of the Federal Security Agency, U.S. Office of Education, and U.S. Department of Labor, Division of Labor Standards, Bulletin No. 9; Washington, D.C.: Government Printing Office, 1947.

Leonard, J. Paul. "The Nature of Work Experience," NASSP *Bulletin*, No. 111, January, 1943.

————. "Work Experience in Secondary Education," NASSP *Bulletin*, No. 123, May, 1944.

National Association of Secondary School Principals. "The Business Education Program in the Secondary School," *Bulletin*, No. 165, November, 1949.

————. "Home Economics in the Secondary School," *Bulletin* No. 196, October, 1953.

National Society for the Study of Education. *American Education in the Post-War Period*. Forty-fourth Yearbook; Chicago: University of Chicago Press, 1945. Part I, "Curriculum Reconstruction"; "Providing Work and Service Experience for Post-War Youth," by W. C. Seyfert, pp. 139–166.

Olson, Clara M., and N. D. Fletcher. *Learn and Live*. New York: Alfred P. Sloan Foundation, 1946.

Passow, A. Harry, and others. *Planning for Talented Youth*. New York: Bureau of Publications, Teachers College, Columbia University, 1955.

————. "Talented Youth: Our Future Leaders," *Teachers College Record*, December, 1955.

Prosser, Charles H., and Thomas H. Quigley. *Vocational Education in a Democracy*. Chicago: American Technical Society, 1949.

Rakestraw, Clarence E. *Training High School Youth for Employment*. Chicago: American Technical Society, 1947.

Seyfert, W. C., and P. A. Rehmus, eds. *Work Experience in Education*. Harvard Workshop Series No. 2, Cambridge, Mass.: Harvard University Press, 1941.

Struck, F. Theodore. *Vocational Education for a Changing World*. New York: John Wiley & Sons, Inc., 1945.

U.S. Office of Education. Home Economics in Public High Schools, 1938–1939. Vocational Division, *Bulletin* No. 213; Washington, D.C.: Government Printing Office, 1941.

————. *Vocational Education in the Years Ahead*. Vocational Division, *Bulletin* No. 234, General Series No. 7; Washington, D.C.: Government Printing Office, 1945.

Chapter 11

SCHOOL ACTIVITIES AND
STUDENT ORGANIZATIONS

O NE OF THE DISTINGUISHING characteristics of the American high school is the number and variety of student organizations and activities that require an increasing amount of the time and attention of staff and students. Whether civic, recreational, or social, or appealing to some special interests, they come under the general classification of extracurricular activities. Although opinions vary concerning the appropriateness of the terms "extracurricular" and "student activities" and although theoretically, perhaps, there should be no differentiation between "curricular" and "extracurricular," these terms are generally used to describe particular areas of school activity.

Whether or not specific school activities are scheduled, are recognized by the granting of credit, and are supervised by school personnel depends upon the particular school. It is difficult if not impossible to define extracurricular activities in terms of any single criterion; yet there is reasonably common agreement regarding the majority of activities coming under this general classification. In general "extracurricular" refers to the activities directed and supervised by the school in addition to the regularly organized, recognized, and scheduled class offerings. In practice, the secondary school program does not typically divide itself into two sharply defined areas but rather presents a continuum ranging from scheduled credit classes to informal group organizations with a loosely defined program and schedule. Midway between these extremes are many activities that might be termed "semicurricular," such as physical education, music, and journalistic activities. Part of these programs may be scheduled curricular activities and part may be quite informal, credit may or may not be granted for them, and they may be scheduled partly within and partly outside the school day. Time and effort spent in trying to arrive at exact distinctions and classifications are not particularly productive. However, it is generally true that when any activity is accepted as "curricular" it is scheduled in the regular school day, gives credit toward graduation, is paid for out of the regular school budget, and is in charge of a teacher qualified to teach it. When none of these criteria apply to a learning activity carried on by a school, it is "extracurricular." As one or more do apply to the activity, it moves in the direction of being accepted into the curriculum. Thus the difference lies not in the nature of the activity but in the status accorded it by the school's faculty and administration and by the school's public.

The educational experiences of the secondary school student ought to include a planned selection from all that goes on under the stimulus and supervision of the school. All such directed activities are part of the total educational program and hence are the responsibility of the school, which is also responsible for seeing that each activity has the status it deserves in the educational program. Whatever the school gives express or tacit approval to as part of a student's program should be neither penalized nor rewarded because it is regarded as extracurricular or curricular. Critical evaluation of the educational purpose and results of school activities, experimentation to develop more educationally effective activities, and the development of guiding principles to give direction to student organizations and activities are much more necessary than bootless wrangling over arbitrary and changing distinctions that have no connection with the educational effectiveness of a given program of activities.

The Function of School Organizations and Activities

The fact that student activities have grown beyond organized class activities indicates a radical change in the concept of the functions and purposes of youth education. Some degree of student organization and informal activities has always characterized youth schools, of course, since almost inevitably a social group such as the student body of a school will form various social and special interest groups and, unless it is rigorously controlled, will devote some time to them. Such groups and activities may, however, exist in spite of, rather than because of, the efforts of those directing the school. McKown[1] outlines three stages in the evolution of extracurricular activities: the period when they were ignored by teachers and administrators; the period when they were openly opposed; and the present period in which they are utilized to achieve recognized educational goals. The rigid intellectualism of our earlier secondary schools, the belief in mental discipline, and the distrust of what was then considered frivolous were all part of one pattern. Not until the studies of child and adolescent growth revealed the importance of the

[1] Harry C. McKown, *Extra-Curricular Activities* (3rd ed.; New York: The Macmillan Company, 1952), pp. 2–3.

total developmental experiences of the student, and the broader concepts of education developed by John Dewey and others began to influence educational thinking was the student activity movement recognized as properly belonging to the total educational program. Although some educators think they receive too much emphasis or doubt the wisdom of specific activities, the majority endorse organizations and activities and look to them as one means of achieving important educational objectives.[2]

This general acceptance of the place of student organizations and activities in the total program, good in itself, has at times led to interesting contradictions and inconsistencies. The educational philosophy that regards the student as a citizen of the school learning through his experiences has been accepted as valid in the area of extracurricular activities but is subject to reservation in the organized curricular area. Thus it is not unusual to find an extensive program of extracurricular activities paralleling a rigid and stereotyped curricular program very much as if the one were a compensation for the other. In practice this device seems to be the only way to hold some students in school, but whether a good educational program can be developed by operating two radically different programs within the same school is certainly open to question.

Occasionally, uncritical acceptance of the idea of student activities without a clear understanding of their underlying purposes and principles has led to an indiscriminate development of all student activities without any attempt to evaluate their objectives. Similarly a school may set up the form of an activity program without ensuring the student the participation that makes such activities educationally effective.

These limitations in a rapidly growing educational movement are not indicative of any fundamental error in the concept of the place of extracurricular activities. Nevertheless, they point to the need for appraisal and a more clear-cut definition of objectives in terms of the total school.

THE PURPOSE OF SCHOOL ACTIVITIES

The purposes served by school activities are not separate and apart from the general purposes of secondary education. Their value and merit lie in their contribution to these broad purposes, to such ends as self-realization, human relationships, economic efficiency, and civic responsibility.[3] By their very nature these activities are especially fitted to pro-

[2] Ellsworth Tompkins, *Extraclass Activities for All Pupils* (U.S. Office of Education, Bulletin No. 4; Washington, D.C.: Government Printing Office, 1950).
[3] See Educational Policies Commission, *The Purposes of Education in American Democracy* (Washington, D.C.: National Education Association, 1938), p. 41.

vide invaluable experiences, particularly in areas related to citizenship and personal development. Goals may be stated in terms of the personal and psychological needs of the individual or in terms of the needs of society, that is, in terms of habits, skills, and understandings. These two approaches are not mutually exclusive, for any valid program must consider the needs of the individual.

PERSONAL NEEDS

Although the needs of the adolescent may be met by different specific activities, they are common and universal. The study of mental hygiene has revealed the crucial nature of the satisfaction of these needs and their relation to the adjustment and developing maturity of the individual. Each individual has a basic need to be accepted, to be identified with a social group. The individual's basic need for a feeling of security demands the satisfaction and assurance that membership in social groups of his own age provides. Each youth wants to be assured that he is like other young people and is accepted by them. It is not enough for him to know that he belongs to such a group as the family. He needs to feel that he has made good with his contemporaries.

It is possible for the individual to feel identity with a total school. This feeling of school membership, however, although it has its place, ordinarily lacks the face-to-face assurance, intimacy, and personal contact gained from the smaller social group. The presence of numerous student clubs and groups, organized for many and varied purposes, offers the individual the needed opportunity to form part of a small group and to associate himself with others of like interest. It also gives him what he usually does not have either in the larger, less specialized student groups or in the regularly organized curricular program—an opportunity to earn recognition from his contemporaries.

Ideally, perhaps, this feeling of identification should be an outcome of membership in all groups in the school and the major concern of class groups. In the elementary school, the single class group that operates throughout the day constitutes an identified in-group from which the pupil can gain security. Some of the experimental, secondary school core programs, which have a longer time schedule, more group enterprises, and some highly specialized selective courses, serve this purpose. However, the curricular program of the typical high school, with its crowded schedule, its series of classes, its constantly shifting class groups, and its often formalized procedure, usually offers relatively little opportunity to satisfy this basic personal need to belong. If satisfaction of these ego or personal needs is essential—and all evidence indicates that it is—then the ultimate aim must be to develop a total school program with many genuine social groups. In the meantime, student organizations play a doubly important role in satisfying these basic needs of adolescents.

It is well to recognize this purpose and function of student activities. From the educational standpoint, the end product, whether it be an athletic event, a musical performance, a school paper, or the development of an exhibit is not as important as the process of learning and the feeling of satisfaction that precedes the ostensible product. For this reason, the evaluation of student activities must always be concerned with whether fundamental human needs are being met. In the larger sense, the ostensible purpose or function of the activity may actually be secondary.

SOCIAL NEEDS

Closely related to these individual needs are what can be termed "social needs," with "social" used in the sense of developing satisfactory relations with others. Each individual feels impelled to develop some competency in dealing with and working with others. This need embodies a series of understandings varying from the relatively simple matter of accepted manners and courtesies to the more fundamental one of comprehending the behavior of others. It is in this setting that the rather elusive traits of leadership are developed. The extracurricular program, with its opportunities for the free association of youth, offers a natural environment for the learning and practice of such understandings.

CITIZENSHIP AND DEMOCRATIC LIVING

In addition to meeting these closely related personal and social needs, the activity program serves as a vehicle for the development of skills, attitudes, and understandings that are accepted as the legitimate goals of secondary education. The extracurricular program offers students many opportunities to meet actual situations calling for group decisions and actions. The development of democratic citizenship requires more than verbal understanding; hence the actual civic habits and attitudes developed by youth may be much more dependent upon these experiences in group living and planning than upon formal knowledge gained in the classroom. As shown in Chapter 17, the extracurricular program that includes a student government organization and its related activities, for example, offers potentialities for providing these experiences in a setting real to youth. The mere presence of a student government organization certainly does not guarantee that these experiences will be available; it must be planned and supervised so as to provide them. The opportunities available for the development of democratic citizenship are almost unlimited in richness and variety. A school that does not utilize them does not have as good a citizenship program as it should have.

DEVELOPMENT OF SPECIAL INTERESTS

The many special interest club groups and activities that have developed as a phase of extracurricular programs stimulate youth to explore potential talents and develop vocational skills and avocational interests in a way that regular curricular programs are not likely to do. A special interest group built around any socially desirable activity is not only a legitimate endeavor of the secondary school; it may offer an opportunity to pursue learning beyond what may be provided in a regular class. This provision for individual development is one of the major functions of the secondary school. It may be argued that if the curricular program were truly oriented to the needs and interests of youth, if class procedure were guided by the individual interests of the students, if the class group were organized on a democratic group planning basis, the need for special interest clubs as part of the extracurricular program would not exist. This argument is a valid one: much may be learned from activities that help to vitalize the curriculum; a common approach to the curricular and the extracurricular programs is a desirable goal. Nevertheless, class loads and programs in a vast number of secondary schools are such that only the extracurricular activities offer the main opportunity for the development of many special interests. Moreover, the flexibility of the extracurricular program makes it the ideal medium to introduce many new interest activities that, even in an extremely dynamic school, would be introduced at a much slower rate if their introduction depended upon their acceptance into the curricular program.

MEETING RECREATIONAL NEEDS

The adolescent needs activities that give him the chance to join his peers in endeavors that ostensibly serve no end except the satisfaction of the moment. These may involve games, dancing, or even nothing more than casual social contacts. The adult or the serious educator may look askance at such activities and wish to substitute something that will presumably lead to some defined, definite, tangible learning or accomplishment. Actually activities that provide primarily for satisfaction at the moment are an essential part of the life of every adult, youth, and child. Not the relatively weak reason of occupying time that might be spent in less desirable ways, but a real purpose lies behind the provisions of recreational opportunities for youth. Their social and personal development, mentioned in preceding paragraphs, demands the social give-and-take that appears in what are primarily recreational activities. Learning in the broad sense of adjustment to life occurs in other than formal intellectual situations.

Purposes Common to the Entire Program

Student activities have been discussed in terms of the contribution they can make toward achieving selected broad objectives of secondary education as well as toward meeting the personal needs of students for self-identification and group membership and for the development of related social skills. The development of democratic citizens, the improvement of individual skills, and opportunities for group recreation are potential outcomes of the extracurricular program. These objectives are not peculiar to the activity program; they are part of the over-all objectives of secondary education, and all the phases of an integrated, well-rounded program of secondary education work for their achievement.

GUIDING PRINCIPLES IN THE ADMINISTRATION
OF STUDENT ACTIVITES

The organization and supervision of student activities, now major responsibilities of secondary school administration, are not without their problems. For one thing, the clean-cut administration of these activities requires that major policies and procedures be carefully defined and understood. The purposes for which these activities exist must be consistent with the general policies of democratic secondary education. To be really effective, the general principles briefly presented here should be interpreted by each school faculty in terms of its local school situation.

The justification for each student activity must lie in the contribution it can make to the learning and development of youth. The practical objective of using student organization and activities to contribute to the operation of the school should never become the main one. Although the production of a good school paper, the maintenance of good order in the halls, the presentation of an effective exhibit, the beautifying of the school grounds are all laudable achievements, they are not fundamental objectives. The learning and development of youth in the process is the only educationally justified goal. Any other outcomes are special or extra dividends, so to speak. In the practical operation of a school, the ostensible outcomes cannot help being important in some measure, but care must be taken lest primary objectives are lost. By the simple device of oversupervising the student and relegating to him routine tasks whose possibilities are soon exhausted, it is possible to sacrifice learning experiences for the sake of achieving practical results.

Public pressure for observable achievement presents the school with a constant temptation to overlook the student. For this reason the learning objectives of the activity program should be the subject of continuous review and study. Otherwise, what should be an educational program may degenerate into an institutionalized affair in which the student's work is directed solely for the aggrandizement of the school.

The activity program for each school should grow out of the life of that school and be adapted to the local situation. The triteness of this statement does not alter its fundamental importance. Activities should always grow out of a job to be done, an interest to be served, or a service to be performed that provides educational experiences. Too often organizations and programs have been copied from other schools, admirers attempting to take them over in full bloom, as it were, from another school. It is small wonder that frequently only the outward form is transplanted, and that this, improperly nourished in strange soil, either withers away or struggles feebly and vainly to keep its former vigor. The variables that exist among communities, staff, and students are unlikely to produce the same pattern of organizations and activities in any two schools. They can learn from exchanging experiences, but the starting point of any activity program should always be the interest and educational needs of their student bodies.

To be vital, the student activity program must be continually changing, dynamic. As in any other part of the educational program, the usefulness of student activities depends upon the active driving interest of students. Clubs are organized because of the interest of a given group of students at a given time. When interest in it disappears, the club should be dissolved. In many activity programs, organizations are carried along from year to year on the assumption that because they are in existence they must have some vital function. If a program of activities is continuously reviewed by students and faculty, as it should be to be a really effective and dynamic program, new groups would be organized and unnecessary ones would disappear.

The duties of student council organizations and service organizations will also change as demands and conditions change. Adjustments in the curricular program will in many cases call for corresponding adjustments in activities. Tradition and continuity have their place, but they should never be the deciding factor in student activities.

Participation in student activities should be equally available to all students with restrictions related only to competency and interest in the given activity. Theoretically, no other policy can be remotely justified in a public school in a democracy, but to assume that present-day practice conforms to it is naïve. It is perfectly legitimate for an interest club to establish certain criteria related to that interest as qualifications for admission. An honor society for recognition of scholarship or a club for the school's letter men by definition has admission qualifications. However, when admission is by secret ballot, which is notably sensitive to the social acceptability of the candidate, equal opportunity for participation in the club is gone. Organizations founded for very laudable purposes, but patterning themselves after the social groupings in society, quickly become nothing more than social cliques concerned only with the ego inflation of their members. The fact that such organizations exist in the adult world is no reason for the public school to copy them.

States that have recognized the incompatibility of secret, self-perpetuating high school fraternities and sororities and similar organizations have made them illegal.[4] In states where they are not illegal, there is no reason why any high school principal or faculty should manifest any approval whatever of these secret, self-perpetuating organizations. Where they do not exist in a high school and the problem seems unlikely to arise, there seems little point in setting up a straw man to knock down. In high schools that seem to offer appropriate conditions for their introduction, steps should be taken to prevent it. Some high school student bodies, for example, have prohibited such organizations in their constitutions and have provided for the disfranchisement of students who accept membership.

If such organizations already exist in a high school, the principal and faculty have the problem of what to do about them. They should not be given any measure of approval or recognition. To ignore them often results in their having privileges that are not accorded the student body as a whole. These organizations can be eliminated only by the united action of students, parents, the board of education, and the state department of education. Many communities, grown more sensitive to undemocratic attitudes and prejudices, have supported a movement to uproot them. Even their student members are sometimes sufficiently aware of their shortcomings to be willing to surrender their charters. If the parents of entering high school students will agree to discourage their sons and daughters from joining such groups, their strength can be undermined at its source, and in a few years their attraction to students will diminish to the vanishing point. Careful planning when the groups are organized, publicly announced admission requirements, guidance of students, and positive measures in support of legitimate social groups are all means of preventing the distortion of student activities.

When activities require more than nominal costs for participation, equality of opportunity likewise becomes more theoretical than real. Activities that require special dues or expenditures for equipment or clothes are in themselves selective.[5] Extra expenditures always present a real

[4] Research Division, National Education Association, "Anti-Fraternity Rules," NASSP *Bulletin*, No. 201 (March, 1954), pp. 80–95.
[5] Harold C. Hand, *How to Conduct a Hidden Tuition Costs Study* (Circular Series A, No. 51, Illinois Secondary School Curriculum Program, Bulletin No. 4; Springfield: State Superintendent of Public Instruction, May, 1949).

problem for the secondary school administrator since funds for the operation of the activity program often are not included in the regular school budget. Keeping fees for clubs at a very nominal rate, providing general tickets that cover most or all activities and that by one devise or another are available to all students, and purchasing out of public funds expensive equipment, such as that needed in musical and recreational activities, are among the methods used to equalize the economic factor.

Student activities should be a recognized responsibility of the school and as such should be planned and supervised. This principle flows logically from the general thesis of the educational values of student activities.

The extracurricular program is an educational program for the development of youth, not simply a device to occupy their time. If it is carried on under the auspices of the school, the school has responsibility of supervising and directing it. Futhermore, as has been remarked elsewhere, desirable educational outcomes do not result automatically; they are achieved only by the application of a basically sound educational philosophy and the careful guidance of the students who participate in the activity. Much of the merit of student activities has arisen from the opportunity offered youth to exercise initiative and assume responsibility; hence supervision and direction by school authorities, instead of lessening these opportunities, must strive to improve them. With the acceptance of the activity program as part of the work of the secondary school has come the realization that its supervision and direction are the responsibilities of the principal and his staff.

There should be a continuous interpretation to the public of the activity program. Those parts of the activity program having to do with athletic or other contests or with public presentations are well publicized and arouse intense interest in the parents and friends of the young people taking part in them.

Superficially it may appear that publicity of this type is all the school needs. However, publicity that emphasizes only public events is likely to present a distorted picture in that the events often overshadow the participants, and those phases of an activity program that do not lend themselves to a public performance are overlooked. In fact, much of the criticism directed at student activities as "fads and frills" has been based on the assumption that these activities had no educational end beyond a debatable recreational aim for participants and audience. If the activity program is thus narrowly conceived and executed, such criticisms are valid. On the other hand, if the program has educational values, then they should be clearly apparent in any public demonstration for parents and patrons.

The orientation of all interpretive activities should be the opportunities the school provides for the development of youth. The activity program should be presented as offering opportunities of genuine value. Public understanding of this program helps build support for an improved curriculum since the same principles of learning underlie both. A program of interpretation should be comprehensive in that the public should know of the activities of all types of student organizations, whether they are of the type that draws audience attention or not.

Interpretation in its broadest sense should be more than a program of information; it should be a program of participation of school authorities and patrons in the development of a better school. Much of the public pressure for what may be already overemphasized aspects of student activities can arise from failure to understand their fundamental objectives. A balanced program requires the cooperation and aid of informed parents and patrons.

Administration of Various Types of Activities

Any survey of the literature dealing with student activities will reveal the enormous variety of student organizations now existing in high school. Not only is it difficult to classify them in other than general categories; the variations in the extent to which certain activities are curricular or extracurricular further complicate classification. The following list includes major categories most typically appearing in various reviews and studies of student activities:

1. Student council and related service organization
2. Departmental and special interest clubs
3. Publication organizations
4. Speech and dramatic organizations
5. Musical organizations
6. Organizations affiliated with national character and service programs
7. Athletic organizations[6]

A later chapter considers activities of the student council related to school discipline and social control. The field of physical education is also reviewed as part of certain special broad fields of the curricular program. The home room organization is often included in a review of student activities, but since it is also generally an essential element of the student guidance program here it will be found under that topic.

[6] See E. K. Fretwell, *Extra-Curricular Activities in Secondary Schools* (Boston: Houghton Mifflin Company, 1931); Galen Jones, *Extra-Curricular Activities in Relation to the Curriculum* (New York: Bureau of Publications, Teachers College, Columbia University, 1935); Harry C. McKown, *Extra-Curricular Activities* (3rd ed.; New York: The Macmillan Company, 1952); and National Association of Secondary School Principals, "Vitalizing Student Activities in the Secondary Schools," *Bulletin*, No. 184, February, 1952.

The following paragraphs present some of the major problems and policies related to the organization and administration of these different types of activities. Each topic has what amounts to a body of literature of its own, from which the secondary school administrator who needs a more detailed discussion should choose.

THE STUDENT COUNCIL

The basic need for organization in the arrangement and improvement of group life in a high school is stressed in a later chapter, but administrative considerations of importance to the principal are included here. The student council, in some form, has become part of the organization and administration of a majority of high schools today. In 1954-1955, the National Association of Student Councils sponsored by the National Association of Secondary School Principals listed a membership of 6,413 schools and the number of schools having some form of student council organizations undoubtedly far exceed this number.[7] Although extreme variations exist in the organization and functions of the councils, the idea of some degree of student participation in the management of the school is firmly established. Excellent publications are available that describe in detail the principles, practices, and examples of student council organization.[8]

The principal function of the student council is to serve as a means of developing democratic citizenship. Whatever other purposes may be ascribed to it, this broad central purpose is the dominant one. An analysis of 110 constitutions of student councils reported in the *Bulletin* of the National Association of Secondary School Principals summarizes the specific purposes mentioned and compares them with an earlier, similar study in 1940 as shown in Table 12.

The development and definition of the responsibilities of the student council are essential to a student council program. More than one student council, well organized on paper, has failed to function properly because of confusion over its responsibilities or because it actually had little or nothing to do that seemed important to students. It must be remembered that although, from the standpoint of the school administrator, the broad purpose of the student council is to further the devel-

[7] For a description of the development and services of the National Association of Student Councils, see Gerald M. Van Pool, "A History of the National Association of Student Councils," NASSP *Bulletin*, No. 213 (October, 1955), pp. 78–104.

[8] Educational Policies Commission, *Learning the Ways of Democracy* (Washington, D.C.: National Education Association, 1940), Chap. 4; Harry C. McKown, *The Student Council* (New York: McGraw-Hill Book Co., Inc., 1944); National Association of Secondary School Principals, "The Student Council in the Secondary School," *Bulletin*, No. 124, October, 1944; and National Association of Secondary School Principals, "Vitalizing Student Activities in the Secondary Schools," *Bulletin*, No. 184 (February, 1952), pp. 43–52.

opment of citizenship, that development will take place only if students have an opportunity to participate in activities and undertakings that seem of genuine significance and importance to them. The individual student is motivated, not by vague theoretical desires to improve his civic understandings and skills, but by the desire to carry through projects that have point and purpose in the here and now of his school life.

TABLE 12. GENERAL GROUPING OF SPECIFIC PURPOSES

PURPOSE	PER CENT	
	1940	1944
To furnish citizenship training	26.4	48.0
To allow pupils to participate in or manage extracurricular affairs	39.5	16.4
To promote student-faculty relationships	11.6	15.5
To promote general welfare	7.0	12.1
To provide for pupil expression	3.6	4.3
To furnish a working model for government	3.6	0.0
Miscellaneous	8.3	3.7

Source: National Association of Secondary School Principals, "The Student Council in the Secondary School," Bulletin, No. 124 (October, 1944), p. 20. Reprinted by permission.

It is impossible to outline any series of specific projects that are equally appropriate for all student councils. Obviously these groups will vary from school to school and from time to time in the same school. Numerous examples of possible activities are cited in the previously mentioned sources, but whatever specific activities are undertaken, these general principles should be observed:

The responsibilities and duties that the council is to have should be clearly defined and understood; ideally, they should be written down in a constitution. Above all, if authority is to be delegated it should be delegated and not kept under the control of the faculty sponsor. There should be no pretending to delegate authority, for sophisticated, intelligent high school youth will not be fooled into thinking they are running an organization that is in reality being managed by the faculty sponsor or the principal. The cynical attitudes frequently exhibited by students toward their student government are the natural outcome of such practices. The error is not the failure really to delegate authority as much as the pretense of doing it. It is well to recognize that the student council can best play an advisory and consulting role in certain fields, and students can find this a responsible and respectable role to play if it is so defined. The experience of student-teacher group planning in curriculum development is an example, and this concept of group planning can well apply to student council activities as well. In curricular areas, in matters of large school policies, and in the general code of conduct of the school, the student council should be one of the participating groups in the evolution of policies and practices. In other areas, notably in the management of school activities, the student council can assume the large part of the responsibility and be the major policy group, directly and by delegation taking a major role in the management of the particular activity.

A clear distinction should be made between activities in which the council participates as a policy body and its actual administrative responsibilities. Considerable variation exists in the role of the council in regard to school control or discipline. Certainly the council should play a large part in developing the morale and the standards of conduct of students in the school. It is the logical agency to review and to propose various regulations and standards of conduct to be established in the school. And it can help to enforce some of the day-by-day routines. Nevertheless, in spite of the success of student courts in selected instances, it is doubtful if the council should become the primary disciplinary agency. The modern concept of the direction of student behavior employs the guidance approach after learning the basic causes of misbehavior. Wise counseling and the treatment of cases individually and privately is more effective than a method that relies on detection and penalties.

Responsibilities and duties should be delegated to the student council as that body develops and as experience and conditions indicate. It is much wiser to initiate a council with a few well-defined responsibilities, adding to them as tradition, experience, and prestige are developed by the group. The error of suddenly creating a full-blown council with an elaborate series of responsibilities has been demonstrated more than once. This, however, is no justification for the slow growth in the level of responsibility permitted the student council that has been the practice in many schools. To forestall this creeping paralysis, any written constitution should be flexible enough to permit development and change.

The particular pattern of organization for student councils and student government has been the subject of much study. Effective programs can be cited for practically any type, but an appropriate organization should provide for the representation of all students and for the performance of its function, and at the same time be no more elaborate than necessary for the execution of its defined tasks. Representation drawn from functioning subgroups in the school such as home rooms has the advantage of providing means whereby representatives can report back to parent groups and vice versa. Committees and special bodies of the council should be organized only as the need for them arises. The practice of patterning the organization after city, state, or federal models may be a practical device for teaching information about the structure of our civil government, but it is likely to create an overcomplicated organization with boards and committees that have no particular relation to the tasks at hand and thus operate in a general atmosphere of make-believe. We show more respect for the intelligence of youth when we name the student governing organization "The Student Council of X High School" and the hall patrol "The Hall Patrol" instead of using such designations as "The Senate" and "The Interstate Commerce Commission." High school youth are realists and we are being unrealistic if we treat them otherwise.

STUDENT CLUBS

Clubs are characteristic of almost every level of American life. No activity in high school is probably so varied, so wide in scope, and reaches so many students as the club program. Other activities may receive greater public attention, but the very variety of an extensive club program can appeal to students of widely different interests and purposes. Although the student council and the special activities in the fields of publications, music, and athletics will appeal to many students, these activities are by their very nature selective and draw those students with particular talents or leadership qualities. The club program, however, provides opportunities for the participation of students who possess less marked special talents and leadership qualities than the other activities require, but who are equally in need of opportunity to follow worthwhile interests.

By its very scope the club program can achieve many varied specific purposes, but in common with other activities it provides opportunities for learning experiences growing out of individual interests, for supplementing and enriching the general curricular offering, for exploring special interests, and for satisfying social experiences.

No precise pattern of club offerings is appropriate for all schools. In general, any club organization established for any socially acceptable student interest should be sponsored and encouraged. Clubs need not have activities closely related to specific subject areas, nor need they be created entirely around intellectual interests. The various types of hobby clubs such as camera clubs, chess clubs, sewing clubs, and modern music clubs are examples of this. It should be remembered that the group planning and the interaction among students in clubs provide one of the more important outcomes of a club program regardless of the particular center of interest that binds the members of each group together.

Typical club programs can be classified according to the type of interest and purpose they represent. Seven types of clubs are presented as appropriate for school sponsorship in the following recommendation from a report of the Committee on Student Activities of the National Association of Secondary School Principals:

1. *Clubs closely related to courses offered in the schools.*—Examples of such clubs are foreign language clubs, mathematics clubs, botany clubs, and so on.

2. *National character-building organizations sponsored by the school.*— Many schools have a Boy Scout troop, the Hi-Y organization, a chapter of the Junior Red Cross, Future Teachers of America or similar organizations.

3. *Local service clubs.*—In this group may be classed clubs organized to perform some special service for the school, such as a "pep club," a "big brother club" (to assist new pupils to get acquainted with the school), a community service club, or some other organization with social service its aim.

4. *Hobby and recreation clubs.*—In this group fall the stamp collectors, the radio clubs, the motion-picture club, and clubs whose aims are primarily social.

5. *Honor societies.*—The most widely recognized club of this type is the *National Honor Society*, originated and sponsored by the National Association of Secondary School Principals.[9]

One of the difficult problems of administration of student clubs concerns the extent to which clubs existing primarily for social purposes should be stimulated and encouraged. Social activities are certainly necessary and desirable for the adolescent, and will ordinarily be a part of most club activities. However, in general, social and recreational activities ought to be developed on a class or total school basis and as a part of organizations existing for other primary purposes. It is very difficult to keep groups whose purpose is entirely social from being exclusive and prestige groups whose total effect in the school will be questionable regardless of the satisfaction the members may derive from the social activities of the groups. Furthermore, the membership criteria mentioned in later paragraphs are very difficult to apply to social groups.

As a general principle a club must undertake some well-defined projects or meet some clearly felt need on the part of its members if it is to maintain any vital life. Presumably it was founded to serve an interest shared by its members. This interest demands activities appropriate to it. Every club and its sponsor face the problem of deciding what particular activities should be undertaken. These projects must grow out of the interest of the student, developed through group planning and carried on largely by their efforts. The sponsor must be fertile in suggestion and able to plan with the students without dominating the program. Experience indicates that the sponsor is perhaps the most important factor in the successful club program, for he must be able to maintain

---

[9] National Association of Secondary School Principals, "Vitalizing Student Activities in the Secondary Schools," Bulletin, No. 102 (December, 1941), pp. 34–35.

that very nice balance of providing leadership and adult counsel without depriving the students of the opportunity to exercise their own initiative and imagination.

The administration of the club program requires clear and well-defined policies. The particular mechanics may vary with schools but the same basic principles are usually applicable. There must be definite criteria for evaluating the desirability of creating a new organization and there must be a definite procedure for bringing it into existence. Club groups that are to be under the sponsorship of the school should not simply appear without some evaluation of their proposed activities, and this evaluation should be based upon a definite philosophy and principle. In general, any proposed student club should be required to show that an adequate number of students have a definite interest in it, that it would serve a defined purpose appropriate to the objectives of the school, and that there are activities by which the group's purpose can be achieved. The student council is the natural body to answer these questions. The school's recognition of the club should be indicated by the appointment of a sponsor, whose new responsibilities should be recognized as part of his professional duties.

Membership policies of all clubs should be clearly established. In general, membership in clubs should be open to all eligible students alike. It is obvious that qualifications for certain club groups must be established, but these qualifications must be related to the purpose and activities of the club. A secret ballot on candidacy of students who meet the pertinent qualifications is an undesirable practice. Social status, membership in certain cliques, and similar extraneous matters can easily become the factors that determine admission. Although fraternities and sororities are banned by law in high schools in most states, a club ostensibly established for worth-while purposes, if allowed to have admission standards unrelated to its purpose, can grow into an organization as undesirable in a high school as if it had originally started out to be socially exclusive and selective. Instances in which "character" organizations or innocuously titled clubs have become exclusive social cliques are not infrequent. Once established, such organizations are difficult to redirect. Clearly defined policies can anticipate such consequences. Social groups organized by students outside the school and carrying on their activities independently of the school, outside of the school day and off the school's property, are, of course, beyond the direct control of the school though not beyond its concern. Steadfast refusal by school authorities to recognize these organizations in any way and a vital program carried on under the sponsorship of the school can keep the influence of such undemocratic groups at a minimum.

The club program, with all of its variations, is one of the richest sources for vital student experience in the high school. And like all parts of the school program, the outcome is dependent upon the guidance and stimulation it is given by the educational leaders of the school. The club program is a genuine professional responsibility of the high school principal.

STUDENT PUBLICATIONS

Student publications are now an accepted part of student life in the great majority of high schools. It is estimated that 24,000 public junior and senior high schools have some type of publication, and many schools have several. It is also estimated that funds expended annually on secondary school publications run into the millions of dollars.[10]

The functions that school publications serve in providing a means of informing the community of the work of the school and in developing morale and unifying the school perhaps account in a considerable part for their rapid development and expansion in recent decades. However, work on student publications provides rich and valuable educational experiences for the student. Spears and Lawshe list the following functions of the school paper as an aid to the school:

1. To educate the community as to the work of the school
2. To publish school news
3. To create and express school opinion
4. To capitalize the achievements of the school
5. To act as a means of unifying the school
6. To express the idealism and reflect the spirit of the school
7. To encourage and stimulate worth-while activities
8. To aid in developing right standards of conduct
9. To promote understanding of other schools
10. To provide an outlet for student suggestions for the betterment of the school
11. To develop better interschool relationships
12. To increase school spirit
13. To promote co-operation between parents and school[11]

That the educational values of work in school publications are recognized is evident in the growing number of instances in which the high school paper is a part of the school curricular program. Galen Jones, studying student activities in 269 high schools, reported in 1935 that the

---

[10] Regis Louise Boyle, "Student Publications," NASSP *Bulletin,* No. 184, February, 1952.

[11] Harold Spears and C. H. Lawshe, Jr., *High School Journalism* (New York: The Macmillan Company, 1949), p. 8.

newspaper was a classroom project in approximately 50 per cent of the schools, the yearbook in 10 per cent, and the handbook in 6 per cent.[12] Three national student press organizations, the National Scholastic Press Association, the Columbia Scholastic Press Association, and the Quill and Scroll have given leadership to and stimulated student publications.

The type of publication produced will necessarily vary from school to school as resources and needs vary. The school newspaper, the most frequent one, presumably provides the most comprehensive and varied educational experience for students in publication organizations. The newspaper may be a printed weekly newspaper characteristic of large high schools or a mimeographed paper issued occasionally by the very small high school. But whatever it is, within its limits, it should represent a carefully planned project embodying the principles of good journalism. Although the student annual may have less interest to the general public, it is of genuine concern to students and often represents a record and memorial of their years in high school. A special, enlarged issue of the newspaper has been used in many schools as a substitute for the more expensive annual. Magazines that offer a medium for the development of creative writing talents of students are a genuinely worth-while educational venture. Difficulties of financing and a more limited audience account for the relatively small number of schools that systematically sponsor such publications. The mimeographed magazine is a possibility for the school that finds it difficult to support a printed magazine. The handbook is quite often a project of the student council and is a part of the orientation program to acquaint students with the regulations, practices, and trad_ions of the school.

The administration of student publications raises its own problems for the principal. For example, the faculty sponsor must be a person trained in at least the elementary principles of journalism, for he must develop a student staff competent to take a major part of the responsibility for the actual publications. Since the program requires time, the faculty sponsor must be allowed enough in the daily schedule to carry it on. For this reason the growing practice of organizing the school newspaper as a cl ssroom project is particularly justified. If it is not undertaken is a classr m project the daily schedule should provide some time for b h sponso ud students to work on publication projects.

he role of the principal in the supervision of student publications particularly the school newspaper, requires judgment and tact. Inasmuch as the newspaper is a public relations project of particular importance, the school administrator will have a particular interest and concern in it. This concern should not extend to the point where the student newspaper becomes nothing more than a publicity vehicle for the school

[12] Jones, *op. cit.*, p. 24.

administrative office, for although such material may be appropriate publicity for the school, it should be issued in a school bulletin. Student responsibility for the publication and student interest in it will be maintained only if these young people have a real part in its direction and operation and if the materials published reflect their interests. The principal should guide and advise students, help determine policies in the selection of materials, and encourage high standards; he should not try to become the editor and rewrite man for the student paper. If the principal is not careful he may find himself accused of restricting what the students regard as the right of freedom of expression and freedom of the press. One of the chief concerns of a publication's sponsor should be to develop enough sense of responsibility in the student staff that it will exercise this right with the judgment that public welfare demands.

The matter of financing a school publication requires careful planning. Advertising can assist in providing funds, but care should be taken that it is sold on the basis of returns to the advertiser and not sought as a charitable donation to assist the school. Part of the learning experience of the student staff should be the planning of a careful budget and the administration of a sound financial plan.

Student publications provide a real opportunity for rich educational experience for students. The great amount of work involved more and more justifies the integration of this activity into the school's curricular program.

SPEECH, DRAMATIC, AND MUSICAL ACTIVITIES

In his study of a sampling of high schools in 1935 Jones found that from 75 to 80 per cent of the music activities and almost 50 per cent of the speech and dramatic activities were organized or a classroom basis.[13] The self-developmental nature of these fields of work has been recognized, and the public has given substantial support to competent work in them. Regardless of how they are classified, because their primary motivation for students is interest and because many of the activities related to their programs are carried on outside the school day, they have some of the characteristics of the extracurricular program. What is important is not whether these fields are offered for credit or scheduled entirely during the school day. Rather, it is the fact that they are recognized as regular parts of the educational program, that specially prepared teachers largely direct and teach them, and that they are scheduled as organized activities. Competent instruction is no longer expected from teachers who have not had definite preparation in these special fields. In his role as administrator, the principal must recognize the basic educational aims of the activity program and share with teachers and pu-

[13] *Ibid.*

pils the responsibility of formulating policies and outlining a developing program. Most of these general principles apply to the whole program growing up around physical education and related activities. They have also become a part of the broad educational program of the school, employ a specially prepared staff, and are thus semicurricular if not wholly curricular activities in many schools.

Some Major Responsibilities in Administering Student Activities

The scope of student activities in the high school of today is such that their administration requires definite policy, organization, and delegation of responsibilities. The time has passed when the principal can direct this program in an offhand manner as an incidental side line. The funds necessary for its operation run annually into thousands of dollars in schools of even modest size, and a large proportion of the student body and staff is involved in the program, in which the public is also keenly interested. Numerous specific problems of policy and practice vary from school to school, but the schedule, the direction and control of funds, guidance of student participation, the selection of sponsors, evaluation, and the organization of the staff to coordinate the program are common to nearly all.

Scheduling Student Activities

A measure of the actual recognition given student activities is the extent to which time is allotted for them in the school day. No particular system of time scheduling would be equally appropriate for all schools. Nor should it be assumed that all of the time for all activities should be in the regular school day any more than it should be assumed that curricular activities should not extend beyond the formal hours of school. However, if activities are genuine educational enterprises, and as such are sponsored and encouraged by the school, then they deserve enough time in the school day to maintain their essential organization and to provide for the principal types of activities.[14]

Obviously, the methods of scheduling must vary. Probably the most frequent practice provides one period in the day for the scheduling of activities, perhaps combining this period with the so-called home room hour. Thus on one day this period may be scheduled for group guidance activities, on another for clubs, on another for musical activities, and so

[14] Tompkins, *op. cit.*, pp. 19–23; and Tompkins, *The Activity Period in Public High Schools* (U.S. Office of Education, Bulletin No. 19; Washington, D.C.: Government Printing Office, 1951).

on for the different types of activities. Assembly programs can be scheduled on such an activity hour. High schools that schedule two or three lunch periods may work in the activity programs around them. For example, each student schedules his lunch so that he is free to participate in the activities he wishes to join. The excerpts from the schedule shown in Table 13 illustrate this method. Some of the major organizations

TABLE 13. EXCERPTS FROM DAILY SCHEDULE OF CLASSES, MAMARONECK (N.Y.) SENIOR HIGH SCHOOL

Periods	8:43 (1) 9:30	9:33 (2) 10:20	10:23 (3) 11:10	11:13 (4) 12:00	12:03 (5) 1:20	1:23 (6) 2:10	2:13 (7) 3:00
Francis 103-A	Eng. 42 103-A	Eng. 4 103-A	Eng. 4H 103-A	Eng. 4 103-A	MTWTh News writing F Assembly		Eng. 4 103-A
Andrews 105-A	Eng. 4 105-A	Eng. 4H 105-A	Eng. 4 105-A		MTWTh 105-A F Assembly	Eng. 4 105-A	Eng. 3H 105-A
Ludwig 207-A		Wor. his. 207-A	Wor. his. 207-A	Wor. his. 207-A	MTTh 207-A F Assembly W St. Coun.	Wor. his. 207-A	Wor. his. 207-A
Devereux 200-A: 101-B	Mech. Dr. 1 101-B	Mech. Dr. 2A 101-B		Shop Related Dr. 1	MTTh 101-B W St. Coun.	Mech. Dr. 1 101-B	Mech. Dr. 2A 101-B
Rentchle 203-A	Rep. 2 203-A	Design 1 203-A	Design 3B & Rep. 3B	Design 2 203-A		Study MTE 104-C	Rep. 1 203-A
Conklin 101-A					M Choir TTh Mixed Glee Club W Male Ens. F Assembly	Music Apprec. 101-A	Harmony 1 101-A
Wells 101-A	Voice Culture 101-A	Voice Culture 101-A			TTh Girls Glee Club 101-A	Music Apprec. 101-A	Harmony 1 101-A
Pinney					M Band Aud.		W Comb. Band 3:00 J.H.S.

are listed on this schedule by name, but minor unlisted ones also meet on various days of the week. This fifth period, which is one hour and seventeen minutes long, actually includes three lunch periods. When not at lunch a student may on different days be in various activity groups in which he has registered, or in a classroom study group. Friday is reserved for assemblies, but they can be moved to any other day of the week or to any other period of the day by interchanging days of the week or periods of the day. Obviously any successful plan must be adapted to the needs of the school. If musical activities are a regular part of the program throughout the day, they may not need to be scheduled with the other activities in this period. The number of schools that have adopted such an activity period is a testimony to its usefulness. It should be assumed that those activities with extensive programs will need to extend their program to out-of-school hours, as noted above, but the allotment of some school time gives official status to the activity and makes possible essential organization and planning.

Whatever time in the school day may be best for the activity period, actually it has been scheduled for any hour from the first period in the morning until the last in the afternoon. Although any given period may have certain advantages over other periods, there is probably no one best time for all schools. The selection of a period in a given school should be determined by the local situation. If the schedule is sufficiently flexible, the hour may be shifted on occasion to take care of particular demands. Likewise, the length of the activity period must be determined by the local school in terms of time and staff available, its belief in the importance of the program, and its administrative practices.

GUIDANCE OF STUDENTS

The various activity programs offer guidance workers in the school both an opportunity and a responsibility. They may obtain valuable insights into student behavior and problems from the observation of performance in different student organizations. The special interest programs give students the opportunity to explore their talents and interests, and the alert guidance counselor will assist them in evaluating their experience and in planning for further participation. The situations in which students perform in student organizations are ordinarily more free and undirected than in the classroom; consequently, the experienced sponsor and counselor can gain understandings of a particular student that might escape observation in the more or less artificial classroom situation.

Its sponsorship of an activity program imposes on the school the responsibility of aiding students in their selection of and participation in different activities. Numerous studies as well as casual observation indicate that means of controlling, or at least directing, the amount and kind of student participation in activities is essential.[15] Completely undirected student participation results in a relatively few students being active in many organizations, a small group controlling and running the student organizations while the large majority of students are inactive

---

[15] Harold C. Hand, *How to Conduct the Participation in Extra-Class Activities Study* (Circular Series A, No. 51, Illinois Secondary School Curriculum Program, Bulletin No. 5; Springfield: State Superintendent of Public Instruction, 1949).

or participate in only a nominal manner. Such a situation can be handled in two radically different ways: regulations can be avoided, but specific counseling and guidance can be undertaken with individual students to encourage those who are inactive and to restrain those who may be considered overactive; or participation of all students may be regulated and the amount of participation by any one person may be limited. Although the guidance approach is the desirable goal, a combination of the two approaches is probably the more effective.

Regulations that require participation are questionable, for the vitality of student organizations lies in the voluntary participation of the students. Finally, the individual personality of each student should be respected. Individual temperaments and needs vary, and to assume the need of or desire for an equal degree of participation in all students overlooks a fundamental fact. However, as student activities are stimulated, as the program is broadened, varied, and made available to all, student participation can be naturally encouraged to the point where the large majority have a part in activities. Regulations that limit the number and type of activities in which any one student may participate can be justified on the basis of the welfare of that student. Often these regulations protect the popular and able student from the excessive load that fellow students will freely delegate to him. However, regulations limiting participation should be broad and flexible. Provisions that tie scholarship closely to permission to enter activities are of doubtful value. If student activities have educational merit and are a means of stimulating student interest in school and vitalizing the curriculum, then to deny these privileges to the poor student hardly makes sense. Where poor scholarship is obviously the result of excessive time devoted to student organizations, controls are justified. The use of point systems that attach numerical weights to memberships and to certain offices in order to set a maximum activity load and the classification of membership and minor and major offices, with a maximum load in terms of combinations, are examples of flexible systems that many schools have used effectively. The high school principal must study the records of the individual students to ascertain the degree and extent of participation in his school. Approaching the problem from the guidance standpoint, he should encourage flexible regulations growing out of the local situation.

THE ACTIVITY FUNDS

The management and the custody of activity funds require system and organization. The time is past when these funds can be kept in a box in the principal's office, the financial records entered on a few loose sheets of paper. The literature presenting specific details for the administration of activity funds is fairly extensive,[16] but the dominant theme is the provision of genuine educational experiences for the students through careful business practices. The principal's responsibilities in connection with student activity funds are the subject of a section of Chapter 21.

Organizing for Supervision of Student Activities

How it will organize its staff to supervise student activities is largely a matter for the individual school to decide in terms of its general organization and needs. In the small high school, the principal will naturally be the director of the program, working with the sponsors of the various organizations and the student representatives. In the larger school, a director of student activities may be assisted by a faculty committee working with student council representatives on general policies and practices. Quite often members of guidance personnel assume special responsibilities in the supervision of the activity program, a sound practice. Basically, administrative organization in this area should follow the general principles of any good school administrative organization: it should provide for the democratic consideration of policy and should delegate authority and responsibility where such delegation is needed.

EVALUATION

Evaluation of the activity program should be continuous, and should include student as well as faculty appraisal. One function of the student council can well be that of appraising certain aspects of student organizations particularly with reference to the reactions of the student body. This is also a responsibility of any faculty policy committee or director of activities.

If evaluation is to mean anything, it must be based upon the measurement of the growth of the students toward accepted goals. But the objectives of student activities are broad and varied, and many aspects of growth are too elusive to measure; hence precise evaluation in this field is difficult. Individual student records containing measures and judgments of development in attitudes, interests, and abilities are one means of appraising activities. Polls and measures of student opinion reveal what students think of the merits of different organizations. The considered opinions of a group of interested sponsors also have value.

An indirect measure is the appraisal of the practices and program of specific activities. Such a measure is based upon the presumably valid as-

---

[16] John M. Trytton, and Walter E. Hess, "Extra-Curricular Activity Funds," NASSP *Bulletin*, No. 184, (February, 1952), pp. 204–229.

sumption that a student organization may have certain observable characteristics which indicate that it will make a worth-while contribution to the education of students belonging to it.

The evaluation criteria of the various accrediting associations can be used by a school staff wishing to appraise its school program. These and other studies may also prove to be a valuable learning experience for the staff.[17]

The following brief outline of a preliminary survey may provide the basis for an expanded evaluation that can be developed by any staff.[18]

ORGANIZATION AND ADMINISTATION OF STUDENTS' ACTIVITY PROGRAMS

TENTATIVE CRITERIA FOR EVALUATION

Purpose: There should be evidence of purpose and plan in the total program of activities.

—— a. The program is an outgrowth of interests promoted by students with faculty participation.
—— b. The program is largely suggested and promoted by the faculty.
—— c. The program is largely the result of chance growth.

—— a. The organizations are chartered only after the activities and purposes have been defined.
—— b. Some of the organizations have defined purposes and recognized activities.
—— c. Organizations appear to exist largely for the sake of organization.

—— a. All organizations are systematically subject to appraisal by faculty and appropriate student groups.
—— b. Major activities are subject to occasional review.
—— c. No consistent appraisal of any activities.

Admission: Qualifications for admission into each activity should be fully presented and defined in terms of interest and appropriate competence.

—— a. Each organization as a part of its charter has a defined and publicly known criterion for admission.
—— b. Admission requirements are generally known by students although not formally adopted.
—— c. No consistent policy.

[17] See Cooperative Study of Secondary School Standards, *Evaluative Criteria* (rev. ed.; Washington, D.C.: American Council on Education, 1950) Sec. E; and Illinois Secondary School Curriculum Program, *What Do You Think about Our Schools' Extra-Class Activities Program?* (Consensus Study No. 1, Inventory A; Springfield: State Superintendent of Public Instruction, 1951).

[18] Developed by a class committee in extraclass activities at Teachers College, Columbia University, New York.

—— a. All restrictive admission requirements are based upon interest and competence in the specific activity which the organization promotes.

—— b. Unrelated requirements (e.g., scholarship for recreational activities) are specified.

—— c. No recognized policy. Closed organizations permitted.

—— a. Membership in practically all activities does not entail expensive dues, insignia and social expenses.

—— b. Very few activities require special expenses.

—— c. The major activities of school entail genuine financial expenses.

Administration: The administrative policies of the student activities are determined by democratic processes.

A. Budget
—— a. A representative student group participates in the formulation of the activities budget.
—— b. Students are occasionally consulted on the activities budget.
—— c. Activities budget is determined by the principal.

B. Club Charters
—— a. New clubs may be chartered by the school council.
—— b. New clubs may be chartered with the approval of the faculty.
—— c. New clubs may be chartered with the approval of the principal.

C. Halls, Cafeteria, etc.
—— a. The regulations are determined by the school council.
—— b. Regulations are determined by faculty committee.
—— c. Regulations are determined by the principal.

School Council: Adequate provisions should be made for pupil participation in school government.

A. Types of Councils
—— a. The school has a school council with clearly defined authority and responsibilities.
—— b. The principal calls student groups together when he feels they can serve a purpose.
—— c. The school has no organization for student participation.

B. Method of Representation
—— a. All student groups and faculty are represented by democratic processes.
—— b. Student representatives are elected by the students but nominated by the principal or faculty.
—— c. Student representatives are appointed by principal or faculty.

C. Activities of the Council
—— a. The school council suggests and undertakes activities for the general welfare of the school.

—— b. The school council undertakes only activities suggested by the principal or faculty.

—— c. The school council does not carry on any real activities.

Scope and Variety: There should be sufficient activities of a varied nature to meet the interests of a heterogeneous student body.

—— a. The program provides activities to meet student interests in school council, games, recreation and social activities, publications, music, dramatics, and many special interests or hobbies.

—— b. The program provides reasonably extensive opportunities in several major activities such as athletics, music and dramatics.

—— c. Only one or two major types of activities are functioning.

—— a. There are sufficient club offerings to permit all students wishing to do so to join some group.

—— b. Club opportunities are available to the more active faction of the student body.

—— c. Club opportunities are available for only a few students.

Participation: An effective activities program should secure the voluntary participation of a high percentage of the students.

—— a. 70% to 100% of boys participate.

—— b. 40% to 70% of boys participate.

—— c. Less than 40%.

—— a. Students attend clubs regularly of their own volition and anticipate each meeting.

—— b. Members must be urged to attend meetings.

—— c. Attendance is poor and irregular.

Accounting: Provision should be made for a systematic accounting of all monies of the activities program with appropriate responsibilities delegated to students.

—— a. All funds are deposited in a central accounting system.

—— b. If an activity wishes, its money can be deposited in a central accounting system; otherwise, the activity handles its own accounts.

—— c. No systematic accounting; each activity is responsible for its accounts.

—— a. The person who handles the central accounting system is bonded, and the funds are insured against thefts.

—— b. The person who handles the central accounting system is bonded.

—— c. No protection is carried on the activities funds.

—— a. Monthly and annual reports are required of each activity with an annual audit.

—— b. Annual reports are required of each activity.

—— c. No reports are required.

—— a. A faculty member assisted by students handles the activity funds.

—— b. A faculty member handles the activity funds.

—— c. Students alone handle the activity funds.

Evaluating and Continuous Study: There should be a continuous cooperative program of study and evaluation.

—— a. A special committee of students and faculty evaluates the activities program at least once each year.

—— b. Evaluation is done sporadically when principal suggests it.

—— c. No real evaluation is ever done.

—— a. There is evidence of pupil growth in the tendency to accept responsibility to an extent markedly greater than they did before experience in the activity.

—— b. Students recognize problems but are hesitant to assume leadership.

—— c. Students are largely unchanged.

Summary

The student activity program has developed to the place where it is accepted as a fundamental part of the educational program. This recognition is and always should be based upon the genuine educational experiences the activities provide students. They exist to serve the students and not the school.

The growth of activity programs has created numerous fields that require trained and competent leadership from the school staff. The basic distinction between curricular and extracurricular activities is gradually disappearing. If activities are actively sponsored by the school and are operated in part in the school day, they become a part of the educational program regardless of whether they are formally classified as curricular or extracurricular.

The same basic policies of good administration apply to the activity program that apply to other areas in the school's program. The goals, too, are the same: democratic education, student development, and efficient operation. Much of value to the educational program has entered it through the medium of student organizations. As long as the activity program is flexible and dynamic, student organizations will continue to make their unique contribution to American secondary education.

Some Points to Consider

1. Make a study of the student activity program of a school you know to decide to what extent each of the activities included can be justified in terms of the guiding principles set forth in this chapter.

2. Is the supervision of an activity by the school likely to make it less appealing to students than if it were not so supervised? How can a school avoid this possibility?

3. What do you think are some of the important strengths and weaknesses of activity sponsors?

4. Does a good activity sponsor over a period of a few years become a more or less indispensable person? How can he work to build a proper relationship to the group with which he works?

5. Outline a talk to parents in which you show what the values of student activities are and how they are realized in a school with which you are familiar.

6. Should students have more responsibility in the handling of student funds than is typically the case? What good arguments for and against increasing the degree of responsibility can you make?

7. Use the evaluation plan included in this chapter to evaluate a student activity program that you know or can get permission to study.

Further Reading

Cooperative Study of Secondary School Standards. *Evaluative Criteria.* Rev. ed.; Washington, D.C.: National Education Association, 1950, Sec. E, p. 191.

Educational Policies Commission. *Learning the Ways of Democracy.* Washington, D.C.: National Education Association, 1940.

———. *The Purposes of Education in American Democracy.* Washington, D.C.: National Education Association, 1938.

———. *School Athletics.* Washington, D.C.: National Education Association, 1954.

Fedder, Ruth. *Guiding Homeroom and Club Activities.* New York: McGraw-Hill Book Co., Inc., 1949.

Fretwell, E. K. *Extra-Curricular Activities in Secondary Schools.* Boston: Houghton Mifflin Company, 1931.

Jones, Galen. *Extra-Curricular Activities in Relation to the Curriculum.* New York: Bureau of Publications, Teachers College, Columbia University, 1935.

McKown, Harry C. *Extra-Curricular Activities.* 3rd ed.; New York: The Macmillan Company, 1952.

———. *The Student Council.* New York: McGraw-Hill Book Co., Inc., 1944.

National Association of Secondary School Principals. "Student Activities in the Secondary School," *Bulletin,* No. 119, January, 1944.

———. "Student Council Handbook," *Bulletin,* No. 89, March, 1940.

———. "Student Council Handbook," *Bulletin,* No. 144, October, 1947.

———. "The Student Council at Work," *Bulletin,* No. 132, October, 1945.

———. "The Student Council in the Secondary School," *Bulletin,* No. 124, October, 1944.

———. "Vitalizing Student Activities in the Secondary Schools," *Bulletin,* No. 102, December, 1941; and *Bulletin,* No. 184, February, 1952.

Scott, Harry A. *Competitive Sports in Schools and Colleges.* New York: Harper & Brothers, 1951.

Spears, Harold, and C. H. Lawshe, Jr. *High School Journalism.* New York: The Macmillan Company, 1949.

Strang, Ruth. *Educational Guidance.* New York: The Macmillan Company, 1947.

————. *Group Activities in College and Secondary School.* New York: Harper & Brothers, 1941.

Tompkins, Ellsworth. *Extraclass Activities for All Pupils.* U.S. Office of Education, Bulletin No. 4; Washington, D.C.: Government Printing Office, 1950.

————. *The Activity Period in Public High Schools.* U.S. Office of Education, Bulletin No. 19; Washington, D.C.: Government Printing Office, 1951.

Chapter 12

CONVENTIONAL SCHEDULE MAKING

TRADITIONAL IDEAS ABOUT the length of the school day and school year, the division of the former into six, seven, or eight short periods, and the division of the latter into two semesters of approximately four and one half months are the natural and logical outgrowths of attempting to fit certain prevailing theories of secondary education into existing conditions. Change these theories and conditions, and the old prescriptions about education are no longer as satisfactory as they once were. We are in the midst of such changes now, and as a result there is more confusion in the minds of the profession about these particular administrative practices than ever before. Consequently, this and the following chapter will attempt, first, to provide the necessary information about daily schedule making according to traditional practice, and then to illustrate and explain some of the newer trends and practices that shifts in educational concepts and in living conditions have made necessary and desirable.

The Origins of Conventional
Daily Schedule Practices

As long as we were almost unanimous in conceiving of education as mastery of the content of certain fields of knowledge, the principal function of the teacher was to check pupils daily to discover whether each one had mastered the last assignment. The daily re-citation periods for each subject had to be long enough to enable the teacher to make this check and to drill pupils further in the content being covered. No doubt in the past most teachers of any subject would have been glad to have a much longer period than was provided by the school, but longer periods were impossible as long as it was generally agreed that each pupil should distribute his daily study time over several fields of equally important knowledge. The division of the school day into several periods of equal length, with one to be devoted to each field of knowledge being studied by each pupil, was a natural—not to say diplomatic—solution to the problem.

As a school improved its program of secondary education it introduced more fields of knowledge into its offering and divided each field into more and more subjects. As this happened, the number of subjects usually required of pupils increased, and since under prevailing conditions the day generally could not be extended, the number of periods in the daily schedule became more numerous and consequently shorter. And so whereas at one time in what was regarded as a poor high school— unable to offer many subjects—a pupil might have a daily schedule of four subjects with some time at school for study, as schools became better— able to offer more and more subjects—a pupil's day was expected to be more nearly filled up with recitations. Home study therefore became not only desirable but absolutely necessary. When the number of subjects reached the point where it was hardly possible for each pupil to recite on each subject daily, the split week was introduced, thus making it possible to have two subjects at one period, one to be recited on twice a week and one three times each week.

MAKING THE DAILY SCHEDULE FIT THIS KIND
OF IMPROVED EDUCATIONAL PROGRAM

Since these changes took place during a prolonged period of rapid expansion of high schools and during a period when many high schools were subject to little effective control by state departments of education or by colleges, a great variety of local practices with respect to the length of daily periods, the length of the school day and year, the number of subjects to be carried at one time by any pupil, and graduation requirements came into existence.

The principal factor in deciding what any particular high school did about these matters was the number of teachers it was able to employ in proportion to its size. If its community was unable or unwilling to provide the school with enough money to employ a relatively large staff of teachers, its program of necessity tended to cover fewer of the fields of knowledge or to offer fewer courses in some of them. It therefore made some of the following adjustments in the organization and administration of its program: (1) it offered only a two- or three-year course leading to graduation; (2) it provided for a shorter school year; (3) it reduced the number of subjects carried by pupils at one time; (4) it increased the fraction of the school day used for study; (5) it increased the number of different subjects taught daily by any one teacher; or (6) it adjusted the number and length of daily periods as much as it could in the light of the number of subjects taught daily by each teacher and the length of the school's day. The net effect of these adjustments was that daily periods tended to be shorter and more numerous, teachers' daily schedules heavier in terms of the number of subjects and classes taught, and pupils' daily and weekly schedules heavier in terms of the number of subjects carried at any one time. The length of the school day, the length of the school year, and the length of the courses leading to graduation were less subject to administrative adjustment, since they were influenced by conditions less under the control of the local schools. The long-time pressure, however, was toward extension of all three of these also. All these pressures prevailed because the accepted concept of a good high school program and of a good high school education for youth tended to be measured in terms of the number of fields of knowledge pupils had had some opportunity to master. What we see today in conventional high school scheduling practices are the current results of the continuing effects of this concept operating under different out-of-school conditions and under more regulation than existed in the last half of the preceding century. What we see in less conventional high schools today are practices born of another concept of secondary education contending with the practices of an older and well-entrenched concept.

Changing Conditions and Concepts of the Present Century

Since about 1900, the high school, along with all other institutions and aspects of our society, has been subject to increased pressures arising from a number of changes and shifts in social and economic conditions. More recently, the high school has also felt the effects of the shift in the concept of its function that has accompanied the popularization of secondary education in this country. Some of these pressures have been influential in changing practices connected with school schedules and calendars.

THE EFFECTS OF STANDARDIZATION

The chaotic conditions that developed during the period of the extremely rapid expansion of the American high school led interested agencies to try to introduce some order into the situation. This movement, led by the colleges and approved by state departments of education, was also participated in by the high schools. It resulted in the establishment of the regional accrediting agencies, which schools and colleges voluntarily joined. These agencies have had many effects upon the high schools, some of which are of doubtful value; but whether or not we approve of all the work of these associations, their motives—to improve high school organization and working relationships—are not so easily questioned.

In this chapter we are concerned only with the actions of these agencies as they influenced practice in daily schedule making, the length of the school period, and the length of the school day and the school year.

These effects grew out of attempts on the part of these associations to set up standards that a good high school should use if its graduates were to be able to enter and succeed in college. The fact that these standards were of little value in producing the desired success in college has nothing to do with how they affected high schools at that time. These early standards were mostly "quantitative" in nature, as the North Central Association of Schools and Colleges admitted when it later was attempting to develop "qualitative" standards. Since they were quantitative they dealt with time and its use by the school. The associations, at least in their earlier days during which the quantitative standards were developed, accepted the concept of the educational program that stresses the covering of the important fields of knowledge. Consequently, their standards tended to be developed in terms of minutes, periods, weeks, and years to be devoted to the study of various parts of those fields of knowledge that were considered to be part of a good college preparatory curriculum in high school. The standards were in terms of units and credits, which were only a thin disguise for the amount of time required to be spent in the study of certain subjects. Thus the basic standard unit of credit was defined in terms of the equivalent of a period of about forty-five minutes a day, five times a week, for a school year.

THE SCHOOL DAY

Although school authorities were able to decide these matters rather independently and thus to begin standardizing the length and number of periods to be devoted by pupils to the study of each subject, they were not in such an independent position on matters that affected the length of the school day and the school year. Yet an exact quantitative unit not only had to prescribe the minutes a day to be spent in the study of each subject but also had to fix the number of weeks, which in turn tended to set a standard school year. The length of the school day was more indirectly but still firmly influenced both by the establishment of the desired length of period and by the number of subjects to be completed each year for college entrance. Out-of-school conditions of life entered here, however, to set limits to what the school might do. Farm and village life and the relatively low level of economic life made the part-time labor of school children before and after school highly desirable and even necessary if the children of a family were to stay in school at all. Consequently, the trend at the high school level was to shorten the conventional elementary school day of nine to four and to close the high school doors earlier in the afternoon. Two other factors were present: colleges did most of their classwork in the mornings and early afternoons, and overworked high school teachers tended to resist long afternoon sessions. The more recent trend to substitute a short lunch period at noon for the hour or hour and a half dismissal for dinner at noon, together with the omission of the quarter-hour morning and afternoon recesses saved some time during the school day and offered an excuse, if not a reason, for an earlier afternoon dismissal. The result of the play of all these factors was to move forward a net school day of about six clock hours. In some states this net six-hour school day has become the law and determines the teacher's day as well as what constitutes full-time attendance of pupils.

This school day of approximately six clock hours was acceptable to school administrators as well as to teachers. It divided conveniently into eight periods, each grossing 45 minutes, which in turn could be divided into morning and afternoon sessions of four periods each. Two double laboratory periods could be held in each session. School sessions starting at nine o'clock and having an hour for a noon dinner were over at four in the afternoon. By starting a half hour earlier and by introducing a half-hour lunch period, the school could close at three in the afternoon. By shaving the length of the periods a few minutes each, where state departments of education and the accrediting associations permitted, further adjustments could be made to local situations demanding a shorter day. Pupils could attend from four to eight periods, depending on the number of subjects carried and the number of double laboratory periods they required. In some schools where crowded conditions require half-day sessions for each pupil, the period is cut to as little as 37 minutes, which, with an early start and a late closing, accounts for two "school" days in nine clock hours. For a seven-period day, periods netting 45 minutes and longer passing periods were used. The chief disadvantage of the seven-period day lay in the fact that it reduced the number of double laboratory periods in a teacher's schedule from four to three, but as the practice of making six periods of teaching the maximum teaching day was introduced, this reduction from four to three was a less serious matter. A school day of less than six clock hours, with a resulting later start or earlier closing, could thus be obtained if desired. The six-period day permitted an even longer period and became popular when the supervised-study idea was in favor. Under this plan, double laboratory periods could be abandoned, since five 60-minute periods meant 300 minutes of instruction weekly, whereas two double and three single 45-minute periods provided only 225 minutes of instruction weekly. Thus in a school day of only six periods it was still possible for any pupil to carry as many as six subjects daily, and as the difficulties of supervising larger and larger study halls increased, the tendency was to encourage pupils to undertake a program that tended to keep them in classrooms throughout the day. These various adjustments thus made it possible for schools to do what colleges expected of them within a school day that was as long as out-of-school conditions would support.

THE LENGTHENING SCHOOL YEAR

Out-of-school influences have also helped determine the length of the school year. How much money the district could raise for the support of high school education was reflected not only in the amount of salary paid teachers each month but also in the length of the school year. Since some districts were financially more able or more willing to tax themselves for high school education than others, the length of the school year varied from district to district. The seasonal nature of the principal industry of an area also affected the length of the school year. Where that industry was agriculture, the school could count on farm boys to troop irregularly into school in the fall as the plowing, seeding, and corn-husking was finished, and to drop out in the spring as moderating weather permitted the resumption of farm work. No matter what it might desire to do about the length of the school year, the school was under pressure to open and close each year in accordance with the stern necessities of the community's economic life. Schools exist even today that have not only the regular summer vacation but also a "cotton" vacation during the year to permit pupils to pick cotton. The length of the school year has been extended as the economic level of the average family has risen and the labor of children has become correspondingly less necessary; as the average number of children in each family has decreased and the available family resources for each child have therefore increased; as the principal occupation of the country has shifted from agriculture to trade and industry and the labor of children has therefore become not only less necessary but even undesirable; as the majority of our people have begun to live in urban rather than in rural homes and the out-of-school life of children has therefore become a more difficult problem for parents; and as the economic and social value of extended education has become more apparent and more parents have therefore become increasingly eager for their children to stay in school longer. The shift from a short school year of about seven months of irregular attendance toward a school year covering most of ten months of fairly regular attendance is one of the sociological bench marks of American life by which we can gauge the progress of a people, committed to a democratic philosophy and endowed with a land of phenomenal productivity, toward the realization of their aspirations for a fuller, richer life for all.

NEW WINE IN OLD BOTTLES

There are still men and women in the high school profession whose concept of the goal of secondary education is the mastery of as much of the many fields of knowledge as is possible and who are confident that the attainment of this immediate goal of mastery automatically insures the attainment of the ultimate goals of character, citizenship, leisure time interests, health, and home membership. These educators are easily satisfied with the little cubicles of time and space that a conventional administration of the school's daily and yearly program provides. But others in the teaching profession begin to be concerned chiefly with the growth and development of boys and girls into young Americans who must be better able to manage in their time and world than their elders have been in theirs. When these more perceptive members of the teaching profession begin to realize that if boys and girls are to grow and develop they must analyze, discuss, and study aspects of the problems of present-day living appropriate to their ages, and must become responsible participants in helping to meet some of the problem situations they encounter in their own personal, school, and community life, then these teachers become dissatisfied with the paper walls of time and space by which tradition has divided the school day and has separated the school from the active life of the world about it. Their classes begin figuratively and literally to break out of the classrooms; the short daily periods seem to make an obstacle race out of the day's work; the essential educational activities of the school continue after the close of the official school day; and projects, activities, and interests generated by the work of the school year cannot well be put into cold storage for the summer just because, according to custom, school is supposed to be "out." And so it is that we are now seeing some protests against the conventional organization of the school's daily and yearly program and find a growing demand for more appropriate administrative arrangements.

The professionally educated school administrator has not tried to put the strong wine of new educational ideas and concepts into old administrative bottles. Instead, he has tried to help devise the new plans, arrangements, relationships, and forms that the new ideas and concepts require if their full force is to be readily available for the improvement of American secondary education. Some of our most modern high schools are reconsidering the whole problem of their organization and use of time. A restructuring would affect the number and length of periods, extend the length of the recognized school day to cover those activities of the school that have spilled over into the "afterschool" periods, and supplement the "regular" school year by a summer program of a rich and varied sort attracting large numbers of otherwise too idle youth. Each of these changes will be elaborated upon in the following chapter. But since many high schools operate upon a subject-schedule type of daily program, and since young high school principals usually begin their careers in school communities where they must show their competence to do the conventional things well, in order to build the confidence that will permit them to introduce innovations in established practices, the next section of this chapter deals with conventional daily schedule making in a subject-organized high school program.

Development of the Conventional Daily Schedule

Most experienced principals are familiar with the standard techniques used in scheduling the conventional subject-organized programs, and many have worked out special adaptations of those they have found useful in their schools. Consequently, this section will probably be of most value to students of education who have not had experience in high school administration, and it will therefore be written with their needs in mind.

PURPOSE AND PLANS

The perfect daily schedule of classes makes it possible for each pupil to have exactly the program that he, his parents, and the school think he should have. Other criteria of success in schedule making include (1) a program for each teacher that assigns to him subjects he feels best qualified to teach; (2) as small a number of different subject fields assigned to each teacher as is possible; (3) a teaching load for each teacher about equal to that of others in terms of the number of pupils taught each day or week; (4) classes as small as the school can provide and as nearly equal in size as possible; and (5) a suitable room for each class—of sufficient size and with proper equipment.

To be able to furnish a high school with a schedule that will meet these tests requires not only considerable planning but planning done in time so that it can be checked and changed as necessary well before the opening of the school year. Failures in schedule making show up at such points as (1) too many large and small classes; (2) poor subject assignments for teachers; (3) poor room usage; (4) unequal pupil loads for teachers; (5) many conflicts between subjects that pupils want or have to take; and, as a result, (6) many changes in registrations and in the schedule itself after the opening of the school year. All of this contributes to a bad start, a waste of time for everyone at the opening of school, and a general disorganization that shows itself in bad feeling between pupils and teachers, among teachers, and between them and the principal.

By speaking of a good start on the year's work, in contrast to a bad one, it is not the intention to imply that no changes or adjustments in pupils' registrations or in the schedule itself, after the opening of school, will ever be necessary or permitted. Changes are bound to occur during the summer months that make it necessary for the school to initiate changes and desirable for the pupils to request them. The schedule that was perfect in May may not be perfect in September, and to "freeze" it as of May may deny in September the very principles of good schedule construction by which one was guided in May. Some principals pride themselves on the fact that they did their work so well in the spring that no changes in schedule or registration are required or permitted in the fall. This is false sense of efficiency and produces a rigidity in the program situation that denies the educational opportunities the schedule was supposed to provide. Some flexibility is a part of a good start on the year's work, but if it means that for two or three weeks pupils are continually changing subjects, hours, and teachers, and that teachers' programs are being frequently reassigned, then flexibility has degenerated into chaos. In between rigidity and chaos is a point that marks a normal start on a year's work, and if a principal's work on a schedule permits this he may consider that he has done a good job.

SOME PRINCIPAL PROBLEMS

With this purpose and with these criteria in mind, the schedule maker will find that in a typical situation he faces several of these important problems:

Providing the most appropriate assignment for each teacher. With the number of subjects to be taught in a school and with the various patterns of teacher preparation that prevail in most high schools, it is often difficult to fit these to each other satisfactorily. Teachers ought not to teach in more than two departments nor have more than three different daily preparations, but in most small schools both of these ideals are generally violated of necessity, and in many larger schools they are occasionally violated for reasons of necessity or convenience. The situation with respect to teacher assignments for the schools of a typical state is shown by Stephen Romine in an article in the *School Review*. His study shows that only about 53 per cent of the teachers are assigned to one field, 33 per cent to two fields, and 14 per cent to more than two fields.[1] The basic principle is to assign to each subject the best-prepared faculty member available, with as appropriate and as equitable a teaching load for each teacher as is possible. The needs of students outweigh the convenience of faculty members. Consultations with the members of the faculty, so that they have an opportunity to see what the problem is and to help solve it, usually result in their seeing that the fairest assignments possible are being made and in their willing acceptance of these assignments.

Ascertaining the needed number of classes in each subject. In an ordinary situation the number of classes in each subject will tend to be the same as the preceding year. Pupils' requirements and choices one

[1] Stephen Romine, "Subject Combinations and Teaching Loads in Secondary Schools," *School Review*, 57, No. 10 (December, 1949), 551.

year in a given school will be about what they were the year before. But if the school is changing in size, if graduation requirements are changed, or if subjects are added or dropped from the school's offering, corresponding changes in the number of classes to be provided in the affected subjects will need to be anticipated.

Eliminating conflicts between subjects required of or desired by any pupil. The good schedule must make it possible for each pupil to take the required subjects, and ought to make it possible for him to take the electives he desires and that have been approved by his parents and the school as appropriate for him. In a large school where there are likely to be several classes of practically all subjects, conflicts between subjects do not present much of a problem. For instance, if in a large school every subject were taught at every period there would not be any chance of conflict between any subjects required of or desired by any pupil. But in most schools conflicts are always likely, and one of the chief problems is to prevent them if it is at all possible.

Providing the best room utilization. In effect this is another type of conflict. In this case the conflict is between two or more classes, each of which needs the same room or same type of room when the number of such rooms in any building is obviously limited. For instance, if there is but one physical science laboratory, chemistry and physics ought to be so scheduled that each class may have access to this room. To force one into a makeshift laboratory situation while leaving the laboratory unoccupied at another period of the day would show poor class scheduling which resulted in poor room utlization.

Equalizing class sizes. This problem arises chiefly when two or more classes of any subject are required in order to accommodate the number of pupils registering for it. If the number of registrants pushes beyond the maximum number desirable for one class, a decision has to be made as to whether to create the second class. These borderline sizes—a few too many registrants for one class but hardly enough for two—have to be settled in terms of the whole school schedule. If a class promises to be larger than desired, but not too large to be accommodated in a suitable classroom, the schedule maker has to consider what effect on the whole schedule the offering of a second class in this subject will have. If these effects seem to him worse than having an oversized class, then he chooses the latter. If not, he creates a second class. In this case, and in all other cases where two or more classes are clearly called for, he needs to schedule each class so that the registration will be about evenly divided between or among them. If one of these classes conflicts with a popular elective or with a subject required of many pupils, and the other one does not, he may expect the latter class to fill quickly and easily and therefore threaten to become too large while the former threatens to be too small.

If this situation is anticipated in the schedule, these classes will be well within the range of the middle 50 per cent of class size and thus result in classes of about equal size and also in fairly equal pupil loads for the teachers.

THE ORDER OF EVENTS

In schools with an enrollment of from about two hundred to two thousand, the order in which the principal decisions or operations need to to be carried out will usually be as indicated below. The situations in very small and in very large schools will be commented upon later.

1. Decide upon changes, if any, that are to be made in the school's offering. Have decisions by the legislature, the state's department of education, the accrediting agencies, the colleges, or the local board of education increased or decreased the required subjects or made desirable the inclusion or the exclusion of any subject? What subjects, if any, not previously offered but which the school is or could be prepared to teach, would pupils and their parents like to see included? What subjects, if any, would they like to see omitted, if necessary, in order that the new ones may be added? An informal opinion poll will help show what the situation is in this respect. With these questions answered, the schedule maker can decide what the subject offering for the next school year will be. Changes and additions or omissions should be approved by the super-intendent and the board of education and discussed with the faculty before being publicly announced as official.

2. Acquaint pupils and, through them, their parents with the official program offering for next year, with what is required of all in each year in each of the school's curriculums, and with what the individual student may elect in any year in each curriculum. Then secure his subject choices as approved by his parents and his home room teacher or other faculty adviser. This information about the school's offering should be furnished each pupil so that it may be studied at school and taken home for consultation. In the home rooms or elsewhere around the school the schedule should be a subject of study; a pupil's past choice of curriculum should be reviewed; success with work in that curriculum should be considered and necessary changes should be made in the light of the pupil's previous performance or in the light of changes in his plans for the future. Furthermore, the pupil should understand the range of elective offerings so that his choice will be an intelligent one. When he has the possibilities well in mind, he should take the material home with a choice-of-subjects blank to be filled out by him and returned to the school with his own and his parents' signatures. Parents who want more information should have the opportunity to obtain it. All of this process should be a matter of educational guidance and should be used by the school as a means of

informing parents about its work as well as a means through which the school learns the reactions of parents to its educational offering.

3. Tabulate the information on these choice-of-subjects blanks to show the number of pupils desiring to register in each subject. This information can be tabulated so as to show also the number of boys and girls, the numbers in each school year, and the numbers in each curriculum desiring to register in each subject. This tabulation can be done on a decentralized basis in home room or in classroom and summarized in the principal's office, or it can be done entirely in this office, the amount of help available in the office being taken into account. If the process is decentralized, part of the work can be done by pupils without requiring so much time of anyone as to approach exploitation. By dividing the total registration in each subject, as shown on this tabulation, by the desired class size, the number of classes in each subject can be determined.

4. Determine the teaching staff needed to handle next year's requested program. Ordinarily the number of classes in each subject will tend to approximate the number needed last year. In this case the present teaching staff will be as well able to care for next year's teaching as it is to handle the current program. If there are wide variations between the number of classes needed in any subject, when compared to those of the present year, the possibilities of meeting next year's needs with the present teaching staff have to be examined. If a need for fewer or more teachers or for teachers with different qualifications should be indicated by this examination, the budget may be affected. This fact alone shows that the scheduling process must be started early enough to meet the dates when budget information for next year is required from the principal by the superintendent of schools. New supplies and equipment may also be unexpected drains on the budget.

5. Make a conflict sheet to determine what subjects cannot be scheduled at any given period if pupils' subject choices are to be respected. A conflict sheet is usually made by listing at the top and in the left margin of a crosshatched sheet of paper the names of subjects in which the registrations show that only one or two classes will be needed. The order at the left and across the top should be the same. Other subjects can be disregarded, since the chance of conflict is reduced as three or more classes of each are needed. By tallying in each square the number registering in any one of these subjects who also want to register in any other one of these, a picture of the number of conflicts likely to develop can be secured. For example, if a pupil has listed on his choice-of-subjects blank physics and Spanish 3, a tally would be placed in the square opposite physics in the left-hand column list and under Spanish 3 in the list across the top of the sheet. Thus it is indicated that this student will have a conflict if these two subjects are scheduled at the same hour.

The number of tallies for any subject in the left-hand margin that appear under any subject at the top of the page shows how important it is for these two subjects not to conflict. The more tallies in any square, the more essential it is to schedule these two subjects at different periods. If two classes of one subject are to be offered, a few conflicts with a single-section subject are not so serious, for these can be cared for in one or the other sections of the subject for which two classes are required.

6. Prepare a tentative schedule. Make a schedule form on a large sheet of paper by ruling it like a checkerboard. Place the names of the teachers across the top and the numbers of the day's periods down the left side. These two can be reversed, but since during the schedule-making process this sheet will be more frequently consulted to see what is offered at a given period than what is offered by a given teacher, and since we read more easily from left to right than up and down, putting the period numbers down the left side is suggested. Place under each teacher's name the number of the room he uses if the same one all day. If he does not, place the room numbers under each of his subjects when they are assigned as called for below. Consult the conflict sheet and the tabulation of information from the choice-of-subjects blanks with special reference to the subjects in which only a *single* class will be needed. Place the name of each of these singles under the name of the teacher who is to teach it and at a period that does not produce a conflict for any student with any other single-class subject. If any teacher is required to perform any nonteaching duty at a certain period, spot it at the proper period because to all intents it is another single. If there are but a few singles, the whole matter can be settled by placing each one at a different period. If there are too many of these singles to make this easy solution possible, then the conflict sheet will show how they can be arranged in the best possible manner. Even so, it may be impossible to schedule the singles so that every student's choice is provided for. In this case a decision must be made as to whether to create two classes of these choices where conflict arises. The decision is based on whether the school can afford it or whether such an addition requires other changes in the schedule that create more problems than they solve. If the decision is in favor of offering it as a single, then some students must make another subject choice, and to that degree the schedule fails of being a perfect one. The choice-of-subjects blanks of the students affected by this unavoidable conflict should be tabbed so that these students can be identified and consulted. The registration summary and conflict sheet will then need to be changed in accordance with their revised choices.

7. After all the singles are as well placed as possible, spot on the tentative schedule sheet any subjects that require two consecutive periods for laboratory work. Watch for room conflicts and do not let these

pile up at any particular periods. At this point, survey the tentative schedule as far as completed and be sure that as good a period assignment has been made for singles and laboratory periods as possible, for much of the success of the schedule depends on the proper placement of these two groups of subjects.

8. Next place on the tentative schedule sheet under the proper teacher's name each of the subjects in which there are to be two classes. Many of these doubles will probably have to be scheduled at periods during which a single is also scheduled. Whenever this happens, make this conflict come between one class of the double and a single usually taken by pupils earlier or later in their school careers. For instance, a double usually taken only by juniors may conflict with a single reserved for seniors without producing many, if any, conflicts. Check with the conflict sheet to see which doubles and singles conflict least. Remember that as much as 50 per cent conflict between one class of a double and a single may do no great harm, for 50 per cent of those in the double can take it at the period when the single is scheduled and 50 per cent of them can take it at another period and thus be able to take the single at the period it is offered.

9. Then place on the tentative schedule sheet under the proper teacher's name each of the subjects for which three or more classes are required. As far as possible avoid placing two classes of a triple in conflict with both classes of a double usually taken by pupils during any one school year. If two classes of a triple usually taken by sophomores conflict with both classes of a double usually taken by them, the fit is so tight that it will be difficult to keep from overfilling the third section of the triple, or the effort to prevent this may develop another oversized class. Usually the flexibility produced by having three or more classes in any subject reduces the danger of conflict to the vanishing point, hence the chief thing to watch in spotting triples is room availability and utilization.

10. When this last group of subjects has been placed on the tentative schedule sheet, the tentative schedule is complete. There will probably be some open squares on this checkerboard in which no subjects have been placed, since in most schools there are more periods in the day than each teacher teaches. These are teachers' free or open periods. If they tend to pile up at any certain periods the schedule maker may want to relocate some of the classes of triples or doubles to reduce this tendency, and with it the danger of oversized classes or study hall at these periods, since the number of pupils going to classes or study halls at any period tends to remain constant and the number of teachers actually teaching at a given period is reduced by the number having open periods. The Douglass teaching load formula can be used at this point to indicate whether teaching loads are approximately equal or not.

This method of schedule making is often called the mosaic plan because one actually builds the schedule by placing one bit of it after another into the over-all checkerboard framework just as one would make a mosaic picture. In fact, some principals use small pieces of cardboard for each class in each subject, fitting these pieces together on a table or tackboard instead of writing upon a large sheet of paper. This method has the advantage of allowing its user to shift subjects about as different combinations and arrangements are tried, without having to erase and rewrite the subject names. However, many adaptations and refinements of this general pattern have been developed by different principals. Usually these tend toward individualizing the process of schedule making so that each pupil's program can be "tailor-made" for him. They generally involve more detailed work on the part of the schedule maker but result in a schedule that accommodates the individual needs of pupils better than the less refined scheduling processes do.

11. At this point it may be desirable to post or mimeograph for distribution to faculty members this tentative schedule in order that each may see what is proposed. Thus any suggestions for changes to suit the desires of any particular teacher may be considered while the scheduling is still in tentative form. Thus, also, any oversights that may have been made are caught, and everyone has a chance to see what his schedule for next year is likely to be. After needed corrections and adjustments have been made, the tentative schedule becomes the official one and the schedules of individual pupils can be made. As has already been indicated, the schedule at this time is not necessarily a *final* one, for doubtless adjustments due to unforeseen events of the summer will make changes necessary. It is, however, the basic framework and actually represents the schedule the school ought to have for the next year if pupils' reasoned choices are to be respected.

12. On each pupil's choice-of-subjects sheet, therefore, can now be written the periods at which each of the subjects he has chosen may be taken. Here again one starts with the singles, then the doubles, and finally the subjects in which three or more classes are offered. If this task is performed at a central point, as in the principal's office, a tally sheet can be kept on one copy of the schedule, showing how many pupils are being assigned to each class and to what extent class sizes are being kept in balance. If this task is decentralized into home rooms or advisory groups, more elaborate arrangements for preventing the development of over and undersized classes must be made. But if the official schedule has been carefully made and if each home room teacher or adviser distributes the registrations in doubles and triples *as evenly as possible* among these classes, while giving to each pupil the program of his choice, the chances are that the inequalities in the various home rooms will balance

each other and all classes will be as nearly equal in size as necessary. At least outsized classes may be reduced to the minimum with a small amount of work in the central office.

If the task is thus decentralized, each home room or advisory group should make a tabulation of its registrations on a copy of the official schedule and send it to the office. The choice-of-subjects sheets may be filled out and this tabulation may be made in each home room by the students themselves, so long as they observe the rule of distributing as evenly as possible registrations in each subject requested by the students in the home room. The tabulation sheet made in the home room will show them how well they have succeeded, and it should not be approved by the home room teacher and sent to the office until it is as nearly perfect as possible. As the tabulation sheets come in to the central office they should be consolidated into a single sheet, which will show to what extent the home rooms have kept classes within size and will show where the home rooms should correct any unnecessary or undesirable inequalities. When the consolidated tally sheet shows a good balance among all classes, the pupil's choice-of-subjects sheet can be regarded as his daily program for the next year.

The home rooms should send their tabulations of registrations to the office from two to four weeks before the end of the school year, for this much time will be needed to make and correct the consolidated tally sheet and to make necessary adjustments in pupils' programs. All the work should be completed while pupils are still attending classes so that they may be consulted if necessary.

13. When the tally sheet shows class sizes to be properly adjusted, pupils' program cards for the following year may be made out from the information on the choice-of-subjects sheets. This may be done in home rooms just before school closes by the pupil himself, who can fill out as many program cards as are needed—one for the home room, one or more for the principal's office and one for himself, if desired. Each pupil then knows what his program will be unless failure or other untoward events make change necessary. If this work is centralized in the principal's office, however, it can be done during the summer so that before school opens in the fall, complete files of pupils' programs will be available. The programs of those who failed, if failure was not anticipated before the close of school, may be revised during the summer, and class rolls for each of the teachers' classes prepared. In the week before school opens in the fall, one or more days may be announced for the registration of pupils new to the system and for adjustments in the programs of registered pupils, if conditions developing during the summer show that such changes should be made. On the first day of school in the fall new students will be assigned to home rooms or advisory groups and others will go first to their last

year's home room or advisory group for their programs and then to their new home rooms and to classes. Of course, some adjustments will still need to be made, but at least a well-organized opening of school can be assured.

Basically the success of the whole operation depends upon the opportunity given each pupil to make a planned and intelligent choice of program and upon developing a satisfactory tentative schedule. If these are well done, a good program for each pupil, each teacher, and the school as a whole is as fully achieved as resources in building, staff, and money permit.

VARIATIONS FOR THE VERY SMALL
AND THE LARGE HIGH SCHOOL

In some respects the task of constructing a good schedule of classes for a very small school is more difficult than one for a larger school because the proportion of single classes is high. On the other hand, the small school has fewer electives, and registration in any of them is either open to anyone in school or restricted pretty largely to the pupils in one school grade. If the electives are open to all, the mosaic plan may be followed, but its operation will be simplified. If the electives are generally open only to pupils of a single school grade, a modified block plan, as explained below, may be followed. In a small school it is possible to give to each pupil in each year a number and to each year a different color of ink. On the tabulation of the choice-of-subjects sheets each student's registration can be shown by placing his number in the space for each subject. If this number is then placed also on his choice-of-subjects blank, he may be easily identified. The use of ink of a different color for each year makes it possible to see at a glance whether the registration in any subject is made up of seniors or freshmen, for example, or whether it is drawn from the school at large. This use of number and color may make a conflict sheet unnecessary. In any case, a number of pupils' programs may have to be handled on an individual basis. The schedule maker has to lay out before him these individual "irregular" programs and, by the process of "cut and fit," evolve a modified mosaic or block plan that satisfies as many of these needs as possible while meeting fully the program requirements of the "regular" pupils.

In a large high school the block plan of scheduling or some combination of it with the mosaic plan is usually followed. The block plan works here because, given a school's offering, given certain required and elective subjects in each curriculum of the school, and given a large student body, the program choices of all pupils will fall into certain patterns. There will be enough registrations of each pattern in each year of each curriculum to form one or more classes or blocks. If registrations for a certain pattern are sufficient for only one class, then they move together as a unit through the day's program. In most large high schools, however, there are enough registrations in most of the patterns to form a block or more than one class. Then each pupil stays within his block all day, but not necessarily with all of the same pupils in each of his classes. For example, if block A in the junior class is made up of classes 1, 2, and 3—all required to take certain subjects and desiring to take the same electives—the students who are in A1 in the first period in English in the second period may be regrouped with some students from classes A2 and A3 for social studies.

Under these conditions, when registrations are tabulated and it is determined what the patterns are, each pupil can be assigned to a block along with other pupils who have chosen the same program pattern. Since this tabulation work in a large high school is a tremendous job, some schools use mechanical means of tabulating. There is no technical reason why any system of coded and punched cards cannot be used in registration activities if it means a great saving of time and expense, but in general the lack of equipment and unfamiliarity with the techniques have retarded the introduction of this method of doing this work. Such cards, however, are being increasingly used even in middle-sized high schools.

After the tabulation has been made, registration plans can be carried out by considering each block as if it were a single pupil; hence if the desired program for each block is provided, the desired program for each pupil in each block is provided. The assumption is, of course, that the pupil's choice is a good one for him. If the school's requirements and regulations are made merely to make registration by the block system easy and possible, then the block system operates to regiment pupils' registration. This is a defect not necessarily inherent in the system, however, but it is a weakness that sometimes creeps into the administration of the plan. Unless care is taken, there will be a tendency to bury the individual in the block. A good opportunity for individual adjustments needs to be provided. There is no reason why these opportunities cannot be offered in a large high school, which has many classes in most subjects and so can enjoy great flexibility in programing. On the other hand, it is hard even for those in charge of a large high school to recognize all the possibilities. Both the mosaic and the block plan can be so administered as to "type" pupils, but they can also be used to meet the particular needs of a given pupil. It all depends upon what those in charge of the plan consider to be of importance. No system is so perfect that, staffed by incompetents, it still turns out a good job. More than good organization and administration are required to make thoughtless and unprincipled people into professional successes. Organization and administration make it easier for conscientious people to turn their thoughts and ideals into programs of action. Thus whether one is making a schedule in a small or a large high school, using one system or another, he still has to face the problem of whether he wants to make the system serve the pupils or to mold the pupils to the system.

Some Points to Consider

1. Examine a copy of the daily schedule of a high school of about one hundred students. Note the subject assignments given to each teacher. Are prospective teachers being prepared to teach in as many fields as these teachers are assigned? If they are not, should they be?

2. Can you tell from studying this schedule which subjects are probably electives? Does the schedule prevent certain pupils from electing any of these subjects?

3. Examine a copy of a daily schedule of a high school of about seven or eight hundred students. How do subject assignments to teachers compare with those in the smaller high school mentioned above? Can you identify the electives in this school? From a study of their schedules what can you surmise about equality of educational opportunity in the two schools?

Further Reading

Davis, Carl D. "IBM Methods in Registration and Grade Reporting," NASSP *Bulletin*, 37, No. 198 (December, 1953), 123–142.

Douglass, Harl R. *Modern Administration of Secondary Schools*. Rev. ed.; Boston: Ginn & Co., 1954. Chap. 5.

Edmonson, J. B., Joseph Roemer, and Francis L. Bacon. *The Administration of the Modern Secondary School*. 4th ed.; New York: The Macmillan Company, 1953. Chap. 6.

Gruenler, A. M. "Schedule Making for an Overcrowded Junior High School," NASSP *Bulletin*, 34, No. 172 (October, 1950), 29–32.

Jacobson, Paul B., William C. Reavis, and James D. Logsdon. *The Effective School Principal*. Englewood Cliffs, N.J.: Prentice-Hall, Inc., 1950. Chaps. 3, 4.

Langfitt, R. E. *The Daily Schedule and High School Reorganization*. New York: The Macmillan Company, 1938.

———. F. W. Cyr, and N. W. Newsom. *The Small High School at Work*. New York: American Book Company, 1936. Chaps. 10, 11.

Newsom, N. W., and Others. *Administrative Practices in Large High Schools*. New York: American Book Company, 1940. Chap. 4.

Research Division, National Education Association, "Teaching Load in 1950," *Research Bulletin*, Vol. 29, No. 1, February, 1951.

Romine, Stephen. "Subject Combinations and Teaching Loads in Secondary Schools," *School Review*, 57, No. 10 (December, 1949), 551.

Chapter 13

THE MODIFIED SCHOOL DAY
AND THE EXTENDED YEAR

The basic purpose of the checkerboard type of schedule described in the previous chapter was to provide an equal amount of time in the pupil's daily program for each of a number of subjects assumed to be of approximately the same importance. But as the typical program offering has expanded to include so many subjects, and as each of these has sought to claim a place in the pupils' programs, the idea of equality has been abandoned. As a result, various modifications in the basic idea of one class, for one period, with one teacher, for each subject, on each day have been introduced. As has been stated, the split week, with two teachers each teaching a different subject two or three times each week at a given period was introduced to accommodate a crowded curriculum. The double period for laboratories and subjects not requiring preparation was not introduced because these subjects were considered twice as important as others, but to provide an amount of time equal to the time given other subjects that were allotted a period at school and supposedly a period of home study. Nevertheless, the fact that the basic time allotment provided in the checkerboard schedule could be changed for these subjects opened the way for other breakdowns of the pattern. The federal policy for vocational classes, which reimbursed local schools for such classes only if three consecutive periods (a half day) were devoted to a vocational subject, rather arbitrarily forced schedule makers to plan programs that did not follow the theory of equality. These departures from the basic plan of the conventional daily schedule have been adopted by many schools, which in the main still give allegiance to the concept of secondary education as the study of certain subjects, the attempted mastery of which is supposed to have a particularly beneficial effect on students. Moreover, they cause these schools to violate this theory in some of their schedule-making practices—as they should—and thus open the way for teachers with other concepts of secondary education to claim that similar and still greater breaks with the basic schedule pattern can and should be made.

NEW DEMANDS ON SCHEDULE MAKERS

In a modern school, where the staff member thinks of his work chiefly as that of guiding and promoting the growth and development of *his* pupils rather than as that of securing mastery of *his* subject, there is a demand for certain opportunities not easily provided unless a quite different approach to schedule making is employed. Dr. Benton Manley, in his "Secondary School Organization and Schedule Making for the Integrating Curriculum," lists the characteristics of the conventional schedule and its shortcomings as follows:

The conventional daily schedule:

1. Includes from 4 to 10 periods; average 6.8.
2. Has periods varying from 35 to 75 minutes in length; average 47.2.
3. Has consecutive single periods that are interspersed with passing periods of from 1 to 7 minutes; average 3.5 minutes.
4. Has double periods for laboratory and shop work when periods are less than 50 minutes in length.
5. Usually includes a home room period, a special period for student activities and for assemblies; average daily time for home room 11.9 minutes; average daily time for extracurricular activities not including assemblies 24.2; average weekly time for assemblies 40.8.
6. Includes a lunch period varying from 20 to 80 minutes in length; average length 50.7 minutes.
7. Organizes a school day varying in length from 4½ to 7½ hours; median 7 hours including all intermissions and the lunch period.
8. Starts the school day 8:00 to 9:04 A.M. and closes it from 1:00 to 4:10 P.M.; median opening time 8:34 A.M.; median closing time 3:33 P.M.
9. Permits students to enroll in from 4 to 6 separate subjects with a minimum of conflict.
10. As a rule, provides no unified relation between consecutive periods and the subjects studied in them other than a time sequence and some arrangement to prevent conflicts in teacher and pupil programs; exceptions would include arrangements such as shorthand followed by typewriting, two science classes arranged in three consecutive periods in order to use the two middle periods for laboratory purposes, etc.

. . . *Briefly these shortcomings are as follows:*

1. The conventional daily schedule lacks flexibility that will:
   a. Permit students frequently to work continuously for two or more consecutive periods.
   b. Provide adequate time for field trips, excursions, etc., without undue interference with other school activities.
   c. Permit students to have access to teachers and teachers to students at periods other than those in which they are regularly scheduled together.
   d. Permit students to be readily shifted from one class group to another.

   e. Allow frequent rearrangements of time and variation in the use of school
      facilities in order to meet the needs of teachers and students.

2. The conventional daily schedule does not permit adequate coordination of
   the efforts of teachers.
   a. No time provided for conferences and cooperative planning.
   b. Lack of such a planning period makes inadequate provision for the in-
      service training of teachers in the new techniques and procedures in-
      volved in a program of education that promotes integration.

3. The conventional daily schedule greatly hampers attempts to make guidance and instruction integral parts of the total learning activity.
   a. In it teachers are, as a rule, primarily concerned with instruction in
      subject matter.
   b. Teachers have little opportunity for conferences with other teachers rela-
      tive to pupil interests and needs and ways and means of meeting them.
   c. As a rule, teachers are not charged with responsibility for meeting the
      interests and needs of students if these do not lite within the compass
      of the subject taught.

4. The conventional daily schedule does not reflect the aims or philosophy of
   the school attempting to develop a program of education that promotes
   integration. It divides the school day and the educational offerings into the
   piecemeal bits which are the outgrowth of the philosophy on which the
   subject curriculum is built.[1]

Manley also reported his inquiry into unmet needs, as listed by
teachers in some modern schools, and found that the principal ones affecting scheduling were to

1. Provide time on the school schedule for teachers of core curriculum groups
   to meet regularly for planning. . . .
2. Schedule for the core curriculum a large enough portion of the school day
   to make it the center of the work program of the pupil. . . .
3. Plan for the same groups of two or more core teachers to follow classes
   in a core organization two or more years.
4. Set up a group of core teachers as a cooperating unit in the faculty with
   a chairman who will aid in keeping the attention of the group fixed on
   the *continuing growth of pupils toward fixed important objectives.*
5. Schedule special interest electives in periods to avoid conflict with the
   core curriculum schedules. . . .
6. Plan for the core teacher to carry out the broad details for guidance and
   adjustment for a limited number of pupils.[2]

The needs to which these teachers gave expression may not have
been voiced by a majority of our high school faculties as yet, but they

----

[1] C. B. Manley, "Secondary School Organization and Schedule Making for the
Integrating Curriculum" (A Type B project, typewritten; New York; Teachers College,
Columbia University, 1941), pp. 141–144.
[2] *Ibid.,* p. 81.

have been felt by thousands of good teachers all over the land as they strive for more effective ways of working with present-day high school populations. Translating some of the principal needs into changes in schedule-making practices we have the following proposals:

1. There is a need for shorter as well as longer class periods than are customarily provided. In practice these should be multiples of the shortest period in the school's daily program: 20–40–80–120–160 minutes or 30–60–90–120–150 minutes. This would merely be a general application of what has been done in relation to vocational subjects and those that do not require preparation.

2. Each teacher who is made responsible for given groups of pupils (not over two groups) should retain these groups for from a quarter or a third up to a half of the day. We now attempt to meet this responsibility when we set up a home room or advisory period in the schedule. The teacher's contact with this group is too brief to permit attaining the desired results. In some schools able to make but a minimum change, this has meant linking the present home room period to the preceding or the succeeding class period. The teacher then has as a home room one of his regular classes. He thus has an opportunity to know them better than is the case now in some schools. Probably less than a quarter of the day would be needed for this amount of integration. There is a little more flexibility in the use of this time, as no bell need mark off the home room period from the remainder of the period. In schools able to go further in the direction of an integrated program for each pupil, the home room period as such might be eliminated from the daily program and its functions better attained as part of the work of an extended period of 80–120–160 or 90–120–150 minutes for the pupils of any grade in any school, as seems best to the staff. This procedure would mean that the school was ready to use such an extended period for some sort of integrated, core, or general education program that included counseling and other types of activity usually carried on in a good home room period—generally because, though their worth was admitted, no place could be found for them in the inn of the conventional subject schedule. In such schools, a "period" of from a third to a half of the day—according to the grade— might be profitably used. The longer the period of time allotted for this part of a pupil's program, the broader the scope of the program undertaken in it should be.

3. There is need for an opportunity for cooperative teaching in the integrated program if and when teachers want it. Cooperative teaching implies that two or more teachers and their classes during this lengthened period may work together for one day or for several. It includes interchange of work and is based upon joint planning for the work of the classes. This requires that the integrated program for the two or more teachers in charge, for example, of the program for the sophomores be

scheduled at the same time. They can thus bring their classes together for visual education, for a demonstration, an excursion, for a talk or a forum discussion. They can also exchange classes if it is desirable for the problem to be broken up so that each teacher handles one part of it.

4. There should be more opportunity for pupil-teacher conferences. Under the conventional schedule these are usually relegated to after school, as it is unusual for the teacher and a pupil with whom he wants to confer to have the same free period. Yet as teachers think in terms of boys and girls instead of subjects, they have more need to confer with pupils individually and in small groups than to refer to textbooks and references. The customary free or open period for a teacher was supposed to provide some time for lesson preparation. But it does not provide time for pupil-teacher conference. Sometime in the day there should be at least one shortened period (twenty-five to thirty minutes) when conferences and nothing but conferences could be scheduled. The conference period should be *during* the day and not at its close, or else attendance takes on the character of being kept in after school. Before, during, or after the lunch periods is a possibility in schools that have a cafeteria lunch service.

5. There needs to be time for teachers' conferences for joint planning. Under the conventional schedule the teacher's free period falls whenever it is best for some reason for him not to have a class. Especially if cooperative teaching is practiced, the cooperating teachers need time for joint planning. Part of this may come after school, but it is the authors' point of view that as much as possible of the work of both pupils and teachers should come within the scheduled day. Why build a schedule that provides for only part of the business of operating a school from day to day and week to week? The better practice would be to make a schedule that includes everything that comes daily or weekly or frequently though irregularly as a part of pupils' and teachers' work in the school. The *scheduled* day then covers the regular workday.

Even if there is no cooperative teaching, it is a good thing for teachers who have the same pupils to be able to meet together to plan for the work of each or all of them. As a teacher transfers his attention from the textbook to his pupils, he wants to know what the whole program of each one is—not just the part of it that he is teaching. Some schools now make it a practice to conduct "grade-level" teachers' meetings. This horizontal type of meeting is a good substitute for the too customary vertical type where all teachers of a department meet. Both are needed, but ordinarily the former is neglected. In the modern school it is one of the most frequent types of meetings.

6. Greater flexibility in the schedule is needed. The objection here is to the fact that under the usual scheduling practices the assumption

is that each pupil and teacher must be in a certain place each period, pre-determined by the schedule maker as much as a year before, and that variations from this are to be the exceptions and approved in the office in advance. Obviously a teacher and class cannot be free to roam as they will about the school and the community. But between these two ex-tremes in scheduling there are ways of allowing a degree of freedom of choice to the class and teacher not provided under the theory and prac-tice of conventional schedule construction. For example, in cooperative teaching under the "school within a school" idea, or under Manley's syn-chronized block plan, there is no reason why the teachers should not know that they are free to regroup their pupils as conditions require, to use one or all of their rooms during the periods of the integrated program, or to do anything else their judgment dictates without securing prior approval of the office, unless what they propose to do involves building space or equipment customarily assigned during these periods to other teachers. Conventional scheduling practice allows a teacher freedom within one period and one room. What is desired is freedom for a group of teachers with a group of classes within a group of periods and a group of rooms, and outside of these rooms, too, if this does not constitute interference with the work of other teachers with their classes. Part of this objective may be realized if the suggestions on scheduling given for (3), (4), and (5) above are followed. The rest is a matter of having a policy in the school that makes a teacher responsible for what he does with his pupils rather than of making the office responsible for what the teacher does with his pupils. If teaching is a profession, then the point at which freedom must reside is the point where professional skill, judg-ment, and ideals are at work teaching boys and girls.

One or more of the above proposals may be found in operation in various schools throughout the country. They are not listed here as new ideas never before thought of or put into practice. Because they have worked where they have been tried they cannot be discounted as mere theory. The trouble is they are usually the exceptions to standard schedule procedures in schools and are more or less reluctantly made. The point stressed here is that schools should use them as freely, quickly, and willingly as they schedule double-period laboratories, for example. They should become part of the accepted techniques that the schedule maker employs to serve the needs of teachers and pupils.

The Changed Schedule Pattern

The schedule maker's concept of what the basic pattern of a schedule should be must be changed if he incorporates into a school's daily sched-ule some of the types of suggestions made in the preceding section. The basic design of the conventional schedule was compared in the preceding chapter to a checkerboard because an equal space was allotted to each teacher on the schedule sheet. The conventional plan is represented by the schedule sheet shown in reduced size in Chart 6.

PERIOD		TEACHER					
		A	B	C	D	E	F
1	8:00– 8:45						
2	8:50– 9:35						
3	9:40–10:25						
4	10:30–11:15						
5	11:20–12:05						
6	12:10– 1:55						
7	2:00– 2:45						

CHART 6. SCHEDULE SHEET

This rigid basic plan must be modified so that we have one which includes the possibility of three or even four lengths of periods, as is suggested in (1) above.

In Chart 7 samples of possible schedules for teachers are shown that illustrate how it is possible to meet a number of the newer demands

PERIOD	A	B	C	D	E	F	G	H	I	J	K	L	PERIOD
8:30													8:30
9:00	Gen. Ed. Core		Gen. Ed. Core		Gen. Ed. Core		X	X	X	X	X	X	9:00
9:30							X	X	X	X	X	X	9:30
10:00													10:00
10:30	Gen. Ed. Core		Gen. Ed. Core		X	X	Gen. Ed. Core		X	X	X	X	10:30
11:00					X	X			X	X	X	X	11:00
11:30	Y	Y	Y	Y	Y	Y	Y	Y	Y	Y	Y	Y	11:30
12:00	Z	Z	Lunch	Lunch	Z	Z	Lunch	Lunch	Z	Z	Lunch	Lunch	12:00
12:30	Lunch	Lunch	Z	Z	Lunch	Lunch	Z	Z	Lunch	Lunch	Z	Z	12:30
1:00													1:00
1:30	Gen. Ed. Core		Gen. Ed. Core		X	X	Gen. Ed. Core		X	X	X	X	1:30
2:00					X	X			X	X	X	X	2:00
2:30													2:30
3:00	Gen. Ed. Core		Gen. Ed. Core		Gen. Ed. Core		X	X	X	X	X	X	3:00
3:30							X	X	X	X	X	X	3:30
4:00													4:00

CHART 7. DAILY SCHEDULE

enumerated above. For example, eight of the teachers shown in this chart —A, B, C, D, E, F, G, and H—have one and a half clock-hour periods for general education core classes. These periods might be used to meet different core classes in the morning and afternoon, or they might be used for each teacher to meet the same class twice each day. The decision would probably depend upon the scope of the general education program: the broader its scope, the larger fraction of the day might logically be allotted to it. In a junior high school, the broader general education program might be more widely used. In a senior high school, probably one and a half clock hours each day would be allotted to general education. The broken lines between A and B, C and D, E and F, and G and H illustrate the fact that the schedule permits cooperative teaching by teacher A with B, C with D, E with F, and G with H. This type of time schedule also permits a broader cooperation in a "synchronized block" of teachers E, F, G, and H whenever it is desirable. Vocational teachers in a senior high school would have schedules similar to those of teachers A and B except that they would have three clock-hour periods in the morning or afternoon.

Four teachers—I, J, K, and L in Chart 7—are shown to have programs that omit core group teaching. They have schedules like those that a convention schedule provides for all teachers—one period for each class. These teachers would teach such special subjects as physical education, art, music, and any elective subjects. Schedules like these would also be assigned to the librarian, to study hall teachers, and to the sponsors of student organizations. It will be noted also that the periods marked X in Chart 7 also include "open" periods. There is no necessity for any teacher working under this type of schedule to teach any more classes than are now taught under conventional scheduling techniques. Some would teach fewer different groups; none need teach more.

The third type of period shown here is three sets of periods of 30 minutes each between eleven thirty and one o'clock. One set of these short periods provides a free conference time when no pupil or teacher has a class and therefore all are free to schedule any needed conferences. A second set of these short periods provides for courses calculated to meet needs and weaknesses that students may have. These include remedial courses in basic educational skills, in corrective physical education, in speech training, and in all other types of courses offered to remedy a critical weakness that, if allowed to persist without an effort by the school to help a youth overcome them, will handicap him all his life. Currently this effort by the school is too meager because no specific time is set aside for it. As a result, many students graduate with weaknesses that could have been removed or at least reduced. What is needed here is a period of drill or practice, a short daily period of concentrated work usually producing more improvement in terms of time spent than a longer period does. These courses interlock with the lunch periods that use the second and third set of short periods. It is easy to see that if a school does not care to include these courses and the conference period in its daily schedule, all can be omitted and an extra X period will be gained, or the daily schedule may be shortened at one end or at both by as much as a clock hour.

If the school day as shown here seems longer than the one we have been accustomed to, it should be remembered that the X periods include student activities that otherwise might come after school and also include at least one open hour for teachers each day so that more of the other work now done by teachers after school can be done within the scheduled day. The idea behind the longer school day is to show as nearly as possible on the schedule all the time actually used by pupils and teachers for schoolwork, instead of showing a short day with a lot of work expected from both students and teachers that must be done after school and at home.

Chart 8 is a fragment of a schedule that was actually in use recently in a twelve-teacher, six-year high school. Only six teachers' programs are shown, since the other six, not being involved in the core program of general education, taught typical 40-minute periods. The purpose here is not to show an ideal program but to show how these teachers and their principal worked out a daily schedule that abandoned the fixed period of standard length in favor of a more flexible one for six of the teachers whose work required it, while retaining the fixed period for teachers not in the core program. These six teachers taught mathematics and commercial subjects (1), agriculture (1), home economics (1), senior high school science (2), and library (1). From this it can be inferred that the core in junior high school covered reading, social studies, science, and health; and in senior high school, reading, literature, and social studies.

The fundamental difference between the work of the maker of a conventional schedule and that of the maker of one of the newer types of schedules is that the former starts to build his mosaic or block schedule with little pieces of time of exactly equal length. The supposition is that these are what he should use for all classes except laboratories. He constructs a design for each teacher which is like that of every other teacher because he has but one-sized block of time. The newer type of schedule starts the schedule maker out with three different blocks of time: a shortened one—25–30 or 35 minutes; a standard or basic block of twice the length of the shortened one; and an even longer block of two, three, or four times the length of the basic one. This type of schedule, with its three units of time, can be adjusted to meet the varied needs of those who teach the broad program of the modern school that stresses growth and development of pupils. It fulfills a function that teachers have said was not fulfilled by conventional scheduling practices.

PERIOD	TEACHER					
	A	B	C	D	E	F
8:30	Activity period Jr. I–II	Core Jr. I–II	Core Jr. I–II	Core Jr. III	Core Sr. III	Core Sr. II
9:55 – 10:35	Typing				Vacant	
10:40 – 11:20	English drill	Mathematics	Mathematics	Glee club	Core Sr. I	Core Sr. III
11:25 – 12:05	Vacant	Library	Physical education			
12:10 – 12:50	Typing	Lunch	Lunch	Lunch		Vacant
12:55	Core Jr. I–II	English drill	Library	Music	Lunch	Lunch
		Physical education	English drill	Music	Core Sr. I	Core Sr. II
2:15		Activity period	Activity period	Vacant		
2:20 – 3:00	Typing			English drill		

CHART 8. SCHEDULE

This type of schedule making is being evolved to cope with the situation produced in modern high schools by present-day social conditions and their demands upon the high schools, by the newer concepts of the function of secondary education in America, and by newer methods and materials of teaching. In time it promises to be as appropriate for these changed conditions as the conventional daily schedule pattern was for the concepts prevailing when it was developed. A good account of how one school went about studying its program to discover its strong and weak points, and of what the results were, is given in *Education Unlimited*.[3] It is pretty good evidence that objectional rigidity in the daily schedule can be largely eliminated.

The above types of changes in the length and pattern of the school day have been introduced in some high schools principally as a way of adapting the school day to changes in the schools' programs which could

[3] Grace S. Wright, Walter H. Gaumnitz, and Everett A. McDonald, *Education Unlimited* (U.S. Office of Education, Bulletin No. 5; Washington, D.C.: Government Printing Office, 1951).

not be easily made within the usual school day with the usual number of equal-length periods. Within the last few years overcrowding in some urban high schools has accounted for modifications in the school day even though no basic changes in the educational program were contemplated. These modifications are usually made to avoid putting students on half-day schedules. In some cases the student body is divided into two shifts one of which makes an early and the other a late start on the school day, and one therefore ends its day earlier than the other. This means that both shifts are in the school building during the middle of the day. But due to the fact that then part of the students are in cafeteria, part can be in an auditorium period and others in large classes which are purposely scheduled at these middle hours; in this way, the whole student body can be cared for at once for a few periods.

In other schools a nine-period day is used with the student body divided into three shifts. One shift is composed of a group of students living near enough to the school to walk to school and to go home to lunch. This shift attends the first three periods, goes home for the middle three periods, and returns for the last three. A second shift starts early and attends the first six periods. The third shift starts late and attends the last six periods. Thus only two thirds of the student body is in the building at any one time.

These types of modification of the daily schedule are in most cases merely administrative adjustments adopted to meet overcrowded conditions. But they prevent schools from going on to half-day sessions and therefore serve a very useful purpose. Also they break with the traditional idea of a relatively short school day and move toward an extended period of daily use of the school plant. Any administrative changes which popularize the idea of more complete use of the high school plant for longer periods of each school day are probably moves in the right direction.

The Extended School Year

It has not been difficult for high school administration to make the few changes required as the typical school year has been extended from seven to eight, to nine, and, in some cases, to ten months. As the public, persuaded in part by the teaching profession, became willing to send children to school longer and to provide the extra money required, schools have simply added the extra weeks and months to the existing school year. The conditions of life in many large, densely populated areas make it unwise for us to close up any of our youth-serving agencies for as long as three months at a time. The loss caused by closing schools is now sometimes partly offset by an expanded program of community recreation, with many on the school staff becoming recreation workers for the summer. This is good as far as it goes, but it still does not use all the appropriate resources of the schools. These resources and facilities are needed all through the year if they are needed at all, because practically all the youth are in the community all year with little but time on their hands. Hence some sort of a longer school year is not so much a matter of education as of public necessity—as well as a public convenience.

The present status of the movement toward a "year-round" school program has been recently reviewed by the Educational Research Service of the National Education Association. This report covers a sample of school systems in cities of over 30,000 and shows little use of the "year-round" or "four-quarter year" idea beyond the typical "summer high school" level. It illustrates the lag between urban need and practice, but one has to remember that in a number of cities other youth-serving agencies such as a recreational commission or the park board often operate a summer program using some of the school's facilities. Some advantages and disadvantages of extending the school year as summarized in this report follow. They illustrate both the degree of comprehension of the problem and lack of it on the part of those who responded.

Advantages of the all-year school organization were:

1. Under the quarter plan, any three quarters attended covered a year's work.

2. Since some parents prefer to take their vacation in the winter months, the plan enabled them to do so without loss of regular school time for children.

3. The designation of the summer quarter as one of the regular quarters of the school year had a tendency to spread the enrolment over a period of 12 months instead of 10, which made it possible to reduce pupil-teacher ratio and to effect a saving in teacher positions.

4. The summer quarter served as an opportunity for slow-learning children; made it possible for irregular pupils to make up deficiencies; permitted some pupils to acquire a greater amount of education before being compelled to leave school for industry; gave prospective college students the opportunity to make up deficiencies and enter college at the start of the regular year; and high school pupils had a better chance to engage in an alternating school-work program.

Disadvantages of the all-year school organization were:

1. Twice as much time was lost in preparation for, and time consumed, in examinations.

2. Some pupils were accelerated in school work to their detriment.

3. The plan interfered with large scale cleaning, remodeling and decoration operations normally done in the summer.

4. A certain per cent of the classroom teachers and principals prefer to study, travel, or rest in the summer.

5. The summer months are not conducive to maximum accomplishment in the learning process.[4]

FURTHER EXTENSION A MATTER OF
MONEY, WEATHER, AND PROGRAM

Keeping school resources fully available on a year-round basis will cost more money, chiefly for the salaries of teaching and operating staffs. Some communities can manage this easily enough; others, because of limited funds, can at best carry on a minimum summer program; and others can afford nothing of this kind. Apparently, some large cities have the most difficulty in continuing to do what they have been doing. It is a strange anomaly when our large cities, which are supposed to be centers of wealth and power, are the first communities to be unable to continue to improve the educational opportunities of their children. Such a situation points directly to the need to overhaul and modernize our system of taxation—not only in behalf of the school but for all other kinds of public works. The questions are: Will communities and states allow those who would like to force a reduction in government activities to use high taxes under present antiquated tax laws and practices as a convincing reason for curtailing all public activities? Or will our citizens come to see that the trouble is not so much *high* taxation as *bad* taxation? Anyone who understands the theory of taxation can suggest changes in tax laws and practices that would tend to equalize the burden of taxation.

At least as far as the cost of education is concerned, we can be sure that out of our present high level of national income as a nation, we are now spending a smaller proportion for education than at any time in this century and a much smaller proportion than many other countries are spending, including even some to which we are sending aid. But even under present taxing limits, many communities have found at least a partial answer and are operating some sort of summer programs that in effect extend the school year.

Summer weather being what it is in many parts of this country, the question is easily raised as to whether, and for how long a period, the school year should be extended. The ready answer is that it is too hot in summer for the schools to begin before the end of the first or second week in September or to carry on long past June first. In some communities this is true, but even there practically everything else operates all summer; moreover, practically all the youth remain in town throughout the sum-

[4] Educational Research Service, *Status of Year-Round School Programs* (Circular No. 7; Washington, D.C.: National Education Association, August, 1952), pp. 2, 3.

mer months. The question is: How much worse off and how much hotter would they be if the schools operated throughout the summer period? The answer depends in part upon the kind of program offered—a matter to which we shall soon come. In the majority of communities, however, summer weather in itself is not the final answer to the problem. Well-built high school buildings are no hotter than many other places in the community. The possibility of air conditioning some parts of the school plant which would otherwise be too hot for summer programs is not beyond the bounds of reason. We air-condition everything else in the community—stores, motion-picture theaters, offices, restaurants, and bars —but are slow to air-condition public libraries, churches, and schools. Even without air conditioning, many high school buildings are as comfortable as the places where youth spend most of the time in the summer when such a program would be in operation. As a matter of fact, summer weather is not generally a valid argument against extension of the school year.

The matter of further extension of the school year actually rests on the question of the kind of program to be offered. Some kinds of summer programs would *not* be worth their cost, but our best summer programs prove that this need not be the case. The traditional use to which high school buildings are put in summer is to house a summer session where pupils who failed some subject during the regular school year may make up their work. Other students who want to earn an extra credit or two are also admitted. Sometimes these students are charged a tuition by the school, which then employs the needed teachers. At other times the right to use the building is granted to faculty members at no or at low cost, and they are permitted to charge a tuition fee to the students who want to come. The possibilities of this being considered a "racket" are easy to see, but if a community can do no more than this, it is better than nothing at all. Nevertheless, many high schools are satisfied to offer such a thin program when they could easily afford the rich one that is so badly needed. It is therefore assumed here that the school's program in the summer ought to be made to include any kind of activities desired by youth to which the physical and personnel resources of the high school can be adapted and which can serve any of the educational needs or recreational or social interests of all youth of the community that are not met as well or as economically by other youth-serving agencies. Obviously the summer program should consider all the children of the community too, but here we specify youth because we are dealing with the high school level of school administration. Such a program could easily be worth its cost to any community and could easily afford a more pleasant and profitable way for youth to spend the summer than is now available to the vast majority.

THE MODERN PROGRAM OF SUMMER SCHOOL ACTIVITIES

The most natural way to extend the school year into a year-round program is to expand the summer session by gradually building it into a program utilizing the resources of the high school to the full extent needed. Some high schools have started doing this—not with the expressed purpose of extending the school year, but for the purpose of serving youth's summer needs for worth-while activities and occupations. As a result, a large proportion of the youth population of the town finds something offered that is of interest to it, and in effect the school operates on a year-round basis. Just as in the older type of high school summer school, a few regular classrooms may be used for required subjects that students need to make up. The summer program also offers students a chance to register for a large number of other offerings that may be regular elective subjects of the winter's program or may be activities that are suitable only for the summer session. Not only the regular classrooms but also laboratories for nature study groups, first-aid classes, radio clubs, camp cooking enthusiasts, and other similar organizations, are open.

The shops will be used by boys and girls who "want to make something." The art studios will be headquarters for students who are on sketching or painting excursions out in the community. The vocational agriculture projects and the programs of the distributive occupations operate, of course, through the summer. The school library will be open for recreational reading. Music studios are the rehearsal centers for beginning and advanced junior community orchestras, bands, and choral groups, which give one or a series of outdoor summer evening concerts. The community's gymnasiums, swimming pools, school playgrounds, and recreation centers are operated for the use of boys and girls as well as adults all day and evening for organized play and competition. There may be summer day camps where boys and girls camp out during the day, returning to their homes for the night, or there may be regular boys' and girls' camps at some near-by recreational center where those not attending the summer camps of other youth-serving agencies may go at a small expense covering the cost of their food. That this summer program does not duplicate the service of most of the other organizations has been the experience of schools that have started such activities. Long trips or cruises are organized for those whose interests are such that firsthand study is desirable. In short, all the physical and personnel resources of the school that can be made to serve any worth-while interest or need of youth are converted to the use of the summer program.

The summer session also offers a chance to do experimental curricular work that cannot be so well or easily done during the regular school session. Sometimes during the regular year a teacher cannot spare the time needed by an experimental undertaking if it is to succeed. Sometimes externally imposed regulations will not permit a really worth-while suggestion to be tried out in the regular school year. The freedom and informality of the summer session facilitates the planning, carrying on, and evaluating of a project, which may then be introduced into the regular session if the experimental summer program establishes its value. In this way the summer session can serve as a sort of curricular vestibule, as have extracurricular activities, into which ideas may enter freely, and, if found to be desirable, may then be admitted more readily into the inner sanctum of the regular school curriculum. A four-quarter school year is thus developed with the fourth quarter using up to ten weeks of what has been the summer vacation period.

The whole cost of some of these programs is borne by the school district just as it is in the winter session. In some cases the cost is shared by the school district, and the city or county government. For others, where a personal expense as for food or travel is involved, a cost charge is made. No teacher need be required to work in the summer program. Some summer teachers may not even be members of the school's winter staff; they may be citizens of the community who are good *teachers* though not certificated ones. Some of the teachers may be from other schools and have special interests or talents not possessed by any member of the winter staff. All should be paid at their regular salary rate, but many may not be working full time on the summer program. Sometimes school credit is earned and sometimes it is not. The purpose of having such a program is not to make early high school graduation possible, nor is the purpose of the summer program served if youth participate simply to earn credit—any more than the school's purpose is served when this happens in the winter session. To prevent mere credit seekers from registering, school credit could be allowed only for making up a required subject. The summer program should be as free as possible from the rules and regulations, from the passing and failing, from the good and poor marks, and from the credit counting of the winter session. It should be a good example to pupils, teachers, and parents of how worth while, profitable, and growth promoting an educational program can be without all the "crutches" that we associate with the regular school program. Such a demonstration might even lead to the actual abandonment of these sterile devices during the winter program as well. Any experienced observer of secondary education who visits a high school campus during the summer when such a program is in full swing will probably sense a level of life and vitality not so generally noticeable in that school in the regular winter session. If it is possible to develop more and more summer school programs in the high schools of this country that are based upon student needs and interests and are free from the academic routines of the regular school sessions, some clever high school principals may be able to feed a few of these summer program vitamins into the winter program and give it more color and life than it has ever enjoyed before.

WELL-ORGANIZED DAY AND YEAR A BASIC ESSENTIAL

It has been said that the only thing about high school administration that distinguishes it from the administration of any other type of school is daily schedule making. This may be such an oversimplification as to be almost untrue, but it at least points out how important daily schedule making is—or appears to others to be—in making a school year a success. Without a doubt a bad schedule or poor administration of other related aspects of the school's daily program, or both, can be a constant source of irritation to pupils, teachers, and even the principal who made the schedule! None of these may realize the source of all the trouble, but the experienced student of high school administration can soon recognize it in a poor daily schedule whose squeaks, groans, and curses cannot be stilled even by large applications of human understanding, courtesy, and good will. A principal owes the community, the students, the teachers, and himself a better chance to do a good year's work than can be done when he has resorted to makeshifts in preparing the school's schedule. The techniques needed to make a good class schedule for any school, the ways of planning for the length of the school day that is most appropriate for a given community, and the history of other modern high schools with an extended school year are all known or easily available to both the experienced and the inexperienced high school principal. Each high school's schedule and calendar should be systematically studied and improved under the direction of the high school principal until every year a vast majority of the school population will say that the school's use, management, and assignment of time on both the daily and the yearly basis are the most satisfactory and effective it has ever had.

Some Points to Consider

1. Is there anything about the modified type of schedules illustrated in this chapter that makes added cost inherent in them?
2. Will the average teacher load in terms of the number of different pupils met daily or weekly be heavier or lighter in these modified schedules?
3. What are some of the reasons—good and bad—why parents usually want their children to have home study to do?
4. If a school extended its day and reduced its demands for study at home, what worth-while activities might it encourage its pupils to undertake to replace the old type of home study?

5. Is having a large number of papers to take home to read at night an essential to good class teaching? Can it be managed otherwise?

6. Would it be a good policy for a board of education to encourage teachers to pursue recreational activities during the school year? How might this policy be implemented?

Further Reading

Alberty, Harold. *Reorganizing the High School Curriculum.* New York: The Macmillan Company, 1953.

Collins, LeRoy D. "How We Solve Our Teen-Age Problem," *The Saturday Evening Post,* Philadelphia, April 24, 1956.

Corey, Stephen M., and others. *General Education in the American High School.* Chicago: Scott, Foresman & Company, 1942. Part II.

Educational Policies Commission. *Education for All American Youth: A Further Look.* Rev. ed.; Washington, D.C.: National Education Association, 1951.

Educational Research Service. *Status of Year-Round School Programs.* Circular No. 7; Washington, D.C.: National Education Association, August, 1952, pp. 2, 3.

Manley, C. B. "Secondary School Organization and Schedule Making for the Integrating Curriculum." A Type B project, typewritten; New York: Teachers College, Columbia University, 1941.

National Association of Secondary School Principals. *Planning for American Youth.* Washington, D.C.: National Education Association, 1951.

Shedd, Arthur B. "To What Extent and in What Ways are the Plants and Personnel of American Public High Schools Used for the Education of Youth during the Summer Months?" Unpublished doctoral thesis; New York: Teachers College, Columbia University, 1950.

Shipp, Frederic T. "A Flexible Daily Schedule for a Modern High School," *American School Board Journal,* October, 1945.

Wright, Grace S., Walter H. Gaumnitz, and Everett A. McDonald, *Education Unlimited.* U.S. Office of Education, Bulletin No. 5; Washington, D.C.: Government Printing Office, 1951.

Chapter 14

THE HIGH SCHOOL'S SPECIAL SERVICES:
LIBRARY AND HEALTH

Whenever a group of people come together to carry on activities of any nature, there is a need for other kinds of activities and services not necessarily related to the ones for which the group gathers. Thus, at any country crossroad and at Grand Central Station enterprising individuals find it profitable to offer a variety of goods and services for the convenience of those who gather there. A well-organized and well-managed enterprise expects these auxiliary services to be needed and therefore plans for them to operate on some basis satisfactory to all. A high school which brings together a group of boys and girls primarily so that they may receive instruction in certain educational programs may expect to find that across the street from it and down on the corner a number of enterprises have sprung up to furnish goods and services to students which the proprietors expect—or at least hope—the high school will not supply. So also the high school will itself embark upon a number of activities that meet some of the common, special, related, or auxiliary needs of the students and faculty. These may be closely connected with the business of educating boys and girls or they may be as remote as taking orders for class rings. In any case, a good high school is organized to care for these auxiliary services and special needs in a satisfactory way. Obviously, the principal of a good high school is primarily concerned to see that the instruction provided for students is of the highest type, but he is also responsible for seeing that there is good organization and management of all the needed special services as well. In fact, it is the authors' belief that if the very best results are to be achieved from the educational program these services must be well operated and their educational possibilities fully utilized. They are not necessary nuisances; instead, they should be regarded as splendid opportunities for student participation in the democratic and efficient organization and management of group life and thus as a most important element in the school's total educational program.

The next two chapters will therefore be concerned with some of the important auxiliary needs and services and their organization and operation so that they not only effectively serve the students' needs but offer a good illustration of, and experience in, well-organized, democratic group living.

The Library Service

The library service is so closely connected with the educational program that it might well be regarded as a part of it, yet it is generally classed as an auxiliary service. And it should be regarded as a service—not just a specialized room in the building. It rises to its highest potential when it is a real service to the school as a whole. The library has been called "the heart of the school." If this expression means that the library pumps books and other graphic materials to every part of the school, then the library is performing a real service. If, however, the expression simply means that the library is a place to which pupils must frequently resort if they are to be educated, then it implies that being educated is a sort of academic process which cannot go on unless one reads many books. Reading books is not the heart of an education: it is an activity which may frequently be auxiliary to becoming better educated. The library, therefore, is perhaps better described as an auxiliary service to education than as "the heart of the school."

BROADENING THE LIBRARY'S BASIC FUNCTION

The library is customarily responsible for securing, circulating, and maintaining in good usable condition the graphic materials needed to supplement and enrich the school's educational program. Graphic materials, in the sense we are using this broad term here, include books, magazines, charts, pictures, and other printed materials. In some schools they also include textbooks and audio-visual materials, which in this chapter are treated as separate services because, although these services are related to each other and ought to be coordinated, each is a service in itself and can be best discussed here as such. This statement of the library's function presumes that some basic reading materials, a text or texts, will be used in many courses and will be either owned by each student or made available to him. But beyond this it is assumed that good instruction will occasionally require the reading of other materials that need not be constantly present in the classroom nor available in the school in a quantity sufficient to supply each pupil with a copy when they are being used. This statement also assumes that classroom instruction will incite pupils to read beyond what is required, and that no matter how good a public library service the community may have there is a need for a special school supply of the kinds of reading materials most likely to be voluntarily called for by pupils. If any or all of these assumptions are unwarranted in respect to any particular high school, then either the authors have made faulty assumptions about the functions of a school library service, or else the school needs to consider why its instructional program does not require and lead to such reading.

As stated above, library service will be treated in this chapter as a separate service to be coordinated with those involved in supplying textbooks and audio-visual materials; yet we should be able to look forward to the time in many high schools when the library and the person in charge there will be regarded as the one service center of instructional materials in the school. The library was the "heart" of the school when books were almost the only instructional materials. If it is still to be so regarded, then its concept of function must be broadened. A better school organization would be created if the library's function is broadened until it is the one instructional materials center of the school and not one of several coordinated centers for texts and audio-visual materials. It would be more convenient for students and teachers if the library were the center to which they went for all business connected with instructional materials, rather than to perhaps as many as four centers for library books, instructional supplies, texts, and audio-visual services. This is not to say that all these types of supplies must be stored for use in the library and adjoining rooms, but wherever they are housed they should be organized and operated through the library and the persons in charge of it. It may well be that in the near future we may expect that what was the library will become the one instructional service center of the school. Librarians then generally would be trained not only in library techniques but also in the high school curriculum, as a few already are.

SPACE PROVISION FOR THE LIBRARY

Such a library service as is envisioned here will require a whole suite of rooms in a high school of almost any size. In addition there will be auxiliary rooms, not necessarily adjoining the library, where instructional materials and aids may be stored and serviced. The size of the school will determine the size of the suite but will not, even in a small high school, reduce the need to one room. The suite needs to provide (1) storage places and equipment for all the kinds of materials supplied to classrooms; (2) work spaces for library administration and book repair; (3) a conference room (or rooms) where a teacher may take all or part of a class for group library work; and (4) a general reading room equipped for checking out books to pupils, teachers, and the general public if the school library serves as a community library as well. Most high school library plans seem to have provided more adequately for the general reading room than for the other three types of space, if the number of vacant seats usually found in such reading rooms and the cramped and inadequate quarters allowed for the work of the librarians is any evidence on this point. The large general reading room in the high school library is probably traceable to college library planning, where it can be assumed that students will have and perhaps use about two hours in the library for each hour spent in class. This situation does not prevail in the high school, where, generally speaking, pupils spend at least four fifths of their time in assigned classes. If such large general reading rooms are provided, there should be some assurance that pupils' programs will be such as to make it possible for them to go in and out of the library as college students do, or that the room will be used as a study hall so that a good average room utilization will prevail. Librarians, however, frequently object to the library being used as a study hall. Such objections are well taken unless conference rooms for group use of the library are provided and unless another teacher or an extra assistant to the librarian is provided to supervise the pupils who are in the library to study. But if these conditions are met, it would seem that objections to the practice should be overruled. If it is decided not to use the library for study, then in planning the building, other study halls should be provided to care for students who under any type of program will have a free period in their schedule. Usually the large size of the general reading room in the library reduces the space left for work, conference, and storage. The argument here is not for less space in the building for the library, but for a different allocation of that space among the types of work to be done there.

The insistence on adequate space for conference rooms for group library work does not imply that every time a class wants to do "supplementary" reading it has to come to this room (or rooms) for it. It is assumed that the library will be organized to send out to classrooms a set of supplementary reading materials that may be retained in any classroom for several days at a time, thus providing "classroom libraries" without having the classroom full of books that are used for only a month or six weeks of any school year. In many schools portable bookshelves or movable bookcases mounted on rubber rollers make it possible to move books in and out of the library easily. On the other hand, when certain types of library work must be done by classes, it is best for all or part of a class to resort to the library conference room where this group work may be done without bothering the rest of the class or the other pupils in the library. Here again, before such conference rooms are provided in a new building, teachers should be consulted to determine whether their plans for teaching are such that this type of room is actually needed. If teachers are unwilling or unable to conduct instruction in any way except from a single textbook, then the proposed conference room might as well be converted into an extra classroom adjoining the library until the instructional plans of the faculty require its use as a library conference room.

LIBRARY PERSONNEL

Someone with at least some library training can be available in even a small school if the need is kept in mind when vacancies are filled. For larger high schools it is assumed that one or more fully trained librarians will be on the staff with the status and salary of regular teachers. The custom which prevails in many schools of paying librarians on a lower salary schedule supplies a pretext for not requiring that they be well or fully trained as *school* librarians. By placing them on the regular teachers' salary schedule, the school is able to ask them to be as fully prepared for their work in the high school as are the other staff members. Hence in addition to having had basic library training they can be expected to have enough understanding of the problems of secondary education to serve on school curriculum committees with other teachers. A really competent high school librarian is often the difference between full use of the library in the school and failure to make more than superficial use of it. Much depends on the attitude of individual teachers toward education, but even the best teachers need the full and interested cooperation of the school librarian. Just as there are some teachers who are mere school-keepers, so there are librarians who are mere book-keepers. The best librarians not only are trained in library techniques and know something about modern secondary education, but they understand how to encourage pupils and teachers to make maximum use of the library.

As a way of making sure that the library and its resources are capable of maximum service to the school, an advisory library committee composed of teachers and students is a good adjunct to the regular library staff. It should have a voice in determining accessions and should also be able to advise with respect to the daily operation of the library. Students who sit on such a committee should not be selected by departments wholly because they have major interests in one of these departments. In this case, they are likely to be no more than rubber stamps in the hands of the teachers in the departments they represent. Rather, they should be appointed to the committee from the student council and responsible through it to the whole student body. The students are the real customers of the library, and their ideas about how it could be run to be most helpful and convenient for them should be heard and usually acted upon. Thus the school's library service may become something for which students are in part responsible; if it does, a quite different attitude on their part toward the library can then be built up.

This participation by the students in the operation and management of the library acquires added importance when it is proposed that a large part of the work of managing the daily operation of the library should be in the hands of students. They can be volunteers who are accepted by the library advisory committee either on the recommendation of the librarian or not, as may seem best. Or they can be members of a class that is studying library service and they will thus serve a sort of part-time apprenticeship in connection with the course by getting work experience. Some may be paid assistants. If both paid and volunteer workers are used, those who are paid must be selected on a basis of known competence, so that all realize that the salaries are being paid to those of demonstrated ability. These student workers should be an organized group—a club perhaps—with student officers and with a librarian as sponsor. The head of this group might well be known as student librarian and responsible under the general direction of the librarian for the organization of this group of student workers. Quite a few schools use student assistants in the library, but in very few is this group organized to discharge a definite budget of responsibility.

In this way a larger degree of responsible student participation may be secured, and with it a larger measure of growth and development for those directly involved. When well operated, such a plan, which enlarges the part played by students in the school's library service, results in good student attitudes and secures a degree of cooperation and interest not otherwise attained. The principal of the high school and the school's librarian should be much concerned to see that the library materials themselves serve to improve the educational opportunity the school can supply; they should also organize the library so that its operation and management are sources of educative work experience for a large number of students.

TEXTBOOK, AUDIO-VISUAL, AND
INSTRUCTIONAL SUPPLY SERVICE

Ordinarily the supply service in a high school is not clearly differentiated; nevertheless it is an important one. In small schools or in schools where texts are not furnished by the board of education or the state, this service may be fused with the library service; even more likely, it is handled in a not too systematic manner directly from the superintendent's or the principal's office. In larger schools, and in those where texts are furnished to pupils, the supply service becomes more important; hence it is more likely to be a separate one. In any case, however, the organization and distribution of texts and instructional supplies are either a direct or an indirect responsibility of the high school principal.

THE PURPOSE TO BE SERVED

The supply service exists to requisition, care for, distribute, repair, and account for texts and general instructional supplies that are the property of the school district. Special instructional items for use in a particular department are usually not its responsibility. Such matters are usually handled directly with the principal by the teacher or the head of the department involved. Where texts as well as general supplies are furnished, the supply service requires the part-time assistance of a responsible person who may be a teacher or a clerk working directly under the direction and supervision of the principal, whose authorization is necessary for charges against the budget and for recommendations for the budget proposed for the ensuing year. Teachers' requests for the use of texts and supplies should be honored by the person in charge without the principal's specific approval. Where the books are issued by the home room or the classroom teacher for pupils to use outside the classroom, the latter should sign a receipt for them, the signatures being filed with the person in charge of this service. Books that are damaged or lost are customarily paid for by the pupils responsible for them, who should settle these liabilities directly with the person in charge of the supply service. At the close of the year, as texts are returned for summer storage, they should be examined to determine whether they need repair or replacement during the summer so that the necessary arrangements may be made.

In some high schools the supply service includes responsibility for audio-visual supplies and equipment. This growing field has become a specialized type of service in large high schools and school systems. In many others, however, it has been integrated with the general instructional supply service which, with a broadened program of library service, may economically provide the organization and management required if audio-visual supplies and equipment are generally used in the classrooms of a school. The person in charge of these materials must be well trained in the use and repair of equipment and familiar with sources of supply of free and rental films. A faculty committee representing the various classrooms where large use of films is made may help make the service more effective. A corps of student assistants can be developed who will do well and with great satisfaction much of the work required in this particular field. In an increasing number of high schools, audio-visual materials are in such general use that no one who is not competent in this area should be in charge of the instructional supply service.

If this instructional supply service is to operate directly from the principal's office, then a suitable room convenient to this office is required. If free texts are supplied by the school, the space needs to be adequate for the storage of the number of books in use, as well as for the storage of general supplies. The best practice in city school systems calls for the amount of general instructional supplies within a building to be held to the minimum with the larger stock for the system as a whole held elsewhere. In smaller systems, the high school instructional supplies may be issued from a room where the supplies for the whole system are stored, or the high school supplies for the entire year may be stored in a separate room. If the school is large enough to permit the separation of this service from the high school principal's office, then a good light, dry room elsewhere in the building should be sought.

In the matter of free textbooks, high school pupils have a direct experience in the use and care of public property. If they are ever going to learn to use and manage it well, they must learn on such relatively small things as textbooks and instructional supplies. A high school principal who feels a minimum responsibility for the use and management of these kinds of public property by the students of the school either has little concern for whether they ever learn that public property is entitled to good care and use, or has not yet recognized how learning occurs. As a representative of the public which owns the property, he has a responsibility for seeing that it is not misused or abused; as an educator, he has a responsibility for seeing that youth learn how and why public property should be used and cared for as they are using it.

The High School Health Service

The amount and character of the health service supplied in a high school may vary according to its size, but some of the largest high schools are the most inadequately supplied, whereas some small schools that have effected a good relationship with county health units have the best service. Where the service is inadequate, shortage of funds is the usual explanation; yet it may well be that part of the difficulty lies in the fact that the school has failed to sense the size of the responsibility for health that is assumed when large numbers of youth are brought together into congested school living. The school may also have failed to recognize how important a good school health service is as a way of teaching good health. The practice in small systems varies: the health service center may be outside the high school building; it may be at the superintendent's office and serve the whole school system; or it may be that there is no separate *school* health center, the service being supplied from some local or county public health center. But any high school large enough to have a gymnasium, an auditorium, or a library is large enough to have a health center of its own. It may be able to afford only a part-time school nurse, but it should have a center in the building where she can work when on duty and which is in the care of some other competent person at other hours. It is a service that must be always available, for its influence ought to be constantly present in the lives of high school youth.

THE FUNCTIONS TO BE SERVED

The principal function of the health service is to protect and promote the physical and mental health and safety of the high school's pupils and staff. An auxiliary function of no less importance is the teaching of health habits, appreciations, and skills by affording the individual encouragement and opportunity to avail himself of the health service. This supplementary function, in fact, is part of the principal function when that function is said to include the *promotion* of health, but it is important enough to be represented separately as a coordinate function. The health service should be coordinated with—or, better yet, be incorporated into—the high school's health education program. But even the most efficient health education program in a typical high school situation is not enough to cope alone with the health need. A health education program is likely to be weighted with a *study* of health—which is a good thing to study—but for best results a health service center is needed where pupils are encouraged and assisted to learn about health in the process of caring for and improving their own health and the health conditions of the community. The health education program with a coordinated or integrated health service is the ideal setup for achieving the school's health objective.

TYPES OF SERVICE

The most obvious type of service to be rendered by a good high school health service is ordinarily thought of as "first aid." Accidents, sudden illness, and emergency health situations occur daily in a high school of even average size. If the school cannot afford full-time nurse service, someone must be on hand who is competent to meet the ordinary emergency situation. Health teachers, physical education teachers, and shop teachers are among those likely to have had some first-aid training and experience; hence one of these teachers may be the logical person to direct the health service when the regular nurse is not present. The school cannot afford not to have someone in charge whenever the building is open to the public for school affairs. Accidents ranging from minor to severe and emergency health situations arise whenever groups of people come together. Usually they involve only one or two people, but if someone with first-aid training is available—and knows it is his responsibility to take charge—the situation can be met well enough to bridge the gap until professional medical service can be secured.

There is also the disaster situation to be prepared for. Fortunately, disasters do not occur frequently in any one school or community, but every so often a hotel fire, a school fire, a flood or storm emergency, or a panic in a school or theater serves to warn those who are in charge of public meeting places of the need to be prepared for such catastrophes. A part of being prepared for disaster situations is to prevent their occurring or to reduce this danger to the minimum. In a well-organized school, a periodic check on the kinds of preventable conditions that may cause disaster is a responsibility of the health service. Everyone who uses a school building and its equipment under conditions where a disaster might develop—at games, parties, or assemblies, for example—should know that the head of the school's health service is responsible for inspections that reduce risks to the minimum. Some industrial communities have developed disaster organizations. Where such an organization exists, the school's health service should be in touch with it, both to get assistance in a hurry and to put the school's own emergency service and equipment at its disposal.

A much less spectacular but more constantly and generally needed type of health service is that which pupils and staff should have when they complain of feeling not up to par. Such service, if pupils are taught to use it freely, helps prevent the spread of contagious diseases and may reveal chronic illness while it is still in an early stage. The health service should be able to make the ordinary preliminary tests usual in such circumstances and to isolate, send home, or summon medical aid, as seems best.

The whole attitude of the school should be that no one who is not feeling well should be in a classroom or office until such tests have been made by the health service. Too often the school's attitude is just the reverse—a false sense of duty calls for the teacher or pupil to stay at his job when actually his duty is to make sure he is a fit person to be allowed to associate with other people. If it is the school's policy to encourage those who do not feel well to remain at home, some pupils and some employees may take advantage now and then, but in the long run it is better to err on the side of safety. Teaching the care and promotion of health is one of the principal objectives of a school, and it cannot by example belittle health just because some may take advantage of the situation created by its interests in health, any more than it can afford to stop the teaching of reading just because some pupils take advantage of the school's tolerant attitude toward reading and sneak into the school's library with "pulp" magazines. No high school really interested in achieving its health objective can show by its attitude toward health care that really its "heart is in the highlands" of mastering academic content, rather than in the down-to-earth business of keeping and promoting good health.

Closely connected with the function of checking health is that of counseling with pupils and staff upon health problems whenever such counsel is desired or seems necessary. The health service should make provision for this to the extent that the local situation requires. If counseling of this kind can be easily secured at public health centers or at an industrial medical care service that includes the families of employees of the major industries of the community, then this function of the school's health service is less important than it is where such service is not readily available from other sources. Regardless of how much or how little of this type of service the school renders, it requires quarters where the counseling can be done on a personal basis. It should be generally understood that the school is willing and able to render such service, for which certain specified hours are set aside. Pupils and staff should feel that it is a service to which they are entitled by reason of their membership in the school's organization. The scope of what is undertaken in such personal conferences will depend upon the competence of the counseling staff. If the school's health staff includes a physician, he will know what his limits of competence are. If it includes only a registered nurse, she, too, will know what she can do and when to refer the patient to a physician for advice. If the school health service does not include either of these, then its consultant service is limited to that narrow field in which an adult can advise a younger person; thus most cases will have to be referred to the family doctor, if any, or to someone whom the school knows to be professionally competent. The school's sincere interest in health should prompt it to limit what it undertakes in this area according to the professional qualifications of those in charge of its health service. As in any other of its professional activities, the school cannot let its enthusiasm get the better of its judgment.

THE HIGH SCHOOL HEALTH SERVICE AND MEDICAL CARE

Whether the high school health service should provide any medical or dental care or not depends upon local conditions. It may not need to do so because such care is already fully provided either by the city or county health service or by private practitioners. Under such circumstances it would be an unnecessary duplication of cost if the high school also began supplying such care. Wherever numbers of youth are not being cared for because not enough such service is available—or is not available at a cost they can afford—the local board of education may decide to provide it at low or at no cost. The basic concern of the public high school principal at this point is that health care be provided when and as it is needed so that youth will have a chance to grow and develop into the best American citizens they are capable of becoming. Who renders the service or under what conditions are matters of secondary importance to the principal so long as the result effectively meets youth's need for health care.

The presumption underlying the initiation of any of these auxiliary activities and services by the high school is that the school, acting under authority of the local board of education, deems it necessary to initiate and conduct them in order that it may best do its main job of educating boys and girls. The school does not assume any auxiliary activity merely because it wants to complicate its work, enlarge its activities, or increase its budget. On the contrary, it first seeks the assistance of all other agencies supposed to be equipped to help youth, and urges upon them the importance of fully meeting these needs as they develop. If these agencies are unable to modify or expand their services so that the needs are fully met, then the school considers whether the situation justifies the creation of an auxiliary service or the extension of an existing one. If the decision is in the affirmative, then, with the approval of the board of education, the school institutes or extends an auxiliary service.

These policies in one community may mean that the high school health service will not need to provide medical or dental care. In another community they may mean that it should do so. But the right of the community to decide through its legally constituted board of education when, how, and to what extent the high school health service shall provide medical care is not one that can be logically denied, wisely abrogated, or safely curtailed.

THE HEALTH SERVICE STAFF

The range of service necessary for this staff to offer determines its size and the character of its qualifications. Each member must be fully and legally qualified according to accepted health and medical standards to perform the services he is employed to perform. It is a disservice to youth to establish an auxiliary agency to help meet youth health needs and then staff it with personnel not qualified to render the contemplated service. Nor is it good for its reputation if the school claims to be able to render a particular kind of service and then does it badly. If it is at all possible, one or more members of the health staff should be employed on a full-time basis. Arrangements should be made with local professional people for part-time specialized counsel and service where the need for such service can be fully met by such a plan.

This staff should work in the high school under the general direction of the high school principal, just as do all other employees of the school assigned to this building. The fact that the members represent a highly specialized and professionalized kind of service does not exempt them from this rule. On the other hand, it is not logical for the school to employ such professional people and then allow the principal, who is a layman in the field of health and medicine, to overrule their judgment and decisions, just because as principal he is head of the high school. The law prevents this whenever it makes it the duty of school health officers to report directly to the city and county health authorities. In other cases the respect of one professional man for another will prompt the principal to be judicious in interposing his judgment into matters of health. Usually a good relationship with city, county, or state health authorities or with local medical and dental groups will afford the principal an opportunity for a conference with them and the school's health staff which will clear up points to the satisfaction of all, especially when the enthusiasm of the school health staff leads its members to insist upon refinements in health and safety measures that the principal regards as impractical.

STUDENT-FACULTY COOPERATION

An advisory committee on health and safety composed of students and faculty should be a part of the school's organization for the maintenance and improvement of health and safety conditions. This committee should operate under the general supervision of whoever heads up the school's health service—even if the school can afford only the part-time service of the teacher on the staff who is most competent in and concerned about health and safety. This committee can help integrate the health service and health education programs. It can suggest policies and practices that the school ought to institute; it can popularize health education and health service with the student body. It can help convince the community that the school is sincerely interested in the personal health problems of youth and in the community's health and safety situations as they affect the health and safety of youth. The student members of the committee should represent the student council's interest in health, first aid, and safety, and should be in charge of any organized student effort or activity designed to maintain or improve these conditions around the school. Such student assistants as are used in the health center or elsewhere around the building in connection with the school's health, first-aid, and safety program should be recommended by this committee, which should also organize and manage them. The student members thus serve in an advisory capacity on the committee but are actively and responsibly involved in the conduct of the school's program in this area.

Some Points to Consider

1. Is it sound policy to organize a high school so that pupils carry some of the responsibility for and do some of the work connected with their life in a school?

2. If you answer the above in the affirmative, why not arrange for them to do all the work of a school except that for which they lack technical competence or that which involves positive danger?

3. Is there danger of exploitation? When is a pupil being exploited? When does exploitation enter in and how could the principal avoid it?

4. Can you justify asking or expecting a pupil to take time from his study to work around the school?

5. If the use of pupils reduces the number of paid employees around the school, is this practice good or bad?

6. In some states child labor laws are strict, and schools are liable for accidents unless they result from work directly connected with classwork for which the pupil enrolled. How can a school proceed in such circumstances?

7. Why is it important to have pupils on committees created to help operate special services? Should teachers be members of such committees?

Further Reading

American Association of School Administrators. *Health in the Schools.* Twentieth Yearbook; Washington, D.C.: National Education Association, 1942.

————. *Safety Education.* Eighteenth Yearbook; Washington, D.C.: National Education Association, 1940. Chaps. 10, 11.

Brem, P. "Ours Is Pupil-planned and Pupil-operated." *National Elementary Principal,* 31 (September, 1951), 212–216.

Coward, G. "We Point with Pride: Library of Myers Park High School, Charlotte, N.C." *Library Journal,* 77 (December 15, 1952), 21–22.

Fargo, L. F. *The Library in the School.* 4th ed.; Chicago: American Library Association, 1947.

Hall, E. "Librarians Are Getting Younger Every Year," *National Elementary Principal,* 31 (September, 1951), 102–109.

Kilander, H. F. "The Administration of Health, Physical Education and Recreation Programs in Secondary Schools," NASSP *Bulletin,* 37, No. 195, May, 1953.

————. "Administrative and Personnel Aspects of School Health Services," *Journal of School Health,* 22 (June, 1952), 155–162.

Olsen, Edward G., ed. *School and Community.* 2nd ed.; Englewood Cliffs, N.J.: Prentice-Hall, Inc., 1954.

Olson, Clara M., and Norman D. Fletcher. *Learn and Live.* New York: Alfred P. Sloan Foundation, Inc., 1946.

Wilson, Howard. *Education for Citizenship.* New York: McGraw-Hill Book Co., Inc., 1938.

Chapter 15

THE HIGH SCHOOL'S SPECIAL SERVICES:
CAFETERIA, TRANSPORTATION, AND
STUDENT AID

Less directly connected with the pupils' regular educational programs than library and health services are the services to be dealt with in this chapter. But here, too, it will be maintained that opportunity for responsible participation by pupils and by teachers is essential to good group living, to sound education, and to good administration of the school. This chapter will undertake to show what the special functions of these three services are, how they can best be performed with teacher-pupil participation, and why the principal has an obligation to attempt to organize them so that opportunity for such participation is provided.

The Cafeteria Service

Arrangements for some sort of lunch service are more and more the rule in high schools. Pupils have always brought their lunch to school, but schools have not always considered themselves obligated to make more than the barest of accommodation available for them. As the size of high school attendance units has increased, a much larger proportion of the pupils are unable to return to their homes for their midday meals. In many towns and cities the main meal of the day is the evening meal; consequently, most families in these communities prefer to have their children stay at school for lunch. With the growing demand for a school lunch service, the attitude of the high school has changed; instead of working to reduce to the lowest possible number those pupils having lunch at school, the school fully accepts the responsibility for as many pupils as want the service and urges all to use it who would not otherwise get a regular noon meal.

STATEMENT OF FUNCTION

As mothers and teachers have learned more about the relation of diet to growth and health, this responsibility is of a higher order than

322

it was when lunches came to school in half-gallon syrup cans and dinner pails. It now requires that the school be able to serve at least one hot dish, well cooked, as well as a variety of other foods, including milk. Not only must the school be responsible for furnishing good foods, it is also expected to encourage youth to select an adequate, well-balanced lunch from what is offered and to acquire desirable social learnings. In addition, knowing as we now do how emotional factors enter in to affect one's health, we expect the school to provide a lunch or cafeteria room that is not only clean and warm but as pleasant, attractive, quiet, and orderly as it can be when used by large numbers of people. In our best high schools these standards are always in the minds of those in charge of the lunch service, even though in many what can be done with the space and equipment available falls far short of these goals.

GOOD PHYSICAL ARRANGEMENTS REQUIRED

Before a school undertakes to operate on a lunch-period schedule or to increase the number of pupils using the lunch service, it should be sure that adequate space and equipment will be provided. Unless these arrangements are satisfactory, it would be wise to delay any marked change in the school lunch service. Many schools operate a poor lunch service, either because boards of education have inadequately provided for it or because the school's administration has not been able to organize the lunch program well. As a result, the lunch period is often the most hectic one of the school day.

The size of the cafeteria room obviously varies with the size of the school, but it also depends upon the quality of the management in the cafeteria, where the arrangements for service lines can be good or bad, as well as in the school at large, where the plans for releasing pupils for lunch can either create short, high peaks of demand or provide a continuous, even flow of pupils down the service lines. The number of periods to be set aside for lunch is an important factor in determining how large the cafeteria room must be. Each extra lunch period provided, for example, reduces the possible peak load in each period. But since lunch must come near the middle of the day, and since at least thirty minutes are needed for each period, a school with more than four lunch periods must send some pupils to lunch rather early and, what is worse from their point of view, not send some of them until very late. Hence, the size of the cafeteria room must accommodate from 25 to 35 per cent of the size of the group to be served with some change above or below this figure as the efficiency of other arrangements is high or low. If the dining space seats 250, and from 12 to 15 students can be served each minute, about 1,000 can be served in three thirty-minute lunch periods. Good standards for the guidance of those responsible for school cafeteria construction, operation, and management are available.[1]

In general, the best arrangements are those that keep the needed size of the cafeteria down. If the room is small, the original cost of space is reduced and there is not the confusion in operation that is more or less inevitable when large groups are brought together. On the other hand, equipment and service in a compact cafeteria may be more expensive than in a larger one; certainly the former demands more ingenuity of administrators responsible for organizing the school at the lunch periods. The best results obtain when there are as many lunch periods as are feasible, when there are enough service lines so that the length of the standing line is usually short, when there are enough assistants behind the service counters so that each pupil is served at each point without delay, when the flow into the cafeteria is continuous, and when the number of seats available (or the size of the room) is sufficient so that as a pupil leaves the service line he can find a place to sit. Proper coordination of these factors affects not only room size but also the orderly and satisfactory operation of the service. Further details on cafeteria size are supplied in a later chapter on school buildings.

The cafeteria director is chiefly responsible for the arrangement of most of these factors, but the one involving the continuous flow of pupils is a problem of general high school administration. An even flow can be produced by releasing rooms to the cafeteria at short intervals during a lunch period, rather than all at once at its beginning. For example, let us assume that a school has four lunch periods thirty minutes long, and at every one of the four periods, fifteen rooms of about 30 pupils each are to be served. These fifteen can be released at one time at the beginning of the period, thus throwing about 450 pupils into the cafeteria within three or four minutes, or three rooms can be released each six minutes, thus tending to reduce to 90 the maximum number headed for the service lines at one time. With two service lines, there will be 45 in each line. The service available will need to be sufficient to move 7 or 8 pupils past any point in each service line every minute if the last one of this group is to be served by the time the next group of rooms is released. This example is scaled to a large high school, but the principle of continuous flow of students to the cafeteria applies even to a small school with only one lunch period. Waiting in line will thus be reduced, and short periods of rush in the service lines, followed by periods of idleness, will be eliminated. In effect, this plan of continuous flow blends the four lunch periods

---

[1] See Mary De Garmo Bryan, *The School Cafeteria* (2nd ed.; New York: Appleton-Century-Crofts, Inc., 1938); also Blanche A. Tansil, "Feeding Children at School" (Unpublished Ed.D. project; New York: Teachers College, Columbia University, 1946).

into one or subdivides each period into five—however one chooses to regard it. The pupils in each of the three rooms released at one time learn as easily when they are due back in their classrooms as they do when a whole fourth of the student body returns to class at once as, indeed, it tends to do when a continuous flow plan is not used. This continuous flow of pupils from classes to the cafeteria and from it back to their classrooms is usually much more satisfactory than the pell-mell rush of large numbers of students into, through, and out of the cafeteria in a relatively short period of time.

That good equipment and service for the service counters must be available is evident from what has just been said. A good kitchen arrangement is also a requisite. It needs to be well separated from the lunchroom itself. Actually, the best arrangement is secured when not only the kitchen but also the serving lines are separated in some manner from the lunchroom itself. Thus the noise and confusion of the kitchen and the service lines are not added to the buzz of conversation in the lunchroom. Such a division affords an opportunity for better ventilation of the kitchen service areas. The desirability of keeping the odors from food preparation out of the rest of the school building suggests the location of the cafeteria in a one-story wing of the building or on the top floor. Either of these locations, if equipped with good exhaust fans, will reduce these odors to the minimum; which will be chosen will depend upon the local situation. Nevertheless, the problem of combating the inevitable odors of cooking must be successfully met somehow.

The cafeteria room during the lunch period is bound to be one of the noisiest places around the school. For this reason, it is important that, where possible, noise be reduced or eliminated. Any realistic program of reducing noise starts with the character of the construction materials used in the cafeteria. Not until rather recently have builders of school buildings paid enough attention to noise abatement to use the requisite amount of good sound-absorbing materials in floors, walls, and ceilings. As a result, we have thousands of high schools that are veritable soundtraps, catching, holding, and even magnifying every sound. The cost of quiet in a school building is one that many people can argue themselves into believing is an unnecessary expense, in spite of the fact that business and industry are willing to afford it for themselves. But new high school buildings are reflecting this trend—not only in the auditorium, gymnasiums, corridors, and cafeteria, but in classrooms and offices as well.

Even in a well-constructed building, however, a standard of conduct must be established that reduces unnecessary noise in the cafeteria to the minimum. It is important to maintain a natural, normal situation in the cafeteria with pupils free to move about and to converse with one another. The problem is how to achieve this and at the same time prevent the overexuberant from creating needless noise and confusion. A well-constructed cafeteria room, good arrangements for service, and a well-established set of standards of conduct that students have developed and helped maintain—these are essential to a good program of noise abatement in a school cafeteria.

GOOD HEALTH STANDARDS TO BE EXEMPLIFIED

Everything about the cafeteria should illustrate to the pupils the health teachings of the school, assuming, of course, that the school is doing what it should be doing in teaching health. If the school is doing this, it would be foolish for the cafeteria to violate all this teaching. And if the school is not doing what it should in health teaching, it is all the more essential that pupils see good practice exemplified in the cafeteria. In our best high schools the health and home education programs of the school and the cafeteria service are consistent with one another. In the classrooms and laboratories a pupil learns what constitutes good food selection for him, when he goes to the cafeteria he has a chance to—in fact, he is encouraged to—practice what he has learned. Everything about the cafeteria should impress the student with its cleanliness. The order in which food is presented to him in the service line should suggest the desirability of balancing his diet. A fairly accurate criterion of the sincerity of the school about its health teaching is the kind, amount, and location of candy on the service lines. There is a good margin of profit on candy—and it comes ready to serve, so that practically no work is involved in its sale. If large amounts and many varieties of cheap candies are placed near the entrance to the service line, one may legitimately conclude that the cafeteria is chiefly concerned with making as much money with as little work as possible regardless of the teachings of the school's health education program. If, on the other hand, candy is placed at the exit from the service line, and the quality is of the best, it is safe to say that health standards and principles are in the minds of those in charge, for under this condition candy sales are known to be reduced, since they catch only the left-over nickel or dime—not the first one.

Another quick but effective check on how health standards are emphasized in most school cafeterias is the number of pupils who are drinking milk. If one looks over the tables when lunch is being eaten and finds them thickly spotted with the white of milk bottles, he can assume that the drinking of milk is being encouraged. If, on the other hand, "pop" bottles are the rule, the conclusion must be different. This is not to imply that carbonated beverages are harmful. As far as these authors know, they are not; but the price asked is high for a little sweetened, colored water. Much better food values for the money ought to be presented in school cafeterias, and pupils should be encouraged to demand them.

It is questionable whether it is good policy to ban the sale of candy, "pop," and other popular foods of low food value for the money. Such regimentation may backfire, doing more harm than good. In some communities the school may easily be able to omit such "food" altogether. In others, where the community attitude is not so good or where there is an unfortunate history in matters of this kind, perhaps the best plan is to reduce their sale as much as possible while encouraging good practice to the full. Various plans for discouraging the one practice and encouraging the opposite are in use. The location on the service line is one. Some schools limit what each pupil can spend on candy and such items. Others do not allow them to be sold until the last ten minutes of each cafeteria period. Schools often combine these restrictions with positive teaching in class and with posters in the halls and cafeteria pointing out the low food values and high cost of some food items as compared to others. The fundamental policies that should guide educators will tend to be constant from school to school, but the levels of practice will have to be adjusted to different communities, with each school working to raise its level by all the legitimate means open to those who believe that education is the most effective means of social progress.

THE CAFETERIA PERSONNEL AND RELATIONSHIPS

The significance that has been attached to good standards and service in the foregoing sections leads to the inevitable conclusion that the cafeteria's operation must be in the hands of a professionally trained person. In a large high school the director of the cafeteria will be a full-time employee and fully responsible for its operation. All who work in this cafeteria are responsible to this director. Under such conditions this director should qualify for, and be a regular member of, the high school faculty. In smaller school systems the actual head of the cafeteria in each school may be but a part-time employee of the school system, with the professionally trained cafeteria supervisor in general charge of the cafeterias in all the schools of the whole system. The part-time employee at the head of each unit, however, must have had enough training or experience to understand and know how to apply the best ideas and highest standards of food selection and service. Similar criteria should guide the selection of all cafeteria workers, each of whom must pass periodic physical examinations. Whoever directs the cafeteria service for the high school or for the school system should be at least partly responsible for administering these examinations, for interviewing prospective employees, and for any further in-service training that may be needed. Where civil service regulations control these appointments, the job descriptions should reflect these types of qualifications for cafeteria positions, and only those who fully meet these qualifications should be appointed. If student employees are used, their selection should be governed by the same standards that apply to other workers.

The cafeteria director in a high school should be responsible to the principal. Where the cafeteria is the only one in the school system, this relationship is simple and direct. Where there is a system of school cafeterias in operation under the general direction of a cafeteria supervisor, and the high school cafeteria consequently operates as a unit in the system under city-wide policies, the relationship is not so direct and simple. In the latter case, it should be assumed that the high school principal has had a chance to help develop the city-wide policies or at least has had a chance to express his views on them. He cannot ask the high school cafeteria director to suspend from operation city-wide policies because he may not think they fit the situation in his particular high school. If he should want them suspended his appeal should be to the city-wide supervisor of cafeterias, and, if necessary, to the assistant superintendent in charge of high schools or to the superintendent of schools. On the other hand, he should be able to expect that the high school cafeteria director will work out and discuss with him the particular practices by which these city-wide policies are to be put into effect in the high school. Both the principal and the director have a chance to appeal, as necessary, to those in general charge of secondary schools and cafeterias if their help is needed in settling details.

CAFETERIA FINANCE

The expense of installing and operating the cafeteria in a high school is a legitimate charge against the school's budget and is therefore a responsibility of the board of education. In some states, actions of the legislature or the state department of education set financial controls for cafeteria operation, but the trend is to recognize it as a school budget expense in the same category with school transportation. The high school cafeteria should not be operated by the principal and director as an independent financial adventure. Neither is it good practice for the cafeteria to be operated as a part of the student activity fund. In the first place, the cafeteria should not be operated for the purpose of making a profit for anybody, nor in such a way as to tempt anyone to try to make a profit. In the second place, the principal's or the director's professional status should not be affected by whether the high school cafeteria makes money or not. Good health standards should be followed and good servings provided for pupils even if there is an unavoidable financial loss. The ingenuity that some high school principals and cafeteria directors have used to provide good cafeteria service in the space and with the equipment available to them is to be commended, but their success should not be used as an argument for perpetuating the failure of many boards of education to assume their rightful financial responsibility for cafeteria service.

Customarily, the charges made to pupils for cafeteria service approximate the cost of the food and its preparation. The charge usually covers the cost of food purchased in quantity and the salaries of those who prepare it, but not the salary of the director of the high school cafeteria or of the city supervisor of cafeterias. The trend is toward the assumption of all salary and wage costs by the school budget. The laws in some states specify rather exactly what cafeteria charges may or may not be covered by the price charged to pupils. These charges against the users of cafeteria service are made in amounts sufficient to cover these costs on the same theory that even where textbooks are furnished free, pupils are often expected to supply at their own expense such consumable items as pencils, pens, and notebooks. As good an argument can be made for furnishing these items free to pupils and for furnishing needed food free in the cafeteria as can be made for supplying free transportation to school pupils. The basic policy is that educational opportunity shall be effectively free to all children and youth, and in the absence of specific prohibitions by the legislature, a board of education may pay any reasonable cost that it deems necessary to produce this result. But it is the custom, however, to make a charge for lunch service, and it is questionable whether a doctrinaire advocacy of free school lunches for all would serve any purpose in many communities. The best general practice probably obtains when as large servings of good food are provided as pupils will eat; when the charge for these servings covers only quantity purchase of the foods and actual wage costs of preparation; when these costs are lowered by the acceptance of food subsidies from any available sources—local, state, or federal; and when a system is in operation that furnishes free lunches (or a chance to earn them) to pupils who need such assistance.

COOPERATIVE OPERATION OF THE CAFETERIA

Supervision of the whole cafeteria space including the dining room should be the direct responsibility of the director of the cafeteria, but since the satisfactory operation of the cafeteria is of concern to practically everyone in school, students should have some responsibility for it. Where adequate, well-equipped quarters are provided, the school authorities can easily create a situation in which students exercise almost complete control of those who use the cafeteria. It is pretty largely a matter of developing a group acceptance of certain standards of conduct. Once the student body has set and accepted appropriate standards, its committees can be pretty largely responsible for seeing that these are respected. Where standards have not been set, or where the task of development is still going on, some assistance from appointed faculty members may be necessary. In most schools, however, students will increasingly take over and the need for faculty assistance will be reduced to the barest minimum.

A cafeteria committee appointed by the student council should be the official point of contact between the students and the cafeteria director. If there is a separate faculty dining room, the faculty may want a similar committee of its own. Some schools have a joint student-faculty committee. These groups should have the opportunity to discuss with the cafeteria director any matters in which they are interested— menus, servings, personnel, student conduct, and other details of operation. Without such an opportunity to discuss complaints and suggest changes, feeling often builds up over small things until the effect is out of proportion to the cause.

When the views of students on the operation of the cafeteria are listened to with respect, they feel that they have a share in the successful functioning of the enterprise, and when changes are proposed they realize that they will be expected to have a part in carrying them out. There are a number of ways of participating in the work of operating the school cafeteria for which students can qualify as well as adults, and students should have the opportunity to perform the work on a volunteer basis or for wages if they want to do so. The jobs range from operating the mechanical dishwashers to acting as cashier. Volunteer tasks include acting as hosts and hostesses to care for details of student conduct assumed by the students' cafeteria committee. The whole group of student workers should be organized under its own elected leadership and be allowed to participate along with the student council cafeteria committee and faculty members in meetings where cafeteria matters are under discussion. As students are made more responsible for the operational arrangements affecting them, the more they will understand what is involved in proposals for improvements. In addition, the cafeteria affords opportunities for training in group leadership and for real work experience.

The lack of student participation and the evidences of student irresponsibility in some high schools tempt one to believe that a high school has to be operated like a penal institution. It takes a visit to a high school where a student body has been taught over the years to accept responsibility, and to act responsibly on its own, to restore one's faith in the possibilities of the high school as a training center for the kinds of young adults America needs. To find an explanation of the differences between two such schools one naturally looks to the community and its homes. There are often differences there that can serve as explanations and excuses; more often, however, the true explanation lies in what each high school's administration expects from its students and in its concepts of what constitutes good school organization and administration. The cafeteria is one of the places where these differences are revealed.

Transportation Service

A number of factors have made the organization and administration of the school transportation service a part of the operation of many high schools. The increased size of high school attendance units, especially in centralized or consolidated districts where in some western areas the extent of the district is such that excessively long trips to school are sometimes required, has been an important one. Some urban districts where other means of travel are available to most pupils still need to furnish transportation for a minority of pupils from outlying sections. Then, too, the modern tendency to regard walking as outmoded—except on a golf course—probably accounts for the existence of part of our school transportation service. It therefore may be classified as both a necessity and a convenience.

Under prevailing conditions in many high school districts, not to make some arrangements for school transportation service would be equivalent to a denial of educational opportunity to those whose homes are such a distance from the school as to make it impossible for them to walk there, or so inconvenient as to make it practically impossible. The same line of reasoning argues for the provision of public school dormitories on the school campus where daily trips between home and school are out of the question. The alternative to the transportation service, if equal educational opportunity is to be assured, is the building of more smaller high school units. These, however, as they usually work out, do not provide as good programs as the larger consolidated high school does and therefore also tend to deny to their students the educational opportunities that are possible in the latter type of school whose pupils largely depend upon the school transportation service. The most practical, economical, and satisfactory solution is for the school to take the initiative by making some sort of arrangement for the transportation of pupils.

TRANSPORTATION SERVICE A SCHOOL BUDGET OBLIGATION

Since this country is committed to equality of educational opportunity, a moral obligation rests on each board of education to arrange for transportation of pupils if the lack of it operates to deny this opportunity. In many states the law expressly requires or permits boards to do so. Not to act upon this responsibility because individual parents do not demand it, or because they are willing to make their own transportation arrangements for which they pay, means that a board is not as eager to provide educational opportunity as the traditions of local initiative and local control of education assume it to be.

The responsibility for the transportation of pupils is discharged under a number of different kinds of arrangements. In a state like North Carolina the transportation of pupils is an enterprise of the state, all the equipment being owned by the state, and its operation being highly centralized. In states where boards own, maintain, and operate their own fleets of school buses the high school principals do not have direct responsibility for organizing and administering the service. In some instances where the high school district is a much larger one than the elementary school district, transportation is provided only for high school pupils. The transportation service is then often a direct responsibility of the high school principal. In some districts the service is contracted for with private companies that furnish equipment and personnel and are usually paid for on the pupil-mile basis. Sometimes the contract is with the community's regular public transportation system, which furnishes estra equipment and schedules as needed for special trips for school pupils. A modification of this plan is one by which the board of education pays to the public transportation company the bus fare of pupils who need to be transported, but the company does not make extra trips. Where the need is not great or affects only a few pupils in widely scattered outlying areas, payment is sometimes made to parents who are willing to supply transportation in their private cars for the neighboring children. Several such plans may often operate in a single district in order to provide adequate service at the most reasonable cost.

In some states the law and the regulations of state departments of education amply safeguard the health, safety, comfort, and welfare of pupils while on school buses. Standards covering the construction and operation of the school transportation equipment and the qualifications for drivers and other personnel involved in school transportation have been carefully developed. Normally, the board of education in a school district has the responsibility of knowing about and applying these standards to their transportation service. Even where the management of school transportation arrangements has not been specifically assigned to his office, the high school principal also has a professional responsibility for knowing that the transportation service being provided the pupils of his school conforms to the best standards and practices. For his own protection, if for no better reason, he cannot afford to allow a board to sleep unmolested on its rights and duties. In the absence of such laws or regulations he should undertake to put into effect, with the board's consent, local regulations based upon approved practice.

PRACTICAL LIMITS OF SCHOOL CONTROL

When high school pupils are transported in equipment owned, maintained, and operated by the high school district under the immediate supervision of the principal, the school is in a position to control it completely and to provide fully for the safety, comfort, health, and welfare of its pupils. Under these circumstances, too, the equipment is freely available for use on such special trips as the educational program of the school requires. Although other arrangements for pupil transportation may be dictated by the conditions prevailing in any particular district, the plan of district ownership and operation is to be preferred because it does not lead to the division of authority and control inherent in the other plans. Under district ownership the school has the chance and the duty of putting into effect the best standards governing equipment and operation; moreover, it is also responsible for the pupils. The school no doubt would be glad to have others assume these added responsibilities if it can satisfy itself that others are willing to assume them and actually do assume them. Otherwise, to the school will fall the burden of providing a district-owned service, since if it institutes a transportation service at all, it cannot afford to be a party to willful neglect of the safety and welfare of its pupils. When the equipment is district-owned and -operated, the high school principal can draw up regulations for the board of education, if this has not been done in the superintendent's office, and with the board's approval can make these regulations official for all employed personnel and for pupils. Assuming that this is a responsibility of the high school principal, he should make the regulations cover standards for equipment, its care, inspection, and operation; the qualifications and duties of personnel; and the conduct and control of pupils. If such regulations are carefully drawn and are known to all, there can be little excuse for violations that involve the safety, health, comfort, or welfare of pupils.[2]

When any type of equipment and service not owned or operated by the district is utilized, the problem of divided responsibility and authority always arises. If the person operating the service is wholly responsible and cooperative, a very satisfactory standard of service can be provided. To the extent that he is not, problems appear which the school has difficulty in meeting. That the school cannot brush these thoughtlessly aside, even if it so desires, is apparent when one recalls

[2] See Marcus C. S. Noble, *Pupil Transportation in the United States* (Scranton, Penn.: International Textbook Company, 1940).

the court decisions touching upon the responsibilities of the school for pupils en route to and from it. These make it clear that the school has the legal authority to enforce reasonable regulations covering the safety, welfare, and conduct of pupils while en route from school and is entitled to the full support of parents in putting these into effect. Even without legal authority its natural concern for its pupils would make the school feel morally responsible for attempting to safeguard its pupils until they had been returned to the supervision of their parents. Therefore, when a school district, in order to implement its duty to provide equality of educational opportunity, finds it necessary or desirable to institute or arrange for a school transportation service, it simply modifies the conditions under which it exercises the already existing control over pupils en route to and from school. Since by establishing such a service the school chooses to enter more actively into this situation, the community may logically expect its administrative officers to be so much the more concerned to see that good standards are proposed, encouraged, and enforced.

School transportation is an area where, in some communities and states, increased pupil responsibility has been tested and found satisfactory. In these situations older boys and girls are employed as drivers and are in charge of the bus and its occupants. Their safety record is better than that of adult drivers and they have less trouble with their passengers. When questioned about how he handled school bus discipline where there were pupil-drivers one principal said, "Riding the bus is a privilege not a right. If unruly pupils are denied the privilege for a day or two they give the driver no further trouble." So in every area of activity where pupil responsibility is increased if students understand that the students carrying the responsibility have the full backing of the student council, the student body, and the faculty they will render more than satisfactory service and all will learn in the process.

Student Aid Service

In practically every high school some pupils occasionally, and a few pupils frequently, need the kind of service known as student aid. The standard of living in this country, on the average, is high, but at one extreme even in "good times" there are likely to be some pupils who will need help in meeting the unavoidable expense of attending high school. For even though we say we have *free* public education, this is, of course, only relatively true. For a large family whose principal wage earners are able to obtain only minimum wages, there is not money enough to supply even the modest needs of a high school pupil attending a high school where every effort is made to keep down the incidental costs of attendance. In times of depression these few pupils in many high schools become numerous, and ways of meeting their needs on a state and federal basis have been found to be necessary.

All the legitimate candidates for such student aid do not come from large families where the total income is low. Some are orphans whose subsistence needs are being cared for by someone or by an institution and who need additional funds for the incidental expenses of high school attendance. Most states either make so meager an allowance for widows and orphans or administer it so badly that the funds do not suffice to meet the incidental expenses of school attendance. Some students help out at home by working after school to such an extent that their schoolwork suffers. These need enough aid in some form to permit a reduction in their work hours so that they can do their schoolwork well. Some need aid temporarily because of sudden and unexpected family misfortunes. Some come from broken homes; others, from homes that are not sympathetic with their desire to stay in school and consequently do not provide the money that attendance requires. A study of the situation in many typical high schools will reveal that this need for student aid is more widespread even in normal times than many suspect.

WHAT SCHOOL CONDITIONS PRODUCE THE NEED

Studies of the absolute minimum amount of money needed to buy the things that attendance requires have shown an average expense of ten dollars a month. This figure is probably now meaningless, for costs have risen sharply since the studies were made. They show, however, the widest of extremes from school to school, as one familiar with American high schools would expect. The costs are affected by whether or not books and supplies are provided from public funds, by the cost of transportation, by the cost of school lunches, by the cost of participating in student activities, by the cost of graduation, and by the standard of dress set by the student body. In some high schools the costs of attending the school and being a part of its life and activities without embarrassment reach twenty-five dollars a month and over; and in some of these schools such figures are considered moderate because the family economic level is high and they are thus easily met. In others, these costs are automatically kept at a very low figure because the families in the community cannot generally afford to send their children to high school without a considerable sacrifice. The community itself sometimes sets a high or a low level with which the school does not interfere, since it seems to work no hardship on anyone. But in many other communities, especially in towns having only a single high school, attended by all the youth of the city, wide ranges of family income exist, and unless the school works to simplify the demands of student life, those who are economically able will set the standards, the cost of which automatically excludes from participation many of the economically less fortunate. Schools therefore should appraise the situation and where necessary intervene to encourage pupils and their parents to accept simple ways of carrying on life at school which keep the costs more nearly within reach of all. To all intents and purposes, these costs constitute a hidden tuition cost of attending what is supposed to be a free school.

Of course, there are still those who, pointing with pride to the difficulties and deprivations they surmounted in their youth, argue that it is good for a youth to have to endure the "slings and arrows of outrageous fortune." But those who have studied the psychology of adolescence or are simply understanding observers of the life of the youth about them will recognize that for each such shining example of the beneficent effects of penury there are many others whose lives and personalities are being deeply creased and distorted by the frustrations produced by living in a situation where economic conditions cut them off from a fair share of participation in the life of the group. If we are to have *free* public high schools and urge or even compel attendance, then we have some obligation to see to it that youth really have a chance to *belong* to the social groups of which they are supposed to be a part.

PLANS FOR MEETING THE NEED

But even where the costs of student life are moderate, and the best of arrangements exist for holding these expenses to a reasonable level, it is necessary for the high school to be organized to meet these needs unobtrusively as they appear. In some high schools the situation is so simple that some teacher who is interested in such activities, cooperating with a committee of the parents' organization, can in an informal way handle all such problems that arise. In many others, however, a more formal organization needs to be set up by the school administration. This can take the form of a student-faculty committee or of a faculty committee acting without students, if that seems preferable. If such a group exists, its work should be correlated with the school's guidance activities so that as needs are discovered by those who counsel most with students, the information can be transmitted to the committee immediately. The desirability of overlapping membership between such a group and the guidance workers is thus indicated. Some people may argue that students should not serve on such a committee, as it would be embarrassing to them and to the pupils served if their "cases" were considered by other students. This reasoning is logical, but some way of getting the students to help, both in discovering the needs of others and in finding ways to meet them, is required. Such channels of communication could be developed without having the student members of the committee aware of every detail of the arrangements made for each pupil. Even the faculty members need not have all this information if the chairman of the group is given some responsibility for carrying out the decisions of the committee. It is important that students see and understand how the decisions of a group affect individual members of that group; participation in some way in a student aid service is one way of acquiring that understanding.

The committee on student aid should also correlate its activities with those of other public and private social agencies of the community. The records of many of the families from which these high school pupils come are in the files of these nonschool agencies. The school should know what actions they have taken, and they, in turn, should know what the school has done or plans to do. The school frequently secures the necessary financial assistance for its students from these public and private agencies. Civic clubs and organizations, for example, are often justifiably proud of the assistance they give to pupils. They like to know that the school is watching for these needs and is willing to certify to their genuineness, and that the school recognizes their concern for such youth. As far as possible, the willingness of all such groups to help students should be encouraged and used, both because they have the means of obtaining funds and because their participation in such activities is good for them, the school, and the pupil.

In most schools the student aid committee, however, will need funds of its own, or at least funds at its own disposal, so that it is not always dependent upon other groups. It should therefore be authorized to receive gifts of money or materials likely to be needed. One way of building up funds for the committee's use is to "tax" some student activity, the receipts from games or public performances, for example, if the student body approves it. Benefit performances given by student groups or student activities carried on for money are other possible sources of funds for the committee. Wherever the money comes from, accurate records should be kept, filed each year with the principal, and open to inspection by anyone who is entitled to see them.

The committee should follow the principle of self-help as far as possible, but it should not be required to see that each pupil it serves has earned what he receives. To pupils who are able to work it should suggest the names of those in the school or the community who could use part-time student help. The school can create regular student assistantships for which pay is given, and students who need part-time work and are qualified for these types of work should be given preference. When work experience programs are as well developed in many high schools as they should be and are fully integrated with the programs of students, it is possible that the needs of all students can be legitimately met by self-help. But until that time, the student aid committee will need to be able to make outright grants of school supplies, clothing, other school necessities, and even money for school expenses, when self-help is not practical or desirable.

The student aid committee should direct the participation of the high school in any programs of student aid supported by the state or federal governments. This country seems today to recognize more clearly the importance of educating all its youth than ever before. Our leadership position in the free world has created a shortage of well-educated young people and there is now great concern that none of our youth grows up without having his abilities developed to the full. Able youth are permitted to defer their military service in order that they may go to college. More scholarship aid is available than ever before. The armed services are spending large sums to increase the supply of skills which are in short supply. All of these affect chiefly youth who are beyond high school age, but we know that about one out of five of our most able youth are dropping out of high school for lack of money with which to meet the necessary expenses of attendance. These programs of aid for college and young adult students presume that all able youth have been able to finish high school. This condition does not, of course, prevail, and if it is desirable for all able youth to have the highest level of training of which they are capable, it will be necessary for such aid programs to reach down to sustain some youth while they are in high school. Scholarships to able high school graduates, now more freely available than ever before, are part of the answer to this problem, but not the whole answer. The report of the President's Commission on Higher Education shows that it is within the realm of possibility that in the years just ahead we may embark upon such programs. The evil effects on youth of the depression years were mitigated to some extent by the high school and college student aid programs of the National Youth Administration. Some such plans may be needed again. One does not have to approve all that was done in those years in the name of the NYA to maintain that its student aid funds were a godsend to thousands of high school and college students. The worst feature of the programs is known to have been its bad administration, often at the local level, by the school and college officials in charge of it. Nevertheless, the principle underlying the creation of these student aid funds—that worthy students should not be denied their educational opportunity by reason of the financial condition of their families—is still sound. As long as this condition operates to deny such opportunity to some students, it will be in the national interest for them to receive aid in some form or other. Every high school should be organized to meet these needs as fully as it can from the available resources and to handle effectively any additional funds that may become available under state or national student aid plans.

THE HIGH SCHOOL SHOULD EXEMPLIFY
WELL-ORGANIZED GROUP LIFE

The theme of utilizing school and community resources for the growth and development of youth by arranging for youth to participate responsibly in community and group life runs throughout the book. These two chapters on the school's special services illustrate how students can participate in their operation. In closing this section, however, the authors desire to re-emphasize the general principles rather than to summarize operational details involved in their administration.

The high school is an educational institution not only because it offers given programs but because it is also a place where youth live. It is truly an educational institution when these two aspects of school life complement each other in furthering the growth and development of its pupils. In actual practice, what is supposed to be learned from the program is sometimes belied by what is lived in the school. The pupils are expected to learn in the classroom to appreciate and revere the moral and ethical concepts and ideals that underlie personal and group living of the highest type, but they sometimes see these so little practiced or praised in the school life of which they are a part that they easily come to the conclusion that these concepts and ideals are not the real dynamics of modern life. In most high schools, however, they do see some attempt to make the life and influence of the school consistent with its teachings. At its best, the American high school exemplifies in spirit and in services to its pupils the real *concern* of a democratic institution for the welfare and well-being of each person belonging to it or affected by it. The American high school, at its best, teaches that institutions in a democratic society should be evaluated in democratic terms. At its best, it shows American youth—and therefore teaches them—that institutions can be so planned, organized, and operated by the people who compose them that each member is better off working in and through these institutions and in living under them than he could possibly be outside of them. The high school teaches youth not only that democratically organized community and institutional life successfully attains the *end* of personal and group welfare for all, but also that active, responsible participation in the work of building and operating such institutions is the best *means* for attaining the high level of personal growth and development to which each person naturally aspires. The individual student thus has an opportunity to see and to learn that as each has a chance and sincerely tries to use his abilities to improve the life of which he is a part,

that life does become better. Moreover, he learns that active participation in this process contributes to the full, well-rounded growth and
development of each member of the group. The basic virtue of democracy
is that its survival depends upon its developing every personality it
touches into the most nearly perfect person that individual is capable of
becoming.

To plan, organize, and to operate a high school in which life and
living approach this goal requires that care and thought must be exercised by principal, faculty, and students, to the extent that they are
entrusted with any degree of leadership in the life of the school. Thus a
high school program and life can be rounded out by cooperative action
until it provides its members with all the kinds of services—the need
for which has been created by the fact of the school's existence. It thus
becomes truly most educative as well as most democratic. It cannot
be one and not the other. If this thought and care are not exercised, the
high school becomes such a poor example of organized group life as to
be wholly unsatisfactory to all and a living argument against the theory
as well as the practice of democracy.

Some Points to Consider

1. Is cafeteria work too menial to ask pupils to do?
2. It is a good policy to expect every student to make some service contribution to the school?
3. When should wages be involved and when should they not? If
a school pays wages to pupils for some work, can it expect others to do other
work on a service basis?
4. The head of the school cafeteria service says, "I don't want these pupils
messing around in my cafeteria." As the principal of this high school, what
would be your response?
5. The high school principal's annual report to the superintendent contained these sentences: "Our cafeteria made a nice profit this year which we
expect to spend installing a new ventilating system in the cafeteria kitchen.
This will not only make the kitchen more comfortable for those who must
work there but tend to keep food odors out of the remainder of the building."
When this was read to the board, some members approved; others objected.
Why could this difference of opinion have existed?

Further Reading

Bryan, Mary De Garmo. *The School Cafeteria.* 2nd ed.; New York: Appleton-
    Century-Crofts, Inc., 1938. Chaps. 1–6.
Butterworth, Julian E. *Administering Pupil Transportation.* Minneapolis, Minn.:
    Educational Publishers, Inc., 1941.
————. "Organization and Administration of the Local School System; Pupil

Transportation," *Review of Educational Research,* 13 (October, 1943), 359–362.

Featherstone, E. G. "Recent Developments in Pupil-Transportation," *American School and University,* 1951, pp. 368–370.

Miller, P. R. "Students Share Responsibility for the School Lunch," *Nation's Schools,* 46 (July, 1950), 64.

National Commission on Safety Education. *Our School Buses.* Washington, D.C.: National Education Association, 1948.

Noble, Marcus C. S. *Pupil Transportation in the United States.* Scranton, Penn.: International Textbook Company, 1940.

————. "School Bus Safety," *NEA Journal,* September, 1946.

————. "The School Bus Standards," *School Life,* April, 1946.

————. "Transportation, Past, Present, and Future," *Senior Scholastic,* February 26, March 26, April 30, 1945.

Page, David R., and Grace Parle. "Model Lunchroom as Seen by Pupil, Mother and Health Inspector," *Nation's Schools,* 53 (April, 1954), 94.

Peabody, Marie. "Let the Children Help in the School Lunch," *Practical Home Economics,* 32 (November, 1953), 45.

Schreiber, Joseph. "Pupils Learn as Well as Eat," *Nation's Schools,* 52 (August, 1953), 76.

Stack, Dorr. "School Transportation—a Look Ahead," *American School and University,* 1953, pp. 387–390.

Tansil, Blanche A. "Feeding Children at School," Unpublished Ed.D. project; New York: Teachers College, Columbia University, 1946.

Thomas, O. M. H. "Plan with Faculty and Students for a Successful School Lunch," *American School Board Journal,* 126 (February, 1953), 60.

Waldrep Reef, and others. "Centralized Operation Pays Off in Oak Ridge," *Nation's Schools,* 46 (September, 1950), 72.

Beside the professional staff relationships dealt with in Part Two the high school principal also has the responsibility for developing and maintaining good pupil personnel relations and conditions. These are closely related to the school's educational program when it is broadly interpreted, as in Part Three. Part Four discusses the organization and administration of some of the principal aspects of the school that are directly related to student welfare and to students' educational programs. Without good policies and practices at points where the school's program and its administration directly touch the students, the work of the school can hardly be regarded as a success.

Part Four

THE PRINCIPAL AND PUPIL PERSONNEL ACTIVITIES

Chapter 16

ENTRANCE, PROGRESS, AND GRADUATION
POLICIES AND PRACTICES

THE AMERICAN ELEMENTARY SCHOOL has traditionally been regarded as the common school and the high school as a selective institution. Today, however, there is a marked tendency to regard the American high school as a part of the common school. It is in a transitional period as it moves toward the point where (1) it will admit as regular high school pupils all adolescent youth who fall within the wide ranges of normality and (2) it will assume normal progress and eventual graduation for all who try to profit from the learning activities that it provides. Many high schools have already reached this point; many others are on the way. Schools and communities that subscribe to this point of view do not assume that all their high school graduates have attained minimum standards in subject matter or have mastered prescribed blocks of subject matter. They assume that the school has done its best to prepare each student for living and that each student has made a reasonable effort to gain from his school experience. These schools have collected detailed evidence that is available to prospective employers, college deans, and anyone else who is interested, so that each graduate may be assisted in finding an appropriate opportunity when he leaves high school. College admissions officers and employers have no right to demand that a high school force its graduates to meet a fixed standard that is inappropriate or even impossible for many. They do have a right to be truthfully and completely informed about any graduate or former student, what kind of a person he is and what he can do. When considering a particular graduate, they are entitled to expect the school to supply information about his experiences, attainments, strengths, and weaknesses, whatever they may be. The fact of high school graduation has never guaranteed much in particular about any graduate, and time has done nothing to assure the world that graduates have attained a common fixed standard of acceptability.

The reasons for the authors' point of view have been developed in other chapters in this book; here they will be briefly mentioned. Knowing what we do about individual differences, and committed as we are to universal secondary education, a wide range of competence in high school graduates is easy to understand. High school principals and teachers are realizing that all pupils can and do continue to learn throughout their high school careers, though some of them learn much more slowly than others. In comparison with abler students, however, slow pupils appear to be at a lesser disadvantage in later adolescence than they were earlier.[1]

State laws related to compulsory schooling reflect the fact that in an industrial democratic society, there is nothing that society can do with youth except send them to school. And increasingly employers, as well as organized labor, are saying that there is no place in modern industry for workers of high school age.[2] Consequently, the school must provide adequate and appropriate opportunities for different kinds of learners. The lay public, therefore, cannot reasonably expect these youth to graduate from high school all alike in anything. The high school principal has the responsibility for educating the public to accept these facts and for seeing that the school has adequate personnel records that can be consulted by those who are legitimately interested in them.

Bases for Entrance

The laws of five states in the Union require full-time attendance at school until the age of 18; four states require full-time attendance at school until the age of 17; the remaining thirty-nine states require full-time attendance at school until the age of 16, with exceptions for some unusual cases. Under certain conditions where part-time or continuation schools are maintained, fourteen states require part-time attendance until the age of 18.[3]

Not only is school attendance required in all states up to specified ages, but the right to attend public schools until they are 20 or 21 years of age is assured to all youth. Teachers, administrators, and school board members can be forced by law to admit to full-time school membership any normal youth whose behavior is acceptable. Obviously all

[1] David Segel, *Intellectual Abilities in the Adolescent Period* (U.S. Office of Education, Bulletin No. 6; Washington, D.C.: Government Printing Office, 1948), pp. 8, 9.

[2] Elizabeth S. Johnson, Unpublished manuscript concerning Louisville study (Washington, D.C.: Child Labor Branch, U.S. Department of Labor).

[3] U.S. Office of Education, *Compulsory School Attendance and Minimum Educational Requirements in the United States* (Circular No. 440; Washington, D.C.: Government Printing Office, March, 1955.)

states and state legislatures consider as secondary pupils all youths up to the age of 16, and many states consider as secondary school pupils all youths up to the age of 18 and even 20. In short, all adolescents have become charges of the public school system.

CURRENT PRACTICE CONFLICTING

Because the high school is in the process of changing, even in a single school admission practices are often varied and conflicting. Theoretically and traditionally, the basis for entrance to high school has been graduation from the eighth grade as determined by subject matter achievement. Actually, admissions are generally based upon both subject matter achievement and social and chronological age. Some state departments of education provide written examinations that may be used to determine entrance to high schools, and in some places pupils completing the elementary school must pass written examinations prepared in the office of the county superintendent of schools before being admitted to high schools. However, in the great majority of school systems, students automatically pass into the high schools upon the satisfactory completion of their elementary work. Although it is usually expected that students will have "passed" in all required elementary school subjects before being promoted to high school, most schools quite properly make exceptions to meet the needs of individuals. As a result, many overage, retarded elementary pupils are allowed to enter the junior high school or the traditional four-year high school in spite of subject deficiencies, the majority of them responding favorably to the change in environment. A practice growing more and more common is for the high school to accept any pupil whose elementary principal recommends him because it appears that the pupil's best interests will be served by the change in school environment, even though he has achieved much less than his age-mates have. This does not mean assigning him credits he has not earned —the records should be kept accurately for guidance purposes; it merely means placing him where he can learn most. The question is not, "Should this pupil be penalized by failure or honored by being promoted to the high school?" but rather, "In what school can this pupil learn and develop and grow most?" Generally this will be the school in which he will be associated with others of comparable social maturity.

SOCIAL MATURITY AS A BASIS

The elementary school is adopting the practice of grouping children by chronological age and by social maturity. Social maturity is determined by teachers through observation of the pupil's social interests, the games he likes, the reading matter he enjoys, and the ages of the pupils with whom he prefers to associate.[4]

Obviously, the improvement of social skills is a worth-while educational goal that is emphasized by grouping upon the basis of social maturity. In addition, and of great importance, such grouping provides situations that allow other types of learning to take place readily. Teachers find that social maturity is a cue to many similar interests and abilities in children and that it is a fundamental factor in different aspects of growth. An overage pupil who is retarded because of a lack of subject matter achievement is frustrated by being unable to share common interests and activities with those of his own age. Being returned to association with those whose interests he shares is an important step toward improving his emotional state so that he can more readily make educational progress.

Since both the elementary school and the high school are parts of America's common school, it follows that their policies and practices should be consistent with one another. Like the elementary school, the high school should be a school for all where each student can find a program adapted to his needs and capacities. Just as the elementary school has already done, the high school should adopt a forthright policy of admitting students upon the basis of social maturity. Intelligent parents want the elementary school to be a school for small and preadolescent children and expect the junior high school and senior high school to be schools especially adapted to younger and older adolescents.

The only sound reasons for differences in policy between the elementary school and the secondary school are those that grow out of the fact that there is a difference in the maturity of the two groups of pupils. This difference explains why we have the two levels of schools. It may justify a grouping of pupils in the elementary school into early and late childhood groups. It may justify creating junior high school and senior high school groups. On the other hand, where a school is small, all twelve years can be organized into one school housed in one building but with appropriate differentiation in program according to the increasing maturity of its pupils. Here, at least, it will be clear that every teacher throughout the school has the responsibility for meeting the needs of all children or youth of the level of maturity to which he is assigned. The high school entrance policy should be based squarely on a recognition of this fact and its program should be adapted to whatever levels and types of ability or interests are to be found in the group entitled to enter it under this policy. But no matter how their populations are grouped or divided, both elementary and high schools now have

[4] Ruth Strang, "Manifestations of Maturity in Adolescents," *Mental Hygiene*, 33, No. 4 (October, 1949), 563–569.

a common purpose: that of providing appropriate educational opportunity for all the pupils of a community of certain levels or degrees of maturity.

Practices Affecting Promotion

Theoretically in most schools, and actually in many, students are promoted or failed chiefly on the basis of their achievement in each subject. There was a time when grade promotions in secondary schools were common, and a student was required to repeat an entire grade if he had failed to pass a single subject. At the present time, promotion by subject is almost universal in all four-year and senior high schools. The practice is not so common in junior high schools because the greater number of required subjects makes it more difficult to administer there, but practically no high school requires the repetition of the work of a whole grade. Each year a considerable number of high school students receive failing marks in one or more subjects, but with the increase in the heterogeneity of the high school population, promotion standards have grown more flexible. This trend is a natural consequence of attempts to adapt instruction to the ranges of ability and interest now found in our high schools.

FIXED VS. FLEXIBLE STANDARDS

In required subjects, the question that should determine promotion for each student is: How much has he achievecd in terms of his ability, even though the resulting achievement as compared to others is very poor? In elective subjects, this question is not so appropriate. Since no one is required to take shorthand, for example, in this subject there is no point in the student's being promoted unless he has enough facility in it so that it is useful in a personal or vocational situation. In elective subjects, adapting the program to the student includes exercising care in determining whether to permit the student to elect the subject or not.

If the program of the school is adapted to the students and care is used to see that each makes a wise choice of program, there is little reason for it to fail with him, or for him to fail with it. Both the school and the students should succeed. Regular progress from the seventh year to the twelfth should be possible and the rule for all who work for it. If the school does its best to adapt its offerings to each student and each student does his best with the program offered him, the school should accept his efforts as satisfactory. Obviously it is unfair to require a student to come to school, require him to take a particular course, and then inform him he has failed it if he has done his best. If the course was not well adapted to the student and even his best was therefore not very good, he still should pass. It is the school community that has failed by not providing an appropriate educational opportunity. Society, community, and student—all three are penalized when the school is unable or unwilling to provide a program that offers each student in it the opportunity to grow and develop. We know that society, community, and student gain little when a student is required to repeat a subject which was unsuited to him in the first place. There is also an inarticulate but persistent and general social pressure to make promotion standards flexible enough to permit students who work to be promoted. Society will not support schools well or willingly in which youth are unable to achieve success.

Many forward-looking teachers and administrators, therefore, actively and vigorously oppose the practice of requiring pupils to repeat subjects. Generally, in elective subjects there is no point in such repetition. In required subjects, teachers make use of trial or conditional promotions with such good results that failure is infrequent. They do not maintain that no student should ever fail, but they do hold that the school should aid every student in building the habit of success rather than that of failure, and they find that a student often fails because a teacher does not know him well enough to help him succeed. They attempt to provide for every student courses adapted to his needs and abilities, arguing that there is no point in forcing any student to repeat a required course if his performance in it has been on a level commensurate with his ability. Such a program does not mean merely the abolition of fixed promotion standards and the establishment of a policy of universal promotions; it means developing standards for each student based upon an adequate assessment of the progress he is making toward goals that are appropriate for him. Helping the student set his goals and then helping him to evaluate his progress toward them is time consuming, but it should not be considered an extra or additional task for the teacher; it is an important part of the teaching. But if a student refuses to make a reasonable effort on an appropriate program he should fail. Failure to do one's best when presented with a reasonable task is failure anywhere in life and ought to be in school. Flexible promotional standards should not be assumed to mean a "no-failure" policy. But failure will be but a small problem in a school that makes every effort to adapt its program to its students.

STANDARDS FOR TALENTED STUDENTS

Flexible standards mean higher standards for the more gifted and talented students than many schools now set. Our best students do so easily what many schools require that they are not sufficiently challenged to provide them with the best opportunities for their full growth and development. In many schools they receive the highest marks and other honors when they know they are not putting forth their best efforts. Bad work habits and attitudes result. This is a result of an inflexible standard which has not been fully adapted to their level of ability. It is not the result of the use of flexible standards, but rather a result of the incomplete use of the principle of flexibility in standards. Many schools need to study the problem of how the comprehensive high school with its doors open to all of the community's youth can better adapt its program and methods of teaching to its talented youth as, for example, the high school at Upper Darby, Pennsylvania, has done.[5]

The school that is serving all adolescents of the community cannot hold them all to identical standards of achievement. The achievements of each must be planned and evaluated in terms of the ability that he has. This procedure has long been held as an ideal by forward-looking educators. Putting it into practice means that teachers help pupils to set goals for themselves that are appropriate for them and are therefore ones toward which they can make progress and so be entitled to feel that they are succeeding. In reviewing the investigations pointing in this direction and in suggesting future lines of action, David M. Trout says,

> The most difficult requirement to be met by the schools is that of putting into practice teaching methods and guidance procedures which will keep each student's aspirations adjusted to his ability. The analysis of level of aspiration by Lewin and his associates, together with the nondirective counseling practices proposed by Carl Rogers, point the way to this objective. The major aim will be to prevent frustrating failure on the one hand, and facile malingering on the other. In place of teacher-made assignments will come pupil-planned group-evaluated performances by all persons—teachers as well as pupils—who are members of the group. Self-evaluation will also have a large place in such a program. It is, indeed, through such evaluations scientifically done at frequent intervals that the adjustment of the level of aspiration to reality is democratically accomplished.

> Grades, promotions, graduations and degrees, all of which are creations of the aristocratic conception of success, need to be gradually eliminated in favor of age and interest groupings in which both individual and group planning will be freely done in response to the self-recognized problems, needs, and interests of the learners.[6]

[5] Upper Darby Committee for the Study of the Gifted, *Guidance for Our Gifted* (Upper Darby, Penn., School District, September, 1952). See also A. Harry Passow and others, *Planning for Talented Youth* (New York: Bureau of Publications, Teachers College, Columbia University, 1955); and U.S. Office of Education, *Teaching Rapid and Slow Learners in High School* (Bulletin No. 5; Washington, D.C.: Government Printing Office, 1954).

[6] David M. Trout, *The Measurement of Student Adjustment and Achievement* (Ann Arbor: University of Michigan Press, 1949), pp. 213–215.

GROUPING AND FLEXIBLE PROMOTION STANDARDS

To group students in secondary schools so that learning takes place most readily is extremely difficult. Students of the same chronological age are often as much as five years apart in physiological development, and the fact that girls grow more rapidly than boys for a time accentuates their difference of interests. In any school of more than average size many students in the ninth grade will surpass half of those in the twelfth grade in their ability to read or in their ability to make arithmetical computations. To the degree that the school succeeds in enrolling and serving all youth in the community, the complexity of the problem increases. Many administrative arrangements are made to reduce the heterogeneity of particular classes or sections. One of these is the organization of multiple curriculum programs such as the college preparatory, commercial, and home economics curriculums, with a series of courses prescribed for each. Another more flexible general plan is the constants-with-variables program, where certain courses are required of all students and elective or variable courses are offered in addition. Often when a student elects a subject, he places himself for part of the day with others with his interests or degree of maturity; if he finds himself ill-suited to an elective course he may change from it. In large school systems there are special classes for the definitely subnormal, for certain types of the physically handicapped, and for pupils who for a time require more intensive individual work than regular classroom teachers have the time to provide.

Most schools large enough to do it attempt to reduce the extent of differences among students in each class or section of the constant subjects by means of some kind of grouping. Ability grouping has been the object of much controversy, and the evidence concerning its effectiveness is not clear. Some educators are violently opposed to any kind of grouping. Presumably a school that uses grouping is doing so because it thinks it thus creates a better learning and teaching situation. If by grouping students we plan to segregate one group of pupils from contacts with other groups, then it must be opposed as any kind of segregation should be opposed. Yet any high school that permits students to elect certain subjects is allowing them to group themselves. If a school requires those in one curriculum to take certain subjects not open to students in other curriculums, it is practicing grouping even if it says it is opposed to the practice. Grouping as now practiced usually does not really segregate one group from another. There are many chances to intermingle, and there are regroupings during each day. It is simply a way of making it easier for a teacher to adapt instruction to his students than he could otherwise. Class size being what it is, it is desirable to shorten the range of ability appearing before the teacher in a given group so that he can more easily adapt instruction to it. If class size could be reduced enough, the teacher would have time enough for each student so that extreme differences in the class could be met and grouping would not be necessary. Grouping is therefore an effort to help solve by organization of the school a teaching problem that at present cannot be solved by reducing class size. By such a plan it is possible to reduce heterogeneity in a class in one respect, in ability to read, for example; but of course in typical high schools it is not possible at the same time to organize many other teaching groups that are homogeneous in a number of other respects.

Many school administrators have concluded that for a particular purpose it is practical to segregate only comparatively small groups of pupils at the extreme ends of a scale. For example, for twelve sections of tenth-grade English, there is no point in attempting twelve different adaptations in tenth-grade English, but it may be practical to arrange for two adaptations for sections at the upper levels of ability in English, and for two sections at the lower levels, with the eight remaining sections following what is considered to be the regular tenth-year program. Obviously, grouping separately by subject will result in less heterogeneous groups than if a certain grouping of students holds for all subjects. Grouping by subject also has the advantage of providing for students a less easily recognized classification. It is very difficult, however, to attempt such grouping in each required subject, even though only the groups at the upper and lower levels are differentiated.

In a number of schools, groups are organized that cut across subject matter lines. Probably the most common combination is English and social studies. In some cases, science is added to these two; in others, science and mathematics are combined. In still other cases, art, music, and literature are joined. In some small schools, pupils from two or even four grades are able to work together in some subjects. Thus, an English class may contain pupils from more than one grade just as has often been the case in art and music for many years. However, creating groups or combining subjects works no wonders. It may help in meeting the problem of adapting the educational program, but it still expects the teacher to make a good deal of adaptation to individual needs.

GROUPING AN AID TO INDIVIDUAL TEACHING

The authors believe that social maturity, as evidenced by a pupil's social interests, the reading he enjoys, and the pupils he selects as associates, is the best single basis for grouping. This policy tends to bring together those whose level of development gives them a basis for working together and for profiting from association with each other. Within this framework, however, students may well be grouped for part of a day on the basis of ability to read or on the basis of interest in general science, for example. Through this arrangement each student can be offered the greatest challenge he is capable of meeting. The arrangement should be so flexible that a student can be changed from one group to another if he needs to be at any time. It scarcely needs to be added that students in each group must have numerous opportunities in other sections of classes for contacts with the entire range of the student population. The sole aim of grouping according to social maturity should be to provide a learning situation in which students of different abilities and interests can work together with other students on content and at a rate adapted to them, thus making it possible for students to succeed with what was expected of them and therefore be eligible for promotion.

Both ability grouping and a good constants-with-variables type of program help to meet individual differences, but they do not solve the whole problem. They merely reduce the range of differences that exist in a class and set an improved stage upon which teachers can work in individualizing standards as to content of the program, learning time, and results anticipated. General administrative arrangements for grouping and promotion, even when they are flexible, are much less important than the individualized arrangements of the classroom teacher.

Trends in promotion practices give evidence of the increasing acceptance of this point of view, which stresses the importance of the teacher-pupil relationship. There was a time when some school systems had regular promotions four times during the school year, with consequent frequent breaks in this relationship. Some school systems still have semiannual promotions, but even this arrangement is now regarded as less and less essential by a considerable number of large as well as small school systems. Because they tend to reduce the number of very small classes, financial considerations were often a factor affecting the decision to change to annual promotions in small school systems. In addition, administrators and staffs have reasoned that when teachers are attempting to meet individual needs of students it is wasteful to change schedules in the middle of the year. Ordinarily the teacher can become better acquainted with a student in a whole year than in a half year, and it is more important to help the teacher learn about the student than it is to form new classes and thus attempt to reduce heterogeneity in a section in some particular respect. Moreover, a teacher who knows it well can often deal more effectively with a somewhat heterogeneous group than he can with a more homogeneous group whom he does not know. Organization can help solve the problem of regular school progress, but the classroom situation is still the crux of the matter.

In reviewing the professional literature of early adolescent education, Dan H. Cooper and Orville E. Peterson summarized their findings on the problem of grouping and promoting thus:

b) The classification of students on the basis of social maturity has been found to be useful in junior and senior high school as a way of bringing together those likely to benefit from association with each other.

. . . . .

g) The problem is one of constantly evaluating the experiences of students during the process of satisfying some needs while simultaneously creating new needs or stimulating new lines of inquiry. Evaluating in this manner demands a teacher who is keen enough to observe behavior signs in the students which will indicate the kinds of experiences needed. The program for each group will still depend on the make-up of the group. Adjustments in the grouping should be made in the cases of pupils who get on badly with the teacher in charge. The key to intelligent grouping is flexibility. Both optimum learning and good social adjustment are dependent upon a feeling of belonging to the group and of acceptance therein.

h) Adequate research on this problem has proved that children gain too little (sometimes nothing) and lose too much in courage and self-esteem to warrant the school in "failing" them. In rare instances only is grading on achievement alone warranted. In the elementary grades grouping by chronological age has been found very useful. However, in the secondary school (especially the seventh through the tenth years) when students are entering the period of rapid growth, grade placement on the basis of chronological age is not very helpful. As has been pointed out, students of the same age can be as much as five years apart in physiological development during these years. The error of expecting a little boy and a mature man to profit from the same educational experiences just because they have both lived thirteen years is quite evident.[7]

SCHOOL MARKS AND PROMOTIONAL PRACTICES

Many investigations have established the fact that teachers' marks are unreliable. A mark of "A" does not mean the same thing in different schools or to different teachers in a single school or to a single teacher at different times. Recent studies show that teachers are unconsciously influenced in marking students by such things as social class and sex. A study by Heintz[8] shows that comparable normal children studied who belonged to families of lower occupational status received more than their share of low marks and less than their share of high marks, while for children of families of higher occupational status the reverse was

[7] Dan H. Cooper and Orville E. Peterson, *Schools for Young Adolescents* (Chicago: Superintendents' Study Club, June, 1949), pp. 33–34.
[8] Emil Heintz, "His Father Is Only the Janitor," *Phi Delta Kappan,* 35 (April, 1954), 265–270.

true. Another interesting report on this situation was presented by Heimann and Schenk.[9]

To most parents marks are evidence of ability or lack of ability to succeed either at the high school or at the college level. The typical American mind translates school marks into the probability of success or failure in later life. And in fact, in spite of their unreliability, marks earned in high school seem to be the best *single* index of success in college, though they apparently have little relation to success in out-of-school life. The explanation of this paradox is that ability to succeed in college is not a suitable basis upon which to judge students when the great majority of them are not going to college. As assigned traditionally by teachers, marks ignore many abilities and characteristics of growth that are of great importance in life in our democracy.

During the second quarter of the century many secondary schools attempted to improve their marking and reporting systems, but they found it extremely difficult because of an inherent conflict in the purposes served by marks. Many educators are agreed that the basic function of marks is as a means for improving instruction and guiding a student in his educational work, but because marks are highly regarded by employers and by college admissions officers, students tend to regard them as ends in themselves. If a student is working primarily for a mark, it becomes difficult for him to know what his real interests are. The intrinsic interest that an activity holds for him is obscured by his attention to the teacher's mark, which becomes his real motivation. To the extent that marks become motives and ends in themselves, they tend to hinder rather than improve instruction.

Following through on their efforts to use marks to improve instruction, many educators hold that each student should be judged in terms of his abilities, and that a mark should neither discourage a poor student who has done his best, nor encourage a bright student who has not done his best. However, all students are sensitive to the prestige value that parents, college admissions officers, and employers place on marks, and even when school workers try to build a sensible attitude, they have great difficulty in preventing marks from encouraging and discouraging students falsely.

Those who have made the most progress have differentiated their marking devices for students, parents, and for college admissions officers and employers. They have asked students to evaluate themselves systematically with check lists designed for that purpose, and in conferences with students they have helped them to judge their achievements in terms of their abilities. However, they cannot use the student evalua-

[9] R. A. Heimann and Q. F. Schenk, "Relations of Social-Class and Sex Differences to High School Achievement," *School Review,* 62 (April, 1954), 213–221.

tions in reporting to parents because they have not yet been able to get most parents to take the time necessary to understand this type of reporting. Therefore the reports to parents may continue to carry the traditional marks. In the guidance files of the school is collected a reservoir of information concerning each student, which is available for a college admissions officer or an employer. Some of the information here has not been emphasized in reports either to the student or to the parent. Records indicating the comparative standing of students may be considered necessary for college admissions officers, but for each student the most important information is that which indicates the progress he has made from where he started. This should be conveyed to parents and pupils, but whether to report the reasons underlying progress or the lack of it to parents should be a matter of discretion and should depend on the attitude they are likely to take toward the school and the student.

Recording and reporting progress is unavoidably complex because a single reporting form will not serve equally well for students, parents, and employers or college admissions officers. Forms should be kept as simple as possible, and every effort should be made to avoid overwhelming teachers with clerical duties. Worth-while efforts to simplify clerical work include issuing marks to parents over a brief period instead of on a single day and issuing them less frequently during the year. There is no reason why all marks should come out on the same day; they may be issued, for example, during a two-week period. And if a longer period between marks means a more accurate and complete recording of progress, marks should be issued four times during the year instead of six. Reporting may be still further reduced in the case of students who have consistently done good work in the school. The work of computing and reporting semester averages for every student taking year subjects can also be eliminated.

In spite of the conflicting purposes for which marks are used, and in spite of the difficulties resulting from these conflicts, most secondary school faculties that have attempted to improve their marking and reporting systems have considered their efforts worth while. They have found an improved marking system a convenient handle to grasp in taking hold of their curriculum problems, defining their objectives, and enlisting the interest of students and parents in the attainment of objectives. Parents and students, as well as teachers, are interested in school marks and what they mean. William L. Wrinkle's *Improving Marking and Reporting Practices,* a comprehensive statement of the efforts to improve marks in a single school over a ten-year period, provides an excellent point of departure for any faculty interested in a similar project. To change the attitude of a faculty toward marks and to get it to help create different attitudes toward them in students and parents is not an easy task for the high school principal, but considering the harmful effects of bad attitudes, it is not a task that many principals can afford to ignore.

MODERN PRACTICE IN EVALUATING PUPILS' PROGRESS

Judging by the sampling study included in the National Survey of Secondary Education[10] and by similar researches made since, most secondary schools issue marks in the form of letters or other symbols representing a multiple point scale. It appears that the greatest single outcome of the studies showing unreliability in teachers' marks has been a general conclusion by teachers that they have more confidence in a letter mark representing a range of percentages than in a number mark in the form of a single percentage. This plan increases the reliability of the mark because it is easier to classify students roughly than it is to make the fine distinctions the percentage system requires. Many schools use a five-point scale with no attempt to allot a fixed percentage of marks to each level. Although such a marking system may be necessary, it is not sufficiently helpful to the individual student, who needs aid in formulating his own goals and in finding out how far he has progressed toward achieving them. Other more descriptive achievement records are necessary.

A few high schools have limited their reporting symbols to two points, such as "Satisfactory" and "Unsatisfactory," but this plan has not proved good enough to encourage its wide adoption. Such schools have generally found it necessary to enter on permanent records for placement purposes much additional information, and parents have often insisted that marks be reported in as many as five different symbols. A two-point scale, however, removes almost entirely the incentive to work for marks and reveals to a faculty that uses it the extent to which students are customarily stimulated to learn through the use of extrinsic pressures. It avoids discouraging poor students, but it also removes any extrinsic incentive for a student to work for an "A" instead of a "C." Thus it can be used effectively only if the curriculum is so reorganized that students more generally have intrinsic instead of extrinsic motives for trying to succeed with their schoolwork.

Dr. Wrinkle reports that in an unpublished research by William R. Ross in 1939 "it was found that 87 per cent of the elementary-school report forms and 23 per cent of the secondary-school forms listed traits of character or personality to be checked by the teacher in reporting on the student." [11] Initiative, industry, dependability, and self-direction are examples of traits often checked by teachers in order to provide an emphasis on personal characteristics of significance. Such outcomes are likely to be neglected in marks given in subjects, and any attention that can be given them is worth while. However, listing them on report cards is of more value when the traits have been carefully defined so that each trait mentioned has more nearly the same meaning for different people. Such items are of the greatest usefulness when they represent specific outcomes in terms of behavior that the staff members have agreed are desirable.

Probably the most effective way of reporting to parents on the progress of students is through parent-teacher conferences. Possibilities for misunderstandings are reduced and reports can be amplified as situations demand. Next to a personal conference with a parent, the most useful instrument of communication is a well-written, informal letter. However, both devices are time consuming and provide individualized records that cannot be readily systematized. For these reasons, although they are used by a few schools that can afford the time for them, for the great majority of public high schools they do not provide a practical solution to the marking problem; consequently most schools continue to use a five-point scale of marks.

Accurate statements telling what a student did are useful in marking a student's progress, in helping him to view his own actions objectively, and in reporting to others as well. College admissions officers and employers are showing more appreciation of evidence of this type. If they can get accurate statements telling what a student has done, they are in a position to form their own opinions about him, and they prefer doing that to receiving secondhand the opinions about him that someone else has already formed. However, teachers, unless they have had special instruction, have difficulty in reporting accurately the actions of students. Arthur E. Traxler's statement of the characteristics of an item in a good anecdotal record, in part, is as follows:

Objective records are generally held to be much more valuable than subjective ones. One of the prime requisites of an anecdote is that it be highly objective. It is possible to prepare anecdotes that possess a high degree of objectivity but untrained observers do not easily write in this way. It seems natural for many of them to obscure the report of what they observe with subjective statements of opinion concerning interpretations and treatment, thus:

"In a meeting of her club today, Alice showed her jealousy of the new president by firing questions at her whenever there was an opportunity. She tried to create difficulties by constant interruptions throughout the period. The

[11] William L. Wrinkle, *Improving Marking and Reporting Practices* (New York: Rinehart & Company, Inc., 1947), p. 52.

other students showed their resentment by calling for her to sit down. It is apparent that she is a natural trouble maker, and I think her counselor should have her in for a serious talk."

The phrases "showed her jealousy," "tried to create difficulties," and "showed their resentment," and the entire last sentence are matters of opinion that have no place in a report of the incident itself. An objective report of what took place would read somewhat as follows:

Incident.—In a meeting of her club today, Alice fired questions at the new president at every opportunity. She interrupted many times during the period. On several occasions the other students called for her to sit down.[12]

EXAMPLES OF NEW TYPE FORMS

The form of marking and reporting that offers the greatest promise of resolving the inherent conflicts and difficulties met in using most marking systems makes use of a check form upon which a student is rated on a number of categories or objectives for each subject being taken. Form 1 is a rating form for social studies used in the University High School, University of Chicago. Such a form should be used only after the teachers have determined their objectives for the school and for each course and activity in the school.

A check list for each subject can be mimeographed and used for both student and teacher evaluation in the classroom. These evaluations need not be sent home to parents, but they can be of great service in marking each student in terms of the ability that he has and in helping each student make a realistic adjustment to his achievements. At the College High School of the Colorado State College of Education at Greeley, after experimenting with a number of different forms over a period of several years, the faculty was able to abandon the use of separate forms for each course and combine all of them into a single form reproduced here in Form 2.

Although it is stated at the bottom of the form that the achievement marked on a five-point scale is to be detached before the report is issued to the student or his parents, Professor Wrinkle states that at the request of the students, this practice was discontinued and the complete report was sent to the homes.[13]

REPORTS RELATED TO SCHOOL AND COURSE OBJECTIVES

Check lists based upon objectives of the school and the activities in the school offer great promise for improving marking practices and evaluation. To be of greatest usefulness, the objectives should be stated

---

[12] Arthur E. Traxler, "The Nature and Use of Anecdotal Records," *Educational Records* (Supplementary Bulletin D; New York: Educational Records Bureau, October, 1949), pp. 4–5.

[13] Wrinkle, *op. cit.*, p. 113.

FORM 1

Rating Form for Social Studies

THE UNIVERSITY OF CHICAGO

The Laboratory School

SEMESTER REPORT, SOCIAL STUDIES IV

Student_____ Date_____
          Last Name   First Name

Purposes	Rating	Comments (if any)
1. Courtesy and cooperation in group situations		
2. Understanding of social studies vocabulary		
3. Sense of historical perspective		
4. Habit of keeping up with current affairs		
5. Ability to interpret social data		
6. Tendency to attack problems systematically		
7. Ability to use social research techniques		
8. Recognition of basic democratic values		
9. Effectiveness in oral expression		
Habits of Work		
10. Persistence in overcoming difficulties		
11. Tendency to work independently		
12. Promptness in completing work		
13. Application during study		
14. Attention to class activities		
15. Participation in class activities		
16. Effectiveness in following directions		

Pupil's Grade_____   Instructor_____

FORM 2

EVALUATION OF STUDENT ACHIEVEMENT

(College High School of Colorado State College of Education at Greeley)

Evaluation of Student Achievement

COLLEGE HIGH SCHOOL OF COLORADO STATE COLLEGE OF EDUCATION AT GREELEY

Student _____

							Date of This Report _____, 194____

	1	2	3	4	5	6	Date of This Report
			Secondary School Year				2½ 5 10 15
	6	8	12	36			

Course or Activity _____

Weeks Enrolled	Regular Periods Each Week

GENERAL OBJECTIVES: The evaluation of the student's achievement of the twelve general objectives which follow is made in terms of what normally might be expected of students of similar age and school placement. O—OUTSTANDING. S—SATISFACTORY. N—NEEDS TO MAKE IMPROVEMENT. U—UNSATISFACTORY. X—INSUFFICIENT EVIDENCE OR DOES NOT APPLY. SPECIFIC BEHAVIORS ESPECIALLY RESPONSIBLE FOR O, N, OR U EVALUATIONS ARE CHECKED. SPECIFIC COMMENTS PARTICULARLY WITH REFERENCE TO O, N, AND U EVALUATIONS ARE WRITTEN ON THE OPPOSITE SIDE OF THIS SHEET.

____ 1. HE DIRECTS HIS INDIVIDUAL ACTIVITIES EFFECTIVELY ( ) begins work promptly ( ) makes good use of time ( ) requires minimum of supervision ( ) does more than the least that will be accepted ( ) meets responsibilities promptly

____ 2. HE FOLLOWS PLANS AND DIRECTIONS ( ) listens to and reads directions carefully ( ) follows and completes plans and directions which have been set up

____ 3. HE GETS ALONG WELL WITH OTHERS ( ) is considerate of rights and wishes of others ( ) is courteous and tolerant ( ) controls his temper ( ) conforms to reasonable social standards

____ 4. HE TAKES AN ACTIVE PART IN GROUP LIVING ( ) participates in group planning ( ) volunteers his services ( ) does his share in group activities

____ 5. HE SPEAKS CORRECTLY AND EFFECTIVELY ( ) speaks clearly ( ) adjusts his voice to the size of the group ( ) uses adequate vocabulary to express himself interestingly ( ) speaks with ease and confidence ( ) uses correct grammatical forms

____ 7. HE OBSERVES ATTENDANCE REGULATIONS ( ) is regular and prompt in attendance except for approved cause ( ) arranges in advance for absence when possible ( ) takes initiative in making up work missed ( ) makes proper use of school health service

____ 8. HE READS WITH EASE AND UNDERSTANDING ( ) selects important ideas ( ) understands and evaluates what he reads ( ) reads with reasonable speed

____ 9. HE EXPRESSES HIMSELF CORRECTLY AND EFFECTIVELY IN WRITING ( ) expresses ideas clearly ( ) uses correct grammatical forms ( ) punctuates correctly ( ) spells correctly ( ) writes legibly

____ 10. HE UTILIZES AVAILABLE SOURCES OF LEARNING MATERIALS ( ) selects and uses appropriate sources of information ( ) uses library and library tools effectively ( ) effectively engages in interview and observation

____ 11. HE USES THE PROBLEM SOLVING METHOD ( ) recognizes problems ( ) states problems clearly ( ) collects and records appropriate information ( ) arrives at sound conclusions

—— 6. HE TAKES GOOD CARE OF PERSONAL AND SCHOOL MATERIALS AND EQUIPMENT ( ) shows respect for property ( ) does not waste or damage materials or equipment ( ) returns things when due ( ) reports breakage and loss

—— 12. HE USES THE BASIC SKILLS IN MATHEMATICS ( ) uses accurately the simple fundamental combinations ( ) computes with reasonable speed ( ) uses fractions and per cents correctly ( ) selects correct processes

SPECIFIC OBJECTIVES: The specific objectives of each course and activity have been discussed with the student and used in classroom instruction and evaluation activities.

HIS ACHIEVEMENT OF THE SPECIFIC OBJECTIVES OF THIS COURSE OR ACTIVITY HAS BEEN:

□ better than □ consistent with □ poorer than what reasonably might have been expected of him in terms of his background and ability.

□ Such that full credit is not recommended on administrative records.

□ Such that he cannot be recommended for admission to college courses or training programs to which this course is prerequisite.

Such as to justify encouraging him

to enroll in _____

not to enroll in _____

_____
Supervising Teacher

This section is for record purposes and is to be detached before the report is issued to the student or his parents.

	OUTSTANDING	ABOVE AVERAGE	AVERAGE	BELOW AVERAGE	VERY POOR*
ACTUAL ACHIEVEMENT:	□	□	□	□	□
EXPECTED ACHIEVEMENT:	□	□	□		

* Adjusted credit recommendation (in full year courses only): ⅓ ½ ⅔ regular credit should be allowed.

Source: William L. Wrinkle, *Improving Marking and Reporting Practices* (New York: Rinehart & Company, Inc., 1947), pp. 108–109. Reprinted by permission of the publishers.

in terms of behavior. The statements need not reflect overt behavior that can be easily observed. Thinking effectively and forming conclusions on the basis of evidence are behaviors, just as are fair play in a basketball game and observing traffic regulations in driving an automobile. However, experiences in school are worth while only to the extent that they make a difference in what boys and girls do and are. Knowledge is important, but the reason for its importance is that it is fundamental to action. If it makes no difference in behavior, how can one be sure that is has served any function? It is not easy to set up objectives in terms of behavior, but after such objectives have been stated, determining the extent to which they have been achieved is easier than when objectives are stated in more traditional terms. Sharper statements subject to less misunderstanding can be made about behaving than about knowing. The following are some of the specific objectives of this type which were set up by the teachers of the College High School of the Colorado State College of Education at Greeley:

Music

1. He reads music at sight, with accuracy as to tone, rhythm, and interpretation.
2. He sings or plays with good tone quality.
3. Into group discussions he brings music information based on reading and listening.
4. He works consistently for the purpose of developing better performance.
5. He asks for help when he needs it to improve his performance.
6. He listens to radio musical programs and attends musical shows and concerts.
7. He participates in community music activities.
8. He chooses suitable music for his own performance.

Red Cross First Aid

1. He correctly applies digital pressure for severe bleeding.
2. He uses the tourniquet properly.
3. He correctly applies bandages, splints, and compresses.
4. He decides when it is necessary to use artificial respiration.
5. He correctly applies artificial respiration.
6. He correctly identifies what not to do at the scene of an accident.
7. He analyzes symptoms and circumstances with precision, and applies the proper first-aid measures in cases of accident or illness.
8. He meets the requirements for eligibility to a certificate issued through the National Red Cross.

Social Studies

1. He constructs and reads maps, graphs, and charts.
2. He locates places referred to in the study of current problems.

3. He explains current problems by recalling correct, significant, related historical information.
4. He recognizes propaganda and prejudiced or otherwise unreliable information.
5. He reads newspapers to secure appropriate information concerning current problems.
6. He reads magazines and pamphlets to secure appropriate information concerning current problems.
7. He listens to radio programs and speakers to secure appropriate information concerning current problems.
8. He expresses ideas by drawing or interpreting cartoons and pictures.
9. He constructs bulletin boards and displays.
10. He expresses ideas by using music, dramatics, or literature.[14]

The Curriculum Planning and Development Committee of the National Association of Secondary School Principals has set up for each of the "ten imperative needs of youth" statements characterizing a school seeking to meet these needs.[15] These are not all stated in terms of pupil behavior. Some simply state a feature or facility that a high school should have. But even these reflect an intention to seek certain kinds of pupil behavior, and so knowledge of these check lists should be useful in helping schools formulate statements of behavior goals in terms of youth needs, and in evaluating course objectives to see to what extent different courses and the school as a whole are helping their youth to meet these needs.

Throughout this book, in discussing all activities of the school, the authors have emphasized the importance of setting up objectives. In activities to be carried on by individuals or by groups, both in the community and within the school, the key to all planning is the answer to the question: What are you trying to do? It is impossible for a school staff to assign marks that mean something to all concerned and that have any degree of accuracy until it has first determined what it wants students to do and be like as a result of their school experiences. Reports of progress in school will not be as good as they should be until they record evidence of what a student can do and what he is like as a person as well as what he knows.

What Should Graduation Mean?

It has always been difficult to know precisely and specifically what was meant by the high school diploma and by graduation from high

---

[14] *Ibid.*, pp. 102–104. Reprinted by permission of the publishers.

[15] William L. Ransom, "How Well Does Your High School Rate on the Ten Imperative Needs of Youth?" NASSP *Bulletin*, No. 164, October, 1949. This is a revised and validated edition of the lists that appeared in preliminary form in the April, 1949, issue of the *Bulletin*.

school. Even when all subjects were prescribed in secondary schools, there were variations in requirements from one school to another. Since students have been allowed to choose many of their subjects of study, variations in programs have existed for individuals within each school. A total of at least fifteen units has usually been necessary for graduation from any approved high school; in fact, this is the only minimum constant requirement for all diplomas.

As of January, 1948, most of the states required a total of sixteen units for graduation from high school; in California eighteen units were necessary for graduation; and in a few states only fifteen units were demanded. However, there was considerable variation in the particular subjects required in the different states. For example, in Michigan the only specified requirement was one-half unit in civics, but in Missouri eleven units were required in designated fields.[16]

In spite of these variations, the high school diploma has traditionally served as a selective instrument by representing quality in academic achievement. Even at the present time, since approximately half the young people of the nation are not graduated from high school, the diploma is often wrongly used by employers as a crude sieve for the selection of employees. That it is not only a poor sieve but that its use is unjust to many nongraduates is known to all; we recognize that some able youth are among those who drop out of high school. Therefore, school staffs are realizing that the diploma is less and less a guarantee of quality and that this fact is an unavoidable and even a desirable concomitant of the high school's having become an institution in which all youth belong.

The fact of graduation never was much of a guarantee of general, all-round, high-level ability, and it certainly ought not to be so regarded now either by the school or by the lay public. It is evidence only that a youth and his school have worked with reasonable diligence over a period of years, now ending at the twelfth grade, to make the most out of him that they could. It is not an opportunity that ought to be denied to any youth and is one which, when accepted by more and more youth, ceases to be the mark of distinction that it once may have been.

Some schools attempt to make the diplomas more meaningful by using different forms of diplomas for graduates of different curriculums such as the college preparatory, the commercial, and the industrial. Other schools write in an appropriate place on the diploma, or on a certificate which may be attached to it, information about the activities a student has participated in, the subjects he has taken, and the marks he

[16] U. S. Office of Education, *Requirements and High School Students' Programs* (Circular No. 300; Washington, D.C.: Government Printing Office, February, 1949).

has received. Still other schools differentiate between the diploma as recognition of thoroughly satisfactory work and the certificate of completion, which recognizes less satisfactory work, or even the certificate of attendance, which recognizes nothing except actual attendance and reasonably good behavior. On the other hand, many schools hold that differentiated diplomas are not consistent with democratic procedures and for this reason issue the same diploma to students well prepared for college and to those whose actual achievements are comparatively low. As long as the differences in the diploma are calculated to indicate differences in the kind of educational opportunity pursued, they probably do little harm. When they begin to be nothing more than counterfeit diplomas, as attendance certificates usually are, they imply that there is such a thing as first- and second-class high school graduation.

Although graduates of high school are not as highly selected as they were fifty or a hundred years ago, there is reason to believe that as many students with superior academic achievements are graduated from high schools each year as were ever graduated in any previous year. However, in addition, there are graduated many students whose strengths are not in academic pursuits, and the high school graduate body, like the student body, has grown more heterogeneous. Comparable studies of high school graduates of Philadelphia in the years 1928 and 1938 indicated that such a situation existed in that city.[17] Scores made on the same examinations by two groups of students, separated by an interval of thirty years, indicated that such a situation existed in the high schools of the state of Ohio.[18] The same situation was indicated by the scores made on the same eighth-grade examinations by students of Boston in 1845 and by students in sample cities of the United States in 1919.[19] Our best graduates are as good as ever, but the typical graduate of a nonselective modern high school cannot be expected to be as good as the typical graduate of a selective school. This, however, is no reason to withhold the diploma from him or to offer a substitute in its place.

GRADUATION SHOULD BE WITHIN REACH OF ALL

The evidence of these and other similar investigations is reassuring to those who take the time to evaluate it, but even if there were no such evidence, the function of the American high school would still be to serve all American youth. When the question is asked about who should be graduated from the high school which serves all American

[17] Philip A. Boyer and Hans C. Gordon, "Have High Schools Neglected Academic Achievement?" *School and Society,* 49 (June 24, 1939), 810–812.
[18] Ralph W. Tyler, "How Can We Improve High School Teaching?" *School Review,* Vol. 56, No. 7, September, 1948.
[19] Otis W. Caldwell and Stuart A. Courtis, *Then and Now in Education* (Yonkers, N.Y.: World Book Company, 1924), pp. 84–97.

youth, the answer is obvious. Just as all who work reasonably well should make regular progress through the school, so in the end they should be graduated from it. Yet high school staffs and communities that actually adjust graduation requirements and practices to all youth face many complex problems. If they want all youth to be graduated, they also want each one to achieve the highest standards of which he is capable. If they are willing for the high school diploma to have a less specific meaning than formerly, they want to be certain that appropriate persons and agencies understand as clearly as possible just what achievements are represented by each diploma.

A community's professional and lay leaders should work together in developing sensible and consistent graduation policies and practices. Businessmen and employers should be told frankly that high school graduation does not mean precisely what they may have supposed it to mean in the past, but they should also be told how they can find out what it does mean, and their suggestions for improving graduation policies and practices should be solicited.

PRACTICES THAT SHOULD BE DEVELOPED

Each school staff should persistently and systematically attempt to define in terms of the behavior of students its objectives for the school and for each of the curriculums in the school. The defining of objectives, a difficult task requiring constant attention, is one that can easily consume too much time; furthermore, there is no point in developing objectives unless something is going to be done about them. The need is to get a few objectives accepted by teachers, students, and patrons so that they can be continuously redefined, better understood, and more effectively implemented. Two fundamental aims that should be accepted by all are to prepare each student (1) to do his part as an effective citizen in the community, and (2) to do some kind of work or to pursue further study in another educational institution. These and similar objectives should receive attention and thought from teachers and from all groups interested in the school, so that the objectives could serve as aids to understanding and as guides for action. Most people in the community are interested in how well the school is doing and how much it is achieving, but they have only a slight basis for judging unless they know first what the school is trying to do.

For each young person who leaves school without graduating, but especially for each graduate, the school staff should accept the responsibility of informing employers and college deans of his progress in attaining his objectives and those of the school, so that his future work or study will be appropriate. No high school graduate should be admitted to college or employed on a job merely because he has a high school diploma, and the general public should understand this. At the same time, however, the public should understand that the school staff has a professional judgment about each graduate's capabilities and is prepared to give this judgment with supporting evidence to appropriate persons and agencies.

In 1935 Francis T. Spaulding suggested that each high school diploma should become in fact an open letter of recommendation telling what the graduate is good *for* in terms that the out-of-school world will value.

In part he said,

It should be noted that this diploma does not call upon the school to certify the absolute completion of a pupil's education: it involves only the school's statement that the pupil is prepared to make a competent beginning in some recognized form of out-of-school work or further study. The value of the diploma will obviously depend, however, on the definiteness of the school's recommendation. Hence, the school should make every effort to insert in the diploma a description of a type of work or study which is really definite: "Stenographic work in a business office," for example, or "Automobile repairing as a helper," "General household service," "Retail selling in a small store," "Further study in a liberal arts college" (naming the college), "Further study in a training-school for nurses" (naming the school).[20]

There are good reasons for the failure of many high schools to approve Spaulding's suggestion of making each diploma an open letter of recommendation. More specific information than he proposes is needed, and unless employers have helped develop these letters of recommendation, they are not likely to pay attention to them. There are advantages in issuing the same diploma to all graduates as a recognition of effort and in using other instruments for placement purposes. The same sort of rapport and understanding is needed between each high school and the employers of the community as now exists between many high schools and the colleges, which have learned by experience that they can depend upon the recommendations that the high school principals and guidance workers make about individual students.

Any company that employs youth merely on presentation of a high school diploma as proof of graduation has no reason to criticize the school. The reflection is rather upon the employment practices of that company, for well-organized personnel offices in industry gather much more comprehensive and detailed data on their new employees than can possibly be made a part of a diploma. Many of these data, however, are available to any representative of industry from the school's guidance officers if he has a legitimate reason for wanting to see them.

[20] Francis T. Spaulding, "Graduation without Equivocation," *Harvard Teachers Record*, 5, No. 3 (June, 1935), 152.

That all who have attended school and worked with a reasonable degree of diligence should be graduated does not mean that standards will be lax, but that they will be different for individuals. Each student should be held to what are, for him, high standards of achievement, but he will not grow and develop unless the challenges presented are within his capacities to achieve. Graduation therefore cannot mean that a fixed minimum achievement in anything can be attained by all; it should mean that each has achieved in terms of his capacity. If appropriate educational opportunities are offered and a student will not make a real effort to profit from them, he should not be graduated. If the compulsory school age has been reached, he may withdraw from school or he may be required to withdraw when he fails to make a respectable effort, or when his presence in school is a threat to the welfare of other students.

Graduation exercises and practices in the American universal secondary school should be as appropriate to their purposes as traditional graduation practices are appropriate to the European selective secondary school. Granting the same diploma to all graduates will tend to make one curriculum as respectable as another and to reduce the influence of the diploma as an extrinsic motivating influence. The awarding of indistinguishable diplomas is an actual step in eliminating extrinsic motives. A student may more easily choose a curriculum because of his intrinsic interest and without regard for the amount of prestige that the general public may accord it.

Each graduate who represents the attainment of any important kind of adult competence should be honored. Social, civic, occupational, and recreational competence should be recognized, along with the ability to perform on paper-and-pencil tests. The evidence of the competence of graduates should be as objective as possible, and, lacking valid tests, the school should be slow to distinguish among graduates for fear of discriminating against some of them. To be graduated with honors should mean that one has shown willingness to enter the initial stages of community citizenship and that one has, when compared to other young adults, comparatively high ability to participate in the major activities of adult life.

The graduates should have a vital part in planning the graduation exercises as a means of interpreting their activities and progress to the community. The community is much more interested in the graduates than in an outside commencement speaker, and it is interested not only in academic activities but in all the activities of the school. Student representatives on the program should be chosen on the basis of leadership and their ability to speak or demonstrate competence in a worth-while accomplishment. The graduation activities themselves should serve as a rich learning experience for young adults and as a means of representing to the community the many-sided activities of its most important institution.

American secondary-school men and women have a body of ideals and theory from which to develop a really appropriate concept of what graduation means. That they have begun to develop practices in harmony with such a concept everyone knows who is familiar with what many secondary schools are doing to provide normal and regular progress of all willing youth through high school to graduation. That a different concept of graduation is being accepted by many schools is also apparent to one who inquires into the new and unique character which some schools are giving to their graduation exercises. What is most needed is a more vigorous educational leadership that will accelerate the rate at which faculties and communities are able to formulate and accept educational programs and practices that are as appropriate to the new American universal secondary school as the older ones were to the European selective secondary school.[21]

Some Points to Consider

1. If a school rigidly followed a system of promotion based on achievement in subjects, what would be the effect on the age range of students? on retardation? on withdrawal from school?

2. If a school rigidly followed a system of social-age promotion what would happen to the age range of students? to the range of achievement in subjects? to retardation? to withdrawal from school?

3. What happens with respect to the above in schools that simultaneously use both of these bases for promotion?

4. Is there a difference between "flexible" standards and no standards of promotion?

5. What points would you make in speaking to a group of citizens of a community in favor of or in opposition to making high school graduation freely available to all who attend high school and make a reasonable effort at their schoolwork?

6. By what line of reasoning could a school defend a policy of denying graduation to a student on account of a low standard of citizenship? What would you suggest as indicating such low standards of citizenship as to constitute grounds for refusing graduation?

Further Reading

Boyer, Philip A., and Hans C. Gordon. "Have High Schools Neglected Academic Achievement?" *School and Society,* 49 (June 24, 1939), 810–812.

Cooper, Dan H., and Orville E. Peterson. *Schools for Young Adolescents.* Chicago: Superintendents' Study Club, June, 1949.

[21] Will French, "What Should Graduation from the Secondary School Mean?" NASSP *Bulletin,* No. 94 (December, 1940), p. 51.

French, Will. "What Should Graduation from the Secondary School Mean?" NASSP *Bulletin,* No. 94, December, 1940.

Heimann, R. A., and Q. F. Schenk. "Relations of Social-Class and Sex Differences to High School Achievement," *School Review,* 62 (April, 1954), 213–221.

Heintz, Emil. "His Father Is Only the Janitor," *Phi Delta Kappan,* 35 (April, 1954), 265–270.

Jewett, and others. *Teaching Rapid and Slow Learners in High School.* U.S. Office of Education, Bulletin No. 5; Washington, D.C.: Government Printing Office, 1954.

Odell, C. W. "Marks and Marking System," in Walter S. Monroe, ed., *Encyclopedia of Educational Research.* Rev. ed.; New York: The Macmillan Company, 1950, pp. 711–715.

Passow, A. Harry, and others. *Planning for Talented Youth.* New York: Bureau of Publications, Teachers College, Columbia University, 1955.

Ransom, William. "How Well Does Your High School Rate on the Ten Imperative Needs of Youth?" NASSP *Bulletin,* No. 164, October, 1949.

Segel, David. *Intellectual Abilities in the Adolescent Period.* U.S. Office of Education, Bulletin No. 6; Washington, D.C.: Government Printing Office, 1948.

Smith, E. R., and R. W. Tyler. *Appraising and Recording Student Progress.* Vol. 3, "Adventure in American Education Series"; New York: Harper & Brothers, 1942.

Spaulding, Francis T. "Graduation without Equivocation," *Harvard Teachers Record,* Vol. 5, No. 3, June, 1935.

Strang, Ruth. "Manifestations of Maturity in Adolescents," *Mental Hygiene,* 33, No. 4 (October, 1949), 563–569.

————. *Reporting to Parents.* New York: Bureau of Publications, Teachers College, Columbia University, 1947.

Traxler, Arthur E. "The Nature and Use of Anecdotal Records," *Educational Records,* Supplementary Bulletin D; New York: Educational Records Bureau, October, 1949.

Trout, David M. *The Measurement of Student Adjustment and Achievement.* Ann Arbor: University of Michigan Press, 1949.

U.S. Office of Education. Education Unlimited. Bulletin No. 5; Washington, D.C.: Government Printing Office, 1951.

————. *Requirements and High School Students' Programs.* Circular No. 300; Washington, D.C.: Government Printing Office, February, 1949.

Upper Darby Committee for the Study of the Gifted. *Guidance for Our Gifted.* Upper Darby, Penn., School District, September, 1952.

Wrinkle, William L. *Improving Marking and Reporting Practices.* New York: Rinehart & Company, Inc., 1947.

Yeager, William A. *Administration and the Pupil.* New York: Harper & Brothers, 1949. Chaps. 20, 21.

Chapter 17

BUILDING STANDARDS OF
GROUP CONTROL

THE REAL END OF DISCIPLINE in the school is to help each student grow into a responsible, self-controlled person, able and willing to play his part as a potential homemaker, worker, and citizen. There are high schools where a high level of individual self-control is in evidence and where it is the fashion for student groups to exercise a large measure of responsibility over their life and activities. Parents are eager for their children to enter such a school and be influenced by it. Such a school does not become an outstanding example of American democratic living at its best because of obedience to snappy commands issued in military fashion or because of stern punishments meted out to all who dare to break institutional regulations. It is probable that such a school grew gradually into this type of institution under the farseeing leadership of a wise principal and an intelligent and sympathetic faculty. It is also likely that these faculty members did not start out with discipline as their foremost objective. They simply encouraged students to set more worthy goals toward which to work. They kept students busy doing things in which they were interested. They gradually made students more and more responsible for the organized life of the school, and the positive approach came to pervade the entire institution. Disciplinary crises were avoided, few disciplinary problems and situations appeared, and as a by-product good discipline became the rule. In all probability, neither the student body nor the teaching staff regarded the principal as a disciplinarian, although a part of the reputation of every high school principal rests upon his success in encouraging good discipline. Everyone gives it a high rating among the objectives he wants the school to achieve, and no one claims that a high school can be considered a success unless it has good discipline.

When we say a high school has good discipline, what do we mean? To most principals and teachers this means it is a quiet, orderly school in which the rules and regulations are seldom broken. In such a school, adults who quite generally are afraid adolescents will get out of hand can live more comfortably and securely. What it ought to mean is that the students of that school are learning to use with some success the large measures of individual freedom which we in this country accord each citizen. They are learning to discuss, decide, carry out, and abide by group decisions democratically reached. In short, they are learning "to live as responsible citizens in a free society." As Dean Virgil Rogers of Syracuse University once said, when he was superintendent of schools at Battle Creek, Michigan, "Discipline is not the absence of noise but the presence of purpose." Discipline in this newer sense is our concern here.

What Good Discipline Is

Discipline has so many different meanings that it needs to be defined before it is discussed. To some it means submissiveness to order and control; to some it means drill; to some it means training through punishment and suffering; to some it means simply consciously planned behavior and is called good or bad discipline as the behavior is approved or disapproved. At times it may properly be any one or a combination of these different concepts. However, because discipline has to be learned and because it involves the total of personality, the development of discipline in a person or in the groups that make up a high school student body is a slow, gradual process. The best standards of discipline are attained only if the individual or group realizes that certain practices are necessary for growth and achievement, and, accordingly, is willing to practice self-discipline. An individual has self-discipline when he can set a goal for himself and then make whatever sacrifices and efforts are necessary to attain it. Discipline is the control of behavior in the light of purpose. This is likewise true of a group. Discipline is manifested whenever the thoughts and actions of a person or a group are controlled so that nothing interferes with the attainment of a goal. If the goal sought by one group is a worthy one, we may approve the discipline exhibited in its attainment. If the goal is unworthy, however, we may not be inclined to approve the evidence of discipline manifested in what may actually be the same conduct. For instance, if a class moves quietly through a corridor to another room to pursue its work we approve the evidence of control. If it does the same thing to avoid doing its regular work, we would not approve this evidence of control. Even when a goal is worthy, no person or group should feel entirely free to organize thoughts and actions in any possible way that is effective in attaining that goal, for there are wrong as well as right ways of attaining worthy goals.

Goals and methods of attaining them vary enormously. At different ages an individual's goal may be a pocketknife, a bicycle, an automobile, a house, or a college education for his children. Any one of these goals could be acquired by theft or by well-directed effort and the diligent husbanding of resources. The more mature individual is able to wait longer for the achievement of his goals, and his eventual satisfactions are likely to be more complex and socialized. The goal of a group may be winning a fight with a gang from another neighborhood, winning a ball game, presenting an assembly program, building a better community, or improving world citizenship. Good discipline means one kind of behavior if the goal of the group is to present an assembly program, and another if the goal is to win a ball game. In the same way, running and shouting in a school corridor between classes is evidence of poor discipline because it interferes with the current goal of the group, but it may be appropriate behavior for a small group eager to fill a commitment for the high school band on a Saturday afternoon. It is often difficult to determine whether discipline is good or bad until we know its purpose.

Establishing good discipline, then, is a dual problem. First, there is need for getting the acceptance of the best goals that it is possible to have a person or a group accept. Then there is the problem of pursuing the goal by means which do not violate the rights of others. Every game has its rules—different from those of all other games—but the rules for any particular game have been developed because they make that game better than it would have been under different rules. Just so in the pursuit of any particular goal by a person or a group in a high school, there are appropriate ways of seeking the goal that do not violate the rights of others and do not conflict with moral, ethical, and spiritual standards underlying our whole way of life. Goal seeking by ways that do not take these matters into account is not legitimate, no matter how effective the means may appear to be. Thus the best discipline is exhibited in a school when all its members have fully accepted the best goals and when these goals are sought under self-imposed controls that take the "general welfare" into account. No wonder *good discipline* in a high school is so much more of a problem than it was in the day when it was thought of as nothing more than blind obedience to authority.

Some Concomitants of Good Discipline

The best authorities in military, industrial, and educational organizations agree on certain principles, ideals, and methods of discipline and reject others. However, *as a matter of practice,* the approved principles, ideals, and methods are often violated by those who are actually in charge of discipline. All have the problem of putting their professed high standards of discipline into actual practice. Principals should realize that all authorities want the same kind of discipline that they themselves do and that disciplinary methods as practiced leave something to be desired. Those who are responsible for discipline in any kind of an organization may, by the attitudes with which they approach this responsibility and by the way they discharge it, actually create as many disciplinary problems as they solve. The disciplinarian himself may be part of the reason for poor discipline in any organization. Some of the important understandings and attitudes with which he should approach his work follow:

1. *Leadership, an outgrowth of confidence.* It is especially true in the high school that leadership depends upon confidence rather than upon fear. Leadership cannot really be assigned on the basis of status; it must be earned through service in cooperative activities. When teachers and students have learned through experience that a principal works for the good of the group, recognizes and encourages the special abilities of members of the group, makes more wise decisions than bad ones, and abides by group decisions in problems that concern all the group, he exerts a leadership based upon confidence. This is a justifiable basis for obedience, whereas fear of consequences as the chief basis for control of the school is neither justifiable nor effective.

2. *Frankness in admitting error.* Many beginning administrators, and teachers as well, fear to lose dignity and the respect of others through being wrong or through being ridiculed. Anyone who makes decisions makes some mistakes and cannot be expected to be always right. A confession that one is uninformed, unless it must be made too frequently, is disarming, and a request for help in securing information is an excellent basis for good teamwork. The fear of ridicule often causes disciplinary problems where a sense of humor and a willingness to laugh at oneself would dispel them. If motives and purposes are good, real respect and leadership in the school do not melt away when students discover that they can occasionally correct mistakes of teachers and administrators.

3. *Fairness and poise.* All conferences between a principal and a student should be conducted with firmness but with fairness and an attitude of good will. Until the facts that can be agreed upon reveal the student's responsibility for a mistake, he should be dealt with as though he were entirely innocent.

The principal should be generous in accepting the word of a student unless it is known to be false. It is better that he be imposed upon than that he make the mistakes of being overly suspicious and of accusing falsely. If he does distrust a student, he should not let the student be aware of his distrust but should seek other means of discovering the truth. Students generally have a keen sense of justice that will grow and flourish in a favorable environment. However, it will shrink in an environment where fairness is lacking in any degree. All these facts are, of course, as true for every member of the staff as they are for the principal. The principal seldom asks one student to give information about another because he believes that there is greater chance of a student's being dependable in the larger communities of his city, state, and nation if he first develops loyalty and dependability in his most intimate relationships. It requires considerable skill to select the few and extreme occasions on which a person ought to give information because he believes it would be greatly harmful to the group if he does not give it.

If a disciplinarian does not maintain his self-control he loses face and becomes merely another disturbed individual. Students understand very well that those who give way to anger are demonstrating weakness. Moreover, an angry disciplinarian is likely to exhaust his resources for improving behavior by immediately prescribing an extreme procedure that he may later be unwilling or unable to carry out. He should do and say as little as he can and still get results. If some procedures or punishments are always kept in reserve, the disciplinarian continues to be a resourceful person of influence in any negotiations that follow.

4. *Using commendation.* Discipline and morale should be positive rather than negative. They are not improved by scolding and thus magnifying the importance of undesirable actions, but rather by emphasizing, commending, and encouraging activities which are well done. And yet praise must be discriminating to be of value. Principals and teachers are not fair to students if they fail to provide objective appraisal of mistakes and successes and to encourage students to evaluate their own activities as well. Usually signs of disapproval are shown too quickly; on the other hand, evidence of approval is too slowly and too seldom shown.

5. *Accepting responsibility.* The self-discipline of the principal and teachers is more often tested than that of students. They have more opportunities to express their loyalty to the school, their willingness to sacrifice for it, and their capacity for assuming responsibilities. Presumably decisions in a school system are made after due consideration and with appropriate consultations, but when they have been made, the principal and teachers should accept full responsibility for carrying them out, and withhold any criticisms until there is a proper time and place for expressing them.

Teachers and administrators tear down their own discipline if by direct statement or by innuendo they fail to support one another. The ideal of professionally ethical conduct is a united front to students and to the public, with appropriate opportunity provided for the expression of differences of interest or opinion.

6. *Obedience based upon understanding.* Wherever people live and work, some rules and regulations are needed so that necessary activities can be carried on effectively, whether these activities are studying, writing, talking, or mining coal. However, conformance should be based upon an intelligent understanding of the reasonableness and desirability of the

rules and an appreciation of the need for authority in our social structure.

In the school the emphasis should be on voluntary subordination based upon an understanding of the goals of the group. Loyalty to a cause well understood and confidence in the team provide a framework within which initiative and resourcefulness can grow and function effectively. When even the leaders of the military subscribe unequivocally to intelligent obedience based upon understanding of the goals or objectives to be sought, what high school principals can legitimately demand blind and unquestioned obedience from teachers and students?

7. *Reform, the objective of punishment.* In the school, when a student misbehaves, the problem of the teacher and the school is not how to punish the student but how to devise learning experiences that will influence his behavior and growth as well as the behavior of the group to which he belongs. It is impossible appropriately to influence the behavior of students by "slot machine justice" or by a prescribed form of punishment for every specific misdemeanor. Each student differs from his fellows, and learning experiences should be fitted to the individual by considering such factors as his age, home conditions, and personal characteristics. High school students generally are alert to variations of conditions for individuals within a group, and usually can see the justice involved in different prescriptions for what appears to be the same offense. If the group has a real question about the justness of the handling of a student's problem, probably the group should be given some understanding of the situation. At times the whole group may be drawn in to assist in planning for the improvement of conditions to aid a single individual.

There is an occasional conflict between what seems best for the individual and what seems best for the group. In such cases an attempt should be made to find a solution that is harmful to neither, but, if this cannot be found, the best interests of the largest number should be served. Unfortunately, this sometimes makes it necessary to remove an individual in order to save the team. However, it should be recognized that efforts to serve the welfare of the group must still respect the "inalienable" rights of each individual. This problem is considered at greater length later in this chapter.

The Foundations of Good Discipline

The foundations of good discipline are deeply imbedded in the program and life of the school. A well-housed school with a well-taught educational program adapted to its pupils has the basic attributes that contribute to good discipline. The lack of any of these tends to produce a bad disciplinary situation that no amount of hard work on the part of principal and faculty can completely offset. Good and bad disciplinary situations are by-products of good and bad school situations. Even in "bad" neighborhoods well-disciplined schools are often found. They are schools which the pupils and parents have come to recognize as serving their needs well. The principal who seeks to lay a sound foundation for really good discipline in his school will look deeply into its program and practices. So also one who seeks the fundamental cause of poor discipline will look far past the immediate situation if he is to discover the real causes.

DEVELOPING SCHOOL-WIDE ATTITUDES
AND POLICIES ON DISCIPLINE

One way to begin to improve a poor disciplinary situation is for the principal to lead the staff of the school in the developing of common understandings and working agreements concerning disciplinary aims and policies. If teachers have—and express by their actions—widely divergent opinions about these matters, students will be confused, just as children in the home are confused when these conflicts arise between parents. Young people must come to feel that there are certain standards to which they must conform and certain limits within which they are free to act. It will seldom be possible to get agreements among teachers concerning the disposition of unusual problem cases, but it will be possible to get agreements on more common ones as a basis for better team-work. A starting point for the building of these common understandings can be found in a discussion of such questions as the following:

1. Considering the aims of our school, what is best and what is worst about our discipline?

2. What are the minimum regulations that are needed to govern traffic in the halls, absences, tardiness, safeguarding of property, and the like?

3. What part should be played by the students in establishing these regulations?

4. What part should be played by the principal, by the teacher, and by students in enforcing these regulations and in extending self-government opportunities?

5. What opportunities for self-government of the student body are being overlooked or too little utilized?

Since this entire book deals with high school management, there is a sense in which everything in it has a bearing on discipline. However, the quality of the management is especially relevant. Careful planning that allows school to begin on the first day with a minimum of confusion makes it easy for each student to begin his work with purpose and enthusiasm. A systematic procedure for checking absences, which causes every student to be reasonably certain that he will be asked to explain each of his absences, is a much greater encouragement to regular attendance than is a system of severe penalties. Opportunities for pilfering or cheating should be as few as possible. The use of exits and halls should be planned to prevent congestion likely to lead to disorder. Both extremes of too much or too little organization should be avoided throughout the school.

The principal should make special arrangements to encourage good disciplinary situations. For example, substitute teachers should be given careful descriptions of past, present, and future activities of the classes they are to meet, and students should be encouraged to take pride in aiding substitute teachers with their difficult assignments. Where each class has its own elected student officers who regularly assist the teacher and who take charge in the teacher's absence, the classwork usually suffers less at the hands of a substitute teacher. Unless some such plans and arrangements are made, it is to be expected that many classes taught by outside substitutes may respond to the situation by temporarily transforming themselves into small mobs. Group meetings of students should be encouraged to define and develop the ideals of the school, and assemblies should be used to encourage good citizenship and school spirit. Successful achievements of the school and of individuals formerly or at present in the student body should be recognized in ways that encourage good citizenship.

Group rivalries that stimulate all students to do their best for the benefit of the group can be used to build loyalties and to raise standards. However, they are an instrument easily overemphasized or wrongly emphasized. In the case of rivalries between schools, it is difficult to avoid building antagonisms toward other schools.

EXTRACLASS ACTIVITIES

A broad program of extraclass activities which provides opportunities for all students to engage in interesting activities, to practice self-control and self-direction, and to release energies and enthusiasms naturally, helps to prevent and alleviate behavior problems. Athletics allow students to release pent-up energies on the play field instead of in the classrooms. Because they provide a legitimate, worthy release, students do not seek a less satisfying one. Every student who acquires a skill or expresses an interest in any kind of wholesome activity adds to his satisfactions and reduces his frustrations. The worst behavior problems are found in those students who have few skills in which they can take pride and few wholesome interests in which they can lose themselves. The weakness in most programs of extraclass activities lies in the fact that there are students whom the programs fail to reach. Especially in large schools it is easy for some students to be overlooked and for the entire program of extraclass activities to be judged successful because of the performance of a few talented students.

GUIDANCE

An effective guidance program reduces behavior problems simply because it makes certain that someone takes an interest in each student. Industry has found that some production increases can be explained in no other way than by workers' response to the interest and concern shown for their welfare as individuals. An effective guidance program reveals the direction in which the instructional program should be adjusted to avoid the weaknesses described in the following section. And finally, if dissatisfactions do exist and if behavior problems do occur, an effective guidance program should be helpful in adjusting them because it studies causes as well as symptoms. Moreover, it discovers the facts needed as a basis for proceeding intelligently to the tasks of adjustment.

THE INSTRUCTIONAL PROGRAM

It has long been recognized that good teaching decreases problems of discipline. In recent years there has been increasing realization of the destructiveness of boredom and fatigue and of the part played by individual teachers in avoiding these poisons. For each teacher in each class situation it is a complex problem requiring careful thought and planning. George V. Sheviakov and Fritz Redl have suggested that any disturbance in the satisfaction children get out of the work they do with their teachers is likely to reveal itself in the production of problem behavior. Some examples of problems of behavior due to poor instructional method which they cite follow:

Subject matter much too easy. Too much of the work ability of the students remains unchallenged and has to search for other outlets.

Subject matter much too difficult. The emotion of frustration accompanies great stretches of the work. Research has proved beyond doubt that exposure to the frustration of not being able to do things well will produce tremendous aggression or restlessness in *normal* children. The result will be unavoidable diversions, taking pokes at each other, dropping and throwing things, irritability, and I-don't-care attitudes, which lower behavioral inhibitions all over the place.

Language of teachers too remote from the child's developmental level, or from the native tongue ordinarily used on his social plane. If that is the case, the child feels out of place, not really wanted, or even looked down upon, and begins to show signs of social-outcast reactions and protest.

Load of assignments too light. Then the feeling of progress in learning is lacking, which again reflects itself in a growing unwillingness to do any work for that subject because the time spent on it does not seem profitable in the end.

Assignments badly planned, poorly explained, unfairly judged—with the result that typical "resentment behavior" pops out in little irritations. . . .

Type of work or way of presentation too advanced—not clicking with the developmental needs of the children. For instance, lectures on nature in general are given at an age where a strong curiosity about animals' bodies could easily be utilized for motivation.

Type of work and presentation too infantile, compared to development level on which children happen to move emotionally. For instance, talks about sex and the flowers are too childlike, when youngsters are full of pride about their newly acquired pre-adolescent daring in sex exploration on a very different level indeed.

Activities too much on a merely verbal level, leaving the normal motoric needs of growing children unchallenged for long stretches of time. Thus, we frequently find restlessness, noise, shuffling of feet, falling of chairs, and pushing each other where too much discussion or lecturing substitutes for real participation and manipulative activities.

Work badly scheduled as to sequences of different types, or ill-placed in terms of exhaustion and fatigue. For instance, the English poetry class is at the end of a long day after a baseball game, at which moment it seems to be especially hard to excite manipulation-greedy sixth-graders about Shelley or Keats.[1]

GOOD TEACHING METHODS

When classes begin promptly and vigorously, when teachers are skillful in arousing and holding interest, and when teachers systematically hold every member of the class responsible for all that takes place during every minute of the class period, students have little time for misbehavior.

If students are made aware of the goals in each subject they are studying, and of the fact that their progress toward those goals can be evaluated, they will even have an interest in a testing program. Achievement on a standardized test or scale can be set as a goal in any class or in all the classes of a particular subject in the school, but before agreeing on such an objective, teachers and students should make sure that such a goal is the one toward which they really wish to work. In the case of rivalries among classes, it is important to make sure that each group of students feels that the teacher is on its team.

Young people learn to make decisions by experience in actually making decisions; they learn to assume responsibilities by actually carry-

[1] George V. Sheviakov and Fritz Redl, *Discipline for Today's Children and Youth* (Washington, D.C.: Association for Supervision and Curriculum Development, N.E.A., 1944), pp. 45–46. Reprinted by permission of the National Education Association.

ing them; they learn to respect others, to cooperate, to make compromises, and to be adaptable to changing conditions by actually participating in group projects that involve all these activities. Cooperative class planning between pupils and teacher gives a wonderful opportunity for democratic action in the classroom. The teacher can always be the leader in the classroom, but the sooner students learn to be leaders, the better for them. Wherever students learn good citizenship by practicing it, sacrifices are made in routine efficiency and teachers spend much time in guiding students to do things they themselves could do with greater ease and dispatch. Training students to take the initiative in the work of the classroom, giving them the experience of finding the question as well as the answer—these are not easy assignments for a teacher, but they are a part of a teacher's responsibility. And this procedure can pay big dividends. In the long run, students grow more from their own doing than from that of their teachers.

STUDENT PARTICIPATION IN SCHOOL GOVERNMENT

Because students grow and learn most from activities that they plan and carry out, student participation in developing and controlling the life of the school is the most effective means of achieving good discipline. This does not mean suddenly allowing the students to govern themselves and their group activities, although after a period of practice and experimentation this result is not only conceivable but highly desirable. It means giving students practice in self-direction in small areas at first and allowing them to assume greater responsibilities as they demonstrate ability to carry them. Young people learn to be good citizens by practicing the activities good citizens carry on, just as they learn to be effective speakers by practice in speaking. The amount and degree of responsible self-direction that a student body exercises through its elected officers and bodies should be gradually increasing in any high school. Only thus can a school hope to provide the maximum amount of opportunity for self-direction that is the end of all good discipline.

It is essential, however, that each area which the students are going to control be clearly defined and that they be given the responsibility for success or failure in it. Otherwise the responsibility will not be a real one for them, and they will not take it seriously. It is important that at any one time students be given only those responsibilities which they understand, which they are ready and willing to undertake, and at which they have a better than even chance for reasonable success. Complete failure sometimes teaches a good lesson; experienced too often, it leads only to more failure. Student participation cannot be imposed; it should be offered and encouraged to grow into vigor and self-reliance.

During the twenties a large high school in the Middle West had successful self-governing study halls that enrolled almost all the students in the school. Students selected their own proctors, who excluded those who interfered in any way with the conscientious work and study that were the accepted standards in each study hall. In general, those who were excluded keenly felt the reproof by their peers, whose judgment they respected and whose favorable opinion they sought. Visitors who came to observe the study halls saw a project in student participation that had the enthusiastic support of the entire faculty and student body. It was difficult for them to realize that it had begun as a very small project involving just a few students; that ten years or so had been required for it to grow slowly and soundly into the thought and action patterns of the entire school; and that students were administering discipline to their peers only in the form of temporary exclusion from the group. Excluded students were not reported to the principal for further discipline.

These characteristics are typical of most successful projects that provide for student participation in school government. Although a good over-all organization, generally called a student council, should be representative of every student in the school, there is no point in organizing such a council until students understand its function and recognize the need for it, and until the principal and faculty are willing to see it begin to be and to become a representative and responsible self-governing agency. It takes a good deal of experience in informal projects, involving a small number of students in each, to bring a student body to the attitudes and understandings that will make possible the success of an all-school council. Students and faculty must have a clear understanding of the organization, its scope and functions. Definite areas of student responsibility, and hence authority, should be set up. These areas should expand from year to year as competence to accept responsibility and discharge authority increases. They must understand the areas where students have real authority and responsibility and recognize other areas where they are cooperating with the principal and board of education in carrying out state law or the board's policies in the schools under its control. The procedure in developing student participation should be slow enough so that all can be prepared for each successive step, but the usual danger is that principals are so slow in developing student participation that many opportunities for building self-control are neglected.

A decision to assign responsibilities for disciplinary action to student boards or groups should be made with great caution. Students often resent disciplinary action imposed by their peers much more than they resent it when imposed by faculty members. Parents also frequently resent it and may add many complications. Students are likely to be severe in their judgments and ruthless in carrying them out, even when they are trying to be fair and objective. They may tend to settle cases on a personal basis. Even where penalties are left to the principal, the onus of detecting and reporting offenses is unpleasant and likely to divide students into antagonistic groups. Though there are examples of schools where it has been successful, in most schools where it has been tried, student assumption of responsibilities for direct disciplinary action has been unsatisfactory chiefly because serious misbehavior is a problem to be solved by individual diagnosis and counseling rather than by assessing penalties.

To the extent that the assumption of responsibility for disciplinary action encourages students to think of their self-governing body as a punishing agency, they are forming a warped idea of the function of self-government. The functions of the "police state" are punitive and restrictive, whereas the functions of democratic government tend more and more to be positive and releasing. In a modern democratic state and in a technological age government can fulfill its aims in no other way. Policing becomes relatively less and less its principal purpose and activity. If high school students get the idea that their own government is principally a police force because they feel its presence most often as a punishing agency, they are not being educated for participation in democratic group life as well as they could be.

THE STUDENT COUNCIL AS A CONSTRUCTIVE DISCIPLINARY AGENCY*

If a student body is to participate in school government in any organized way, the student council or its equivalent will be needed. To the extent that a student council helps the student body set standards, adopt goals, and plan ways of working to reach them, it is concerned with guiding and controlling conduct and hence is an agency of school discipline in the most constructive sense. Its importance as a part of the high school's educational program is stressed elsewhere; here it will be considered only as an agency for improving group life in the school. There is a voluminous literature concerning the methods of organizing student councils, the steps in the process, and suitable activities for the councils. In addition to a national association of student councils, state associations exist in many states. The publications of the National Self-Government Committee are available in the Division of Secondary Education of the United States Office of Education, and the office of the National Association of Secondary School Principals in Washington offers special helps for workers with student councils. The *Bulletin* of the latter organization listed a set of five criteria of a good student council in one of its

* See also the discussion of the student council in Chapter 11.

issues.[2] The five standards, or criteria, with three especially pertinent subpoints for each criterion, are as follows:

CRITERION ONE

A good Student Council possesses power, authority, and responsibility.

2. It proposes and carries out activities for the improvement of the school. . . .
3. It co-ordinates the extracurriculum activities of the school, enlisting the entire school personnel in so doing. . . .
5. Its source of power lies in the delegation to it by the Principal of authority and responsibility for action within specific or general areas; . . .

CRITERION TWO

A good Student Council practices accepted democratic principles in its operations; its Constitution and By-Laws are carefully planned and democratically conceived. . . .

3. Student units which elect representatives must be small enough so that they can keep close contact with the activity of their representatives. . . .
11. The Council accepts responsibility for its failures as well as its successes. . . .
17. Planning in a democratic manner on the part of leaders precedes the initiation of most activities. . . .

CRITERION THREE

A good Student Council is supported on the part of the faculty and Principal by a true understanding of the Council's role; in addition, the attitude of the Principal and faculty is sympathetic. . . .

2. The necessary means are taken to keep the faculty continuously informed of the role of the Council. . . .
3. The Principal and faculty demonstrate their faith and confidence in the Council by calling upon it for assistance. . . .
4. Steps are taken whenever necessary to acquaint the entire student body with the Council's purposes, functions, problems, and activities, to the end that it will receive maximum student interest and support. . . .

CRITERION FOUR

A good Student Council has a sound functioning organization. . . .

1. The Council operates by the authority and according to the provisions of a Constitution formally adopted and regularly ratified by the student body. . . .

[2] From Robert C. Vanderlip, "Standards of a Good Student Council" (A study for a doctoral dissertation; Washington, D.C.: School of Education, George Washington University); reprinted in the NASSP *Bulletin*, No. 124 (October, 1944), pp. 105–115. Reprinted by permission of the National Education Association.

7. The Adviser or Sponsor of the Council is its Counselor; he is expected to aid the Council in ways to promote its success although he is to maintain a secondary place when it makes decisions; he cannot veto action of the Council, except in cases in which the Principal is also the Adviser. . . .

8. The Council must be given the opportunity to experiment, to be on its own; it has the right to fail as well as succeed. . . .

CRITERION FIVE

An effective Student Council has prestige, and enlists the ready cooperation of the student body. . . .

2. The student body understands the purposes of the Council. . . .

7. Student Council projects are worth while and challenging. . . .

14. The Student Council encourages students to:
    a. Be free to express opposition to any project which, in their opinion, is open to serious question.
    b. Be alert to weaknesses in the school and show their concern in a cooperative way to do something about such weaknesses.
    c. Develop a sense of civic duty that will encourage them to carry out all assignments.

Student councils which meet these criteria will generally be more effective agencies for building good standards of group control than if they do not possess these characteristics.

Meeting Disciplinary Emergencies

The all-important work of the principal should be to establish a fundamentally sound school situation from which good discipline is a natural outgrowth. Obviously, this is a long, hard task. In the meanwhile, a reasonably orderly social situation must be maintained by almost any means, or there is no hope of even the beginning of a good disciplinary situation. The principal has the responsibility of protecting the health, welfare, safety, and comfort of the great majority of the students against the minority as best he can, pending the time when an improved school situation will begin to generate its own discipline. The temptation is to be satisfied with the externally enforced discipline that may be necessary at times of emergency, and, instead of accepting it as a temporary means of reaching a really good disciplinary situation, to begin accepting it as an end in itself. This kind of disciplinary situation always has to be understood as the *semblance* of good discipline and not as the really good discipline with which this chapter is concerned. Too many high schools operate constantly under what Sheviakov and Redl call "surface discipline." It is imposed on students and they comply. But it is not teaching them self-control. Neither is it teaching them how to organize as groups for the management of group life activities.

METHODS—REMEDIAL PROCEDURES

Even in the best situation, needs will arise for remedial treatment and for the discouragement and prevention of unsocial behavior. A healthy adolescent should be expected to present behavior problems from time to time during his struggles to attain status as an adult. In his efforts to establish new relationships with his age-mates of both sexes, an adolescent is likely to be thrown occasionally into a situation where to react healthfully is to be a behavior problem. Administrators and teachers should be careful students of the needs and characteristics of the adolescent youth with whom they work.

SOME BASIC PRINCIPLES

There are at least three principles that should be basic in the thinking of administrators and staff members as they deal with young offenders and attempt to improve their behavior. First, problems that indicate social and emotional maladjustments of students are more serious than those that denote active disturbance of school routine. Many teachers are inclined to be sensitive to behavior difficulties that directly frustrate adult purposes or annoy adult susceptibilities. Actually, offenses such as lying about others, inattention in class, and careless work habits indicate a lack of personal adjustment and are much more serious than misdemeanors that irritate teachers, such as whispering, impertinence, and smoking.

Second, the source of disciplinary problems arising from maladjustments often cannot be judged by what students do and say. What a student says is disturbing him may not be the real factor at all, and antagonism expressed toward a teacher may really be antagonism toward a member of his family or of his gang. Apparent insolence may be merely a complete lack of good manners.

Third, because people vary greatly and because the same individual does not always react in the same way, it is very difficult to generalize about disciplinary problems. Each one demands a separate analysis and procedures designed to bring about improvement that will be slow and gradual at best.

GROUP ANALYSES

Although those who speak and write about disciplinary problems generally focus their attention upon the individual, two careful students have made the following generalization about the disciplinary difficulties of individuals and groups:

Only about 10 percent of all cases of school discipline are simple cases of "individual disturbances" clear and proper. About 30 percent of the cases at least are cases where problem behavior is produced entirely by *group psychological* inadequacies of school life. About 60 percent of the cases seem to us to involve both personal case history of the individual and some deficiency in the *psychological structure of the group.* This means, then, that at east 90 percent of all discipline cases are in dire need of group *psychological analysis* and consideration.[3]

Probably most high school principals would disclaim any ability to provide group psychological analysis. And yet there are many fundamental questions affecting groups that professionally trained principals are well qualified to answer. Are dissatisfactions within the group being caused by bad curriculum planning? Are standards for group behavior too high or too low? Does the group feel too much autocratic pressure, or is too little leadership being provided? Is the group under a strain because of sudden changes in the school or in other aspects of the environment? Are there enough common interests or background experiences in each of the various groups as they are organized? These are questions that principals can answer and do something about.

Many group difficulties, however, are more complex. Tensions and frictions between individuals or cliques are neither easily understood nor readily improved. Frictions may come from bad leadership within a group, from an overemphasis upon competition, or from a natural and normal situation in which individuals are competing with one another for places of leadership. Group life for adults does not always run smoothly, and there is good reason to expect even more friction among youth as they try themselves out in the process of growing up.

Sometimes groups of students behave as if they were personally antagonistic to everything about the school and to the principal in particular. It may be necessary for the principal to take steps which will achieve a change in surface behavior, even though he knows that thereby he is making no progress in changing fundamental attitudes. In any event, the principal should maintain the attitude of a physician and persistently probe for the causes of misbehavior. Students do not suddenly become possessed by demons. In some way they have learned the behavior they are exhibiting. No one has taught it deliberately, but it has been taught inadvertently. In all probability the personal antagonisms to the school that seem to exist are not real but are surface expressions of difficulties which are much deeper. Someone about this school should know each individual and group and make intensive efforts to analyze each situation and to find the real causes of difficulties.

The prescribing of punishments for groups offers many difficulties,

[3] Sheviakov and Redl, *op. cit.*, p. 44.

and experienced principals tend to avoid it unless the offense is of an extremely serious nature and unless every member of the group is definitely involved. It is a mistake to punish the many for the mistakes of the few. Group conferences are often effective because they make it possible for all facts to be brought into the open and for all issues to be defined. They dispel false rumors and provide a sound basis for the building of an intelligent public opinion. Social disapproval is the greatest deterrent to misbehavior. Students are very sensitive to the opinions of their age-mates, and strong school pride and loyalty create uncomfortable conditions for offenders who have harmed the school.

School strikes are an outgrowth of unrecognized group tensions. They may be expected to occur in high schools in a country that is as yet unable to settle some adult difficulties without them. They are very annoying to faculties, to school executives, and to parents, especially when they occur in upper-class communities where it is customary to regard a strike as a screen for subversiveness. School strikes are to be deprecated because they usually reveal an arbitrary and unjust act or position on the part of someone in authority; a sudden change in policy or plan without prior efforts to have student understanding of a matter which is of more importance to students than the adults realized; or sudden and intemperate action on the part of student leaders with little or no effort to get a situation settled by "peaceful" means. Too often, "student" strikes are aided if not fomented by adults in the community who ought to know better. They can usually be prevented where any degree of understanding has been built up between student leaders and the school staff. When they occur they have to be settled by arbitration and conciliation just as any strike must be settled. Expressions of horror, browbeating tactics, and arbitrary acts by adult authorities calculated to put "children" in their places are of no avail. Someone who is willing to go into the matter calmly and patiently with representatives of the striking students has to enter the picture and work out the best solution possible. A more fundamental study of the underlying causes then needs to be made to reduce the chances of future strikes.

DEALING WITH INDIVIDUALS

A properly conducted personal conference is the first step in analyzing a student's problem and in helping him to see it from the standpoint of others. Even where the misbehavior of a group is involved, the most effective procedure involves a personal conference with each member of the group. It should be conducted by one staff member so that no individual student will feel that he is being placed at a disadvantage by a "gang" of teachers. For first offenders, especially, many problems can be adjusted by persuasion and suggestions.

In difficult cases a personal conference may be nothing but the first step and a means of beginning to secure the facts upon which procedures for adjusting a student's behavior may be based. Dr. Elmer H. Garinger, when principal of the Central High School at Charlotte, North Carolina, listed different types of devices which have been effective in that school, as follows:

Devices directed toward the student are:

a. Persuasion and suggestion
b. Improving the health of the pupil
c. Frequent reporting to parents
d. Providing food and clothing for the pupil when needed
e. Assignment of the problem pupil to some one teacher for guidance
f. Asking some adult in the community to accept responsibility for guidance of the pupil.

Devices directed to the school environment are:

a. Adjustment of the entire program of the pupil to his capacities and abilities
b. Encouragement of the pupil to join a club
c. Giving the problem pupil a position of some responsibility
d. Change of course or of teacher
e. Use of school funds to encourage known but underdeveloped interests
f. Transfer to another school.

Devices directed to the outside environment are:

a. Visiting the home of the pupil
b. Obtaining work for the problem case
c. Recommending a change in methods of control to the parents
d. Securing a camp scholarship or membership in an outside school organization for the pupil.[4]

Dr. Garinger believed that among the most effective of these devices were improving the health of the pupil, assigning the pupil to some one teacher for guidance, adjusting the program to the pupil's capacities and abilities, and visiting the home of the pupil.

KEEPING RECORDS OF MALADJUSTMENTS

For each student the school should keep a cumulative record of the evidences of his maladjustment and the efforts made at adjustment. Perhaps this record should be destroyed when the student leaves the

---

[4] Elmer H. Garinger, quoted in N. W. Newsom and others, *Administrative Practices in Large High Schools* (New York: American Book Company, 1940), pp. 536, 537, 538.

school, but it is essential for both preventive and remedial work. A periodic survey of the records will show the frequency of reported offenses. An analysis of an individual record will show the progress being made with an individual and the success of the measures that have been used. In a large school it is impossible to deal with a student and prescribe for him as an individual unless records are kept. In many schools it has been found helpful to let a student contribute to this record by writing a full and accurate account of his offense, including an analysis of its bad effects and a proposal of his own for doing something about it.

CONFERENCES WITH PARENTS

Many principals find it helpful in dealing with problem cases of discipline to ask the parents to visit the school for a personal conference. It should be made clear that the purpose of such a conference is not to embarrass either the parents or the student but to throw light on the problem at hand and to work out a way of cooperation to achieve a common objective. No one should leave the conference with resentment because he has lost face. If parents happen to be the rare ones who do not wish to cooperate, the school should know it. Conferences between parents and principals should certainly not be limited to a consideration of disciplinary problems. It is to be assumed that any school has a number of ways by which members of the school's faculty as well as the principal make occasional but systematic contacts with parents when no unpleasant incident needs to be discussed.

PENALTIES

If responsibility can be definitely fixed, restitution for damage done is an effective penalty because it appeals to the student's sense of fair play and because it is so closely related to the misdeed. However, the penalty should be governed by the situation. Sometimes an entire group is reponsible for damage done by an individual, and sometimes damage is done by accident and not by conscious misdeed.

Requiring pupils to make apologies even in private to a teacher or pupil against whom the offender has transgressed seems clearly unwise. Being forced to make an apology is more than likely to lead to hypocrisy, to the feeding of fires of resentfulness, antagonism, and vengeance. Some pupils will regard the apology as an easy way to escape any significant punishment, and the procedure becomes education in hypocrisy.

If the pupil, however, is brought to see that he has been wrong, has done an injustice, or has been discourteous, a subtle suggestion that he can regain the good will or respect of the victim by a statement that he is sorry, or that he now sees that he was in the wrong, possesses none of these limitations. If safeguarded from exploitation by deceitful pupils, it can do no harm.

Educational writers generally consider it bad policy to detain students after hours for their misdeeds and offer these reasons: it causes students to dislike school; it offers a routine, superficial way for teachers to take action and may easily become a substitute for a more fundamental solution of problems; and it makes an unnecessary demand on the teacher's time. Detention after school has consequently been abandoned in many high schools and in a number of junior high schools. The pupil detained does not feel that this punishment is much to be feared. It affords him much time to rationalize his conduct and a stimulus to nurse his resentment and dissatisfaction. In many schools, however, it is employed apparently with some success as punishment for minor offenses, and is so managed that the pupil has the feeling of being a good sport in "taking his medicine" as a matter of course. Nevertheless it seems to be a dubious practice and there is nothing to show that it improves school discipline over what it would otherwise be. The plan of "demerits" is equally open to question.

Suspension and expulsion from school are rarely justifiable. The former causes the student to fall behind with his work and for disinterested students may be a reward rather than a punishment. The latter does not solve a problem but merely transfers it from the school to an environment in which there is even less likelihood of a favorable solution being achieved. In the few cases where leaving school appears to be an advantage to the student, it should be possible to make the situation clear to him and his parents so that a voluntary withdrawal rather than a suspension would result. A short suspension is occasionally useful while a student's case is being investigated, and expulsion may be unavoidable if the facts show that a student is clearly a corrupting influence. The high school has a responsibility for retaining every student as long as it can contribute to his growth and development. On the other hand, it has to protect other students from the acts of a few. The high school is a school for normal youth, and when an individual shows that he is persistently unable or unwilling to be normal he has to be removed from the group. However, these penalties are so serious that they should be used only after thorough investigation and the accumulation of convincing evidence.

Although corporal punishment was common during pioneer days, it is uncommon now. It is increasingly regarded as a confession of professional inadequacy, a physical indignity which should not be inflicted on any individual nor particularly upon one who is immature, a hazard to the morale of the school, and a source of lawsuits that can be avoided. It has no place in the American high school.

This chapter can perhaps best be closed with excerpts from two sources. From *Helping Teachers Understand Children,* we quote the following:

Our analysis indicates that teachers who understand children show the following characteristics: (1) they think of children's behavior as caused by a series of factors that can be identified and they therefore believe that boys and girls are understandable and educable; (2) they are able to accept every child emotionally and to respect and value him as a human being; (3) they recognize that every child is unique and therefore they constantly seek information about each of their pupils that will enable them to know the factors that are influencing their development and behavior; (4) they know the common developmental tasks that all children face during the several phases of their growth and what complications often arise as individuals with varying characteristics and backgrounds work at those tasks; (5) they know the more important generalizations that describe and explain human growth, development, motivation, learning, and behavior; and (6) they are well accustomed to methods of gathering and organizing relevant information about a child, of finding the scientific principles to which this information points as explaining the particular individual's maturity level and overt actions, and of using these explanatory principles—together with the pertinent data—as the basis for helping the youngster meet his problems of growing up.[5]

Dr. Percival M. Symonds underscores the importance of the principal in school discipline when he says,

One should not dismiss this topic of punishment without stopping to consider what discipline and punishment mean to the teacher. Unfortunately, many teachers who would like to adopt a more constructive attitude toward the problems of classroom discipline and control are prevented from doing so by the conditions under which they must teach and the attitude of their superior officers and the community. In the first place, control is a difficult matter at best when one has charge of a class of forty or more children, however high a teacher's ideals may be. In spite of various suggestions, most teachers are reduced to rather rigid and autocratic methods of management and control of large classes over a long period of time. Second, discipline in a school is a function of the administration. The principal sets the pattern for the social relations in a school by his philosophy and interpretation of the meaning of education. If he takes a positive and constructive point of view toward education he makes possible a constructive attitude for his teachers, but if he is a believer in authoritarian control and repression he makes the teacher's task difficult. If the principal places great emphasis on order, system, and quiet in the classroom, it is the unusual teacher who is able to achieve these standards by

[5] Division on Child Development and Teacher Personnel, *Helping Teachers Understand Children* (Washington, D.C.: American Council on Education, 1945), pp. 19–20.

which he is to be evaluated without using methods that are in a degree repressive. The tone and morale of a school go back to the psychology of the principal and the principal, in so many cases, calls the turn for his teachers. It is true that each teacher in a school will reveal his individual personality in his relations with the class, but limits are set on what he can accomplish by the standards and expectations of the principal.[6]

This whole chapter is an indictment of the concepts and methods of discipline prevalent in too many high schools in which a negative approach to the behavior of individuals and groups is made. In these schools the stress is on repression, and while the result may be a sort of surface discipline, the habitual behaviors it produces may in reality be worse than those it suppresses. This chapter calls for a positive rational approach to conduct: one that seeks changes in the school situation which encourage and produce good personal and group reactions; one that looks past overt acts to their causes in the school, at home, or in the community at large; and finally one in which the principal and faculty, with the assistance of the students, their parents, and citizens, join together to produce a suitable environment for youth and a school program in which the patterns of conduct learned and the underlying standards adopted are more in harmony with what a democratic society with our moral and ethical ideals approves.

Some Points to Consider

1. It is the authors' belief that, the ages of pupils taken into account, higher levels of responsible participation in school life and operation are to be found in good elementary schools than in good high schools. Do you agree? Explain your position.

2. In your experience would you say most high schools have good "surface" discipline or fundamentally good discipline? How would you improve this situation where surface discipline exists?

3. Do current figures on juvenile delinquency illustrate that present-day youth are an undisciplined generation?

4. Why is it important to work for *responsible* student participation? What differences does it make to insist on this word?

5. Some principals say they do not want student councils because they want to work for self-control of each student as an individual. What weakness in their concept of the student council do they exhibit?

6. High School A is attended by a typical group of students from a typical community. Getting good discipline seems to be a principal worry and chief activity of the faculty and administration. In High School B, attended by a similar group from a similar community, good discipline seems to be a minor concern of all; yet, if anything, discipline is really better here than in High

[6] Percival M. Symonds, "Classroom Discipline," *Teachers College Record* (December, 1949), pp. 153–154.

School A. How might the difference be explained? What might High School A introduce from High School B to improve its situation?

Further Reading

Baruch, Dorothy. *New Ways in Discipline.* New York: McGraw-Hill Book Co., Inc., 1949.

Blos, Peter. *The Adolescent Personality.* New York: Appleton-Century-Crofts, Inc., 1941.

Caruthers, Thomas J. "Discipline as a Means of Development," *Phi Delta Kappan,* December, 1953.

Cohler, M. J. "A New Look at the Old Problems of Discipline," *School Review,* 56, No. 8 (October, 1948), 468–475.

Division on Child Development and Teacher Personnel. *Helping Teachers Understand Children.* Washington, D.C.: American Council on Education, 1945.

Edgar, Robert W. "Discipline and Purpose," *Teachers College Record,* October, 1955.

Educational Policies Commission. *Learning the Ways of Democracy.* Washington, D.C.: National Education Association, 1940.

Fedder, Ruth. *Guiding Homeroom and Club Activities.* New York: McGraw-Hill Book Co., Inc., 1949.

Hill, Arthur S., Leonard M. Miller, and Hazel F. Gabbard, "Schools Face the Delinquency Problem," NASSP *Bulletin,* No. 198, December, 1953.

Hymes, James L., Jr. *Behavior and Misbehavior.* Englewood Cliffs, N.J.: Prentice-Hall, Inc., 1955.

———. *Effective Home-School Relations.* Englewood Cliffs, N.J.: Prentice-Hall, Inc., 1955.

Kelley, Earl C., and Roland C. Faunce. *Your School and Its Government.* New York: National Self-government Committee, 1945.

Lewin, Kurt, Charles E. Meyers, and Joan Kalhorn. *Authority and Frustration.* Iowa City: University of Iowa Press, 1944.

Mahoney, John. *For Us the Living.* New York: Harper & Brothers, 1945. Chap. 13.

McKown, Harry C. *Extra-Curricular Activities.* 3rd ed.; New York: The Macmillan Company, 1952. Chap. 4.

———. *The Student Council.* New York: McGraw-Hill Book Co., Inc., 1944.

Meek, Lois H., ed., Committee on Workshops. *The Personal-Social Development of Boys and Girls with Implications for Secondary Education.* New York: Progressive Education Association, 1940.

Morris, Glyn. *Practical Guidance Methods for Principals and Teachers.* New York: Harper & Brothers, 1952. Chap. 9.

National Association of Secondary School Principals. "Student Activities in the Secondary School," *Bulletin,* No. 119, January, 1944.

———. "Student Council Handbook," *Bulletin,* No. 89, March, 1940.

———. "The Student Council in the Secondary School," *Bulletin,* No. 124, October, 1944.

National Education Association. *It's High Time*. Washington, D.C.: National Education Association, 1955.

Partridge, E. D. *Social Psychology of Adolescence*. Englewood Cliffs, N.J.: Prentice-Hall, Inc., 1938.

Sheviakov, George V., and Fritz Redl. *Discipline for Today's Children and Youth*. Washington, D.C.: Association for Supervision and Curriculum Development, N.E.A., 1944.

Smith, Joe. *Student Councils for Our Times*. New York: Bureau of Publications, Teachers College, Columbia University, 1951.

Symonds, Percival M. "Classroom Discipline," *Teachers College Record*, December, 1949.

Tomajan, John S. "The Test: Obedience to the Unenforceable," *New York Times Magazine* (July 3, 1955), p. 8.

Vanderlip, Robert C. "Standards of a Good Student Council," in "The Council in the Secondary School," NASSP *Bulletin*, No. 124, October, 1944.

Yeager, William A. *Administration and the Pupil*. New York: Harper & Brothers, 1949. Chap. 16.

Chapter 18

GUIDANCE AND RECORDS OF
PUPIL GROWTH

Pupil personnel work, an important part of high school administration, includes all that the school does to help it know its pupils well enough —and to help them know themselves well enough—so that the school's educational program and life will be of maximum service to each student. It includes study of and work with individual students. It also includes work with small face-to-face groups, since it is sometimes possible to achieve in such groups the results that otherwise would have to be sought through individual counseling. All that we know about individual differences points up the need for a high school to check carefully to see that each student's educational experience is the best for him. All that we know about youth points to the need for each student to have a chance to consult and advise with his parents and with his teachers about how to make his high school experience of most benefit to himself. We know that students need and want help in finding the answers to their personal, social, and educational problems. They do not want to be told the answers and it does not help them learn anything but the memorized answer if this is done. They learn to solve their problems best when the teacher or counselor is free with hints, clues, and suggestions while the student is discovering the answer for himself. They generally learn least and slowest when left wholly to their own resources. Guidance and counseling therefore serve a very positive function in increasing the amount of learning derived from a given experience.[1] We also know that although in a very small high school the personal relationship between principal, staff, and each pupil may be close enough so that a minimum of formal organization and administration is required, in typical high schools best results will be attained only where the administration and staff have given careful thought to planning the school's pupil personnel program.

[1] Robert C. Craig, *The Transfer Value of Guided Learning* (New York: Bureau of Publications, Teachers College, Columbia University, 1953).

The Scope of the Pupil Personnel Program

The scope of a high school's program of pupil personnel work tends to be set by the school's concept of its function and the related concept of the function of secondary education in modern America. The program will also be influenced by the extent of the responsibility the school accepts for its students. If the school regards secondary education, perhaps unconsciously, as chiefly concerned with providing able and ambitious youth with a better chance to get ahead in life, then the personnel program will center around those who show themselves to be the most able and ambitious. The school's interest in the others will naturally be less, for at heart the school questions whether those of less ability and ambition really belong in the student body. If such a school believes it should help the able and ambitious to get ahead in life mainly by providing them with an opportunity to study and master certain fields of knowledge, then its personnel work will be a narrowly conceived program of educational guidance and counseling. It will leave to the home and the church most of the tasks of advisement in other matters essential to a youth's advancement but less closely related to this restricted concept of education. Such a school's personnel records will therefore be mainly a matter of teachers' marks in subjects, credits earned, achievement scores in standard tests and perhaps in a few tests diagnostic of ability in certain subjects. Indeed, many high schools that would deny they accept these circumscribed concepts of the function of the American high school and of education itself show by the fact that their records are almost exclusively of the type described above that they are still clinging to the older patterns of practice. You can tell something about where a high school's heart is by the records it makes and treasures in its fireproof vault.

BROADER CONCEPTS FIND INCREASING FAVOR

More and more high schools in this country are trying to develop educational programs and concepts of the school's function in keeping with the demands of modern American life and the needs of our youth. They are beginning to accept a responsibility for helping youth, their parents, and the community with the all-round growth and development of all the youth in the community. They deny that such growth and development as a school can help provide for youth is a privilege which goes along with the social and economic status of his family. They tend to hold that in this country, and everywhere that the principles of our type of democracy are being accepted, secondary schools, along with the homes, become principal agents of society in assuring it of that continuing supply of well-grown and fully developed youth that its preservation and development require. There are therefore no youth in such a high school's community whose needs, interests, and abilities can be legitimately neglected as the school plans and develops its program and work. There are no youth to whom its counsel and advice need not be freely available in matters affecting their growth and development.

These points of view result in a broad concept of the scope of the school's pupil personnel work and records. As the school's program and work broaden, the relative importance of pupil personnel work increases. If the school's educational program is very narrow, the pupil's choice of subjects is limited. The program he selects may be good or bad for him, but there is less that can be done as the result of personnel work than can be done if the school offered him an opportunity for a wider choice of subjects. Where there is opportunity for a broad choice of educational and school-life experience, guidance and counseling can help the youth to see better what the full opportunity for him in the school's broad program really is. Thus a good educational program and effective counseling service go hand in hand. It is discouraging both to the youth and to his counselor to plan for the former's needs when both know that the school's program is too narrowly conceived to make such a plan practical. But it is just as unrealistic to assume that if a school provides enriched offerings all youth and their parents can, unassisted by the resources of the school, plan and carry out programs of school experience that are absolutely the best for each. Only when both a broad educational program and an intelligent counseling service are available can the school discharge its function well.

AREAS OF PUPIL PERSONNEL WORK

The growth and development of a youth is, of course, an integrated affair of the whole person. Best results cannot be expected if one kind of growth and development is sought while another is neglected. The emotional poise and stability we seek in older youth, for example, is not a goal to be attained at the cost of physical health and fitness. Yet in discussing, studying, planning, and conducting personnel work, it is necessary to break the total program down into parts, each of which aims at producing one of the kinds of growth and development that we see as a part of the all-round growth in youth. In the organization and administration of pupil personnel work programs, it is essential to have elements of the program designed to foster the several areas of growth that the school decides to encourage and promote. The principal has the additional and more important duty of being sure that these elements are so interrelated with one another that a balanced program is attained. Here, as elsewhere, the real work of the top executive in an institution often becomes one of correlating the work and activities of specialized workers so that the ends for which the specialized activities are carried on are not lost sight of.

Each of the important specialized types of pupil personnel work might be thought of as another form of the special services to which two previous chapters have been devoted. All are, however, like the educational program itself, so basic and inherent a part of the school's work that they ought not to be thought of as comprising a special service more or less auxiliary to the school's main concern. Actually, guiding, counseling, and teaching a student are such interrelated processes—and good results are so dependent upon interrelationship—that guidance cannot be thought of as a special *auxiliary* service. In other words, school guidance programs seek to help pupils make wise choices so that a larger and better measure of growth and development may result from the experiences available to him in a school. For every kind of growth and development for which the school feels enough concern to provide pupils an opportunity for experience, some kind of pupil personnel work will no doubt be done. However, schools commonly consider certain areas of so much importance to all pupils as to require formal organization and administration. Chief among these areas are (1) educational guidance, (2) vocational guidance, and (3) social-recreational guidance. Various other types of guidance activities, such as civic and moral guidance, are usually carried on by the school without formal organization. Health guidance, another type offered by many high schools, is so closely related to the school's health service, which was included in a previous chapter, that this chapter will be centered on consideration of the other three types mentioned above.

Educational Guidance

This aspect of pupil personnel work can be so broadly defined as to include all kinds of guidance except perhaps vocational; here it will be regarded as a program developed by the school to help a student make the best possible choice as to curriculum, subjects, and daily schedules, so that he gets the full advantage of what the school's educational program has to offer him. The high school's responsibility for such guidance and counseling begins when a youth is still in the upper grades of the elementary school and does not end until he has had help in selecting a school at a higher level or in finding his place as a young adult in the community.

ORIENTATION PROGRAM

This phase of this work is concerned with acquainting prospective students with what the school's educational offerings are. Explanatory printed materials are prepared that give an over-all picture of the total school program—curriculums available, the purposes served by each, the subjects required and elective each year, the extracurricular activities, and the procedures necessary for an entering student to follow at the time of his initial registration. These materials are usually prepared to serve the needs of students entering any year of the program as well as those of the whole group who are entering the school for the first time. They are also useful to parents of new students and ought to be made freely available to them as well as to the entering students. In well-articulated school systems these materials are placed in the hands of teachers in the sending schools well in advance of the date when the students will enter the high school so that they can be studied and discussed there. Usually this orientation period acquaints the prospective students with more than the high school's educational offering. These other aspects will be touched on later when social-recreational guidance is being discussed. Often the orientation work of the sending schools is rounded out by informal meetings conducted by a guidance worker or counselor from the high school, where questions of interest to the entering group may be answered. Meetings of parents with representatives from the high school, attended at least by the parents who have not had children in the high school before, ought to be arranged, preferably by the sending schools. Out of these conferences should come decisions as to each prospective student's program for the next year and some tentative decisions as to his whole program. The chapter in which daily schedule-making procedures are outlined assumes that such orientation activities as are mentioned here have been carried out by the schools. Chapter 23 also stresses the importance of close relationships between elementary and secondary schools. They form a sound foundation for subsequent educational guidance activities in the high school that can be laid in no other way.

IN-SCHOOL PROGRAM

When a student begins to attend a typical high school, some one of his numerous teachers must assume responsibility for further educational guidance. In many schools this guidance is provided in a home room or in a similar group. Unfortunately, the home room plan of guidance often allows too little time for the performance of the guidance functions and pays too little attention to the teacher's readiness to perform this service. The educational aspect of guidance, however, is probably the phase of the program that the typical teacher is best prepared to handle. In the early weeks of the school year, and especially in home rooms in which are those students who are just beginning their career in the high school, a further period of orientation to the school's educational programs and related practices is usually in order. Changes in daily schedule, conflicts in classes, marking systems, reports to parents, home study requirements, and many other details need to be known and understood by these new students. Later on, if unsatisfactory work is being done by any pupils, this fact is usually brought to the attention of the home room teacher in the hope that some constructive proposals may evolve from conferences between him and the students. If it seems desirable, the home room teacher may give or arrange for prognostic or aptitude tests, or both, as a means of developing a better basis for judgment as to what needs to be done in special cases.

Preparation of the students for registration for next year is another phase of educational guidance often centered in the home room. If students have made over-all plans for their full high school career there is need to decide whether changes are indicated as a result of this last year's experience. If changes are to be made, which ones can be made and which ones the students, with their parents' approval, want to make are problems that can be thrashed out in the home room. In fact, the whole process of advance registration can be so handled in the home room that it is a guided educational experience for the students and not the performance of routines with no recognition of their full meaning.

For juniors and seniors, a good educational guidance program includes an effort by the school to place each student who plans to continue his education beyond the high school, whether this means regular pre-professional college courses, shorter full-time programs in technical or business schools, or part-time evening courses which all but the smallest high schools and communities ought to be expected to make available as they are needed. In all these cases, either in the home rooms or in special group meetings for those students interested in particular types of schooling after they leave high school, full information ought to be provided so that the choices and decisions made will be as wise as possible. If the educational guidance program has been operating effectively since these juniors and seniors first entered the secondary school in the seventh year, and if some of the basic records illustrated later in this chapter have been made, the school will be able to offer good counsel to its students, both in pursuing their programs in high school and in preparing for higher educational levels after they leave it.

Vocational Guidance

The importance of making a wise choice of a lifework is so great for practically every youth that it is hard to conceive of a good high school that does not plan to offer such counsel and guidance to its students. The character of this program may vary with such factors as the socio-economic levels of the families served, but there are few high schools where it can be legitimately said that no effort need be made to assist their students in vocational planning. This matter is so important to a large majority of youth that in most high schools a much larger proportion of the educational program ought to be devoted to preparation for lifework than is now the case. But even where such a program exists—and we may even say that because it exists—a well-developed program of vocational guidance is all the more essential. This statement should help make it clear that there will be a close relationship between the educational and vocational aspects of a school's guidance program. But one cannot take the place of the other, nor can an enriched educational program be expected to make guidance programs anything but more essential.

VARYING DEGREE OF EMPHASIS ON VOCATIONAL GUIDANCE

The extent to which vocational guidance will need to be stressed, the amount of separation from educational guidance, and the point at which this separation and stress should begin will vary from one school community to another. In a community where practically all youth remain in school until graduation and a very large proportion go on to college, the stress on vocational guidance as distinct from educational guidance will be much less than in a community where there is a tendency for many to drop out of high school as soon as the law allows and where a high proportion of dropouts and graduates take up adult life in the community immediately on leaving high school. In between these two extremes are many variations, with other factors operating to change the stress and character of vocational guidance. By studying its own situation any high school can decide what to do about vocational guidance and when to do it. Where such a study reveals a large dropout at the minimum legal age, the beginning of vocational guidance service needs to be moved down in the school to reach the years when all are still in school. For the same reason pre-vocational education courses such as those in occupations need to be moved down. Regular vocational courses on a full- or part-time basis should immediately follow these in order to be open to youth at the time or just before the time they would otherwise discontinue their education. As the compulsory education age rises or the supply of jobs open to youth is restricted and only older youth are needed, these programs should be deferred to later years and the educational offerings of the earlier school years enriched with the addition of more courses of the exploratory type, such as those in applied and industrial arts, business, and homemaking, all of which are basic to various types of lifework.

SPECIAL VOCATIONAL GUIDANCE SERVICE NEEDED

Although the nature of educational guidance may make it relatively easy for typical classroom teachers to learn to counsel students with respect to their educational plans and decisions, this is not true of vocational guidance. Even a small school needs at least one teacher who is qualified to teach vocational guidance courses or regular vocational courses and also to assist home room teachers in matters of vocational guidance. If information about the various techniques, processes, activities, and basic records essential to good vocational guidance is available to home room teachers and their students, the level of accomplishment in vocational guidance will be raised far above what it is likely to be where this minimum of service is not available. Every community expects its high school principal and faculty to be able to help students make wise choices with respect to their educational plans and programs. Most communities endorse the high school program of extracurricular activities and the school's practice of assigning one or more teachers to advise and guide students participating in them. It is equally vital that in the important area of lifework the school provide competent guidance and counsel for its students.

The culminating activity of this specialized service for most students is a chance to go to work on a suitable job. It is not up to the school to find him a job, but at least the pupil needs to feel that the school has taken an active interest in his efforts to place himself. Moreover, it is to the school's advantage to have its graduates feel that everything reasonable was done to help them find employment. This service is covered at some length in a subsequent chapter; it is mentioned here only to round out the concept of a good vocational guidance program.

Social-Recreational Guidance

Just as a high school's program of general education needs to be complemented by an educational guidance service and its specialized program of lifework education needs a complementary program of vocational guidance, so the program of extracurricular activities needs a parallel program of social-recreational guidance. Maximum benefits from all three programs will result only when a planned effort on the part of the school results in a better experience for students with all three than would occur were every student left without the help that a school faculty can and ought to give. Many opportunities for social-recreational guidance grow out of the school's extracurricular activity program, but those opportunities related to the more unorganized group life of the school ought not to be neglected. The mere fact that a student has membership in the student body and in its small classroom groups creates opportunities for the school to call attention to desirable and undesirable social standards and practices and to encourage students to choose better ones.

INFORMATION NEEDED BY NEW STUDENTS

The orientation phase of the social-recreational guidance program for new students ought to give them a chance to know the scope of the extracurricular activity program and to begin to get acquainted with the school's standards. Just as they need to know the full possibilities of the school's educational program, so they also need to be acquainted with those of the extracurricular activity program. Early in their entering year, students should be informed in their home room about the objectives of the whole extracurricular activity program and of the purpose of each organized group or activity, the membership qualifications, the rules for membership and participation, and the meeting schedules. They also need to know about the school's student government and about the school's standards for personal and group conduct in classrooms, corridors, assemblies, and at games and social affairs. All these and similar matters are now often covered in a student handbook, which can be used as a reference in the home rooms and in other meetings where social and recreational guidance is being carried on.

NEED FOR CONTINUOUS PROMOTIONAL PROGRAM

With a large turnover in the student body of around 25 per cent or more each year due to graduation, dropout, and transfer, it is impossible to supply this guidance and information at the beginning of each year and then assume that it is done for the year. Moreover, the maintenance of personal and group patterns and standards of student conduct requires the continuous program of support and approval of appropriate members of the faculty and student officers. One of the causes of the decline of interest in the social and recreational activities of a high school is the lack of a sustained effort to keep students informed of what opportunities for participation are developing and where. The recurring annual round of events and activities may get to be an old story to the faculty, and it is easy to forget that students need to be continuously informed and encouraged to participate in them. Personal and group standards which become so well established that the faculty relaxes its efforts and does not encourage student leaders to inform new students and urge their acceptance of them have a way of being forgotten, and new and sometimes lower standards appear first as an exception and soon as the rule. The steady work of years in developing high standards of student conduct at athletic contests, for instance, can be undone in a short time if student leaders and appropriate faculty members do not seize upon every occasion to give approving support to those standards. Desirable traditions persist longest without anyone's active support in a static society. An American high school is a fluid, unstable, and dynamic social organization, and only a well-planned and continuous effort at social-recreational guidance can maintain and develop its activities and standards.

This chapter opened with a statement that a broadly conceived concept of the responsibility of the high school for the growth and development of its students was required to support as broad a program of guidance as is encompassed by the three areas proposed earlier in this chapter. By now it should be evident that the successful operation of such a program means that a school must really make it possible for members of the faculty to know their students. This would appear to require special concern for two points that in many modern schools are somewhat neglected. The first is a truly adequate opportunity to know students better than the typical teacher's day now generally permits. To meet this situation, better chances to meet students in small face-to-face groups and better opportunities for individual conferences must be more freely provided. The home room has been mentioned in this chapter as a center for guidance services. A more adequate amount of time for the home room, however, has been suggested. More will be said on this point in the last section of this chapter, where the over-all organization of the school for guidance service will be discussed.

In addition to improved opportunities for contacts with small groups, a second requirement is a functional system of personnel records. Even when they are given a good home room organization, teachers cannot be expected to remember all the data about each student which ought to be considered when conferences or discussions are being held on the basis of which students are to be encouraged to make decisions. Teachers must be able to refer to a continuing record of pertinent facts about the students' lives and records and to use these facts as the basis for what they say in conferences or group discussions. We must therefore consider the question of what constitutes good systems of personnel records.

Types of Pupil Personnel Records

As is indicated earlier in this chapter, a school's records tell something about the breadth of its concern for the growth and development of its students. A school may have broad concerns and incomplete records for lack of staff time or money. This is unfortunate, for no matter how great a school's concern is, it cannot act on this concern wisely unless pertinent records are at hand. More often, however, the lack of records is indicative of the lack of concern or at least of a low level of concern. Records need to be broad and deep. That is, they need to cover many phases of growth and development, and they need to reach back to earlier years to give a moving picture or at least a series of snapshots. A student's present growth can be interpreted well only in the light of the past.

In this section are presented several types of forms that illustrate what is meant by breadth and depth of records. In Chapter 16, we have already supplied some samples of forms used in reporting to parents. These forms included here have not been selected as the best records of their types, for we have no way of being sure what is the best record of any type. They do illustrate that some high schools are enough concerned about various aspects of the growth and development of their students to make records to guide them in future counseling with any student. These forms also illustrate particular items they have thought important enough to include. For example, Form 3 shows the details one school seeks about the health status of its students. A study of it shows that this school has available the pertinent health information it might need to consider in advising a student on any problem or decision. The cumulative records that follow later as Forms 7–10 also illustrate how health knowledge is incorporated into the over-all record of each student. Probably a few high schools can support health records as complete as some of these, but child health is so vital to this nation that the day should not be far off when such complete health records on every boy and girl in each community ought to be available. In many places the best agency to make and use such records is the school, and money from federal and state sources ought to be available if it is needed to enable local schools to develop, use, and keep a record of our national child health resources.

Another important kind of record deals with students' competence to find and hold jobs. Vocational counseling exists to help a youth appraise his own abilities in terms of what various kinds of jobs demand, to help a youth prepare by education for what is for him a suitable kind of work, and to help him make an initial adjustment to the world of work. Form 4 illustrates records used by high schools in connection with their efforts to aid in job placement. The cumulative records shown as Form 7–10 include items concerned with work-experience, interests, aptitude tests, and work plans, all of which builds up a substantial budget of information for use in vocational counseling.

Numerous items on the cumulative records shown here as Forms 7–10 provide information designed to be useful in counseling students on personal and social matters. Such a wide variety of information is so useful here that it is difficult to draw it together on one form as is done on the health records. Personality and character traits tend to indicate how a student reacts in social and group situations. Work habits as revealed in school and on a job add a significant sidelight. Factual statements on the amount of participation in the activities of the school and the degree of responsibility assumed indicate ability and willingness to enter into group activities. Forms 5 and 6 illustrate records made of particular kinds of participation. Form 6 attempts to get a record of service rendered, of responsibility carried, and the attitudes and traits exhibited while the student was at work. Such records can make the generalized items on a cumulative record more realistic.

The cumulative record shown as Forms 7–10 is the master record for each student. Such forms are often made up in a folder or packet of letter-file size so that the contributing records such as shown in Forms 3–6 can be filed in them. It is not always desirable to bring all records into this file until a student is graduated, since such a record as the health record, for example, may be needed frequently in the school's health center. This raises the problem of whether to centralize all of a student's records at one point so that anyone needing fuller information about a student can see the complete file in one office, or whether to keep a student's records in various locations near their source on the theory that to do so promotes frequent use of them. Some schools resolve this situation by retaining the original record at its source and sending a copy to the central file. Such duplication increases clerical work, although the use of modern carbon copy forms can reduce this a great deal. Other schools retain the records at their points of origin and send only a warning note to the central file, calling attention to certain unusually significant items on these various records and to the need to see them. Another plan is to break up the central cumulative file into sections, which are then placed in the offices of the teacher-counselors. This practice makes the records more accessible to the counselor and the home room teacher likely to be involved in matters concerning any pupil, but from the principal's point of view it is a disadvantage in that the record is not near his office. Since the record is kept for the benefit of the student, and since he benefits most when a large share of responsibility for counseling is carried by a staff member who knows him well, it is probably better to

410

FORM 3

MONTCLAIR PUBLIC SCHOOLS
SCHOOL RECORD OF HEALTH

Name____ Address____ Date of Birth____ Sex____

Grade	
School	
Date	
Age	
Nutritional status	
Subcutaneous tissue	
Muscles	
Bone	
Weight is	
Weight should be	
Height	
Eyes	R L
Vision	R L
Ears	R L
Hearing	T P
Teeth	
Gums	
Nose conditions	
Throat conditions	
Glands Lymph	
Thyroid	
Others	
Skin	
Heart	
Lungs	
Posture	
Orthopedic defects	
Speech defects	
Nervous condition	
Physician's sig.	
Nurse's sig.	
Parent present	
Teacher's sig.	

Code: o—Satisfactory; X—Correction needed (referred); V—Minor defect (not referred); #—Improved not cured; ‡—Cured
+ —Previous correction; — —No information obtained; Z—Parents cooperating; *—Follow-up

Parent's Name _____ Address _____

Observable Health Habits

Cleanliness body, teeth,
face, hands, nails, neck
Neatness of clothing
Adequate clothing
Mental Hygiene

Health Habit Interview with Parent

Nourishing Food
Milk, tea, coffee
Has tooth brush
Amount of sleep with window open
Elimination
Mental stability at home

School Attendance

Disease	Date	Convalesence
Diphtheria		
Chicken-pox		
Whooping cough		
Mumps		
Poliomyelitis		

Disease	Date	Convalesence	Others	Date
Measles				
Scarlet fever				
Pneumonia				
Small-pox				
German measles				

Immunization	Date
Small-pox	
Diphtheria	
Schick—Neg.—Pos.	
Scarlet fever	
Dick—Neg.—Pos.	
Typhold	

Home and Follow-up Visits (Corrections, Home Cooperation, Improvements)

Date

FORM 4

TULSA CENTRAL HIGH SCHOOL

EMPLOYMENT APPLICATION

Name: _____ Address: _____ Date _____ Class _____

Last Name   First Name

Phone: _____ Age: _____ Height: _____ Weight: _____ Nationality: _____

Father living? _____ Who supports your family? _____ Business of father _____

What work can you do? _____ Bicycle? _____

What Experience? _____ Drive a car? _____

Office Record of Placements

	SCHEDULE OF CLASSES	
Do not write below	PERIOD	ROOM NO
1.	H.R.	
2.	2	
3.	3	
4.	4	
5.	5	
6.	6	
	7	
	Underline	Study Hall

decentralize the cumulative file than to centralize it. In any case, of course, locked fire-resistant files are necessary. It may be assumed that the frequency of use of a record varies with the square of the distance between a teacher who needs the record and the point at which it is filed. Only in small schools, therefore, can the records be centralized at one place in the school without cutting down on their usefulness. In larger schools they should be decentralized or adequate arrangements should be made for placing copies at or near the places where they can be easily accessible to those who serve as the counselors for each group of pupils. More use will probably be made of these records if decentralized for the convenience of counselors than if conveniently centralized in the principal's office.

The cumulative records shown here illustrate variations in form and in scope of items covered. The California form (Form 7) was devised after a careful study of items considered to be the most valuable by the principals and guidance workers of that state. The headings on this record were selected by the State Committee on Cumulative Records appointed by the State Superintendent of Public Instruction. Comparable forms for use in the elementary school and the junior college and a handbook are also available.[2] Form 8, a copy of the state form of North Carolina, was developed under the leadership of the state department of education. A manual for the guidance of those using the record is also available. A comparison of this form with that of California will show points of difference. The former covers under sixteen general heads the full school career of a pupil, but it includes many of the same items found in the California form. Form 9 is a copy of a cumulative form prepared by a committee of the NASSP and recommended for use on a national scale by this organization. It gives relatively more space to academic achievement records than do the California and North Carolina forms and consequently less to other items. It is more in the nature of a summary of records of personality traits, health, work interests, and plans, and presumes that supplemental records for these facts will be filed in this cumulative folder. It probably represents as complete a record as can be proposed for national use with any hope that high schools generally will be able to use it.

A proposed form more elaborate than any of these has been recently prepared by the Department of Supervision and Curriculum Development of the National Educational Association. Reprinted here as Form 10, it covers the elementary and secondary school years. It probably represents the most outright application of the growth and development theory of education to the cumulative record, with the California form a close second. It is included here as indicative of how trends in

---

[2] *Handbook on California Cumulative Records* (Sacramento; State Department of Education, 1955).

FORM 5

RECORD OF EXTRACURRICULAR ACTIVITIES

CENTRAL HIGH SCHOOL, TULSA, OKLAHOMA

....   *Last Name First*   *Boy or Girl*   *Year of Graduation*

Name of Organization for which Report is made..

SERVICE	LEADERSHIP	CHARACTER AND ATTITUDE
Record of Volunteer or Committee Service	Record of service in elected offices	

Date..................................   Sponsor..................................

(Over for added space)

FORM 6

TULSA CENTRAL HIGH SCHOOL

STAGECRAFT ASSIGNMENTS RECORD

Name...Week Beginning..................

DAY	NATURE OF WORK	Worked		Total Time	O. K. by
		From	To		
Mon.					
Tues.					
Wed.					
Thurs.					
Fri.					
Sat.					
TOTAL TIME					

Remarks:

educational psychology and in curriculum thinking affect the make-up of cumulative records and are a source of ideas of those who desire to improve the records they are using.

DEVELOPING AND USING RECORDS

No school should install any type of record illustrated here, or any other for that matter, without a full study of what its needs are and how the form under consideration meets these needs. These record forms are printed here to show what some schools have decided were useful. It is hoped that they came to this decision as a result of careful study of what was actually needed in their schools. If this study is made by representatives of the groups who will be keeping, making, and using the records, the records will probably be better and the objection to their use in the school sharply reduced. To be of greatest value, the data entered on the records must be compiled by workers who believe them worth gathering and so enter the information more promptly, willingly, and accurately than they would otherwise. Moreover, they are then more likely to use the records wisely when occasion suggests their use. Before major record forms are designed and adopted for use, the principal should set up some plan whereby a committee, if not the whole faculty, may determine what items of information are called for, may study available forms critically, may select or create one best adapted to the local situation, and may work to develop in the school community an understanding of its use and value. The whole system of forms and records should be occasionally reviewed to see if each item is as essential as it was when it was originally introduced into use. Often such a review will result in the elimination, combination, or simplification of existing forms and records and will prevent a cumulative piling up of the unnecessary record work that reduces the staff's willingness to see a new record form added.

The use of such complete cumulative records as are illustrated here involves the making and keeping of many types of supplemental records, too numerous to be reproduced here. The principal must decide how complete the pupil personnel records of a high school can be without overburdening the staff to the point that it makes so many records that no one has time to use them. The best high schools tend to individualize their approach to each student. Hence they need individual case histories of each student just as a doctor needs a case history of each patient whose health he is supposed to care for. The keeping of numerous case histories requires an adequate clerical staff, which should be supplemented by students where possible; moreover, records should be simplified and their scope reduced to the point where they do not constitute a burden on the available staff. On the other hand, the staff has no legitimate reason for thinking that the making of pupil personnel records is a waste of time or an imposition. The making of such records is part of a teacher's professional responsibility; because it often requires the exercise of professional judgment it cannot be left to clerical workers and students. No professionally minded person whose work influences the lives of others as much as education does will expect to avoid the necessity of making, keeping, and using detailed and accurate personnel records. They are part of a scientific, professional approach to teaching in the modern school.

Staffing for Pupil Personnel Service

The proper performance of the duties necessary for a pupil personnel program of the scope indicated in this chapter will require time and ability from any high school's staff which will not be available without careful staff organization and administration. Even then, many small high schools or those with low limits on their expenditures for each pupil will have to curtail the program and services beyond desirable minima and rely on less well-trained service than should be provided. The task here is not only to sketch types of organization for pupil personnel work which have been found useful in schools where a good organization has been provided but also to indicate something about how schools with much less time and money available for this service can trim it down to what is practical for them.

THE HOME ROOM AS A BASIS OF ORGANIZATION

Some rather small grouping of students is an essential. If a program of pupil personnel work rises above mediocrity it will be because there is a basic working group small enough so that the teacher or teachers can really get acquainted with each member of the group for which they are responsible. In many schools the home room group or a similar group is an answer. In the typical high school it is almost impossible for teachers to get the kind of acquaintance and understanding of each of a group of students which he needs if he is to be their counselor and guide without such an arrangement. Too often, of course, the home room fails to live up to its possibilities because of the inadequate amount of time allowed or because of the encroachment of other matters. In schools that do not have home rooms, and sometimes in those that do, if the results have not been satisfactory, the home room and its teacher are assigned a relatively unimportant place in pupil personnel work and the principal responsibility is transferred to one or more all-school special workers. The problem here is for these workers to know all the students well enough to be able to advise them. Such a system often leads to the making of a multiplicity of records in the hope that if one of these workers can refer to enough facts about each student he can do a better job than he otherwise would. This is probably a safe assumption, but there is no substitute for the intimate knowledge of a teacher who knows the student as a person. Some plan of organizing the student body which provides a face-to-face grouping of pupils for each counselor, as is found in the home room, and also allows the counselor time for working with this group and each member of it, is a basic essential.

In some schools the home room occupies a regular full-length, daily period. This period is one of each teacher's daily assignments and it is not added to what is ordinarily considered to be a full-time, daily teaching load in such a system. It is also recognized as a regular part of each student's daily program and his classwork is adjusted accordingly. Group guidance and counseling not provided for in such courses as "occupations" goes on in the home room. Self-initiated group activities there give the teacher a chance to see the members in action in social situations. The size of the group, the time allotment, and the work and activities included all contribute to such a home room serving a real function in the pupil personnel program.

MODIFIED HOME ROOM BASIS

In schools unable to make such a regular home room provision or where some teachers are unable to handle the home room acceptably, a modified plan has been used. The home room is still the basic unit, but some of its activities and duties are shifted to a larger counseling group consisting of four or five of the home room groups. This larger group is put in charge of one of the teachers who was most successful in the regular-sized home room. The whole school is thus divided into counseling groups of the size of four or five home room groups, and the best home room teacher out of each group of four or five teachers is put in charge. It has been found that these good home room teachers can do successfully with these larger groups many of the things they did so well in their own smaller home rooms. These teachers become home room teacher-leaders or teacher-counselors and supervise the other teachers whose home rooms compose the larger counseling group. Some types of personnel work are still done in the regular home room. Some are planned for in the counseling group and then carried out in the home room groups. Some are entirely removed from the home room and assigned to the counseling group. Thus the average level of success of the work of the home room is raised because more responsibility is carried by those teachers who by personality, training, and interest are best able to succeed with it. Much of the most difficult individual counseling is shifted, either partially or completely, from the regular home room teacher to these counselors.

Schools which now have class sponsors or advisers for each year's class can incorporate this group counseling into the work of the class sponsor. A class may be the counseling group where its size runs less than approximately 150 students. The regular auditorium or a small room accommodating the four or five home room groups and their teachers may be used on a rotating schedule that makes it available to each counseling group once or twice a week. These teacher-counselors are in reality supervisors of a part of the school's pupil personnel program. As such they are not regular class teachers, and the salary schedule of the system ought to provide a salary in proportion to the added responsibility and extra specialized training required. The whole plan is a development which recognizes that at present not all teachers are equipped by personality, training, or by desire to develop the relationship with individual pupils that a well-functioning pupil personnel program requires. Yet at least a quarter or a third of the faculties of most schools are so equipped. This plan seeks to utilize these abilities for the benefit of a larger proportion of the whole student body.

Another variation in organization by which schools are able to allow a teacher to be personally acquainted with those whom he advises is through an integrated core of general education. If a school has a program of general education that permits one teacher to teach one class of pupils for up to half of the school day, during part of this lengthened general education period pupil personnel work can be accomplished. In reality it becomes the student's "home" room—the center of his school life—and this teacher naturally knows him better than high school teachers in the more conventional systems ordinarily can. With the older student who goes into vocational education courses where half of the day is spent with a vocational teacher, this period too becomes the center of his school day and this teacher has the best chance really to know him; hence pupil personnel work naturally centers here. Thus in schools where an integrated program of general education is provided, or where older students are in vocational education courses, a teacher has an unexcelled opportunity to work closely with a small group, and a home room period for pupil personnel work is not needed.

SPECIALIZED GUIDANCE SERVICES

Small as well as large schools can organize so that some sort of face-to-face group is available for pupil personnel work. Even schools with meager financial resources can do it, although, of course, inadequate buildings, the inexperience of teachers, or low levels of professional preparation will limit the success of the program and interfere with its operation. It is at the point of providing needed special services that small or impoverished schools find it difficult to keep up the pace. The large school

FORM 10

Cumulative Record

Public Schools

Photo   Photo   Photo   Photo

Last Name	First	Middle	Sex	Race
			M / F	W / N / O

Date of Birth Mo. Day Year	Place of Birth City State

ACADEMIC RECORD—ELEMENTARY SCHOOLS

Date Entered	School	Teacher	Grade or Year in School	Days in Attendance	Units of Work	Knowledge	Co-operation	Responsibility	Social Concern	Creativeness	Reading	Oral Expression	Written Expression	Number Skills	Personal Adjustment	Promoted To	Date	Transferred To	Date

Key
S=Superior Growth and Adjustment.
M=Medium or Normal Growth and Adjustment.
L=Needs Special Help and Guidance.

SUMMARY OF ANECDOTAL RECORDS—SIGNIFICANT ASPECTS OF STUDENT GROWTH

Date	Elementary Record	Date	Junior High School Record	Date	Senior High School Record

Date	Outstanding Activities and Experiences	Date	Work Experiences	Date	Follow-up Record
					First Year
					Third Year
					Fifth Year

Grade	SEVENTH														EIGHT
School	Entered Left														
Date	19							19							19
Semester	First							Second							Fir
Subject	Units	Knowledge	Co-operation	Responsibility	Social Concern	Critical Thinking	Work Habits	Units	Knowledge	Co-operation	Responsibility	Social Concern	Critical Thinking	Work Habits	Subject
Total Units															Total Units

Grade	TENTH														ELEVEN
School	Entered Left														
Date	19							19							19
Semester	First							Second							Fir
Subject	Units	Knowledge	Co-operation	Responsibility	Social Concern	Critical Thinking	Work Habits	Units	Knowledge	Co-operation	Responsibility	Social Concern	Critical Thinking	Work Habits	Subject
Total Units															Total Units

Date of Graduation from High School

No. in Graduating Class   Rank in Class

Name of High School from which Graduated

ECONDARY SCHOOLS

									NINTH														
Entered									Entered														
Left									Left														
19								19		19													

Work Habits	Units	Knowledge	Co-operation	Responsibility	Social Concern	Critical Thinking	Work Habits	Subject	Units	Knowledge	Co-operation	Responsibility	Social Concern	Critical Thinking	Work Habits	Units	Knowledge	Co-operation	Responsibility	Social Concern	Critical Thinking	Work Habits
Second									**First**							**Second**						
								Total Units														

								TWELFTH														
Entered									Entered													
Left									Left													
19								19		19												

Units	Knowledge	Co-operation	Responsibility	Social Concern	Critical Thinking	Work Habits	Subject	Units	Knowledge	Co-operation	Responsibility	Social Concern	Critical Thinking	Work Habits	Units	Knowledge	Co-operation	Responsibility	Social Concern	Critical Thinking	Work Habits
Second								**First**							**Second**						
							Total Units														

Transcript Sent To	Attendance Record					
School or College	Date	Absence	Tardy	Date	Absence	Tardy

INFORMATION CONCERNING HOME

Name		Lives With	Phone

	Nat'l	Sep.	Dead	Religion	Language Spoken	Education
Father						
Mother						
Step-Father						
Step-Mother						

Date	Home Address	

Siblings	Older	Younger	Date	Father's Occupation	Mother's Occupation
Brothers					
Sisters					
Others in Home					

SUMMARY OF TEST DATA

EDUCATIONAL TEST DATA—ELEMENTARY

Date	Name of Test	Form	Score	% or G. P.	Norm

*

EDUCATIONAL TEST DATA—JUNIOR HIGH SCHOOL

Date	Name of Test	Form	Score	% or G. P.	Norm

EDUCATIONAL TEST DATA—SENIOR HIGH SCHOOL

Date	Name of Test	Form	Score	% or G. P.	Norm

TESTS OF MENTAL MATURITY

Date	Name of Test	Grade	Form	CA	MA	IQ

*

PERSONAL AND SOCIAL ADJUSTMENT INVENTORIES

Date	Grade	Name of Inventory	Results

Date	Grade	Name of Inventory	Results

*

SIGNIFICANT PHYSICAL AND MENTAL HEALTH INFORMATION

Date		Date	

*

*More space may be allowed here, if needed.

can justify the full-time director of guidance and the assistant principals or deans for boys and girls who make up the group that takes the lead in the all-school program of pupil personnel work. These workers often have the part-time services of specialists such as a psychologist, a medical doctor, a supervisor of tests and measurements, a vocational counselor, visiting teachers, and psychiatric workers. Some schools set up clinics attended by as many of these specialists as are needed for special cases and for a thoroughgoing study of them. In such a school, the director of guidance coordinates all the available resources and makes them readily available as needed to home room teachers and other full-time workers in the high school.

In most high schools, however, few of these special services are available, and even the number of full-time staff members that can be assigned to this service is limited. In smaller schools the principal and three or four teachers who serve as advisers for each year's class and as home room teacher-leaders or teacher-counselors have to carry most of the load. The scope of the over-all program must then be restricted to basic general activities in the areas of educational, vocational, and social-recreational guidance. It means the program centers on what can be done through group guidance, with individual guidance reduced below a desirable level for lack of time and the specialized types of training often needed by particular types of pupils. In some instances very small high schools have been able to secure some of these special services through cooperative arrangements. For example, under the leadership of county superintendents of schools, county guidance services have been set up with each high school contributing to the expense. A group of specialized workers is thus made available, on a rotating schedule, to each of the small high schools in the county. At present it is not possible for each of our many high schools to do as good personnel work with its students as they require, but the principal can by planning and study apply the full power of whatever resources there are in the faculty and community to the task and thereby get better performance than otherwise would be the case.

GUIDANCE PROGRAMS WRECKED ON CURRICULAR ROCKS

The interrelatedness of the programs of guidance and education has been stressed in this chapter. Many high schools, recognizing that all was not well with their students, have sought to meet the situation by expanding their guidance staffs. This may give the school a temporary lift, but sooner or later a schism of major or minor proportions develops between the guidance staff and the teaching staff. It may be between the guidance workers and the principal himself. The guidance workers may feel that the teachers and even the principal do little or nothing to change the bad adjustment between the school's educational program and what the guidance workers have discovered to be the needs of the boys and girls. The teachers, on the other hand, may regard the guidance group as too critical of what the school is doing, and as expecting the impossible in the way of adjustments to boys and girls. Eventually this state of affairs results in the frustration of the guidance group, which takes refuge in a testing program, the recording of results, the keeping of other records, and the making of whatever minor adjustments for individuals that can easily be made. In the end the school is little better off than it was before the guidance services were expanded.

The crux of the difficulty is that if those who work in the pupil personnel area take their work seriously they are bound to discover that the educational program of a typical high school needs a thorough overhauling if it is to meet the needs of boys and girls. Unless the school is then willing to go the second mile and work to develop the school program and life indicated as desirable by the findings of the guidance workers, guidance in the school is no more than window dressing that makes the school look more interested in the all-round growth and developments of its students than it really is. The high school principal, therefore, has the job of encouraging those responsible for pupil personnel work to indicate where the school's program, activities, and practices fall short of what is needed while helping those responsible for developing and teaching the program to modify it in the directions revealed by pupil needs.[3] If a school stresses pupil guidance, presumably it is concerned for the welfare of pupils; but if its educational program is "a stern and rock-bound coast"—unchanging and unyielding—then sooner or later the wreckage of what was once a good guidance program will be piled high upon it. The principal of a typical high school is responsible for strong leadership which presses for the development of a school program and a climate conducive to the kind of all-round growth and development that pupil personnel work seeks to help youth achieve.

Some Points to Consider

1. There has been criticism of the Life Adjustment Education program on the ground that it seems to assume that the home, church, and community are to be pretty largely left out in the process of growing a new adult generation. Should the high school expect to be a major factor in this process? Should it "take over"? How would you think a high school should plan to work in a community?

2. Having in mind a high school you know well, list what it does to help its students with decisions in the areas of health, social and personal

[3] Will French, "The Role of the American High School," NASSP *Bulletin,* 39, No. 1 (February, 1955), 1–62.

growth, and educational achievement. Indicate what you think it does very well, fairly well, and poorly or not at all.

3. At what points, if any, is this school's educational program inadequate if there is to be action taken as the result of counseling decisions in these three areas?

4. Make a collection of all the record forms used by a selected high school and show how they contribute to the over-all picture the school has of each of its students. Relate them to part of the cumulative record used by this school.

5. Examine the cumulative record folders (or packets) of some students in a high school to see how complete the information on them is. Inquire about the use of these records and form an opinion as to whether they are organized for easy and frequent use.

6. Select one of the cumulative record forms illustrated in this chapter and make lists of supplemental forms you think would need to be made by one or more members of the staff in order to provide the information called for under some of the main headings on this cumulative record form.

Further Reading

Aikin, Wilford M. *The Story of the Eight-Year Study.* New York: Harper & Brothers, 1942. Chap. 4.

Commission on Research and Service, Southern Association of Secondary Schools and Colleges. *Educational Records and Their Uses.* Atlanta, Ga.: The Association, 1954.

Fedder, Ruth. *Guiding Home Room and Club Activities.* New York: McGraw-Hill Book Co., Inc., 1949.

Forrester, Gertrude. *Methods of Vocational Guidance.* Boston: D. C. Heath & Company, 1944.

French, Will. "The Role of the American High School," NASSP *Bulletin,* 39, No. 1 (February, 1955), 1–62.

Germane, Charles E., and Edith G. Germane. *Personnel Work in High School.* New York: Silver Burdett Company, 1941.

Gesell, Arnold, and others. *Youth: the Years from 10 to 16.* New York: Harper & Brothers, 1956.

Hill, A. S., L. M. Miller, and H. F. Gabbard. "Schools Face the Delinquency Problem," NASSP *Bulletin,* 37, No. 198 (December, 1953), 181–218.

Hoppock, Robert. *Group Guidance.* New York: McGraw-Hill Book Co., Inc., 1949.

Jones, Arthur J., Leonard M. Miller, and Galen Jones. "The National Picture of Pupil Personnel and Guidance Services in 1953," NASSP *Bulletin,* 38, No. 200, February, 1954.

Meek, Lois H., ed., Committee on Workshops. *The Personal-Social Development of Boys and Girls with Implication for Secondary Education.* New York: Progressive Education Association, 1940.

Morris, Glyn. *Practical Guidance Methods for Principals and Teachers.* New York: Harper & Brothers, 1952.

National Society for the Study of Education. *Adapting Secondary School Programs to the Needs of Youth.* Fifty-second Yearbook; Chicago: University of Chicago Press, 1953. Part II, Chap. 11.

Segel, David. *Cumulative Records: State Laws and State Department of Education Regulations and Services.* Mimeographed Guide-Lines No. 5; Washington, D.C.: Office of Education, May, 1955.

Smith, Eugene R., and Ralph W. Tyler. *Appraising and Recording Student Progress.* Vol. III in "Adventures in American Education Series"; New York: Harper & Brothers, 1942.

Strang, Ruth. *Child Development and Guidance in Rural Schools.* New York: Harper & Brothers, 1943.

———. *Counseling Techniques in College and Secondary School.* New York: Harper & Brothers, 1937.

———. *Pupil Personnel and Guidance.* New York: The Macmillan Company, 1940.

———. *Role of the Teacher in Personnel Work.* New York: Columbia University Press, 1946.

Super, Donald E. *Appraising Vocational Fitness by Means of Psychological Tests.* New York: Harper & Brothers, 1949.

Traxler, Arthur E. *Techniques of Guidance: Tests, Records, and Counseling in a Guidance Program.* New York: Harper & Brothers, 1945.

Chapter 19

THE SCHOOL'S RESPONSIBILITY FOR POST-HIGH SCHOOL PLACEMENT

Any secondary school is always interested in the success or failure of its graduates and former students. The public high school is no exception to this rule, but like other secondary schools it often assumes, with respect to most former students, the role of an interested and sympathetic bystander. As the high school has expanded its program, and as its student body has begun to include the representative groups of American youth that it now does, it is more than ever necessary for the high school to see that its students make a good adjustment after they leave it. As a result, although we still have some high schools that continue the attitude of the benevolent bystander, others are organized to render whatever help they can in the placement of their former students—both graduates and early leavers—in the social, economic, and educational life of the community.

Today's conditions do not make for the easy, automatic absorption of school-leaving youth into community life that was once the rule. Youth are no longer, generally, the economic assets to a family or to a community's industrial life that they formerly were. Even in the era in American life when we were so eager for a labor supply that we had almost no immigration restrictions, many youth found their best chance for a start in life through homesteading a claim of 160 acres of government land. In an earlier day communities were smaller and more simply organized. Now it is easier than it once was for a youth to live in a social-cultural community without being a part of it. Youth-serving agencies of many kinds have therefore been developed, of which the YMCA and the YWCA, the Boy Scouts and the Girl Scouts are outstanding examples. So many of these center on younger youth that communities are not generally as well prepared to meet the social-cultural needs of older youth who are practically young adults, as they should be. The high school is thus the logical agency for communities to use to improve their facilities for absorbing older youth as they leave high school and become candidates for entrance into adult activities and organizations in the community.

Scope and Purposes of This Activity

The main idea behind an effort at postschool placement is usually a vocational one: most boys and girls leaving high school need and want a job, and the high school ought to be interested in seeing that they get it. For the boys and girls who are going to college the shift that takes place when they leave high school is not a distinct break. But so far the majority of youth leave high school without expecting to become students in any other school; for them, leaving high school is a complete break in the life pattern they have been following. As high school pupils they were members of a well-recognized social group in the school community, which had its own activities and interests in which they participated. Once that school connection is broken, they are out, they do not belong, they have lost their place in what was their world. Some graduates try to maintain it by enrolling as postgraduates. Some who left before graduation try to regain it by re-entering school after a brief whirl at the "outside" world. Others hang around the high school building before and after school and during lunch periods. But even for these there is no return to "the good old days." In a sense they are "displaced persons" in current American life.

If the school's program is well integrated with the life of the community, so that while they are still in high school pupils can begin to take their places in the life of the community, this break is much less sudden. But even in the best of high schools now, in spite of all that is done to prevent it, there is still an out-of-school versus an in-school situation, which means that pupils enter another world when they leave high school. The school's placement efforts should take into account this whole need to make an adjustment of out-of-school life—not just the vocational placement aspect, important though it be. The service should be organized to assist all former students—those who left before graduation and graduates, whether bound for college or not—to find places in and become adjusted to whatever is to be their life and world. What is involved in this program will be developed in succeeding paragraphs.

POST-HIGH SCHOOL EDUCATIONAL PLACEMENT

Perhaps less needs to be said about placement in college than about any other aspect of the placement responsibility, because many schools are already doing this well. Nevertheless, as a larger and larger percentage of youth graduate from high school and plan, or at least hope, to enter some kind of a college, the need for an effective program of college placement becomes greater and greater. Too many schools concentrate too much of their efforts on placing a few good students in a select list of colleges. This is what the responsibility used to be—not what it is. Now we must add to this aspect of the job the responsibility of helping a large number of youth, who are not especially good students, to find at a higher level an appropriate school in which they can hope to succeed. They may or may not be the sons and daughters of the socially and economically elite of the community, they may never graduate *magna cum laude* from any institution, but they want "to go to college," and they have abilities and interests that can be further developed in schools primarily for older youth. In many parts of the country college entrance is now freely open to high school graduates. So there the problem is not so much of entrance to college as of success as a college student. If the high school's placement service, in conjunction with the school's guidance program, will spend more time in teaching this group (and their parents) to make a good choice of college and less time in trying to prepare them for it through the conventional "college preparatory" program, high schools will not need to worry so much about whether their students will succeed in college or not. Indeed, the so-called "college preparatory" curriculum is not the best preparation for college for many of the high school students who do go on to post-high school educational institutions. Parts of it are essential to success in the work of some college for some high school students, and parts of it are not. At best the "college preparatory" program is a college *entrance* program because many colleges have arbitrarily refused to accept any high school graduate who has not taken it in high school. This practice is less and less true today, for the colleges as well as the high schools recognize the accumulating evidence that success in no one program of subjects in high school is highly correlated with success in college. The success of veterans in college who were not high school graduates and the results of the Eight-Year Study showed that success in college did not depend upon the pattern of subjects taken in high school. This Study also seemed to indicate that students whose high school program departed most from the accepted college preparatory pattern were the most successful in college. All this evidence also tends to invalidate the use of many subject matter tests as predictive measures of success in college.

Many colleges have therefore begun to use other measures for predicting the probable success of high school graduates in college. Segel, in *Predicting Success in College*, a pamphlet from the United States Office of Education, shows that the best predictive measure of success in college is made up of the combination of average high school marks, a group intelligence test, and a comprehensive English test. Other factors, such as intellectual competence, cultural development, practical competence, character traits, emotional balance, social fitness, and physical fitness, enter into college success. Many colleges are attempting to get more comprehensive data covering these factors on prospective college entrants. Most of these efforts involve closer cooperation between high schools and colleges, so that the college has a chance to get more information about prospective students than it can obtain without the full cooperation of the high school. Michigan, under the leadership of the state department of education, in cooperation with the Michigan School-masters' Club, has produced "The Michigan Agreement," the principal portions of which are these:

1. It is proposed that this Agreement be extended to include any ac-credited high school whose staff will make the commitments noted below in Section Two. The Agreement is as follows: "The college agrees to disregard the pattern of subjects pursued in considering for admission the graduates of se-lected accredited high schools, provided they are recommended by the school from among the more able students in the graduating class. This Agreement does not imply that students must be admitted to certain college courses or curricula for which they cannot give evidence of adequate preparation."

Secondary schools are urged to make available such basic courses as pro-vide a necessary preparation for entering technical, industrial, or professional curricula. It is recommended further that colleges provide accelerated programs of preparation for specialized college curricula for those graduates who are un-able to secure such preparatory training in high school.

2. High schools which seek to be governed by this Agreement shall as-sume responsibility for and shall furnish evidence that they are initiating and continuing such procedures as the following:

    a. A program involving the building of an adequate personal file about each student, including testing data of various kinds, anecdotal rec-ords, personality inventories, achievement samples, etc. The high-school staff will assume responsibility for developing a summary of these personal data for submission to the college.

    b. A basic curriculum study and evaluation of the purposes and program of the secondary school.

    c. Procedures for continuous follow-up of former pupils.

    d. A continuous program of information and orientation throughout the high-school course regarding the nature and requirements of certain occupations and specialized college courses. During the senior year, to devote special emphasis to the occupation or college of the pupil's choice. . . .

4. It is understood that high schools which cannot or will not make and observe the above commitments (see Section Two) will continue to employ the major and minor sequences for those students who wish to attend college.[1]

----

[1] Leon S. Waskin, "The Michigan Secondary School-College Agreement," NASSP *Bulletin*, No. 159 (January, 1949), p. 51. Reprinted by permission of the National Education Association.

The trend throughout most of the nation is toward a more rational approach to the matter of college entrance, and individual high school principals and their state associations, as in Michigan, should take positive and united action, in cooperation with the colleges, to develop better bases for college entrance.

The willingness of colleges to participate with high schools in the work of the School and College Study of Admissions with Advanced Standing[2] and other similar projects is further evidence of increasing flexibility in college entrance arrangements. This is a study of the possibility of offering in high school, to selected students, subjects usually regarded as "college" subjects for which advanced standing in college may then be secured.

But even when this is done, the need still remains for the high school to help each college-bound student and his parents make a wise choice of college. There are so many types and levels of colleges that unless the student makes a study of his own abilities and interests and relates these to what the colleges have to offer he may find that he does not succeed in the college to which he goes because of having made what was for him a poor choice. The better high schools have therefore begun to see that college-bound students and their parents have an opportunity to become more fully informed about the various colleges before they decide on one. It is as important to include the parent group in this effort as the students themselves, for often the prejudices of the former in favor of certain colleges are quite unreasoned and if allowed to settle the matter of college choice may result in needless college failure. The high school has to do its best to show parents that all the sons or daughters of all the graduates of a given small, exclusive private college cannot be entered there as long as the college exercises its right to remain small and exclusive. Parents also have to learn that there are many excellent colleges outside the northeastern part of the United States that can give their sons and daughters the best of college training.

Some high schools have found it practical to set up each year a series of "college days" or a "college week," during which representatives of various colleges have a chance to meet interested prospective college entrants, and the latter have a chance to ask questions about life and programs at the various colleges. In fact, unless the principal develops a definite plan for managing the visits of these many college representatives they become almost a nuisance in some high schools. Sometimes trips to typical colleges where students can see what the colleges are

[2] School and College Study of Admission with Advanced Standing, *Bulletin of Information* (Philadelphia: The Study, 1952). See also *Bridging the Gap between School and College* (Evaluation Report No. 1; New York: Fund for the Advancement of Education, 1953).

like and talk to students and representatives are helpful. The guidance officers and home room teachers often gather a wide range of published materials for use by interested students. A few schools arrange for a more comprehensive approach to this problem by setting up a period of several weeks' study in the junior or senior year, when a well-organized unit of instruction on how to select a college is offered to college-bound students. Other students may use this time for a study of their lifework choices. Sometimes this study takes the form of a re-evaluation of the personal decisions on their lifework which they may have made as a result of their work in ninth-year guidance or occupations courses. As a result of such study and appraisal, under the guidance of the school and rather late in their high school career all interested students will have a chance to consider thoroughly their probable status when they leave school. The college-bound group can develop its plan of study in such a way that various groups interested in engineering, medicine, or education, for example, may study together what various colleges have to offer them and what they, as individuals, have to offer these colleges. This period of study can be included in the general education program of high schools having such a curricular organization, or it can be incorporated into English or "modern problems" courses, or into home room programs, taking the place, if necessary, of other material of less immediate value and concern. When an auxiliary opportunity for parent education and for individual conferences on college selection is offered so that such matters can be discussed by parents and children at home, against a common background of information, many of the problems of "preparing" for college can be more easily solved because the school can count on a more intelligent selection of colleges being made.

Currently the high school principal's problem in this area is one of discouraging the faculty, the parents, and the school's community from measuring the school's success in college placement primarily by the good record of a few outstanding students in a few exclusive colleges, and of encouraging them to measure its success in terms of how able it is to get large numbers of its graduates who want to go to college to select institutions whose offerings are most appropriate to their needs and abilities. Only then can a high school really claim to be rendering a good college educational placement service.

POST-HIGH SCHOOL JOB PLACEMENT

This is another aspect of placement to which schools have long given some attention. Technical, commerical, and vocational high schools and departments generally have some kind of contacts through which they place at least their best graduates. This is good as far as it goes, but to the degree that this program fails to try to make a good placement of the ordinary graduate and the student who leaves before graduating, it is not a well-rounded program. These latter groups of pupils not only are in as much need of jobs as are the really good graduates, but are doubtless more in need of the school's help if they are to find appropriate ones. The lack of a good vocational adjustment immediately after leaving high school causes the vast majority of these young people to shift from one type of job to another in the first year or two out of high school in a way that clearly indicates vocational floundering. Though many of the graduates and other former students may not be able to acquire the vocational competence the school might wish, there are many kinds of jobs which require limited levels of competence and into which the school can help these former pupils fit. With them the principal task of the school is to provide as much initial employability as possible and then to help these young people find a job at which they can succeed while acquiring additional competence in it. The *Occupational Adjustment Study,* sponsored by the National Association of Secondary School Principals, showed that high schools, by their offerings and their guidance, could increase the initial employability of these students and thus reduce the characteristic floundering from job to job of so many former high school students during their first two or three years out of school.

A really successful program of vocational placement means that all youth leaving high school and not going to college who want employment are helped to find suitable job possibilities where they can make a start in becoming economically self-supporting. On the basis of this job training, plus what the school ought to offer them in evening courses or part-time classes, they should make a good adjustment to a place of their own in the work life of the community.

The task of job placement probably cannot be expected to be well done as long as a school's program is built upon the idea that these job-seeking pupils should be in school full time until they are out of school full time. The various types of programs mentioned above for former students who are on the job ought to be preceded for many of them who are still in school by work experience in distributive education, in diversified occupations, or in similar programs. Many should begin getting some training in work on the job under the supervision of the school while they are still considered to be in school full time. This arrangement means school credit for work experience outside school in industry or in various forms of public service in the community. Only when high schools arrange to combine opportunity for part-time job training for full-time students before they leave school with part-time educational offerings for them as full-time workers after they leave school, have high schools fully bridged for their students and former students the gap between school life and postschool life in the field of work.

OTHER TYPES OF POST-HIGH SCHOOL PLACEMENT

Making an occupational adjustment of this type is the best assurance there is that students who do not go to college will make a complete adjustment to community life when they leave school. If one has a place in our economic world he finds acceptance in other aspects of community life. Nevertheless there are activities the school can carry on that will assist former students in this process of becoming fully accepted into young adulthood. A good general rule is that for every type of interest and activity which the school's educational program promotes there should be connecting outlets into community organizations where these interests and activities may be carried out by former students of the school in company with other older adults with similar interests. For instance, high school pupils who are members of school musical organizations often get much real pleasure and satisfaction from them, only to find themselves without this opportunity the moment they sever their school connection. In some places community musical organizations are open to them, and in others connections with musical groups of a church or lodge are possible. But many of these young people are unable to establish these contacts. Why should the school not try to see that these pupils know more about how they are to reach the community's musical groups? Why should not the school see that these musical groups know more about the interests and abilities of former students? Why not an organized plan for a smooth transition from school to community musical groups? The same questions could be asked about drama and art groups and other special interest groups represented both in the school and in the community. A few high schools have found ways of helping youth make these transitions. All need to work at the task.

If there are no such community groups, perhaps the school should promote their establishment around a nucleus of former high school students, thus enriching the community's recreational life. If existing groups are too rigid, too old, or too "stuffy" for the younger adults of the community, new organizations should be formed. Just as junior chambers of commerce have been developed by young businessmen into organizations where young men can play prominent parts, so we need a number of other "junior" organizations in various other fields of interests that young adults can run. This whole area of specialized recreational interests and activities cultivated by the high school for its own students while they are in school is an area where an organized effort on the part of the school should result in a more complete and satisfactory adjustment to community life for former high school students.

Another break occurs in the student's social life when he leaves school. Formerly he belonged to social groups that are part of the school, but when he leaves school he also leaves these. Some high school students also have out-of-school social groups that gradually take the place of the school groups when they leave school. But for many there is an almost complete loss of social contacts. Young people's groups in the community should look on the youth who leave school as potential additions to their membership lists. These groups should know who these young people are, because the high school should have a way of informing them. The YMCA and YWCA are examples of groups in cities which ought to be watching for former school youth who are in need of new connections with social groups. To some extent they are—as are the young people's groups in the various churches. But in typical high schools and communities the membership of former high school students in social groups is left to chance and is therefore not very satisfying. The high school should be the agency helping to make contacts between each year's group of former students and the existing organizations in which youth can join for social contacts.

The high school alumni association may be able to serve a really useful function here. If there is any purpose in having such an organization at all, it should be other than the Christmas vacation social affairs often sponsored by this association for high school graduates who are home from college and who have very slight if any need for the social contacts thus provided. An alumni association should concern itself most with graduates who do *not* go to college but who stay in the community. It should be a rallying point for their social life and activities. If their social needs are not met by other organizations of the community, then the school's alumni association could perform a useful community service by carrying on throughout the school year a varied group of social and recreational activities centered about the school's recent graduates while they gradually find their places in the community. The high school in a community that has few organizations open to youth could promote through its placement service such an alumni association as a way of rendering a real service to its former students.

The Indicated Organization

In a high school that has a fully developed guidance program the placement activities may well be an integrated part of this program. Ultimately a guidance program is tested by how well students of a high school are able to get along after the school guidance service no longer plays a large part in their lives. Its influence, however, should not cease abruptly when the student graduates or leaves school. The high school's guidance service should follow up the former student long enough to be sure that he is making out well enough on his own, or if not, to determine what else it can do and why what the school has done has not resulted in a good adjustment to the community.

In high schools whose guidance programs are more limited in scope, the part-time service of a faculty member may be required. He will need to have access to records that show what pupils' hopes and plans are when they leave school. He will need to know well the occupational, institutional, social, and recreational life of the community. He should be responsible for instituting community surveys of various types that provide factual data upon which he can rely. On the basis of these data, he will be able to advise with youth, their parents, employees, representatives of other youth-serving agencies of the community, and colleges. He can be a sort of coordinator of the various persons in the community who have a special interest in youth between their departure from school and their complete induction into the young adult life of the community.

Under existing conditions, these young people are in what might well be considered a civic-internship period. Supposedly, each has left school because the school has done about all it can to start him on a career as a young adult citizen. He is not, however, old enough to be *fully* accepted into young adult life. He is ready to spend a larger part of his time in direct participation in the life activities of young citizens than the high school program afforded him. But in most of the states he must be twenty-one years of age before he is fully and legally accepted as an adult. During this internship period the head of the placement service in the school and the leaders of other community organizations with special interests in older youth should constitute themselves as a council to work with elected representatives of these youth to see that as much is accomplished by each youth toward becoming completely qualified for full participation in adult life as is possible for him. Each year the twenty-one-year-old group of each community should be formally inducted into full citizenship at a civic induction cermony and welcomed by distinguished representatives of the older adult groups. Do we not have in many communities an annual ceremony of induction of new citizens who have taken out their last citizenship papers during the last year? Why should not the much larger group of native-born new citizens be included on this occasion? Under these circumstances high school graduation would be regarded as the *commencement* of an induction period that is brought to a conclusion with a community-wide ceremony of induction into the full rights and duties of American citizenship. Such an induction would help all youth to realize that the United States of America bestows upon every youth at age twenty-one an honor that is not to be compared with the titles, ranks, orders, or decoration conferred by some other governments only upon a selected few. The American high school has not fully met its obligations to this country or to its students until it has a well-developed organization for placement that reaches into the high school where the potential workers are to be found and out into the life of the community into which they are being drawn. This is an auxiliary service whose embryonic roots are to be found in most high schools. It is a service, however, not generally as fully developed by high schools as the conditions confronting present-day older youth require.

Some Points to Consider

1. If a youth leaves high school before graduating, why should the high school feel any special responsibility toward him?

2. Make a list of the organizations in a community you know which profess a special interest in the youth of that community. Do these groups have any arrangements for coordinating their programs? What useful purposes, if any, would be served if the community had a youth council that brought these organization leaders together for discussion and planning?

3. What job placement services are carried on by any high school with which you are familiar? How is this done? What records has the school which will help it render a good service to youth who want jobs, and to employers? What other records should it have, if any?

4. If an effective employment service for young people exists in a community, what should be the relation of the high school to it?

5. Are the employers of a community justified in expecting the high school to be able to supply pertinent information and other assistance that will help them find good young workers?

6. Suppose a high school adopts the attitude that it will do nothing about helping its former students find jobs because it would then be compelled to make choices among them and thus lay itself open to charges of favoritism. What could you say to counter such a position?

7. What does a high school with which you are familiar do to help its graduates get accepted by colleges?

8. Some high schools charge a fee for copies of the transcripts of the high school record of graduates if more than two or three are requested by one person. Why do they do so? Can you think of a better way of meeting this situation?

9. What does any college whose practices you know do to supply prospective students with information that will help them make a wise choice of colleges? Is this effort adequate?

10. Compare the entrance requirements of several representative liberal arts colleges. Is there anything to show that the colleges with the most rigid entrance requirements graduate young men and women better qualified to succeed in life than those graduated from other colleges?

11. A home for the aged accepts for residence only old men and women who are in the most robust health. In its advertising it points to the fact that its old people during their residence enjoy good health and generally

live to an exceptionally advanced age. How much credit should it be given for this situation? What connection is there between the practices of this home and what some colleges are doing?

Further Reading

Aikin, Wilford M. *The Story of the Eight-Year Study*. New York: Harper & Brothers, 1942.

Everson, Syrilla. "Highland Park Explores Work Fields," *American School Board Journal*, 114 (March, 1947), 31–33.

Fine, Benjamin. *Admission to American Colleges*. New York: Harper & Brothers, 1946.

Hollingshead, August B. *Elmtown's Youth*. New York: John Wiley & Sons, Inc., 1949.

Jacobson, Paul B., and B. L. Dodds. "Work Experience and Secondary Education," NASSP *Bulletin*, No. 120, February, 1944.

Landy, Edward, and Others. "The Occupational Adjustment Study," NASSP *Bulletin*, No. 93, November, 1940.

Leonard, J. Paul. "Can We Face the Evidence on College Entrance Requirements?" *School Review*, Vol. 53, No. 6, June, 1945.

Pattillo, M. M., Jr., and L. Stout. *Cooperation between Secondary Schools and Colleges*. Lincoln, Neb.: North Central Association, n.d.

President's Commission on Higher Education. *Higher Education for American Democracy*. Report; Washington, D.C.: Government Printing Office, December, 1947.

School and College Study of Admission with Advanced Standing. *Bulletin of Information*, Philadelphia: The Study, 1952.

Segel, David. *Prediction of Success in College*. U.S. Office of Education, *Bulletin*, No. 15; Washington, D.C.: Government Printing Office, 1934.

Story, Robert C. *Residence and Migration of College Students, 1949–1950*. U.S. Office of Education, Misc. No. 14; Washington, D.C.: Government Printing Office, 1951.

Waskin, Leon S. "The Michigan Secondary School-College Agreement," NASSP *Bulletin*, No. 159, January, 1949.

*Part Five deals with an auxiliary but very important aspect
of the high school principal's responsibility. It may be possible to have a fairly good educational program in a poor
and badly operated school plant, but certainly it is not easy
to do so. Good plant operation and management can improve the climate in which staff and students work. Helping to create the best possible physical setting for this work
is a responsibility that no really competent high school
principal neglects. Another managerial responsibility which
heads up in the principal's office is that of maintaining
good working relations with other educational agencies and
institutions.*

Part Five

THE PRINCIPAL AND PLANT MANAGEMENT AND INSTITUTIONAL RELATIONS

Chapter 20

THE PRINCIPAL AND SCHOOL PLANT
MANAGEMENT

THE PRINCIPAL HAS A RESPONSIBILITY for leading teachers, students, school custodians, and even patrons to accept and to maintain high standards of housekeeping in the school. If each person understands the responsibility that belongs to himself and to others, and if all work cooperatively toward common goals of cleanliness, safety, efficient utilization, and preservation of property, there is a good prospect of achieving these goals. Sharing responsibilities for the use and care of the school plant helps to build better standards of practice and better appreciations in the school and in the community.

Housekeeping Responsibilities
Widely Shared with Others

Every teacher should feel some responsibility for the general care of the entire school building and grounds. The principal and teachers should systematically inspect different parts of the building early in the morning before students have entered the building. If corridors, stairs, classrooms, toilets, and other rooms are unclean before students arrive, it can be concluded that custodians either have been careless in their work or in some way have been prevented from doing it. Significant details to be noticed are the condition of blackboards and chalk troughs; the care with which desks and chairs have been dusted; the condition of the floor about the base of desks; and condition of soap dispensers, towel containers, and other fixtures; and the condition of safety devices, such as fire alarm systems, fire hose, and panic bolts on doors.

The principal should conduct periodic inspections after teachers and students have left the building and before custodians have swept it. Each teacher should keep in reasonable order his books, papers, models, projection equipment, and similar teaching materials. Custodians should not be expected to be responsible for the condition of books left strewn over desks and tables or of expensive equipment left where extra care must be exercised in cleaning around it. When chairs have been rearranged for some special purpose they should be replaced by students.

Teachers should have some knowledge of the custodian's working schedule and should respect it as far as this is possible. For example, while classes are going on he has much more time for extra tasks than he has after school hours when he is cleaning the classrooms. The ordinary care of a building and grounds—cleaning, heating, ventilating, caring for minor repairs, and the many additional duties that make up the work of the custodian—will occupy all the custodian's time even if the school community gives him the best of cooperation. When this cooperation is lacking, undue burdens are thrust upon him, and he may develop a resentful attitude because he cannot maintain his regular work schedule.

STUDENTS

Most boys have some experience in marking on desks, defacing doors and statues, or breaking windows, activities that are carried on where children are experiencing frustration for one reason or another. Since the school is not responsible for all the frustrations that children experience, it cannot eliminate all offenses against property. Yet most students can be taught that the destruction of property is an offense against the group, a mark of immaturity and bad taste, or an evidence of poor sportsmanship. Such practices are matters of school or community custom or tradition. There are some high schools in which such actions seldom occur, and there are some colleges in which they are frequent. They occur least in schools where the students have had real responsibilities in the activities of the school and have come to identify those activities with their real interests.

In schools where students have been actively involved in cleaning and painting corridor or toilet walls, in making over a classroom into a more satisfactory setting for classwork, and in making the school grounds more beautiful, it is the common experience that the students take a greater interest in keeping up the appearance of the school than before. Under these conditions, damage to the property of the school becomes an obstacle to their own interests and activities.

Teachers should be alert to opportunities for encouraging students to learn by doing—through serving in groups that are responsible for the systematic inspection of all conditions affecting safety and through taking part in campaigns to improve cleanliness. Biology students can learn more about shrubs and flowers while carrying on projects that beautify the school grounds than they can out of a textbook. Each student is then more likely to realize that he has a responsibility for preventing damage to shrubs, flowers, and grass than otherwise would be the case.

In establishing standards of practice that will protect property, nothing succeeds like success. If custodians keep the building clean and quickly erase markings and other evidences of depreciation, the students are likely to respect school property. If they can be encouraged to plan and carry out inspections and clean-up campaigns, and if they actually feel that the success of these campaigns reflect credit upon them, they are likely to take pride in the appearance of their school. And if marked or carved walls mean extra work for those who have done the damage and not for the custodians, the tendency to deface or destroy will be curbed. It cannot be expected that the varied activities carried on in a school will leave the building spotlessly clean and in perfect order, but if all who create disorder and debris during their legitimate work will clean up reasonably well at its conclusion, the premises will be kept much cleaner and in better order than if everyone depends upon the custodian for all of this work. Students who get the idea that helping to keep their school building clean is a low grade of work to which they cannot stoop need a few lessons on just what it is that makes work honorable.

In many school cafeterias, students work for their lunches. Students are also employed in some schools as part-time custodians. In a school where many students carelessly litter the floor and expect paid workers to clean it up, the practice of using part-time student custodians is less defensible than it is in a school where everyone feels a responsibility for the cleanliness of the building. During NYA days, principals were careful to see that no student worker displaced a regular employee. During the war, with its attendent labor shortage, this problem was non-existent. The possibilities for students to get work experience through cleaning the building will vary with time and place, but most schools are in a position to give regular employment to students who need part-time work. In all schools there are opportunities for groups to launch specific projects, such as cleaning up the study hall, cleaning out lockers, ridding the campus of dandelions, or cleaning the shelves and tables in the library, where many volunteer hands make light work.

SCHOOL CUSTODIANS

The last twenty years have seen an increasing recognition of the importance of the work of the custodian or custodian engineer. Efforts have been made to dignify the position. There is a National Association of Engineers and Custodians. Many school systems have provided uniforms for their custodians; many have provided systematic instruction for them; some have helped them to draw up and adopt a code of ethics. In some systems such positions come under civil service, a practice that ought to be nation-wide. In some states custodians are now being granted tenure and retirement benefits. These endeavors have been made because of a clearer realization of the responsibilities of the custodian. In addition to cleaning, preserving, and protecting the school building, he is responsible for safety and health, and must maintain harmonious relationships with teachers, students, and the general public.

The alert custodian can prevent many hazards to safety. He can eliminate others, and he should report to his superiors those he cannot eliminate. His activities in the interest of safety are many and varied. He must clear winter sidewalks of ice and snow and see that sand or cinders are scattered over icy spots on steps or walks when they are needed. In extremely cold weather, he will find it necessary to maintain fires over week ends or during holidays. Obstructions in hallways or stairs must be removed, and worn stair treads or boards, protruding nails, broken or splintered handrails must be repaired or replaced. Electric circuits must be in safe condition at all times. All other precautions against fire, such as the removal of trash and proper disposal of oily rags, must be taken. Fire-fighting equipment must be checked periodically and overhauled. When a fire does occur, the custodian is expected to help sound the alarm, get students out safely, and protect property by cutting off the gas and electricity. Boilers and gauges must be examined periodically and kept in excellent repair to prevent explosions. The list of duties is of sufficient length and significance to require the services of workmen of character, energy and ability.

The custodian should be able to secure the cooperation of teachers and students in keeping the building clean and free from marks. He will be expected to perform many little tasks that will improve classrooms for teachers. If such requests become too numerous he can request teachers to secure the approval of the principal before he varies his schedule to perform nonroutine tasks. The custodian usually has no disciplinary responsibilities, but students should understand that he is responsible for certain supplies and for certain parts of the school property. In some schools he exercises some police functions. In his relationships with students and teachers he should be friendly, truthful, dependable, and wholesome.

In his relationships with the public, the custodian should promote understanding of the school system and good will toward it. He should refrain from casting any reflection upon the management or the work of teachers. He should understand that his vocational responsibilities are to his immediate superior and to his school principal rather than to members of the school board or to influential citizens.

THE COMMUNITY

Since students tend to imitate their elders, the conduct of adults when present at school for a meeting, dinner, play, athletic contest, or other gathering serves as a model to the younger generation. For this reason, public gatherings at the school should be properly supervised and athletic contests there should not be conducted in an atmosphere suggestive of public wrestling matches and prize fights. It is difficult to keep neat, orderly school grounds in a neighborhood where nothing else is orderly, but this condition has often been remedied by neighborhood beautification campaigns carried on by the school. If the school grounds are well kept and handsome, any community will take pride in their appearance. Patrons and friends of the school should be encouraged to contribute to its improvement. Criticisms and suggestions offered by neighbors of the school should not be ignored, even though the neighbors may be more discriminating in their judgments about the school property than about their own.

Organization and Direction of Custodial Service

One often hears of a school custodian of sterling character who has lent great dignity to his position by the quality of service he has rendered through the years. Occasionally there is one whom students and teachers alike have sought out for counsel and advice. It is difficult to attract such men to custodial work, but if they would make the effort, most boards of education could improve their programs for recruiting and retaining custodial workers.

WAGE SCALE AND WORKING CONDITIONS

Custodians should be paid on a scale commensurate with the prevailing level of wages offered by local establishments for the same responsibility, type of work, and ability. If the prevailing wage scale can be exceeded, it will provide a wider choice of candidates from which to fill a vacancy. Provision should be made for annual increases in pay, two-week vacations with pay starting after a year's employment, and sick leave privileges similar to those granted teachers. The best practice requires that all school employees who are not certificated by the state be listed as "classified" employees and put under civil service rules. Custodians should be employed on a twelve-month basis, both to reduce the turnover in the staff and to make possible the annual repairing and refurbishing of buildings, grounds, and equipment. To the extent that custodians are employed on a nine- or ten-month basis, necessary repairs and improvements must be accomplished during the school year, and a larger staff is essential during that time. However, under this arrangement there is little or no saving in the total cost of school housekeeping and less satisfaction for everyone concerned.

The length of the workday and the workweek for custodians should be the normal one. Where more than one man is employed in a building, the hours when the men are expected to be on duty may be alternated. In some school systems a special squad of workmen takes over night duties in all small buildings in the city. Custodians assisting with meetings, plays, athletic events, or other affairs outside school hours should either be paid for their time or be given an equal amount of time off during the school day. Arrangements to this effect should be city-wide and so well established that assignments to these outside duties will cause no resentment. The schools should pay custodians according to the prevailing wage scale. If School A pays more an hour for outside duties than School B in the same system does, or if School A pays for the extra time and School B staggers the work assignments to compensate for extra assignments, resentments will arise. A community activity should pay for this extra help, as should a school activity that is self-supporting; otherwise the school system should assume the cost and budget for it accordingly. When an emergency such as a broken pipe occurs, a conscientious custodian will be willing to work overtime whether he is paid or not, but if any considerable amount of overtime is required, he should be paid for it. He certainly should receive pay for any work after hours that is scheduled in advance.

In any event the actual payment for extra services to the custodian should be made by the board of education. Even though an out-of-school group is providing funds for extra services, the group should make payment to the board of education and not the custodian.

Custodial service and building protection should be made available whenever the building is in use by groups of people. If pupil groups use the building at night or other out-of-school hours, the teacher in charge of the activities should be responsible for pupil supervision during such occupancy.

PLANNING THE WORK

The principal should aid and encourage the custodian in analyzing his job and in developing a schedule of work. Some tasks may be done when routine activities are demanding a minimum of attention. Yards, sidewalks, drinking fountains, stairs, basements, and toilet rooms may be cleaned during school hours. Closets, urinals, and toilet fixtures should be cleaned daily. Classrooms and cloakrooms should be swept daily after school is dismissed. Some activities should be carried on weekly, such as the scrubbing of toilets or the sweeping of engine rooms. At less frequent intervals during the school year, windows should be cleaned and many classrooms scrubbed. Most painting and repairing will be done during the summer vacations but some of it can be done during other brief vacations. The custodian will always need to save some of his time for emergencies and to make repairs and replacements as need for them arises. However, a systematic schedule will enable him to work more efficiently if it reduces his peak loads of work during certain hours and assigns more tasks to his slack periods.

In aiding a custodian to determine his work load and plan his schedule, the principal will use such standards as the number of classrooms, floor area, and the number of pupils enrolled. Such standards are helpful but, unless many other factors are recognized, they do not constitute an adequate basis for making comparisons between the tasks assigned different custodians. N. E. Viles suggests twenty factors that administrators should take into account in studying the work load of each custodian.

1. Where only one man is employed, hours of service are not easily alternated.

2. If special men are employed for repair work, night service, or early morning firing, the work of the regular janitor is made easier.

3. Buildings in smoky areas are harder to maintain in a satisfactory manner.

4. Old buildings usually present problems not found in modern plants.

5. The lack of scrubbing machines, brushes, mops, etc., and of the proper cleaning materials, increases the time required for cleaning.

6. Old wood or pitted concrete floors require more cleaning time than do smooth surfaces.

7. Small glass panes, although having other advantages, require more time for cleaning than do large panes.

8. More time is spent in temperature control in an area where the temperature is below freezing for many days during the year.

9. There is usually more night work in junior and senior high school than in elementary school buildings.

10. Ash hoists, automatic temperature control, and stokers now do many of the tasks once done by janitors.

11. Gas and oil fuels require less labor and cause less dirt than does soft coal.

12. Old enamelware plumbing fixtures check and require more attention than does the smooth surface of porcelain.

13. The large areas now recommended for playgrounds with their ornamental planting require care and attention.

14. Muddy grounds or surfaces covered with gravel or cinders permit the tracking in of material injurious to schoolroom floors.

15. The use of the building at night, particularly by non-school organizations, calls for extra care and attention on the part of the custodian.

16. Work shops, science rooms, and rooms where cooking is done are usually difficult to maintain.

17. Small fixed seats with multiple legs are factors in the time required for daily cleaning.

18. Smooth glazed wainscots absorb little dirt and require less cleaning time than do rough surfaces.

19. In some areas the water is impregnated with minerals that accumulate on plumbing fixtures and in heating systems, thus involving more work on the part of the janitor.

20. It is necessary to know the amount of assistance that the janitor will give in toilet room supervision or in other non-cleaning jobs.[1]

THE PRINCIPAL AND THE CUSTODIAN

In most of the larger communities, the rules and regulations of the board of education give some attention to the duties and responsibilities of the school custodian. The tone of these statements generally reflects the point of view of the administrator, with little consideration for the point of view of the custodian as an employee. A recent commendable tendency, in keeping with the modern trend toward greater participation by all employees in school planning, is the practice of inviting school custodians to aid in setting up a statement of approved practices for them. Why should not the head custodian, for example, attend meetings of faculty members or of students where building problems and housekeeping practices are being discussed.

The principal is responsible for upgrading the efficiency of the custodian, but that responsibility cannot be discharged solely by rigid inspections. The custodian enjoys working with the principal as well as for him and appreciates commendation for a task well done. The authors of *The School Custodian's Housekeeping Handbook,* a book addressed to the school custodian, suggest what the relationship of the principal to custodian should be.

In a sense, the custodian is the principal's right-hand man. The principal needs his assistance, and he counts on him to a very great degree. He usually realizes the importance of the custodian's position and appreciates the fact that a clean, well-kept, properly heated and ventilated building favorably affects the teachers in their teaching and the children in their learning. He knows that the employee can gain good will for the school through his good work and his friendly attitude toward pupils, teachers, and visitors. He appreciates the employee who is courteous, dependable, and cheerful, who can be counted on to do his work without constant supervision and direction, and who is always willing to do the countless small tasks that must be done.[2]

---

[1] N. E. Viles, *The Custodian at Work* (Lincoln, Neb.: University Publishing Company, 1941), pp. 34–35. Reprinted by permission of the publishers.

[2] Henry H. Linn, Leslie C. Helm, and K. P. Grabarkiewicz, *The School Custodian's Housekeeping Handbook* (New York: Bureau of Publications, Teachers College, Columbia University, 1949), p. 8.

Repairs and Replacements

Many school districts practice false economy by neglecting to repair and maintain school buildings and equipment. During the depression of the nineteen thirties maintenance budgets were kept at a minimum and needed repairs allowed to accumulate; consequently, when the repairs eventually had to be made at inflated prices, their costs were abnormally high. Neglected repairs are always expensive because they reduce the number of years during which buildings and equipment can be used, and because shabby buildings contribute little to the spirit of the school and the community. The principal should use his influence to assure the budgeting of ample funds so that the building can be kept in good repair.

Most large school districts maintain in a central shop a regular force of repair men who do all the needed work in the district. In the smaller districts, where this arrangement is not feasible, it is all the more important that each custodian be a skilled workman. However, in all but the smallest districts it is possible to have at least one or two skilled men with all-around mechanical skills who can go from one building to another assisting with the more critical problems of maintenance and repair.

Each custodian should be able to make immediately the minor repairs and replacements needed in the school, such as a leak, a broken shade cord, windowpane, or piece of furniture. In a few large school systems, division of labor is carried to such an extreme that a special workman has to be called for each separate type of repair or maintenance. This arrangement may be necessary when only the lowest grade of unskilled labor is employed for the work of the custodian, but it can be avoided if better workmen are hired and given any necessary on-the-job training so that they can be entrusted with much maintenance and repair work. Students are responsive to the housekeeping done in the building, and efforts to keep the building in the best possible repair should be so unremitting that students cannot fail to be impressed by the care and attention given to all school property. Under the guidance of the teachers of physics, chemistry, arts and crafts, or practical arts, students may assist in the making of minor or emergency repairs that do not involve any hazards. More extensive repairs, such as painting and decorating schoolrooms and furniture, replacement of flooring or repairs to shower rooms and toilet systems, should be made during vacations or on Saturdays, depending on the extent of the repair and the emergency. Whether the custodian does the work or not, it is his responsibility to know when it is necessary and to inform the proper authorities.

Appropriate repairs and replacements often make great improvements in heating, lighting, and ventilation. For example, merely painting a drab ceiling with flat white may increase the illumination in certain parts of a classroom by as much as 100 per cent. Comparable improvements in lighting may be effected by the proper finishing of floors, desks, and equipment. A light-colored chalk board is now available which, in many classrooms, interferes with good lighting less than does the conventional blackboard. Sliding panels can be installed to cover conventional blackboards with lighter colored surfaces during the periods when they are not actually in use. These examples indicate the importance of consulting experts in many different fields to make sure that repairs are properly made with correct materials. Repairs of a complicated nature should not be undertaken by regular school custodians. Included in this category may be those involving heating, ventilating, masonry, roofing, brickwork, concreting, and plumbing. These should be made by special maintenance workers employed by the board of education or should be let out by contract to private firms.

The primary requisite for a successful maintenance program is planning. Instructors or department heads should periodically report repair and maintenance needs to the principal. The custodian should make up a yearly calendar in the form of a check list of inspections and should schedule a definite amount of time for inspection each month, week, and day. Frequently inspection will disclose the development of weaknesses that can be repaired before they actually become serious and costly. The repair of a weak spot on a composition roof may save a leak that would ruin the decoration and equipment of several rooms. The repair of a crack occurring from settling may add years to the life of the building.

The principal should organize the faculty members as well as the custodians in annual, thorough inspections and occasional informal ones to determine what is necessary to maintain and repair the building and equipment.

Building Utilization

DURING SCHOOL HOURS

To high school teachers and administrators it seems that the buildings in which they work never offer sufficient space. Most high school buildings are crowded at some period during the day. When a room becomes available, almost every member of the staff has a different suggestion for using it. This situation suggests to administrators the importance of knowing the extent to which buildings are utilized and the methods by which utilization can be increased. Fortified with facts, they can make decisions based on educational needs rather than on the persuasive powers of individual teachers.

When systematic studies are made, principals are often surprised at the amount of unused classroom space there is in the buildings they supervise. In 1926, Morphet[3] found the average percentage of room utilization to be only 75.4 for fifty-eight high schools, and in 1936 Scott[4] found the percentage to be only 79.2 for twenty-eight high schools.

Such evidence shows that the school administrator should exhaust every means of providing more effective building utilization before seeking additional school facilities. His basic data will consist of (1) the number of student stations (seats; space at tables, apparatus, or machines; and areas of floor space to which students may be assigned for stated periods) provided in the space available, and (2) the extent to which these stations are utilized in the periods provided in the school schedule. His means of improving building utilization are (1) increasing the number of student stations without violating standards of good health and hygiene, (2) keeping class sizes up to the standard accepted by the school, and (3) increasing the number of periods in the school day so that the available student stations can be used more often.

AFTER SCHOOL HOURS AND DURING VACATIONS

Under pioneer conditions the school was inevitably a community center. As the country developed, the school lost this role, but it seems to be regaining a part of its former position of serving the entire community. This recent tendency has grown for many reasons, one being the very apparent waste that exists when school buildings stand idle while civic or community agencies are hard pressed to house worthwhile community activities. Moreover, schoolmen have realized that since other agencies as well as the school have educational functions, it is reasonable for these agencies to use the facilities of the school. They have also realized that it is good public relations to encourage wide use of school facilities and to cultivate the habit of regarding the school as a community center. In a school which is being used as a community center, many nonstudent groups will be making use of the auditorium, gymnasium, shops, arts and crafts rooms, cafeteria, library, clubrooms, science laboratories, commercial rooms, little theater, playgrounds, social rooms (and their facilities for serving), rifle range, music rooms, health unit, and field house facilities. Communities that are getting the

[3] Edgar L. Morphet, "The Measurement and Interpretation of School Building Utilization" (*Teachers College Contributions to Education*, No. 264; New York: Bureau of Publications, Teachers College, Columbia University, 1927).

[4] Ralph S. Scott, "The Utilization of Building Space in Secondary Schools" (Unpublished master's thesis; Chicago: Department of Education, University of Chicago, 1936).

maximum use out of their school buildings keep school facilities at work during the summer vacation periods to serve both youth and adults. In many instances, boards of education finance and control such extensions of school services as classes and activities for adults, afterschool activities for children and out-of-school youth, and summer recreational programs. Teachers are often employed for evening or summer work and are paid extra for such extra duties.

USES OF THE BUILDING BY AGENCIES
OTHER THAN THE SCHOOL

Often an arrangement is made whereby responsible agencies use school facilities over a long period of time; examples are a park board using a school playground in its summer recreation program or a business or industrial organization using school classrooms to house an instructional program carried on in evening classes. Most high school buildings are rented to community groups for occasional or regular meetings of patriotic, religious, business, racial, political, civic, vocational, or professional, health, and parental groups. In some states, boards of education are required to open buildings free to civic and educational groups for meetings where an admission fee is not charged.

Practices in renting school facilities are not uniform. In some districts the responsibility for the supervision of the building is placed entirely upon the renting organization and its officers; in others it is retained entirely by the school board. Fees charged usually vary from a small one for groups of school age to a large fee for a profit-making venture.

Some boards open high school buildings free or for a very nominal fee to responsible community groups who will use them for open meetings or affairs that contribute to the enrichment of the community's cultural, civic, religious, or educational life.

There are numerous examples of cooperation between school boards on the one hand and park boards or recreation commissions on the other which make school plants and grounds available for community recreation programs on a year-round basis. The authors hold that it should be easy for any responsible community group to get the use of a public school facility. Obviously, school officials will wish to make sure that (1) the activities of such nonschool groups are in harmony with the broad purposes of the school, (2) the regular pupil activities are not displaced, and (3) the protection of property is assured. Regulations should be developed for the use of the building by out-of-school groups, and such groups making application for building facilities should make it on an application form that carries an agreement to observe the building regulations.

Recent studies have shown that school buildings are kept open for use by the pupils and community for an average of sixty-nine hours a week. Many administrators are prepared to assume key positions in developing the concept of the wider use of the school by the community. Indeed, in most large cities, school workers have felt the need for a greater community of interests among the patrons of large high schools. Atlanta, Georgia, has attempted to meet this need by establishing enough junior-senior high schools so that each serves a comparatively small geographical area, the residents of which have some community of interests. In such a situation it is easier to identify and encourage the common interests of students, parents, and members of the community, and to increase the community use of a city high school to the point where it approaches what is to be found in many small urban and rural communities.

Provisions for Safety

In many schools, provisions for safety are worked out or supervised by safety councils composed of students and teachers. Sometimes custodians serve on such councils. The activities of such a council should supplement those of responsible school officials, but they are often effective not only in educating students and teachers to safety needs, but also in improving physical conditions affecting safety. Safety promotion is a natural field in which students may assume a large measure of responsibility. They can survey existing conditions, make recommendations for their improvement, and then see that their recommendations, if approved, are carried out.

FIRE PREVENTION

Some mention has already been made of the custodian's responsibility for good safety practices. It is impossible to divorce this subject from comment about boilers, furnace room hazards, and fire hazards from faulty wiring. Unless there are city-wide programs of instruction in these matters for custodians, it is the principal's responsibility to see that custodians are fire-conscious and that their practices are calculated to prevent fires. Great care should be exercised in the use and storage of inflammable materials or those that might cause spontaneous combustion. As few oily rags as possible should be kept on hand, and these should be stored in metal boxes that are *not* close to wooden walls. Paints and varnishes should be kept in fireproof lockers or in an outside building separated from the school. No piles of sawdust or other debris should be allowed to accumulate except in fireproof bins. Few schools have found the baling and sale of waste paper to be economically worth while, but if paper is collected, it should be stored in a fireproof room. All fire-fighting apparatus should be regularly inspected and tested. Unannounced fire drills are as valuable for the custodial staff as for the students.

SAFETY IN CASE OF FIRE

The principal should make sure that in case of fire there is a definite plan for the passage of students from each room to the outside of the building. In many states he is legally responsible for such a plan and for emergency exit drills. An explanation of this plan and brief directions for leaving should be posted in a convenient and conspicuous place in each room in the building, preferably where they can be read easily as students are leaving the room.

In arranging for periodic fire drills, the principal should go far beyond a perfunctory observance of the law. Drills should be carried out at all times of the day and from every room in the building including the auditorium and the lunchroom. Student committees should supervise traffic in each section of the building during these emergency exit drills, and the flow of traffic should be directed to assure orderly passing and to save time. Stairways and exits should not be used beyond their capacities.

Each floor of the building should be equipped with an inside fire hose or with fire extinguishers, and a number of teachers and students should be trained to use this equipment. It is recommended that no one should have to travel more than 100 feet from any place in the building to reach an extinguisher. Fire hoses should be checked for efficiency and the extinguishers should be recharged at regular intervals. The principal should know what the state laws covering fire prevention require with respect to school buildings and what the local ordinances are; he should report any noncompliance until the condition is remedied.

ACCIDENT PREVENTION

Apparently it is impossible to eliminate accidents entirely in school activities. It is possible, however, to eliminate unnecessary hazards and keep the accident rate at a minimum. The following are some precautions listed by Viles, which custodians can take to eliminate needless accidents in special rooms:

1. Watch all gas heaters for fumes. Flexible hose contacts should be permitted only between the shutoff cock and the burners. Even then, a rigid connection is preferable.
2. Watch gas for possible leakage. Gas purchased from service com-

panies usually has in it a malodorant that a leak may be detected easily. All canned gas purchased in pressure tanks should also have in it a malodorant.

3. Have fixed racks for acid carboys.

4. In chemical laboratories keep a woolen blanket to use in smothering possible fires in clothing or elsewhere.

5. Treat tops of chemical laboratory tables to make them acid resisting.

6. Have all machine guards in shops fastened securely.

7. Remove rubbish from around power machines. Eliminate slick floor conditions from around power machines.

8. Keep boiler room clean. Have fire doors free acting. Do not block fire door openings.

9. Watch boiler steam pressure, also water level in boiler. Even "popping off" of the boiler has been known to give alarm to pupils in the building.

10. Pick up soap in shower rooms.

11. Remove all obstacles that might cause tripping around swimming pools.

12. Regulate hot water flow in showers and laboratories.

13. Place handrails on ramps for swimming pool.[5]

Accidents occasionally occur in physical education classes. To assure the safety of students and to reduce accident rates, Mabel Lee suggests consideration of the following points:

1. Proper supervision of facilities and equipment.
2. Direct safety instructions to pupils and student leaders.
3. Full-time teachers of physical education.
4. The use of students as squad leaders.
5. Classification of students by age and ability.
6. Proper inspection of equipment and apparatus at regular intervals.
7. Athletic fields smooth and free from obstacles where injury might occur.
8. All indoor surfaces provided with nonslip surfaces.
9. Enforcement of safety rules in the natatorium.
10. Satisfactory officiating for games in which rough play might result in injury to pupils.
11. Sufficient lighting for dressing rooms, halls, and gymnasiums.
12. Passageways and gymnasiums free of equipment, apparatus, and projections of any type.
13. Require eyeglass protectors for students who must wear glasses during activity.
14. A physical examination for all pupils in order to avoid pupil participation in activities beyond their physical capacity.[6]

[5] Viles, *op. cit.*, pp. 148–149.

[6] Arranged from Mabel Lee, *The Conduct of Physical Education: Its Organization and Administration for Girls and Women* (New York: A. S. Barnes & Company, 1937), pp. 251–252.

The school should be so organized that first aid can be administered immediately and professional service provided in the shortest possible time after accidents do occur. A complete report should be made and kept of each accident.

SUPERVISING STUDENT TRAFFIC WITHIN THE BUILDING

The prevention of accidents is one of the reasons for building good standards of orderly passing in corridors. No one would expect the principal to insist upon formal marching or to prevent students from laughing or chatting as they pass in the halls from one classroom to another, but it is essential to prevent running or hurried passing that might cause injury to others. It is essential to avoid unnecessary noise and confusion from banging lockers or from loud talking that frays the nerves of teachers and students alike. It is important to establish attitudes of poise and consideration for others and to avoid a noisy, boisterous atmosphere in which acts are likely to be impulsive and ill-considered. When all students are encouraged to take pride in their maturity and self-control, student bodies learn to set good conduct patterns that contribute to the pleasure and happiness of all.

In many schools, teachers are assigned to hall stations for supervision of student traffic, and, in most schools, there are brief periods when this practice seems useful. However, if students come to feel that the matter of safety is involved, they will, through the proper student organizations, set up good standards and their own ways of enforcing them.

Teachers and students have many opportunities to study the flow of traffic between classes and to plan to improve traffic conditions. A little study should make it apparent to all that traffic rules are needed in a crowded school just as they are in crowded downtown streets. It often saves time and distance if students use particular stairways in going to certain sections of the building. The clanging of locker doors is of no importance in a section of the building where classes are not meeting, but it may be a source of great annoyance in other sections. Often the reassigning of classes to different rooms will reduce considerably the traffic congestion in parts of the building.

Student bicycles and automobiles present safety problems, many of which students can solve in their own intelligent self-interest. There are walks and paths near the school where bicycle riders constitute a menace. There are busy intersections where careless pedestrians endanger themselves and others. Confusion and thefts result from irregular or unsupervised parking places. Such problems should be presented to student committees or student-teacher safety committees, with an assurance that the committees will be given any authority necessary to discharge their responsibility.

In schools where students are not ready for such responsibilities, teachers and principals devise plans and regulations to minimize the problems arising from the bicycles, motorcycles, and cars that bring students to school. If it can possibly be done, regular parking places should be established for bicycles and automobiles. In some schools a parking place is marked, numbered, and assigned to each car necessarily driven to school. A permit from the principal allows a student to use his assigned parking place so long as he observes the regulations that have been established for student drivers. In addition to the usual traffic regulations, other rules apply to loafing in cars while school is in sessions, taking a car from its parking place before school is out, overloading cars, riding on running boards, and lending or borrowing cars. When students apply to the principal for permits to assigned parking places, they file complete information about their cars so that the information will be available in case of theft.

Such detailed plans involve much clerical work and painstaking effort, but they are usually effective in reducing carelessness, trespass, theft, and reckless driving. They reduce the student's feeling of being unknown and therefore not accountable for what he does; they build a sense of responsibility and accountability.

PLANT MANAGEMENT AND SPECIAL SERVICES

Every special service operated by the school has its own maintenance and operation problems. Its equipment, supplies, building management, and hours of operation will probably be different from those required by the classroom program; yet custodians usually think that the building belongs to teachers and pupils from first bell to last bell and after that, to them. The library, health center, and cafeteria, on the other hand, often operate on different schedules, and require different types of maintenance work, which must permit the full and free operation of these special services and be satisfactory to those in charge of them. Even pupil transportation, especially when school-owned and -operated buses are used, requires special building and service arrangements. As these services multiply, the need for a competent head custodian increases, as does the need for the development of a high level of coordination between the head custodian and principal if the instructional staff and the building maintenance staff are both to be able to do well the duties expected of them.

Summary

The principal must see that everyone connected with the school assumes appropriate responsibility in the management of the school plant;

and must define clearly the responsibility that each individual has. Teachers, students, and community members, as well as custodians and principals, should contribute to school housekeeping and management. Periodically, experts should aid in inspections of the plant to make sure that the research findings of specialists are being utilized. Everyone connected with school has a stake in good school housekeeping because the objectives of comfort, beauty, efficiency, health, and safety are of concern and benefit to all.

Some Points to Consider

1. What are some of the important policies that boards of education should have with reference to employees responsible for the maintenance and operation of school buildings?

2. When, if ever, should a school custodian exercise disciplinary control over students?

3. What are the needs for, and the advantages and disadvantages of, having any or all custodians deputized as police officers?

4. What policies and practices can a high school principal institute that tend to increase the pride and self-respect of maintenance and operation employees?

5. What attitudes toward the unionization of these workers should school executives take?

Further Reading

Brainard, Alanson D., and others. *Handbook for School Custodians*. Lincoln, Neb.: University of Nebraska Press, 1948.

Bryan, Mary De Garmo. *The School Cafeteria*. 2nd ed.; New York: Appleton-Century-Crofts, Inc., 1938.

Cubberley, E. P. *The Principal and His School*. Boston: Houghton Mifflin Company, 1923.

Jacobson, Paul B., William C. Reavis, and James D. Logsdon. *Duties of School Principals*. Englewood Cliffs, N.J.: Prentice-Hall, Inc., 1950.

Lee, Mabel. *The Conduct of Physical Education: Its Organization and Administration for Girls and Women*. New York: A. S. Barnes & Company, 1937.

Linn, Henry H., Leslie C. Helm, and K. P. Grabarkiewicz. *The School Custodian's Housekeeping Handbook*. New York: Bureau of Publications, Teachers College, Columbia University, 1948. Chaps. 1–3.

Moehlman, Arthur B. *School Administration*. 2nd ed.; Boston: Houghton Mifflin Company, 1951. Chap. 17.

Morphet, Edgar L. "The Measurement and Interpretation of School Building Utilization," *Teachers College Contributions to Education*, No. 264; New York: Bureau of Publications, Teachers College, Columbia University, 1927.

Scott, Ralph S. "The Utilization of Building Space in Secondary Schools." Unpublished master's thesis; Chicago: Department of Education, University of Chicago, 1936.

Viles, N. E. *The Custodian at Work*. Lincoln, Neb.: University Publishing Company, 1941.

——. *Improving School Custodial Service*. Office of Education, Bulletin No. 13; Washington, D.C.: Government Printing Office, 1949.

——. *School Fire Drills*. Office of Education, Pamphlet No. 103; Washington, D.C.: Government Printing Office, 1948.

——. *School Fire Safety*. Office of Education, Bulletin No. 13; Washington, D.C.: Government Printing Office, 1951.

Chapter 21

BUSINESS ACCOUNTING AND
HIGH SCHOOL ADMINISTRATION

LIKE HUSBANDS, SCHOOL EXECUTIVES must be good providers. They must secure funds for the operation of schools and then spend these funds wisely, always making sure that expenditures do not exceed incomes. For many reasons, these are important functions of secondary school administrators. Our society places a high valuation upon financial competence and responsibility.

When a high school principal and his faculty have agreed on some modification in program that they can fully justify and about which they are very enthusiastic, it is a bit disheartening to be faced with the unromantic question of "How much will it cost?" Yet that is exactly what happens, and since most ideas, plans, proposals, or improvements are likely to call for some expenditure of money, the final decision as to whether a particular project can be carried out or not rests on its value and its cost in relation to the value and cost of some other proposal. In this sense the educational program is determined by financial considerations, and the principal needs to be prepared to show that anything he recommends is well worth the money it will cost.

Administrators must know and understand the sources of school revenues at local, state, and federal levels. They should also help teachers and patrons to understand what these sources are. Not only do high school administrators need to administer honestly and efficiently the internal funds in connection with extraclass activities, but they also must be able, at all times, to prove that their administration of such funds has been honest and efficient. Although these basic principles have been emphasized in school administration courses for a generation, financial problems have grown more complex, and the need for their emphasis is greater now than ever. Many high school principals who have been honest in their handling of student funds have found themselves in difficulty because they were unable to prove their honesty. And they have learned by bitter experience the importance of well-kept financial records.

Board of Education Finances

High school principals have important parts in the preparation and administration of school budgets. In Illinois, for example, where some high schools are operated as distinct units under separate boards of education, the principal is the administrative officer of the board of education and assumes full charge of all financial procedures. Where the high school principal is responsible to the superintendent, as he usually is, he works directly with the superintendent rather than with the board of education. The larger the school and the more professional the outlook of the superintendent, the more likely is the principal to have distinct responsibilities in connection with the budget. Even in the smallest school he should have certain responsibilities in making estimates of expenditures and in rendering accounting records for expenditures made.

IMPORTANCE OF THE BUDGET

The budget is a financial statement of the estimated revenues and expenditures of a particular school situation for a given year. Its preparation involves (1) an agreement upon the program that should be undertaken in the school situation, (2) a determination of the funds available and what restrictions if any must be placed upon their expenditure, and (3) the relation of the proposed program to the funds available. After the budget has been prepared and adopted, it provides a guide for administrative action. Decisions can be made quickly upon the basis of budgetary plans and with the knowledge that they are based upon mature group judgments rather than on off-the-cuff impulses. If the budget is organized in approximately the same form from year to year, data will be comparable, and each year the budget planning should be an improvement over that of the preceding year.

CRITERIA FOR THE BUDGET

A number of years ago Raymond G. Campbell analyzed the literature on budgetary procedure and concluded that there are six chief criteria of excellence. These criteria are for the total budget and hence were designed to cover items beyond the responsibility of the principal. Nevertheless, they have value for anyone who is interested in budgetary procedures, whether they are related to over-all plans or to such limited areas as expenditures for a department or for the activity program in a large school.

1. *Inclusiveness.* The budget presents a complete picture of the financial plan for operating the schools. . . .
2. *Balance* (articulation of ends with means). The budget considers

the needs of all legitimate activities in the school system in relation to each other and to the organization as a whole; it contemplates the total expenditures for all purposes from the standpoint of the anticipated income. . . .

3. *Responsibility.* The budgetary procedure definitely places the responsibility for directing the preparation, the presentation and defense, and the execution of the budget on the executive head of the school system and the responsibility for its review and adoption on the board of education. . . .

4. *Fiscal Control.* The budget serves as an instrument in controlling income and disbursements. . . .

5. *Flexibility.* In providing for financial control, the budgetary procedure recognizes the possibility of emergencies which necessitate such change from the original financial plan as is compatible with its safeguarding as a whole. . . .

6. *Publicity.* The budgetary procedure includes adequate provisions for informing the public of the proposals contained in the plan for carrying on the school operations; it offers the opportunity of criticism and suggestions to parties interested in the conduct of the schools.[1]

BUDGET FORMS

The provisions of the budget should conform to these criteria. There are advantages in using forms similar to those used by other schools so that data can be compared readily. In fact, in most states there are statutes regulating these matters. The most commonly used headings or divisions of the budget are as follows: (1) general control (salaries of superintendent and his office assistants: their clerks and supplies); (2) instructional service (salaries and teachers' supplies); (3) auxiliary agencies (library, health service, and so on); (4) operation of plant (custodians' salaries, fuel, and so on); (5) maintenance of plant (painting and repairs); (6) fixed charges (telephones and rents); (7) debt service (bond maturities and interest charges); and (8) capital outlay (land, buildings, equipment, and so on).

Sources of income are commonly (1) local taxes; (2) sale of lands; (3) state aid (from state taxes and from state-administered federal funds); (4) tuitions (for students living outside the district); and (5) fee and rents (laboratories, books, lockers, auditorium, gymnasium, and so on). These sources vary from time to time, and the proportion of the total derived from each varies from place to place. For example, during recession years tax collections are slow, and increased pressures bring about changes in both local and state tax structures. It is important for all school administrators and teachers to keep continuously informed about these sources of school revenues. All citizens know when their

[1] Raymond Guy Campbell, *State Supervision and Regulation of Budgetary Procedures in Public School Systems* (New York: Bureau of Publications, Teachers College, Columbia University, 1935), pp. 14–18.

taxes increase, but they know little about where their taxes go, and they are not likely to know unless those within the system assume the responsibility of serving as a news source for these matters.

PREPARING THE BUDGET

During the course of the entire school year, as desirable changes are indicated by emergencies and as requests are made by staff members, the principal should make notes and records that will be useful in the actual preparation of the budget. However, each year his intensive work should be done on a regular time schedule. If the principal's reports have been properly prepared and include recommendations for the educational program in the forthcoming year, they will be helpful in indicating what the expenditures ought to be. A review of the old budget in terms of the proposals that are under consideration will indicate which ones can be included in the report submitted to the superintendent of schools.

WIDE PARTICIPATION

In doing the work assigned to him on the budget, the principal should confer with representatives of all departments in the school and if possible with every member of the staff, each of whom will have a point of view worthy of consideration. Many school administrators have found it advisable for every staff member to participate in the preparation of the budget. One way of achieving this is to place a budget box in the school where every staff member can turn in his written suggestions concerning his own needs and those of the school. Department heads should consult teachers within their departments before submitting their departmental estimates. When the budget for the high school is finally approved, it should provide for a free sum of money to be spent for schoolbooks, equipment, or supplies and subject to the requisition of any staff member within the limits set by the board of education. Another way of securing participation is for the board to determine the amount available for a certain purpose, for example, audio-visual equipment and supplies, and then request the teachers to recommend a formula for utilizing this special fund. Such wide participation in the making of the budget deepens the interest of staff members in the whole school enterprise and usually improves the budget. Informed about these school problems, they can enlighten their friends and the public generally. Participation in the making of the budget improves the relationship between the business office and the individual school because it helps staff members to realize that sufficient funds are seldom available for all desirable proposals. Thus when choices are made, staff members are likely to understand —whether or not they approve—the reasons for the decision.

Because uniformity in business procedures can lead to desirable economies, in school business matters there is a temptation to practice uniformity for its own sake. Wide staff participation can uproot and guard against this evil. Teachers can be helpful in eliminating red tape, in improving requisition forms, and in developing ways of effecting economies in the classroom use of materials.

Before the budget is finally adopted by the board of education, the principal is usually informed by the superintendent of the maximum appropriation his school can hope to receive and may be asked to eliminate some items from his requests. Hence, before presenting his requests for the consideration of the superintendent and the board, the principal should study the various items and be ready to rate them in their order of importance. When eliminations must be made, staff members should have the same voice in the decisions that they had in developing the tentative budget. Teachers can be invited to classify individual budget items or even categories of items as most important, important, or least important.

VALUES OF COST STUDIES

Cost studies are of value when budgetary decisions are made. However, factors affecting cost vary so widely that general studies must be carefully analyzed. Comparative studies of carefully defined per pupil costs in a few similar schools may be very informative. For example, the item of instructional costs now typically constitutes over 70 per cent of the total budget, and most administrators strive to keep the percentage as high as possible. Other general items vary from 1 to 9 per cent each, but if they are clearly out of line with practice in similar schools, they should be scrutinized carefully. Common practice is not always best practice, but an administrator should thoroughly understand and be prepared to justify any wide deviation from the mean.

Within a school system or even within a single school, unit cost studies provide a good basis for the development of the budget. They generally show a high cost for such desirable features of the modern secondary school as shop and laboratory courses, increased health services, the single salary schedule, and decreased student loads. The longer school day and year and the increased use of the school plant lower unit costs if the total costs of the school plant are taken into account. Whatever the studies show, they should be made because they lead to more intelligent budget decisions. Here again staff participation is generally helpful in determining the what and the how of cost studies that should be made. To be of most service, unit costs for the preceding year should be available by the following fall.

Data that should be available for making budgetary estimates upon

the basis of cost studies include total and school population, anticipated enrollments, pupil-teacher ratios to be maintained, anticipated
pupil loads, extensions or contractions in program, equipment and supply quotas, salary schedules, facts about economic trends, and receipts
and expenditures for preceding years.

The library budget should be a special concern of the principal because it represents an important part of the school that will be neglected
unless it has a vigorous advocate. An allowance for fuel will be in the
budget whether the principal recommends it or not, but books for the
library may be overlooked unless the principal remembers them. A regional accrediting association, before postwar costs hit their peak, recommended a library-book expenditure of 75 cents a student a year in
schools of at least medium size, with a larger allowance for small
schools and a total expenditure not less than $200 even in the smallest
schools. The total library budget should be broken down into separate
budgets for each department or division, with some funds reserved for
general purposes.

Before the budget is finally approved by the board, it is customary
to make the proposed budget available to all who are interested. Printed
or duplicated copies are distributed as widely as necessary, and its salient
facts are usually discussed in the local newspaper. The principal should
lead in helping teachers and patrons to understand the budget. Those who
support the school have a right to know the nature of its expenditures;
if they understand its budget, they are much more likely to be favorably disposed toward it.

OPERATION OF THE BUDGET

The accounting system must be closely related to the budget if
the latter is to be well administered. Requisition forms should contain
the information needed for proper endorsement and intelligent purchasing. One copy of each form used should be kept available for reference and
for the building of permanent records.

The procedures should be standardized and the channels for forms
and procedures well established so that transactions are routine in character. The complexity of both forms and procedures usually varies directly
with the size of the school. For example, in a small school requisitions on
the budget are not numerous enough to be burdensome to the principal, and he probably should receive them from teachers, department
heads, or custodians whenever needs arise. In a larger school, requisitions
may be so numerous that the principal is justified in requesting teachers
and others to anticipate their needs and submit all requests to him on a
particular day of the week or month. Accounting procedures should require as little attention from the administrator as possible. However,

an accurate record for a comprehensive audit and a dependable basis for investigating comparable costs must be provided.

The principal, or the one to whom he has delegated the responsibility of making requisitions, should keep memorandum accounts that will enable him to determine quickly whether or not requisitioned items can be secured within the limits of unspent budget balances. In some systems such budget information is provided at intervals from the superintendent's office. However, two routine checks of budget items are by no means a waste of time, and the principal will gain in effectiveness if he is self-reliant in discharging his budgetary responsibilities. Clerks in other administrative offices are more conscientious in their duties if they know they are dealing with someone who is accurately informed about items within his control.

In many schools it has been found necessary for the principal to administer a petty cash fund provided for in the budget. This account should be as small as possible, and each month the principal should render a completely itemized statement for it. It should cover expenses that are small and unexpected but easily justified; it should not be a catchall for large expenses or for those that can be anticipated.

INVENTORIES

Many schools find it advisable to maintain perpetual inventory forms for all supply items. The forms include spaces for the name and description of each item, its specifications, the names of the departments using it, and its unit cost. Spaces are also available for recording purchases, the distribution to teachers, and the quantity remaining on hand. Such a record should be checked occasionally by an actual physical inventory. If the record is accurate, it will show at once the quantity of any item available for the remainder of the year. Such information is helpful in anticipating shortages and in estimating annual purchases. Periodic inventories of equipment should also be made for insurance purposes.

The principal should be friendly and cooperative in his relationships with business representatives of the superintendent's office. Occasionally in larger systems antagonisms arise between business officials and representatives of instructional staffs because of the difference in their particular functions. Business officials should constantly remind themselves that their function is to spend money efficiently, according to the provisions of the budget as it was approved by the board of education. It is not their function to restrict expenditures in order to build up big budget balances at the year's end. High school principals, on the other hand, should remember that through the years conservative business administrators have served an important function in building confidence in public schools and boards of education. Employees in the business offices of school boards are expected by the board and the public to scrutinize expenditures to see that prices charged are right, that the item is in the budget, and that a sufficient balance is on hand to cover each expenditure. The whole process of the final budget formulation and expenditure should be recognized by all as a proper function of the office of the superintendent of schools.

Financing Extraclass Activities

No longer is it possible for a host of special organizations to operate their finances independently. The income from dues and from the sale of materials and tickets runs into very substantial amounts. If the school sponsors these activities and assumes responsibility for them, then their funds should be as carefully and scrupulously handled and accounted for as any public funds.

About one fourth of the states have considered it necessary to enact legislation designed to safeguard pupil funds and to provide for the supervision of their expenditure.[2] In another fourth of the states, regulations designed to achieve the same purposes have been adopted by state departments of education.[3] Such legislation and regulations aid high school principals in their efforts to develop businesslike procedures in the management of these funds.

In states where activity funds are not controlled by statutes, the principal's personal responsibility for them is generally much greater than his responsibility for the regular funds of the board of education, for usually the board of education accepts much less responsibility for the internal funds than it does for the regular funds. The board should accept equal responsibility for raising and spending both types of funds. Even if the board is unwilling to contribute to activity funds, it should pay for an annual audit. Too often activity funds are ignored entirely by everyone in authority except the high school principal. He is and should be responsible for them, but they are so important and complex that policies for their management merit the consideration of the board of education whether or not the state holds the board responsible for them.

THE CENTRAL TREASURER

Specialists in extraclass activities and successful principals recommend that all activity funds be deposited with a central treasurer for the high school as a whole, who maintains separate accounts for all or-

---

[2] Wilson H. Ivans and Helen I. Anderson, "Extra-Curricular Funds Accounting in the Various States: A Preliminary Report," NASSP *Bulletin,* No. 38 (March, 1954), pp. 128–130.

[3] *Ibid.,* pp. 131–133.

ganizations and for special events. Each organization makes its deposits in the central fund as it would in a bank; upon being properly directed, the treasurer disburses the funds of any organization. Under such an arrangement it is possible and desirable to follow the best budgetary and accounting procedures.

Important standards often found in legislation and generally found in state department of education regulations and recommendations of professional educators include the following:

1. Each person responsible for the final receipt of money should be bonded.
2. There should be an approved depository.
3. All disbursements should be by bank check and with supporting voucher.
4. Accurate and detailed accounts of all receipts and disbursements should be kept.
5. There should be monthly reconciliations of bank statements and periodic reports of financial condition.
6. There should be an annual audit by a qualified accountant.
7. Each separate account should be operated under a planned budget as largely as possible with the cooperation of the pupils of the school.

The fact that activity funds must be handled systematically, strictly accounted for, and regularly audited does not mean that there is no place for the students in this operation. The handling and management of the activity funds is in itself a valuable educational experience for them. There are two levels of operation in the handling of funds: one determines the general policy to be followed in raising and disbursing funds; the other is the mechanics by which funds are actually collected and disbursed. The principal cannot avoid final responsibility for the funds, but he should confer with a student finance committee on the general policies to be followed in their use. A central policy committee with student representation can establish regulations governing the use that separate organizations may make of funds, but these organizations should be allowed to decide how their funds are to be obtained and used as long as their decisions do not conflict with school policy.

The budgeting of student funds by the students themselves provides excellent experience in the assuming of real responsibility. Any other procedure is shortsighted as well as undemocratic, because it denies to those whose money is being spent a voice in how it should be spent or an appeal from any decisions that may have been made. Those who earn money should participate in deciding how it shall be spent; unless they do they are likely to lose interest in earning it. In recent years there has been an increased emphasis on the budgeting of student activity funds, an emphasis that seems likely to continue.

In helping to make school policies concerned with activity funds, students often have opportunities to improve school practices which are particularly within their control. Numerous studies of hidden tuition costs have shown that students spend surprising amounts not only for such items as laboratory fees and physical education equipment, which are controlled by the board of education, but also for such items as admission fees to school events and orchids for the junior prom, which depend largely upon the fashions set by the pupils themselves. Studies have also shown that pupils from families of the lowest economic status in a particular community participate least in extraclass activities. In some schools, student policy committees have reviewed the findings of such surveys and then systematically attacked the task of reducing costs in student activities.

Of the many specific problems arising in the management of activity funds, a frequently recurring one is the extent to which funds collected or earned by a given activity should be used exclusively for that activity. Certain activities are much more productive of income than others which may be of equal or superior merit educationally. It has long been a recognized broad principle in educational finance that funds are disbursed in terms of educational need rather than according to the source of their collection. An activity budget that in net effect draws funds from one source and spends them for another perhaps not closely related undertaking is educationally justified, but in practice such a policy must be judiciously administered. In some states it is forbidden by law. The high school principal should never privately and alone take the responsibility for such decisions. A finance committee, with faculty and student representation, should carefully review budget needs as presented by each organization. It should then propose a budget for each organization and hold public hearings at which the organizations can present arguments for changes in their proposed budgets. When this committee finally fixes a comprehensive budget and recommends it to the student council or to the principal or to both, then not even the principal should be able to violate it except with the approval of this committee. The procedure outlined above should not only make students familiar with accepted methods of budgeting funds, but convince them that in this instance, at least, the allotments have not been determined by individual caprice.

RAISING FUNDS

The raising of funds for the support of extraclass activities presents a problem if so much money is required that there is a continual demand made on students and their parents for it. The time and energy of students and teachers are often spent in campaigns, drives, and ticket-selling contests, whose sole purpose is to raise money for some activity of real educational significance. No one would expect students to sell tickets so that history could be taught, but in many schools it is the usual practice for students to raise money so that other educational acivities of great importance may be included in the offering of the school. It is often recommended that such activities be financed by boards of education, and support from this source is actually considerable if account is taken of the fact that facilities and faculty sponsors are provided. Boards of education often pay staff members extra for sponsoring after-school activities, and the amount of support for extraclass activities supplied indirectly and directly by boards of education is on the increase. Nevertheless, few school boards support these activities entirely, and many support them not at all. Most funds come from ticket sales, special sales, membership dues, advertising or contributions, bookstore profits, and the like. Sometimes profits from the cafeteria are used to finance worthy enterprises, but this is a very dubious procedure. Many schools have some form of activity budget under which one fee paid by a student covers the cost of most of the activities for a year. Few have been able to use a single fee for all student activities, and perhaps it is not necessary that they should, since no person is likely to be interested in every activity.

Regardless of how funds are collected and by whom, they should be strictly accounted for, preferably under some centralized control. Many schools have found it advisable to make one faculty member responsible for the supervision of the entire activity program, including all activity finance and ticket sales. After the principal or his representative has approved a proposed ticket sale, representatives of the group concerned submit an order for tickets to the faculty sponsor. The tickets should be numbered serially so that a check can be made on all tickets and on the persons who handle them. The sponsor is guided in his supervision of the sale by the information provided on the ticket order. Most of the activities are carried on by students under the supervision of the faculty sponsor, who knows at all times the accountability of each student and holds him responsible for accuracy in his accounts. Through the years those who manage ticket sales secure insights into the particular problems of different organizations and are able to make recommendations that increase efficiency and add to the educational values of the activities. The school has no right to conduct the sale of tickets in such a way that students learn that it is easy to be dishonest about the money they collect. The school generally finds it advisable to give the greatest possible publicity to the accounting of student funds. Wherever possible it gives responsibility to students under its supervision, a procedure that builds respect for businesslike accounting for public funds.

Miscellaneous Business Responsibilities

Principals have additional responsibilities for business management that are related to both the activity funds and the regular funds of the board of education. Each of these funds should be organized separately according to accepted business practices, so that no confusion between board funds and board property and student funds and student property results.

Even in the smallest school systems there are advantages in centralizing all purchasing in one person, as is almost invariably done for the expenditure of the regular funds of the school board. Occasionally, however, even in large high schools, teacher-sponsors or student representatives of organizations make purchases for student activities as the needs arise. This lack of organization often leads to waste and inefficiency. In some schools, a single, trained person is given the specific responsibility for all purchasing. As he gains experience and sees, in their proper perspective, all the purchases that are made throughout the school, he will eliminate much duplication and establish economical practices. In other schools, purchase orders are issued by one person, but the actual purchases are made by a sponsor or a student. When a considerable amount of money is involved, it is often wise to purchase on the basis of competitive bids.

RECEIVING AND STORING SUPPLIES AND EQUIPMENT

There should be a systematic procedure for receiving and checking supplies and purchases charged to board or student funds. Checking can best be done in a room where all supplies are received and by the purchasing agent or someone working under his supervision. Often a storage room can serve both the board of education and student activity organizations. Whoever receives all purchases should be a responsible and careful worker. Without careful checking, even in a small school, enormous waste occurs through shortages in shipping, the receipt of goods in bad condition, and theft or damage of packages not promptly checked.

In another chapter in this book the importance of adequate storage places for unused supplies and equipment has been emphasized. In many school systems, supplies are stored in a centrally located building and distributed several times a year to individual schools. Even with such an arrangement, the principal should install a simple system for safeguarding supplies and accounting for them, but if large quantities of supplies are stored at the school, the problem is more complex. Supplies and equipment should always be kept in locked rooms, cases, or cabinets, keys being available only to those who are responsible for their safekeeping, distribution, or use. In order to prevent deterioration and waste, supplies left over from a previous year should always be used before those more recently received. It is better to keep the amount of supplies in each classroom reduced to what is essential for immediate needs. If this is not done, a surprisingly large quantity of materials will accumulate without anyone being able to say what is in short supply and what is not.

In schools which furnish free or rental textbooks and in those which lend laboratory or athletic equipment to pupils, there is need for a record of each item lent each pupil. These records can be kept on cards or on record books in each department. The record should show for each pupil and each piece of equipment the date of issue, the date of return, the condition of the equipment upon each occasion, and the charge made, if any.

MONEY COLLECTED BY TEACHERS

Many boards of education have regulations preventing or regulating the collection of money from students in connection with regular classroom work. It is also desirable that controls be established over collections for outside agencies. Even when a request for such a collection seems entirely reasonable to the principal in a particular school, generally it should be submitted to a committee of teachers and students for consideration. Teachers should not collect money from students unless it is for a cause that has been thoroughly scrutinized and approved. Sometimes collections are approved for the purchase of instructional materials, though the board of education ought to meet all such expenses from the budget. Sometimes students organize their own community chest drive and participate as a unit in the larger city-wide enterprise. Various other occasions warrant the participation of the school in fund-raising activities. When such collections are made, however, records should be kept that will protect everyone concerned from the consequences of carelessness, and from rumors of negligence, waste, or misappropriation. There is no way of having this protection without keeping a record of the payments made by each student. However, much time can be saved if teachers issue to students receipts made in duplicate and pay all money received to a chief clerk. The clerk can issue receipts to the instructors and keep a ledger of receipts and disbursements adequate for ready reference to payments made by any student or group of students. If it is not possible to organize itself well enough to provide a good check on all the money it handles, then the school should not undertake the activity at all.

BOOKSTORE AND CAFETERIA

When bookstores, cafeterias, and other enterprises are operated in high schools, they should be managed for the convenience, economy, education, and health of pupils and not for profit. They should be started by schools when a real need exists for them, and they should be operated in such a way as to provide educational experiences for some pupils while serving the needs of all. All such activities offer advantages to students because of a pooling of purchasing power, but the cafeteria manager has unusual opportunities in this respect. For each of these projects, business procedures should be centralized and built into a routine in order to save time for wise purchasing and to make the experiences of student workers of maximum educational value. The students and the public are entitled to all the facts about business transactions in these activities, and annual audits are essential. Student advisory boards often help in keeping the public informed and in giving the students experience in management. Such projects offer opportunities for students to learn through work experience, but in the cafeteria, especially, there is a need to guard against employing students in a routine, noneducative manner. The principal needs to give all such enterprises careful supervision, and his office should be a clearinghouse through which businessmen and parents can come to understand the need for them in the school and to approve the policies and practices under which they operate.

THE PRINCIPAL'S ANNUAL REPORT

Each year the principal should make a brief report to the superintendent of schools to report the activities and achievements of the school and to make recommendations for the coming year. To the extent that it deals with the management activities of the principal, the report is an index to the business administration of the school. It should survey activities and define objectives. Ordinarily it should include data concerning enrollments, funds handled, learning activities organized in each department, extraclass activities, the parent-teacher association, the plant and equipment, the library, and the cafeteria. It should not be encyclopedic in nature but broad enough to provide a direction for future activities. If it seems to be a basis for growth and movement, it will be read. It need not treat all aspects of the school with equal thoroughness each year; rather, it should take them in rotation. If it is also a careful summary of the immediate objectives of the school, it may well serve as the first preliminary step in budget making.

Summary

As head of a high school, the principal is also a business manager. Since public schools spend public money, the high school principal, as one of its administrators, shares the responsibility for seeing that the public gets its money's worth. This is not to say that he is responsible for running the school cheaply—for *saving* money. Rather, he is responsible for *spending* wisely. He must always be able to prove that he has done this well. He should follow approved business and accounting policies and practices in the management of school finance, and should carry on the business of the school from a glass pocketbook. The preparation and the operation of budgets constitute good tests of teacher and student participation because the activities are of a fundamental nature. If teachers and students can take part in these activities, administrators can feel reasonably sure of their interest and of their ability to participate successfully in other activities. They can also be sure that the budget is probably a better one than would be prepared by the principal working it out alone. Underlying the preparation and operation of budgets for student activities are the same principles that underlie the preparation and operation of any budget. The high school principal should be given responsibility by the superintendent for the operation of the high school budget and for the supervision of all the financial accounts of student activities. When given this responsibility he has the concurrent duty of providing close supervision of all school funds.

Some Points to Consider

1. "Our practices in student activity finances grow out of our policy of utilizing every possible opportunity to develop the ability of individual students and of the student body as a whole to participate widely and responsibly in the management of their affairs." Draw up a set of practices to be followed in relation to student activity finances consistent with this high school's policy.

2. "It is our practice to assign teachers to duty wherever money is to be handled in order to prevent students from being presented with temptation which they might be unable to resist." Draw up a statement of policy consistent with this high school's practice.

3. Do you think it would be a good plan to admit all high school students free to athletic games and other all-school activities with an admission fee only for "outsiders"? What alternative plans are there and what are their relative merits?

4. To what extent, if at all, should the school budget as approved by the board of education cover student activities? What arguments support your position? Draw up a statement of policy for whatever practices you approve.

5. To what extent should student organizations be encouraged to try to "make money"? What are the arguments for and against it?

Further Reading

Campbell, Raymond Guy. *State Supervision and Regulation of Budgetary Procedures in Public School Systems.* New York: Bureau of Publications, Teachers College, Columbia University, 1935.

Coleta, Sister M., O.P. "Cumulative Records for a High School of 250 Students," *Catholic School Journal,* Vol. 49, No. 6, May, 1949.

Donovan, Bernard E. "Building A Budget," *High Points,* 34 (May, 1952), 5–11.

Eaves, C. W. "Central Treasury for All Activities," *Clearing House* (September, 1954), pp. 30–34.

Greider, Calvin, and W. E. Rosenstengel. *Public School Administration*. New York: The Ronald Press Co., 1954. Chaps. 18–20.

Halley, Robert R. "Criteria of a Good Student Body Budget," *Clearing House* (September, 1951), pp. 28–29.

———. "A Student-Body Budget in a Small Rural School," *American School Board Journal*, 119 (July, 1949), 28.

Hand, Harold C. *How to Conduct a Hidden Tuition Costs Study*. Circular Series A, No. 51, Illinois Secondary School Curriculum Program, Bulletin No. 4; Springfield: State Superintendent of Public Instruction, May, 1949.

Hendrix, E. L. "Supervision of Student Body Accounting," *California Journal of Secondary Education*, 26, No. 2 (February, 1951), 110–112.

Ivans, Wilson H., and Helen I. Anderson. "Extra-Curricular Funds Accounting in the Various States: A Preliminary Report," NASSP *Bulletin*, No. 38 (March, 1954), pp. 122–136.

Jacobson, Paul B., William C. Reavis, and James D. Logsdon. *Duties of School Principals*. Englewood Cliffs, N.J.: Prentice-Hall, Inc., 1950. Chap. 20

La Franchi, Edward H. "The Administration of Student Body Funds," *California Journal of Secondary Education*, 25 (October, 1950), 352–356.

Moehlman, Arthur B. *School Administration*. 2nd ed.; Boston: Houghton Mifflin Company, 1951. Chaps. 18, 30.

Shane, Harold G., and Wilbur A. Yauch. *Creative School Administration*. New York: Henry Holt & Co., Inc., 1954. Chap. 16.

Thompson, G. B., and M. W. Stout. "What Is Effective Administration of Pupil Activity Finances?" NASSP *Bulletin*, No. 33 (April, 1949), pp. 287–300.

Trytten, John M., and Walter E. Hess. "Extra-Curricular Activity Funds," NASSP *Bulletin*, No. 36 (February, 1952), pp. 204–229.

Chapter 22

BUILDINGS FOR THE FUTURE

ANY SCHOOL BUILDING REFLECTS an educational philosophy of some kind or the lack of one, and that influence usually lasts for fifty or seventy-five years after the building is erected. School buildings should be designed by architects who have made a study of the problems of this special field, and each building should meet the educational specifications drawn up by members of the school staff who have carefully scrutinized every aspect of the present and probably future educational program of the community in which the proposed building is to be located.

Administrators readily accept these principles, but in most high schools the educational program is actually cramped by existing building limitations of some kind. Many such limitations exist because of subsequent changes in educational programs, some of which could have been foreseen. Many exist because educational specifications were not developed, were developed too hurriedly, or, if developed, were not followed. Other limitations are due to the fact that the educational planners were unaware of the purposes, methods, and long-time trends of modern education.

Although this chapter is to be primarily devoted to new high school buildings, it may be useful to stress the point that much can be done to make an old high school building much more useful and pleasant than many are. Just because a school cannot have a new modern building is no excuse for enduring the inconveniences of an old building if they can be removed without too great expense. In many communities where a new high school building is out of the question for a long time to come the question is whether to make the best of the present building or to continue to endure it in its present antiquated state.

Probably not much can be done at reasonable cost to the external appearance of an old building. Really bringing it up to date in appearance may be almost as expensive as building a new structure. But there are a number of ways of treating the interior of an old building that will

478

make it a much more satisfactory setting for a good school than many old buildings now are and at such a reasonable cost compared to a new building as to make it a bargain. Lighting is often bad in an old building. The windows may be too small in proportion to floor area. Modern artificial lighting can be installed that will at least materially reduce this shortcoming. Floors in classrooms and corridors get old, dingy, and dirty-looking. New floors can be laid or the old ones covered at a gain not only in appearance but also in the reduction of noise. Plumbing and heating systems can be worked over. Some antiquated school plumbing ought to be condemned for health reasons and new fixtures installed. Yet some communities will allow this old equipment to remain long after it has been replaced in every house in town. Old heating systems are often noisy, inefficient, and costly to operate. The new type of heating and ventilating systems will be more healthful as well as more economical.

A careful study of space allotment in an old building will often show how the removal or shifting of nonbearing walls will create a much more efficient working space. As a rule, old buildings were not well planned internally for even an old-fashioned program of education; hence some remodeling to meet the needs of a modern program can be easily justified. A remarkable improvement in classrooms can be made if good judgment is used in repainting walls and woodwork. Cheerful color, for example, can do much for classrooms. Add to this better lighting, some modern school furniture, and arrangements for darkening the room for the use of visual aids, and the old classrooms will hardly be recognizable.

This may sound like an expensive program, but if by undertaking it a community is providing itself with a reasonably good school plant, it does so for much less than the cost of a new building. There is no reason why a high school principal should not expect a community to do what it can to keep its high school plant as nearly up to date as possible. He cannot, however, expect the community to assume this obligation unless he makes some well-planned recommendations as to what the needs are and what he thinks can be done about them.

Over-All Planning

Planning a modern high school building is an extended, time-consuming, and complicated process. It is much more than requesting an architect to design a building with a number of standard classrooms, having attached an auditorium and gymnasium; it is rather the task of planning a physical expression of the educational philosophy of the school. There are many obvious examples. Even the seats used in the school reflect the thinking of the faculty; moreover, the decision as to the types of seating to be used in various parts of the building is not so simple that it can be left to architects and builders alone. The type of seat needed in the English class is different from the one required in science laboratories. In English classes one type of seat is needed if students learn by listening to lectures from teachers, whereas a different type of seat is needed if students learn by using the classroom as a laboratory. In science classes one type of seat is needed if all students learn by conducting experiments, but a different type is required if students conduct only occasional experiments, most experiments being demonstrated by the instructor.

In classrooms where students use many books instead of single textbooks, additional space is needed for the storage of supplementary materials. In classrooms where core or common learnings are taught, greater and more varied storage space is needed than in classrooms in which are taught only the specialized subjects of English or history or science. To the extent that the school has long class periods in the daily schedule, the building should have more classrooms and less space in libraries and study halls. Thus the methods of learning to be used, as well as the breadth of the offering, affect the design of the building.

WIDE PARTICIPATION IN PLANNING

All those who are going to operate and use the new facilities should have a part in planning them. Teachers and staff members are aware of defects and shortcomings that should be avoided in new buildings, and if they share in the planning of new features they can use them to maximum advantage because of a complete awareness of their potentialities. Pupils, parents, custodians, and any adults who use the school frequently can also make significant contributions in planning facilities for current and future educational adequacy. In a large school it will be advisable to organize participants into special committees dealing with particular types of facilities such as commercial rooms or recreational facilities, with an over-all committee to advise in coordinating the reports of the special committees.

There should be a coordinator (who may or may not be the principal) to serve as liaison representative between the architect and the interested groups which present their views. The coordinator should have authority to allocate space and location; he should be responsible for assembling the educational specifications and presenting them through proper officials to the architect. Such educational planning requires an awareness of the educational philosophies and trends to be followed and it is generally time consuming. However, in addition to the contribution to the resulting product, wide participation in cooperative planning helps to create a feeling of partnership and responsibility.

PROVIDING FOR ADAPTABILITY

Each committee should consider not only the operation of the present program but also the needs of the foreseeable future. Will the school eventually provide junior college facilities for the youth of the community? Will adults increasingly use the school for recreation, public gatherings, and for the improvement of community health? What particular kinds of education for lifework does the school need to add to its present offerings? Many of these questions cannot be answered finally and for all time, but they can be answered at least in terms of immediate and probable future needs. It is sound economy to plan new buildings so that they may be adapted to changing program offerings, teaching methods, and pupil groupings with reasonable cost and effort. In most cases it is desirable so to design a building that anticipated additions are easily made and that the central area and service systems are planned to care for such additions.

SELECTING ARCHITECTS

Since public schools are built with public funds raised by taxation, many boards of education are tempted to follow the old practice of dividing the work of designing school buildings among all the architectural firms of the district. Other boards of education, more conscious of the specialized nature of schoolhouse construction, have preferred to use only architects who have specialized in the designing of school buildings. Some districts are large enough to employ specialists in school architecture as permanent members of the staff. Others employ specialists directly or work out plans whereby consulting specialists may assist the local architect, who has received the commission by virtue of his competence as a local taxpayer of influence and prominence. Whatever the demands of local politics, districts will be better satisfied if they secure the services of architects who have some special competence in the designing of school buildings.

DETERMINING PRESENT AND FUTURE NEEDS

A survey to determine needs should be one step in planning for a new building or new building facilities. However, for the principal who has been serving in this position for some time, this should never be a first step but merely one of many in his continuous evaluation of the needs and trends in his school. The enrollments of the school for years past, the enrollments in grade schools in the district, the recorded births in the district, the interests and abilities of the student body, and the subsequent careers of members of previous student bodies provide basic data for estimating the needs of the prospective high school population and hence the size and character of the new building.

Most high school communities have reason to anticipate substantial secondary school enrollment increases during the next one and a half decades. The most important factor which will contribute to this increase is the sustained record of live births in the United States. It is indicated that the public high school enrollments, grades 9–12, will increase by about 26 or 27 per cent between the school years 1954–1955 and 1959–1960. A report by the Ruml Committee indicates that the total population of fourteen- to seventeen-year-old youth will increase from about 9,000,000 in 1954 to something over 14,000,000 in 1965.[1] Even greater increases than these are indicated by the fact that each year, 1951 to 1954 inclusive, set an all-time record of live births which reached 4,100,000 for the continental United States for the calendar year 1954.

A second factor contributing to increased enrollments is expected to be the improved holding power of the schools particularly as it is affected by district reorganization and the establishment of reorganized secondary schools. School building needs should probably be considered an important factor in accounting for the recent accelerated establishing of junior high schools and junior-senior high schools. If it is desired to provide facilities in home economics, industrial arts, and so on, for seventh- and eighth-grade pupils, such facilities can probably be provided and utilized more economically in some kind of a reorganized secondary school than in an eight-grade elementary school.

Estimates of anticipated increases in population in various areas of a school district can be obtained from public-utility corporations— telephone, gas, water, and power companies—which take into account economic factors such as the closing of some shops and industries and the opening of others. The high school principal will also need to consider the effect of the establishment of new high schools in neighboring districts, changes in tuition laws that may increase attendance from neighboring districts, and changes in the nature of the population that may affect school attendance. Some allowance should be made for increases in the proportion of the population attending high school, which will continue to increase although much more slowly in the future than it has in the past. By using all available data and taking into account all influences that seem to bear upon school enrollments, it is possible to forecast reasonably accurate estimates of the future high school enrollment for a given district.

[1] National Citizens Commission for the Public Schools, *Financing Public Education in the Decade Ahead* (2 West 45th St., New York: The Commission, December, 1954), p. 45.

CHARACTERISTICS OF THE BUILDING

The size of the building will be determined by the number of students to be served, the extent to which adults will use the building, and the types of services to be provided. In small schools a useful estimate of the classrooms needed can be made by a simple inspections of the sections that must be offered in each subject in order to provide for the respective enrollments. In a school of five hundred or more, for each department and for the entire school, Paul C. Packer's[2] room formula may be used to estimate the number of rooms required. Adjusted to a weekly basis, the formula is as follows:

$$\frac{\text{No. of students registered in subject} \times \text{No. of class periods or subjects a week}}{\text{Average size of section} \times \text{No. of periods in school day} \times 5}$$
$$= \text{No. of rooms required}$$

Since many classes, such as home economics and woodworking, require special rooms, it is necessary to calculate the number of rooms required by each department. More detailed and specific methods of estimating the space needs for schools of different sizes are to be found in *Planning Secondary School Buildings*.[3] It is obvious that possible although not necessarily desirable ways of decreasing the number of rooms required are to decrease the number of class periods each week in a subject, to increase the average size of the sections, and to increase the number of periods in the school day. These methods are entirely within the control of the principal of the school, but he should be fully aware of the effects of using them.

Standards accepted by experts concerned with fire protection make it possible for one-story buildings to be of ordinary construction if exit facilities are adequate. It is preferable that two-story buildings be of fire-resistive construction. However, buildings not over two stories in height, but with some combustible partitions and floors, are approved in some areas providing the floors, walls, and ceilings of all corridors and stairs are of fire-resistive construction. Buildings of more than two stories, if erected, should be of fire-resistive construction throughout.

There is no advantage in tall buildings, and they should not be built except in congested areas of large cities where nothing else is possible. In fact, these areas can have the advantage of the best we know

[2] Paul C. Packer, *Housing of High School Programs* (New York: Bureau of Publications, Teachers College, Columbia University, 1924).

[3] N. L. Engelhardt, N. L. Engelhardt, Jr., and Stanton Leggett, *Planning Secondary School Buildings* (New York: Reinhold Publishing Corp., 1949), Chaps. 6–7.

about school sites and school buildings only at prohibitively high costs. The authors therefore recognize that many of the suggestions that follow cannot be applied to buildings to be erected in the congested areas of large cities unless wholesale reconstruction of the neighborhood is contemplated. The authors, however, assume that the trend is toward less congested urban living and a lessening of the strains of congested institutional life. The building and site standards quoted here have been developed to help cure some of our urban ills rather than because they can be cheaply and easily attained.

There are advantages in an open rather than a massive design and in ample window spaces. The building need not be symmetrical but it should have balance. It should be located at least 150 feet from the street in order to be free from traffic noise and obstructions to sunlight. The plant should be planned so that if necessary it can be adapted to future changes in educational requirements. It should be possible to make additions to and alterations in the plant without destroying the association of related units and the efficiency of traffic flow. The use of non-bearing partitions and interchangeable or multipurpose units will contribute to this objective and eventually to the economical upkeep and operation of the plant. Both the original cost and the operation of the plant should be economical in terms of the resources of the district and the existing educational needs. No plant should cost so much that it causes the curtailment of other educational programs needed in the district.

In the state of California, where the population has grown rapidly in recent years, many school buildings have been required to keep pace with enrollments; consequently a good deal of experimentation in school design has been possible. In some regions of the nation, because of climatic conditions, the rather radical buildings developed in California may be impracticable; nevertheless they suggest directions in which adaptations can be made in any climate. A pioneer school in this state that planned simply to house a modern program, and to serve children rather than civic pride, has been described as follows:

The architects worked out six main principles, four of which deal with the critical factor of windows and daylight. (1) A one-story plan replaced the conventional multistory plans, eliminating stairs, heavy foundations, and fireproofing. It also opened the way to having windows on both sides of the

---

WEST CHARLOTTE HIGH SCHOOL, FRONT ELEVATION OF ACADEMIC AND ADMINISTRATIVE BUILDING. ARCHITECTS GRAVES AND TOY, CHARLOTTE, NORTH CAROLINA. PHOTO BY JOSEPH W. MOLITOR. A SENIOR HIGH SCHOOL BUILDING FOR 1,500 STUDENTS, ON A FIFTY-ACRE SITE

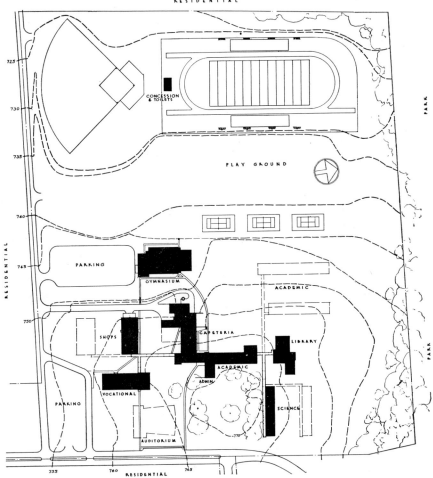

RESIDENTIAL

725

730

735

740

745

750

755   760   765

RESIDENTIAL

CONCESSION & TOILETS

PLAY GROUND

PARKING

GYMNASIUM

ACADEMIC

SHOPS

CAFETERIA

LIBRARY

ACADEMIC

VOCATIONAL

ADMIN

SCIENCE

PARKING

AUDITORIUM

-770

RESIDENTIAL

PARK

PARK

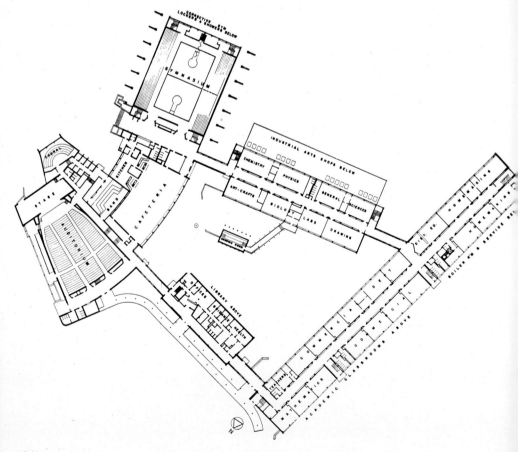

room. In later development, the one-story type was to prove capable of admitting still more light through the top of the roof. (2) A long corridor, flanked by classroom wings—a "backbone with ribs"—supplanted the quadrangle plans commonly in use. At Acalanes, these wings have open side-corridors—merely a canopy roof on steel posts—so that each classroom has direct access on both sides to the out-of-doors. Cross ventilation as well as two-sided lighting is thus facilitated. Quick escape of all pupils, in less than a minute in case of fire or emergency, is possible without the hazard of stairs or the cost of fireproofing the building. (3) Orientation of all rooms is uniform, so that all alike face in the best direction for light and sun—an arrangement not possible with the "closed" plan, with its meandering corridors and random orientation of rooms. It also permits the addition of new units with a minimum of structural alteration to the existing plant.

(4) Multisource daylight is provided to insure good visibility throughout all parts of the room. The corridor canopy is dropped from the roof level to permit the classrooms to have dormer windows above it on the south, while larger windows facing the opposite direction gain unobstructed north daylight. In the old-fashioned school, the pupil at a desk near the corridor receives perhaps one-one hundredths as much daylight on his desk as the pupil next the window wall. At Acalanes, the light for both is ample, and very nearly equal. (5) Classrooms are standard in size and shape and easily interchangeable in terms of the school's activity programs. To enlarge or decrease the size of the rooms, interior partitions of plywood-covered framing can be easily moved and remounted. (6) Complete separation of the different systems—structural, partitional, storage, heating, and lighting—from each other makes all of them easy to get at for repair and maintenance, and for quick changes when there is a shift of program. Acalanes classrooms have, as a matter of record, been enlarged or made smaller by shifting partitions in half an hour, with no upset whatsoever to lighting, heating, or wiring.[4]

TOWARD PREFABRICATED STRUCTURES

The suddenness of enrollment increases in the face of rising construction costs has forced some communities to use "temporary" units, but it has also sparked a trend toward the development of prefabricated school buildings. By using some of the newer finishing materials and utility service units, some temporary buildings can be made to provide usable housing for emergency periods. Such housing units can be provided to serve as advance or temporary housing at a proposed new secondary school or they can house an overflow of pupils in existing centers.

[4] "Pioneer School," *Architectural Forum*, 91, No. 4 (October, 1949), 104. Reprinted by permission of the *Architectural Forum*.

EAST HARTFORD HIGH SCHOOL. ARCHITECTS NICHOLS AND BUTTERFIELD, WEST HARTFORD, CONNECTICUT, AND PERKINS AND WILL, CHICAGO. A JUNIOR-SENIOR HIGH SCHOOL FOR 1,500 STUDENTS

One type of temporary construction consists of cheap masonry units, sometimes unfinished, meeting minimum construction standards but erected at an economical cost. These are not necessarily movable and are not always adaptable to changing needs. Some schools have erected such temporary units to serve as lunchrooms or as shops and later, after new buildings were erected, converted these temporary units into storage and service areas or in a few cases to bus storage. A second type of temporary housing is termed "portable," although usually they are never moved. These buildings are often limited to single classroom sizes, are of frame construction, and are so designed that they could be loaded and trucked to new positions when needed. Another kind of portable is the "demountable," which is usually made up with movable panels for walls, floors, and ceiling or roof. The panels are so arranged that the building can be erected as a single room, or several rooms can be assembled as one building.

A third type of emergency construction is the prefabricated unit which has been developed by factories after the fashion of the prefabricated house. Some prefabricated units are of metal construction and some are of other types of materials. There are also prefabricated units in which the manufacturer has developed panel members in fixed modules which can be assembled into buildings of various sizes and with various arrangements. Thus classrooms can be arranged in varying sizes. Such prefabricated units have not been used extensively and are still in the experimental stage, but England has developed some very useful and attractive designs and at least one large manufacturer of prefabricated housing in this country has entered the field of schoolhouse construction. The need for speedy relief, for low costs, and for flexibility in the face of rising high school enrollments may easily lead to rapid improvement in design and to more general use of prefabricated schoolhouse construction, just as has happened in home building and in industrial plants.

SELECTING THE SITE

Most public-spirited citizens feel they are well qualified to select a school site, and many are quite willing to do it. Sometimes individuals and small groups have selfish interests in influencing the location of public buildings. For these reasons the selection of school sites probably stimulates as much controversy and as many mistaken decisions as any other aspect of the entire school plant program. Most school sites are too small, although those purchased in recent years are much more adequate than those acquired before 1900 or even during the first quarter of the twentieth century.

For junior and senior high schools, it is suggested that there be provided a minimum site of 10 acres, plus an additional acre for each 100 pupils of predicted ultimate maximum enrollment. Thus a high school of 500 pupils would have a site of 15 acres. For secondary schools accommodating grades 13 and 14, it is suggested that there be provided a minimum site of 30 acres plus an additional acre for each 100 students of predicted ultimate maximum enrollment.[5]

This minimum should permit expansion of the building to meet future needs and provide adequate playground, athletic, planting, and parking facilities, and outdoor space for types of classwork that cannot be carried on within the building. If this minimum will not meet these needs, it should be exceeded. Sites of from 75 to 100 acres are being secured for some high schools; such space can be used to advantage in comprehensive and well-planned programs. "If there is one aspect of future secondary school programs that can be predicted with reasonable assurance, it is that the out-of-doors will increase tremendously in significance in the educational pattern."[6]

The site should be in a suitable environment where it will be convenient and accessible with the fewest hazards for the students who are going to attend the school. Ordinarily comparatively few sites of sufficient acreage in any community will meet the criterion of convenience and accessibility. However, to ensure adequate consideration of all the factors concerned, a school site should be decided upon only after a careful survey has been made under the guidance of trained and experience educators. Once the site has been selected it is as necessary to plan for traffic, parking spaces, recreational areas, and planting as it is to plan for the building itself. Reliable standards for evaluating school sites are available and their use in connection with proposed sites will reveal any undesirable characteristics.

Instructional Space

UNSPECIALIZED ROOMS

All classrooms should be workshops or learning laboratories, and as far as possible each room should have its individual character. However, much can be done through furnishings and equipment to individualize a room, and many academic or recitation rooms can be constructed so that they are interchangeable.

For certain types of secondary school programs, where academic classrooms were equipped with tablet-arm chairs and used only for lecture and

[5] National Council on Schoolhouse Construction, *Guide for Planning School Plants* (rev. ed.; Nashville, Tenn.: State Department of Education, 1949), p. 19.
[6] Engelhardt and others, *op. cit.*, p. 6.

recitation, the old standard of 18 to 20 square feet per occupant was probably adequate. The trend, however, has been to lengthen the class period and to use a portion of the period for directed study. This type of classroom procedure requires more desk space for texts, reference books, and notebooks. There is also a tendency toward more informal small-group activities within the classroom, especially in the core subjects. These modern practices require informal seating and floor areas of 25 to 30 square feet per pupil. In small high schools, with considerable variation in class size, space utilization can be increased by providing classrooms of different sizes.[7]

The size of each room will depend upon the type of activity planned for it. About three fifths of the academic classrooms should accommodate from thirty to forty students, but about one fifth of the rooms should be built for larger groups, and about one fifth of them should be planned for smaller groups. It is hoped that classes of over thirty pupils will be less the rule in the future than now. If so, classrooms designed for these enrollments will still not be too large, considering the trend in methods of teaching. Small high schools have a large proportion of small rooms, whereas large schools are likely to need more large rooms than small ones.

Some of the rooms should be provided with chalkboards on three sides. However, requirements for chalkboards, bulletin boards, storage cabinets, and shelves for teaching supplies will vary with subjects and methods, and in providing for them are to be found some of the opportunities for individualizing rooms. In large high schools it is desirable to plan so that classes in each department may unite for some activities and may have at least one conference room and a library of special materials. All rooms should contain outlets for audio-visual teaching aids.

SCIENCE ROOMS

Three types of arrangements for science facilities have been widely used: (1) separate rooms for recitation and laboratory; (2) a large laboratory in which one portion of the room is equipped for recitation and another for laboratory; and (3) a single laboratory equipped with a demonstration desk and science tables that face one way so that the room may be used either for demonstration and lecture or for student experimentation. The third type is now most used and is especially satisfactory for all-purpose science rooms in small schools with only one science teacher.

Science laboratories should be planned with special care. Equipment usually includes a demonstration table provided with a sink, run-

[7] American Association of School Administrators, *American School Buildings* (Twenty-seventh Yearbook; Washington, D.C.: National Education Association, 1949), pp. 93–94.

ning water, gas, and electricity. The necessary floor and wall connections for equipment and services should be provided at the proper locations during the basic construction. The size of the laboratory will be determined by the maximum size of classes and the different sciences to be taught. A minimum of 30 square feet of floor area is needed for each student exclusive of storage and other accessory space.

For general equipment and supplies and for individual materials the storage space should be safe, secure, and adequate, with chemical supplies stored separately.

SHOPS AND ART STUDIOS

School shops should be located in a separate building or on the ground floor in a section of the building which has been acoustically treated so that the noise will not disturb students at work in other courses.

The character and location of the shops should permit changes and expansion, especially if the school is located in a rapidly growing community. Shops present many problems to the architect; they need special wiring, plumbing, and ventilating systems. Moreover, their storage rooms should be convenient to delivery service and to the shops themselves. Safety for students and teachers demands good lighting, fire protection, and adequate space for each activity. Because of the individual character of the instruction and the nature of the machinery and equipment used, a minimum of 75 square feet is not too large an area for each student.

The general shop allows students to have exploratory experiences with work in wood, metal, electric power, printing, and ceramics. It is the most commonly used shop room in small and large schools alike. Rooms for specialized kinds of shopwork can be planned to meet any existing needs.

Toilet and washing facilities, student lockers, tool and supply cabinets, and storage racks for lumber should be provided in connection with the shops. General storage and supplies for all shops may well be concentrated so that they can be economically and efficiently handled.

An adjacent classroom, drafting room, or combination class and drafting room should be available to shop students, all rooms being adequately lighted for evening classes.

Studios should be planned for the contemplated program in art and located near the shops. These rooms need special lighting and decoration, ample storage space, special tables, sinks with running water, wall cabinets and bulletin boards, storage space for unfinished work, and equipment for visual aids. A minimum of 30 square feet of floor space a student is needed exclusive of storage.

HOME ECONOMICS

In home economics rooms, as with science laboratories, the trend in recent years has been toward a general all-purpose room. This arrangement is commonly used in the small high school with only one homemaking teacher, but it exists in schools that have the two departments of clothing and foods. The room is usually equipped with from two to five unit kitchens each, designed to accommodate four girls. Thus the room is a combination kitchen, laboratory, and classroom. Storage space and wall cabinets for supplies are necessary. An all-purpose room should contain 40 square feet of net floor space for each student and have attached a small accessory room.

In schools large enough to maintain two rooms for home economics, the second room may be equipped for teaching all phases of clothing, home nursing, home decoration, and child development. Family relationships and consumer buying may be taught in either room. In large high schools special rooms can be planned for these specific phases of the home economics program.

There should also be a laundry center with equipment for washing, drying, and ironing. The exhibit type of housekeeping suite cannot be justified, but there is justification for a bedroom that is used as a clinic room for child care and home nursing and for a room that is often used as a dining room by students and adults.

MUSIC STUDIOS AND DRAMATIC ROOMS

Specific areas planned for the music program are essential in the modern secondary school. In the small school this may mean merely arranging for built-in wall cases and adequate storage room for equipment near the auditorium, which can be used as the music room. In large schools at least one separate room large enough for band, orchestra, or chorus is essential. Desirable also are small rooms for small ensemble work and practice rooms for as few as six or eight students in instrumental and vocal classwork.

In any case it is desirable to locate music studios near the auditorium stage and in such a way that they are easily accessible to each other. They should not be located in basement areas.

Music studios should receive special acoustical treatment so that sounds coming from them will not interfere with work either in another music room or in a quiet area of the building. If the acoustical treatment is carried out during the course of the construction of the building, it will be comparatively inexpensive. In music studios it will also be comparatively easy to reduce the reverberation period without going below the point necessary for brilliant musical effects. Soundproof double doors are essential for shop and music rooms and in corridors leading from these rooms.

Speech and dramatic activities have secured a permanent place in the program of the modern secondary school and require facilities in addition to those afforded by a single auditorium. A little theater with a well-equipped stage and seating space for a small audience is a better training ground for students in dramatics than is a large auditorium. Such a theater has an additional advantage for students because, being used less by the community than a large auditorium, it is nearly always available. If it is impossible to build both an auditorium and a little theater, it is generally better to provide a little theater that can be expanded to seat about five hundred and that has an adequate stage than to build only a larger auditorium.

Many large schools have at least one classroom that is large enough to seat one hundred students and that has a small stage or platform at one end. It is also possible to place a stage at one end of a study hall or to set up temporarily a portable stage for rehearsals in the cafeteria or the gymnasium. Or two classrooms separated by folding soundproof partitions can be thrown together when occasion demands.

It is desirable to have a few special rooms that may be used by such groups as the staff of the annual, the newspaper staff, or the student council, but these rooms need not be especially designed. Regular classrooms that have special equipment and are free at designated periods during the day will serve such purposes satisfactorily. There should be at least one conference room for small groups of students, teachers, parents, and members of the community.

General Space

It is difficult to plan for high utilization of large rooms such as the library, auditorium, gymnasium, cafeteria, and study hall, which are used for general purposes. For this reason these rooms are ordinarily expensive to operate, and many schools have attempted to effect economies by planning for a multiple or at least a combination use of a single unit. Years of experience and trial and error have improved considerably the effectiveness of these combination efforts. Many architects and boards of education consider these combinations unavoidable. However, high school principals generally regard these combinations as makeshifts and hold that, even though they are expensive, the library, auditorium, gymnasium, and cafeteria are essential in the modern high school.

LIBRARY

The library has often been called the heart of the school. Though this statement may be less true of high schools as their concept of education revolves less and less about the conventional academic subjects, still the library will always be one of the important centers in a good school, and its physical arrangements and plan of organization should be carefully thought out. The principal can secure reliable standards and regulations for library design and arrangement from state and regional accrediting agencies and from the American Library Association. He can delegate much responsibility to the properly trained school librarian. However, if he is to be a professional leader of the staff he will need to give particular attention to planning the library facilities and its services and to evaluating their effectiveness in relation to all the programs that the education of modern youth requires. If the broadened concept of library function proposed in Chapter 14 is adopted, a novel space provision for the library will need to be made.

In many schools, particularly in small ones, the library is combined with the study hall. In some schools the central library is small and serves merely as a clearinghouse for the classroom libraries, which are emphasized. In most large high schools there is but one library, and books are regularly sent from it to classrooms on light trucks. The high school library should be located in an area which is most convenient to all the rooms in the building. Auxiliary libraries make books more readily accessible to students, but they are costly because of duplication in books, supervision, and management.

A combined school and community library demands much more space than does a school library, in order to meet the needs of adults as well as students. It should be located on the first floor with an outside entrance to the adult reading room.

Engelhardt, Engelhardt, and Leggett state that

no high school should be planned with such a small enrollment that it will not need a library for at least a capacity of 50, and no library capacity should be less than 10 percent of the total enrollment. Percentage figures of this kind are, however, deceptive because the library is constantly taking on new functions and should not be planned in such a restricted manner as to prevent the fulfillment of all desirable functions. In a school of 1,250 pupils it ought not to be unreasonable to have a library that will house 250 students. Study halls would be eliminated in the planning and true learning functions would be stressed.[8]

Only after careful analysis of the scheduling of proposed offerings can the need for seating capacity be accurately determined. In most high

[8] Engelhardt and others, *op. cit.*, p. 125.

schools without study halls, it is estimated that the library reading room should seat about one sixth of the enrollment. Where there are study halls or where the lengthened period tends to reduce their importance, the needed seating capacity of the library reading room depends largely upon whether library work during the school day is to be done in the library or whether it is to be done in the classroom. In the former case the classes are brought to the library and more seating space, preferably divided by glass partitions, is needed. In the latter case "room libraries" are provided—the books going to the pupils and not they to the books. The library reading room can then be smaller. The teaching staff has to decide how it plans to coordinate library usage and instruction before the size of the library reading room can be determined in any school.

Not more than six students should be accommodated at each table in the reading center. The chairs should encourage proper posture, and the tables should be arranged so that readers will not be forced to face windows or other unshielded sources of light. There should also be some chairs for informal reading without a table. Most of the books should be on open shelves around the reading room. A workroom, a librarian's office, and stock rooms for materials not in current use are essential. In small schools the librarian's office and the workroom can be combined. Other special rooms, as indicated in the following quotation, are desirable:

> One or more well-lighted and well-ventilated small rooms should be provided for conference, group study, and committees. Each of these rooms should be equipped with table, chairs, and shelving. Conference rooms may be separated from the main reading room by clear glass partitions.[9]

STUDY HALLS

If study halls are separate from the library they should be convenient to it. Large study halls create disciplinary problems. Some principals meet these problems by assigning additional teachers so that there are never more than fifty students for each teacher in any study room. A few have created a study hall for English and another for history with appropriate books and materials in open shelves. The lengthened period reduces the need for study halls and is doubtless one reason for the trend in its favor. If a section of the cafeteria is insulated from the noise and odors of the near-by kitchen it can relieve a crowded study hall during the periods it is not being used as a dining room. However, without such acoustical construction a cafeteria is ill suited for study, and in any event the study hall is usually most crowded just when the cafeteria space is being used for lunch.

There are satisfactory seats that can be used either in an auditorium or in a study hall and that make possible the conversion within a period of

[9] American Association of School Administrators, *op. cit.*, p. 113.

fifteen minutes, of an auditorium into a study hall with half the seating capacity. However, even half the seating capacity of an auditorium is too much seating capacity for a study hall, and the auditorium is generally far from the reference books and study aids. There is no inexpensive solution to the problem of the study hall. The regular classroom is large enough for the study groups to which most teachers can give effective aid and supervision. The school's daily schedules and the pupils' daily program should move in the direction of making many large study halls in a school unnecessary.

AUDIO-VISUAL AIDS

The library may well be the service center for the audio-visual aids used in each large classroom. One classroom should be the *minimum* total space for screening, hearing, and storing these materials. This room should be longer than it is wide. It should be well ventilated and should have lightproof window shades, seats at least 6 feet from the screen, and no seats on the side of the room in the front rows. The walls should be acoustically treated. The storage of catalogues, correspondence, and supplies will require cabinets of some kind. The film storage cabinet should be of metal or tin-lined wood and should be placed away from the source of heat. A large school may require additional projection rooms, but one central service and storage center will be needed. The regular classrooms should also have needed electrical outlets for the audio-visual equipment. Television facilities should include an extra and larger conduit line or an amplified type master antenna system.

Audio-visual aids include a wide variety of materials, but at present schools are increasingly using projected picture materials. The various devices and machines used to project picture materials include the stereoscope, opaque projector, glass-slide projector, microprojector, filmstrip projector, motion-picture projector, and sound-picture projector. Since pictures will be shown in classrooms as well as in the projection room, there should be additional projectors that can be moved around to all the classrooms in the building.

AUDITORIUM

The smaller schools often have an auditorium that combines economically, if not effectively, such functions as school assembly, community theater, gymnasium, cafeteria, study hall, social room, and classrooms. Folding chairs and equipment of various types are stored under the stage at one end of the room. A few schools have reported the auditorium-gymnasium as satisfactory, but it has not worked well in schools that must change the room frequently to perform one function or the other.

Ideally, an auditorium should have no functions other than as assembly room and theater, but the most desirable size for it is difficult to determine. An important factor is the extent to which adequate auditorium facilities are available in the community. The high cost of building is forcing an acceptance of school auditoriums of smaller and smaller seating capacity. Large high schools find it increasingly difficult to defend the cost of an auditorium that seats all or even a major part of the student body. A smaller auditorium can fill most of a school's needs for an assembly. The stage of a little theater will serve dramatic students better than the stage of a large auditorium. If large crowds must be accommodated only on occasions, other community facilities can be used, or the gymnasium can be converted temporarily into an auditorium. Even in a very large high school, it is difficult to establish the value to students of an auditorium seating more than 1,700. In fact, a large auditorium can usually be justified only if it is needed for community affairs, and in that case it should be clearly understood that the school is bearing a cost in building and in operating a large auditorium as a convenience to the community, and that a smaller one would serve the school's purposes as well. However, unless the community has a suitable auditorium it should be encouraged to include one in the high school building.

The auditorium should be on the ground floor with direct exits from both the front and the rear. It should be in a separate wing of the main building so that it can be isolated for community affairs during the day and for all functions at night. It should be conveniently located with respect to the parts of the building used for music and speech.

The stage should be from 28 to 30 feet in depth, and the proscenium opening should be from 24 to 30 feet wide. Many stages are built with insufficient off-stage space. The combined area of the two wings should be equal to the width of the proscenium opening times the depth. There should be wide doors opening from the stage for moving large properties. Two large dressing rooms equipped with lockers and toilet facilities are desirable, but adjacent classrooms and general toilet rooms can be used. Ample space will be required for the storage of stage properties.

Formerly orchestra pits were built in the auditorium, but current practice economizes by using an unseated section of the floor next to the stage to provide space for the orchestra. Connections should be installed for a sound-picture projector with a speaker cable from a place near the screen to the projector. The larger the auditorium, the greater the need for special acoustical treatment. Since provision must be made for the best possible artificial lighting during evening use, natural lighting is not necessary. Good ventilation is essential.

If a large auditorium is built as a social center of the community, and if it is also the place where group activities of the school are presented before community audiences, the auditorium becomes a very important part of the school's physical plant. It should be planned carefully and managed with efficiency after it has been constructed. Its management should be a responsibility of the high school principal under the general policies set by the board of education. If the auditorium is used much by the community, in order to make sure that both school and nonschool activities are provided for, a calendar of activities should be prepared so that it is possible to schedule events as much as a year in advance. In a large school the principal usually delegates the direct management of the auditorium to a teacher, who spends part of his time as manager and supervisor. Students build stage properties, manage the curtain, shift scenes during performances, and serve as ushers and ticket takers. In the auditorium the school is so often on dress parade that both students and teachers will be interested in securing and preserving appropriate furnishings and properties.

GYMNASIUM

The basic suggestions made concerning the location, design, and utilization of the auditorium are applicable to the gymnasium as well. It should be on the ground floor, readily accessible to students and the public, and in a separate wing of the main building so that it can be isolated for community use. Unlike the auditorium, the gymnasium requires sunlight and good natural lighting, and should be located so that its noise will not interfere with the quiet areas of the school. The gymnasium should be planned primarily to provide sufficient space for a good physical education program for all students and not to provide seating space for a maximum number of spectators for basketball games. If the community has use for a great basketball arena, it should be justified on that basis rather than on an educational one.

A school with an enrollment of five hundred or less can be served very well by one gymnasium. Its dimensions will be determined by the number of classes in physical education and their activities. A room 76 by 96 feet will provide space for a regulation basketball court, safety zones, and enough folding bleachers to seat five hundred people. When the bleachers are down, the space can be utilized for class activities. If the school is so large that additional space is needed for physical education, a second and smaller gymnasium without bleachers provides an economical arrangement.

Many schools use gymnasiums with rooms for boys and girls separated by folding doors or steel curtains, and which can be thrown together in one large space for certain occasions. The boys' and girls' classes are conducted in the main gymnasium on alternate days to allow for variety in activities. Acoustical treatment, desirable when there is only one gymnasium, is strongly recommended when two rooms are separated by a folding door. In all but the smaller schools there is a need for one or more small physical education rooms of approximately classroom size for remedial and corrective work. How many of these rooms will be required will depend upon the size of the school and the extent to which the physical education program of each student is based on a careful medical examination. It is of great importance that the gymnasium floor be resilient and free from slipperiness. It should be laid so that there is ventilation under it. The windows should be placed at least 12 feet above the floor.

Because it is impossible to keep basement lockers clean, dry, and well ventilated, lockers and showers should not be placed in basements. They should be on the floor level of the gymnasium, accessible to it and to outdoor play areas. If the playing floor is on the ground level, the seating galleries can be on the sides and the lockers and showers can be under the galleries. If possible the gymnasium should be in a one-story wing of the building where plenty of overhead sunlight can be provided. There should be enough lockers for street clothing to accommodate the largest class, and enough small lockers for gymnasium clothing to accommodate all students enrolled in physical education classes. Near the lockers should be common shower rooms for boys and common shower rooms for girls, with at least one shower head for each group of four students. Towel rooms should open into drying rooms located at the exits from the showers in order to keep the floors of the locker rooms dry. The floors of these rooms should be of nonslip tile or other nonabsorptive material.

A swimming pool is a valuable adjunct to a modern health and physical education program. Experiences in World War II and statistics on causes of death among adolescents indicate that the ability to swim might well be a requirement for high school graduation. Swimming pools should be built where funds are available for their proper construction and operation.

There should be an office with lavatory, toilet, and shower for the instructors of boys and another for the instructors of girls. Near the instructors' offices should be equipment and apparatus rooms provided with double doors that will accommodate large equipment.

In some cities community needs have stimulated the building of large field houses that seat great crowds at basketball games and provide for indoor track, baseball, and football. The field house may serve as a great auditorium or be combined with a large grandstand for the football field. Many cities need one such structure, and in such instances it may well be associated with the schools. Here again, as with the school auditorium built to accommodate the community, the public needs to recognize that the cost of building and operating such a facility is being charged to the budget of the board of education. Under such circumstances, the community should expect the school to be in charge of the facility it has built, rather than some unit of the local government.

CAFETERIA

Probably the best location for the cafeteria is on the first floor, near a service driveway. Odors are likely to be least offensive when food is prepared and served on the top floor, but it is time consuming to move supplies there, and any except the ground floor is inconvenient for community use. A one-story extension of the first floor to house the cafeteria makes a good solution of this problem, especially if satisfactory exhaust fans are used. Like the auditorium and the gymnasium, the cafeteria should be situated so that it may be used by adults when school is not in session and without the necessity of opening the entire building. If the cafeteria is in a separate building it should be accessible to students by a covered passageway.

By careful planning of the various stations and the rooms in which the food is prepared, all waste in transportation and much confusion can be eliminated. For example, in a large cafeteria a station for receiving soiled dishes set up in the center of the dining room causes much noise and confusion; it is much better to place such a station in the kitchen, or near it, where the dishes can be quickly and quietly removed, perhaps to a moving belt. Provisions should be made for the comfort and convenience of employees and for the maintenance of sanitary conditions.

The size of the dining room and the length and number of food counters will depend upon the number of students who will be served at any one time. The size of the kitchen and storage rooms will depend upon the total number of people who will be served at all lunch periods. The dining room should contain from 10 to 12 square feet for each student seated in the room during the most crowded lunch period. The kitchen area should contain about 1½ square feet for each meal served, with a minimum total of 300 square feet.

The dining room should receive acoustical treatment; if it can be separated by a soundproof partition from the kitchen and service area, it can be used for many other purposes, including social programs, music instruction, and audio-visual demonstrations. In such instances, however, special provisions should be made for the storage of equipment used in the other activities. In a large school it is also desirable to install folding doors that will make possible one or two private dining rooms.

ADMINISTRATIVE FACILITIES

In even the smallest high schools it is essential that there be an outer office and a private office for the principal. Since one reception room can serve all visitors and since one set of records can be used by the entire staff, in larger schools there should be a comprehensive office suite for all the administrative and guidance officers in the school. The most desirable location for this suite is on the ground floor near the main entrance.

In the general office there should be a waiting room and space for the clerical assistants. The former should be easily accessible to the public as well as to the school, and in large schools it may be necessary to have a separate waiting room for the public. Many details and routine matters can be transacted over a counter separating the outer office from the clerical office. The latter should contain a fireproof vault and electrical control stations. The principal's office should be adjacent to the general office and the corridor. Without being inaccessible or uninviting, it should afford protection from those whose questions can be answered by clerks and, upon occasions, privacy from any distractions. It should be large enough for small group conferences.

Also communicating directly with the general office should be the offices of any administrative assistants. The placement office, offices for the guidance counselors, and the student aid office should be in the general suite or located close to it. The guidance center's arrangements should be such as to provide for private conferences. The health office may be a part of the counseling suite or a part of the health and physical education department. Minimum facilities should include a waiting room and an examination room. Desirable additional facilities are a nurse's room, rest rooms, dressing booths, dental clinic, doctor's office, and a classroom for health education classes.

Although it is impossible to provide an individual office for each teacher, there should be teachers' workrooms where each can work effectively and have access to filing and drawer space in addition to what is available in the classrooms of the building. These workrooms should be equipped with typewriters, duplicating machines, worktables, and professional books and materials. There should also be adequately equipped rest rooms for teachers.

Because the advantages of a school store are greatly appreciated by students and parents, much of the opposition of local merchants to this institution has disappeared. If local conditions make such a store necessary and desirable, space should be planned for it somewhere on the main floor of the building away from the central office and near an exit to the street. There should be a stock room, a window and booth for ticket sales, a business office, and a room where supplies may be sold over counters. Such a store should be planned as a laboratory for the business education department.

General Service Facilities

Science teachers may be depended upon to plan science laboratories carefully, and teachers of music and dramatics will take a deep interest in the planning of the auditorium. But no specialist or group of specialists is particularly concerned about stairways, toilet rooms, and service systems that affect all the school in indirect ways. For this reason, the principal should give special attention to these facilities in a new building.

TOILET ROOMS

There should be one or more separate toilet rooms for boys and for girls with adequate washing facilities on each floor of the school building. Many schools have enough toilet fixtures but few have sufficient adjoining space equipped for washing and supplied with towels and mirrors. The ventilation of toilet rooms should be separate from the ventilation of the remainder of the building. The doors should be so arranged that the interior of the rooms will not be exposed to view when the outer door is opened. Walls, partitions, and floors should be of nonabsorbent, washable materials.

ROOMS FOR CUSTODIANS

In the basement and on each floor of every large building should be facilities for the custodial staff. In at least one such location there should be an office and workshop; in all of them there should be toilets and lavatories, lockers, and storage space for tools and supplies. If the custodial office also serves as a receiving room, it should be on the first floor. In a large school it is especially important to prevent losses by checking in at one station all goods that have been purchased by the board of education or by any department of the school.

STUDENT LOCKERS

Each student in the school should have a locker. Oversized lockers are desirable, but most schools find it necessary to economize with a locker 12 by 12 by 72 inches, with a shelf for books and hat. The lockers should be built into the walls of the halls and should be carefully distributed so that they will not cause congestion in the corridors. Placing some lockers on each floor of the building is preferable to putting double tiers of lockers in any corridor. High-grade combination locks should be furnished by the school, and only one student should know the combination to each lock. Locks are more serviceable if the combinations can be changed when necessary.

CORRIDORS AND STAIRWAYS

Economies can be attained by planning corridors of varying widths. On the first floor in the central sections of the building, corridors from 10 to 16 feet wide will be necessary in order to provide ample room for traffic in both directions. On upper floors and in remote wings of the building, corridors from 8 to 12 feet wide can accommodate the flow of traffic. Both ends of the corridors should have natural lighting. Each corridor should terminate at or near an exit. The extension of corridors beyond exits or stairs should not exceed 35 feet.

Stairs should not be located in the corridors but at right angles to the corridors. Stairways should be placed near exits and the entrance to stair wells should be hooded. The capacities of both stairs and corridors should be computed on the basis of standards set in the Building Exits Code of the National Fire Protection Association or the recommendations of the National Council on Schoolhouse Construction.

If a section of the corridor on the top floor is given overhead lighting it may be used effectively as an art gallery. All the main corridors should have molding near the ceiling from which pictures may be hung. Small lobbies and display windows at the corners of corridors are appropriate for exhibits of classwork. There should be at least one drinking fountain on every floor of the building, preferably at points in corridors where traffic congestion is unlikely to occur. At least one fountain for every seventy-five students in the school is the recommended ratio.

HEATING AND VENTILATING

The type of heating and ventilating to be installed should be the subject of special study and careful planning. The six general types of heating and ventilating commonly used in schools are (1) direct or warm air heating with natural ventilation, (2) direct heating with window supply and gravity exhaust, (3) direct heating with window supply and fan exhaust, (4) unit ventilators, (5) forced warm air with central or zone fans, and (6) radiant panel heating. So little radiant heating has been used in schools that its effectiveness is not fully known. Any one of the other five types will give reasonably satisfactory results if regional climatic conditions are considered properly in the selection and if the system chosen is properly installed, operated, and maintained.

Heating and ventilating systems, together with their thermostatic controls, should be zoned so that such spaces as the auditorium, gymnasium, cafeteria, library, and administrative offices can be heated independently of those portions of the building not in use.

In large schools safety and cleanliness are often achieved by separating the heating plant from the main building. Wherever they are located, boiler rooms should be large enough to allow for possible increased boiler capacity in the future and so planned that future additions can be readily serviced. Within boiler rooms boilers should be placed where they may be cleaned and repaired easily.

The air must be kept moving at all times in all parts of the building. Attic spaces under flat roofs should have openings sufficient to allow a free circulation of air. Wardrobe spaces should have a direct means of ventilation through grilles to the exhaust ducts. There should be exhaust fans appropriate to the type of heating system in use to draw air from corridors and classrooms.

LIGHTING

During recent years in no aspect of the school plant has more progress been made than in the field of lighting. The most light is not necessarily the best light. Lighting engineers have shifted their emphasis from the quantitative "How much light should we have?" to the qualitative "How well can we see?" Brightness balance is considered the key to visual comfort and efficiency, and the semidirect and indirect types of lighting have been found best for high schools.

If it becomes necessary to compromise between two artificial lighting systems, one of which produces high intensities with excessive brightness and the other produces a reasonable intensity with comfortable brightness, decisions should favor comfort.

In schoolrooms used for night classes, provisions should be made for an artificial lighting system that will produce the desired intensities and brightness conditions without daylight. In choosing a lighting system, one should keep in mind that during night use the highest brightness in the room is the immediate area of the lighting unit.[10]

When buildings are designed, careful plans should be made for adequate electrical wiring that will care properly for the present load and for any foreseeable future load. It is simple and inexpensive to make such plans during construction and thus avoid dangers from overloading or the added expense of later rewiring.

Students of lighting no longer hold that unilateral lighting is the best solution to the problem of crosslighting. New developments in structural design and in the control of daylight from many sources have made possible a more adequate visual environment for each room in the school building. Light can come from the east, west, north, and south— if it is properly controlled.

Building window heads as near the ceiling as possible and window

[10] National Council on Schoolhouse Construction, *Guide for Planning School Plants* (rev. ed., by W. D. McClurkin, George Peabody College for Teachers; Nashville, Tenn.: State Department of Education, 1953), p. 158.

sashes at least as high as the tops of desks and tables contributes to an adequate visual environment. When schoolroom surfaces in a new building are being finished, it costs no more to use colors and finishes with the proper reflection factors than it does to use traditional colors and finishes.

Fortunately there is an agreeable acceptance of light colored interiors, and a reasonable supply of materials. Floors can and should be 20 to 25 percent reflectance; furniture 40 to 60 percent; walls 60 to 70 percent; ceilings 85 percent; and chalk boards 15 to 20 percent. Surface finish should be matte rather than specular because the specular surfaces image bright areas, thus introducing high brightness contrasts into the visual field.[11]

It is not possible for every school administrator to become an expert in school lighting, but he should understand the problem well enough to know whether or not the community is receiving expert professional service in school lighting from the architect or the illuminating engineer.

ACOUSTICAL TREATMENT

During recent years, great progress has been made in conditioning schoolrooms for hearing ease and noise control. It should be assumed that everywhere throughout the building sound-absorbent materials have been used, but acoustical treatment involves more than applying anywhere in a room enough materials of high sound absorption to reduce noises. Where the materials are applied is important. The size and shape of rooms also affect their acoustical properties. Changes in parallel wall or ceiling surfaces may improve the acoustics in a room. A competent acoustical engineer has many resources for reducing the noises in a building that is yet to be built.

The inclusion of many noisy activities in the daily work of the schools takes a heavy toll from the energies of teachers. The administrator who is planning a new school building should make sure that his community is receiving expert professional service from a competent acoustical engineer as well as from the architect and illuminating engineer. The criterion for the selection of each of these services is specialized professional skill and not political prestige.

Summary

Planning for the school plant cannot be separated from any of the activities carried on in the school. It is a part of the over-all planning and evaluating that should be carried on continuously in connection with guidance, the school's educational offering, and the resources of the com-

[11] "Pioneer School," *loc. cit.*, p. 149.

munity. Planning a new building should not mean a sudden redirection of staff efforts but an analysis of evidence already secured and a maturation of plans long in the making in the different departments of the school. Although such plans should grow from continuous evaluative efforts, they should be forward looking. The remodeling of an old building should be carried out only in terms of long-time plans for the future. It is possible for remodeling to be, in the long run, actually detrimental to the progress of the school. The effectiveness of a new school plant depends upon the alertness of the members of the staff in defining their purposes and in evaluating their own efforts to achieve them. The planning of the school plant is an integral part of this entire process in which the principal is responsible for a leadership that helps the community get the very best out of its building investment.

When building costs rise rapidly as compared to rather fixed tax and bond limits, communities have great difficulty in financing high school buildings that are at all adequate to their needs. To whatever extent this means that high school buildings of the future have less of the costly ornateness that characterized the exterior of some of the buildings of the past, we have a net gain. Buildings of exterior simplicity cost less and are beautiful. If this need for care in spending money results in fewer marble-lined corridors, we have lost nothing. We can spend more of the available money on functional utility and still have attractive interiors. If this forced economy means that we do not try to design buildings and use materials that will last a century or so, perhaps we will be better off. Most high school buildings outlast their usefulness. If the cheaper designs and materials we are compelled to use still give us a safe building for the foreseeable future, we have bought all the durability we need. Beauty of functional design, utility of interior arrangements, and safety for those who use a building are what we need to buy. If high costs force us to plan carefully for these essentials, we may get more for our money than otherwise. If they deny us any of these, then the costs are high indeed. Only the most careful attention on the part of school administrators to these details of building planning and construction and to improved means of raising revenue for schoolhouse construction can assure us that the high school buildings of the future—many of which are now in the planning stage—will be as much better than those of the past as they need to be.

Some Points to Consider

1. Consider the program of some high school with which you are familiar. Then check the building facilities to see to what extent the building is suitable for the program.

2. Consider some desirable additions to the program offered the youth

of that community. Could these additions be accommodated in the building?

3. For what elements of a desirable school program are many typical school plants poorly adapted? For what elements best adapted?

4. Some good high school buildings include a room or rooms specifically set aside for students' social use. Can you defend such use of space?

5. Study some of the plans to be found in the references cited in this chapter. What features do you find that represent advanced thinking in the planning of high school plants?

6. Should high school buildings be planned to allow various community groups to use them? What typical changes in plans would be required?

Further Reading

American Association of School Administrators. *American School Buildings.* Twenty-seventh Yearbook; Washington, D.C.: National Education Association, 1949.

The American School and University. Twenty-first Yearbook; New York: American School Publishing Corp., 1948–1949, 1949–1950.

Barrow, J. M. "New High School Campus Zoned for Public and Academic Use," *Nation's Schools* (March, 1954), p. 55.

Caudill, W. W. "Housing the Secondary School of Tomorrow," *Teachers College Record,* April, 1955.

Cocking, W. D. "School Building Competition," *American School and University,* Vol. 24, 1952–1953.

———. "Secondary School Plants of the Future," *School Executive* (February, 1955), p. 7.

Engelhardt, N. L., N. L. Engelhardt, Jr., and Stanton Leggett. *Planning Secondary School Buildings.* New York: Reinhold Publishing Corp., 1949.

Engelhardt, N. L., Jr. "Laboratories for Learning," *School Executive,* November, 1954; and *School Executive,* September, 1954, School Plant Section.

Fowlkes, J. G., and L. B. Perkins. "What Are the Trends in Planning and Constructing Junior and Senior High School Buildings and Plants?" NASSP *Bulletin,* No. 163, May, 1949.

Illinois Library Association. *Planning School Library Quarters: A Functional Approach.* Chicago: American Library Association, 1949.

Koopman, George Robert. "Changing High School Programs and Their Implications for Design," *The American School and University,* 1955.

Lee, Ata. *Space and Equipment for Homemaking Programs.* Office of Education, Misc. No. 9; Washington, D.C.: Government Printing Office, 1950.

Lynch, J. M. "A Junior High School with a Built-in Program," *American School Board Journal* (January, 1955), p. 55.

Moore, Hollis A., and W. W. Caudill. "Designed for the Early-Teen Ager," *Nation's Schools* (January, 1955), p. 55.

National Council of Chief State School Officers. *Planning Rural Community School Buildings.* Prepared under supervision of Frank Cyr and Henry Linn; New York: Bureau of Publications, Teachers College, Columbia University, 1949.

National Council on Schoolhouse Construction. *Guide for Planning School Plants.* Rev. ed.; Nashville, Tenn.: State Department of Education, 1949.
———. *Guide for Planning School Plants.* Nashville, Tenn.: National Council for School Plant Planning, 1953.

National Facilities Conference. *A Guide for Planning Facilities for Athletics, Recreation, Physical and Health Education.* 1201 Sixteenth Street, N.W., Washington, D.C.: American Association for Health, Physical Education and Recreation, 1947.

National Fire Protection Association. *Building Exits Code.* 12th ed.; 60 Battery-march Street, Boston, Mass.: The Association, 1952.

"Pioneer School," *Architectural Forum,* Vol. 91, No. 4, October, 1949.

Reid, "The Secondary School Plant of the Future," *American School and University,* Vol. 24, 1952–1953.

Saylor, Galen. "Secondary School Buildings," *NEA Journal,* April and May, 1956.

School Planning Laboratory. *Planning Tomorrow's Secondary Schools.* Palo Alto, Calif.: Stanford University Press, 1954.

U.S. Office of Education. *Science Facilities for Secondary Schools.* Bulletin Misc. No. 17; Washington, D.C.: Government Printing Office, 1950.

Viles, N. E. *School Buildings—Remodeling, Rehabilitation, Modernization, Repair.* Office of Education, Bulletin No. 17; Washington, D.C.: Government Printing Office, 1950.

Wilson, Russell E. *Flexible Classrooms.* 51 West Hancock, Detroit, Mich.: The Carter Company, 1953.

Chapter 23

INSTITUTIONAL RELATIONS

So far the chapters of part five have been devoted chiefly to problems of institutional management, leaving to this chapter the institutional relations aspect of this part of the text. These institutional relations with other schools and colleges and with educational organizations and associations are important to any high school. This importance sometimes arises out of the effect good relations can have on the students and graduates of the school and sometimes out of the fact that understanding, cooperative relations are always better for a high school than their opposites. In either case the principal as the official head of the school bears some personal responsibility for maintaining and improving these relations or, at least, for seeing that the school is well represented in contacts which it has with these other groups.

These relations embrace a wide variety of educational institutions, organizations, and associations. Some are to be found within the school system to which a high school belongs and in the local community, some operate at the state level, while some are regional and national in character. Some of these relations involve schools which are lower or higher in the educational ladder than a junior or a senior high school. These are especially important relations because, as has already been pointed out in other chapters, there should be no sharp breaks in the student educational programs which would interfere with a smooth and comfortable transition from one school to another higher one.

Local School Relations

A local school system in a town, city, or county should be a *system* of schools, not merely a group of neighboring schools. This text has pointed out the reasons why each school should have a large degree of autonomy, but it has stressed the necessity of this freedom being exercised within broad policies set by the local board of education. The children of any community pass through its schools from the lowest to the highest grades and from elementary through secondary schools. For them it is or should be a continuous school experience with a high degree of continuity and consistency. For example, the promotion practices of the secondary schools of a system should not vary sharply from those followed in its elementary schools. One should not find that in the lower schools of a system no home study was expected and then find that in the junior high school or in the senior high school students, all at once were required to embark upon a heavy program of home study. If home study is expected in a system it should be assumed that there will be a gradual increase in its amount as one moves from earlier to later years in the system. When there is consistency in practices among the schools of a system or when there is a smooth transition for students from lower to higher schools within a system we usually say that the schools are well articulated. Problems of *articulation* are usually the joint responsibilities of the heads and staffs of all the schools and especially of the superintendent. Basic policies and practices should be worked out and instituted on a system-wide basis reflecting a unified philosophy of education, with each school retaining the right to vary practices so long as they are not inconsistent with the basic policies of the system. The principal of a high school cannot legitimately expect to maintain or institute practices independently of other schools of the system simply because it is the "highest" unit in the system. To do so produces bad articulation and this is indicative of weakness in the school system. The criterion is whether the experience of a student in the system is a continuous, consistent experience, with the gradual introduction of new practices as he progresses, or whether he is subjected to sudden, new demands and expectations perhaps inconsistent with each other as he moves from a lower to a higher school within the system.

RELATIONS WITH THE BOARD OF EDUCATION

This text has made it crystal clear that the high school principal's relations with the local board of education are to be carried out through the office of the superintendent of schools where such an office exists. This should not however result in such a distant relationship between him and the board that the latter is prevented from having a clear understanding of the program and problems of the high school. Good superintendents usually facilitate such contacts between principals and the board and between the individual schools of the system and the board as will enable the board to understand each school's program and problems. Superintendents do this by asking principals to join with them in presenting reports and proposals to the board. They are eager for the board to make firsthand contacts with each school's program, facilities, activities, principal, and staff so that the board can form its own judgments and thus make wiser over-all decisions.

The high school principal will utilize this willingness to help the board become acquainted with the school by inviting the board's presence in the school and by helping the superintendent prepare and present reports, proposals, and recommendations affecting his school. He will not utilize these contacts to initiate special appeals to the board as a whole and certainly not to an individual board member whom he thinks might be willing to make representations on behalf of the high school at the expense of other schools. This first mentioned relationship with a board promotes good articulation within the school system, while this second one would lead to disunity and ill will in the system. In discharging his responsibility for good relationships between the high school as an institution and the board, the principal has the responsibility for considering the need for good relations between the board and the school system as a whole, not just between his school and the board.

RELATIONS BETWEEN "HIGHER" AND "LOWER" SCHOOLS

The advent of the junior high school as an intermediate unit between what was the eight-year elementary school and the four-year secondary school raised a fear among some school people that two "breaks" in a local school program, rather than one, would result. The existence of this fear is indicative of our recognition that any break or point of inarticulation in a school program is undesirable. All schools have had and now have one, if not two, points of transfer where students move from one school to another. The need therefore to bridge the potential gaps still exists and perhaps is even greater today than it used to be.

Traditionally there has been a tendency for the higher school to dictate to the lower school what its program should be and what standards its students should reach before they could enter the higher school. This is a result of the application of the selective principle in education. It justified a higher school in assuming that no student should enter its rarified educational atmosphere unless he could show that he had properly prepared himself in a lower school by studying certain subjects and showing high levels of proficiency in them. Those who had not done so could not enter at all or were soon dropped out if they revealed weakness in their preparation. This principle may have given the higher school some right to make demands on a lower school, but, in a system which embraces the idea of universal education through high school, each school at every level of universal education has the responsibility for adapting its program to the age group for which it is designed. They can criticize each other only for failure to make the best adaptations to its student body. As this text has already indicated, the senior high school can no longer dictate to the junior high school or the junior high school to the elementary school. Instead they have the joint responsibility of cooperatively developing programs that are so closely articulated that students are able easily to make necessary adjustments as they move from a lower school designed for younger students to a higher one designed for more mature students. Some detailed suggestions as to how this can be done will be listed presently.

RELATIONS WITH OTHER LOCAL SCHOOLS

Practically every high school exists alongside other local schools which are not a part of the local school system. Some of these are private or parochial elementary or secondary schools and some are specialized schools such as business and music schools. There is usually a transfer of students and graduates between these schools and the public high school. They may also be full- or part-time training programs conducted by hospitals, businesses, and industries. All of these are in reality part of the educational opportunity available locally to the community's youth.

While it is the position of these authors that the public high school's program should so completely meet the needs of youth as to make some of these other schools unnecessary, yet public school administrators cannot legitimately take the attitude that education is a field into which private enterprise should not enter nor, of course, can they hold that parents have no right to send their children to other state-approved non-public schools if they prefer to do so. The basic policy controlling the attitude of the public secondary school principal toward these other local educational institutions and programs, therefore, can only be one of mutual respect and cooperation. Some of these offer instruction of a character or quality which only the best of high schools offer; for example, nurse's aide programs in a hospital, advanced voice or instrumental music education, or the specialized training required in a large local industry. In such cases it should be relatively easy for a high school student to arrange his program to permit part-time attendance at another local educational institution. The idea, for instance, that all music lessons must be taken in afterschool hours when the type or level of instruction desired is not available in the high school is a practice that prevents youth from taking full advantage of locally available educational opportunity. Consultations among those in charge of these schools and programs ought to result in mutually agreeable arrangements which would provide more flexibility of operation than sometimes prevails.

Such a policy on the part of the public secondary school should not mean, however, that the principal did not recognize that there are sometimes certain "fly-by-night" schools in some communities which offer little or no education to young people while charging high tuition. As experience identifies such schools to a principal he should withdraw cooperation. Sometimes appeals to the state department of education will make it possible for it to act to improve the situation. Sometimes all that can be done is to discourage students from attendance by giving them *general* advice to beware of this type of "school."

RELATIONS WITH INSTITUTIONS OF COLLEGE GRADE

These are the relations which have been of the greatest concern to high schools, and as the number of graduates who continue their education in institutions of college grade increases these relations will continue to be important concerns of the high school principal. The term "institutions of college grade" is one used to denote the types of institutions which require high school graduation for entrance and which sometimes specify all or part of the subjects to be taken in high school if a student is to be accepted. These include, of course, two- and four-year colleges as well as a variety of other educational institutions that do not necessarily go under the name of a college.

The traditional relationship between secondary schools and this group of institutions has been one of control by the colleges. Sometimes this control·was exercised delicately, sometimes brusquely, and always somewhat effectively. Under the conditions of the past it was natural for the institutions which were not only higher but older and better organized to assume such control. As high schools have become larger and better organized and as they have begun to serve other purposes than that of college preparation, control by the higher institutions has lessened.

THE CARNEGIE UNIT

One of the principal instruments of college control has been the Carnegie unit. A unit was defined as one academic subject studied for a year. One hundred and twenty clock hours were assumed to be required for a year's work in such a subject. Later, nonacademic subjects were evaluated in terms of this unit and where these required no home study sometimes a "double period" of recitation was expected. Strangely enough this unit was developed by the Carnegie Foundation for the Advancement of Teaching as a means of identifying institutions that were to be regarded as "colleges" and therefore eligible for participation in its retirement income plan for college professors. Only institutions which required four years of high school work amounting to at least fourteen Carnegie units as defined above and which met certain other requirements were to be considered colleges. A side effect of this decision was that a high school should be a four-year institution. Subsequently by action of various colleges, the Committee of Ten (1893), and the Committee on College Entrance Requirements (1899), this unit was used to control still further what the high school did. For example only certain subjects were recognized as college entrance subjects, and in the case of some of these, specified content had to be covered during a year's work before it could be considered as worth a unit of credit. So while the Carnegie Foundation did not create the Carnegie unit primarily as a means of college control of high schools, yet the subsequent actions of its board of trustees, composed largely of college presidents, tended to make it so and it is still one of the most influential controls exercised by many colleges over the high schools in large areas of this country.[1]

In an earlier chapter it is proposed that each normal youth, his parents, and the school should agree each year on what is a full-time load for each student. This would be determined as a part of the counseling and guidance service offered by the school. When he has succeeded with these yearly programs for the number of years of secondary education offered by the school he should be ready to graduate. This is to say that the school's program, as constituted, should have then done all for that student that it can do. The number of "units of credit" completed by him will have been right for him. If the school and community survey their graduates and are not satisfied with the results in that their patterns of behavior are not those which they think should result from completing secondary education, then the remedy is not to require more "units" for graduation, but rather to appraise the school's offering in the light of the desired behavior patterns and make such changes in the program as seem likely to produce better results. In the end, graduation would then represent not the "taking" of a fixed number of Carnegie units of work, but as much progress by each student toward certain kinds of desirable behavior patterns as it is possible for a good program of secondary education to accomplish. This of course requires that high schools more generally and more consistently identify the behavioral outcomes which they seek as a result of secondary education and develop programs of educative experience calculated to be of maximum assistance to youth in acquiring these behaviors. Then the importance of Carnegie units in secondary education will automatically decline.

However, the idea of the "unit" as a measure of progress through high schools has now become so thoroughly ingrained into secondary school administration that it is hard to see how it will be displaced, even though there is general willingness to agree that it is a poor measure of what ought to constitute progress toward graduation from high school. Since it is certain to be used until better measures of progress are developed and popularized, it probably will continue for some time to come to be a large influence in the relations between high schools and colleges.

[1] Ellsworth Tompkins and Walter H. Gaumnitz, *The Carnegie Unit: Its Origin, Status and Trends* (U.S. Office of Education, Bulletin No. 7; Washington, D.C.: Government Printing Office, 1954).

The high school principal is easily able to make the contacts necessary to the maintenance of cordial relationships with the responsible officers of higher institutions which are located in or near his own community. These contacts usually result in understandings which become the
basis of working arrangements. These direct contacts and the acquaint-
anceships which they develop usually create mutual respect which makes
it possible more easily to adjust difficulties as they arise. The principal
should approach these officials with the expectation of being received as
a full partner in the joint enterprise of providing appropriate educational
opportunity for local youth. At least such an approach shows that he
does not regard the heads of other institutions as his rivals in performing
the task and so he encourages a cooperative attitude. These personal contacts coupled with mutual community interests and the general desire
of the local community, which often is largely responsible for the support of both the high school and the local college, usually result in good
relations among these institutions.

The problem is somewhat different when the relations with nonlocal
higher institutions are considered. The problem these relations present
to a high school principal varies a great deal according to the section of
the country in which he is working. In the area east and north of Ohio,
West Virginia, and Maryland, higher education is not as freely available
to high school graduates in proportion to their number as in southern,
central, and western sections of the country. This northeast area has,
of course, many colleges and some of the best; but it also has a density of
high school population, fewer large state universities, and higher average
college tuition charges. Many of these "eastern" colleges enjoy a fine reputation which enables them to be more selective, thus further reducing
the immediate availability of college education to high school graduates
of this area. The relative scarcity of opportunity for higher education
in this area accounts for the large annual exodus of college-bound youth
to the west and south each fall. There is a reverse flow, too, but studies
of this situation show a strong flow south to Maryland and other colleges
to the south and an even larger volume to the west—to Ohio, Michigan,
Minnesota, Wisconsin, Indiana, Illinois, and Iowa.

This relative shortage in the supply of opportunity for higher education easily available to youth in this area creates a "seller's market"
which permits the colleges to make demands on these high schools which
they otherwise could not. This places many of the high school principals
of this area in a position of having to "cultivate" good relations with the
admissions officers of the colleges of this area. This is true also of the principals of high schools located in high economic level suburbs in other areas
of the country where a larger number of graduates hope to enter these
"eastern" colleges. They capitalize upon their friendship with the admis-

sions officers and with members of college faculties, upon the good records on the College Board Examinations which their graduates make, upon the good records students from their high schools have made in these colleges, and upon the connections various laymen in their communities have with some of these colleges. These relations are all carried on in the most dignified manner by both colleges and high schools, but there is no assumption on anyone's part that the relationship is one of equality. The basis for a truly cooperative approach therefore does not really exist.

ESTABLISHING COOPERATIVE PROGRAMS

This situation has been principally responsible for several efforts on the part of secondary schools to establish these relations on a better basis. The Eight-Year Study was one of these. It sought to show—and did show—that secondary schools could have more freedom in planning the high school programs of college-bound students without sending them to college less well prepared to succeed there than under present practices. More recent efforts by smaller groups of schools, such as a representative group from the Metropolitan School Study Council in the New York City area, have tried to set in motion arrangements which would be more satisfactory to them. Mutual understandings reached by this group are indicated by the following:

1. The secondary schools and colleges—public, private, two year, and four year—have a job to do in educating our youth, which can best be done when the basic policies underlying youth education are cooperatively agreed upon and accepted as the basis for action at both the school and college levels.

2. The secondary school and college must each be responsible for implementing these policies at its own level, but they should consult with each other regarding these programs so all will be informed and the two coordinated.

3. Admission to any college is a privilege and the responsible authorities of each college have the right to decide which candidates for entrance the college will accept.

4. The basis for this decision should be the best obtainable evidence of the candidate's competence to succeed in the college, as considered in terms of its offerings, standards and policies.

5. Acceptable evidence of ability to do course work and of ability to profit from and contribute to the out-of-class campus life of the college will vary from college to college.

6. The weight to be attached to evidence of ability to do work in any particular field of study will vary with the candidate's major fields of interest and with his plans for a career.

7. The pattern of high school courses which will produce the best evidence of competence to do college work may well vary with the candidate's

major fields of interest, his plans for a career, and the college to which he seeks admission.

8. Colleges and high schools have a responsibility for working out together the kinds and level of competence desired by the colleges so that high schools and prospective students may be fully informed.

9. Competence to read, write and speak English well is an important prerequisite for successful work in college and it is the responsibility of the high schools to develop this competence.

10. Candidates for entrance into professional schools or into any department requiring special competence should show the necessary special competence to an extent appropriate for freshman work. How a candidate secures this required level of special competence is not of major importance.

11. General intelligence as shown by the results of intelligence tests, competence to read, write and speak English well, and a good scholastic record in a challenging high school program are good predictors of success in college for persons of normal emotional balance and maturity.

12. Evidence of ability and willingness of a candidate to profit from and to contribute to out-of-class campus life is ordinarily best shown by the activities in which he has engaged in his school and community, the responsibilities he has borne, and the interests he has manifested while a student in the secondary school.

13. High schools have the responsibility of conferring frequently with students and their parents, of keeping them fully advised as to whether the student's work in their opinion seems to be of a character to qualify him for consideration by the college of his choice, and, if not, of suggesting alternatives. This responsibility implies that the schools should seek and colleges provide information which will help in the effective discharge of this obligation.

14. High schools have the responsibility for arranging programs for each student each year so that he has what is for him the maximum educational opportunity which that school can provide. As high schools are freed from blanket course prescriptions for college entrance, this responsibility is increased and the opportunity for discharging it enhanced.

15. High schools have the responsibility for maintaining counseling service adequate enough to give them detailed and exact knowledge of their students so that (1) they can properly advise them as students and (2) so they can supply factual information to the colleges on the basis of which colleges can, in part, make their decisions.

16. Adequate counseling implies that high schools will have the services of counselors properly trained in test administration, and that they will put into the student's records during his residence in the school, on their own initiative, the results of various standard tests which promise to be helpful in the process of (1) assisting him to plan his high school program; (2) assisting him to select a college that would serve him best; (3) assisting him to select a field of educational interest; and (4) assisting colleges to determine his desirability as a candidate. Colleges can assist in recommending useful practices.

17. High schools which do not as yet have adequate counseling staffs,

whose records are incomplete, and whose programs do not provide opportunities for students to develop specialized types of competence in keeping with their interests and abilities, should expect that colleges will necessarily require of the graduates of such high schools other evidence of competence to succeed in college than the schools are able to provide.

18. It is recognized that many secondary schools have extensive and adequate programs of testing and guidance under trained and experienced counselors. When such schools can present descriptions of their candidates for college admission in such terms as to satisfy the admissions officer of the college concerned, and when the schools have established with this college a reputation for accuracy, then these candidates should not be required to present additional evidences of their competency to do successful college work.

19. High schools should be responsible for assisting the colleges in making their decisions about whether or not to accept any student by supplying all pertinent information they can about each student, and by helping the colleges to interpret the available information. But neither high schools nor their principals should be asked to make routine categorical recommendations of acceptance or rejection.

The National Association of Secondary School Principals has created a Committee on School and College Relations to work on this problem on a national basis. Much of the work of the regional association, to be discussed later in this chapter, has had improved cooperative relations in mind. The Pattillo-Stout document, cited in the chapter bibliography, is illustrative of this effort in the North Central Association. The Southern Association has administrative arrangements for bringing high schools, state departments of education, and colleges into harmony on matters affecting high schools and colleges in this area. In the far west the University of California has exercised an undue influence not only upon high schools but upon junior colleges. Not all of this influence has been bad, of course, but few would claim that the relations which have been established are the results of free cooperation among these institutions. In sections of the country outside of the north east, high school principals have generally started from a more favorable position. In some states public colleges are required by law to accept high school graduates as college students. Stated thus, this would seem to be an unwise statute. But in operation it has not proven so to be. The high schools assume the responsibility of informing their students about requirements for success in various kinds of colleges. The colleges exercise the right to determine whether the student is competent in the fields basic to the kind of college education he seeks and, if not, he is required to register in college courses which will help him become competent. A high school student who anticipates attending an engineering college, for example, is informed by his high school how important competence in science and mathematics is. The college satisfies itself that the entering student has the required competence or registers him in courses which he needs in order to become competent. Failure to do so properly restricts his opportunity to continue his work toward a degree in engineering. Better transition between high school and college is thus made possible. At least under such a law both the colleges and the high school are mutually responsible and come to occupy a coordinate position in the process of providing educational opportunity for the youth of the state.

In other central, southern, and western states the supply of higher educational opportunity has in the past been more abundant in proportion to the demand, and consequently the colleges were not in as good a position to dominate the situation as they might have been. The result has been some ability on the part of the high schools to initiate and prosecute movements which have given them more freedom to plan the programs of their college-bound students than has been the case. The Michigan Agreement, quoted in Chapter 19, is a case in point. Under this the member high schools are released from certain college entrance requirements provided they develop their guidance programs and their personnel records so they are better able to plan the high school programs of their students and better able to show Michigan colleges in more detail what kinds of competence their high school graduates possess. This is a good example of high school principals, under the leadership of the state department of education, acting to secure the responsibilities and to accept the obligations of developing and conducting their own college entrance programs as equals with the colleges in so doing. The levels and types of relations between these colleges and these high schools naturally become quite different from the older, more dominating position of the colleges which tends to persist.

Improving Institutional Relations

Principals use a number of techniques and devices to improve articulation among the various institutions responsible for a youth's education.

1. The principal adopts for himself, and cultivates among the staff, the attitude that every other school is as eager to do good work with its students as he and they are. This is the basis for eliminating the tendency to find fault with pupils who come in from other schools and to speak disparagingly to them and their parents about other schools. This fault-finding attitude is simply an effort to build up one's own institution by tearing down another and it does not pay.

2. When an attitude as suggested above comes into control of the conduct of the principal and staff, the basis of a cooperative approach to other schools has been established. Joint action can then be taken by

persons and groups on problems, and mutually satisfactory solutions are far more likely to result. For this purpose joint committees are often set up: conferences between or among opposite "numbers" in the other schools are arranged. These bring together those carrying various types of administrative or teaching responsibilities in the different schools for the purpose of developing greater integration of practices and program. Each must be willing to make adjustments until workable plans are formulated.

3. Representatives of the staff of the receiving school make contacts with incoming students in their present schools. These schools welcome such contacts and adjust their programs to permit them. This begins the process of orienting these students to what will be their new school. Information is presented in oral and written form and every effort is made to increase the student's pleasurable anticipation of entrance into the new school. Meetings with their parents in the semester prior to entrance as well as just after entrance are sometimes helpful. One high school has used such a parents' meeting as a way of meeting some of the problems growing out of high school fraternities by pointing out the need for, and types of, home and school cooperation called for under these conditions.

4. Opportunity is sometimes provided for incoming students to visit the receiving school in the semester before actual entrance. Where such students have no other way of becoming acquainted with their new school building this arrangement often makes them feel much more at home. This is often made the occasion for a welcome of the new students by representatives of the student organization of the receiving school. Sometimes new schedules of classes are far enough developed so that it is possible for these students to be shown the classrooms in which they will have their classes. This can easily be done if an "orientation" period is held for new students prior to the regular opening of school. It not only helps to banish the "lost" feeling that new students often have but helps get the school off to a good start the first day of the new semester.

5. Efforts are made to establish a friendly attitude of welcome to new students among the entire student body. This is in contrast to the practice in some schools of taking advantage of incoming students' unfamiliarity to play crude jokes on them and to engage in hazing. There is little use in having the student council extend a welcome to new students unless the general attitude of the great majority of students is friendly and helpful. There is no place at all in a high school for some of the types of hazing which still occur in a few schools.

6. Careful coordination of content, methods, and level of expectation in such continuing subjects as reading and English, arithmetic and mathematics, arts courses, and health and physical education helps

to create the feeling in a new student that he is ready and able to begin succeeding in his new schoolwork. Failure to do this results in a feeling of maladjustment which is often reflected in poor discipline, unnecessary absence, and early dropping out of school. Standards of acceptable school conduct in a higher school should also tend to develop out of those of the lower school.

7. Good sets of cumulative records that follow the student up through his entire school career are an absolute essential. The reasons for this and desirable types to be provided have already been presented in this text so they only need to be mentioned here.

8. Factual reports from the higher school—college, senior, or junior high school—to the lower sending school on the success of its former students in the higher school are helpful if it is clear that they are sent in a spirit of helpfulness and not in dissatisfaction. That is why they should be factual in nature with a minimum of opinion or interpretation. Let the lower school interpret them and ask for the judgments of the higher school if it wants them. If such reports can be sent and received in good spirit they can become the basis for conferences which can result in improvements in programs and practices in both the higher and lower school. Accounts of good current practices are to be found in the *National Elementary Principal* for February, 1952. The Day Junior High School (Newtonville, Mass.) has a booklet entitled *Entering* which has attracted considerable attention. (See Chapter 23 bibliography.)

9. Arrangements for contacts with employing firms for whom school-leavers and non-college-bound graduates go to work can be made the basis for changes in school programs, which will mean that the school has contributed more to initial employability and thus helped its former students get a better start on a job. Where a school conducts a diversified occupations or distributive industry program this task falls naturally into the hands of the coordinators of these programs. Learning to work on a new job in industry is a very real part of a youth's education. In some industries he goes through an industry-run program of work education. There is no more reason for being willing to accept inarticulation between educational programs on the job and in the school than between units of the school. Where such efforts are made, initial employability increases and job turnover and youth unemployment decrease. During the depression, Salt Lake City enjoyed the lowest level of youth unemployment partly because the schools made an effort to establish a close coordination between the schools and the city's industries, which were employing recent students or graduates of the high schools.[2]

[2] J. L. Bergstresser, "Counseling and the Changing High School Curriculum," NASSP *Bulletin*, 24, No. 91 (May, 1940), 1–100.

These indicate some of the important ways in which individual principals and high schools can proceed individually to develop better relations between and among the schools and institutions which all together are responsible for the education of individual youths. Other ways exist by which groups of schools work together so that a more completely unified educational experience may be enjoyed by youth generally. We turn to these next.

Relations with Regional Associations

There are six regional associations which together blanket the country: the New England, the Middle States, the North Central, the Southern, and the Western Associations of Colleges and Secondary Schools, and the Northwestern Association of Secondary and Higher Schools. The general purpose served by these six is to provide a method by which the secondary schools and the colleges of these regions may reach some common understandings on problems of mutual concern in each region. The principal differences among them arise out of the amount of initiative taken by each of the associations and the degree of control exercised over individual member colleges and secondary schools. The New England Association, true to the traditions of its region, has been disinclined to exert more than a mild influence on the conduct of any individual college or high school. The North Central Association, followed closely by the Southern Association, has enforced its ideas on member high schools and colleges to the point of taking disciplinary action against them. The tendency toward such activities on the part of a regional association seems to have been associated with the stress on standardization and accreditation. Where and when an association assumed a great deal of responsibility for raising the standards in schools and colleges and used withholding of accreditation as a means of enforcing standards, it has tended to act both as its own law enforcement officer and judge. Where and as the accrediting function has been left to state departments of education, where in a number of states it legally belongs, the associations' influence tends to be of a more professional nature. The trend in all of them is toward the latter, but on occasion the exercise of something like police power by an association over its members seems still to serve a good purpose. A recent example is that of the North Central Association, which has undertaken to control abuses in college athletics in its region. A good example of the more professional approach to the problem of the improvement of secondary schools is the development of the *Evaluative Criteria* by the combined action of all these associations. These criteria serve as self-evaluation instruments by which a high school faculty can study its school and determine the strong and weak points as compared with other good high schools. The faculty can then decide at what points it thinks efforts at improvement should be made.[3]

As the various committees and commissions of the regional associations conduct research, issue reports, and conduct discussions dealing with the problems of concern to their colleges and high schools they become a forum before which high school principals can bring matters of mutual concern to the colleges and high schools. Any high school principal or a group from any state thus has a place to which they can repair with any problem of institutional relations which requires consensus of agreement among schools or colleges. These associations thus can serve as media for the improvement of institutional relations among large groups of schools and colleges over a wide region where the efforts of individual principals not acting as a group would be far less effective. Membership of a high school in a regional association therefore gives the principal another effective means to use in his efforts at improving institutional relations.

Relations with the State Department of Education

The legal fact of the states' responsibility for education within their borders is fully considered in Part One of this book. The corollary of this is the responsibility of local schools to the state through the state department of education. A principal, as the head of a high school together with the superintendent of schools, is often made responsible for carrying out locally the decisions of the legislature and/or state department of education. He has no choice in many of these matters and the state departments of education often are clothed with power by the legislature to see that these duties are performed by local school administrators. The principal is at least jointly responsible for carrying out the state's program of education. If instruction in the evils of alcoholic beverages is required by law or regulation of the state department of education, if a specified number of minutes per week of physical education is required, if driver education is required, if American history is required in specified years, the principal bears a responsibility for seeing that in his school these requirements are fulfilled. So also is the case with matters relating to enforcement of compulsory at-

[3] For an account of how the *Evaluative Criteria* are used in Indiana, see C. G. F. Franzen, C. W. Jung, Otto Hughes, and others, *Use of Evaluative Criteria in Indiana Secondary Schools* (Bloomington: School of Education, Indiana University, 1954). A different plan is presented in California Association of Secondary School Principals, *Procedures for Appraising California High Schools* (Sacramento: The Association, 1954).

tendance laws, with attendance reports, with teacher certification, with fire drills, with bus operation, with sanitary conditions in the building, and with reports called for in connection with reimbursement of money spent locally on programs supported in part by federal or state funds. No experienced principal needs to be told that he has many relationships with his state's department of education.

The proper discharge of these and similar responsibilities together with the maintenance of instruction at a good qualitative level are usually necessary before a high school is placed on the state's list of accredited high schools. This is a program begun about seventy-five years ago which has spread to many states. Being a high school accredited by the state means that the school and its graduates enjoy certain standings not available to nonaccredited high schools. In some states graduates of accredited high schools may enter public higher institutions in that state without examination. In some of the regional associations, state accreditation is essential for membership and membership means that a school's graduates are more readily accepted by out-of-state colleges. Accreditation also means in some states full participation in any state aid funds available. It is generally regarded by a community as a sign that its high school is a good high school and is therefore a standing which no high school principal is willing to have his school lose.

Most state departments wich accredit high schools set up some system of inspection to be complied with by all high schools desiring to become or remain accredited schools. Sometimes this is done by requiring certain reports; sometimes by a personal visit from a member of the state department, and the principal is usually the local school official to whom he looks for cooperation. A record for prompt and efficient cooperation is of value not only to the principal personally but also to the school system of which he is a part. On the basis of confidence thus built up, it is often possible for the school to get approval for projects and activities which it wants to undertake but which may require some modification of the procedures or programs usually found in accredited schools. Or it may lead to the inclusion of the school in a group which, under state department of education leadership, is undertaking some more or less experimental procedure. For in spite of being shorthanded, the better state departments try to find time not only to carry out their mandatory duties concerned with seeing that high schools reach minimum standards but also to exercise some leadership in helping high schools to become better schools. As is indicated in Part One, this is a function of state departments of education which ought to be paramount. It is a counterpart to the theory advocated in this text that the high school principal reaches his highest level of professional competence as he devotes his energy to activities designed to improve the

the school rather than those designed merely to keep it operating smoothly.

A good relationship with the state department of education is desirable then not only because it may succeed in getting or continuing the accredited standing of a school, but also because it may secure approval for the initiation of projects or programs of special value in a particular school or may result in the inclusion of the school in a group selected to act as "pilot schools" in improving secondary education in the state. In either case the way is opened with approval of the state department of education for creative activities or for innovations which keep the school and its staff alive and alert to new developments in education. More and more the better state departments of education are inclined to improve their state programs of secondary education by inviting the high schools of the state, or representatives thereof, to join with it in making decisions about projects to undertake and about how to organize to accomplish whatever is decided upon. They less and less resort to the power to compel compliance which they undoubtedly have. Less and less do we find them announcing decisions and securing compliance by threats to withhold funds or accreditation. Under these improved working relationships principals have a much better chance to initiate suggestions than ever before and to secure opportunity to participate in the process of developing the plans required to put them into force.

Stronger State High School Principals' Associations Needed

In this situation state associations of high school principals have a new and enlarged opportunity. State departments of education find it increasingly difficult to ignore suggestions made to it which have the backing of such a state association. They are also increasingly eager for such contacts with state associations. So state high school principals' associations have less excuse than ever for being as ineffectual as many of them have been.

In the past the tendency has been for such associations to exist on paper with officers and dues and to hold only an annual meeting at which a few talks were given. Those which were a year-round working organization with a program were the rare exceptions to the rule. Some states only now are developing any such organization at all. In some states, where small high schools predominate, principals report that superintendents have not welcomed the idea of an association of high school principals. But now most states have the beginnings of an association and the problem is to make all of them into effective year-round organizations. Their principal purpose should be to provide an agency through which principals could study and act on problems of importance to secondary education in the state. The officers—at least the president —should be chosen because he is known to be an energetic proponent of improved educational opportunity for all youth in the state. There should be a working executive committee to help decide upon the activities upon which the state association should concentrate. There should then be committees which would be working throughout the year upon important problems. These should be action committees responsible for more than making a report at the state-wide meetings. The state-wide meetings held at least once a year would then become action-planning and decision-making meetings with plenty of discussion, rather than sessions devoted to listening to the presentation of a series of unrelated topics from which seldom comes any incentive to action. The work of such an association commands the respect of state departments of education, of the state superintendents' associations, boards of education associations, and of the schools of education in a state.

The Life Adjustment Education movement brought an increased activity to a number of state associations. In Kansas an active state committee got behind this idea and promoted it on a state-wide basis. The California state association operates through a number of state-wide committees. North Carolina, with a state association which is just getting on its feet, is an example of one whose work centers on problems of a professional nature rather than on high school athletics, state contests, and other more incidental matters. Michigan, Illinois, New Jersey, and several other states furnish good examples of active and forceful state associations. Properly functioning state associations of high school principals present an avenue through which the state-wide group of principals can develop relations and exercise influence as a group on matters where principals working singly and individually on improving institutional relation cannot be expected to be fully effective.

DISCUSSION GROUPS AND STATE ASSOCIATIONS

Most states are too large for it to be possible for the high school principals to meet more than once or twice a year as a state group. Even when they do the size of the group often operates to make full discussion of problems and issues difficult. Opportunity for full and free discussion is desirable, for it brings out various points of view and new ideas. It also serves as a learning experience as each member of the group has an opportunity not only to contribute from his own thinking and experience but to enlarge his own perception of the situation by hearing the other members of the group. The desirability of such discussions among groups of principals who work in neighboring high school districts prompted the National Association of Secondary School Principals some years ago to promote the organization of discussion groups on a nation-wide basis for the purpose of considering the reports of its national Committee on Issues and Functions of Secondary Education. Many such groups were then organized and some still continue and there was general agreement as to their value.

This experience prompts the suggestion that, since state-wide meetings of the high school principals' associations are not frequently possible, these associations should utilize this technique and promote the creation of such a number of discussion groups in each state as is necessary in order for each principal to be a member without too long a trip from his home base. These groups could then meet from three to six times each year for a late afternoon session, dinner, and an evening meeting which closes early enough to permit getting home that evening. The discussions should generally grow out of some professional matters which are of real concern to each particular group, rather than from a set program prepared by the state association. Nevertheless on occasion this association could ask these groups to give attention to state-wide problems on which it is formulating policy and planning action. The result would be more unity of thought and action among the principals of the state and its components and a closer association among principals in these discussion group areas. A strong state association program for advancing the interests of secondary education within the state could be developed and, given the support of a state department of education which was willing to work on a cooperative basis, could account for sound and rapid improvement in secondary education in the state.

The values in promoting understandings and good institutional relations inherent in these discussion groups are such that, where it is not possible for a whole state to organize them, it would be desirable for more neighboring groups of high school principals to initiate action toward creating them. A good example of this is the organization of the suburban high school principals around Philadelphia. There, with the cooperation of the colleges of the area having teacher education programs, such a locally initiated group exists, which meets several times a year. Committees are appointed to work on problems. They usually meet at three or four o'clock (prior to the dinner meeting of the group) and from time to time report to the group during the evening, and discussion ensues. It would be a good thing if in many areas of the country some of the leading high school principals would get together and call an initial meeting of all the principals of the area to see if the formation of such a group in the area for consideration and discussion of pertinent professional matters would not serve a useful purpose. The resulting degree of mutual understanding, good will, fellowship, and professional growth over a few years would astound the more skeptical principals in the area.

BUILDING INSTITUTIONAL RELATIONS A TEAM JOB

The concentration of attention in this chapter on the principal's function in creating and developing good relations between and among the other institutions with which it is associated, should not be interpreted to mean that this is a one-man job. This book is devoted to the work of the high school principal, and hence his function in this matter is emphasized. Other members of the staff, however, also have important roles to play in building good institutional relations with the various types of organizations with which their particular work in a high school throws them in contact. The good high school principal recognizes this and urges other members of the school staff to share this responsibility. He sees himself as a sort of coordinator of a school-wide program designed to establish and improve the working relations with all the local, state, regional, and national groups whose programs and activities have a bearing on those of the school which he heads. He recognizes that the direction of improvement in this school and the rate at which he and the staff can make progress is influenced by what other educational institutions are thinking and doing. No school "lives unto itself alone" and therefore is, and ought to be, influenced by, and be an influence upon, other people and groups who have a sincere interest in the education and welfare of American youth. Developing good institutional relations therefore become an important aspect of school administration.

Some Points to Consider

1. Try out one or more sections of the *Evaluative Criteria* on some high school with which you are familiar.

2. Use a section or more of the Ransom Check List mentioned in the text in another connection in the same way.[4]

3. Considering the sections of the two which are most closely related to the high school's program, what differences are there in the type of information about the school each seeks to evaluate?

4. Of what importance to a school system are city-wide meetings of the high school principals and teachers in a city school system? Of what importance are meetings of the principals and teachers of elementary and junior high schools with the principal and/or teachers to which the students of the former

[4] W. L. Ransom. "How Well Does Your High School Rate on the Ten Imperative Needs of Youth?" NASSP *Bulletin*, No. 164, October, 1949.

two usually go? Which kind of meeting usually occurs the most frequently in most school systems? Is this good?

5. How do European schools, which do not use the Carnegie unit, determine progress and graduation?

6. Under what if any conditions, would you favor the use of such a system in this country?

7. Some vocational schools use "clock hours of instruction" instead of the Carnegie unit and allow "credit" in a course if a minimum number of jobs are satisfactorily completed. Is this a better plan on which to base progress and graduation than on units?

8. If Neuberger is correct in the article cited in the reference list for this chapter, what are some of the things we must get done if we want better state departments of education?

9. How do you rate your state department of education on leadership? on efforts at cooperative action with the schools of the state? on its tendency to dictate to local school systems?

10. Does your state have a strong high school principals' association? What are some of its best recent achievements? What committees does it have at work between its meetings? Can you suggest some areas where the work of a state-wide committee of the high school principals' association might do some good?

Further Reading

California Association of Secondary School Principals. *Procedures for Appraising California High Schools.* Sacramento: The Association, 1954.

Cooperative Study of Secondary School Standards. *Evaluative Criteria,* Washington, D.C.: American Council on Education, 1950.

Day Junior High School. *Entering.* Public Schools: Newtonville, Mass.

Department of Elementary School Principals. "Orientation of Pupils for the Secondary School," *National Elementary Principal,* 31, No. 4, February, 1952.

———. "Public School Students Excel at Princeton," *E.J.S. Developments,* Vol. III, No. 3, March, 1955.

Franzen, C. G. F., C. W. Jung, Otto Hughes, and others. *Use of Evaluative Criteria in Indiana Secondary Schools.* Bloomington: School of Education, Indiana University, 1954.

Neuberger, R. L. "The Decay of State Governments," *Harper's Magazine,* October, 1953, pp. 34–41.

Ransom, W. L. "How Well Does Your High School Rate on the Ten Imperative Needs of Youth?" NASSP *Bulletin,* No. 164 (October, 1949), pp. 8–46.

Tompkins, Ellsworth, and Walter H. Gaumnitz. *The Carnegie Unit: Its Origin, Status and Trends.* U.S. Office of Education; Bulletin No. 7; Washington, D.C.: Government Printing Office, 1954.

In Part Six the authors have assumed that a typical American community is intensely interested in its youth and its school and in itself as a place where its youth live and grow. Part Six therefore considers some of the community activities in which the school may take the lead. It also suggests some of the studies that the school and its students may undertake on the basis of which better plans can be made for the development of the community and its school. The high school principal ought to be among the leaders in such a program of school-community betterment; certainly the quality of his suggestions and evaluations should increase the community's respect for him as a person, for the school he heads, and for public education as a means of sound social progress.

Part Six

THE HIGH SCHOOL AND ITS COMMUNITY

Chapter 24

THE SCHOOL STUDIES THE
COMMUNITY AND ITS YOUTH

> The democratic problem in education is not primarily a problem of
> training children; it is the problem of *making a community* within which
> children cannot help growing up to be democratic, intelligent, disciplined
> to freedom, reverent of the goods of life, and eager to share in the tasks of
> the age. A school cannot produce this result; nothing but a community
> can do so.[1]

THE SCHOOL is but one of many educational agencies in the community;
in many respects, parents, friends, motion pictures, radio and television,
and newspapers influence students more than teachers do. Yet high
school faculties often proceed as if they were the only educative influence affecting youth in the community and as if, irrespective of all other
educative influences and of even the youth themselves, a high school must
be a good high school if it is a carbon copy of other high schools. Each
high school, to be good, has to be as different from other high schools
as the needs of its community and its youth require. In communities
where the great majority of the high school students enter college the
success of the school in preparing students to enter the colleges of their
choice may be one of the important criteria for judging the effectiveness
of the school. However, in general, good public high schools are not
necessarily good because they succeed in having a few of their superior
students admitted to highly selective colleges. They must also help all
their students to success in their current living, provide appropriate
learning activities for them in terms of the experiences they have already had, and help them to adjust satisfactorily to the situations in
which they are going to be placed. This requires that every school
study its community and its students because no community with its
student body is exactly like any other. Externally good high schools

[1] Joseph K. Hart, *The Discovery of Intelligence* (New York: Appleton-Century-
Crofts, Inc., 1924), p. 383.

may look alike, but actually there are real differences born of the social setting of which each is a part.

There are industrial centers where working mothers are the rule rather than the exception. There are villages where mothers seldom work outside the home. There are college towns where adult interests are chiefly intellectual, and many communities where adult interests range widely but only occasionally touch the intellectual. In areas not widely separated, there are cities with a breezy western culture, and others colored by a German or a French background, or by the traditions of the Deep South. There are cities where most of the high school graduates move away to make their lives and their homes. There are others where most people remain to live out their lives in the communities where they attended high school. In some communities children have learned to play together successfully and have acquired wholesome interests; in others they have not. Externally these towns and cities may look alike; yet they differ from each other in ways that a really good high school must take into account.

Need for Local Studies

STUDY THE YOUTHS' COMMUNITY

To make certain that the school supplements instead of duplicates the educational experiences students obtain in the community, and to know what learning activities are appropriate and meaningful to students in the environment in which they live, the staff of the school must study both the community in which the youth live and the youth who live in the community. Serviceable schools grow out of the economic, social, and cultural soils of their communities. Unless high schools in America can gear their programs into community life, they will idle along in neutral until other institutions will rise up to take their places just as the academy replaced the Latin grammar school and the high school replaced the academy. Students are what they are because of what their experiences have made them—each is the effect of these experiences on his particular self. To be most educative, the activities of the school program must be based upon the students' experiences, their achievements, and their interests, and upon the cultural pattern of the community. Just as a skillful teacher probes to find what a student knows and understands in order to determine the most profitable approach to use in presenting subject matter to him, so will the staff of a good school study the students of the school and their community backgrounds to determine the broad outlines of the educational program. The high school needs to know and to take into account the effect on its youth of such significant facts about the community as these:

A. Population Characteristics

1. Nationality pattern and racial composition of all people
2. Historical and geographical backgrounds
3. Percentages of different age groups in the population
4. Numerical ratio of males to females
5. The number of children in public, private, and religious schools
6. Health and safety statistics
7. Stability of family life
8. Mobility of families
9. Occupations of the people
10. Educational status of the people

B. Institutional Relations

1. Between the schools and the park and recreation boards
2. Among youth-serving organizations
3. Between management and labor groups
4. Between urban and rural agencies

C. Value Systems

1. Attitudes toward religious and spiritual values
2. Attitudes toward secondary and higher education
3. Recreational interests of the people
4. Quality of citizenship (toleration of crime, delinquency, and political corruption)
5. Aesthetic appreciations of the people

D. Social Stratification

1. Groups growing from economic status
2. Minority groups
3. Degree of cohesion and cooperation among the people

E. Power Structure

1. The places where power resides
2. Leadership groups and individual leaders who make fundamental decisions
3. The influence of radio stations, television stations, and newspapers
4. Patterns of interpersonal relationships
5. The way in which public opinion is formed

F. The Physical Setting

1. Natural resources and how they are used
2. Industrial, residence, or slum areas which are changing
3. Static industrial, residence, or slum areas

Information concerning such items is especially significant for the student of the local community, but it is significant as well for the student of the state, federal, and international community. For example, when sociologists observe a lack of balance in numbers between the sexes in any community, they look for the effect of this imbalance upon the stability of family life. In the same way many students of the national community point to the increase in juvenile delinquency which has accompanied the drafting of young men for military service and the resulting nation-wide imbalance between the sexes of draft age.

As local communities become less self-sufficient and more interdependent, individuals and institutions become interested members of larger and overlapping communities. As education is increasingly considered a state function to be supported by the state, persons interested in local schools feel a deepened sense of belonging to the state community. While controls were exercised by the federal government during the war and immediately afterward, everyone knew that he belonged to the national community. At the present time most of us are aware of the place of our nation in a world community. Thus the concept of community education is dynamic rather than limited and provincial. It serves as a unifying and not a divisive force.

Other Youth-Serving Agencies

The study of the community should certainly provide for the identification of its other youth-serving agencies and an analysis of the services provided for youth by each of them. Education and the school are so often considered synonymous that the part played in youth education by the many outside agencies is often overlooked or, at least, only partially recognized. Certainly the high school is the central institution, and in most communities the only institution, devoted solely to the organized education of youth. In spite of this, the high school should not, and in the final analysis cannot, operate in isolation from the total life of the community.

In our earlier and more simply organized society the everyday work and life of the community outside the school provided a very real educational laboratory for the growing adolescent. The school was for many if not for most youths a supplementary agency. With the growing complexity of modern social and economic life, organized agencies have of necessity arisen to achieve what in an earlier age was accomplished in the simple, direct living of the small community. The expansion of the school is an example of this growth. Parallel to this is the initiation and growth of a multitude of other youth-serving organizations of a recreational, character-building, religious, or service nature operating under private or public auspices. Although their primary purpose may not be strictly defined as educational in the sense that the purpose of the school is educational, yet these agencies, by the very fact that they provide activities for youth and supervise and direct the use of some fraction of the youth's time, are a very definite part of the program of youth education in any community.

In appraising the educational program of the community, the critical high school principal must not only evaluate the activities of the school but recognize as well all of the other educative agencies and influences of the community. In a typical town this appraisal will generally involve a complex pattern of agencies and activities. The simplest first approach to the problem is to observe the places and the ways in which adolescent youth spend their time. A sample list of this nature can be revealing, for it will bring to light the part-time work experience available to youth in the community with its educational implications. It will show the religious organizations and their varied programs of character education. Numerous organized youth groups, such as the Boy Scouts, the YMCA and YWCA, local recreation groups, will be in the list, as will the numerous commercial and semicommercial agencies such as the theaters, dance halls, skating rinks, pool halls, the corner drugstore, and other local hangouts. All of these, whether we like it or not, affect youth's education.

YOUTH-SERVING AGENCIES MANY AND VARIED

It is no simple matter to describe or even classify the many organized agencies that in one way or another may serve the needs of youth in any community. Every community will have its own pattern of organizations that differs to some extent from that of any other community. The services provided by the schools vary between communities and states. The services provided by a particular agency or organization may differ considerably from community to community as the communities themselves vary in structure and organization. A brief overview of the numerous types of organizations characteristic of typical communities is not offered as a specific pattern, but it at least points out the wealth of resources ordinarily available to youth.

An impressive number of national youth organizations extends throughout the nation, and there is scarcely a community that does not have one or more of these local youth groups. Prominent among the national agencies are what may be termed the character organizations represented by the Boy Scouts and the Girl Scouts of America, the Camp Fire Girls, the Hi-Y and Gray Y of the Young Men's Christian Association and the Girl Reserves of the Young Women's Christian Association, the Catholic Youth Organization, and the Young Men's Hebrew Association. Serving primarily rural youth are the extensive 4-H Clubs, the Future Farmers of America, and the Future Homemakers of America.

Service organizations such as the Junior Red Cross are active in all parts of the country. All the churches sponsor young people's organizations. Naturally some local groups are more vigorous and attract more young people than others do, but here again the picture changes with each community. Besides these local units of national organizations, most communities have their own active youth groups of one kind or another.

In addition to youth organizations, numerous public and private agencies provide particular services for youth. Some governmental agencies include types of health service in their programs. Recreational facilities or activities are provided in many communities by both private agencies and special governmental organizations. Welfare agencies, public and private, offer various types of special services for youth. Although many communities may be without youth-serving agencies, it is safe to say that the limitations in youth services in most other communities are more likely to arise from failure effectively to use and coordinate the existing services. This raises the whole question of policy in the direction and coordination of youth-serving agencies.

DIVERSITY OF CONTROL OF YOUTH-SERVING AGENCIES

The secondary school principal who accepts the broader aspect of his responsibility and becomes concerned over the lack of coordination among the youth-serving agencies of his community immediately faces the fact of the diversity of control of these agencies. Only in the school or in very closely related agencies will the principal have direct supervisory responsibility. Whether or not he believes that the school should have the entire responsibility of providing for youth education and welfare in the community, the fact remains that the political and social philosophy of the people of the United States has consistently supported the practice of diversity of control of our educational and welfare organizations. Although this diversity often creates problems of coordination and results in duplication of efforts, in practice there are substantial reasons why our democracy has supported it.

To those who are enamored with simplicity of organization and the seeming neatness and precision of centralized administration, the vision of the school as the single and over-all organization directing all youth activity in the community has great appeal. Such central control is presumed by many to have the merit of efficiency, but in spite of what may appear to be its advantages, the gain in efficiency in the long run may be questioned. The American philosophy of freedom for the individual and for groups to develop in their own ways has permitted and even stimulated the growth of private youth-serving agencies and organizations.

Although it appears that the complexities of modern social and economic conditions and our expansion of the concept of education have resulted in the steady increase or broadening of the activities of the school, it would be an error to assume that the school or, indeed, any other agency will gain control of the many other youth-serving organizations. There is much evidence that the vitality and the flexibility of American community life have arisen from the freedom of many leaders to exercise initiative and imagination. Certainly decentralization and coordinated effort have provided a protection against totalitarian controls. One has but to examine the authoritarian and single control of all youth activities in the Communist nations to recognize the total incompatibility of such a system with the spirit and practice of American democracy. The variations in the American community youth services from place to place and from time to time are part and parcel of a dynamic social organization.

The role that private organizations have had in pioneering new youth services is often not fully recognized. Many services now performed by schools were first initiated by private groups. Recreational activities and selected aspects of vocational education and health programs are examples of this. Many services are today performed by cooperative efforts of the schools, other governmental agencies, and private organizations. Private agencies are often in a better position than the schools to pioneer a service and help develop a public realization of the need for it as a part of the school program.

DEFINING THE FUNCTIONS OF DIFFERENT AGENCIES

In a general way the functions of different national youth organizations, the school, and other governmental and private agencies are defined by the purpose for which they were established and by their existing programs. However, there is a great deal of flexibility in the specific activities that any agency may perform in any local community. The policy of most organizations not only permits but encourages flexibility and adaptation to local needs. Thus an effective program in any local community largely depends upon the degree to which different organizations adapt their programs to the needs of the local area and upon the degree to which the activities of these organizations supplement one another in order to provide an integrated and comprehensive program of youth services for the community.

Many examples may be cited to illustrate variations in the functions undertaken by the school in different communities in conjunction with other organizations. Recreation is a typical one. Many different coordinated programs have been developed in this field: joint municipal and school programs; privately sponsored associations functioning in a cooperative relation to the school; a comprehensive program initiated by the school but drawing into a coordinated program many private organizations; and coordinated recreation programs of school, church, and other organizations.

Likewise, the health program of the school will need to be determined by the total services furnished by other organizations. The primary objective of any group of community organizations should be to provide the most comprehensive program of services of which the total resources of all agencies are capable.

Although the total community program must be a coordinated program with all agencies cooperating, the school is the central agency in most communities. Certainly it is responsible for the largest body of services, and for this reason the school authorities may appropriately take the lead in undertaking local coordination. The type of coordination here suggested will not, ordinarily, occur by accident. Local organization and machinery for coordination and integration of services are usually needed. Who besides the high school principal in a community can see more clearly the importance of effective coordination or be more eager to help the community's youth get the full benefits of a well-rounded, closely articulated program of education and welfare?

ORGANIZING FOR EFFECTIVE COORDINATION

The methods by which a better local coordination may be secured must be adapted to the particular community. In the small community the informal personal contacts between people who are active in different organizations and groups can provide a reasonably effective integration among the different agencies without much systematic formal organization. Certainly the high school principal, as the head of the most comprehensive youth-serving agency, should take an active part in initiating such activities and organization as are needed. Much will depend, of course, upon the degree to which the school staff and particularly the school administrators already share in these activities and in the general life of the community. The active school administrator will often be called upon to serve on community committees and councils sponsoring various youth activities. Participation in the activities of service clubs, churches, and other community organizations provides school people with many opportunities for informally developing a better understanding with those who may be active in developing varied nonschool youth services.

However, as communities become larger in size and more complex in structure, personal acquaintance and informal relations between the personnel in schools and in other youth-serving groups may no longer be adequate. The very variety and number of agencies may make it desirable to organize planning groups to study the total community youth needs, develop wider knowledge and understanding of the function of each organization or agency, and establish some allocation of responsibility for an integrated program. The structure and scope of such planning bodies may take many forms. Community recreation councils have been organized in many localities. Somewhat broader in purpose have been the youth councils established in numerous communities. The Council of Social Agencies typically provides the coordinating force in welfare activities. Whatever form such councils may take in meeting the needs of a particular community, they can and do perform a necessary function in the modern complex community life. Basically such councils are not and should not be administrative bodies but should be a means for seeing that the various operating agencies fulfill their responsibilities. They should provide for the representation of all groups that can contribute in any way to youth service in general or at least of those in the area of the service toward whose coordination they are working. Although specific situations may prove exceptions, in general the actions of such councils are strengthened if the membership includes lay citizens as well as professional workers. And in any such council the representatives of the school are in a central position.

There is no formula for knowing when to start a community youth council, but an intelligent school administrator certainly should be among the first to discern the need if it exists and is the logical person in the community to take the lead in forming such a coordinating body.

THE DIRECTION OF UNORGANIZED YOUTH ACTIVITIES

The alert high school administrator has other opportunities besides providing active leadership in coordinating and encouraging the work of the organized youth-serving groups in the community. He should also be influential in directing, and perhaps assisting in, the establishment of controls over the unorganized youth life in the community. A considerable part of recreation and amusement in American communities is offered by private commercial enterprises. The relatively high degree of freedom extended American youth, together with the range and anonymity of action made possible by the automobile, places a real responsibility on the commercial amusement agencies to enforce reasonable moral and social standards. By and large, commercial agencies probably wish to do so, but frequently neither the individual operator nor the community at large has defined such standards or made any concerted effort to reach agreement on them.

The high school principal working with students, parent groups, and other community agencies can provide the necessary leadership in the formulation of standards. Parents as an unorganized group are often not in possession of the facts regarding the commercial amusement centers in the community and are slow to get into action even when they think that "something ought to be done." It is not the job of the high school principal to set himself up as an amateur policeman or to supplant the parents in the direction of youth, but he is responsible for ascertaining the facts about his community; he can insure that accurate information is available to parents, can take the lead in encouraging some uniform attitude among them, and can urge them to take group action.

The principal should also work with the youth in the school in influencing their use of commercial amusement in the community. The proprietors of commercial establishments are very often willing to cooperate with school and parents in setting and enforcing reasonable moral and social standards if they are defined and agreed upon. The high school principal is the liaison between these groups. When the standards are violated, he will be able to mobilize public opinion and, in extreme cases, to see that the community or legal controls are enforced.

Study the Community's Youth

Chapter 18 of this book indicated that the school staff should gather information concerning such items as the attendance, health, native ability, and achievement of its students. In addition, the staff that studies the community relationship of its students will be interested in such items as these:

1. Elimination from school and its local causes
2. Retardation in school and its local causes
3. Work experiences of students
4. Jobs or colleges that the graduates and former students enter and their success there
5. Social adjustment of students and graduates
6. Likes and dislikes of the students
7. Goals the students hold for themselves
8. Scientific attitudes held by students and graduates
9. Civic competence of students and graduates
10. Recreational interests
11. Interests gained in the school that are retained
12. Families established by the graduates
13. Proportion of high school graduates who remain in the community
14. Framework of values established by the students and the graduates

EXAMPLES OF YOUTH AND COMMUNITY STUDY

Many readily available investigations have been carried on that illustrate how a community may be studied as the social setting for its youth. Others are examples of how a school may study the youth themselves to see what some of the effects of such a setting on the youth have been.

In a typical middle western community during the school year 1941–1942, Hollingshead studied 735 adolescent boys and girls, their family backgrounds, their behavior, and the community's social structure. He observed their social behavior in seven major areas: the school, the job, the church, recreation, cliques, dates, and sex. He found considerable evidence that the social behavior of adolescents was related functionally to the position their families occupied in the social structure of the community. He also found evidence that some teachers catered to the social status of individual students instead of to their educational needs.[2]

Social status of students can be estimated by means of an index which involves the ratings by parents or guardians on (1) occupation, (2) source of income, (3) type of house, and (4) dwelling area.[3] Students who are in need of social skills and lacking in friendly relations with others can be identified by means of sociometric techniques of varying complexity.[4] A comparatively simple procedure is to use a brief questionnaire by which students may anonymously indicate those among their associates whom they would choose first and second in a number of situations such as serving on a committee, eating lunch, going to an athletic contest, or working in a shop.

Common problems and interests of students can be identified by using check lists and inventories which are available[5] or by using questionnaires designed for a particular school. In Colorado, a check list submitted to 1,800 boys and girls in grades 9 to 12 indicated that a topic of most interest in each of the four grades was "How to act—manners and etiquette for business, parties, dates, and so forth." A topic of least interest in each grade was "Labor, management, unions, and related problems." [6] A questionnaire submitted to four thousand students, grades 7 through 9 indicated that most of them had worries concerning their own growth and health and that most of them believed they would be

[2] August B. Hollingshead, *Elmtown's Youth* (New York: John Wiley & Sons, Inc., 1949), p. 480.

[3] W. L. Warner and others, *Social Class in America* (Chicago: Science Research Associates, 1949).

[4] R. J. Havighurst and Hilda Taba, *Adolescent Character and Personality* (New York: John Wiley & Sons, Inc., 1949), pp. 217–219. See also *How to Construct a Sociogram* (New York: Bureau of Publications, Teachers College, Columbia University, 1947).

[5] *S.R.A. Youth Inventory* (Chicago: Science Research Associates, n.d.); *Thurstone's Vocational Interest Schedule* (Yonkers, N.Y.: World Book Company, 1947).

[6] Stephen Romine, *Youth Interests and the Educational Program of the Secondary School* (Boulder, Colo.: Extension Division, University of Colorado, 1951).

542   THE HIGH SCHOOL AND ITS COMMUNITY

inadequate as committee chairmen.[7] Quite often, in responding to such questionnaires, numbers of students indicate a desire to make new friends and an eagerness for social approval.

In a small school in a rural area the teachers investigated the social and leisure time activities of all seventh- and eighth-grade students in the school. Each teacher interviewed ten students and the same items of information were secured in each interview. It was found that no social activities were regularly available to the students except those sponsored by a new religious sect which had recently been introduced into the area.

In numerous schools, studies have been made of hidden tuition costs and teachers have been surprised at the costs of laboratory fees, physical education charges, attendance at school events, and so on. These costs usually range from $75 to $175 per year per pupil. Many investigations of the participation in extraclass activities have been made, also, of students who come from families of low income groups. It has generally been found that participation in extraclass activities varies directly with the income of families. Comparatively brief and simple questionnaires are available for testing the probabilities that either or both conditions exist in any school. The questionnaires with precise directions for administering them were prepared for the Illinois Secondary School Curriculum Program.[8]

During the early 1950's, several state-wide studies of early school-leavers were carried on.[9] Data were obtained through parent and pupil opinion polls, follow-up studies of employment status and experiences, records made in college and other post-high school education, and employer rating polls. In the different states, considerable similarity was found in the reasons given by youth for dropping out of school. In order by frequency these were preferred work to school, was not interested in school work, could not learn and was discouraged, was failing and did not want to repeat the grade, disliked a certain teacher, disliked a certain subject, and could learn more out of school than in. Some reported the need of more money to buy clothes or to help at home. Others cited such reasons as ill health or the fact that their friends had left school.

[7] F. L. Pond, "Determining the Needs of Youth," NASSP *Bulletin*, 35 (October, 1951), 88–97.

[8] Harold C. Hand, *How to Conduct the Participation in Extra-Class Activities Study* (Circular Series A, No. 51, Illinois Secondary School Curriculum Program, Bulletin No. 5); and *How to Conduct a Hidden Tuition Costs Study* (Circular Series A, No. 51, Illinois Secondary School Curriculum Program, Bulletin No. 4; Springfield: State Superintendent of Public Instruction, May, 1949).

[9] U.S. Office of Education, *A Look Ahead in Secondary Education* (Bulletin No. 4; Washington, D.C.: Government Printing Office, 1954), pp. 104–105.

With a view to remedying the conditions which cause students to leave school early, many local schools have made careful studies of their dropouts. The findings at Grand Rapids, Michigan, were not unlike those in many other community studies. Youth dropping out of school came disproportionately from impoverished neighborhoods, from retarded and low I.Q. groups, from emotional deviates and disturbed homes, from families moving about, and from those who disliked either a teacher or the entire school. Some changes made in Grand Rapids schools in an effort to improve holding power were increased attention to extraclass activities for all pupils, improved guidance and counseling through systematic contacts with parents, the introduction of auto repair shopwork beginning in the ninth grade, greater flexibility in scheduling, and special social activities and civic responsibilites for the nonparticipating and socially nonaccepted girls and boys. There is some evidence that these changes improved the holding power of Grand Rapids school during a period of six years.[10] Most local efforts to improve holding power have been successful if they have been systematically planned and carried out. As a factor in achieving success, the interest of the staff seems to be more important than the particular nature of the plan.

Aids in making follow-up studies are readily available. A few high schools, especially those emphasizing vocational training, make follow-up studies of all students—early school-leavers as well as graduates and those who secured employment with or without school assistance. Some schools send a questionnaire to each former student five years after he has graduated or left school. One school requires each student, during a school-leaving interview, to fill in his name and address on a questionnaire which is to be mailed to him five years later.[11] One study of early school-leavers which has significance for educators was made by persons trained in interview techniques. In Louisville, Kentucky, interviews were held with 41 representative employers and 524 boys and girls fourteen through nineteen years of age who were out of school and working or seeking work. Items of particular interest are the following: (1) Dissatisfaction with the high school program appeared to be at least as great a factor in early school leaving as economic need. (2) The majority of employers favored the practice of hiring, for full-time employment, only young people at least eighteen years of age, although currently most of them were accepting some applicants at sixteen and seventeen. (3) In

[10] *Ibid.*, pp. 61–63.
[11] *A Guide for the Study of Holding Power in Minnesota Schools* (St. Paul, Minn.: State Department of Education, 1952); *Follow-up Study of Holding Power* (Albany, N.Y.: The University of the State of New York, 1951); and *Improvement of Holding Power through a Continuous Study of Youth in School* (Albany, N.Y.: The University of the State of New York, 1952).

general, the youngest workers had the poorest jobs, the greatest difficulties in getting jobs, and the fewest job satisfactions.[12]

Probably in few high schools will resources be available for carrying on comprehensive surveys through depth interviews by well-trained interviewers. However, in any high school some seniors, after being appropriately instructed, can interview some employers or some workers who are former students of the school. If some information is collected systematically each year,, it will serve as a valuable resource, even though it is not possible to interview all employers or all school-leavers at one time.

SECURING COMMUNITY FACTS

Much pertinent data about communities can be secured from such sources as previous surveys, the federal census, court records, market research agencies, public utilities, and chambers of commerce. Increasingly, business and community agencies are aiding schools to study local communities. For example, in Indianapolis, local business institutions supplied data which the school staff used in preparing instructional materials for pupils relating to such topics as banking, department stores, and manufacturing in that city. The Atlanta, Georgia, public schools used a text called *Atlanta Builds for the Future,* which was prepared cooperatively by businessmen and educators. Published by the University of North Carolina, the text includes significant data about Atlanta which were compiled as a basis for city planning.

Much pertinent data about the community can be gathered by the students themselves. In some communities, by interviewing older residents and by consulting uncommon records, students have written a history of the community or have made contributions to one which had already been written. The possibilities of surveys in many departments of the school are illustrated by the activities carried on at the Wells High School in Chicago.

Our community surveys conducted by subject-field classes particularly developed potentialities for uncovering both community educational facilities and social backgrounds of pupils. Each subject field uncovered information suited to its peculiar needs. The fine-arts classes began to discover opportunities for pupils to participate in music and art activities of the community and to enjoy appreciation of community manifestations of music and art as these were evidenced in community life. Our English classes probed the opportunities of the community for recreational reading, amateur theatricals, wholesome motion

---

[12] *Hunting a Career: Study of Out-of-School Youth, Louisville, Kentucky* (U.S. Department of Labor, Labor Standards Bureau, Bulletin No. 115, 1949; Washington, D.C.: Government Printing Office, 1950).

pictures, radio programs and the like. Likewise, our commercial classes surveyed the commercial life of the community; the industrial arts, the industries; the social studies classes, the housing; the science groups, the sanitation facilities; and the physical education classes, the possibilities of participation in athletic sports and games for pupils. The value of such data for classroom implementation of effective living of the pupils was incalculable.[13]

Numerous articles and guides are available for teachers and students who wish to study the community and its resources.[14] A survey may reveal or document the existence of community needs which point to changes which should be made in the school program. For example, school administrators in a midwestern city spotted the incidence of delinquency upon a map and found that juvenile offenses were most frequent where real estate values were lowest and where the fewest recreation facilities were available. This finding was in some measure responsible for the subsequent expansion of the afterschool recreational program in parts of the city. Sometimes a survey reveals or documents needs which clearly cannot be met by the school alone. Upon the basis of facts gathered by a junior college in a rural area with a declining population, it was concluded that (1) the area was being by-passed by mechanization, and (2) mechanization of cotton production in a neighboring area had increased unemployment in the immediate area. These facts were of considerable significance for the school, but the school alone could do little about them. Community action outside the school was needed.

Beginning in 1946, an in-service program of community study was carried on during a number of years for the teachers in the Baltimore city schools.[15] The first year of the program was concerned with understanding the community as an environmental influence affecting the child in his relation to the school and to learning. The second year was concerned largely with curriculum revision and the use of community resources. The third and fourth years were concerned mainly with efforts to bring about important community improvements. Schools did make important community changes in Baltimore, but better understanding of the

[13] Paul R. Pierce, *Developing a High School Curriculum* (New York: American Book Company, 1942), pp. 188–189.
[14] U.S. Office of Education, *An Outline of Steps to Be Taken in a Community Occupational Survey* (Mimeograph; Washington, D.C.: Government Printing Office, 1955) 7 pp.; *Basic Community Survey* (Bulletin No. 3014, Instructional Service Series; Lansing, Mich.: Department of Public Instruction, 1939); Edward G. Olsen, ed., *School and Community* (2nd ed.; Englewood Cliffs, N.J.: Prentice-Hall, Inc., 1954), pp. 250–276; Charles L. Robbins, *The Small Town and Its School* (Bulletin No. 348; Iowa City: State University of Iowa, 1934); and *Your Community Looks at Itself* (Atlanta, Ga.: Southern Regional Council, Inc., n.d.), 68 pp.
[15] Edward G. Olsen, ed., *The Modern Community School* (New York: Appleton-Century-Crofts, Inc., 1953), pp. 161–178.

community and closer contact with it brought about important changes in the school, also, as many teachers "saw children's dirty faces in an entirely new light."

Collecting information about youth and the community, and securing insights into the problems of youth are long-time jobs requiring patience and persistence. However, a portion of the time and energy of every principal and his staff should be spent upon such research. Other agencies and individuals in the community can be encouraged to help. In regular classes, students can carry on investigations that are fruitful not only because they learn by doing, but also because they uncover facts as well. Student clubs, honor groups, and even graduating classes have sometimes undertaken investigations as special projects. When information has been secured, it should not be filed away and neglected in office files.

Purposes Served by Community Study

Two large and interrelated purposes may be served by studying the community: (1) improving the conventional program of the school, and (2) improving the community.

IMPROVING THE CONVENTIONAL
PROGRAM OF THE SCHOOL

Learning experiences for boys and girls can be vitalized through the study of the community. Students are given opportunities to learn by doing. Opportunities are uncovered for capitalizing upon the present interests of students and for providing them with immediate satisfactions. This is true of health, occupations, citizenship, family life, and leisure time activities. It is true of each of the ten Imperative Needs of American Youth. Instead of studying about health, recreation, and occupations only in the abstract, it is possible also to study them in a specific situation in the local community. Studying about health rules, proper rest, and adequate diet should be supplemented by analyzing the local situation to see how health is actually determined by community sanitation, the availability of medical services, and the habits and attitudes of the people. Finding out what recreational facilities there are and can be in the community should supplement merely studying about recreation. Finding out the characteristics of all the jobs that have been filled in the community during the past year and what is required for success in them should supplement studying about occupations from a book.

The conditions of modern life do not encourage the building of the social understandings and skills necessary for its successful continuance.

Whether we look at the international, the federal, the state, or the local community, the great weakness of people is their inability to understand the evolving culture and to get along with each other. It is difficult to develop social understandings and cooperative skills strong enough to withstand the strains of modern living. Many of our problems are too complex to be easily understood, but every community contains comparatively simple aspects of all of them.

High school students who study their community have an opportunity to see their tasks in adjusting to the community as it is, as well as their problems in making it over into what they think it should be. They have opportunities to plan cooperatively and actually carry out their plans. In many high schools, students under the direction of guidance workers have investigated the jobs that have been filled by youth in a community during a given period of time. They have also gathered data concerning the effectiveness of the employment service at the school and both the strengths and the weaknesses of the candidates the service has succeeded in placing in jobs. Not only do such investigations provide excellent experience and valuable information for those doing the investigating, but also, when the results are retained through the years, they provide excellent content for courses of study. Numbers of students can profit from them and improve their attempts to adjust to the community as it is, whether or not they had anything to do with the original investigations.

Studying a particular community and taking part in its activities is obviously helpful to students who are going to remain there. It is also helpful to those who are going to live in other communities because it encourages them to establish roots and interests regardless of where they live and how temporary their residence may be. People who adjust best in new and strange communities are those who have had previous experience in adjusting to other communities.

Some schools build social understandings and skills for old and young alike. During vacations and evenings, their gymnasiums and playgrounds are used for appropriate seasonal athletic activities by out-of-school youth, their auditoriums are used for meetings, lectures, and discussion groups, and their practical arts and craft shops are used by interested adults. Regular classes for adults are held in academic classrooms. Youth clubs of various kinds and rural life organizations hold meetings at these schools. Community dances, ice-cream socials, and holiday celebrations are held there. But there are not enough of these community-centered schools, and they are seldom located in urban areas. Yet school workers, as well as the public, have come to realize that it is wasteful to maintain the traditional concept of the school plant as only a place where children come to learn lessons during the regular school hours.

Support is growing for the idea of extending the school year, as advocated in Chapter 13. There is also a conviction that it is not sensible for park boards and similar authorities to duplicate school facilities that stand idle most of the time. It will take time for park boards and school boards to develop practical working relationships and agreement concerning the assumption of various responsibilities, but there is little doubt that school plants of the future will be used more hours each day and more days in the year than those of traditional schools have been. The beginnings of the all-year programs for youth in which school plants and personnel are utilized are to be found in many communities that maintain good schools; they mark a trend that we may expect to see developed in the years to come.

Close study of the community affords teachers superior understanding of the backgrounds of their students. They know better the learning activities for which their students are ready, and are better able to avoid duplicating them. They know how to present new material to students so that it will be significant and meaningful, because they know where the students can use this new information or where they can see it being used. They have an improved conception of what should be taught and when, because they know what the students have already learned and how, and what they *need* to know.

As a result of the study of the community by the school there can be desirable changes in the school's educational program—in the specific content of courses in the program, and in the methods of teaching employed. Using the schools as community centers also has its effect on students' attitudes toward school. In formal, traditional schools, high school students even find it difficult to catch the spirit of play at school parties after school. To them, the school has always been a place clothed in formality and restraint. It is a good thing for them to have pleasant experiences at the school and to know that adults are eager and willing to gather there for community activities. Although such experiences may not cause youth to go eagerly to school for learning's sake, they should reduce the lagging of their steps.

Teachers who know of the student's educational experiences outside the school will have a better understanding of his problems as a learner. They will be able to help him find integration and unity in all his learning experiences, many of which seem inconsistent. Or better still, they may be able to prevent his being faced with conflicting points of view and inconsistent experiences. Just as quarreling parents exert a bad influence upon a child because they place him in conflict, so do school, home, and community often place a child in conflict because none of them understands what the others are doing. A student may be working with the same persistent problem in his home, his school, and at his job. A little thought and cooperation on the part of the three agencies, initiated by the school, may make possible a more coordinated approach to the problems of this youth.

IMPROVING THE COMMUNITY

The basic reason for the study of the community by the high school is to improve the work of the school and thus to promote better growth and development of youth. When this task is well done, the community is improved thereby and the improved community makes possible the further betterment of the school. Hence although it is not the primary purpose of the school to make the community better, when the school discharges its primary function well, the community *is* made better. This close school-community relationship can start an ascending and expanding spiral of school-community development. Whether it does so depends largely on the leadership of the high school principal and faculty.

School administrators and staffs should first seek to improve themselves and their programs. Such efforts have generally required students to study the community and to make excursions and field trips. Often they have been motivated to carry on community activities under the supervision of adults. In many communities, as teachers have gained skill and as students and laymen have gained insight into the learning and growing process, students have been more directly responsible for bringing about community improvement. For example, in Des Moines, Iowa, high school students initiated a campaign for a city-manager government and secured 4,500 signatures to a petition before turning the campaign over to adults. In the Holtville High School in Alabama, students during World War II had the satisfaction of knowing that they were helping to meet food needs that were greatly increased by the war and by the necessity of feeding the peoples of Europe after the war.

In an effort to inform the people of the community about the possibilities of canning food, they [the teachers and pupils] published a list of vegetables to be grown for this purpose, telling when to plant and how much. In the summer of 1942, approximately 8,500 cans were filled, and because of the increased need for food preservation, plans are being made to can at least 15,000 this summer. Canning now is done by school girls in home economics classes. They learn how to can meats, fruits, and vegetables. There is also a volunteer canning group composed of fourteen girls who are available to do canning at odd times when whole classes cannot stop to do it.

. . . Before this plant [a meat-processing and refrigeration plant] was installed, farmers in this section lost about 25 per cent of the meat they killed because they could not handle it properly. Besides helping them save their meat, this plant will do all their work for them, from the slaughtering on, for the payment of a small fee. In the past eleven months we have handled 94,200 pounds of pork and 5,901 pounds of beef, serving 655 customers, these figures almost doubling those of any previous year.[16]

It is difficult to generalize about student activities for community improvement. Activities that may be successful in some communities cannot be carried out in others. The most successful begin with some real need felt by the community for an improvement in its life. It may be the need for better recreational programs for youth, for better health service, or for a program to help prevent soil erosion. There are communities that derive much pleasure from their little theater groups, community orchestras and glee clubs, literary clubs, and athletic clubs, whose members are almost entirely the recent graduates of the local high schools. There are communities where it is common for groups of adults to enjoy bird hikes and hunts for plants and flowers, largely because they acquired these interests in high school. The same can be said for photography, woodwork, leather work, and the enjoyment of good music. The community's greatest need may be economic, social, civic, or cultural; but whatever it is, the school in its own interest should make a positive and substantial effort to help meet it.

Every experienced teacher has observed the improvement of health attitudes and practices in entire families and communities because children in school became conscious of the need for improvement and talked about it at home. In all areas are opportunities for students to improve adult life. Group prejudices must be avoided and discriminating consumer habits must be established, however, if the school can vitalize its work sufficiently to set fashions.

In recent years we have come to realize that the enormous natural resources of our country are being depleted. Especially during World War II did the tremendous drains on our reserves indicate the necessity for careful spending and conserving of our resources. In many of these areas, such as flood control, conservation of minerals, and preservation of wild life, effective actions must be planned by our state and federal governments. However, there are other areas, such as soil conservation and reforestation, in which it is important for every citizen to be aware of conservation problems and alert to the contribution he can make to their solution. In most communities there is at least one type of our natural resources that needs to be conserved, and when high school students become interested in and concerned about these needs, their parents and neighbors are likely to also.

Examples of the school's serving and improving the community are

[16] Whilden Wallace, James Chrietzberg, and Verner M. Sims, *The Story of Holtville—A Southern Association School* (Nashville, Tenn.: Cullen and Ghertner Company, 1944), p. 147.

not difficult to find; they are very common. But they should be deepened and extended and interpreted to the public. As the public comes to
understand clearly their nature and value, it will be easier to make them
central and vital parts of the school's program rather than mere append-
ages.

Trade schools made an enormous contribution toward training the
manpower for our war and postwar production. Guidance departments
are providing valuable assistance to business and industrial concerns in
helping them assign their employees to the posts in which they will be
most useful and successful. Employers are being saved great amounts of
time and money by the effectiveness of school placement services.

School shops are repairing furniture and equipment for homes and
farms, and home economics departments are aiding in the planning and
redecorating of homes and in making clothes for the family. Schools are
carrying on campaigns for community beautification. In many rural communities, farm equipment repair programs have been instituted in order
to keep necessary farm equipment in repair.

Edward G. Olsen has listed a number of activities to illustrate those
commonly centered in the public schools of many rural districts, villages,
towns, cities, and metropolitan areas throughout the United States:[17]

Community Groups Which Meet in School	Community Activities Held in the School	Community Service Functions of the School
Garden club	Choral group	Audio-visual center
4-H Club	Civil defense instruc-	Arts and crafts studio
Mothers club	tion	Baby clinic
Parent-Teacher	Concerts	Canning equipment
Association	Conservation planning	Community theater
Pet association	Family play nights	Creative writing
Photography club	Forums	laboratory
Boy and Girl Scouts	Hobby exhibits	Home repair shop
Service clubs	Pageants	Immunization center
Stamp club	Rhythm band	Library
Toastmaster's club	Square dancing	Science laboratory
Town athletic teams	Vacation Bible School	Youth employment center

To suggest that helping to improve the community is one of the
tasks of the school does not mean that the school is to assume the tasks of
other successful institutions in the community. It implies a survey of
community needs, an analysis of the work of other community agencies,
and a careful defining of the work of the school. The school should provide leadership in studying the youths' community, in studying the com-

[17] Olsen, ed., School and Community, p. 406.

munity's youth, in finding out how and where the school's efforts are
most needed, and in helping to integrate the programs of all institutions
and agencies in the community.

Ruth Strang summarizes common features of the most comprehensive programs of community betterment as follows:

1. A person with vision gives the people of the community initial impetus and inspiration.

2. A mass meeting is held to lay the foundation for community organization.

3. Small, informal study groups work on different parts of the program
and carry out their plans. The most important personal relations and community
planning often take place in the small group or sub-group.

4. The use of consultant service, printed material, radio talks, visual aids,
or financial assistance helps to increase efficiency, sustain effort, and get results.

5. Recognition of achievement is given in the form of objective evidence
of improvement and, in some instances, by published reports of progress.

6. Personal development of individuals is achieved through the experience of working successfully with others for the welfare of all.

7. The philosophy of the program includes belief in the untapped potentialities of people, acceptance of their points of view and values, and emphasis
on the importance of translating good ideas into action.[18]

PROCEDURES FOR FACULTY STUDY

There is no one formula to be followed by a school in its study of
the community and its youth. Many school staffs have regarded such
study as a part of their regular tasks in improving the effectiveness of
the school or in improving the community. The following outline indicates in some detail what a school staff can do to find out the needs of its
youth:

1. Study pupils now in school, utilizing guidance facilities and techniques.

   a. With the cooperation of the pupil, find for each one the answers to such
     questions as:

     What is his home background?
     What are his interests and abilities?
     Are his abilities comparable with his hopes and plans for the future?
     What are his major out-of-school activities?
     In what school activities does he participate, and how successful is he?
     What estimates do his employer and other out-of-school associates place
       upon his general dependability and competence?

[18] Ruth Strang, in National Society for the Study of Education, *The Community
School* (Fifty-second Yearbook; Chicago: University of Chicago Press, 1953), Part II,
pp. 168–169.

How is he regarded by his peers?

What are his ideals?

When will he be equipped for reasonable competence in out-of-school life or in some higher institution?

What are his major educational problems?

b. Analyze for both individuals and groups findings covering the areas of personality traits, economic and cultural background, physical status, achievement, mental traits, outside school activities and interests, and occupational goals.

c. Study pupil participation in school activities outside the classroom, in the school, and in the community. Collect data on the range of available activities, the number of students taking part, and the characteristics of participants and nonparticipants.

2. Study the accepted principles of growth and development in youth, such as those of mental growth, development of personality traits, differentiation among traits, changes in types of reasoning by age and general mental ability, and so on.

3. Study out-of-school youth of school age, utilizing guidance facilities and follow-up surveys.

a. Obtain as nearly as possible information to parallel that obtained about in-school youth.

b. Ask about every dropout such questions as

When did he leave school?

Why, according to his own account, did he leave?

Why, according to his parents, did he leave?

What efforts did the school make to help him prepare for his present activities?

What efforts did the school make to hold him in school?

What could the school have done to help him in his present activities?

What services could the school offer him now?

c. Summarize findings to discover

What proportion of pupils were eliminated from school before graduation, and at what school level did they drop out?

What were the characteristics of the pupils who dropped out?

d. Formulate conclusions as to steps the school could take to increase its holding power, and so reduce dropouts.

4. Utilize guidance facilities and community surveys to study the graduates and former pupils of a class which was graduated about ten years ago, in order to collect information about their first ten years after high school. Find answers for each class member to such questions about his adult life as

To what kind of job did he go?

How long has he held his present job? earlier jobs?

Is he married? How long has he been? How many children are there in the family? Is he divorced?

What civic activities does he engage in?

What public offices has he held?

What community organizations does he participate in?

What does he consider to have been helpful features of his school experience?

How, in his opinion, could the school have been more directly helpful to him?

5. Make surveys of various phases of community activities to discover data which will help identify the life needs of youth. Include such areas as recreational facilities and practices, medical facilities, health status of various population groups, crime statistics, housing facilites, record of employment or unemployment over the past fifteen years, and so on.

6. Make a survey of pupil opinion, covering such questions as (a) why do students drop out of school, (b) what are the strengths and weaknesses of the existing school, and (c) how could the school be changed to better meet student needs.

7. Make a study of hidden tuition costs in the school to discover how much and what kind of payment students must make to attend school and take full part in its activities.

8. Make a study of the adequacy and effectiveness of the pupil personnel or guidance program.

The staff of the Parker District High School, Greenville, South Carolina, prepared the following statement of its objectives:

1. To develop better citizenship in both children and adults (acceptance of responsibility, leadership, personality)

2. To meet the individual need of our people (health, basic skills, vocational self-sufficiency)

3. To work in and with the community for improved living (better homes, worth-while leisure-time activities, cooperative work, people fitted into proper roles in community life) [19]

At the Central Michigan College at Mt. Pleasant, Michigan, the study of community life problems began with the asking of the following questions:

1. If it were in your power to change this community, what changes would you make?

2. What needs have the people in this community?

[19] Parker District High School Faculty, *Parker High School Serves Its People* (Greenville, S.C.: Parker District Schools, 1942).

3. What plan of action would you suggest that the school undertake to meet these needs?
4. What changes in the curriculum would you make so as to meet their needs? [20]

After discussing the questions, the faculty decided

1. To study housing, land use and conservation, food habits, and recreation in two contrasting counties
2. To study the vocational, cooperative buying and marketing needs of the Indians in the area
3. To study the housing needs of seven of the surrounding counties
4. To develop a manual for the preparation of warm lunches in schools
5. To prepare a list of similar problems that should be considered in the preparation of instructional material to be used in the area[21]

Obviously these two schools believed that a high school's program of study should be more sharply focused on the improvement of living in the community than is usually the case, or they would not have asked these questions or have come to these conclusions. How did they come to this belief? The answer to this question can be found only in case studies of these and similar schools. Case studies made by the authors of this book have usually shown that there is at least one person in the group with unorthodox ideas about the function of youth education. Perhaps the ideas of these people may not be more unorthodox than those of others, but at least they are more willing and eager to see these ideas go to work in the school. Practically all principals and teachers want to gear the school and their teaching to the community and its youth, but whatever adaptations they make do not fundamentally alter orthodox school practices and teaching content. The persons who lead such schools to make basic changes in their programs of youth education as suggested by various studies of the youth and their communities are willing and eager to go the whole way. Sometimes they work in situations where the gap between a conventional high school program and the youth life of the community is so wide that the ridiculousness of the situation is sufficiently obvious to make agreement on a new program easier. If these leaders are successful they are able to inspire confidence in their own sincerity, good judgment, and good intentions, and, as a consequence, willingness in others to follow them.

At first there are but a few such people in the community or on the faculty, but they are able to introduce small changes. Perhaps the commercial program of the school will be more closely related to the

[20] Clara M. Olson and Norman D. Fletcher, *Learn and Live* (New York: Alfred P. Sloan Foundation, Inc., 1946), p. 93.
[21] *Ibid.*

skills and knowledge required by the kinds of jobs actually secured by students when they leave school. Perhaps home economics courses will begin to include instruction aimed at meeting the needs of home life exactly on the level of homes in the community: better-balanced meals out of the narrow range of foods actually available in the homes of the students or the quick-freezing of foods for storage in the community cold-storage plant. Perhaps it is health instruction that gradually grows into good sex education. Many schools have made such starts and contrive to carry on these innovations but, having made a start, they, like Lot's wife, look back and then are able to go no further. In a few schools, however, the leaders do not let these gains satisfy them; but instead, they launch a second round at once, and then a third until the process becomes continuous. The twenty-ninth annual report of the supervising principal of Toms River, New Jersey, is a sort of cumulative record of several years of such work in this school. *The Thread That Runs So True*[22] is shot through and through with illustrations to support Jesse Stuart's conviction that schools in the Kentucky mountains ought to raise the level of youth and community living, and describes his continuous efforts to change them.

In general, schools that develop functional school-community programs have interested leadership somewhere in the group. If it is not in the principal's office, at least the principal is a firm supporter of the work. Such schools work at the job over a period of years, usually without any spectacularly rapid developments. Their success rests on conviction and hard work rather than on genius or luck or an ample budget.

Educational workers and laymen can generally see the value of community study and activities in industrial, rural, and marginal areas, but they are slow to recognize the value of these activities in college preparatory high schools and in communities of higher economic status. There is nothing to show that both these students and these communities cannot profit by such study. Community study and activities are appropriate for academic as well as the so-called nonacademic students. College-bound students need practice in sharing community responsibilities as they grow into adulthood; they also need to grow in their understanding of our evolving culture through realistic contact with segments of it in the local community. By providing this direction, principals and teachers who work with selected student bodies can make a great contribution to the functional movement in high schools everywhere. Throughout the history of secondary education in America, schools have been slow to adopt realistic practices because they have been reluctant to depart from the paths trod by the entirely respectable college prepara-

[22] Jesse Stuart, *The Thread That Runs So True* (New York: Charles Scribner's Sons, 1949).

tory schools. If these schools would increasingly study and utilize community resources, the weight of their example would be entirely disproportionate to their numbers.

Students in schools in high socioeconomic communities, as well as those of low socioeconomic levels, can profit from a study of the local community because it is the best way in which many students can begin to acquire the insights and understandings necessary for civic competence in the modern world. Study of the community by the school is one of the most effective ways to start a community toward self-improvement, and study of the community and its youth by the faculty is one of the best ways of discovering what changes need to be made in the school's educational program. Professor Elwood Cubberley used to say, "As goes the principal, so goes the school." To this one could add, "As goes the school, so goes the community."

Some Points to Consider

1. List the institutions in a community you know that claim to be "serving the needs of youth."

2. List the principal activities of each that illustrate the kinds of youth needs they are undertaking to meet.

3. Do you think that some kinds of activities are stressed until there is competition between institutions for the time of youth? What kinds of activities are overstressed? What kinds neglected?

4. Is there any agency for coordinating the programs, the administration, or the budgets of these agencies so that they and the high school provide an integrated program of youth service for the community? Should there be?

5. Does the high school seek to expand its program and to increase its demands on the time of youth for activities and study so that other agencies are crowded out as far as school youth are concerned?

6. Do the other youth-serving agencies serve mostly youth who are not in high school?

7. What would be a good policy for the high school to adopt to govern its relations with other youth-serving agencies in this community?

8. With a community in mind that you know well, make a list of evidences of its need for a better or a different kind of education. To what extent is the high school of this community providing education to meet these needs? To what extent should it? Do older adolescents and young adults exhibit the same degree of need for this better and different education as the older people of the community?

9. List needs for education (for health and physical fitness, for example) that some high school you know is apparently trying to supply, judged by its educational offerings. Do you think it is doing a reasonable job in these areas? What is it doing less well? What makes you think so?

10. Did Dr. Ben Wood have a point when he said, "You can't teach

children until you learn children"? What implications do you see in this for teacher education?

11. Considering matters discussed in this chapter, should a principal plan for meetings of teachers by grade levels as well as by departments? What differences in matters to be discussed would there be in these two types of meetings?

Further Reading

Anderson, W. P. "The High School in the Community," *Teachers College Record*, 56, No. 7 (April, 1955), 377–383.

Biddle, W. W. *The Cultivation of Community Leaders*. New York: Harper & Brothers, 1953. Chap. 2.

Caswell, Hollis L., ed. *The American High School*. John Dewey Society Yearbook, 1947; New York: Harper & Brothers, 1946. Chap. 6.

Educational Policies Commission. *Education for All American Youth: A Further Look*. Rev. ed.; Washington, D.C.: National Education Association, 1951.

———. *Strengthening Community Life*. Washington, D.C.: National Education Association, 1954.

Everett, Samuel, ed. *The Community School*. New York: Appleton-Century-Crofts, Inc., 1936.

Grinnell, J. E. *The School and the Community*. New York: The Ronald Press Co., 1955.

Hand, Harold C. *What People Think about Their Schools*. Yonkers, N.Y.: World Book Company, 1949. Pp. 153–219.

Hanna, Paul R. *Youth Serves the Community*. New York: Appleton-Century-Crofts, Inc., 1936.

Hart, Joseph K. *The Discovery of Intelligence*. New York: Appleton-Century-Crofts, Inc., 1924.

Hollingshead, August B. *Elmtown's Youth*. New York: John Wiley & Sons, Inc., 1949.

Ivins, Wilson H., William H. Fox, and David Segel. *A Study of the Secondary School Program in the Light of the Characteristics and Needs of Youth*. Bulletin of the School of Education, University of Indiana, Vol. 25, No. 6, November, 1949.

Johnson, Elizabeth S., and Caroline E. Legg. "Why Young People Leave School," NASSP *Bulletin*, No. 158, November, 1948.

Leonard, J. Paul. *Developing the Secondary School Curriculum*. Rev. ed.; New York: Rinehart & Company, Inc., 1953.

Morrill, M. B., and B. C. Douglass. *Improvement of Living through Education*. University of Vermont and State Agricultural College; New York: Alfred P. Sloan Foundation, Inc., 1954.

National Association of Secondary School Principals. *Planning for American Youth*. Washington, D.C.: National Education Association, 1951.

National Society for the Study of Education. *Adapting the Secondary School*

Program to the Needs of Youth and *The Community School*. Fifty-second Yearbook; Chicago: University of Chicago Press, 1953. Parts I, II.

Ogden, Jean, and Jess Ogden. *Small Communities in Action*. New York: Harper & Brothers, 1946.

Olsen, Edward G. *The Modern Community School*. New York: Appleton-Century-Crofts, Inc., 1953.

———, ed. *School and Community*. 2nd ed.; Englewood Cliffs, N.J.: Prentice-Hall, Inc., 1954.

Olson, Clara M., and Norman D. Fletcher. *Learn and Live*. New York: Alfred P. Sloan Foundation, Inc., 1946.

Parker District High School Faculty. *Parker High School Serves Its People*. Greenville, S. C.: Parker District Schools, 1942.

Pierce, Paul R. *Developing a High School Curriculum*. New York: American Book Company, 1942.

Quillen, I. James, and Lavonne A. Hanna. "Using Community Resources in Social Studies Instruction," *Education for Social Competence*. Chicago: Scott, Foresman & Company, 1948. Chap. 11.

Stuart, Jesse. *The Thread That Runs So True*. New York: Charles Scribner's Sons, 1949.

U.S. Office of Education. *Improving School Holding Power—Some Research Proposals*. Circular No. 291; Washington, D.C.: Government Printing Office, 1951.

———. *A Look Ahead in Secondary Education*. Bulletin No. 4; Washington, D.C.: Government Printing Office, 1954.

———. *Why Do Boys and Girls Drop Out of School, and What Can We Do about It?* Circular No. 269; Washington, D.C.: Government Printing Office, 1950.

Wallace, Whilden, James Chrietzberg, and Verner M. Sims. *The Story of Holtville—A Southern Association School*. Nashville, Tenn.: Cullen and Ghertner Company, 1944.

Chapter 25

THE SCHOOL AND COMMUNITY PLAN
FOR YOUTH EDUCATION

IN MOST NATIONS THERE IS LITTLE NEED for educational planning at the local level because planning for all educational programs is done by national ministries of education. In the United States there is no national system of education; there are, instead, state and local systems. National associations, conferences, and committees offer guides of various kinds for those who wish to use them. Similar resources are available in states, but the educational plans which affect youth most are those made in each local community for the youth of that community. Obviously such plans could be made by educators alone. However, educators increasingly recognize that education is a community-wide, as well as a school, function; that citizens may be helpful to school programs by serving as resource persons; and that citizens who understand a school program because they have shared in developing it are very likely to support that program. Laymen increasingly are concerned with the school program because the existence of various disintegrative forces in society bring a new appreciation for the educational influences of good schools and good communities. As a result, since World War II especially, in many communities educators and laymen have worked together in planning for youth education. Stimulating and leading such planning are prime responsibilities of the high school principal.

Since it was founded in 1949, the National Citizens Commission for the Public Schools has stimulated the formation of hundreds of local citizens' committees which have worked with boards of education in improving local schools. The national commission is composed of prominent laymen from many sections of the nation, and reflects different views on education. It has no professional connection with education, religion, or politics. The Commission has been financially supported by foundations interested in education and has not sought to present a program of its own. It serves merely as a clearinghouse for local experience and prepares materials relating to current educational problems designed to be helpful to local committees. Quite properly it has urged local committees to work with and through local boards of education. The basic principles of the Commission have been stated as follows:

> The problem of its children's schools lies at the heart of a free society. None of man's public institutions has a deeper effect upon his conduct as a citizen, whether of the community, of the nation, or of the world.
>
> The goal of our public schools should be to make the best in education available to every American child on completely equal terms.
>
> Public school education should be constantly reappraised and kept responsive both to our educational traditions and to the changing times.
>
> With these basic beliefs in mind, the National Citizens Commission for the Public Schools has set for itself two immediate goals:
>
> To help Americans realize how important our public schools are to our expanding democracy.
>
> To arouse in each community the intelligence and will to improve our public schools.[1]

Most states have had experience with state-level citizens' educational councils or committees of some kind. In some states, as in Connecticut, the committee has arranged for state conferences of educators and citizens. In a number of states, as in Florida, a citizens' committee has stimulated improved educational legislation. In Illinois a steering committee representing thirty-two lay and professional organizations sponsored a curriculum revision program which reached communities in all parts of the state. In Michigan a representative advisory committee aided in planning the Community-School Service Program, which was initiated by the State Department of Public Instruction and financed by the Kellogg Foundation. In New York the Council on Readjustment of High School Education, composed of nineteen leading citizens of the state, assisted the State Department of Education and local school leaders in planning readjustments in the secondary school curriculum necessary to meet the life needs of all youth. Generally, a primary objective of state committees has been to aid the local community as it planned for youth education. Undoubtedly, the work of such committees has served to strengthen the grass roots of American democracy.

Local Planning for Education

In the preceding chapter were described a number of ways in which the school could collect facts about the community and its youth. These facts could be used (1) to provide guidance for a few educational leaders in their planning of the educational program, and (2) as evidence in a

---

[1] National Citizens Commission for the Public Schools, *How Can We Organize for Better Schools?* (2 West 45th St., N.Y.: The Commission, 1953), p. 64.

campaign to induce teachers and the public to accept the program as planned by the educational leaders. It is to be regretted that the results of surveys are sometimes so used. Such information should serve as the basic material for educational planning by teachers, parents, students, and administrators working together. Teachers and principals may be expected to provide leadership by suggesting a problem to be attacked or a list of possible solutions to a particular problem. However, such proposals should merely be starting points for the work of different individuals and groups. A committee of citizens and teachers may cooperatively build a priority list of problems to be attacked and develop plans of action for attacking them.

For the most part the contributions of citizens should be in determining goals for the schools, and for the most part the contributions of educators should be in determining methods and procedures. However, educators are citizens and should have a part in determining goals. Similarly, laymen are often resourceful in developing methods which the school can use. If a committee has been appointed by or with the authority of the board of education and if it has arrived at consensus after systematic procedures, its recommendations should be respected.

OPINION POLLS

How to take the first step in interesting citizens in school and community planning for youth education is a troublesome question. In many communities school staffs and parent-teacher associations have answered this question by using check lists and inventories which have been designed to find out what people think about the school program, the particular aspects of the school program they would like to improve, and how they would like to go about it. For example, in Illinois were developed three separate inventories designed in such a way as to help parents and teachers accomplish three things:

1. To come to an agreement concerning what parents and teachers should be doing together in the development of a better school program
2. To come to an agreement concerning the things parents and teachers want to start working upon together in order to better the school's program
3. To work out your own plan for cooperation and to devise ways that parents and teachers may work together most effectively in the development of a better school program[2]

Similar instruments have been made available by the Superintendent of Instruction in Illinois for helping teachers and parents in a local

[2] Illinois Curriculum Program, *What Do You Think about Parents and Teachers Working Together for Better Schools?* (Consensus Study Number 8, Inventory A; Springfield: Superintendent of Public Instruction, 1952), pp. 3, 17.

school to build consensus in a number of subject matter areas such as English, science, and health. In each area the procedure used has been to fill out in turn each of the three inventories, tabulate the results, and arrange group meetings to discuss the results. A discussion of the tabulated opinions is universally interesting and often parents and teachers are able to agree upon efforts to improve which should be carried out cooperatively. For example, in one school it was revealed that both parents and teachers believed that more attention should be given to preparation for marriage, homemaking, and parenthood. However, each group had been reluctant to move forward for fear of opposition from the other. The reports of the inventories and the discussions which followed encouraged them to cooperate in developing the desired program.

Other communities have used check lists drawn up by juries of specialists in secondary education[3] to ask themselves, "Which of these practices do we consider most desirable?" "Which of the desirable practices do we wish to establish or improve in our own school?" and "How shall we proceed to attain our objectives?" Having decided what they wanted to do and how they wished to go about it, they were then in a position to call in experts and use them for specific purposes. They were not in the position of asking experts what the local school and community should be doing.

A less complex technique was used by the Superintendent of Instruction in Michigan in sampling opinions of citizens in that state, but the results probably aided planning for education in many communities. The Superintendent reported to the governor and the legislature in January, 1952, that according to his investigation most of the citizens believed the schools were doing a good job and most of them were agreed on the necessity of vocational education and education for home and family living. This tended to encourage local schools to endeavor to improve these programs.

Fact Finding by Citizens

In numerous communities local educators have worked cooperatively with other community agencies and leaders in conducting fact-finding studies. A survey of one community grew from the work of the high school principal in a service club which was discouraged because it had no specific plans other than to cooperate in whatever worthy cause chance brought to its attention. The planning of many school buildings has been

[3] William L. Ransom, "How Well Does Your School Rate on the Ten Imperative Needs of Youth?" NASSP *Bulletin,* 33, No. 164 (October, 1949), 8–46; and State Commission, United Forces for Education, *Education in North Carolina* (Report; Raleigh, N.C.: The Commission, 1948), pp. 149–163.

preceded by surveys of job opportunities conducted jointly by the school and other community agencies. In many communities the school and community have jointly studied recreational practices, health conditions and services, and housing conditions.

In Midland, Michigan, the board of education invited and secured broad citizen participation in a community self-study survey. Four study committees were appointed which gathered facts, analyzed them, and made resulting recommendations in the following areas:

1. *The Nature of the Midland School Community*
   Its history, industrial life, cultural status, educational level, recreational interests, census data, birth rates and trends, home construction, school construction, school enrollments and financial status.

2. *The Physical Plant and School Sites*
   Condition of buildings and fixed equipment, repair and maintenance needs, life expectancy, feasibility of additions, and adequacy and location of sites.

3. *Educational Offering and Organization*
   The operating philosophy and objectives of the school system; principles of learning; scope, sequence, and content of the curriculum; organization of the schools with respect to the educational offering; relation of the educational offering to the needs of the learners and to life in the community.

4. *Special and Extended Services*
   Criteria for an extended service program, education of deviates, services to staff personnel, services to pupil personnel such as health services, lunches, recreation and sports, handling of supplies, facilities for maintenance, transportation, and administration quarters.[4]

Many community surveys have been less comprehensive. In one-room rural schools, students and their parents have made crude community surveys of population facts such as where the people lived, whether they were owners or tenants, whether they had gardens, what their housing conditions were, and how much fruit and vegetables they canned at home. Such information has served as a basis for the curriculum and for educational planning in a rural school.

CITIZENS' ADVISORY COMMITTEES

The gathering of facts and the analyzing of them should lead to recommendations for action. Whether the recommendations can be carried out depends upon the strength which can be mobilized to support them in the community. For this reason, some business leaders, habitually op-

[4] Ernest R. Britton, "Making the Community Self-Study Survey," NASSP *Bulletin*, No. 194 (April, 1953), p. 390.

posed to increasing taxes, are often included in the membership of committees to study school finances and make recommendations concerning them. Sometimes such reluctant taxpayers are less reluctant to support adequate school budgets when they thoroughly understand school financial situations and needs.

In most schools temporary or continuing citizens' advisory committees are needed. Such committees have lent strength to the federally aided vocational program in high schools since its inception. Local farmers advise the vocational teacher of agriculture concerning the course that he teaches. Skilled workmen and representatives of employers advise the instructors who are teaching skilled trades. Wherever the high school prepares youth for life in the local community, there are similar opportunities for citizens' advisory committees.

A publication of the Educational Policies Commission describes six examples of school-community action which illustrate the wide range of purposes which citizens can serve in planning for community improvement and for youth education.[5] In the Bronx Park Community of New York City,

. . . literally, thousands of citizens, teachers, and school children had the experience of working together on community-wide projects. Numerous community groups were formed to promote joint action. The Unmet Needs session had, for example, alerted school people and lay citizens to the importance of mental health. The district guidance coordinator, a committee of supervisors, and a group of parents made a guidance survey in which parents interviewed other parents. The findings stimulated attempts to meet the emotional needs of children more effectively by parents in homes and teachers in schools. A curriculum group, similar to the one on guidance, considered ways and means of presenting the achievements and current problems of the schools to the district.[6]

There is significance in the fact that the Bronx Park illustration exemplifies the work of citizens' advisory groups in a community which is part of a larger city school system. It illustrates a different pattern of lay participation than is presented by citizens' advisory committees representing a city-wide school district. Obviously there is need for such city- or district-wide citizens' committees. They do not however make lay committees attached directly to a high school unnecessary. Each high school in a city system needs lay groups working with its staff on the particular problems which it has in providing good education for its own students. If there is to be lay participation in, and real local control of, education, it will show itself at the local school-community

[5] Educational Policies Commission, *Strengthening Community Life—Schools Can Help* (Washington, D.C.: National Education Association, 1954).
[6] *Ibid.*, p. 41.

level—the attendance unit level—as well as at the school district level. In smaller single high school communities it is possible that this local high school representation on the community's citizens' committee may be secured by having one of its subcommittees composed of citizens who are especially interested in the local problems of youth education. But even in these smaller communities some such plan for involving laymen in *direct* efforts at improving the high school's program needs to be in operation. The existence of a city- or district-wide citizens' advisory committee does not provide the full benefits of such lay participation. Each high school principal and staff needs to be working hand in hand with a representative group of its own students' parents.

COORDINATING COUNCILS

The most effective school and community action programs have been coordinated by community councils of some kind. These coordinating groups are called community councils, youth councils, social welfare councils, neighborhood councils, and the like. Their function is to develop continuous and cooperative planning on the part of all agencies interested in improving the community; for example, homes, schools, churches, welfare agencies, service clubs, business groups, labor unions, women's clubs, and youth agencies. Coordinating councils operate by securing facts about the community, developing understanding of problems, developing action programs, securing public support for these programs, and carrying out plans for cooperative action. Where they are successful they conserve human energies and financial resources by preventing bickerings, jealousies, duplication, and waste among the community agencies. Where they are not successful it is often because they have not tied themselves in to the power structure of the community and involved the real community leaders in their plans. It has been estimated that

in the 38,000 communities of the United States there are about 11,000 community councils. Of these, some 1,000 are general community councils; the others are specialized in terms of particular aspects of community life.[7]

One of the first coordinating councils was organized in Berkeley, California, in 1919, by the superintendent of schools and the chief of police in order to mobilize all the agencies of the community in meeting the problems of youth in that city. It is not probable that many coordinating councils have been organized without the schools being represented. The school is the one agency in the community which reaches the great majority of children and youth and, as such, is a great factor in

[7] Edward G. Olsen, ed., *School and Community* (2nd ed.; Englewood Cliffs, N.J.: Prentice-Hall, Inc., 1954), p. 451.

the future of the community. Many of the problems faced by community councils are educational problems, and school representatives have particular contributions to make toward their solutions. High school principals and teachers should welcome opportunities to participate in coordinating councils or to initiate their organization where such councils do not exist. The coordinating council should be developed as an agency through which representatives of the school and community citizens may maintain active and continuing cooperation in planning school policies.

High school principals and teachers can make a particular contribution to community councils by seeing to it that youth have opportunities to work shoulder to shoulder with adults in community activities. Youth of high school age are eager to grow up and attain adult status. Their two chief avenues for doing it are by earning money on a job and by participating with adults as equals in tackling tasks of importance in the community. Working with adults in the solution of community problems provides worth-while learning exercises for youth, but youthful ideas and enthusiasms also make real contributions to community life. For example, housing surveys conducted by youth have provided the basic foundation for housing projects that were actually carried out.

Following are examples of cooperative activities carried on by the school and other government agencies in one community as a result of joint planning arranged by a coordinating council:

1. The school and the state employment service worked together to bridge the gap between full-time school and full-time employment.

2. The school and the welfare services pooled information for the guidance of youth and for initiating action for dependency allotments when they were needed.

3. The school and the health and welfare departments worked together in securing medical, dental, and psychological assistance for individuals who needed it.

4. The school and recreation, park, conservation, and youth agencies worked together in providing a broad recreation program (including camping, swimming, and outdoor activities) for all youth.

5. School guidance personnel worked closely with the police and with probation officers in providing assistance to youth who had been involved in crimes or misdemeanors.

These examples illustrate the opportunities which exist in most communities to achieve greater efficiency by coordinating activities already going on. Actually most coordinating councils which are sucessful go far beyond the coordination of traditional ongoing activities. They are creative in developing ideas for new and distinctive activities for youth education and for community betterment.

Numerous aids are available for school staffs interested in working with citizens' advisory committees or with coordinating councils.[8] Leaders who have had experience caution that (1) it takes time to build public understanding, and (2) key leaders in the community must be involved. One way to find out who the leaders are is systematically to ask people in different geographic, economic, and social groups.

In any typical community there are those who can be interested in all the tasks of planning for youth, in gathering facts concerning present status, in formulating ideals to be attained, and in designing and effecting plans of action. The responsibilities of the high school principal and teachers are to interest these people in the tasks, to keep them at their work, and to be willing to work alongside them as copartners in the community's most important public undertaking.

Organized labor is, and has always been, deeply interested in public education. Ministers, physicians, judges, social workers, and social hygiene groups are interested in education for family life; physicians and workers in county and state health agencies are interested in health education; musicians, artists, sport fans, and service clubs are interested in leisure time activities; businessmen, women's clubs, executives, and workers of all kinds are interested in vocational counseling and in education for lifework. Parents are interested in their own children, and adults are interested in young people whom they happen to know. The high school principal should organize these resources for improving the program of the school.

PARENTS AS PLANNERS

The greatest contribution that a group of parents or adults in the community can make to a school is not in connection with the raising of funds to purchase new equipment for the stage in the auditorium or to buy uniforms for the school band. Their best service lies in building an intelligent public opinion based upon an understanding of the needs of youth and the purposes of the school. Also they very properly may, and do, help define the general objectives of the school and of the educational program for youth in the community, while giving intelligent support to the work of the professional staff. As Thomas H. Briggs has often said, "Many of the problems connected with the school are matters of common sense, and teachers have no monopoly on common sense."

Parent groups should be introduced to the study of the character-

[8] Bureau of Adult Education, *Adventure in Cooperation: Community Building in a Central School* (Albany, N.Y.: The State Education Department, 1949); *Citizens Advisory Committees: Avenues to Better Schools* (Albany, N.Y.: The State Education Department, 1952); Arthur Hillman, *Community Organization and Planning* (New York: The Macmillan Company, 1950); and Clarence King, *Organizing for Community Action* (New York: Harper & Brothers, 1948).

istics of adolescents, the steps by which youth grow into adulthood, and the educational effects of out-of-school experiences. Unless they are informed in these and other matters basic to youth education, the results of their work on school problems may be beside the point. It is not an easy matter to interest parents of high school youth in such group study projects. They have many interests to take their time. During the years their children were in elementary schools, they were under great pressure from the children to attend parents' meetings, and some of them feel they have already attended enough such meetings to last them a lifetime. Now that the children are in high school, the parents are inclined to remain away from the school and place them on their own. The children themselves, now in high school, are feeling an urge for independence and a reluctance to have their parents visit the school. The parents' study of these basic matters will probably, therefore, have to be incidental to participating in the solution of problems that they see as directly connected with the life of the school and particular boys and girls in it.

Parents can most readily be interested in a definite project, such as a plan for vocational guidance, college guidance, or social activities in the school. They are willing to be of service if they can be shown some need they can help meet, such as improving physical facilities or contributing to community understanding and morale. In many schools, because they have found that such meetings are almost invariably helpful to parents and teachers alike, principals and teachers plan carefully and work earnestly to get parents to come to the school for personal conferences.

In a school in which one of the authors was principal a number of years ago there was much waste of time and effort because, although individual daily schedules had been carefully made for the students in the spring before summer vacation began, most of the students at the opening of school in September seemed to think their schedules must be changed. Merely in order to reduce the number of these requests the rule was established that no change would be made unless a parent were interested enough to make a personal call at the school and ask for it. There was a great decrease in the number of requests for changes, but there were surprises as well. Most parents who came to the school did not want the schedules changed when they understood all the factors involved; most parents gained information about the school that they considered helpful; and most of them contributed helpful information about the home life of students. Thereafter, the principal was constantly devising methods to induce parents to call at the school for personal conferences about the progress of their children. And he did more thinking about what the school could do for parents and less about what parents could do for the school. If a parent can see a complete record of the student's progress, including teachers' marks, reading test scores, achievement test scores, an interest record, interest inventory test results, and record of extracurricular activities, he is likely to see a pattern in the complete picture. He is also likely to develop a lively interest in his child's growth and a deeper appreciation of what the school has been able to contribute to it.

If a school does not have a parent-teacher association, a parents' association, or a fathers' club, the principal should either organize one or provide some other systematic method of calling parents together to work on school problems and to discuss school affairs. To be without some such group is to attempt to operate the school in a vacuum. The fact that some organizations of this type have been badly guided by individuals for personal or partisan purposes is no evidence that they should not exist. It is evidence, instead, that the principal and his staff should have done a better job of explaining the school to the parents and of enlisting parents' aid in determining the purposes of the school. If there are criticisms of the school, it is much better to have them channeled into the parents' association than to have them broadcast in social gatherings and in the marketplace. Criticisms should be received objectively as evidences of a need for careful investigations and not as personal affronts. For example, if there is criticism of the school cafeteria, a committee of parents and teachers should be appointed to make a careful firsthand investigation and to recommend remedial changes if the criticisms prove to be well founded. In this way, the group serves as a safety valve that often prevents an explosion. Innovations may originate, or proposed innovations may be explained and criticized in meetings of parents, where their final formulation and interpretation may be much improved. If the program, the policies, and the progress and achievements of the school, its staff, and its students are well understood by such groups, they will in turn inform the general public.

The relations of the principal with such a group should always be kept on a friendly but professional level. He should be reluctant to guide the control of a parents' association into the hands of his friends or even away from those who are unfriendly to him. His efforts would be better directed toward interesting larger and larger numbers of parents in the school and in its policies. If he is energetic, effective, and forthright, his administration will fare well enough at the hands of those who happen to gain positions of leadership in the parents' associations.

The principal and members of the staff can often help to make the meetings sufficiently attractive to secure good attendance. Parents are interested in the teachers of their children and often appreciate arrangements that permit a period just before or after the meeting when they can visit teachers in their classrooms and offices and confer with them about the progress of the children. They like meetings whose programs are centered around problems of the school. If these problems have been the subject of a period of work and study by a smaller group that is proposing a solution to the problem at the meeting, so much the better. Parents are also interested in programs that include large numbers of students or programs extremely well done by a few students. They are interested in programs that help them meet family situations arising during the growing pains of their adolescent children. Fathers-and-sons nights, or mothers-and-daughters teas often become rallying points for large groups. In general, programs related directly to the welfare of the youth of the school and not to abstract educational problems are the ones that capture and hold the interest of parents. If an alumni organization or a fathers' club exists in the school, either the principal or some members of the staff should spend enough time with it to make it an aid rather than a hindrance to the education of youth in the community.

TEACHERS AS PLANNERS

The nation's appreciation of its schools was deepening during World War II as teachers carried on Red Cross work, civilian defense projects, scrap drives, manpower registration, rationing, and other wartime activities. Hereafter it should be easier to think of the school—its plant as well as its personnel—as a community resource to be used in carrying on the community's peacetime activities. Many teachers made acquaintances and built understanding relationships in the community that still enhance the public's opinion of its schools and their teachers.

There are opportunities for all teachers, in their community relations, to contribute to the enrichment of community life. Usually they are eager to be accepted by the community as full-fledged partners in helping the community become a better place in which youth may live. They are not, however, willing to have other adults of the community turn the whole job over to them. American Legion posts, women's clubs, and community clubs of all kinds have energies they are willing to spend for the benefit of youth, but they sometimes fail to see their opportunities or misdirect their efforts entirely, because they have overlooked the contributions that members of the high school staff could make to their programs. Improved community recreational programs, boys' clubs, girls' camps, scholarships, and better understanding between workers, businessmen, and farmers are examples of the kinds of achievement that teachers have helped to accomplish when accepted as members of key adult groups at the right place and the right time.

Teachers have also stimulated groups of parents to accept responsibility for chaperoning dances and parties that had grown up without sponsorship and control in the community. They have discovered educational experiences going on in the community that were duplicating those of the school, thus making it possible for the school to turn its energies in another direction. Communities that utilize the abilities of teachers without attempting to exploit them have found them willing to make the kind of contribution for which their professional training has fitted them.

People who become teachers are themselves assets to most communities, and their influence on other adults in the community as teachers and as persons is probably as important as many of their activities in the classroom. They should be encouraged to be active in the community. There is a limit to the time they can spend in community activities, just as there is for other busy adults; but, as the teachers are given a chance to serve them, communities will come to realize that teachers who are leaders in the community as well as in the classroom are a good investment. The school should be able to make adjustments in teachers' programs to permit participation in the civic acitvities of community groups.

A teacher who is a full-fledged participant in community activities will find that he needs to have a clear understanding of the purposes of the school and the activities of those in different departments in order to be able to interpret the school to the public. If a layman or a patron inquires of a teacher of Latin about a particular policy that he has observed in the financial administration of the school and the teacher is unable to explain or defend the policy, a chance to build understanding of the school and its program has been lost. Before teachers can be expected to understand a policy and explain it to others, they themselves must have had an opportunity to understand it. The first step toward the community's being able to get full benefit out of the abilities of the high school faculty is taken when the school administration makes it possible for teachers to plan and help develop the school's policies and program. An informed group of teachers who understand the school and its program is always a force in the community.

Through speaking, writing, and the arranging of forum or panel discussions, members of the faculty should be encouraged to help the public understand the school's problems, to think about the problems, and to help work out solutions for them. Many times individual teachers are more effective in these group situations than the principal is, for each of them is acquainted with some group with which he is especially influential. Every teacher should be encouraged to make an effort to influence the community and to lead it in its study of some school problem.

Many have surprised themselves, as well as others, as they discovered unsuspected abilities that opened for them new interests and rich satisfactions in worth-while achievements.

In our American society the most significant educational planning is done at the local, rather than the state or national, level; it is done when teachers, students, and citizens work together. Among the high school principal's chief responsibilities are those of looking to the future and planning for youth education. He will need to know the community and its youth and how youth learn and grow. He will need to work with people to coordinate and stimulate their planning. He will need to keep constantly in mind the goals of the school and the ways in which other community agencies advance or hinder those goals.

Underlying the efforts of the high school principal and his professional staff to develop good school-community relations should be the point of view that the best school that can be developed and maintained in any community is the one built on the kind of public understanding that grows only out of active and widely shared participation in the process of creating and operating it. Efforts based on another philosophy, though at first marked by rapid progress, will sooner or later bog down in a morass of public ignorance, misunderstanding, lack of confidence, and ill will. The school and the community will hold together under the strains of continuous school operation only when they are welded by the kind of understanding that is born of experience. Educational administrators, who presumably know that in a democratic society enduring public support comes only from public understanding, should be the last to expect to get and to keep the support of a community on any other basis.

Some Points to Consider

1. What are some of the ways in which citizens can serve the school as resource persons?

2. What advantages and disadvantages may possibly be realized when administrators use opinion polls to find out what the people think about their schools?

3. What are some of the cooperative activities affecting youth which a coordinating council might stimulate among business groups and voluntary youth-serving agencies in a community?

4. Give examples of contributions and mistakes which have been made by citizens' advisory committees. What steps might have been taken to improve the work of these committees?

5. If schools plan, should they confine themselves to planning for the location and size of new buildings? What other aspects of their growth and development need more planning than they commonly receive?

6. Can you find any evidence of planning or lack of planning in any high school that you know?

Further Reading

American Association of School Administrators. *Community Leadership*. Washington, D.C.: National Education Association, 1950.

————. *Lay Advisory Committees*. Washington, D.C.: National Education Association, 1951.

Biddle, W. W. *The Cultivation of Community Leaders*. New York: Harper & Brothers, 1953. Chaps. 1, 4.

Britton, Ernest R. "Making the Community Self-Study Survey," NASSP *Bulletin*, No. 194, April, 1953.

California Association of School Administrators. *The People and the Schools of California*. Pasadena, Calif.: The Association, 1950.

Campbell, R. F., and Ramseyer, J. A. *The Dynamics of School-Community Relations*. New York: Allyn & Bacon, 1955. Chaps. 5, 6.

Doddy, Hurley H. *Informal Groups and the Community*. New York: Bureau of Publications, Teachers College, Columbia University, 1952.

Educational Policies Commission. *Citizens and Educational Policies*. Washington, D.C.: National Education Association, 1951.

————. *Education for All American Youth: A Further Look*. Rev. ed.; Washington, D.C.: National Education Association, 1951.

————. *Learning the Ways of Democracy*. Washington, D.C.: National Education Association, 1940.

————. *Strengthening Community Life—Schools Can Help*. Washington, D.C.: National Education Association, 1954. 42 pp.

Havighurst, Robert. *A Community Youth Development Program*. Chicago: University of Chicago Press, 1952.

Hayes, Wyland J. *The Small Community Looks Ahead*. New York: Harcourt, Brace & Co., Inc., 1947.

Hechinger, Fred M. *An Adventure in Education*. New York: The Macmillan Company, 1950.

Hillman, Arthur. *Community Organization and Planning*. New York: The Macmillan Company, 1950.

Hollingshead, August B. *Elmtown's Youth*. New York: John Wiley & Sons, Inc., 1949. Part II.

Illinois Curriculum Program. *What Do You Think about Parents and Teachers Working Together for Better Schools?* Consensus Study No. 8, Inventories A, B, and C; Springfield: State Superintendent of Public Instruction, 1952.

King, Clarence. *Organizing for Community Action*. New York: Harper & Brothers, 1948.

Mackenzie, Gordon N. "Community Cooperation in Curriculum Planning," *Teachers College Record*, 51. (March, 1950), 347–352.

Matthews, Mark S. *Guide to Community Action: A Source Book for Citizen Volunteers*. New York: Harper & Brothers, 1954.

National Citizens Commission for the Public Schools. *What Do We Know about Our Schools?* 2 West 45th St., N.Y. 19: The Commission, 1953.

National Society for the Study of Education. *The Community School.* Fifty-second Yearbook; Chicago: University of Chicago Press, 1953. Part II.

Olsen, Edward G., ed. *The Modern Community School.* New York: Appleton-Century-Crofts, Inc., 1953.

————. *School and Community.* 2nd ed.; Englewood Cliffs, N.J.: Prentice-Hall, Inc., 1954.

Roberts, O. H., Jr. "The Community and Secondary Education," *Improving Work Skills of the Nation.* New York: Columbia University Press, 1955. Chap. 11.

The State Education Department. *Adventure in Cooperation: Community Building in a Central School.* Albany, N.Y.: The Department, 1949.

————. *Citizens Advisory Committees: Avenues to Better Schools.* Albany, N.Y.: The Department, 1952.

Washington State Superintendent of Public Instruction. *You Can't Do It Alone.* Olympia, Washington: The Superintendent, 1951.

Whitelaw, John B. *The School and Its Community.* Rev. ed.; Baltimore, Md.: Johns Hopkins Press, 1951.

Chapter 26

LOCAL PLANNING AND
PUBLIC RELATIONS

THE SCHOOL THAT HAS STUDIED the community and its youth and planned with the community for its youth has in those processes used the most fundamental techniques available for attaining the ends of a good public relations program. As an aspect of those processes, however, it is necessary to keep the community informed concerning the activities of the school and those who plan with it. Even if the entire community were disposed to participate in planning for youth education, a systematic information program would be necessary so that activities could be coordinated. Actually many people are completely absorbed in their own interests and, in periods of increasing tax budgets and more complex school programs, some people are unfriendly to schools. Keeping the community informed is a part of democratic administration that serves to aid the community in planning, developing, and evaluating the most effective program of secondary education for its youth. As the Metropolitan School Study Council has indicated,

> The emphasis in the past in publicity has been to tell the people how good the community's schools are; to try to "sell the schools" as they are to the public. A newer emphasis is a presentation of a picture of the schools as they might be, the kind of education that could be secured if "our schools were as good as they ought to be" despite whatever hindrances exist against achieving this.[1]

The basic reason for developing a good public relations program should be to speed up the rate at which the school can advance from its present level toward being a better school. The assumption is that the best rate of progress will be reached and maintained when it results from the joint efforts of interested laymen and the leadership of its schools. Efforts to improve the school made by the public without good educational leadership will be halting and sporadic. Efforts made by educational

---

[1] Metropolitan School Study Council, *What Schools Can Do* (New York: The Council, 1945), p. 218.

leaders that do not involve the public cannot succeed because the public will not support leaders or programs that it no longer understands. The best way to get the community to support a better school program is to have the community understand it. The best way to have the community understand a better program is to get it to help decide what is a better program and to help develop it. A modern public relations program for a school is the sum total of all the activities undertaken in such a way as to bring the public into such close, active touch with the school, its program, and its various activities that real public understanding is developed and public support is gained. Such a modern program produces a realization on the part of the members of the staff that almost every contact the school has with its public can be made into an opportunity for building understanding of the schools. It is responsible for the school's initiating some activities because they promise to be good ways of developing that understanding. It changes the emphasis on some activities and the character of others. In the end it becomes not only a program that is carried on in order to encourage public participation in school affairs but a way of so conducting all the activities of the school that every chance to extend and increase community contacts, cooperations, and relationships is utilized.

Psychological Aspects of Public Relations Activities

There are principles of social psychology that are basic to all relations with students, parents, and the general public. They have been followed by many successful administrators who have learned through experience that they are practical and effective. In his *Techniques of Appeal and Social Control*,[2] Merl E. Bonney stresses some often neglected techniques that have proved useful in developing understanding and in promoting cooperative activities. Among these are the following:

1. Encourage individuals and groups to make their own decisions. Many enthusiasts for a cause arouse antagonism by insistence and high-pressure methods. Other leaders, just as determined and just as enthusiastic, secure wholehearted cooperation by carefully respecting the rights of others to make their own decisions.

2. Present all the facts and present them in detail. Unless this is done, there will be a lack of interest and understanding as well as a suspicion among some people that information is being withheld for ulterior motives. Presenting all the evidence inspires confidence because it implies confidence in those who are receiving it.

[2] Merl E. Bonney, *Techniques of Appeal and Social Control* (Menasha, Wisc.: George Banta Publishing Company, 1936).

3. Avoid frontal attacks on well-established points of view and attitudes. Because it leads to a careful consideration of objectives, revising the report card may be an effective method of attacking more fundamental curriculum problems. The expression "teacher-pupil planning" antagonizes many teachers who might tactfully be led to allow their charges to make decisions about class procedure. Building units of work that require more school time may serve, as no verbal argument would, to bring people to appreciate the value of a lengthened class period. Using a lengthened period temporarily during a summer school may cause teachers to see values in a permanently lengthened class period.

4. Encourage wide participation on the part of the public. The public as well as students and teachers should be encouraged to participate in school activities on the level of responsibility and degree of educational advancement for which they are ready. They will grow in understanding and ability to assume responsibility as well as in their loyalty to the school.

5. Establish many firsthand contacts in the community. Direct contacts stimulate interchange of ideas, and understanding and sympathy. If the program of the school is valid, those who know it well will approve it. If it is not valid, those who know it well can help change it.

6. Use familiar terms. When it is necessary to use new terms, definitions should be frequently repeated.[3] Students of semantics have shown us how difficult it is to communicate with people unless we do it in terms of common experiences. Educators find it necessary to coin new terms to facilitate their thinking, but by neglecting to define them carefully they often confuse one another and befog the general public. Even with such a well-known term as "guidance," it is better to avoid using the word itself and speak instead of aiding children in selecting subjects, jobs, activities, and so on.

7. Use specific incidents and projects rather than abstract generalizations. To tell the public that the improved social adjustment of students is an aim of the school will probably make little impression. However, the story of a boy with a particular problem in getting along with his own age-mates and the procedures used by the school in helping him solve that problem will stimulate interest and understanding. In the same way, demonstration lessons and student performances before civic groups arouse more interest and understanding than carefully prepared generalizations about the learning activities of students.

8. Carefully prepare illustrative material which is so varied that it will appeal to different groups of people. Since the patrons of the school have varying backgrounds, different types of material will appeal to different people. Pictures, charts, and graphs, dramatizations, stories,

[3] *Ibid.*, pp. 334–341.

and community celebrations are examples of mediums that may be effective in a program designed for the general public. Usually the greater the variety of these, the more effective the program will be. Repetition in varied forms is a pattern which business and industry have used with such great success that the schools may well follow their example.

9. Use emphatic and unequivocal language.[4] Simple language, vivid illustrations, and forthright presentation are effective procedures both within and without the classroom. Occasionally educators, in efforts to be entirely fair and absolutely accurate, make the mistake of mystifying audiences by presenting so much material that their principal issues are lost in the process. Teachers can learn from the professional baseball player who, when invited to explain the process of learning to play baseball, gave this terse instruction: "Go out there and throw the ball."

10. Do not oversimplify the issue.[5] In using forthright and unequivocal language, educators should resist the temptation to oversimplify. Unless they do resist this temptation they will either (1) build a narrow and inadequate public understanding, or (2) make themselves vulnerable to critics who may call attention to neglected aspects of the situation and make it appear that the public has been intentionally duped and misled.

Avenues of Public Understanding

It is not practicable to catalogue all the ways of reaching the public that are available in the high schools of this country, for they vary to a great extent according to the community. There follows, therefore, some discussion of a few typical channels that can be better utilized toward this end than they commonly are.

TEACHERS AND PUBLIC RELATIONS

While consideration was given in a preceding chapter to the importance of teachers in community planning for youth education, it is worth repeating here that teachers have difficulty in understanding, interpreting, and supporting an educational program unless they have had a part in developing it. For that reason an elementary step in public relations for the school administration is to make it possible for teachers to help in developing the school's policies and program. A second step for the school administration is to make sure that in dealing with the public it represents adequately the professional and personal interests of the teaching staff. In many respects the public relations of the teaching

[4] *Ibid.*, p. 341.
[5] *Ibid.*, p. 342.

staff are merely a reflection of the state of morale and *esprit de corps* which exist within the staff.

Following is a public relations check list drawn up by a committee of classroom teachers in Sheboygan, Wisconsin, in 1955:

TEACHER CLASSROOM PUBLIC RELATION CHECK LIST

(If you can check "yes" to most of these items, the Sheboygan school system says you rate high in public relations. If "no"—well?)

1. Does your classroom radiate friendly and cheerful surroundings?
2. Do you give the appearance that you like your job?
3. Do you have in your classroom a climate and spirit inducive to learning?
4. Do your classroom experiences dovetail into home activities?
5. Are you aware of the fact that what you say and do during the day is constantly being carried into the home?
6. Do you praise your students for commendable action?
7. Do you know your children well enough to say some nice things about every one of your students?
8. Do you convey to parents an accurate interpretation of your class aims, your students' accomplishments and their needs?
9. Do you give a lift to the struggling youngster with a smile and a "Hi"?
10. Are you turning tomorrow's voters into enthusiastic boosters of public education?
11. Are you applying classroom acquired knowledge to life problems and situations?
12. In your classroom are you an executive or a policeman?
13. Does your classroom provide opportunity for each individual to exercise self-discipline?
14. Do your students feel that your class is doing something for them?
15. Are you a Sphinx of your real self who has gained mutual respect of the students?
16. Do the students appreciate the fact that you too are a competent learner?
17. Do you adjust yourself easily to new situations without reflecting your likes or dislikes upon the members of your class?
18. Have your children acquired a sense of "belongingness"?
19. Do you avoid sarcasm in the classroom and any other outworn procedures which create bad public relations?
20. Do you help your children acquire moral and spiritual values which give them the balance between the urge of freedom and the necessity for dependency?

STUDENTS AS INTERPRETERS AND PLANNERS

Probably the high school students constitute the group that is most effective in interpreting the school to the public. Many parents and friends of students hold no opinions concerning the school except those they have acquired by listening to the students or observing them.

Enthusiasms about teachers, recreational activities, the success of the school's graduates, assembly programs, school publications, and classroom activities are readily communicated to parents and friends. Resentments and ill will that arise out of real or imagined grievances are communicated just as readily.

Hence it is important from a public relations standpoint, as well as sound educationally, to share with students the building of educational plans and policies. It is well to be sure that students understand the existing policies and program of the school, but it is even better if they understand because they have had an active part in evaluating and in helping to improve them. The principles that are sound in relations with the general public are valid in student relations as well.

Students are busy with their own interests even as adults are, and, unless they are informed about the achievements of the school, an entire student body lacking in understanding of the school and in enthusiasm for it may grow up in a few short years. Teachers are entirely aware of the fact that they have to teach 7B or 10B English to every group of students that enters the school, but they tend to feel that some matters of group guidance or of interpretation of the school can safely be neglected as annual projects. This is not so. Building group morale is a continuous, never-ending task that must be faced each time new students are inducted into the school.

It can be done in English classes, in common learnings classes, in home rooms, in assemblies, through bulletins, and through school publications. The school newspaper, in addition to informing students, informs parents and friends, for it goes into the homes and is often read there with interest. The social studies courses should contain units designed to build understanding and appreciation of the contribution the public school system has made and can make to American life and culture and to the local community. The same is true of the school annual, which may use themes dealing with the history, resources, or occupations of the community. In some high schools, student writers for the school newspaper regularly prepare news stories which are made available to the local papers. Pictures are provided by student assistants serving as school photographers or by members of a photographers' club. Taking part in such activities, as well as reading the completed stories, is a means of educating students about the policies and usages of their school.

COMMENCEMENT EXERCISES

The commencement exercises offer an unusual opportunity to develop in those who are present a better understanding of the aims, methods, and accomplishments of the school. At no other single occasion are so many people gathered in one audience with such a deep personal interest in the product of the school. Since those present are chiefly interested in the graduates, the program should be centered on them and should provide the audience with a sense of satisfaction rather than the feeling of frustration often stimulated by an unrelated, even though admirable, discourse delivered by an outside speaker. The occasion is for the graduates, so the spotlight should be kept focused on them. The part played by others should be incidental. The program, which should have a theme of some social and educational significance, should be planned well in advance under the direction of those in the school who are best at arranging effective public occasions. Moreover, it should be so planned that a representative number of the graduates participate. The use of groups in musical organizations, pageants, verse choirs, and discussion panels raises the number participating far above what it will be if two or three graduates give talks. By combining emotional appeal with factual data, with explanatory material, and with forthright statements of the principles underlying modern, democratic education, an increased public understanding and faith in the work of the school can grow out of the occasion. Not only the commencement program itself but all the events of the graduation season should be planned and organized to fix the place of the school and of education in the public mind; in short, full advantage is taken of the fact that at this season of the year it is very easy for the high school to get the interested and sympathetic attention of the typical American community.

RESOURCE PERSONS AND AGENCIES IN THE COMMUNITY

As members of the community study youth and the work of the school, they grow in the appreciation of the significance of the problems of youth and of the functional nature of the school's work. The laymen most interested in the school are not necessarily those to whom the school has given the greatest service; they are those who have done the most for the school and have therefore become interested in it. They have served on citizens' advisory committees for a building program, vocational courses of study, student service clubs, or student safety councils. They have served as resource persons to inform groups of students and to advise individuals concerning the advantages and disadvantages of certain occupations. They have visited the school to inform students about local history or industry. They have received groups of students in their businesses and industries and attempted to show them what makes the wheels go around. When laymen study and serve the school, they have so much to give it that staff members should carefully consider all offers of cooperation in order to find some arrangement that can be made to contribute to the fundamental purposes of the school. Many individuals and groups sincerely desire to be of service.

Others may have motives of self-interest but at the same time offer real opportunities for the education of youth.

The National Association of Manufacturers is sponsor for the organization of chapters of Junior Achievement, Inc., throughout the United States. Under the personal guidance of a business leader and his firm, a group of high school boys and girls is encouraged to form a business, each member of the group being a shareholder and a worker in the corporation. These members of the firm are paid by the hour for the work they do and receive dividends on their shares according to the profits earned. Doubtless one of the purposes of the NAM is the building of favorable attitudes among youth toward the traditional practices of American business. However that may be, other worth-while concomitant learnings occur as a result of experience in rather advanced and democratic practice in American business, since every worker in Junior Achievement, Inc., is also a shareholder with a voice in the management of the business in which he is engaged. This rather unusual approach to the problem of youth also interests adult leaders in youth at a time when it is extremely difficult to find enough of them for youth activities both inside and outside the school. The school should retain general control of such activities, but it should not lose the advantages of such cooperative undertakings because it fears that the promoters may have some personal and noneducational motives for offering to participate in the activity.

Many schools have been successful in recruiting volunteer or paid lay workers to supervise social activities, sponsor clubs, and teach skills to youth in afterschool classes. They have been careful to see that lines of responsibility are clearly defined, and, where the school maintains responsibility, some measures of control and supervision have been established.

When the principal and members of the staff begin planning with other agencies for the education of youth, they see again the absolute necessity of a clearly defined and generally accepted statement of objectives for the school. Proposals for cooperation are continually coming to the school from advertisers and from groups with varying degrees of disinterestedness. Some of these proposals would exploit youth; some would help them grow into maturity. Many, however, are so controversial or so antagonistic to the principles supporting our public school system that they cannot be accepted. Yet it is impossible to reject all proposals or to accept them all. In an area for which many proposals have been made, for example, a program should be drawn up and those proposals accepted that contribute to the program and those rejected that do not.

This policy is recommended in the Consumer Education Study, which states,

The two criteria proposed, one positive and one negative, represent general agreement by a considerable number of representatives of business and of education, who, meeting in separate groups, considered the whole problem of the use of commercial materials in schools. They have also received written approval by a still larger number of representatives of education and of business who have considered them individually. . . .

The criteria proposed:

1. *Contribution to the Educational Program.* To be usable in classrooms, commercial supplementary teaching materials must contribute positively and effectively to promoting without distortion the educational program approved by the responsible educational authorities of the school.

2. *Absence of Sales Promotion.* Commercial supplementary teaching materials must not contain direct promotion of sales. The name of the donating firm should appear, but not with such emphasis or repetition as to subordinate the educational content, and it is also permissible for the donor to list unobtrusively his important products or services. But there should be no boastful claims for them, no efforts to persuade, no urges to buy or to try.[6]

Many principals have been guided by these criteria in approving competitions for scholarships sponsored by manufacturing and distributing companies. Worth-while scholarships for able students represent such an urgent need that principals have approved such scholarships, so long as the products advertised have been useful and the advertising involved has been incidental to the projects.

A policy of discriminating between proposals and agencies aids in the formation of public opinion. Many dubious proposals cannot be decided upon until they are tried out, and the school serves a constructive purpose by accepting or rejecting them and thus bringing them to public attention. Such tryouts need not be extremely dangerous ones, because there are always community groups and forces ready to support the school in rejecting a proposal that is definitely questionable. Probably the lack of a clear program of objectives and policies has been responsible for much of the school's traditional aloofness from the community. Lacking a set of criteria for allying the school with cooperative ventures, school administrators have sought safety in attempting to avoid all such commitments.

NEWSPAPER AND BROADCASTING RELATIONSHIPS

An important educational agency, and one of the most important channels through which the public receives information about the school, is the local newspaper. Because many people have no personal associations

[6] National Association of Secondary School Principals, *Supplementary Teaching Materials* (Consumer Education Study; Washington, D.C.: National Education Association, 1945).

with students and teachers, the newspaper is largely responsible for the community's favorable or unfavorable attitudes toward the school. For this reason, the high school principal should do his utmost to establish relationships with representatives of the local papers that in the long run will ensure an informed reporting of what is going on at the school. He will not succeed in establishing these relationships by adopting a servile attitude or by attempting to control the stories that are printed; rather, he should keep in mind the functions of the newspaper in the community and the reporter's point of view toward school news.

An honest newspaper is the greatest weapon that an honest public official has. Political corruption, vice, and blackmailing by pressure groups are not so likely to thrive in communities where newspapers print all the news objectively. Therefore, the school principal should be cordial to the representatives of the paper that is eager to secure all the news fit to print. Such a policy may occasionally cause the school to appear in a bad light, but if the principal is efficient, honest, and forthright, it will in the long run do the school more good than harm. An objective newspaper will deter those with dishonest motives, unclean hands, or insufficient evidence from attacking the school. Many hard-pressed schoolmen have been saved by their willingness to allow an aggressive newspaper to look at all the available evidence and by the willingness of the newspaper to print all the facts, even though some of them were unsavory.

The school is a public institution, and the newspaper has a right to full information about the events that happen there. Incidents occurring at the school are not private matters to be withheld or made available as the principal sees fit. The news is made when the incident occurs and not when it is written up in the newspaper. No reporter should expect a school principal to report an unfavorable incident about the school, but if the reporter hears of it and starts investigating, he has a right to expect the principal to answer his questions accurately and truthfully, even though reluctantly. Often school principals are tempted to regard newspaper reporters as sadists or cynics who enjoy writing stories that cause their victims to writhe and squirm. Occasionally, perhaps, there is such a reporter, but more often they are ambitious workers, eager to earn a living for themselves and their families, and anxious to build a career. Schoolmen who help them get stories are their friends, and those who make it difficult for them to do their work are not. Securing sympathetic treatment from news representatives is often as simple as that. The principal should show a willingness to help reporters with their work. He will not only increase the amount of news space devoted to the school, but he will improve his understanding and appreciation of what the reporters consider news; and, having helped the reporters with their work, he may reasonably expect them at times in the future to help him with his. At least the high school principal must proceed on this basis until, in an individual case, he finds that it does not hold true.

Newspaper representatives can help the principal to a better understanding of what is news. Often when a reporter inquires for news, he is told that nothing of importance has happened simply because the principal knows so little about news values that he does not realize the possibilities of an event until a week or so after it has occurred. Talking to reporters will help him to develop alertness and awareness in connection with the news values of events that occur in his school. Moreover, many schoolmen have acquired from reporters a sense of timing that has aided them in the introduction of innovations, in the announcement of appointments, and even in the planning of future policies and activities for the school. The very fact that newsmen know what is going on in every stratum of the community makes them valuable allies and tutors for the schoolman who would be a leader of his community. Often the schoolman can broaden even an editor's point of view in local affairs and increase his appreciation of the school's usefulness. The schoolman and the newsman are really fellow educators, and each can be of help to the other. Sometimes the principal, the superintendent, some members of the staff, or a high school journalism class will assume the responsibility for regularly supplying school news to the local newspaper. Whoever writes these bulletins or news stories should write them carefully and accurately and in such a way that they will interest local readers. Aimless general statements interest nobody or are misunderstood by the few individuals who happen to read them. A continuous flow of news stories and pictures illustrating and documenting what the school is trying to do builds a reserve of public understanding upon which the school can draw as it continues to seek the aid of the public in the improvement of its program.

An educational magazine editor includes the following among his suggestions on how to work with reporters:

1. Be available.
2. Be willing to dig up information requested.
3. Give advance notice to the press when you can.
4. Don't clam up on ticklish matters.
5. Don't exaggerate a story's importance.
6. Don't complain bitterly over editing.
7. Respect exclusiveness but don't play favorites.
8. Don't make the reporter swear to when and how the story will appear.
9. Don't tell the reporter how to write his own story.[7]

[7] Hollis A. Moore, Jr., "Let's Go to Press" (Washington, D.C.: National School Public Relations Association, N.E.A., 1955).

Those who gather news for radio and television broadcasting have more or less the same attitudes toward their work that newspaper reporters have. They also are entitled to information about any events connected with the school. Radio and television stations devote a certain amount of their time to public-service programs and are glad to have good programs presented by students whether from local or distant high schools. People are interested in programs of many different types so long as they are well done. They are especially interested in music, dramatics, and programs that give them practical information, such as how to buy meats, fabrics, or household appliances. Radio and television thus offer many possibilities for varying the mediums through which people are informed about their schools. They also offer opportunities for youth to acquire experience and poise for public performances.

CAPITALIZING ON INDIVIDUAL CONTACTS

Everyone connected with the school should develop skill and effectiveness in dealing with patrons and representatives of the public who come to visit it. Each visitor should be made to feel that he has received courteous and fair treatment, and that the matter he is interested in was approached with an open mind. If a father is disturbed about his child's record in school, he is made more disturbed by the conviction that a decision about this problem has already been made and the incident is closed. He should first be convinced that the school's interest is in the welfare of his child and not in reaching a stereotyped, ready-made solution. Then he and the representative of the school should engage in an honest search for a solution that will be for the best interests of the youth concerned. This is not to say that belligerent parents should be allowed to impose their wills upon the school, but that principals, teachers, students, and patrons, in their relationships with one another should develop techniques of open-mindedness and skill in reaching a mutually satisfactory solution through discussion. Most people enjoy having a part in making decisions that affect them; actually, in the long run, little is gained by forcing decisions upon anyone or trying to convince him against his will. An individual grows most and can be influenced most when he shares the responsibility for a decision made jointly.

Every single contact that a student or an employee of the school has with a member of the community is significant. The school is judged by the conduct of students on their way home, the reception accorded visitors, and even the effectiveness of the telephone service. In a city high school of which one of the authors was once principal, it was the practice to have a clerk telephone, wherever possible, the home of each student who was absent. This was a service much appreciated by many parents, but it was possible for a clerk to evoke a variety of responses from parents according to whether he was rude or courteous over the telephone. For example, anger and annoyance were the customary response to a demanding and peremptory "This is Central High School. We notice that John is absent this morning and we want to know the reason why." On the other hand, gratitude and appreciation invariably followed a courteous, sympathetic "We notice that John is absent this morning. We hope he is not ill." To argue that these individual contacts are unimportant because they affect but one person at a time is to be totally unconscious of the fact that all public or group understanding develops out of individual understanding. The "public" never understands anything except as the individuals who compose it come to understand. So any public relations programs that seek public understanding and appreciation of an ongoing school program must utilize the principles and techniques of good teaching. In short, particular, individual members of the public must have a chance to learn, so that they will help teach others. A good public relations program is only a complex assortment of teaching situations in which individual members of the public have a chance to learn about the school. Every contact the school staff has with a member of the public in which the center of interest is the school is therefore a miniature public relations program in action, and the success of the whole program is pretty well measured by the success of each of these individual contacts.

The Anatomy of a Community

In his *The Governing of Men*,[8] Alexander H. Leighton records how a group of several thousand persons thrown suddenly together at the Poston Relocation Center during World War II gradually evolved into a community. At first there were only thousands of people and nothing to make them into a community. The only social organization there was the family. There was none of the organization or social structure we expect to find present where so many people live together in a large group. But the needs of these people in this new physical setting began to make social or community structures necessary, and so they began to grow. The book shows how these structures developed in answer to commonly felt needs and how conflicting needs and ideas created rival and conflicting solutions that had to be harmonized. The book is of interest to those who work in and with local communities, because it is a picture of a community being formed and born. In a way it is a study of community embryology and contributes the same insight into com-

---

[8] Alexander H. Leighton, *The Governing of Men* (Princeton, N.J.: Princeton University Press, 1945).

munity life that human embryology contributes to the study of the human organism.

THE STRUCTURE OF A COMMUNITY

When one puts a community under a social microscope, however, it becomes clear that what appeared to be a fairly well-integrated social organism turns out to be only a loosely knit aggregate of social groups, no one of which is in reality as much of a unity as the use of the term "organism" implies. If a school administrator looks through this microscope at what he thought was "the public," he will find it is composed of many publics; and if he thought he could identify a "school-public," he will find it to be composed of many publics, each of which has fairly continuous but not common reasons for being interested in the schools. There is seldom what we call a "public opinion." More often it is better described as the opinions of the various publics. For the school administrator there turn out to be the opinions of the publics about the school and not an opinion of a single public about the school. Only very infrequently do critical events and conditions unite a whole community into what can be properly described as a single public opinion on the school or on anything else. Just because, for example, both the American Legion and the American Association of University Women may have expressed their interest in education by having local committees on education, it does not at all prove that, as soon as they are given a chance to understand it, they are ready to join to support a program that the faculty has endorsed. Both may be "interested" in education but for such different reasons that the principal cannot assume that they form part of a "school-public" ready to mass behind any proposal as soon as they recognize its merit. The best that can be hoped for is that their interest in education will cause them to be willing to join together with other local groups interested in education to study the local school's program, to plan for the solution of its problems, and to participate in the work required if the problems are to be solved. Out of this working together a united school-public may be built, but no principal can assume that a school-public interested in education exists and is therefore ready and willing to form a single unified opinion on school matters as soon as it is given an opportunity to consider them. There is no ready-made school-public willing to understand, to approve, and to have a public opinion on school affairs. There are only loosely constructed social groups, some of which are interested in education. Out of these groups a school-public can be built through cooperative action, and in the process it will come to have a public opinion on school affairs. But this public will keep falling apart and back into its several groups unless it is continuously used in the process of developing a better and better school.

Anyone who works with a community as if it were a rather stable, unified, enduring entity needs to make a thorough study of the anatomy of democratic communities. They are dynamic, changing, loosely knit aggregates of other smaller groups that are largely free agents. They form and dissolve, split up and reunite in an unending process and in a changing pattern. They are capable of joining in unifying thought and organized action, but it does not come natural to them. The school administrator can best capitalize on these possibilities by providing plenty of opportunity for responsible participation in the processes by which a better school is built. If he continually does this, he will find that he has helped the community to build a school-public, and that there is a public opinion or mind about the school and its affairs that will carry it forward from year to year.

GROUP LEADERS SHOULD BE IDENTIFIED

Such a fluid, unstable picture of the structure of community life may make the task of planning and conducting a school-community public relations program seem an impossible one. Still closer study of these community organizations, however, reveals something to build on. If one studies the anatomy of one of these community groups, he discovers that it is centered about a nucleus of group leaders who really give the organization its character and guide its activities. Each organization is composed of the membership at large, which enjoys the contacts it provides and which approves in general of its purposes. If the group is organized for an educational purpose, then all its members share this interest to a degree, but its officers and executive committee are the ones who are deeply interested. If it is not primarily an educational organization, but is enough interested in education to have an education committee, then the members most actively interested in education will tend to be associated with this committee.

The school administrator who is concerned with a public relations program ought to be willing to give each of these groups, as groups, all the time and attention they will give him, and ought to be ready to include as many group members as are willing, in active work in the school enterprises that the public relations program exists to foster. But he will know that actually he will have succeeded very well if, though he gets only a minority to accept an active part, he has succeeded in arousing active interest and support from those who make up the nuclei of leadership in these various community groups. The administrator may find it profitable to make up a list of all the organizations in the community that are strictly educational, such as the City Teachers Club and the Parent-Teachers Council; those that are allied to social service agencies; those with an interest in child welfare; those that have a standing committee on education; and those with a committee on the school budget. Here is the group of organizations in the community whose leadership is from time to time and for one reason or another interested in education. The members who are the officers, the executive committee, and the committees on education or child welfare are the leaders of the particular organizations in the community who have the most initial interest in the school and its program and are most likely to respond to an invitation from the school to participate actively in the school development program. Once such people as these have taken part in the program, they will contribute a great deal to it, understand it fully, and be able to explain it to the membership of organizations. A study of these lists of leaders will show interrelationships that further simplify the situation. Some will be found to be school employees but active leaders in organizations not directly identified with the school. Someone who is a member of the executive committee of one organization may be the chairman of the education or child welfare committee of another. This interlocking of leadership reduces the number of different people in the community who are interested in education and at the same time are group leaders. The school's program of public relations should seek the active identification of this group with some aspect of its effort to improve the school. Through the ability thus developed, through the understanding thus created, through the good will thus generated, the school can be sure that progress toward the best possible school for its community is being made at the best rate that can be maintained.

"PUBLIC RELATIONS" INTRINSIC TO EDUCATIONAL DEVELOPMENT

Such programs can be launched and guided more intelligently if school principals have made a close enough study of the anatomy of the community and its organizations to understand their structures and functions. This study will enable them more effectively to exercise leadership in planning and launching programs calculated to improve the local school. It is assumed in this chapter that the principal and the faculty are sincerely interested in improving their school in the most satisfactory way. Thus they must know their own community and its youth, since the effectiveness of the school is best measured by how its work helps students fit into and improve their community. To know their community as thoroughly as they should, the principal and the faculty must study it objectively. Inviting students, parents, and citizens to participate in a community-wide study is a most effective method because it draws upon their knowledge of their community and because, through helping in the study, local citizens become even better informed about it and the place of the program of the school in the general pattern.

Some valuable and timely hints for high school principals on desirable and undesirable attitudes and practices in the area of public relations are to be found in a study, completed in 1955, in which were reported the opinions of 725 qualified observers concerning acceptable and unacceptable practices of high school principals. The observers were selected individuals who, in a variety of schools, had been in good positions to evaluate the character and work of one or more high school principals. In interviews they were asked to answer in detail and by means of descriptive incidents the following question: "Thinking back over your observations and experiences in connection with the high school, what do you believe the high school principal must do or avoid doing to meet your expectations?" Insofar as the replies related to public relations the acceptable and unacceptable practices were summarized as follows:

V. ENLISTING THE SUPPORT AND COOPERATION OF THE COMMUNITY

Acceptable Practices	*Unacceptable Practices*
1. Establishes a personal acquaintance with many individuals in the community, particularly through informal, friendly contacts.	1. Does not get around in the community enough to develop personal acquaintance and understanding with local citizens.
2. Keeps the community informed—through news releases, speeches, casual contacts, and other such means—of what the school is doing and what it needs.	2. Displays an attitude of superiority and indicates desire for aloofness from "non-professional" people of the community.
3. Invites laymen to participate in cooperative planning to improve the school, always welcoming suggestions from those that do not take an active part.	3. Does not establish procedures to keep the community informed of what the school is doing, what it needs, and what it is planning.
4. Urges staff members and students to tell people in the community what the school is accomplishing and planning.	4. Uses terms and expressions that lay citizens fail to comprehend.
5. Collaborates with other community leaders, explaining how cooperation between the school and their groups or organizations may enhance educational opportunities for	5. Shows more concern for the children of certain families in the community than he does for the offspring of other families.

youth and, in turn, yield benefit
to the community.

6. Adapts his speech and actions to a
mode that is readily understood by
the various individuals and groups
with whom he associates and com-
municates.

VIII. PARTICIPATING IN COMMUNITY AFFAIRS

Acceptable Practices	*Unacceptable Practices*
1. Participates, according to interest and time available, in activities pertinent to religious services, business matters, industrial problems, recreational pursuits, and other affairs incident to the life of a responsible citizen.	1. Becomes involved in so many community activities that he does not have sufficient time nor energy to perform well his responsibilities in the school.
2. Takes part regularly in at least one local civic organization.	2. Joins a number of community groups but contributes little or nothing to their activities.
3. Takes advantage of opportunities to diffuse information about the school during his contacts with citizens in community groups and activities.	3. Isolates himself from activities of the community.
4. Avoids becoming involved, if at all possible, in local inter-group contention over non-school issues.	4. Seeks positions in local organizations primarily for the purpose of getting publicity or other personal gain.
	5. Aligns himself with factious community groups that are engaged in discord over non-school problems.
	6. Spends most of the time and energy which he devotes to community affairs in working with the same group of people.[9]

Such cooperative study, planning, and evaluation should improve
both the community and its school. This, in fact, is the ideal relationship between the community and the school. Where this cooperative
relationship exists, a natural, unforced, and dynamic "public relations
program" exists and the school does not need to create an artificial and

[9] David B. Austin and James S. Collins, "A Study of Attitudes toward the High
School Principalship," NASSP *Bulletin*, January, 1956. Reprinted by permission.

extrinsic program through which to inform and educate the public. Such a public relations program is the best channel through which to effect improvement in the school. Although it is a natural bulwark against unjust criticism of the school, defense of the school as it is ought never be the reason for the development of a public relations program. The real reason for building a good working relationship among teachers, students, parents, and the community is that these relationships ensure the maximum rate of continuous improvement in the program of the school. More public understanding of change and more willingness to accept it in the local school are generated by methods that are educationally sound than by any other methods. If public education is as important to a democratic society as school administrators usually tell the public it is, then they should be the first to recognize that the education of the public is the best protection for any public school and the best guarantee of its continuous improvement.

Some Points to Consider

1. Why is a program for maintaining good public relations an essential activity of a secondary school? If a school is a good school, why is a public relations program needed? Compare the public relations problem of a high school with that of a local business of comparable size. What similarities and differences do you discover? What are the factors that may cause a high school principal and his staff to give less attention to public relations than they should?

2. What are the purposes of a public relations program? List as many legitimate purposes of a public relations program as you can. Are there any possible purposes that are not legitimate? How do you compare these purposes in order of importance? May the order of importance vary from school to school? If so, why?

3. Are "school publicity" and "public relations programs" synonymous?

4. If you were principal of a high school which had never made an effort at building any public relations and about which there was no particular criticism, would you try to develop what you considered to be a good program of public relations? Why? If so, what are some of the types of activities you would consider most important?

5. What sort of educational planning underlies the idea that a public relations program should undertake to "sell" the principal's plans to the community?

6. How would you evaluate a school's public relations program and reach some decision as to how good you thought it was?

Further Reading

American Association of School Administrators. *Paths to Better Schools.* Twenty-third Yearbook; Washington, D.C.: National Education Association, 1945.

————. *Public Relations for America's Schools.* Twenty-eighth Yearbook; Washington, D.C.: National Education Association, 1950.

Association for Supervision and Curriculum Development. *Building Public Confidence in the Schools.* Washington, D.C.: National Education Association, 1949.

Austin, David B., and James S. Collins. "A Study of Attitudes toward the High School Principalship," NASSP *Bulletin,* January, 1956.

Bakkegard, B. M. "Public School Music as a Public Relations Agent," *Music Educators' Journal,* 39, No. 1 (September, 1952), 61–63.

Biddle, W. W. *The Cultivation of Community Leaders.* New York: Harper & Brothers, 1953. Chaps. 9, 12.

Blackwell, Gordon W. "A Sociologist on School-Community Relationships." *Annals of the American Academy of Political and Social Science,* 302: 128–35 (November, 1955).

Bonney, Merl E. *Techniques of Appeal and Social Control.* Menasha, Wisc.: George Banta Publishing Company, 1936.

California Congress of Parents and Teachers. *Teaching Today's Youth.* Los Angeles, Calif.: 1954.

Division of Press and Radio Relations, National Education Association, *The 1952 "PR" Guide.* Washington, D.C.: The Division, 1952. A where-to-look handbook of aids for your school public relations program.

Fine, Benjamin. *Educational Publicity.* New York: Harper & Brothers, 1943.

Gustavson, B. C. "The Open House as a Medium for Public Relations," NASSP *Bulletin,* 34, No. 167 (January, 1950), 195–197.

Hamlin, Herbert M. *The Public and Its Education.* Danville, Ill.: The Interstate Printers and Publishers, 1955.

Harp, John A., Jr. "Public Relations in the Secondary School," NASSP *Bulletin,* 38, No. 204 (October, 1954), 117–133.

Leighton, Alexander H. *The Governing of Men.* Princeton, N.J.: Princeton University Press, 1945.

Mathes, G. E., and G. D. Lange. "What Need for a Public Relations Program for the Secondary School," NASSP *Bulletin,* 34, No. 170 (April, 1950), 73–82.

Metropolitan School Study Council. *What Schools Can Do.* New York: The Council, 1944, 1945.

National Association of Secondary School Principals. "Education for Improved Community Life," *Bulletin,* No. 139, May, 1946.

————. *It's High Time.* Washington, D.C.: National Education Association, 1955.

————. "Public Relations in Secondary Schools," *Bulletin,* No. 152, February, 1948.

————. *Supplementary Teaching Materials.* Consumer Education Study; Washington, D.C.: National Education Association, 1945.

National School Public Relations Association. *It Starts in the Classroom.* Washington, D.C.: National Education Association, 1951. A public relations handbook for classroom teachers.

————. *Teaming Up for Public Relations.* Washington, D.C.: National Education Association, 1952. A handbook for leaders in public education.

National Society for the Study of Education. *The Community School.* Fifty-second Yearbook; Chicago: University of Chicago Press, 1953. Part II.

Olsen, Edward G., ed. *The Modern Community School.* New York: Appleton-Century-Crofts, Inc., 1953.

————. *School and Community.* 2nd ed.; Englewood Cliffs, N.J.: Prentice-Hall, Inc., 1954.

Patterson, N.S. "School Yearbooks as Public Relations for Education and Training Media for Youth," *School and Society,* 74, No. 1923 (October, 1951), 296–298.

Reller, Theodore L. "Some Paths to Coordination," *Annals of the American Academy of Political and Social Science.* 302:143–48 (November, 1955).

Tuttle, Edward M. "All the Facts All the Time," *Phi Delta Kappan,* 33 (November, 1951), 115–117.

Xavier, Sister Mary, O.P. "Relationships of the (Catholic) Secondary Schools with the Community and with the Public Schools," Proceedings and Addresses, Forty-sixth Annual Meeting; National Catholic Educational Association, Washington, D.C., 1949.

INDEX

Index

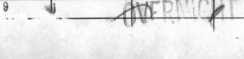

All youth need to develop saleable skills and those under-standings and attitudes that make the worker an intelligent and productive participant in economic life. To this end, most youth need supervised work experience as well as education in the skills and knowledge of their occupations.

All youth need to develop and maintain good health and physical fitness.

All youth need to understand the rights and duties of the citizen of a democratic society, and to be diligent and competent in the performance of their obligations as members of the community and citizens of the state and nation.

All youth need to understand the significance of the family for the individual and society and the conditions conducive to successful family life.

All youth need to know how to purchase and use goods and services intelligently, understanding both the values received by the consumer and the economic consequences of their acts.